Muslim–Christian Romance in Times of Captivity

International Research in General and Comparative Literature

INTERNATIONALE FORSCHUNGEN ZUR ALLGEMEINEN
UND VERGLEICHENDEN LITERATURWISSENSCHAFT

Series Editors

Norbert Bachleitner, *Universität Wien*, Austria
Juliane Werner, *Universität Wien*, Austria

Founded by

Alberto Martino

Editorial Board

Rüdiger Görner, *Queen Mary, University of London*, UK
Stephanie M. Hilger, *University of Illinois at Urbana-Champaign*, Illinois, USA
Achim Hölter, *Universität Wien*, Austria
Manfred Pfister, *Freie Universität Berlin*, Germany
Sven H. Rossel, *Universität Wien*, Austria

VOLUME 216

The titles published in this series are listed at *brill.com/favl*

Muslim–Christian Romance in Times of Captivity

By

Eva Simmons

BRILL

LEIDEN | BOSTON

Cover illustration: Codex Manesse 251r Bruno von Hornberg.

The Library of Congress Cataloging-in-Publication Data is available online at https://catalog.loc.gov
LC record available at https://lccn.loc.gov/2025012273

Typeface for the Latin, Greek, and Cyrillic scripts: "Brill". See and download: brill.com/brill-typeface.

ISSN 0929-6999
ISBN 978-90-04-71226-3 (hardback)
ISBN 978-90-04-71228-7 (e-book)
DOI 10.1163/9789004712287

Copyright 2025 by Koninklijke Brill BV, Plantijnstraat 2, 2321 JC Leiden, The Netherlands.
Koninklijke Brill BV incorporates the imprints Brill, Brill Nijhoff, Brill Schöningh, Brill Fink, Brill mentis, Brill Wageningen Academic, Vandenhoeck & Ruprecht, Böhlau and V&R unipress.
Koninklijke Brill BV reserves the right to protect this publication against unauthorized use. Requests for re-use and/or translations must be addressed to Koninklijke Brill BV via brill.com or copyright.com.
For more information: info@brill.com.

This book is printed on acid-free paper and produced in a sustainable manner.

To Paul

Contents

Preface XIII
Acknowledgements XVI
List of Figures XVIII

Introduction: Muslim–Christian Romance in Times of Captivity   1
1   Slavery from Ancient Times Onwards, and Its Documentation   4
2   Slavery and Love   7
3   Early Islamic Perspectives (Chapter 1)   12
4   Mediaeval Christian Romances (Chapter 2)   14
5   Lived Experience of Slavery in North Africa and the Mediterranean: Development of the Mediterranean Slave Trade (Chapter 3)   16
6   Slavery and Romance in 16th–17th Century Novels and Plays of Spain (Chapter 4)   18
7   Slavery and Romance in 16th–17th Century Literature of England and France (Chapter 5)   19
8   The 18th Century and Beyond; and Conclusion (Chapter 6)   20
    8.1   *Gender-Role Reversal and the Lure of the Desert: Genteel Heroines and Commanding Arab Heroes*   21
9   A Caveat   22

1 Early Islamic Perspectives   24
    1   The Coming of Islam: Slavery, Sexuality, and Religious and Cultural Difference   24
        1.1   *The Qurʾan and Slavery*   27
        1.2   *One Thousand and One Nights (Alf Layla wa Layla)*   30
        1.3   *Greek Influence*   31
        1.4   One Thousand-and One-Nights: *Analysis*   32
    2   *One Thousand and One Nights*: Stories   34
        2.1   *The Story of Nur al-Din Ali ibn-Bakkar and the Slave Girl Shams al-Nahar*   34
        2.2   *The Story of the Slave-Girl Anis al-Jalis and Nur al-Din Ali ibn Khaqan*   36
        2.3   *'Occidentalism': A Response to 'Orientalism'*   37
    3   *One Thousand-and One-Nights* Stories with Love between Muslims and Christians, and Religious Conversion Themes   39
        3.1   The Tale of King ʿUmar ibn al-*Nuʿuman* and His Sons Sharkān and Zau al-Makan (Nights *45–145*)   39

		3.2	*The Story of Ali Nur al-Din and Miriam the Sash Maker* (Nights 863–94): *Plot and Analysis* 43
	4	Some Shorter *Nights* Stories 48
		4.1	*The Tale of the Abbot Who Converted to Islam* (Nights 412–14) 48
		4.2	*The Story of the Christian Princess and the Muslim* (Nights 477–78) 49
		4.3	*The Tale of the Muslim Hero and the Christian Girl* (Nights 474–77) 49
		4.4	*The Man from Upper Egypt and His Frankish Wife* (Nights 894–96) 50
	5	*Tales of the Marvellous and News of the Strange* (16th century CE?) 52
		5.1	Sīrat Dhāt al-Himma 57
	6	Poetry 59
		6.1	*Slave Motifs in the Poetry of Al-Andalus* 60
		6.2	*Ruler-Poets* 62
		6.3	*Poetry and Religion* 64
	7	Ibn Ḥazm 65
	8	Yusuf and Zulaikha 74
		8.1	*Jami's* Yusuf and Zulaikha 75
2	**Mediaeval Christian Romances – Cultural Borrowings** 81
	1	Arab Origins of the Idea of Courtly Love 84
	2	*Digenes Akrites:* Product of a Muslim-Christian Frontier 88
	3	Two Mediaeval French/Middle English Romances 95
		3.1	*Floire et Blanchefleur* 96
		3.2	*Spiritual Kinship of Muslim and Christian* 100
		3.3	*Possible Sources of* Floire et Blanchefleur 105
		3.4	*Aucassin et Nicolette* 107
		3.5	Floire et Blanchefleur *and* Aucassin et Nicolette: *Analyses* 112
		3.6	*Ethno-Cultural Kinship* 113
		3.7	*Comparisons* 117
	4	The Charlemagne Narrative Tradition 118
		4.1	*The* Chanson de Roland/Song of Roland 118
		4.2	*The Character of Baligant* 119
		4.3	*The Character of Bramimonde* 121
	5	Other Charlemagne Texts 125
		5.1	*Rouland and Vernagu* 125
		5.2	*Turpin's History of Charles* 125

        5.3   *Otuel*   126
   6   The Character of Floripas in Medieval French and English
        Literature   127
        6.1   Fierabras *and* Sir Ferumbras   127
        6.2   *The Sowdone of Babylone*   132
        6.3   *Charles the Grete*   134
   7   The King of Tars   142
   8   Boccaccio and His Successors   145

3   **The Lived Experience of Slavery in North Africa and the Mediterranean – Development of the Mediterranean Slave Trade**   148
   1   The Lived Experience of Slavery   155
   2   Conversion and Religious Practice   157
   3   Personal Narratives of Enslavement   160
        3.1   *Father Jeronimo Gracián*   161
        3.2   *Diego Galán*   164
        3.3   *Fra Diego de Haedo/Dr Antonio de Sosa*   166
        3.4   *Emanuel (Emmanuel) d'Aranda*   168
        3.5   *Jacques Philippe Laugier de Tassy/John Morgan*   172
   4   Morgan's Additions and Comparisons with de Tassy's Account   177
   5   Miguel de Cervantes   180
   6   Women Slaves and the Harem   185
   7   Thomas Pellow   188
   8   Lady Mary Wortley Montagu   193
   9   Lived Experience and Literature: Some Concluding Remarks   196

4   **Slavery and Romance in 16th–17th Century Novels and Plays of Spain**   198
   1   A Shared Culture in Spain   199
        1.1   *El Abencerraje*   202
        1.2   *Pérez de Hita,* Guerras civiles de Granada (Civil Wars of Granada)   205
   2   Changing Fortunes of the Moriscos   212
        2.1   *Ozmín y Daraja*   216
   3   Cervantes: 'Moorish' Themes, in Prose Fiction and on the Spanish Stage   221
   4   Cervantes's Works   224
        4.1   El trato de Argel   224
        4.2   *La Historia del cautivo/The Story of the Captive*   227
        4.3   *Los Baños de Argel* [*The Dungeons of Algiers*]   233

		4.4	*El Amante Liberal* [*The Generous – or Liberal – Lover*] 242

       4.5   *La Gran Sultana* [*The Great Sultana*] *Doña Catalina de Oviedo* (*Published 1615*)   244

  5 Other Cervantine Texts   252

       5.1   *El Gallardo Español* [the Gallant Spaniard], *Published 1615*   253

  6 Summary   255

  7 Cervantes's Literary Heir: Lope de Vega   257

5 Slavery and Romance in 16th–17th Century England and France   259

  1 'Moorish' and 'Turkish' Themes in 16th–17th Century England   259

  2 Tragicomedy   262

       2.1   *Robert Greene (1558–1592)*   263

       2.2   *Greene's* Orlando Furioso *(1589? Printed 1594)*   263

       2.3   *Greene's* The Comicall Historie of Alphonsus, King of Aragon *(1599)*   268

       2.4   *Philip Massinger,* The Renegado, *(Licensed 1624, Published 1630)*   272

  3 Growth of 'Moorish' and Muslim Themes in France during the 17th Century   281

       3.1   *Almahide*   284

  4 Some Other 'Moorish' and 'Turkish' Themes in French   285

       4.1   *Zaïde/Zayde*   286

       4.2   *Jean-François Regnard,* La Provençale *(Published Posthumously in 1731)*   291

  5 The 'Moorish' or 'Turkish' Text in England after the Restoration   296

       5.1   *John Dryden:* Almanzor and Almahide, Or, The Conquest of Granada   299

       5.2   *The Fair One of Tunis*   302

       5.3   *Some Other Post-Restoration Texts in French and English*   309

       5.4   *Aphra Behn/Thomas Southerne* Oroonoko   312

6 The 18th Century Onwards   314

  1 Galland and the Spread of Orientalism   314

  2 England   315

  3 Continuation of Slavery and Romance Themes   316

  4 Slavery and Romance in the 18th Century Theatre   319

       4.1   *George Colman the Younger*   319

  5 Nineteenth Century   322

       5.1   *Ann Lemoine*   322

	5.2	*Lord Byron* 323
	5.3	*François-René de Chateaubriand and Washington Irving* 324
6	Sadomasochism and Its Commercial Lure 326
7	Twentieth Century and Beyond 328
	7.1	*Gender Role Reversal and the Lure of the Desert: Genteel Heroines and Commanding Arab Heroes* 328
8	The 21st Century: Tables Turned 332
9	Slavery and Romance in Entertainment of the East 334
10	Summary and Conclusion 335
	10.1	*The 'Other' and the 'Same'/ 'Them' and 'Us'* 338
11	Post Script: Two Tales of Mixed-Faith Romance in the 21st Century 342
	11.1	*Haret al-Yahud* [*Jewish Quarter*] 342
	11.2	Gader Haya [Borderlife, *Initial English Translation, Later Changed to* All the Rivers] 343

Appendices   345
Bibliography   352
Index   380

Preface

The year is 2019, the venue a puppet theatre in Palermo. The lights dim, the curtains are drawn and the show is about to begin. On stage two life-like marionettes appear in full mediaeval armour with swords drawn. Orlando and Rinaldo are cousins and best friends, so why are they fighting? They are duelling for the love of a pagan princess: Angelica (often identified as 'Saracen' – Muslim); their romantic passions override their love for one another. All are characters in a story based on two Italian epic poems: *Orlando Innamorato* (1483) by Matteo Maria Boiardo, and its successor piece *Orlando Furioso* (1516) by Ludovico Ariosto, themselves inspired by the 11th century French epic, *La Chanson de Roland*. The theme's survival in a puppet show in 21st-century Sicily attests to the enduring appeal and adaptability of the 'love for the other' motif, and specifically between a Muslim and a Christian – supposedly enemies, but drawn inexorably together as lovers and spiritual kin. It is with this fascination that my book is concerned.

FIGURE 0.1 A flyer advertising the puppet show in Palermo, Sicily, 2019
PHOTOGRAPH BY THE AUTHOR

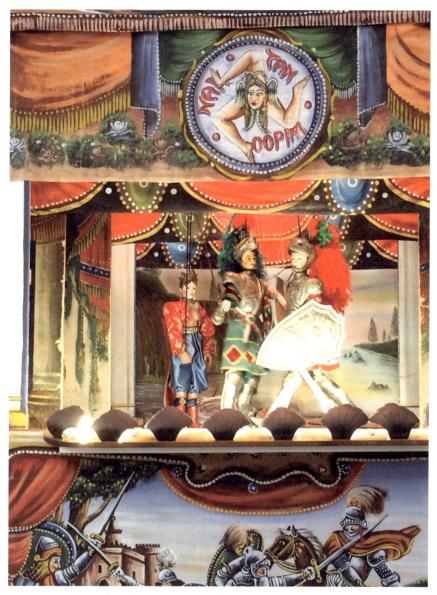

FIGURE 0.2 A scene from the action, showing duelling knights Orlando and Rinaldo with the Saracen princess Angelica (in trousers) in the background
PHOTOGRAPH BY THE AUTHOR

Acknowledgements

This book began as a preoccupation with certain words in the plays of Aphra Behn (1640–89), subject of my PhD thesis. Those words included 'slavery', and 'honour', obsessively recurring throughout her work. I puzzled over what they 'meant' in the context and why slavery was used almost interchangeably to refer both to its literal manifestation and, metaphorically, as an expression of an emotional state: a perception of helplessness in love. My supervisor, the late Inga-Stina Ewbank of Bedford College (now absorbed into Royal Holloway University) led me to explore Behn's sources, and thence to the 17th century French novels of d'Urfé, La Calprenède, and Mme. de Scudéry and others, and plays and novels of 'Golden Age' Spain.

Years later, reflecting upon all that I had learned, I decided to make the background (to Behn's plays) into my foreground for further study. So my first debt of gratitude is to Inga-Stina, whose wide view of literature fed into a broadening of my own.

A Cambridge friend, the late Dr Nita Mandel, invited me to join a small literary group she was involved in running, to which I then contributed a paper on my researches thus far, called 'A Slave to Love: Captivity and Romance in Early Novels'. Afterwards, two academics who were present, Dr. Hilda Davidson and Prof. Leo Salingar, urged me to turn the paper into a book and offered to help me publish it. Sadly, they both died far too soon to see this book in print, but I here acknowledge my debt to them as well as to Nita.

Study at the Woolf Institute, Cambridge, introduced me to interfaith relations and learning about Islam. Friendships I made there, and in Arabic-language classes, have endured, especially with Samia Baig, with whom I have had numerous discussions on subjects related to this book and with whom I subsequently worked on interfaith presentations in schools. These experiences have been very important to me.

In 2018 I contacted the late Prof. Malcolm Lyons who, with his wife Ursula translated into English and edited the definitive modern edition of *One Thousand and One Nights,* to which I have referred so often in this book that I have lost count. They also translated numerous other originally Arab-language works previously unknown in the West. Prof. Lyons turned out to be a most delightful man who wore his erudition lightly and introduced me to his great friend Sir Roger Tomkys who, like Malcolm, gave me great encouragement, as well as leading me to the late Iradj Bagherzade, founder/owner of the wonderful publishing house I.B. Tauris. Iradj read the book and gave me the first positive feedback I had received from someone outside my immediate circle who had actually read it. Meeting him was a great pleasure and, again, I am sad that he died before this publication. To all these scholars I am profoundly grateful.

My alma mater for my B.A, Lucy Cavendish College in Cambridge gave me a Visiting Scholarship, 2021–23, with space to work and access to all college facilities. I give warm thanks to them, especially to Alison Vinnicombe and Tom Hawker-Dawson, who were most instrumental in offering me the award and encouraging my work.

From Prof. Miri Rubin I received invaluable advice on various aspects of academic research and the quest to find a publisher. Thank you Miri, for sharing your experience and knowledge with me.

Dr Rachel Meller proofread and commented on a late draft: thank you so much Rachel for all you have done, and for your enthusiasm.

My anonymous peer-reviewers gave me important feedback on my writing, for which I am most grateful.

My thanks too go to the editors, Iulia Ivana and Masja Horn at Brill, publishers of this book, who assisted me during the process of submission, and to Victoria Parrin who proofread the final document.

Finally, I hesitate to use the cliché that friends and relatives who have provided support have been 'too numerous to mention', but I have had so many conversations and received so much interest in the book from them, that it is hard for me to name one (or three) without inadvertently omitting someone else.

A few individuals stand out, however: my mother, the late Ilse Meyer and my sisters Sylvia Armit and Dr Marion Kant, expressed sustained interest in my work, as did my brother-in-law Andrew Armit, and nieces and nephews Jakob (Jascha) Kanev, Rachel Kanev, Monty Kanev and Zoe Armit. My mother in particular, followed my progress with keen interest and, burrowing in the British Library on my behalf, 'found' what became one of 'my' stories: Ann Lemoine's *The Beautiful African; Or, Love and Slavery: An Interesting Tale* (1805).

My most profound gratitude goes to my partner Paul Crossley, to whom this book is dedicated. During countless discussions, he helped me find my way through the mass of material I have consulted for this book, read and helped me shape innumerable drafts, and offered unfailing support and inspiration over many years. In addition, he kept me fed and watered (when I might have skipped meals in order to keep working), as well as providing stimulating and informed companionship throughout the process. I thank you, Paul, from the bottom of my heart.

Figures

0.1   A flyer advertising the puppet show in Palermo, Sicily, 2019 (left)   xiv

0.2   A scene from the action, showing duelling knights Orlando and Rinaldo with the Saracen princess Angelica (in trousers) in the background (right)   xv

1.1   Set design by Leon Bakst for the ballet, *Sheherazade,* performed by the Ballet Russes, with music by Nicolai Rimsky-Korsakov in 1910. Bakst collaborated with Sergei Diaghilev, co-founding the Ballet Russes, for which he was the artistic director and he also designed the costumes. The original cast included Ida Rubinstein, Vaslav Nijinsky, Enrico Cecchetti, and Bronislava Nijinska. Image in the public domain   33

1.2   Abriza Defeats Sharkān, illustration for the 1897 edition of *The Book of the Thousand Nights and a Night* by Albert Letchford. Image in the public domain   41

1.3   Miriam the Girdle-Girl, wood engraving, Denning Fink publisher, Pforzheim, 1842   45

1.4   Map of Expansion of Caliphate, source. Image in the public domain   57

1.5   Image of Ibn Ḥazm on a Spanish postage stamp dated 1986, value 12 Pesetas. Image by Sergei Nezhinskii   67

1.6   Monument to al-Hakam II in Córdoba (Spain)   73

2.1   Floris en Blancefloer, produced by the Dutch engraver, printer and translator Jan van Doesborch, ca. 1517. Image in the public domain   98

2.2   Flore and Blanscheflur discovered in bed together, illustration by Konrad Fleck, Hagenau, Workshop of Diebold Lauber, around 1442–1444. Image in the public domain   99

2.3   Aucassin and Nicolette, oil on canvas painting by Marianne Stokes (1855–1927). Image in the public domain   109

2.4   Hürrem Sultan – Roxelana, 'La Sultana Rossa', painted by Tiziano Vecelli or Vecellio (Titian) ca 1550. Image in the public domain   114

2.5   Bust of Abd-ar-Raḥmān III, displayed in a restaurant in Córdoba – formerly a 16th century palace   116

2.6   Battle of Roncevaux Pass in 778 CE, 15th century anonymous painting. Image in the public domain   119

2.7   The giant Fierabras. Engraving from the 1497 edition of Jehan Bagnyon's *Roman de Fierabras le Géant* (P. Maréchal et B. Chaussard, Lyon), BNF RES-Y2-993. Image in the public domain   129

2.8   Floripas listens outside the prison. Image taken from f. 94 of *Roman de Brut,* a verse epitome (begins imperfectly) with continuation to *Edward III; Destruction de Rome; Fierabras.* Written in French. Image in the public domain   133

FIGURES   XIX

2.9   A mediaeval wedding (The Marriage of Louis de Blois and Marie de France in
      1360): Master of the Getty Froissart (Flemish, active about 1475–1485), Bruges,
      Belgium, about 1480–1483, Tempera colours, gold leaf, gold paint, and ink on
      parchment   140
3.1   Map of Algiers, 1602, engraving by Giovanni Orlandi (active 1590-ca 1613)   149
3.2   The Barbarossa brothers, Aruj (Oruç) (died 1518) and Kheir-ad-Din (Hayreddin)
      (died 1546), engraving, Dutch school, 17th century   150
3.3   Portrait of Emmanuel d'Aranda (anonymous artist, Brugge? 1642): collection
      Musea Brugge Groeningemuseum. Image in the public domain   168
3.4   Statue of Cervantes by Joan Vancell Puigcercós, 1892, in Madrid   181
3.5   Miguel de Cervantes Saved by the Fathers of the Redemption, 1580, colour
      engraving, French school   185
4.1   Muhammad XII's family in the Alhambra moments after the fall of Granada in
      1492, painting by Manuel Gómez-Moreno González, c. 1880: Salida de la familia
      de Boabdil de la Granada [The Family of Boabdil leaving Granada]. Image in
      the public domain   202
4.2   The Hall of the Abencerrajes, Alhambra, Granada, where according to tradition
      30 members of the Abencerrage clan were murdered. Painting by Leon Auguste
      Asselineau (1808–89)   210
4.3   Mateo Alemán Oil on canvas, by Manual Cabral y Aguado-Bejarano (1827–1891),
      Gallery of the University of Seville. Image in the public domain   217
4.4   Safiye Sultan, also known as Valide Sultan (1550–1618), artist unknown. Image in
      the public domain   245
5.1   Angelica Carving Medoro's Name on a Tree, fresco by Giovanni Battista Tiepolo
      (1757). Image in the public domain   264
5.2   An Algerian Ship off a Barbary Port, oil painting by the 17th century Flemish
      marine artist, Andries van Eertvelt   293
5.3   Portrait of an Unknown Woman, traditionally identified as Nell Gwyn (1650–
      1687), playing the original Almahide in Dryden's *Almanzor and Almahide*,
      Workshop of Sir Peter Lely. Image in the public domain   302
5.4   Edward Kynaston (c. 1640–1712), The first Boabdil in *Almanzor and Almahide, or,
      The Conquest of Granada*, by John Dryden. Image in the public domain   303
6.1   Illustration from *The Arabian Nights* by Dutch artist David Coster (1686–
      1752): Shahrazad tells her story to Shahryar, while her sister Dunyazad is
      listening. Image in the public domain   315
6.2   Flyleaves for Vol. 1 of the second edition (1729), of Samuel Croxall's *A Select
      Collection of Novels and Histories*   318
6.3   Poster for the film, *The Sheik*, 1921, showing Agnes Ayres, as Lady Diana
      Mayo   330

INTRODUCTION

Muslim–Christian Romance in Times of Captivity

Few things can be more terrifying for a free person than to be enslaved. If you were at sea, there would be the sudden shock of seeing a pirate vessel rapidly approaching; the mounting dread as the marauders reached and boarded your ship; and finally, the overwhelming horror, as it dawned on you that you were in those alien people's power. Alternatively, you might be sold as a slave or else be captured in war. Whichever way it happened, you would be wrenched from your friends, family and familiar surroundings, and carried off to face a completely unknown and unforeseeable future, probably in a foreign land. Many first- and second-hand accounts of such capture scenes testify to the rapidly changing emotions, and terror, of the victims. One characteristic account has come down to posterity from a Portuguese merchant, João Mascarenhas, delineating the terror and mounting horror experienced by someone newly-enslaved and waiting to learn their fate.[1] A parallel description is offered by Jean-François Regnard who, like Miguel de Cervantes was himself captured and enslaved by pirates, and drew on these events for his fictional *La Provençale*.

And yet, from these desperate circumstances, generations of storytellers in many diverse countries and cultures fashioned narratives in which the capture and enslavement, or existing slave status, of the victim became subordinated to a romance motif: the love that developed between the captive and another person encountered in the new environment. The language associated with literal captivity and slavery metamorphosed into a metaphorical system of relating the emotions of fictional protagonists.

Thus, over many centuries, the concept and metaphor of being 'a slave to love', or variants in other languages, became indispensable ingredients of romance, but also essential parts of the vocabulary, in many works of European and some non–European fiction, so that situation and parlance became fused: in poetry, prose and drama. Throughout this book I am trying to address this conundrum: how the horror of enslavement could be thus narratively transformed into entertaining romance.

A *topos*, or motif, became commonplace in literature, of romantic passion between two people, where one of them is literally a slave and the other is

---

1   Quoted by Robert C. Davis, *Christian Slaves, Muslim Masters*, 2003 (repr. Basingstoke, Hants. and New York: Palgrave Macmillan, 2004), 69.

not. A variant of this theme involves love between two captives, both attempting to become free. Frequently the slave/captive and his or her lover belong to different religions: usually Muslim and Christian, or it appears that their religions diverge. Both Christian and Muslim societies discouraged, or altogether forbade the enslavement of co-religionists, meaning that a slave, initially at least, would probably have a different faith from that of their captor. Frequently in European literature, the love interest is between a male slave, usually a Christian, and a technically free woman who may be betrothed or married to another man, often a Muslim, and thus subject to the strict Muslim restraints on women. In this sense, she too is represented as being, in effect, a captive. In various stories, slaves and especially slave women are integral to the plot, influencing one or more of the main protagonists.

Embedded in many of the stories is the ethno/religious hybridity of one or both of the protagonists: typically, a Muslim turns out to have been born of Christians; or to have secretly converted to Christianity before the events of the story; or to have mixed parentage (Muslim/Christian). The denouement generally involves either the consummation of such interfaith love, or the revelation that a supposed 'Muslim' is really a Christian. Where there is a genuine difference in religions, in European literature the Muslim almost invariably converts to Christianity. This is a reversal from some early Muslim works, in which the Christian converts to Islam.

Not all the episodes of enslavement occur through piracy but, invariably, the love affairs between Christians and Muslims take place against a backdrop of conflict. Historically, the two faiths confronted one another, and fought skirmishes and battles, on long and shifting frontiers in various parts of the Mediterranean world, as well as inland: in Armenia, for example, and, internally, in Spain. But they also traded, and shared cultures across borders which, though divisive, were also porous, allowing for the throughflow and exchange of goods, ideas, and people. Many of the works in this study are associated with actual border areas; and the narratives, as we shall explore, often reflected actual events, where Muslims and Christians not only clashed, but also intermarried extensively.

The idea that an individual venturing on the high seas, or even following his or her trade near the shore, could be captured and enslaved – as well as the possibility that this same person might be freed at any time – accorded with notions about rapid reversals of fate: the wheel of fortune turning, so recurrent in European literature and philosophy from ancient times onwards. A Spanish text, translated into English in 1651, observes:

> Hee [sic] that is once embarqued upon the Sea, and arrives happily to Shoare, is much bounden to his fortune; and he confideth in her too much, that putteth himselfe a second time upon that fearfull element. For my part, I thinke there is no greater proofe of courage, then [sic] to enterprise to passe a Gulf without necessity, or without thereto being incited by covetousnesse. Fortune bears sovereign sway over four things, which are, Marriages, great Mens Favourites, Warres, and Navigations. But according to the opinion of many, the last is the most perillous.[2]

This general observation acts as a preamble to an episode in which the Christian hero Don Fenise is shipwrecked and lands upon the Barbary shore, where he falls in love with an enslaved woman.

Religious and secular authorities on both sides, concerned about 'cultural hybridity and miscegenation', cautioned against interfaith matches.[3] But still the love affairs and marriages took place, and the stories continued to be told and written. And, since one of the principal ways in which individuals from the two religions could meet, apart from on the battlefield, was when affiliates of one faith were captured by forces of 'the other', in many narratives of love between people from warring nations, one or both of them becomes enslaved at some point. In some mediaeval literature, as well as in Cervantes and Regnard for example, we find captive Christian heroes encountering Muslim women who are effectively kept prisoner by incarceration in harems or other female quarters. Love affairs between these protagonists often follow. Later works draw heavily on such originals, for ideas, plot-lines, and characters, and all are saturated with the language (including metaphors) of captivity and notions of personal hybridity.

Many of these stories conform to stock romantic patterns in that the love interest is central; heroes and heroines are idealised, and there are few features to distinguish one from another: they are all handsome or beautiful, charming, brave and adventurous (women as well as men); and they experience strong emotions, including tender passion (both sexes), and rage (mostly the males). Certain standard themes and settings also recur: courtship in a beautiful garden; a heroine held captive in a tall tower;[4] disguises – including gentlemen

---

2 'Francisco de las Coveras' (i.e. Francisco de Quintana), *Experiencias de amor y fortuna*, tr. into English as *The History of Don Fenise*, 1651, 141.
3 Cf. Sergio La Porta, 'Conflicted Co-Existence: Christian-Muslim Interaction and Its Representation in Medieval Armenia', in Jerold C. Frakes, *Contextualizing the Muslim Other in Medieval Christian Discourse* (New York: Palgrave Macmillan, 2011), 103–123, 113 and passim.
4 See Appendices 1 and 2: Tower and Garden.

and women masquerading as slaves; and, especially, religious conversions. By the 17th century in France, and in some English literature of the period, the terminology of captivity and enslavement had become ossified into a series of linguistic flourishes. However, the pattern of romantic love between individuals from opposing camps, with the enslavement of one or more characters, had its roots in real events, and remained popular for long afterwards.

1   Slavery from Ancient Times Onwards, and Its Documentation

Slave-taking is an ancient practice and slavery is among the oldest of human conditions: references to it may be found in some of the first known writing, such as the Sumerian *Code of Ur-Nammu*, and the *Hammurabic Code*;[5] and so it seems reasonable to suppose the practice extended well back into prehistoric times. In the Mediterranean, piracy and the slavery associated with it were rampant long before the Islamic era.[6] Acquiring power over another individual holds out the attractive possibility of the 'owner' having to work less – or not at all – without any of the disadvantages of having to pay for the work or the slave's welfare: slaves could, if the 'owner' wished, be forced to subsist on minimal rations and in mean conditions. In addition, it could make desirable 'foreigners' sexually available: part of the attraction of sexual slavery is undoubtedly the power wielded over the slave by the 'owner', as well as the tantalising cultural 'difference' between slaver and enslaved.

Conflicts between neighbouring peoples were mostly about land, but also about who would do the hardest and most undesirable jobs such as construction, farm labour, and domestic work. One way to acquire a cheap and malleable labour force was to capture it and take it back to one's own territory: in the ancient world it was customary not only to kill but also to enslave members of defeated populations. Thus, for much of recorded history victorious armies would often destroy a town and seize its surviving inhabitants, killing some and carrying others home to serve as slaves.

Alternatively, one could buy slaves – but all slavery was ultimately underpinned by violence and/or the threat of violence. Such trade was therefore a regular by-product of warfare and to mutual advantage between otherwise

---

[5] *Encyclopaedia of the Social Sciences*, ed. Edwin R.A. Seligman, 15 vols. (New York: The Macmillan Company, 1930–1935, Reissued 1937), transcribed by Andrew Chrucky, March 23, 2004, for http://www.ditext.com/moral/slavery.html [accessed 9/2/2016].
[6] Cf. David Abulafia, *The Great Sea: A Human History of the Mediterranean*, 2011 (repr. London and other locations: Penguin Books, 2012), 194–96.

hostile nations – a practice which continues to this day regarding hostages and prisoners of war. Piracy, with its predilection for snaring individuals (especially those from unfriendly countries) and then selling them into slavery, was similarly widespread. Although slave populations and the slave trade had existed in both pre-Christian and pre-Islamic Arab societies since ancient times, the new religions did nothing to diminish these institutions.[7]

At some point, people began to associate certain kinds of emotional torment with physical slavery, and metaphors of slavery came easily to people living in slave-owning societies. Eventually, these concepts became divorced from the condition of servitude itself and were simply tropes, shorthand not only for conditions of extreme pain and misery, but also of love (or lust) in many cases referencing relationships in which one lover was perceived to hold power disproportionately over the other.

But, for now, let us consider situations in which conditions of literal enslavement mingle with descriptions of individuals 'enslaved' by love. The terms 'captive' and 'slave' when relating to someone who has been captured in, or taken to a hostile country, are here used interchangeably. For although not all captives laboured as slaves, all of them had the status of slaves unless and until they were ransomed or freed by some other means. Some scholars, such as William Phillips, have made a distinction between captives taken in warfare, who might be ransomed, or regain freedom via a prisoner exchange, or even by escaping, and other slaves whose conditions were more permanent.[8] But as far as I am concerned, to be in captivity in whatever circumstances, and however briefly, was to be, effectively, a slave; the captive had no agency or power whatsoever over his or her day-to-day life. Furthermore, he or she could be loaned out or given away, or traded or sold as chattel, at any time. In the Mediterranean, with which so much of this book is concerned, piracy and the kidnapping of individuals were not confined to Muslims: Christians too

---

7   Regarding ancient pre-Christian, early Imperial Christian (i.e. after the conversion of the Emperor Constantine to Christianity), and early Muslim practices, cf., for example, George Finlay, *Greece under the Romans: a Historical View of the Condition of the Greek Nation, from the Time of its Conquest by the Romans until the Extinction of the Roman empire in the East, B.C. 146-A.D. 717*, 2nd ed. (Edinburgh: William Blackwood and Sons, 1857), 8, 17, 39, 60, 94, 103, 105, 114, 183, 184, 241, 242, 246, 464, 475, and 495. For detailed accounts of rival policies and practices of enslavement of Christians and Muslims from the 8th century onwards, cf. George Finlay, *History of the Byzantine and Greek Empires, from DCCXVI to MCCCCLIII*, 1854, 2nd ed., Edinburgh and London: William Blackwood and Sons, 1856, vol I, 27, 65, 104, 106, 122, 130, 159, and 260–61; and vol. II, 317, 328–29, 346, 359–60, 366, 370, 381, 515, 521, 522, and 531.
8   William D. Phillips, *Slavery in Medieval and Early Modern Iberia* (Philadelphia, Pa.: University of Pennsylvania Press, 2014), 5–6, and passim.

were involved in seizing and enslaving Muslim adversaries.[9] Some argue that this was on a smaller scale.[10] Clissold states that, although both Christianity and Islam accepted slavery as an institution, it not only lasted longer but also 'loomed larger, in Muslim societies than in Christian Europe'.[11] More recently, it has been claimed that the numbers were approximately equal, and the two practices were intertwined.[12] Just as many Christians enslaved by Muslims converted to Islam, Muslim slaves of Christians often converted to Christianity.

Although the body of literature detailing experiences of Christians captured and enslaved by Muslims – and, particularly by Barbary pirates – is considerable, and includes both factual (mostly autobiographical) writing, and fiction, there is a dearth of personal accounts on the enslavement of Muslims. Where they do exist, in reports by Muslim travellers, traders, ambassadors and others who endured captivity by Christians, they are primarily factual, and contained within letters, biographical entries, official records and books, rather than existing as stand-alone narratives or stories. Some reports of captivity could be anecdotal, digressive, inaccurate, or even deliberately distorting; but they did not, on the whole take the form of captivity narratives, let alone fiction, in the European sense:

> this [Muslim captivity narrative] material does not belong to a distinct genre of writing with its distinct set of conventions, as in the European tradition, nor to a body of macro-historical documents and treatises: rather, it appears as subtexts, intrusions into larger polemics, hagiographies or histories and religious expositions.[13]

---

9   Cf e.g., Phillips, *Slavery in Medieval and Early Modern Iberia*, passim. And cf. Daniel Hershenzon, *The Captive Sea: Slavery, Communication, and Commerce in Early Modern Spain* (Philadelphia: University of Pennsylvania Press, 2018); Daniel Hershenzon, 'Towards a Connected History of Bondage in the Mediterranean: Recent Trends in The Field', *History Compass* 15 (2017): 1–13.

10 Cf. Linda Colley, *Captives: Britain, Empire and the World, 1600–1850* (London: Pimlico, 2003) 45–46; Robert C. Davis, *Holy War and Human Bondage: Tales of Christian-Muslim Slavery in the Early-Modern Mediterranean* (Santa Barbara, Calif. and Other Locations: Praeger/ABC-CLIO, 2009); Ellen Friedman, *Spanish Captives in North Africa in the Early Modern Age,* (Madison: University of Wisconsin Press, 1983), xviii; Gordon, 106.

11 Stephen Clissold, *The Barbary Slaves* (London: Elek, 1977), 7.

12 Hershenzon, *The Captive Sea*, 4, 18, and Hershenzon, 'Towards a Connected History', 1, 2, 4, 8.

13 Nabil Matar, 'Arab Views of Europeans, 1578–1727', in *Re-Orienting the Renaissance: Cultural Exchanges with the East*, ed. Gerald MacLean (Basingstoke, Hants. and New York: Palgrave Macmillan, 2005), 126–147, 140.

In most of this book therefore my focus will be on the enslavement of Christians and the literature deriving from it, rather than the enslavement of Muslims. But although Muslims rarely or never composed fantasies involving their own captivity in Christian lands, nevertheless, slaves – including Christian slaves – in Muslim territories appear as love objects in numerous lighter works by Muslims, especially early poetry, anecdotes, and stories such as those in *One Thousand and One Nights*, for example. Some of these inspire and inform later literature by Christians, as I shall show.

In Muslim–Christian romances of Europe, the possibility that a captured Christian woman might be taken into some Muslim ruler's harem added to the *frisson* of the oriental motif in general. Moreover, the European perception that Muslim women too, whether wives or concubines, were incarcerated in the harem, further blurred the line between slave and free, dignifying as it were, the state of slavery. This was to feed into the campaigns of European women for greater freedom in their own societies, with the concept of slavery being applied to the state of marriage in Europe from the 17th century onwards.

2   Slavery and Love

This book sets out to trace the impulses, historic, literary, and sometimes psychological, which gave rise to the motif and language of love involving slaves and, especially, love between a Muslim and a Christian 'other'. I shall focus primarily on love between people of these two faiths, with some mention of that between Muslims and Muslims or Christians and Christians in a Muslim setting, as witnessed and described by Christians.

One exception to this general rule is Aphra Behn's novel *Oroonoko* (1688), set partly in Africa, partly in North America: its slave–hero and heroine are both African. But the first part of the novel, nominally placed in 'Coromantien' (identified by subsequent commentators as a trading station on the Gold Coast – modern-day Ghana), owes much in the structure of the court it defines and its descriptive detail to 'Moorish' or Middle Eastern fictional antecedents.[14] Joanna Lipking says the king 'acts like an autocrat in an Oriental tale'.[15] Janet Todd makes the 'Oriental' connection more obliquely, saying Oroonoko's language is best suited for the theatre and a court 'where the king aspired to

---

14   Cf. Christopher F. Loar, *Political Magic: British Fictions of Savagery and Sovereignty 1650–1750* (New York: Fordham University Press, 2014), 256, Note 47.
15   *Oroonoko* (New York and London: W.W. Norton and Co [a Norton Critical Edition], ed. Joanna Lipking, 1997), xiii.

absolute distinction from his subjects – the sort of court which the Restoration fantasised in tales of Turkish sultans.'[16] And Behn, like others speaking of Afro–diasporan people from Shakespeare onwards, refers to her hero as a 'Moor'.

In this book I will also suggest that the power of the trope, 'a slave to love', which recurred to the extent that it long ago became a cliché, may first have resided in the sexual excitement created by the idea of love and passion between slave and non-slave (occasionally also between two slaves) in the original material. The erotic appeal of such situations generally lies precisely in the imbalance of power: the control over life and limb which the 'owner' has over the enslaved person acting as a potent aphrodisiac, potentially on the one being controlled, as well as the one in control.[17] I shall argue that the theme of slavery, used in this erotic fashion in the English novel and play, derives from French sources and/or influences and these in turn were informed by a Spanish literary genre, which Maria Soleded Carrasco-Urgoiti identified as the 'Moorish Novel',[18] but which also gave rise to poetry and plays on Andalusi and Islamic themes. European literature, including that of Spain, was in turn influenced by Arab material, which itself drew upon earlier Greek stories. As Melitzki notes, 'Wherever we find it in medieval literature, the marriage of Christian and Saracen as a literary theme seems to be Arabo-Byzantine in origin and relates in particular to events in Asia Minor, the location of Christian provinces nearest to the Muslim frontier'.[19]

In Greek and Roman literature we already find most of the themes and motifs discussed in this book: shipwrecks and piracy; the capture and enslavement of formerly free people; love between a free person (usually in classical times a man) and a (usually female) slave, even – in the drama – love between people of different ethno–cultural origins (although in the romances lovers are 'the same', rather than 'different'); and the etymological entanglement of literal and metaphorical slavery: the motif of the 'slave to love'. Only the religious aspect, central to later literature, is absent. Greek romances, or novellas,

---

16   Janet Todd, *The Secret Life of Aphra Behn* (London: Andre Deutsch Ltd., 1996), 418.
17   The phenomenal success of E.L. James's novel, *Fifty Shades of Grey* (2011), with its sado-masochistic, dominant/submissive relationship between the two main characters, and its scenes of bondage, corporal punishment and humiliation, demonstrates the enduring appeal of such scenarios. It sold more than 100,000 copies in the first week after its publication, and quickly topped the best-seller lists. The film of it was also an immediate success, earning more than $571 million worldwide.
18   María Soledad Carrasco-Urgoiti, *The Moorish Novel*: 'El Abencerraje' *and* 'Pérez de Hita' (Boston: Twayne Publishers, 1976).
19   Cf. Dorothee Melitzki, *The Matter of Araby in Medieval England* (New Haven and London: Yale University Press, 1977), 137.

long unknown or considered irrelevant were, like the plays, 'rediscovered' during the European Renaissance. Arabs encountered the romances when they conquered Byzantine lands, such as Syria, where these stories were told. The Arabs then conveyed them, along with much other material from the Greco–Roman classical world, to Christians with whom they came into contact. An incidental but pertinent aim of this book is to demonstrate the transference of literary themes and concepts from culture to culture and language to language. For Christian writing, seminal texts in this regard are *Nights* tales, whose structures, plots and norms underlie so many European romances.[20]

Another of my aims is to explore the idea of the Muslim in Christian fiction, usually a woman, not as 'equal' in the modern sense, but as an emotional peer to the European man who comes to love her, his 'other', who is also his spiritual kin, despite her 'alien' origins; and, similarly, the man is spiritual kin to the woman. It is characteristic in works of mediaeval literature, as is acknowledged by Mohja Kahf (who is otherwise deeply critical of Christian fictional treatments of Muslim women),[21] but in later works as well, even into the 19th century. As I argue in Chapters 2 and 4, Muslims and Christians in Andalucia and the Middle East were often quite similar to one another ethnically, especially in the upper echelons of Muslim society, due to substantial intermarrying and also widespread concubinage of women from communities defeated in battle, or 'purchased' as slaves. A precedent had been set by the Prophet Muhammad, several of whose wives were from other religions, and both Umayyad and Abbasid rulers married captive Christian women. Among them was Abd-al-Aziz ibn Musa, Muslim son of the powerful general Mūsá bin Nuṣayr, and himself first Governor of Muslim al-Andalus, who married Egilon or Egilona, widow of the last Visigoth (Christian) king of Spain after the Muslim conquest. Muslims, including captives, were often appropriated by, and sometimes married to Christians, including members of the nobility. Dadson argues persuasively that many Moriscos *did* assimilate and some made their way into the upper echelons of Christian society, partly through intermarriage with Christians. Recent scholarship has shown a significant genetic inheritance from North Africa among modern-day Spaniards.[22]

---

20   Cf. Peter Heath, 'Romance as Genre in *One Thousand and One Nights*', in *Journal of Arabic Literature* 18 (1987), 1–21, and 19 (1988), 3–26; repr. in *The Arabian Nights Reader, ed.* Ulrich Marzolph (Detroit, Mich.: Wayne State University Press, 2006), 170–225.

21   Mohja Kahf, *Western Representations of the Muslim Woman: from Termagant to Odalisque* (Austin: University of Texas Press, 1999), 5.

22   Trevor J. Dadson, 'The Assimilation of Spain's Moriscos: Fiction or Reality?' in the *Journal of Levantine Studies*, Vol. 1, No. 2, (Winter 2011), 11–30.

In addition, one aspect of the long co-existence of Muslims and Christians in Spain was a well-documented merging of their two cultures. Shared tastes developed: in food, costume, and cultural preferences more generally; and much of the Spanish language is infused with Arabic terms and forms, an obvious example being the number of Spanish words that begin with 'al', the definite article in Arabic. Significantly, the Catholic Queen Isabella wore Andalusi Arab dress when she rode into Granada to take possession of the city. This reflected her desire to minimise the alarm felt by the newly conquered people, but was also an expression of her own taste: a convenient fusion of expediency and inclination. However, Muslims too, often adopted Christian styles.[23]

This ethno/cultural affinity is a fact that underlies all texts, which from time to time is made manifest. In *Floire et Blanchefleur* (Chapter 2) for example, the lovers – one Christian, one Muslim – are described as being so similar physically that they are mistaken for siblings. In other texts, such as *la Historia del cautivo* (*The Captive's Tale*) of Cervantes (Chapter 4), the ostensibly Muslim woman has converted to Christianity before the story begins. In the *Guerras civiles de Granada* (*Civil Wars of Granada*) too, the queen of Granada has been predisposed to convert, under the influence of a Christian slave of her father's, although her actual conversion occurs only at the end of the story. Thematically, in both these Spanish works, the Christian slave is an instrument whereby the confined ('enslaved') Muslim woman is enabled to find spiritual freedom through conversion to Christianity.

Thus, these stories, while trading on the exotic and erotic appeal of ostensible 'difference', actually re-unite people who are essentially 'the same': a case of 'difference' masking an innate similarity, or what might be termed *simpatía*: the instinctive recognition of a kindred spirit. Here it may be helpful to refer to Plato's *Symposium*, in which the playwright Aristophanes speaks of the human condition as a state in which each individual is half of a whole that had been split in ancient times, resulting in the two halves becoming separated from one another. The two parts are mutually complementary: different from one another, but together forming a perfect whole. Each person is driven to seek his or her lost 'half' so as, by unifying with it, to feel complete again. This is the quest for love and the discovery of, and bonding with, the 'other' represents finding true love and 'wholeness'.

The idea of an unceasing search for one's 'other half' is a major theme of Western literature. This book is written partly with Plato's parable in mind, but

---

[23] María Soledad Carrasco-Urgoiti, *The Moorish Novel*; Barbara Fuchs, *Exotic Nation: Maurophilia and the Construction of Early Modern Spain* (Philadelphia, Pa.: University of Pennsylvania Press, 2009).

defining the 'other' as differing in religion, culture, and nationality: Muslim and Christian, as well as gender. The two meet, or become 'one', in the context of one or both of them becoming slaves. The denouement occurs when both lovers are once again free and able to marry and live together. But they can only truly become 'one' when they share the same religion, meaning that one of the lovers must convert, or have previously converted, to the faith of the other.

Conventionally, in these stories, conversion usually means converting to the faith of the dominant partner, who is usually the man. This reveals a tacit and less felicitous aspect of the conversion motif: it is symbolic of masculine as well as military and cultural victory, actual or imagined, achieved by the converter's people over those of the converted; in this sense, it represents a spiritual extension of Muslim-Christian warfare: the battle for souls. Historically, victorious armies often forced those whom they had conquered to convert to their own religion. When, in the stories, the converter is the man and the converted individual a woman, there is a double assertion of power: of Christian over Muslim, or vice versa, and of man over woman; the woman's transplantation into a foreign culture will also subject her to new forms of oppression with patriarchal power and influence doubly confirmed. However, in my view, this does not negate ideas of spiritual affinity and 'kinship' between Christian lover and Muslim beloved; rather, it qualifies them, setting them in the contexts of the relevant times and places.

For the purpose of this discussion, I have divided works incorporating themes of captivity and romance into two major categories: captivity with the loss of, search for and eventually, discovery of the beloved who is 'the same' as the seeker, in terms of culture, social standing and, most importantly, religious faith; and that leading to romance with an individual who, on the face of it at least, is 'other' to the seeker. Into the first category fall the Greek romances and most Greek and Latin plays which deal with such themes. Some of the key concepts and terminology in 'slavery and romance' stories originate from the Greek novellas of the 1st-3rd century CE, as well as in ancient Greek and Roman plays. We already find lovers separated, captured by pirates and enslaved in works such as Chariton's *Chaereas and Callirrhoe* (1st or 2nd century CE), and the *Aethiopica* or *Ethiopian History* of Heliodorus of Emesa, also known as *Theagenes and Chariclea* (3rd century CE), for example.

However, religion, if mentioned at all in these texts, is generally only an incidental factor, as when the Oracle at Delphi is consulted, or some god is invoked. Also, in these novellas, rarely is there any ethnic or other 'difference' between the two lovers. Notably, Chariclea's skin colour – white, like that of Theagenes, and unlike that of her Ethiopian parents – is critical to the plotline of the *Aethiopica*, as is her Greek upbringing. The conclusion, in which the lovers are happily reunited, represents the bringing back together of two free people who are essentially the 'same'. In contrast, Roman comedy often features love affairs between free men and slaves, who may sometimes be explicitly signified as 'foreign', but this aspect is not generally important to the action or its outcome and religious difference is not a factor.

European novels and plays about mixed-faith romances involve both patterns of relationship, i.e. same faith/culture and different faith/culture. But where a Muslim man loves a Christian woman, his suit is usually doomed to failure and is often mocked by the author. The romantic plot, in which the lovers' union is destined to succeed, typically involves a Muslim woman and a Christian man. But as in Islamic societies sexual relations between Christian men and Muslim women were strictly forbidden, with harsh penalties prescribed for offenders of both sexes, extreme elements of risk and danger are added to many plots, inviting scenes of life-or-death situations.

Finally, in much of European drama where union is with the 'other', as with the 'Oriental' Medea, or in *Othello* for example, the result is tragedy. Since I am here concerned primarily with works where the union is, seemingly at any rate, a happy one, such tragic outcomes do not generally come into my scheme, except where references to such resolutions are useful.

3 Early Islamic Perspectives (Chapter 1)

With the advent of Islam, the matter of religion becomes central and part of the attraction between people from different faiths lies precisely in the perceived 'otherness' of the beloved. In Chapter 1, I examine some of the earliest Islamic writings, and specifically the Qur'an, for the attitudes expressed therein toward the institution of slavery, as well as some Arab and Persian poetry. The Qur'an, like the Biblical Old and New Testaments, assumes the existence of slavery. It regulates the practice of the institution and thus implicitly accepts it. The Prophet Muhammad and his Companions who could afford it themselves owned slaves; some of them, including the Prophet, acquired more by conquest.[24]

---

[24] Bernard Lewis, *Race and Slavery in the Middle East: An Historical Enquiry* (New York and Oxford: Oxford University Press, 1990), Chapter 1, 5. Cf. also, Hend Gilli-Elewy, 'On the Provenance of Slaves in Mecca during the Time of the Prophet Muhammad', *International Journal of Middle East Studies* 49 (2017), 164–68: https://www.cambridge.org/core/journals/international-journal-of-middle-east-studies/article/on-the-provenance-of-slaves-in-mecca-during-the-time-of-the-prophet-muhammad/B11A052F86EF0061AD9DF

Slavery could generally only arise from three circumstances: (1) being born to slave parents; (2) being sold into slavery by one's compatriots, which could even include one's own parents; or (3) being captured in war, or through a raid. The latter prescription soon became restricted to infidels captured in a jihad. Slaves came mainly from remote places because, 'though a free Muslim could not be enslaved, conversion to Islam by a non-Muslim slave did not require his liberation. His slave status was not affected by his new faith, nor was that of a Muslim child born to slave parents'.[25] This meant that, by definition, large numbers of slaves would be of foreign origin and many would be Christians.

One critical difference frequently occurs between Muslim and Christian texts: although both tend to be set in Muslim countries with Christian slaves being subservient to Muslim 'owners', in Muslim texts, the 'slave' is usually a woman who, in becoming a Muslim, converts to the dominant culture of the land in which she resides. In Christian texts however, the slave is often a man who, escaping from his captors, also removes the beloved woman from Muslim society and takes her to a Christian country. Thereafter, as in Muslim texts, the woman converts to the faith of the dominant male, in this case a Christian.

In this chapter also, I consider another variant to my general scheme: the Persian *Yusuf and Zulaikha* in which, because it is set in Biblical times, there is no possibility of a reference to Islam, but it is the product of a Muslim author and his society, and remains to this day popular in a number of Muslim countries, being re-told in languages including Arabic, Urdu, Kashmiri, Bengali, and Turkish. Moreover, the differences in nationality, culture and class between the protagonists (he is Hebrew and a slave, while she is the wife of a high-ranking Egyptian) are explicit and contribute to the erotic charge of the story, however else it may be interpreted.[26]

Chapter 1 ends with discussions of some early Muslim texts, predominantly tales from *One Thousand and One Nights*, with an outcome involving Christians converting to Islam. Since these are almost certainly earlier than the Christian texts surveyed, I assume that the latter may well have been influenced by the

---

E4C0EB4F5E0 [accessed 16/5/2024], 164; BBC, 'Muhammad and Slavery', *Slavery in Islam*, online, 7/9/2009: https://www.bbc.co.uk/religion/religions/islam/history/slavery_1.shtml [accessed 16/5/2024]. One hadith of Sahih al-Bukhari refers to a specific slave of the Prophet: https://sunnah.com/bukhari:7263 [accessed 23/5/2024].

25   Lewis, *Race and Slavery*, 9.
26   Even though Joseph's story is set in pre-Islamic times, there is a sura of the Qur'an devoted to it, and *Yusuf and Zulaikha* has been the subject of an enormous amount of religious exegesis and academic scholarship, interpreting its significance for Islam in general and Sufism in particular. The Qur'an explicitly states that Joseph was not a Jew, but in *Yusuf and Zulaikha* he is identified as a Hebrew.

Muslim texts. There is now ample scholarship to suggest that some of the *Nights,* at least, were well-known in Europe centuries before Antoine Galland's seminal translations of 1704–17. Gould speculates that during the Middle Ages the 'Oriental Tale' reached Scandinavia and other European countries via warfare in Islamic Spain (232); as well as travel, and in pursuit of trade with Arabs and Persians in Eastern Europe and Asia; and study under the aegis of Arab scholars, the fruits of which were then widely disseminated throughout Europe (246–50).[27] A reference to *Alf Layla wa Layla* is contained in a notebook found in the Cairo Genizah, from roughly 1150 CE.[28] Given the contacts among Jews across many national boundaries, the stories may well have travelled from Cairo to Europe.

4 Mediaeval Christian Romances (Chapter 2)

Some of the earliest Christian stories derive from the borderlands between Christendom and Islam: expansionist early Islam confronting Byzantine Christianity in the eastern Mediterranean and, overlapping with this chronologically, the protracted Muslim-Christian encounter and warfare in Spain. These works relate to the period from the 7th to the 12th centuries CE and human interactions between individuals of the two sides. The chapter begins with *Digenes Akritas* (10th-11th century CE?), one of the earliest Christian treatments of love, slavery and religious conversion, set in what is today Armenia. The epics of this region would merit a separate study; I have touched on them because of the light they shed on cross-border religious and erotic encounters. The title *Digenes Akritas* covers diverse writings, celebrating in verse or prose, the life and deeds of a hero whose name alludes to his mixed parentage: a Christian mother and an Arab father who converted from Islam to Christianity for love.[29] Religious conversion themes recur, both in *Digenes*'s own search for love and in some sub-plots of the story involving other characters.

In a very different spirit are the French romances which happily match Christian hero/ines with a Muslim 'other'. They include the 12th century *Floire*

---

27 Chester Nathan Gould, 'The *friðþjófssaga* an Oriental Tale', in *Scandinavian Studies and Notes*, vol. VII, No. 8, ed. A.M. Sturtevant (August 1923), 219–50.

28 Jonathan Decter, *Iberian Jewish Literature: Between al-Andalus and Christian Europe* (Bloomington and Indianapolis: Indiana University Press, 2007), 113.

29 Digenes Akrites is loosely translated as 'Twyborn the Borderer' (by John Mavrogordato); the 'Two-Blood Border Lord' (Denison B. Hull); or the 'man of double descent' (Elizabeth Jeffries).

et Blanchefleur and 12th–13th century *Aucassin et Nicolette* (themselves possibly originating in Muslim sources). These are followed by discussions of several French *chansons de geste*, beginning with the seminal 11th-12th century *Chanson de Roland* and works based on it, including English romances derived from or modelled on the French. The intrusion into the *gestes*, which are essentially chronicles of bloodshed and slaughter inflicted mutually by Muslims and Christians, of themes involving love across religious and cultural boundaries is striking. William Comfort notes that the '*matière de Bretagne*', meaning romances of King Arthur and the knights of the Round Table, always remained distinct from the *matière de France:* the *Chanson de Roland* and other *chansons de geste:*

> Yet the demand for romance was insistent. How should the conservative school of poets, who prided themselves upon dealing with a situation which they claimed as true and historical, respond to the new literary demand? ... One course lay open: to take the Saracens, ready to hand, and infuse a strong dose of romance into the personal relations of Christian and Saracen.[30]

Comfort then notes the similarities which mediaeval authors perceived between Muslims and Christians. European opinion was immensely (perhaps wilfully) ignorant about Islam, believing it to consist in the worship of devils and assorted idols. However, Europeans were also obsessed with the necessity to convert their opponents to their own faith. Once converted, the former Muslims could take their place in Christian society and marry Christian women. Barring the question of faith, 'a Saracen knight was as good as a Christian knight'.[31] The convert then usually became a devotee of his new faith, zealously participating in the slaughter of former co-religionists. Such converts may be female as well as male. Enter the character of the 'enamored [sic] Saracen princess' who converts because she is sick with love for a Christian, and who then becomes a fighter for Christianity.[32] Such women appear in no fewer than seventeen *chansons de geste*.[33] Comfort remarks, 'To have merely

---

[30] William Wistar Comfort, 'The Saracens in Christian Poetry', in *Dublin Review,* Vol. CXLIX, No. 298 (July and October 1911), 23–48, 29.

[31] Comfort, 'Saracens', 31.

[32] Melitzki, 129, 169–75; Remke Kruk, *The Warrior Women of Islam: Female Empowerment in Arabic Popular Literature* (London and New York: I.B. Tauris, 2014), passim.

[33] Lynne Tarte Ramsey, *Christian, Saracen and Genre in Medieval French Literature* (New York and London: Routledge, 2001), 39.

mentioned the existence of this charming type is to indicate the invasion of epic poetry by romance'.[34]

5 Lived Experience of Slavery in North Africa and the Mediterranean: Development of the Mediterranean Slave Trade (Chapter 3)

Although the Mediterranean slave trade dates back to ancient times, so far as most Europeans were concerned, its effects were sporadic until the 16th century. However, with the exodus of the Muslims (Moriscos) from Spain, beginning in 1492, this situation changed. Many of the émigrés made their way to North Africa where, aided by their local knowledge of European and especially Spanish coastal areas, and spurred on by a desire for revenge, they fostered a thriving trade of piracy in the Mediterranean, thus turning the enslavement of Europeans, especially Catholics, into a lucrative business.

This trade, on which several North African states were to depend for several centuries, represented a transformation of hostilities between Muslims and Christians, from open confrontation to battles of wits and guns, where European nations, Spain in particular, faced lightning raids on their coastal villages and towns, as well as on shipping in the Mediterranean and other seas. These episodes resulted in the capture and enslavement of large numbers of Europeans, who were then transported to slave states bordering the Mediterranean, as well as Ottoman Turkey.

Chapter 3 depicts the institution of slavery in Islamic lands, so far as it is known from factual sources: so much has been written about slavery in Islamic communities that it is often difficult to disentangle fact from fiction. Much of what passes for 'evidence' about the conditions of slaves is fabricated. Even the plays and novels of Cervantes, for example, while clearly informed by his personal experiences as a slave in Algiers for five years (1575–80) must be treated as fictitious, as he left no factual account of those experiences. Nevertheless, fictions have sometimes been misdiagnosed as factual narratives. As an example, Baepler points out in his introduction to the 'History of the Captivity and Sufferings of Mrs Maria Martin' (1807) that the piece, which he describes as her 'gruesome account of her captivity in an Algerian dungeon', is actually fiction masquerading as fact, itself based on another fiction by one Mary Velnet. Martin's account was nevertheless a great success and ran to many editions.[35]

---

34 Comfort, 'Saracens', 38.
35 *White Slaves, African Masters: American Barbary Captivity Narratives,* ed. Paul Baepler (Chicago: University of Chicago Press, 1999), 147.

INTRODUCTION

Moreover, even accounts by freed slaves and their advocates, including priests sent to ransom them and political emissaries which are now generally accepted as authentic, may have been embellished to provoke sympathy from readers, encourage generous donations to fund the redemption of other captives, exonerate the slaves' actions while in captivity (for example, accepting conversion to Islam), for entertainment, or for other reasons.

In discussing the evidence, I have tried to separate fact from fiction, mostly relying on modern scholars' findings from historic documents, letters, and other such artefacts and examining the autobiographical narratives of individuals known to have visited Islamic lands themselves. I consider the fictional accounts separately. However, even apparently factual accounts, such as those of Laugier de Tassy and John Morgan (early 18th century), contain material evidently based on hearsay and gossip. Such accounts – including rumours, legends and myths told to the traveller, or the slave, by people encountered in the slave country – have clear hallmarks of invention and point toward contemporary and subsequent fiction.

North African societies were highly mixed, ethnically and culturally, with Berbers, Arabs, Turks and formerly European renegades dwelling side by side, in addition to the slaves of various origins and occupying various social strata. Most Europeans were unaware of these multiple and often subtle distinctions, and in the resulting literature of this period and later, the terms 'Barbary', 'Algerian', 'Muslim' (and its variants, such as 'Mussulman', Mohammedan, etc.), 'Moor' and 'Turk' are used indiscriminately and often interchangeably in relation to individuals from the North African states.

Sexual relations between Muslim men and captive Christian women were considered normal: Gordon goes so far as to say that,

> The most common and enduring purpose for acquiring slaves in the Arab world was to exploit them for sexual purposes. Islamic law conferred upon the owner of slaves full control over their sexual and reproductive functions, as well as the fruits of their labor. He had fairly complete access to his female slaves and kept for his own kinship group the children he sired with them. These women were nothing less than sexual objects.[36]

References to unions between Muslim men and Christian women abound, often with significant consequences. The feared and celebrated corsair known

---

36 Murray Gordon, *Slavery in the Arab World* (New York: New Amsterdam Press, 1989), 79. There is also copious documentation of male captives, especially young boys, being used for sex, but this is an aspect beyond the scope of the current study.

as Barbarossa (Khair, or Kheir ad-Din), a Greek renegade who became ruler of Algiers (1518–1533), was rumoured to have had a Turkish father and a Christian mother.[37] One legend concerning the fall of Granada to the Catholics relates how its ageing King Muley-Hacén deserted his Muslim wife Aixa for a Castilian (Christian) woman captive. The king's wife retaliated by turning his son Boabdil against him, as well as gaining the support of one of Granada's leading clans – the Abencerrajes. Muley-Hacén was deposed, but the civil strife engendered by these events proved fatally weakening to the whole kingdom. In other words, the kingdom was lost for love – and the love of a slave at that.[38]

6 Slavery and Romance in 16th–17th Century Novels and Plays of Spain (Chapter 4)

In Chapter 4 we come to the 'Moorish' novel and its descendants, tales of the Muslim-Christian frontier in Spain. The earliest of these, including *El Abencerraje* (1561–65) and *Ozmín y Daraja* (1599) feature pairs of Muslim lovers encountering noble Christians; in each story, one of the Muslims is made captive by a Christian. While both stories are set in al-Andalus (Andalucia), the action of *Ozmín y Daraja*, unlike its predecessor *El Abencerraje*, takes place in the period immediately after the conquest of Granada, which completed the process of the *reconquista*, the re-Christianisation of Spain. The emphasis in both these pieces is on the faultlessly chivalrous behaviour of the Christians; in the former, the Muslims are exemplary too. However, in *Ozmín y Daraja* the Christians behave nobly, but the Muslim *Ozmín* is less gallantly depicted. When eventually both lovers convert to Christianity, it is under duress, rather than being inspired by love. This less idealistic portrayal of the Muslim lovers reflects changing circumstances in Spain, with tensions and mutual suspicions rising between Christians and the subjugated remaining Moriscos.

With the *Guerras civiles de Granada* (*Civil Wars of Granada*) (1599) by Pérez de Hita, we are given fictionalised access to events inside Granada in the days leading up to its surrender to the Christian monarchs in 1492. Inhabitants of the doomed city live a sort of *carpe diem* existence, with a courtly veneer thinly veiling bitter feuding. These divisions again reflect a wider historical reality in which Andalusi Muslims steadily lost ground because of schisms and rivalries in their ranks. Meanwhile the Christians succeeded in overcoming their

---

[37] Stephen Clissold, *The Barbary Slaves* (London: Elek, 1977), 22.
[38] Carrasco-Urgoiti, *The Moorish Novel*, 27.

INTRODUCTION

own past differences to launch a coordinated, religiously motivated campaign to conquer the remaining Muslim territories: the marriage of Ferdinand of Aragon to Isabella of Castile laid the groundwork for what would become a unified imperial Spain.

Chapter 4 continues with a study of works by Miguel de Cervantes. I show the transition that takes place between two plays set in Algiers, one written at the start of his career, *El trato de Argel* (1582?), the other, *Los baños de Argel*, published toward its end (in 1615, but probably written some time before that). The horror which overshadows much of the first play has become muted in the second. More importantly, whereas in the first play the love of Muslim for Christian is mocked, with the denouement bringing Christian lovers together, in the second, Muslim and Christian are united, although the Muslim heroine Zahara is revealed to have been a long-time Christian. The religious conversion theme, present also in *la Historia del cautivo* (*The Captive's Tale*, a short story intercalated in *Don Quixote*) has become prominent. In Cervantes's *La Gran sultana Doña Catalina de Oviedo* (published 1615), the Christian heroine marries the Ottoman Sultan. Bucking historical and literary patterns, she is able to retain her Christian faith right up to the psychologically ambiguous ending.

7   Slavery and Romance in 16th–17th Century Literature of England and France (Chapter 5)

Chapter 5 begins with a study of some Renaissance English literature, continues with literature of 17th century France and ends with drama and non-dramatic prose of the English Restoration period. The reason for this sequence is chronological: I wanted to address some slavery and romance works of the 16th and early 17th centuries (i.e. pre-Civil-War period) in England, as well as those of the Restoration period. But the latter were strongly influenced by works published in France during the intervening years.

In the early part of the chapter, I foreground two plays by Robert Greene, *Orlando Furioso* (1589–94), which looks back to the 'Matter of France'; and *The Comicall Historie of Alphonsus, King of Aragon* (1599), set in historical Spain. These plays are remarkable in that both end with Muslim-Christian unions that do not involve religious conversion on either side, a phenomenon rarely seen in European literature of the period. Philip Massinger's *The Renegado* (licensed 1624, published 1630) draws on Cervantine material, and possibly also *One Thousand and One Nights,* for a play set in Tunis.

Following this section, I look at the impact of Spanish, specifically 'Moorish', literature on the French and then the English. With French novels of the 17th century, Islamic settings and themes employed by the *précieuses* and others have become vehicles for elaborate constructions of language and plot in which captivity and slavery themes are exploited for their titillating power. In works such as *Almahide* (1660–63), and Sébastien de Brémond's *L'amoureux Africain, ou, Nouvelle galanterie* (1676), and *L'heureux esclave* (1677), as well as some English translations and works inspired by them, pain mingles with pleasure: at times the two are fused in works that barely conceal a sado-masochistic impulse.

Although English writing adopts many of the conventions of French novels, it is influenced too by neo-classical trends (including the plays of Corneille and Racine). With Dryden's two-part drama, *The Conquest of Granada* (1670 and 1671) in particular, the emphasis shifts to conflicts between love and duty, while romance themes of Muslim-Christian attraction remain. The centrepiece is the fatal clash between the two leading Granadine clans, the Abencerrajes and the Zegries.

The chapter ends with brief surveys of some other post-Restoration texts, including Aphra Behn's *Oroonoko: or, The Royal Slave* (1688) and its reworking in 1696 as a play by Thomas Southerne, which converts her story of love between two Africans into one of love across racial and cultural boundaries.

8   The 18th Century and Beyond; and Conclusion (Chapter 6)

Chapter 6 begins by noting the impact of Antoine Galland's translations of *One Thousand and One Nights*, from 1704–17, on the literature of the 18th century onwards, with a focus on England. Multiple editions of Samuel Croxall's *A Select Collection of Novels and Histories* (1722) attest to the enduring popularity of captivity and romance stories, with which the collection is replete, while George Colman the Younger's musical drama *The Mountaineers* (1793) capitalises on the appeal of Spanish captivity literature, especially that of Cervantes. His opera *Inkle and Yarico* (1787) turns a tragic short story from the 17th century, about greed and betrayal in a mixed-race relationship, into a full re-telling, with many embellishments and a happy ending.

The 19th century sees the survival of 'Turkish' and 'Moorish' literature, made tragic in the hands of Lord Byron and François-René de Chateaubriand. Byron's *The Giaour* (1812–13), *The Bride of Abydos* (1813), *The Corsair* (1814), and *The Siege of Corinth* (1816) all draw on traditional Muslim-Christian romance material, but eschew any romantic 'happy endings'. Chateaubriand's *Les aventures du dernier Abencerraje* (*The Last of the Abencerrajes*), written in 1810 and published in 1826, looks back to *El Abencerraje* and other Spanish stories to fashion a new plot, but one in which the love between its Muslim hero and Christian heroine is destined to remain unfulfilled. In a traditional mode, but with a 'romantic' sensibility and happier outcome, is *The Beautiful African; Or, Love and Slavery: An Interesting Tale*, (1805) by Ann Lemoine; while Washington Irving's *Tales of the Alhambra* (1829), also products of romanticism, are narrated anecdotally and accompanied by the author's philosophical musings.

8.1 Gender-Role Reversal and the Lure of the Desert: Genteel Heroines and Commanding Arab Heroes

At the end of the 19th century a new type of literature emerges, especially in the United States, in which the predominant gender assignments of earlier centuries are reversed. Instead of the enslaved Christian man 'conquering' a Muslim woman, freeing himself and assimilating her into his own culture, we now encounter armies of Christian (or 'Christian') 'white' women encountering darker-skinned, Muslim men and 'taming' their attractive but dangerous wildness to assimilate them into western manners and mores. Typically, the woman is physically captured ('enslaved') by the man, while he is psychologically captivated by her. At first, she resists his advances but at last she succumbs, and the narratives end with the two happily united. An early example, based on the novel, *The Sheik* [sic] (1919) by the Anglo-American writer E.M. Hull, was re-incarnated in 1921 as a seminal Hollywood film with the same title, starring Rudolph Valentino. These books, especially the most recent ones, also tend to be written by women and many are set in the past, and incorporate salacious elements. I examine some of the impulses which serve to render this escapist fiction immensely popular, creating mass markets into the present day. The chapter then looks ahead to the continuation of the Muslim-Christian romance motif into the 21st century and the enduring appeal of captivity and exogamy themes.

Finally, in my Conclusion, I engage in a broader analysis of some of the psychological impulses underlying the works more generally. I consider the complex and often conflicting drives of authors who recognised the existence of kinship between apparently disparate peoples, and yet were in thrall to political, religious and sometimes misogynistic imperatives requiring an explicit display of the hegemony of their own culture and gender. The attraction of opposites and yearning for equality and 'wholeness' through union with the Platonic 'other', represented by individuals from a different faith and the opposite sex, were tempered by an inability to escape the normative constraints of the authors' own cultures: the drive for conquest and the assertion of their own cultural and gender superiority.

Increasingly, literary critics and historians are exploring the complexity of both historic events and attitudes, as well as in literary treatments involving Christians and Muslims. While hostility was indisputably present, palpable and sustained bouts of warfare were coeval with friendlier exchanges which included diplomacy, trade and intermarriage, the recognition of which gives rise to a more nuanced view of Muslim-Christian relations than has often been the case in the past. Discussing such changes from the perspective of mediaeval Christianity, Frakes speaks of a 'multiplicity of ... discourses' regarding 'the Muslim Other' – rather than a 'monolithic anti-Muslim diatribe'.[39]

Hugh Goddard has encapsulated the dual, and often conflicted, attitudes pertaining between Christians and Muslims over time. He contrasts the hostility between adherents of the two faiths, epitomised and most extremely represented by the Crusades, with English people travelling as guests in Muslim lands and appealing to Muslims 'as supplicants' for trading privileges.[40] I suggest that the same kind of conflicted duality is expressed in most of the stories surveyed in this book, occurring simultaneously in both authors and players. Thus, the discourse of conversion is narrated and mediated through the medium of love for the captive, and captivating, 'other'.

9   A Caveat

In the 21st century we are becoming increasingly sensitive to the misogyny and exploitation that motivate and underlie so many of the exchanges between men and women. High-profile court cases and the 'Me-Too' movement have exposed the enormous extent to which many women have, historically, suffered abuse at the hands of men, especially those in positions of power. Captive women in particular, have been routinely subject to sexual exploitation, as scholars such as Montefiore have emphasised.[41]

In addition, the 'Black Lives Matter' campaign has underlined the systemic ill-treatment experienced by Afro-diasporan slaves and the legacies of racism and disadvantage in contemporary society. The scale of the transatlantic

---

39   Frakes, ed., *Contextualizing the Muslim Other*, xviii.
40   Hugh Goddard, *A History of Christian-Muslim Relations* (Edinburgh: Edinburgh University Press, 2000), 1–4. And cf. also Darío Fernández-Morera, *The Myth of the Andalusian Paradise: Muslims, Christians and Jews Under Islamic Rule in Medieval Spain*, 2016 (repr. Wilmington, Delaware: ISI Books, 2017), passim.
41   Simon Sebag Montefiore, *The World: A Family History* (London: Weidenfeld and Nicholson, 2022), 659.

slave trade was so great and its formal abolition so relatively recent, that today the very words 'slave' and 'slavery' evoke images of people from sub-Saharan Africa. But the Mediterranean slave trade, much less known about today, was also on a very large scale (albeit smaller than the transatlantic trade), affecting millions of people.

With these issues in mind, I want to emphasise, firstly, that this study is in no way intended to glorify slavery, or glamourise the power imbalances resulting from any protagonist's captivity. Secondly, it does not attempt to interrogate transatlantic slavery, which is a huge topic well covered by other scholars. Despite their suffering, enslaved people have encountered disparate social situations and experienced, as well as arousing in others, yearning, love and desire. A vast body of literature developed to fictionalise encounters involving enslaved protagonists. Most of these stories are fantasies, designed to appeal to readers' appetites for diversion; they are tales of the triumph of love over adversity, in a particular setting. My focus is on Muslim-Christian slavery around the Mediterranean and the literature associated with it.

Finally, it is important to note that many of the fictional 'slaves' I have selected to discuss are men, rather than women, and that even when it is women who are physically enslaved and the men are technically free, the men are subject to psychological captivity in many of the narratives. As a literary history of a hitherto largely ignored area of study, this book is intended to discuss love stories involving captive men and women – without in any way justifying slavery itself.

CHAPTER 1

Early Islamic Perspectives

> A king am I, subdued, his power humbled
> To love, like a captive in fetters, forlorn!
> EMIR AL-HAKAM I OF CÓRDOBA, al-Andalus, 8–9th CE, to a slave woman[1]

∴

1   The Coming of Islam: Slavery, Sexuality, and Religious and Cultural Difference

Slavery is an ancient institution practised widely in antiquity,[2] and love between free men and slave women is a frequent motif of classical Greek and Roman comedies, particularly those of Menander, Plautus and Terence. Motifs of (temporary) enslavement also feature in Greek romances of the 1st-4th centuries CE. In these works, however, religion is usually irrelevant to the plots and, in the romances in particular, the lovers are culturally and ethnically similar. But with the coming of Islam love and passion between slave woman and free man take on a new potency as a literary theme, with sexual *frisson* accompanying overt or submerged power motifs, and conversion of the beloved to the religion of the dominant partner being an underlying but significant goal.

The institution of slavery was for centuries not only sanctioned but even, according to some interpretations, prescribed by the Qur'an,[3] although most modern Muslims do not consider slave concubines to be acceptable, and slavery was abolished in most parts of the Muslim world during the course of the

---

[1] A.R. Nykl, in *Hispano-Arabic Poetry and its Relation to the Old Provençal Troubadours* (Baltimore: J. H. Furst and Co., 1946), 20. Also quoted by Charles M. Barrack, in 'Motifs of Love in the Courtly Love Lyric of Moslem Spain and Hohenstaufen Germany: In Memory of Ernst Behler', *Monatshefte*, Vol. 105, No. 2 (Summer 2013), 173–200, 181.

[2] Montefiore records the first named enslaved people, in Uruk, ca. 3000 BCE, in *The World*, 11.

[3] Slavery was also, of course, sanctioned in Judaeo-Christian texts, including the Torah/Bible, and in the writings of St. Augustine and Thomas Aquinas. See, e.g., Steven A. Epstein, *Speaking of Slavery* (Ithaca and London: Cornell University Press, 2001), 140.

20th century.[4] As at other times and in other regions, slaves were acquired largely through military conquest: slaves, both male and female were booty, like other valuables. Since only non-Muslims could be enslaved, slaves would mostly be of a different religious and often ethnic background to their Muslim captors and 'owners' (although some Muslims might be born into slavery too). A Muslim man could also enjoy sex with a non-Muslim captive woman without violating the precepts of his faith. Her faith and ethnicity were no impediment to their relations.

In Christian societies on the other hand, a man was allowed no legal outlet for his passions except through marriage (and even then, passion was discouraged by some ascetics).[5] However, in contrast to Islam, there was no absolute prohibition on enslaving co-religionists and sexual abuse of slaves, both Christian and non-Christian (against religious precepts), was practised widely. As both Epstein and Sebag Montefiore note, enslavement could mean (in Epstein's words) 'a lifetime of rape' for some women;[6] although homosexual rape was, of course, also a possibility. But, in some societies at least, women and girls cost more in slave markets than men and boys.[7]

When it came to marriage, the religion and ethnicity of a desirable woman became all-important to both faiths. and a prerequisite for the legalisation of any sexual relations would be conversion of the subordinate partner to the dominant religion. As we shall see later in this and subsequent chapters, poetry and prose fiction may celebrate the attractions of a woman who is 'different', 'exotic', but she will nearly always be 'other', and her status marginal until she is brought into the fold of the faith community.

In addition, many Muslims, like their Christian counterparts, preferred light colouring to dark. White slaves, especially white women, were more expensive than blacks.[8] Interestingly, mutual racial prejudices led to parallel narratives concerning skin colour and religious conversion in both Muslim and Christian literature. According to one Muslim tradition, an Ethiopian tells the Prophet Muhammad, 'You Arabs excel us in all, in build, color, and in the possession of

---

4　Kecia Ali, *Sexual Ethics and Islam: Feminist Reflections on Qur'an, Hadith and Jurisprudence* (London: Oneworld Publications, 2015), 52.
5　For a brief overview of the topic, cf. e.g. Andrew Holt, *Medieval Masculinity and the Crusades: The Clerical Creation of a New Warrior Identity*, Ph.D. dissertation for the University of Florida (2013) published online: https://ufdcimages.uflib.ufl.edu/UF/E0/04/53/51/00001/HOLT_A.pdf [accessed 25/2/2024]. Chapter 2, 'Early Christianity: the Ascetic Ideal', deals especially with the topic of early Christian views on sexuality.
6　Epstein, *Speaking of Slavery*, 21, 59, 64, 106, and 145; Montefiore, *The World,* xxxvii.
7　Epstein, 111–12.
8　Lewis, *Race and Slavery*, 13, 56; Epstein, *Speaking of Slavery*, 80.

the Prophet. If I believe, will I be with you in Paradise?' The Prophet answers, 'Yes, and in Paradise the whiteness of the Ethiopian will be seen over a stretch of a thousand years'. Another Muslim text, *Risalat al-Ghufran,* describes how the skin of a woman changed from black to white when she adopted Islam.[9]

In *The King of Tars,* the Sultan changes in colour from black to white as soon as he is dipped into the baptismal font as part of his conversion from Islam to Christianity.[10] Akbari comments that his is one of two types of 'Saracen' bodies: those that are assimilable [i.e., into the Christian community], and those that are not. Other examples of assimilable bodies are those of Floripas and her brother, the eponymous Fierabras/Ferumbras, of mediaeval legends and poetic texts.[11] Both these individuals, who begin as enemies of the Christian Charlemagne and his forces, convert to Christianity.

Since in Islamic lands sex with a slave was the only legitimate and indeed sanctioned way that a free man could have sex outside marriage, inevitably such relations would occur frequently. Thus, slavery and, by extension, sexual relations with an 'other', became important to life in such countries, as well as in the literature, in which the enslaved beloved is almost always of a different religion and nation, at least initially. In Islam, the idea of sexual relations was first associated with servitude, as well as marriage. The Prophet Muhammad followed long-standing practice in enslaving enemies captured in battle, including non-Muslim women whom he would take for himself, or for his men, as wives or concubines. Two of these were Jewish women: Rayhana bint Zayd, and Safiya (or Sophia) bint Huyayy, made captive following battles with Jewish tribes.[12] A third non-Muslim woman, Mariyah al Qibtiyaa was a Coptic Christian, given to the Prophet as a gift.[13] The women were expected to convert to Islam, although it is not certain that all did.[14] Then, as subsequently in Muslim lands, conversion brought privileges and status to captives, as well as a better chance of obtaining freedom. For the Prophet and his successors, the

---

9   Lewis, *Race and Slavery,* 35–36.
10 Suzanne Conklin Akbari, *Idols in the East* (Cornell, USA: Cornell University Press, 2009), 166.
11 Akbari, *Idols,* 166.
12 There are countless accounts of the Prophet Muhammad's life and his wives and concubines. One that is generally well-regarded is by Karen Armstrong, *Muhammad: A Biography of the Prophet*, 1991 (repr. London: Phoenix Press, 2004).
13 Washington Irving, *Life of Mahomet* (London: Henry G. Bohn, 1850), 112, 121 and 131.
14 Shaykh Muhammad Hisham Kabbani and Laleh Bakhtiar, *Encyclopedia of Muhammad's Women Companions and the Traditions they Related* (Chicago, Illinois, USA: Kazi Publications, 1998), 374–76.

conversion of former enemies was an essential tool for enlarging the empire and binding conquered peoples to their new masters as clients and allies.

1.1   The Qur'an and Slavery

The Qur'an specifically sanctions sex with slaves, defined as *'ma malakat ayma-nukum'* [literally, 'that which your right hand possesses']. Indeed, it allows men sexual relations with only two categories of women: wives, and slave girls or women. The availability of slave women for sexual purposes is spelled out clearly, and repeatedly. One reference will suffice:

> Blessed are the believers ... who restrain their carnal desires (except with their wives *and slave-girls, for these are lawful to them*: transgressors are those who lust after other than these).
>   Qur'an, 23: 1–6 [my italics][15]

The Qur'an's sanctioning of slavery led some commentators to conclude that the institution of slavery was not just legitimate, in line with custom and practice, but even mandatory because it was specifically allowed by God and therefore even illegal to proscribe.[16] A Moroccan Sultan, challenged at the height of the European anti-slavery movement at least to moderate, if not completely to abolish, slavery in his realm responded:

> As to ... the making of Slaves and Trading therewith, it is confirmed by our Book as also by the *Sunna* of Our Prophet, on whom be the blessing and the peace of God – and furthermore there is not any controversy between the *Oolama* [sic] on that subject, and no one can allow what is prohibited *or prohibit that which is made lawful* [my italics]![17]

With regard to slave women, even in the 20th century, the influential conservative journalist and theologian, Sayid Abul Ala Maududi, disputed some

---

15   Quoted from, *The Koran*, 1956, ed. and tr. N.J. Dawood (repr. London, New York and other locations: Penguin Books [Penguin Classics], 1999), 240–41. All further quotations are from this edition.
16   Bernard Lewis, quoting the Qur'an: v: 87, in *Race and Slavery in the Middle East: An Historical Enquiry* (New York and Oxford: Oxford University Press, 1990), 78.
17   'Correspondence Concerning Slavery between Consul General Drummond Hay and the Sultan of Morocco (1842)', *Addendum, Document 4,* to Lewis's, *Race and Slavery*, 156.

modern interpretations of the Qur'an which argued that a man could only have sex with a slave-girl if he married her.[18]

Muhammad's own actions and the Qur'an thus provided sacred precedent and legal precept, respectively, to justify men having sexual relations with slave-women. However, Islam encouraged the manumission of slaves – especially if they had converted to Islam.[19] In addition, the Qur'an, and many subsequent Islamic authorities, banned rape: they stipulated that no man should have sex with a slave-woman against her will. Nevertheless, in situations where the balance of power was so uneven, the rules must often have been broken. In addition, there would have been many ways in which a male owner could have coerced an unwilling slave woman to have sex with him, short of actually raping her. Some authorities have argued that a man could force his slave to marry him, which would in effect mean that she would have to have sex with him.[20]

Conversely, although marriage between freewomen and male slaves was theoretically possible, it was discouraged and in practice forbidden.[21] A story is told about a Muslim woman who, not long after the death of the Prophet Muhammad, had sexual relations with a male slave (the sources are unclear as to whether she married him, or treated him as a male concubine). She mentioned this to the Caliph Umar Ibn Khattab, explaining that she "'thought that ownership by the right hand made lawful to me what it makes lawful to men.'" Horrified by her actions, as well as her rationale, the Caliph sought advice from some of the Prophet Muhammad's Companions – who had known the Prophet personally, and they confirmed, "'She has [given] the book of Exalted God [the Qur'an] an interpretation that is not its interpretation'". Umar banished the slave and forbade the woman from ever marrying any man, thus condemning her to lifelong celibacy. A variant of this story involves a Bedouin woman who took a Christian slave as her concubine. The Caliph ordered the slave to be sold and punished the woman.[22]

---

18   Sayid Abul Ala Maududi, *Tafhim al-Qur'an – The Meaning of the Qur'an*, Section 1494, https://ia802301.us.archive.org/14/items/TheHolyQuranWithColorCodedEnglishTransliterationAndTranslationFaridBookDepot/quran-tafseer-maududi.pdf, [accessed 10/11/2016].
19   Gordon, *Slavery in the Arab World*, 40.
20   Kecia Ali, *Marriage and Slavery in Early Islam* (Mass. and London: Harvard University Press, 2010), 39–40; Kecia Ali, 'Concubinage and Consent', *International Journal of Middle East Studies*, Vol. 49, Issue 1, February 2017, 148–152, 149: https://doi.org/10.1017/S0020743816001203, [accessed 27/3/2018]; R. Levy, quoting Khalil b. Ishaq, *Mukhtasar*, agrees. Cf. Reuben Levy, *The Social Structure of Islam* (Cambridge: Cambridge University Press, 1957), 80.
21   Bernard Lewis, *Race and Slavery*, 8.
22   Quoted by Kecia Ali, *Marriage and Slavery*, 12–13.

Successive authorities maintained that Muslims were not to be enslaved by other Muslims.[23] Only men and women who were either purchased, or captured in war between Muslims and non-Muslims (referred to as *'Kafirun'* – infidels) could be made slaves. Those who were purchased would often have been kidnapped from their home communities by slave-traders or their agents and brought to one of the slave-markets that abounded in North Africa and the Middle East. Leslie Peirce notes that:

> the Islamic ban on enslaving one's fellow subjects, although frequently ignored, resulted in a practice of slavery that incorporated captive peoples from widely diverse origins. Ruling regimes systematically recruited outsiders into the governing class, and domestic regimes made use of slave concubines for reproductive purposes (the offspring of a free male and a slave concubine were considered freeborn).[24]

This means that slave women would almost always be members of another religion, in practice very often members of another people or race. Women of the harem were predominantly of foreign origin. Children born of such unions would usually be acknowledged by the father, and the son of a sultan could succeed him, even if his mother was a slave. Abd al-Raḥmān I, founder of the Umayyad Dynasty of al-Andalus, was the son of a Berber concubine. Indeed, between the 8th and 10th centuries CE, all the Umayyad rulers of Iberia were born to slave concubines,[25] as were most of the Abbasid caliphs from the 8th to 13th centuries: 36 out of 39 rulers.[26]

The mother of the celebrated Abbasid Caliph Haroun al-Rashid (786–809), who figures prominently as a character in *One Thousand and One Nights*, was historically a former slave woman, al-Khayzuran bint Atta. She was kidnapped from her home at Jorash in Yemen by a Bedouin, who then sold her in a slave market near Mecca to the Abbasid Caliph Al-Mahdi. The Caliph fell in love with her and married her. Al-Khayzuran had a strong personality and greatly influenced her husband in his running of state affairs. Her character may be reflected in that of Shahrazad, the teller of tales in *One Thousand and*

---

23 Lewis, *Race and Slavery*, 55, 57.
24 Leslie Peirce, 'Writing Histories of Sexuality in the Middle East', *American Historical Review*, 114, 5 (December 2009), 1325–1339, 1326.
25 Simon Barton, 'Women on the Frontline', *History Today*, vol. 65, (1 January 2015).
26 Adam Ali, 'Slave, Queen, and Mother of Caliphs: the Story of Khayzuran': www.medievalists.net, 04, 2019 [accessed 9/5/2023].

One Nights.[27] Haroun too married the daughter of a slave woman, his cousin Amatul Aziz Bint Ja'far al-Mansur, known familiarly as 'Zubaida'. Her mother was the sister of al-Khayzuran. Like the latter, she came to exercise enormous power over her husband's affairs, as well as those of a subsequent Caliph, al-Mamun. She also features in *One Thousand and One Nights*, in the story 'Haroun al-Rashid and Queen Zubaydah in the Bath'.[28]

In the Ottoman Empire, inter-marriage was 'a crucial aspect of the Muslim-Christian encounter and an … important kind of mixing … that aided the spread of Ottoman control and Islam'.[29] Furthermore, it made for a 'new Ottoman Rumi [Christian] culture [which] was remarkably heterogeneous and polyglot, reflecting the cultural and religious diversity of the Lands of Rum'.[30]

Long associations arose between love and slavery, and love between free men and slave women was celebrated in Arabic life and literature, involving men at the highest level of Muslim society. But embellished and fictionalised accounts of the well-known pre-Islamic Arab poet and adventurer, Antarah ibn Shaddad al-Absi (525–608 CE) reverse the pattern with, unusually, love between an enslaved man and a free woman. The eponymous hero of an Arab romance, *Antar and Abla,* is born in slavery to a free Arab and an Ethiopian woman whom his father had enslaved after a tribal war. He falls in love with his wealthy cousin Abla, whom he seeks to marry despite his own slave status. Antar secures his freedom by distinguishing himself in battle. After many vicissitudes he reaches the empire of Ethiopia and discovers that his mother, Zabiba, is in fact the emperor's grand-daughter. The story has alternative endings, some happy and some unhappy, with Antar being killed fighting.[31]

1.2 One Thousand and One Nights (*Alf Layla wa Layla*)

One Thousand and One Nights, also known as the *Arabian Nights* or simply as the *Nights*, are believed to have circulated orally before, or at the same time as they were written down. They are of variant origin (Indian, Persian, Egyptian, Iraqi, etc.) whose composition dates are unknown. The king in the framing

---

27   André Clot. *Haroun al-Rashid and the World of One Thousand and One Nights,* tr. and ed. by John Howe (London: Saqi) 1989; Tayeb El-Hibri, *Reinterpreting Islamic Historiography: Harun al-Rashid and the Narrative of the Abbasid Caliphate* (Cambridge: Cambridge University Press, 1999), 43–44 and 174–75, and Chapter 2 passim.
28   Clot, *Haroun al-Rashid*.
29   Tijana Krstić, *Contested Conversions: Narratives of Religious Change in the Early Modern Ottoman Empire* (Stanford, Calif.: Stanford University Press, 2011), 65.
30   Krstić, 67.
31   Lewis, *Race and Slavery*, 24; https://en.wikipedia.org/wiki/Antarah_ibn_Shaddad, [accessed 5/5/2023].

story, Shahriyar, may be based on the historic 7th-century CE Sassanian Persian prince of that name, son of Khosrow II, who was murdered by his brother. The Sassanians are said to have enjoyed story-telling, but an early Persian manuscript, *Hazār afsāna* (A Thousand Stories) mentioned in the 10th century CE, has not survived.[32] The earliest known documentation of the stories is a scrap of papyrus from Egypt, in Arabic, and dated 879 CE. The first comprehensive collection, and translation (into French), of the *Nights* was made by the 18th century Orientalist and scholar, Antoine Galland, based on a 14th century Arabic manuscript. His work, *Les Mille et une nuits, contes arabes traduits en français*, was published in 12 volumes from 1704–17. It had an enormous impact throughout Europe and beyond, and was translated into many other languages.

1.3   Greek Influence

The Arabs drew extensively on Greek scholarship, particularly in the fields of medicine, mathematics, philosophy, astronomy and other sciences, as well as astrology. Less well recognised are the literary derivations: *Antar and Abla* has interesting echoes of the Greek-language *Aethiopica* by Heliodorus of Emesa (in present-day Syria) in which, again unusually, an Ethiopian princess falls in love with, and eventually marries, a Greek nobleman.[33]

Many elements of the *Nights* have Greek antecedents: the very framing story, in which Shahrazad 'weaves out an endless tapestry of stories' in order to ward off her fate, recalls Penelope endlessly weaving in *The Iliad*, as Marina Warner points out.[34] The stories provide a link between Classical and Byzantine work on the one hand, and the European late Middle Ages and Renaissance periods on the other. Structural elements, such as the story within a story within a story, the so-called 'boxing' of stories, also recall the Greek novellas.

Grunebaum points to the realistic urban settings of the *Nights*, as well as their classical patterns of style, presentation and emotional conventions, as evidence of Greek precedents. Other possible influences include that of Plautus's *Miles Gloriosus* (based on one or two Greek plays) in which a woman deceives her husband by pretending to have a twin sister, on the *Nights'* story of

---

32   For these and some other details relating to the *Nights* mentioned in the present chapter, see *The Arabian Nights Encyclopedia*, ed. Ulrich Marzolph and Richard van Leeuwen, with the collaboration of Hassan Wassouf, 2 vols. (Santa Barbara: ABC-Clio, 2004).

33   The heroine's race and cultural origins are not apparent, as by a quirk of fate (which becomes central to the plot) she is born white, and then educated as a Greek. Cf. *Collected Ancient Greek Novels*, ed. B. Reardon (Berkeley, London: University of California Press,1989, repr. 2008).

34   Marina Warner, *Stranger Magic: Charmed States and the Arabian Nights* (London: Chatto and Windus, 2011), 2.

'The Butcher, his Wife and the Soldier'; as well as the device of a secret passage between two houses, which recurs in another *Nights* tale, 'Qamar az-Zaman and his Beloved'. In this *Nights* story, the woman meets her lover disguised as a slave. Numerous other Greek plot-lines recur, with small changes, in the *Nights*.[35]

But it is the Greek novel which Grunebaum cites as a particular influence on the *Nights,* and especially how it 'treats the fate of two lovers as an organic unit of dramatic composition.' These lovers are separated after their initial union, made to wander, 'persecuted by fate' and finally reunited. Fate 'rules supreme', Grunebaum adds, and 'There is no action springing from the peculiarities of the characters involved'. Seafaring also plays a part, as do attacks by pirates (in several Greek stories); robbers who kill each other for the possession of a princess (as at the beginning of the *Aethiopica*); and a funeral being held with a mausoleum erected for one supposed dead but still alive (Achilles Tatius's *Leucippe and Clitophone;* Chariton's *Chaereas and Callirhoe;* and *Apollonius of Tyre*).

Other features common to both Greek novels and the *Nights* – as well as some Arabic poetry – include love at first sight; sentimental themes such as suffering for love and misery being considered as a deadly disease; fainting, desperation, madness, etc.; and a glorification of chastity, blended with a latent lasciviousness. It is significant, Grunebaum comments, that factors like these, as well as military imagery such as love wounding, eyes like arrows and similar objects, entered into Arabic poetry, just as Muslim dominion was being extended over Greek cultural territory, especially Syria. The prevalent uses of letters, dreams, and happy endings, are also common to both Greek and Arabic genres.[36]

1.4 One Thousand-and One-Nights: *Analysis*

The framing story of this iconic work involves an early sexual scene between King Shahriyar's wife and her attendants on the one hand, and black male slaves on the other. This ushers in the brutal episode whose shadow hangs over all the subsequent narratives, in which the king has all of the participants in the orgy beheaded due to his disgust and sense of betrayal. Here racism, misogyny and aristocratic class arrogance are fused in an unholy triangle, which culminates in the beheadings of both women and slaves, presenting shocking

---

35 Gustave E. von Grunebaum, 'Greek Form Elements in the Arabian Nights', *Islam and Medieval Hellenism: Social and Cultural Perspectives,* ed. Dunning S. Wilson (London: Variorum Reprints, 1976), 278.
36 Grunebaum, 284–89.

FIGURE 1.1   Set design by Leon Bakst for the ballet, *Sheherazade,* performed by the Ballet Russes, with music by Nicolai Rimsky-Korsakov in 1910. Bakst collaborated with Sergei Diaghilev, co-founding the Ballet Russes, for which he was the artistic director and he also designed the costumes. The original cast included Ida Rubinstein, Vaslav Nijinsky, Enrico Cecchetti, and Bronislava Nijinska. Image in the public domain
SOURCE: WIKIART: HTTPS://WWW.WIKIART.ORG/EN/LEON-BAKST/SET-DESIGN-FOR-SCHEHERAZADE-1910-11

images of carnage to the reader. Only the ingenuity and virtue of the vizier's daughter, Shahrazad, can heal the king of his emotional sickness and murderous intents.[37] Shahriyar and Shahrazad are both Persian names, suggesting they are ethnically and culturally similar, and Shahrazad is not a slave. But her

---

37   In my discussion of the *Nights* I used, initially, the translation of Husain Haddawy, as his source is the Arabic text of the eminent scholar Muhsin Mahdi (1984), itself edited from a 14th century Syrian manuscript, the earliest extant. However, certain stories not mentioned by Mahdi or Hadawy and particularly pertinent to this study are contained in *One Thousand and One Nights* of Richard Burton (1885), and some of them also appear in subsequent editions, including that of Malcolm C Lyons and Ursula Lyons, *The Arabian Nights: Tales of 1,001 Nights*, 3 vols, 2008, (repr. London: Penguin, 2010), to which I refer extensively, as the most comprehensive, scholarly and readable modern edition of the *Nights* in English.

powerlessness in relation to Shahriyar and her physical vulnerability give her, effectively, the status of a slave, although their relationship is not a love story in any conventional sense. Love, absent to begin with, grows on his side over the period of *One Thousand and One Nights*, at the end of which he lifts the threat of execution; her feelings are never made clear.

The story has been re-told countless times over the centuries in countries around the world, and through every medium, including drama, opera and ballet [Figure 1.1]. And many of the tales contained within the framing narrative relate explicitly to slave women as both subjects and objects of desire. Two stories in Haddawy's edition particularly concern the love between a slave woman and a free man: 'The Story of Nur al-Din Ali ibn-Bakkar and the Slave Girl Shams al-Nahar' and 'The Story of the Slave-Girl Anis al-Jalis and Nur al-Din Ali ibn Khaqan'. These are almost mirror-images of each other in that, although both concern forbidden love between a freeborn young man and a slave-girl belonging, or destined to belong, to the ruler, the first is a tragedy about a doomed love, while the second is an adventure story and romance with elements of humour.

2 *One Thousand and One Nights*: Stories

2.1 *The Story of Nur al-Din Ali ibn-Bakkar and the Slave Girl Shams al-Nahar*

This story, told at Shahriyar's request, contrasts starkly with a preceding long cycle of farcical tales. An air of tragedy hangs over it almost from the beginning, when Nur al-Din is present, by chance, as Shams al-Nahar and her entourage enter the shop of his friend, the druggist Abu al-Hasan ibn-Tahir. Nur al-Din is immediately overcome with confusion and almost swoons. Then, punning on that part of her name (Shams) which means sun, he laments that,

> She is the sun that in heaven dwells;
> Console your heart and let it patient be,
> For neither can you to the sun ascend,
> Nor can she descend from heaven to thee.
> *Nights,* HADDAWY ed., 296

She is also described as like 'the full moon' (a conventional image) or 'the rising sun' (326). Some time later Shams al-Nahar summons the druggist and the young man to the palace, where it is revealed that she is the favourite slave and concubine to the Caliph, Haroun al-Rashid.

The room into which the visitors are taken at the palace is explicitly compared with an exquisite chamber in Paradise, leading out to a garden in which art and nature are ideally combined. Into this scene walks Shams al-Nahar, dazzling even in these surroundings, 'as the sun emerges from the clouds'. But in the midst of this beauty and happiness, the youth is already predicting his own end:

> She alone is the source of my pain ...
> Since first my eyes saw her enchanting face,
> Restless my soul has been and no peace known.
> O poor soul, for God's sake, depart in peace
> And let my wasting body lie alone.

Shams al-Nahar then has one of her women echo his words with a tragic interpretation of her own in which 'With bitter tears' the two lovers blame the fates for their predicament. Just as the couple are acknowledging the extent of their love, they are interrupted with news that the Caliph's eunuchs are at the door. What follows is a descent into the tragedy foreshadowed at the outset. The lovers meet only one more time, when robbers attack and kidnap them. Finally, each one dies, essentially of a broken heart.

'The Story of Nur al-Din...' reveals a hothouse society of gossip and intrigue. Its approach is deeply psychological and the narrative unfolds slowly, centring on subtle developments in the lovers' emotions. Much of this process is revealed through poems and songs sung by various women acting as chorus, mystically, intimately and intuitively reflecting the lovers' feelings, but also precipitating events, including, by uncovering her secret in the presence of the Caliph, Shams al-Nahar's death.

Central to the outcome is the problem that the slave-girl is not only the absolute possession, but also the favourite of the Caliph. In other stories in the *Nights*, such as that of Anis al-Jalis (discussed below), as well as some later European stories including Mozart's opera *Il Seraglio* with libretto by Christoph Friedrich Bretzner, the ruler is content for the girl concerned to marry someone else, ushering in a breezy solution and a happy ending. But here the Caliph's devotion to her is too absolute for him to relinquish her.

The couple know from the start that their love is futile, but they cannot live without one another: her name Shams al-Nahar signifies the rising sun (sun of the dawn), while his means light of religion. Light of the sun and the light of religion represent, respectively, two elements without which (in the context) no living being can survive. The Qur'an promises eternal life in Paradise to the believer, eternal damnation to the unbeliever. Nur al-Din has contravened the essential Qur'anic law, enjoining the faithful to restrain their desires except with their own wives and slave-women; by lusting after another man's slave Nur al-Din will, ultimately, be denied the light of the sun.

Meanwhile, Shams al-Nahar, in loving a man who is not her husband or owner, has overturned the right order of things, threatening social chaos. She will be denied the light of religion and will descend into a metaphorical and perhaps literal hell. Love conquers and then destroys them; it is seen as the 'great misfortune' (314) and as having 'so possessed them that it will not leave them alone until they perish' (319). The two are slaves of love and Shams al-Nahar is thus doubly enslaved, but the story charts the loss of Paradise for both of them. From the beginning both grasp the extent of their transgression, which is the cause of their mutual distress and fatalism throughout.

2.2 The Story of the Slave-Girl Anis al-Jalis and Nur al-Din Ali ibn Khaqan

In complete contrast to the story of Nur al-Din and Shams al-Nahar is 'The Story of the Slave-Girl Anis al-Jalis and Nur al-Din Ali ibn Khaqan'. The foreign origin of the slave girl, though not spelled out with regard to Anis al-Jalis, is made clear in a list of nationalities of women being bought and sold in the slave market: they include Nubians, 'Europeans' [sic], Greeks, Circassians, Turks and Tartars and others (357). In other words, they are mostly Christians and all of them are from non-Muslim countries.

As in the story of 'Shams al-Nahar', a high-status young man, a vizier's son, falls in love with a slave-girl destined for the ruler, in this case the king of Basra; indeed, their desire is lustily and hastily consummated. The difference between this story and that of 'Shams al-Nahar' is that their love develops before the king knows of her existence. The piece's atmosphere is even quite comic in places, as in several scenes where Nur al-Din seeks to sell Anis al-Jalis, with her acquiescence, as a way out of his poverty. In addition, whereas in the 'Shams al-Nahar' story, the deepening sense of tragedy derives substantially from the lovers' anguish at their constant separation, here the lovers spend most of their time together. However, the two stories share the protagonists' pervasive fear of offending powerful men in a society where power is arbitrary, and the slightest offence can lead to a cruel death.

As with the preceding tale, a substantial part of the story takes place in the Caliph Haroun al-Rashid's Paradise Garden, the 'Garden of Delight'; but this setting prefigures the paradise the lovers will gain at the end, living the 'happiest and most delightful of lives' until their deaths. When, eventually, the king learns of the lovers' situation, having neither any emotional nor conscious financial investment in the girl (he had forgotten he had previously given his vizier money to buy a slave-girl), he is happy to bring the lovers together permanently. The Caliph's property has not been taken from him, only a prospective possession to which he has not had a chance to become attached. Thus, no religious or social precept has been violated and the resolution can be a happy one.

Various other stories in the *Nights* involve women, mostly slave girls, being given away by generous and wealthy men: often the giver is Haroun al-Rashid himself.[38] Occasionally the gift results in the woman being liberated; sometimes the woman reverts to the giver, whom she loves and who loves her. All these stories foreground the love between a slave woman and a free man but, as with other non-Christian stories we are considering, religious differences between the lovers are not an issue: the important factors are those of class and what is socially appropriate in context.

2.3 *'Occidentalism': A Response to 'Orientalism'*

Ever since Edward Said's ground-breaking and controversial *Orientalism* (1978), commentators have debated the western preoccupation with Islam, much of which he condemns. Less discussed is the idea that both the hostility toward and the fascination with the 'other' could be mutual: Nizar F. Hermes, specifically challenging Said, has studied Muslims' encounter with Christians from the perspective of the East and some Muslim writers' powerful attraction to 'Ifranj' [Frankish Christian] and 'Rûmi' [Byzantine Christian] women.[39] Abbasid interest in Byzantium and the Byzantines anticipates Orientalism, he says and 'one cannot deny the fact that as Orientalism has actively participated in the construction of the Oriental as the Other, of the early/modern European, this older medieval Muslim tradition indubitably bore a similar responsibility in fashioning *al-Rûm* as the Muslim Other',[40] and that, 'if the West has always had its Orient, the East, in turn, has had its own Occident'.[41]

Hermes's study of the *Ifranjiyyat* of Ibn Qaysarani, one of the most celebrated poets of the Middle Ages, provides many examples of his intense attraction to

---

38 For a discussion of these stories, cf. Chester Nathan Gould, 'The *Frithjof's Saga*', 227–31.
39 Nizar F. Hermes, *The European Other in Medieval Arabic Literature and Culture: Ninth-Twelfth Century AD* (New York: Palgrave Macmillan) 2012; Nizar F. Hermes (2017), 'The Poetry of Frankish Enchantment: The *Iffranjiyat* of Ibn Qaysarani', *Middle Eastern Literature*, 20:3, 267–287: https://www.tandfonline.com/doi/full/10.1080/1475262X.2017.1385695, [accessed 10/2/2023]; Nizar F. Hermes, 'The Byzantines in Medieval Arab Poetry: Abu Firas' *Al Rumiyyat* and the Poetic Responses of al-Qaffal and Ibn Ḥazm to Nicephore Phocas' "Al-Qasida al-Arminiyya al-Malʿuna" (The Armenian Cursed Ode)', *Byzantina Symmeikta*, 19, 35–61.
40 Hermes, 'The Byzantines', 40.
41 Hermes, *The European Other*, 8.

Christian women, which he celebrates in verses, some salacious; he even fantasises about being a captive in order to be close to Frankish women:

> Woe to me from a town across the frontier ...
> By it, there are palaces resembling churches
> Inside which the icons do speak!
> In their abodes, I journeyed and left a heart ...
> I have since envied those living in their terrain.
> For the sake of nearness, I have even envied those who [sic] they detain.[42]

The poet imagines himself as a 'victim' of Frankish beauty and elegance:

> A Frankish woman has enchanted me,
> The breeze of fragrance on her does linger.
> In her robe, a branch so tender,
> and in her crown, a radiant moon.
> And if there is blueness in her eye,
> for God's sake, a spear's head is so blue.[43]

This reverse gaze could be manifest, at least in Iran, even in the period when European colonial expansion was at its height,

> The European woman (zan-i Farangi) was the locus of gaze and erotic fantasy for many eighteenth- and nineteenth-century Persianate voy(ag)eurs of Europe. The travelers' recounting of their self-experience provided the material for the formation of competing discourses on women of Europe. With the political hegemony of Europe, a woman's body served as an important marker of identity and difference and as a terrain of cultural and political contestations. The eroticized depiction of European women by male travelers engendered a desire for that 'heaven on earth.'[44]

---

[42] Quoted in Hermes, 'Poetry of Frankish Enchantment', 275.
[43] Hermes, 'Poetry', 276.
[44] Mohamad Tavakoli-Targhi, *Refashioning Iran: Orientalism, Occidentalism and Historiography*, London: Palgrave Macmillan, 2001, 54.

3 *One Thousand-and One-Nights* Stories with Love between Muslims and Christians, and Religious Conversion Themes

The preoccupation with the Christian 'other' as a love object, as well as a target for religious conversion, is manifest in several stories included in later editions of the *Nights,* among them Richard Burton's collection (1885), and the Lyons translation. These feature themes of love between a Muslim (man) and an 'other' (woman) who is explicitly identified as Christian, and some of these stories culminate in religious conversion, always from Christianity to Islam, rather than the other way round as with most of the Christian works surveyed for this volume.[45] But 18th and earlier 19th century editions, including Galland's, omit these stories altogether. The *Arabian Nights Encyclopedia* speaks of literary ties between Arabic and Byzantine epics in particular, citing theories that 'they may have originated simultaneously, probably from a common source'.[46] The editors believe it likely that the epic dates back to the middle of the 13th century or earlier.[47] Robert Irwin states that the epic of *Omar ibn al-Nuʿuman*, to give one example, was among tales probably added (to the original core) at some time 'from the tenth century onwards', which could make it one of the earliest literary treatments of religion as an important element in a romance.[48]

3.1 The Tale of King ʿUmar ibn al-*Nuʿuman* and His Sons Sharkān and Zau al-Makan (Nights 45–145)

This 'sprawling epic'[49] begins in the Baghdadi court of the eponymous King ʿUmar, who has just one son, called Sharkān, despite having four wives and three hundred and sixty concubines. ʿUmar sends Sharkān, accompanied by his vizier Dandan, a Muslim army and 'Byzantine' (Christian) envoys to battle in enemy territory. Separated from the others, Sharkān wanders into a lovely meadow where a girl of incomparable beauty ('like the full moon', which is the highest praise in Arabic literature) is wrestling and overcoming, one by one, a group of 'virgins' [her female companions]. Sharkān tells her he will take them all as booty for himself and his men. She wrestles and three times defeats him; each time he is disorientated by her luscious shapeliness: when he

---

45 Lyons, eds., *Arabian Nights*.
46 Marzolph et al, *The Arabian Nights Encyclopedia,* Vol. 2, 510; cf. also Vol. 1, 435.
47 *The Arabian Nights Encyclopedia*, Vol. 1, 434.
48 Robert Irwin, *The Arabian Nights: a Companion* (London and other locations: Penguin Books Ltd., 1994, repr. 1995), 48.
49 Irwin, *Companion*, 89.

'put his hand on her slender waist, his fingers sunk into the folds of her belly' [Figure 1.2].[50]

Sharkān tells his adversary he is now 'the slave of love ... wretched ... brokenhearted', and invites her to come with him to the 'lands of Islam'. But she informs him that if she fell into the hands of ʿUmar ibn al-Nuʿuman, she would never again be free: an insight which proves tragically prophetic. Instead, she takes him to her 'convent', a gorgeous building with a marble floor, gold-adorned hangings and a throne 'spread with silks'[51] which Sharkān is told to mount. He stays for three days, wined and dined lavishly, and entertained by the young woman, now playing musical instruments and reciting Greek poetry.

The young woman recognises him as Sharkān, technically her enemy, but she assures him she will protect him. He recites from a 7th century poem (*Jamil Buthaina*), suggesting that dying for love is as much a martyr's death as dying in battle:

> They say: "Fight in the Holy War, Jamil, go on a raid."
> But what war do I want to wage except the war of women?
> In every talk of theirs there is joy
> And all their victims die a martyr's death.[52]

Inevitably, the Muslim man and the Christian woman fall deeply in love and she begs Sharkān not to leave her. But, without warning, her father's army approaches, sent to capture him. Guided by the young woman, Sharkān kills more than eighty Christian soldiers and the rest flee. The girl orders him to behead the gatekeepers, as punishment for not warning her of the soldiers' approach. He obliges, and the girl now identifies herself as Abriza, daughter of Hardub, the Christian king of Armenian Caesaria.

Abriza and Sharkān flee separately, arranging to meet in Baghdad. Along the way, he and his men encounter a hundred Frankish (Christian) horsemen who defeat them, but spare all the Muslims' lives. The leader challenges Sharkān, in fluent Arabic, to one-to-one combat. The two fight all day, but just as Sharkān is about to strike his opponent with his sword, the Frank shouts at him 'Sharkān, this is not knightly behaviour, but the deed of a man who has been overcome by women'. His adversary all along has been Abriza, seeking to test him in battle, while the 'Frankish soldiers' were her 'virgin girls' in disguise. Abriza orders the captured Muslims to be released and they all kiss the

---

50   Lyons eds., *Nights,* Vol. 1, 315.
51   Lyons eds., Vol. 1, 319.
52   Lyons eds., Vol. 1, 324.

FIGURE 1.2   Abriza Defeats Sharkān, illustration for the 1897 edition of *The Book of the Thousand Nights and a Night* by Albert Letchford. Image in the public domain
SOURCE: HTTPS://EN.WIKISOURCE.ORG/WIKI/THE_BOOK_OF_ THE THOUSAND_NIGHTS_AND_ONE_NIGHT/ILLUSTRATIONS

ground: the Christians face the Muslims and vice versa. The women change out of their 'Frankish' clothes and they all ride into Muslim territory, where they are escorted to the palace.

The story quite suddenly turns to tragedy. In Baghdad, the Byzantine princess becomes the object of ʿUmar's lust and he drugs her and then rapes her: 'The devil tempted him and ... he was unable to control himself'.[53] Upon waking, Abriza discovers she has been deflowered, goes into seclusion and then flees, giving birth to a son in the desert. A slave tries to force himself on Abriza and, repulsed by her, he kills her. Her father King Hardub discovers her body and vows to obtain vengeance.

Thus, abruptly ends the romance of Abriza and Sharkān. In a later, Christian, story thought to have been influenced by the *Nights* (*Floire et Blanchefleur*), when the Muslim Blanchefleur is kidnapped, the Christian boy Floire abandons his home and braves many dangers until he finds her.[54] In contrast Sharkān passively, perhaps fatalistically, accepts Abriza's disappearance. He ends up becoming Sultan of Damascus and marrying another woman. This initially romantic and entertaining tale is overwhelmed by darkness; and the union of Muslim and Christian, with Abriza converting to Islam, which might have been anticipated, is aborted.[55]

The authors of the *Arabian Nights Encyclopedia* suggest that in the *Arabian Nights*, 'Christians and their roles serve as a negative stereotype' with Christian-Muslim relations being 'governed by religious rivalry and war'. The tale of 'Umar ibn al-Nu'uman is given as an example of these trends. The authors continue,

> As in the European romances of chivalry, the opposing communities from both sides are depicted in a derogatory and contemptible way, as practising foul habits and exhibiting unwarranted pride. Nevertheless, the Muslims acknowledge Christians as a formidable foe who are not easy to vanquish.[56]

But in the Arab story of 'Umar ibn al-Nu'uman, the handling of the 'others', in this case the Christians, varies. The Christian maiden Abriza is depicted as an ideal chivalrous knight, supremely brave and peerlessly skilled at wrestling, sword fighting and other forms of combat; she has pride in her abilities and in her royal status; she has incomparable beauty (which ultimately proves her undoing); and she is intellectually accomplished, with a sophisticated knowledge of Arabic language and poetry (talents most prized in Arab culture), despite her native language being Greek.

---

53   Lyons eds., Vol 1, 340.
54   This story is examined in detail in Chapter 2 of this book.
55   The rest of the epic concerns 'Umar and his children and grandchildren, all of whom die in the course of the narrative, except for his concubine Sophia, his daughter, Nuzhat al-Zaman and grandson Kana-ma-Kana, who is eventually crowned king.
56   *Arabian Nights Encyclopedia*, Vol. 2, 523.

Abriza is shown to be loyal to a fault: to her women and to her beloved, as well as generous, refusing to kill soldiers she and her women have vanquished; she is courteous and hospitable, even to the man who will go on to rape her. She also has a keen sense of morality, several times admonishing Sharkān for his behaviour and instructing him in the correct ways of speech and action. Abriza's women too are accomplished, beautiful and virtuous. Abriza comes out of the story much better than Sharkān: she protects him against all comers and helps him to escape the traps laid for him by her father and others, so he can return safely to his own land. But he entirely fails to protect her when she is in his country, despite having foreseen that his father would covet her, resulting in the losses of both her honour and her life. Sharkān ultimately suffers the same fate as his father: death by poison (on a dagger) administered by Abriza's grandmother. This is not a morality tale in any conventional sense, but a narration of events both comic and tragic, with several people being punished for their crimes, but in which an innocent and virtuous young woman, author of many good deeds, comes to a bitter end.

As we have seen, in the saga of ʿUmar ibn al-Nuʿuman, the love between Muslim and Christian is aborted and both the lovers are murdered in the course of the story. However, several other *Nights* tales bring interfaith and inter-cultural love to fruition, ending with conversion of the Christian to Islam and union of the couple, usually through marriage.

3.2 *The Story of Ali Nur al-Din and Miriam the Sash Maker* (Nights 863– 94): *Plot and Analysis*

The hero of this tale, Ali, is forced to go on the run after a family altercation in which he wounds his father and then escapes, taking with him some of his father's money. He boards a ship bound for Alexandria, where an old apothecary gives him shelter. While waiting for the old man's return, Ali sees a radiantly beautiful girl seated on a mule behind a Persian, who hands her to an auctioneer to be sold [Figure 1.3]. The Persian has promised her the final say on her buyer and she rejects several bidders until, catching sight of Ali, she instantly falls in love with him. Told he is too poor to purchase her, she removes a valuable ring from her finger and with it bribes the auctioneer to effect the sale. She tells the auctioneer that she is 'sell[ing] herself' to Ali Nur al-Din and the deal is concluded.

The slave girl, later identified as a 'Frank' (Christian) called Miriam, is shocked by the meanness of Ali's lodgings and demands expensive food and drink. The apothecary agrees to give Ali some money, but counsels the young man to 'enjoy' his slave girl for a night and then return her to the market. Guided by Miriam, Ali buys silk, wine and food, which she cooks expertly. When he is in a drunken sleep, she uses the silk to make a beautiful sash, which he will later sell for a large profit. Upon his awakening, the couple make love and he finds her to be a virgin.

The couple's life together continues in this vein. Miriam's sashes are all sold and they live contentedly for a year. Miriam makes Ali an exquisitely beautiful cloak, which he wears to go to market. One day Ali wakes to find Miriam weeping bitterly. She predicts that an old 'Frank' with only one eye will be the means of their separation. Falling asleep on a bench at the market, Ali wakes to find nearby a Frank fitting Miriam's description, who first persuades Ali to sell him his cloak, and then – having made Ali truly drunk – Miriam herself, for a huge sum.

Now more is revealed about Miriam's origins and descent into slavery: she is a king's daughter, from 'Ifranja' [France]. Raised in luxury, she is learned and accomplished in 'manly pursuits' such as horsemanship, as well as expert in many crafts; she is 'unparalleled in her age and time' (386). Recovering from illness, Miriam had set out on a pilgrimage. En route, her ship was attacked by Muslim pirates (referred to in the text as 'fighters in the holy war'), who stripped the vessel of its valuables, captured Miriam and sold her to the Persian merchant mentioned earlier. When he fell ill, she nursed him so tenderly that he promised to grant her wish to be sold to a man of her choice whom she could love. She converted to Islam and learned the Qur'an by heart, as well as many Islamic traditions. Thus, she came to live with Ali Nur al-Din. But her grief-stricken father sent the one-eyed Frank – his vizier – to search for her. Ignoring her anguish and rage, the vizier forces Miriam onto a ship bound for her home country.

Meanwhile, wallowing in grief at Miriam's loss, Ali manages to board a ship bound for France. This ship is also overrun by pirates, who take it to France, where they are imprisoned – just as Miriam's ship is arriving. Questioned by her mother whether she is still a virgin, Miriam claims to have been raped. Her father says she can only be 'purified' through the decapitation of a hundred Muslims and so the newly captured men are all beheaded save for Ali Nur al-Din, who is reprieved at the last minute by a twist of fate.

One day, as Miriam and her women are on their way to church to offer thanks for her safe return, Ali sees Miriam by chance and she contrives to be alone with him, reproaching him for having so carelessly sold her. Later, she strips off her clothes and jewels, and she and Ali make love in the chapel of the Virgin Mary. At this, Burton comments,

> This profaning a Christian Church which contained the relics of the Virgin would hugely delight the coffee-house habitués, and the Egyptians

FIGURE 1.3   Miriam the Girdle-Girl, wood engraving, Denning Fink publisher, Pforzheim, 1842
CREDIT ALAMY

would be equally flattered to hear that the son of a Cairene merchant had made the conquest of a Frankish Princess Royal.[57]

The couple's long poetic lament, when the church bell tolls morning, signalling the need for them to cease their pleasures and to part, recalls (perhaps anticipates?) the mediaeval European *aubade* or *alba* in which lovers about to separate following a night of forbidden passion express their sorrow. Speaking alone, after expressing his love and desire for Miriam, Ali adds,

> I swore if ever I was in command
> And was a sultan with the power to rule,

---

57   Richard Burton, *The Book of the Thousand Nights and a Night: A Plain and Literal Translation of the Arabian Nights Entertainments*, tr. From the Arabic by Captain Sir Richard F. Burton, 12 vols. (1885) Vol. 8, 328.

> I would raze all churches to the ground,
> Killing whatever priests there were on earth.[58]

His words reflect his resentment over the murder of his Muslim fellow-passengers, but seem inappropriate for his situation in the company of a woman from a Christian culture. However, they compound the profaning of Christianity, begun with the scene of love-making in the chapel.

Miriam now instructs Ali to wait until the next night, take some valuables from the church, go down to the shore to board a vessel with ten men and await her arrival. Complying, Ali finds the ship's captain, a fierce man with a long beard who, on flimsy pretexts, proceeds to kill all the other men except Ali and set out to sea. Fearful and dejected, Ali is stunned to observe the captain pulling off his beard and being revealed as none other than Miriam in masculine disguise. She had killed the captain and ripped off his beard to attach to her own skin!

At Alexandria harbour, Ali tells Miriam to wait until he can bring her a veil and suitable clothing. Meanwhile, her enraged father swiftly sends a vessel full of armed men, which arrives at Alexandria just after Ali leaves. Captive now, and facing her father, Miriam lies to him again, swearing 'by the Cross and the Crucified' that she had been kidnapped. Unconvinced, the king sentences her to death on the cross. Her life is saved only by the one-eyed vizier pleading to marry her, swearing to lock her in a high tower and to kill thirty Muslims, if he is allowed to have her.

Distraught on discovering Miriam's departure, Ali determines to follow her but is recaptured, only escaping death by claiming to be an expert on horses. He lands in the clutches of the vizier, but by good luck (or divine providence) Ali manages to heal a sick prized stallion and in reward the vizier sets him free and employs him as master of the horse.

Ali spends his days and nights reciting mournful poetry, lamenting his loss and his 'enslaved' heart. The vizier's daughter, pitying the lovers, brings them back together. The couple escape, riding the vizier's stallions. On hearing of this, the incensed king murders the vizier and then sets out after the lovers, accompanied by his sons and other followers. Miriam prepares to do battle, but Ali admits he is incapable of fighting: he is a lover, but not a warrior.

Now follows a dispute on religion between Miriam and her brother Bartaut Ra's al Qillaut. He reproaches her for her apostasy and threatens her with the cruellest of deaths if she won't recant. But she swears that Islam is the true faith, which she will never abandon. She defeats and kills Bartaut in a fight.

---

58 Lyons, eds., *Nights:* Vol. 3, 396.

She then challenges the others to a combat which she defines as a jihad, a holy war, a 'day of glory for the faithful' against the 'enemies of religion ... Idolaters [and] tyrannical unbelievers'. Miriam's middle and younger brothers suffer the same fate as Bartaut.

The despairing ruler, with three sons dead and his daughter apostatised and missing, writes to the Caliph, Haroun al-Rashid, asking for his help and pledging to give the Caliph half the city of Rome if she is found. The lovers are arrested and brought to Baghdad, where the Caliph marvels at their beauty. He tells them of the king's request and challenges them to reply. Miriam responds with a long eloquent speech, avowing her faith as a Muslim and in the Caliph as 'God's regent on earth' to protect her and Ali Nur al-Din from 'unbelievers who associate other gods with the Omniscient Lord, who magnify the Cross, worship idols and believe in the divinity of Jesus, who was a created being'. Twice she recites the Shahadah, the Islamic creed: ('there is no god but God; Muhammad is the Apostle of God').

The Caliph agrees to give the lovers sanctuary and protection and arranges a splendid wedding for them. After a happy stay in Baghdad, the couple return to a rapturous welcome from Ali's parents in Cairo and a life of luxury and enjoyment.

This story shares many aspects with 'The Tale of King 'Umar ibn al-Nu'uman'; one could almost say it shows what might have been, had Sharkān and his beloved Abriza been allowed to stay together and marry. The differences are in the respective characters of both lovers: whereas Sharkān is weak, his love is ineffectual and he neglects to protect Abriza, later seeming uninterested in her eventual fate, Ali Nur al-Din is a flawed but faithful lover, who will risk his life many times in order to be with Miriam, although he lacks both practical and martial skills and leaves most of the thinking, and the fighting, to her.

Miriam too is different from Abriza: whereas both women are clever, accomplished and great warriors, both disguise themselves as men and kill – or order the killing of – fellow-Christians, Abriza has a kinder, more trusting, merciful and respectful nature than Miriam, which ultimately contributes to her undoing. Miriam is tough, suspicious, ruthless and even more resourceful than Abriza: ready to kill anyone who stands in her way without mercy or compunction. She is also determined to carve out a life of her choosing, even though she has been enslaved. She takes the initiative repeatedly, in relation to Nur al-Din and many others, harshly rejecting suitors not to her taste and holding out for a young and attractive man, even though he turns out to be penniless (and feckless). Ali's timidity and tendency to foul things up are at times comical – especially when contrasted with Miriam's pragmatic and unflinching resolve in the face of many adversities.

Miriam's staunch fidelity to Islam, as a relatively new convert, is also striking: at the court of Haroun al-Rashid she recites the creed and much besides in order to save her and Ali's lives. She exhibits a convert's hatred of Christianity, which she depicts as paganism ['*shirk*' – idolatry], in true jihadi style. Her religiosity as a Muslim is similar (but opposite) to the steadfast Christianity which we will encounter later among heroines such as Cervantes's pious, formerly Muslim, converts in *La historia del cautivo* and other works. The scene in which Miriam and Nur al-Din make love in a chapel of the Virgin Mary suggests an inverse relationship to that of Cervantes's Zoraida with her love of 'Leila Marien' and desire to emulate the Virgin. True to mediaeval history, in which rulers often appealed to leaders from other religions for aid, is Miriam's Christian father's appeal to Haroun, across national and faith boundaries. But true to the demands of the plot (and the exigencies of Islam), once he has learned of Miriam's conversion, Haroun rejects the king's arguments, protects the lovers and instead arranges their wedding.

4   Some Shorter *Nights* Stories

4.1   *The Tale of the Abbot Who Converted to Islam* (Nights 412–14)

In this tale, the eponymous cleric, Abd al-Masih, is incidental to the plot concerning a Muslim man and a Christian woman who converts to Islam. The man, whose adoration for the woman is at first unrequited, is attacked and wounded by some boys of her village. The girl feels sorry for him and tells him that if he will convert to Christianity, she will marry him. He refuses and is again attacked by boys, but this time is so severely wounded that he dies. The young woman is distraught. She dreams that if she will convert to Islam, the pair can be together in Paradise. She converts and then starves herself, dying on the Muslim's grave. Muslims and Christians vie with each other to bury her, and eventually it is confirmed that she was a Muslim and should have a Muslim burial, beside the young man's grave. At this, the abbot Abd al-Masih, seeing 'proof of the validity of Islam', also converts, along with all the other monks and the people of the village. The abbot is renamed 'Abd Allah (servant of God).

In this story, the entire emphasis is on conversion and justifying Islam, and the love story is sketchy. The young man gazes at the young woman and tells her that he loves her, but the first attack on him is at her instigation. Only later does she lean towards him, but her love, if it is love she feels, is never actually stated, only that she wishes to be with the young man in Paradise. Two apples play a significant part in the story, reversing the role of the apple in the Biblical story of Adam and Eve [in the Qur'an Adam and Eve are similarly tempted, but the type of fruit they eat is not specified]. Here the apples have an unrivalled flavour and sweetness, representing the sweetness of God or faith, or both, and one of them shines brightly. It is the eating of one of the apples that confirms both the girl and all the other Christians in their desire for conversion.

4.2 *The Story of the Christian Princess and the Muslim* (Nights 477–78)

The story of 'The Christian Princess and the Muslim' is one made familiar to people in both East and West through fairy tales: a princess is desperately ill and her father appeals for help in saving her. But anyone who attempts a cure and fails will be put to death. A Muslim doctor called Ibrahim ibn al-Khawwas, satisfying his curiosity to visit some lands of 'unbelievers', arrives at the city with the sick princess and receives a summons to go to the palace. He enters the room containing the girl's sickbed, concealed behind a curtain.

The young woman immediately knows who her visitor is and tells him his coming has been foretold to her. From other things she says, he understands that she has converted – or wishes to be converted – to Islam, which he welcomes. She is miraculously healed and the doctor is hailed as the curer of her disease. The princess then asks the doctor to take her to 'the lands of Islam'. The next day they depart secretly and reach Mecca, where she lives devoutly beside the Kaʿaba before dying seven years later and being buried in the holy city. Here, once again, the purpose of the story seems to be to relate the circumstances of a religious conversion, and love between the couple, if it exists at all, is never stated, nor is there any reference to a marriage between them.

4.3 *The Tale of the Muslim Hero and the Christian Girl* (Nights 474–77)

More expressly romantic is the story of 'The Muslim Hero and the Christian Girl', which begins with a Muslim siege of a Christian fortress outside Damascus. Two Muslim brothers are ambushed, whereupon one is killed and the other is captured. The prisoner (who is never named) is taken to the fortress commander, who determines to have him convert to Christianity. To that end, the beautiful daughter of one of the commander's officers (also not named) is assigned to the task. Far from converting the prisoner, the girl falls passionately in love with him and offers to convert to his religion. He supervises her conversion and instructs her how to pray. She tells him she has only converted in order to be near him, but undeterred he says that if she can find a way for them to escape together, he will marry her.

The girl convinces her father that the young man will convert to Christianity but cannot do so in the town where his brother was killed. She obtains permission for them to leave and they travel through the night. Pursued by men on horseback, the man becomes afraid, but the woman acts as his conscience, telling him to trust in his God for salvation. The pursuing army turns out to consist of angels on horseback, sent to bless them and witness their marriage and, in the morning, they reach the holy city of Medina. There they meet the Caliph ʿUmar ibn al-Khattab, who orders a feast to celebrate their nuptials. The couple then live 'in the most perfect joy' until death.

4.4   *The Man from Upper Egypt and His Frankish Wife* (Nights 894–96)

The interest of this tale lies in the striking colour of the children born to the couple and its contrast with that of their father. In the *Aethiopica,* the whiteness of the heroine's skin forces her departure from her home and is the cause of all her subsequent adventures and misadventures. The motif of skin colour as a representation of religion interpreted as race exists also in mediaeval literature, notably the Middle English rhyme of *The King of Tars*, as will be shown later (in Chapter 2). In the Arab *Sīrat Dhāt al-Himma* however, a child is born black after its mother, Maymuna, is forced into marriage with a man she loathes, who then drugs and effectively rapes her. The child's skin colour is attributed to the fact that the assault took place while the mother was menstruating.[59]

In 'The Man from Upper Egypt and his Frankish Wife' the emir Shuja al-Din, governor of Cairo, narrates that he once stayed in the house of a man from Upper Egypt, who was elderly and very dark-skinned but had three remarkably reddish-white children. Asked about the cause, the host said it was because his wife was a Frankish woman whom he had encountered while on a trading visit to the Christian town of Acre, during a truce between Christians and Muslims. He had fallen in love with her and taken her captive. She was accompanied by an elderly woman, whom he paid so as to lie with the younger woman.

But when it came to it, he was repeatedly overcome by religious scruples and ashamed to have sex with a Christian woman. The truce ending, the man was forced to leave Acre without her. In Damascus, he achieved commercial success and went into slave-trading. Three years later Saladin, having conquered the Franks, offered him a choice from among Frankish women slaves, in lieu of a final payment. One of these was the girl whom he had loved in Acre. She had been married to a Frankish knight and did not remember the Egyptian. When he reminded her of their previous meetings, she told him she had converted to Islam. The man set about freeing her and they were then married.

---

[59]   Remke Kruk, *The Warrior Women of Islam: Female Empowerment in Arabic Popular Literature* (London and New York: I.B. Tauris and Co. Ltd., 2014), 65.

One day Saladin asked for all the prisoners and captives to be handed back because of a new agreement 'between kings'. The man was heartbroken, but his wife asked him to take her to Saladin, who was seated side by side with a Frankish envoy. Saladin and the envoy asked her what she wanted and she said she chose to stay with the Muslim and to live as a Muslim. Before leaving, the Frank handed her a chest which her mother had sent her as a gift: inside, untouched and still in the same purse, was the money her husband had paid for her company in Acre.

• • •

Many factors in the stories above bear comparison with the Christian texts we will consider later, including chiefly: love of an 'other', religious conversion for love, the pivotal roles played by pirates, episodes of captivity bringing lovers together, as well as the metaphorical resort to images of slavery to describe a lover's passion. As in Greek novellas, ideas of a foreign land as a place of danger and one's own as a place of safety occur frequently. The incarceration of a lover in a tall tower (Miriam locked up by the vizier) is a recurring theme, as is the pitting of youth against unattractive and sometimes criminal old age. Fidelity to the faith adopted by a convert will appear again in the *Nights* and in Christian texts, but in the latter the religion in question will of course be Christianity.

However, an important difference between many of the *Nights* tales (including the story of 'Umar ibn al-Nu'uman, as we have seen above) and Christian ones, is the absence of poetic justice. In the story of Ali Nur al-Din and Miriam the Sashmaker for example, the hero blinds his father in one eye and takes (one might say steals) a thousand dinars from his parents' house. But he is never called to account for this and, at the end, he is welcomed back warmly by his parents, together with his new bride. Miriam, like the Greek Medea, kills a brother in order to further her love affair – in fact she kills three brothers; like Medea, she suffers no punishment for this. Nevertheless, the groundwork has been laid for many a Christian story, adopting and adapting Arab plots and characters for their own ends.

Finally, women like Abriza and Miriam come from a long and vigorous tradition of 'warrior women' in popular Arab literature, with origins not later than the 10th century, as outlined by Remke Kruk.[60] Kruk notes too that similar traditions exist in Persian, Turkish and Urdu literatures of the period.[61] Women

---

60   Remke Kruk, *Warrior Women*, 3.
61   Kruk, 15–16.

wrestling is a frequent trope in such stories, as is the motif of women in battle disguising themselves as men.[62] The *Sīrat Baibars* has a princess named Ward dressing in the clothes of her mortally wounded father in order to threaten their attackers. Not all such warrior women are discerning in their choice of victims: some kill quite casually anyone whom they dislike or who gets in their way. They may have been naturally strong and trained to fight from an early age. They may capture or be captured by men whom they love or despise.[63] But in context, their actions are not censured; as Niall Christie documents, their betrayals of their former (Christian) co-religionists in no way detract from their appeal.[64]

5 *Tales of the Marvellous and News of the Strange* (16th century CE?)

A collection of stories called *Tales of the Marvellous and News of the Strange* has several accounts overlapping with, and similar in style to those of *One Thousand and One Nights*; the date(s) of their actual composition is unknown.[65] The character of Muhammad in 'The Story of Muhammad the Foundling and Hārūn al-Rashīd' resembles that of Yusuf in *Yusuf and Zulaikha* (discussed below) in that his remarkable beauty dazzles men and women alike and he is accused of rape by a thwarted would-be lover.

However, the circumstances of the foundling's birth, unlike those of Yusuf, are unclear and he is adopted by the Caliph Hārūn al-Rashīd. Muhammad's accuser is not a wife, but a lovely 'Rumi' (Byzantine Christian) slave girl bought by the Caliph Hārūn al-Rashīd. Muhammad flees for his life, but the story does not end with her and Muhammad's union. The slave girl is first imprisoned

---

62 Kruk, 23 and 26.
63 Malcolm C. Lyons, *The Arabian Epic: Heroic and Oral Story-Telling*, 3 vols (Cambridge: Cambridge University Press, 1995), Vol. I, 109–18.
64 Niall Christie (2012) 'Noble Betrayers of their Faith, Families and Folk: Some Non-Muslim Women in Mediaeval Arabic Popular Literature', *Folklore*, 123:1, 84–98, 84 and passim: DOI: 10.1080/0015587X.2012.642988, [accessed 25/3/2023].
65 *Tales of the Marvellous and News of the Strange*, ed. and tr. Malcolm C. Lyons 2014, (repr. London: Penguin Classics, 2015). In his introduction to the collection, Robert Irwin cites dates for the stories varying from the fourteenth to the sixteenth centuries CE (xii), although much of the material contained in the tales is clearly of an earlier origin; some of the events and characters in them relate to historical events and people from as far back as the time of the Prophet Muhammad, i.e, the 1st/7th century. The unique manuscript of the tales was discovered by the German Arabist Hellmut Ritter in a library in Istanbul, and he published it in 1933. All further page references relating to *Tales of the Marvellous and News of the Strange* are from the Lyons edition.

and then sold on after having, like Shahriyar's wives in *One Thousand and One Nights,* been intimate with a black slave, who is killed when his story comes out. In fact, after dallying with another beautiful woman while on the run from his accusers, Muhammad is eventually reunited with Hārūn al-Rashīd in Baghdad and is paired with an older man called Khultukh who has befriended him during his period in exile. Muhammad has moved to Baghdad to be near him and the Caliph; the nature of Khultukh and Muhammad's relationship is ambiguous.

Several other stories in the collection feature Christians and pagans converting to Islam, as well as miscegenation, including extraordinary love affairs and even marriages between humans and jinns, or humans and animals. In 'The Story of Mahliya and Mauhub and the White-footed Gazelle', humans are metamorphosed into animals and back to humans, and marry across species lines: in the most extreme case, a woman marries a lion. As Irwin remarks in his introduction to the collection, 'Therianthropy, the transformation of a human into an animal, is usually presented by storytellers as a form of imprisonment'.[66] As with the victims of the sorceress Circe, transformed into swine in the *Odyssey,* the human is trapped in the animal form while retaining human senses and sensibilities. But the hero, Mauhub, despite having been suckled by a lioness, is also in thrall to the Christian princess Mahliya: she, entrusted by her father with his affairs of state when aged only fourteen, is clever and resourceful and, having access to various magic spells, outwits Mauhub at every turn.

First, she initiates the contact between herself and Mauhub. A mistress of disguises, she deceives him by masquerading at first as her own vizier and then as a nun, in a reversal of the *Nights* episodes in which Hārūn al-Rashīd poses as a merchant in order to learn about his people's lives. And when, due to a misunderstanding, they fight each other, the Amazonian Mahliya defeats Mauhub and destroys his army, humbling him by means of her superior planning, while he is naïve and easily led. She is also ruthless, torturing some sorcerers to obtain information and finally crucifying and drowning, respectively, one of the sorcerers and her daughter.

Diversity in 'The story of Mauhub and Mahliya' is presented as desirable: although the hero and heroine are both Christians, they are of different nationalities, he being from Zaba (in the region of Java or Sumatra), while she is Egyptian. In a passage describing the splendour of Mahliya's court, she is said to be flanked by a thousand Byzantine eunuchs *of various races*, as well as

---

66   Irwin, Introduction to *Tales of the Marvellous*, xxvii.

a thousand slave girls *of various races* (432, my emphases). And celebrating her marriage to Mauhub, Mahliya has brought to her women 'from every region' (434). The variety and multiplicity of races and regional origins of these courtly servants seem to underline their value.

As Irwin notes in his introduction to the collection, this and several other stories show some knowledge of Christian doctrine,[67] even though the author appears to have been Muslim. The story ends with praise of, and an invocation of blessings on the Prophet Muhammad. And yet, in a mirroring of ignorant Christian treatments of Islam, here the Christian protagonists pay homage to the pagan god Baal.

In 'The Story of Sul and Shumul' the theology is even more extraordinary, since Sul, although a Christian, needs help from the chief Muslim devil Iblis Abu Marra, who has authority over all other devils as well as jinn, to solve his problems. Sul, in traditional Arab fashion, is deeply in love with his first cousin Shumul, with whom he has grown up. Indeed, his love is expressed as thraldom in poem after poem which he writes to and about her: 'she enslaves men with her loveliness' (229); 'I am bound in fetters of her love' (230); 'How can I forget one who captured me.' (ibid); 'A ... girl, whose love imprisons me' (234); 'her glance captures hearts' (236); and 'I am your ransom' (ibid). He reproaches Shumul for showing 'no pity for my tears' (235) and asks rhetorically, whether she means to leave him dead (236). However, these metaphors are all whimsical and deliberately hyperbolic, part of a game Sul plays with Shumul who is, apparently, just as much in love with him as he with her; it is she who urges him on to ever more extreme flights of fancy, congratulating him repeatedly on his inventions.

Sul is clearly a man destined to suffer. Just when he has been granted his heart's desire and is about to marry his beloved Shumul, an enormous snake carries off the bride. For two or three days, Sul does nothing but weep and appears close to death until, seeing Shumul in a dream, he finds the strength to go and look for her. It is here the devil comes in useful, demanding Sul's service as the price for assisting him and Sul agrees, although he adds, guardedly, 'God alone is omnipotent' (252). This caveat is not enough to deter Iblis, who orders the *ifrits* [cunning types of jinn] to produce Shumul, and the lovers are reunited. Sul recites a prayer to God (even though, it appears God had little to do with the successful outcome of events) and Iblis accepts that Sul is 'a believer' (253). Sul informs Shumul that he must also marry a woman called Al-Nahhada, who has fallen in love with him, which Shumul dutifully accepts,

---

67   Irwin, Introduction to *Tales of the Marvellous,* xxxvi.

acknowledging that al-Nahhada had been good to her. Sul has children with both women and the piece ends, like others in the collection, with a call for blessings and peace for the Prophet Muhammad.

'The Story of Miqdad and Mayasa' is set in the Hijaz in the 6th-7th/1st century, in a period spanning the pre-Islamic era, the so-called *Jahiliya* [Time of Ignorance], and the early Islamic one. The hero, Miqdad, has a historic forebear of that name, who was one of the earliest people to convert to Islam.[68] Like Sharkān in the *Nights'* Tale of King ʿUmar ibn al-Nuʿuman, Miqdad fights a beautiful Amazonian woman, in this case Mayasa. But Miqdad, swearing an oath by the pagan goddess al-Lat, and unlike Sharkān, defeats his adversary, who vows to marry him, swearing an oath by the goddesses al-Lat and al-Uzza (274).

However, Mayasa's father demands an enormous dowry and the rest of the story concerns Miqdad's herculean efforts to amass the necessary wealth, by overcoming huge numbers of men and taking their goods as booty. The only man he cannot defeat is the Prophet's cousin and son-in-law Abu 'l-Hasan ʿAli. Ali recites the Shahada (Muslim creed) and Miqdad recites it after him, accepting Islam. Mayasa, threatened with forced marriage to a man called Malik, whom she hates, knocks him flat, then asks for God's help and is transported, as if by magic, to the Prophet's Mosque in Medina. There she too converts to Islam. Until that point, Miqdad and Mayasa are for a time of different faiths, but from then on, they share the religion of Islam. ʿAli challenges Malik and his brother to convert; when they refuse, ʿAli orders Miqdad to behead them. The couple, reunited, renew their faith in front of the Prophet and Miqdad becomes a champion of Islam, continuing to fight jihad until his death, by the side of ʿAli.

One other story features devoted love between a presumably Muslim man and his, presumably non-Muslim, slave girl: 'The Story of Talha, the Son of the Qadi of Fustat, and What Happened to Him with his Slave Girl Tuhfa, and How She was Taken Away from Him, and What Hardship Befell until there was Relief after Grief'. This story is identified among a group of Arab tales in which beautiful slave women and their devoted owners are separated but then reunited, often through the generosity of new owners ready to relinquish both the woman and the price paid for her.[69] The title gives a pretty comprehensive summary of the whole story, leaving little suspense for the reader, but it is still

---

68 Lyons, *Tales of the Marvellous,* xxxviii.
69 Geert Jan van Gelder lists and summarises twenty such stories in his 'Slave Girl Lost and Regained: Transformations of a Story', in *The Arabian Nights in Transnational Perspective,* ed. Ulrich Marzolph (Detroit, Michigan: Wayne State University Press, 2007), 65–82.

worth telling in more detail. Talha, son of the Qadi of Fustat (Cairo) and 'the most beautiful child ever seen', is given a similarly beautiful slave girl, Tuhfa. The boy and his slave girl are brought up and educated together. Like Miriam, she becomes impossibly erudite, with a 'perfect mastery of all branches of learning', including a complete knowledge of the Qur'an as well as arithmetic, chess, backgammon and the lute, which she plays and to which she sings, delightfully. Talha's father agrees to his marriage with Tuhfa.

Inheriting his father's wealth, Talha squanders it all and sinks into poverty. Tuhfa suggests he sell her, so as to make some money, and reluctantly he agrees. The rest of the story concerns the couple's many abortive attempts to get back together, in the course of which Talha, maddened by grief, is locked up in chains. Eventually, after much suffering and many misunderstandings, as well as a shipwreck which renders Talha once again penniless, and heroic self-sacrifice on the part of Tuhfa's new 'owner', the couple are reunited. The story has obvious echoes of the *Nights* 'Story of Ali Nur al-Din and Miriam the Sash-Maker'. It may also be a predecessor for the mediaeval Christian story of *Floire et Blanchefleur*, which we shall encounter in the next chapter.

Finally, in one story in the collection, ethnicity plays a major role in a tale now bluntly labelled 'racist'.[70] In 'The Story of Ashraf and Anjab' the hero, al-Ashraf, is the son of a beautiful slave girl who was married to the Caliph's cousin, Muhammad. As a baby, Ashraf will not accept milk from his mother, but only from an ugly black slave girl, whose own son, al-Anjab, similarly black and ugly, is raised with al-Ashraf as his brother. Al-Anjab becomes the villain of the piece, pretending love for al-Ashraf and passing himself off as his real brother, despite knowing their true relationship. Falling into al-Anjab's clutches, al-Ashraf is imprisoned and tortured. All comes right in the end however, with al-Ashraf being restored to wealth and al-Anjab beheaded.

Unusually in this collection of stories, 'Ashraf and Anjab' has no central love story: the only marriage at the end is between al-Ashraf's widowed mother and a cook who has rescued Ashraf from his dungeon. It is included here for the light it sheds on one aspect of race relations in a Muslim land.

---

[70] By Genevieve Valentine, reviewing the Lyons edition of *Tales of the Marvellous* … for npr (National Public Radio), on the 18th February 2015: https://www.npr.org/2015/02/18/385193561/tales-of-the-marvellous-is-indeed-very-strange [accessed 18/7/2023]; and Robert Irwin, *The Dark Side of 'The Arabian Nights'* : https://www.criticalmuslim.io/the-dark-side-of-the-arabian-nights [accessed 16/4/2024].

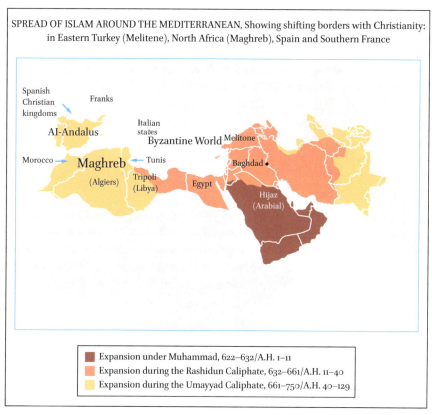

FIGURE 1.4   Map of Expansion of Caliphate, source. Image in the public domain
SOURCE: HTTPS://COMMONS.WIKIMEDIA.ORG/WIKI/FILE:MAP_OF_EXPANSI
ON_OF_CALIPHATE.SVG EMBELLISHED (WITH PLACE NAMES AND OTHER
TEXT) BY THE CURRENT AUTHOR

5.1   Sīrat Dhāt al-Himma

The voluminous epic *Sīrat Dhāt al-Himma*, also known as *Sīrat Ḏāt al-Himma wa-l-Baṭṭāl* or simply *Sīrat Delhemma*, has a number of Christian warrior women and conversions of Christian women to Islam, as well as episodes of captivity, in its many strands of plot.[71] The context of the epic, which was written during or some time after the 9th century, is the Arab-Byzantine wars during the Umayyad and early Abbasid periods of the late 7th and 8th centuries. Caliph Hārūn al-Rashīd appears several times – as in the *Nights*, as do the

---

71 An abbreviated translation of the book has been published recently: Melanie Magidow, ed. and translator, *The Tale of Princess Fatima, Warrior Woman: The Arabic Epic of Dhāt al-Himma* (London: Penguin Books, 2022).

historic Caliphs al-Amin, al-Ma'mun and al-Mu'tasim. Much of the work is set in Malatya (also known as Melitene), in Eastern Anatolia, on the frontier between Christendom and Islam; it was captured by the Rashidun Caliphate in 638 CE and was the base for many Muslim raids against the Byzantines [Figure 1.4]. The eponymous heroine Dhāt al-Himma is Warden of the Marches, that is to say, she is responsible for patrolling the borderlands.

Other locations of the epic include Constantinople. An account of its siege by the Umayyad Caliph Maslama in 717–18 CE is reworked to culminate in a victory for the Muslim armies, rather than the notable defeat which it was in reality; and some scenes are set in the western Mediterranean, in the Maghreb and Islamic Spain.

Among the Byzantine Christian women who appear in the epic are Iftuna, Marjana, Maymuna, Nura, Nur al-Nar and Zananir, who usually but not invariably convert in the service of marriage to Muslim men. The Byzantine princess Nura resists marriage but is repeatedly captured and tied up, and finally forced to marry one of the epic's central characters, the clever survivor al-Baṭṭāl.[72] She tries to poison him on their wedding night but, with the help of Dhāt al-Himma, he overcomes and rapes her, after which her hatred toward al-Baṭṭāl turns to love. By then she has already converted to Islam. Conversely, a slave girl who refuses to convert is killed and in one episode of the *Sīrat Dhāt al-Himma* ten thousand people are killed for refusing Islam.[73] A few characters who have converted, convert back again: Maymuna, a major figure in the narrative, converts to Islam and marries a Muslim prince, but then converts back to Christianity in an act signalling her gradual degradation, downfall and ultimately her violent death. The treacherous villain of the piece, the qadi Uqba, is a secret convert to Christianity and, when eventually unmasked, ends his days crucified at the gates of Constantinople.

A number of Christian women in *Sīrat Dhāt al-Himma* are shown taking the initiative with Muslim men. A Christian princess comes to the tent of the Muslim Arnus, confiding that she is too frightened to sleep and then sits talking to him 'as though she was his wife'. Other Christian girls, 'drunk or sober, try more blatantly to seduce Muslims; narrative convention suggests that the misguided girls must be converted, having been shown the advantages of Muslim marriage'. One Christian woman, Zananir, falls in love with a Muslim named

---

72 Identified as a traditional type of clever and cunning man in Arabic fiction: Malcom C Lyons, *The Man of Wiles in Popular Arab Literature: a Study of a Medieval Arab Hero* (Edinburgh: Edinburgh University Press, 2012).
73 Lyons, M.C. *Arabian Epic*, Vol. 1, 48.

Lu'lu because he has refused to abandon Islam 'and whatever is forbidden is sweet'.[74]

In the next chapter, we shall encounter similarly tough and bellicose women in mediaeval Christian narratives. In these cases, they are Muslims, women such as Floripas and Nicolette, who fight to win the men they love.

6   Poetry

Love between free men and slave women is celebrated in some of the earliest Arab and Persian poetry. The 10th century Persian poet Rudagi boasts,

> How many pretty girls took a fancy to me
> and came to see me furtively by night,
> not daring to come by day
> for fear of their master or of jail.[75]

Rarely is the social relationship between the poet and the woman of whom – or to whom – he writes made as clear as in the verse quoted above. As Lewis points out in the *Introduction* to his collection of poems, the woman in such poetry is often a slave, 'perhaps one of the educated and cultivated singing girls who provided the feminine element in court society and are celebrated by many writers'.[76]

In relatively few of the Muslim poetry and romance texts I have considered is the slave woman's religion mentioned. One which does specify the beloved's faith is a short poem, 'Marguerite', by the 11th-century Andalusi poet Ibn Billita:

Marguerite

> Shining marguerite,
> Flower fair and sweet,
> Golden glow a-glimmer
> On your silver shimmer.

---

74   Lyons, *Arabian Epic*, Vol. 1, 39–40.
75   *Music of a Distant Drum: Classical Arabic, Persian, Turkish, and Hebrew Poems*, ed. and tr. Bernard Lewis (Princeton University Press, Princeton and Oxford, 2001), 98.
76   Lewis ed., *Music of a Distant Drum*, 23.

> Frankish slave, pale-faced,
> Magian faith embraced,
> Mystic fire discerning
> To its altar turning.
>
> Mouth of my adored,
> And, for love's reward,
> Gleaming gold I shower
> In her mouth, my flower.[77]

The title – which is presumably the name of the woman described in this piece – invokes a conceit whereby the poet references a woman's fair skin. Her light colouring, her white and gold, are like those of the flower. The 'Mystic fire' of the middle stanza alludes to the fire worship of the Zoroastrians. The golden colour of the money he gives for her (presumably sexual) services echoes her own.

But there is something deeply troubling in the manner by which he pays her – filling her mouth with gold, thereby subtly comparing her with the avaricious King Midas, whose touch turned everything to gold, even his food. Another allusion could be to the shower of gold, one of the disguises of the god Zeus with which, according to classical mythology, he seduced the Greek princess Danaë. She was sometimes seen as a symbol of the corrupting effect of wealth, which could purchase anything, including female virtue. In later years, Danaë was depicted as a courtesan. These discreet associations lend the poem a strong satiric element, its romantic and elegant imagery notwithstanding.

6.1   Slave Motifs in the Poetry of Al-Andalus

Much of the poetry of Islamic al-Andalus is saturated with oxymoronic imagery fusing love, pain, servitude and death. Poets' awareness in real life of ever-present suffering and death is reflected in their work, often displaced onto erotic relationships. They witnessed the torture and execution of others all around them and were at constant risk themselves, their nominally free state offering them no more protection than if they had been enslaved. In a despotic and rigidly hierarchical society, the ruler held the absolute power of life and death in his hands. Yet life was precarious for all, as he too could be overthrown at any time by one stronger or more ruthless than himself. This insecurity was exacerbated by constant warfare with the Christians to the north, as well as

---

[77] *Moorish Poetry: A Translation of* 'The Pennants', *an Anthology Compiled in 1243 by the Andalusian Ibn Sa'id*, ed. A.J. Arberry (Cambridge: Cambridge University Press, 1953), 77.

between Muslim nation-states (*taifas*), after the collapse of the Caliphate in 1031 CE, followed by successive waves of conquest by Almoravids and then Almohads, from North Africa. Each upheaval reconstituted the upper echelons of Andalusi society, as the invaders usurped incumbent rulers and installed members of their own entourage around them.

Social and political factions abounded, but were also fluid, frequently changing their shape and composition. People vied to ally themselves with the most powerful and when the locus of power shifted, so too did the loyalty of many former adherents. Poets too looked for patronage and support and, in a society which valued poetry and literature above all other arts, their verses could create great opportunities. Witty or flattering lines judiciously conveyed to a wealthy superior could gain rich rewards; some of the more fawning poems addressed to rulers closely resemble love letters. Alternatively, an ill-placed satire or other misjudged lines could mean imprisonment or death. The 12th century poet Abū Ja'far Aḥmad ibn 'Abd al-Malik Ibn Sa'īd loved a woman called Ḥafṣa, an accomplished poet in her own right, who was also desired by Abū Ja'far's employer, the Almohad governor of Granada Abu Sa'id Uthman. One day, after drinking heavily, Abu Ja'far composed some insulting and belittling verses on the topic of his employer. These being reported to the governor, the latter grew incensed and ordered the poet's execution.[78]

The uncertainties and frequent reversals of life were reflected in poetic tropes linking love with sickness, torment, slavery and death. The image of lovers' eyes emitting deadly arrows or beams to pierce the heart or soul foreshadows what would later, and in other places, be known as a type of Petrarchan conceit.[79] Some poems speak of being crazed by love,[80] of being enslaved to or wounded, or made ill by the beloved,[81] or of owing a duty of submission. A 10th-century poet, Ibn 'Abd Rabbih, wrote to his lover reproachfully,

> You are my illness, in your power lies my remedy;
> You can cure me of my pain and suffering:
> My heart is in love with one it does not name,
> Suffers a pain, the greatest of all pains!

---

78 Ross Brann, 'He Said, She Said: Reinscribing the Andalusi Arabic Love Lyric', *Studies in Arabic and Hebrew Letters: In Honor of Raymond P. Scheindlin*, ed. Jonathan P. Decter and Michael Chaim Rand (Piscataway, NJ: Gorgias Press LLC, 2007), 7–16.
79 Nykl, e.g. 207, 243, 249, 342–430.
80 Nykl, e.g. 250, 277.
81 Nykl, 241, 246, 272, 282, 294–95.

> Oh you who blame me, what matters it if you
> Remain alive and I die of my pain? ...
>
> Oh pearl that subdues all minds by beauty,
> Oh gazelle so deft in torturing hearts! ...
>
> In loving you, my passion caused me to befriend pains,
> As if I were their mate and they my friends ...
>
> Love has put fetters on my heart,
> As a herdsman puts fetters on a camel ...
> Oh you, whose eyelids are languid, though free from illness,
> Between your eyes is where lovers find their death![82]

The paradox whereby the free poet becomes slave to the slave woman is exploited by the 11th –12th century Spanish Jew, Yehuda Halevi. He eulogises his beloved, addressing her as one who has 'made me captive with your loveliness and burdened me with great toil in this captivity.'[83] The conceit of love as slavery, with the lover chained, is also developed by the poet Ibn Zaidun, who wrote ever more desperate letters to his disdainful lover the royal princess Wallada, an accomplished poet in her own right. For several months they had enjoyed ecstatic trysts in a darkened garden. But at even their happiest time together, he wrote telling her that love had made him ill and separation from her would mean his death; he refers to himself as her slave, bound by fetters of passion (Nykl, 109 and 110). Their affair did not last. Wallada drew away from Ibn Zaidun and subsequently discarded him in favour of a duller but wealthier man, with whom she lived until his death.

6.2   Ruler-Poets

Poetry is considered the highest artistic form in traditional Arab culture and many rulers prided themselves on being poets; they had the same preoccupations as their subjects. The 8th-9th century emir al-Hakam I, despite achieving several significant military victories, addressed the following subservient lines to some women in his harem, themselves akin to slaves:

> A king am I, subdued, his power humbled
> To love, like a captive in fetters, forlorn! ...

---

[82]   Quoted by Nykl, 38–39.
[83]   Lewis, *Music of a Distant Drum,* 191.

> Excessive love has made of him a slave
> Though before that he was a mighty king!
> If he weeps, complains of love, more unjustly
> They treat, eschew him, bring him near his death! ...
> Humble demeanor behooves [sic] a free man
> Whenever he becomes a slave through love! [84]

In a somewhat similar vein, the 11th century poet-King al-Mu'tamid, 'conformed to a literary convention of the sovereignty of women and compared himself to a lion pursued by a gazelle' in poems addressed to his beloved slave I'timad al-Rumakiyya.[85] Al-Mu'tamid, himself descended from a Christian slave woman, held a lifelong passion for the girl who was, like him, a clever versifier and whom he observed washing clothes by a river. He chose her for his wife, after she improvised some witty lines in response to lines of his. One of his poems refers back to this time:

> How many nights, too, in the river's loop I spent
> With a graceful slave girl for my companion;
> The curve of her bracelet imitated the river.
> She poured out for me the wine of her eyes.[86]

His love for Al-Rumakkiya notwithstanding, Al-Mu'tamid could also admire beautiful boys, as well as other women. Of one youth he wrote that,

> They named him Sword; two other swords: his eyes!
> Both he and those are ready to slay me!
> Would not one slaying by sword have quite sufficed?
> Yet by his eyebrows two further blows were dealt!
> I made *him* captive; his charming eyes in turn
> Made *me his* captive: now we are *both* masters, *both* slaves!
> Oh Sword, be kind toward a captive of love,
> Who asks not, as a favour, to be freed by you.[87]

---

84 Quoted by Nykl, 20–21.
85 Robert Irwin, ed, *Night and Horses and the Desert: An Anthology of Classical Arabic Literature* (London and other locations: Allen Lane and The Penguin Press, 1999), 267.
86 Christopher Middleton and Leticia Garza-Falcon, *Andalusian Poems,* quoted in Irwin, ed, *Night and Horses,* 268.
87 Nykl, 143.

The king was deposed by the Berber Almoravids and imprisoned, along with his household, then exiled with his family in Morocco. Now he was literally a captive and wrote poignantly about it, using images similar to those he had used about love:

> A stranger, a captive in the Magrib: over there,
> The throne will mourn him and the pulpit also,
> Sharp, cutting swords, and the lances likewise,
> Will shed, profusely, bitter tears of grief!
> There was a time when power was his friend,
> A very close one, but today it eschews him.[88]

Finally, the Almoravid ruler Ibn Tashufin, fearing al-Mu'tamid might try to escape, ordered him to be put in chains, in which state his life ended. In his last days, the king wrote verses about his captivity: of 'fetters [which] kindle a fire/Which sets my arms and every joint aflame', of being tortured by grief and the knowledge that his children had been made destitute and were far away, and of the 'corners of the earth' 'filled … with pain' because of his sufferings. He foresees his own death and asks rhetorically, 'how were you vanquished after having vanquished …?'[89]

6.3 Poetry and Religion

Interrogations of slavery and the slave status occur not only in literature, but also ontologically in metaphysical theology, especially that of the Sufis. The 11th-century Andalusi Ibn 'Arabī argues that since humans are the slaves of God, freedom is the perfect form of slavery.[90] In other writing, he warns against slavery to the passions, to one's own desires.[91] Many poems speak of clandestine meetings, abruptly terminated by the advent of dawn, such as a verse by the Syrian Umayyad Caliph and poet Al-Walid II.[92] Such forms are more familiar to us as *aubades* in the work of troubadours and other Christian authors, from the late Middle Ages onwards, such as the songs of Wolfram von Eschenbach and in England, Chaucer's *Troilus and Criseyde* and Shakespeare's *Romeo and Juliet*.

---

88   Nykl, 149.
89   Nykl, 149–52.
90   Cf. *Oxford Dictionary of Islam*, 119.
91   Cf. Muhammad Rahmatullah, 'Slavery and Islam', *Islamic Literature,* Vol. XIII, No. 2, February (1967), Lahore, Pakistan.
92   Lewis, *Music of a Distant Drum,* 48; and Lewis's *Introduction*, 23.

7   Ibn Ḥazm

Love between slave-woman and free man is frequently referred to in Arab textbooks and manuals on love and sex, much of it erotic. Among these are books such as Omar Haleby's *El Kitab*, translated into French as *El Ktab des lois secrètes de l'amour* (*Book of the Secrets of Love*),[93] al-Siyuti's *Kitab al-Izah fi-ilm* (*Book of Exposition*)[94] and *Al-Raud al-atir wa nuzhat al-Khatir* (*The Perfumed Garden*) by the 16th century writer Umar ibn Muhammad Nefzawi, sometimes known simply as Sheikh (or Cheikh) Nefzawi (or Nefzaoui).[95] These books feature anecdotes about love involving mostly female slaves, but also occasionally male, and are referred to enthusiastically by Richard Burton in his edition of *One Thousand and One Nights*,[96] and by Donald McCormick in his *Erotic Literature*.[97]

The most famous of the Andalusi poets was Abū Muḥammad ʿAlī ibn Aḥmad ibn Saʿīd ibn Ḥazm, known in short form as Ibn Ḥazm (994–1064 CE) [Figure 1.5], whose *Ṭawq al-Ḥamāmah* – translated into English as *The Ring of the Dove* is a compendium of observations and anecdotes on themes of love, now whimsical, now discursive, now earnest and moral.[98] Since, as noted above, extra-marital sex, and by extension even flirtation, were only permissible with slave girls in most Muslim societies, a large number of Ibn Ḥazm's anecdotes have at their heart the love of a man for a slave girl or vice versa. This love may be between a slave and her 'owner', or an acquaintance, or just a passer-by. The lover may be a nobleman, an ordinary man, or even a freedman ('freed' man, meaning a manumitted slave).

---

[93] Omar Haleby, *El Ktab des lois secrètes de l'amour / d'après le Khôdja Omer Haleby, Abou Othmân;* traduction, mise en ordre et commentaires de Paul de Régla [Paris], 1838– , 1893.

[94] Jala al-Din al-Siyuti, *Kitab al-Izah fi-ilm bi-it-tamam wa al-kamal*, (*Book of Exposition, literally translated from the Arabic by an English Bohemian*), 1893 (repr. Paris, London and New York: Maison d'editions scientifiques, 1900).

[95] *The Perfumed Garden of the Cheikh Nefzaoui: a Manual of Arab Erotology* (XVI century), Revised and Corrected translation (into English, by Richard Burton), (London and Benares: Cosmopoli, for the Kama Shastra Society of London and Benares, for private circulation only, 1886); digitized by the Internet Archive in 2010 with funding from Boston Public Library: https://en.wikisource.org/wiki/The_Perfumed_Garden [accessed 14/10/2016].

[96] *The Book of the Thousand and One Nights*, ed. and tr. Burton, Vol. 10, 175.

[97] Donald McCormick, *Erotic Literature: A Connoiseur's Guide* (New York: Continuum Publishing Co., 1992), 28–29.

[98] Ibn Ḥazm, *The Ring of the Dove: a Treatise on the Art and Practice of Arab Love*, tr. and ed. by A.J. Arberry, 1953 (repr. London: Luzac Oriental, 1994). All subsequent page references with regard to Ibn Ḥazm relate to this edition.

Ibn Ḥazm was a philosopher, statesman, theologian and historian, as well as poet, and this is his only work on the topic of love. He expounds his ideas under various headings, such as 'The Signs of Love'; 'Of Falling in Love while Asleep' (i.e., through a dream); 'Of Falling in Love at First Sight'; 'Of Falling in Love after a Long Association' and so on. The text takes the form of stories and anecdotes, interspersed with verses of Ibn Ḥazm's own composition, written to illustrate the various themes and stories.

The picture painted is of intense flirtations and love affairs, carried on against a backdrop of desperate political turmoil: a *carpe diem* situation in which poets and political figures (often one and the same person, like Ibn Ḥazm himself) alternated between vying for position and power, and seeking and enjoying love, in a society at first riven with internal strife and then conquered by the North African Almoravids. One terrible story is of a freedman who takes part in a revolt led by the rebel Hishām Ibn Sulaimān Ibn al-Nasir against the Caliph al-Mahdi. Hishām is taken prisoner and killed, whereupon the conspirators, including the freedman Khalaf, flee. However, finding himself 'unable to endure being parted from a slave-girl he possessed in Cordova', Khalaf returns to the capital where he is captured and crucified. Ibn Ḥazm concludes that this incident furnishes 'striking proof of the way in which passion will lead a man into imminent and obvious disaster, recognisable as such by the most sensible and most stupid of human beings' (Ibn Ḥazm, *Ring of the Dove*, 249–50).

Many other instances are given in which the love of a slave woman leads to the misery, or even death, of the lover. It may be his own scruples that are his undoing: one man of high rank, renowned for his piety, sees a slave-girl in the street with her face uncovered. He falls deeply in love with her, but is so fearful of falling into temptation, that he leaves the city for Basra. There he dies of love (226–27). Another man, Marwān Ibn Aḥmad Ibn Hudair, is murdered by his slave-girl Qatr a-Nada (108–09); we are not told why.

Alternatively, it may be the girl's coldness that causes the man pain. In one of Ibn Ḥazm's stories, a slave woman whom he adores repeatedly refuses his advances (208–14). This gives rise not only to his own deep suffering but eventually, he suggests, her own as well. Under the heading 'Of Forgetting', he tells of his vain and 'violent' passion for the singing-girl who, despite their having enjoyed a 'loving friendship' in their youth, consistently rejects him. No matter how hard he tries, he cannot persuade her to give herself to him: being shy, modest and chaste, she always avoids him. After a long separation, the poet sees her again at his father's funeral and his passion is kindled anew. He compares his own feelings of emotional death with the literal death of his father.

EARLY ISLAMIC PERSPECTIVES

After several more years, the narrator encounters the woman again, but this time she is so altered he scarcely recognises her:

> Gone was her radiant beauty, vanished her wondrous loveliness; faded now was that lustrous complexion which once gleamed like a polished sword or an Indian mirror; withered was the bloom on which the eye once gazed transfixed ... Only a fragment of the whole remained.
> *Ring of the Dove,* 213

Ibn Ḥazm concludes that her disdain and her decline are linked: she refused his (and other men's) protection and thereby neglected her own interests, so that with the coming of harsher times she was forced to 'besmirch herself in those inevitable excursions to which her circumstances had driven her, and from which she had formerly been sheltered and exempted'. The loss was a mutual one:

FIGURE 1.5   Image of Ibn Ḥazm on a Spanish postage stamp dated 1986, value 12 Pesetas. Image by Sergei Nezhinskii
CREDIT: DREAMSTIME: HTTPS://WWW.DREAMSTIME.COM/SPAIN-CIRCA-STAMP-PRINTED-SPAIN-SHOWS-PORTRAIT-IBN-HAZM-IMAGE180617931.

> For women are as aromatic herbs, which if not tended soon lose their fragrance; they are as edifices, which, if not constantly cared for, quickly fall into ruin.
>
> If I had enjoyed the least degree of intimacy with her, if she had been only a little kind to me, I would have been beside myself with happiness; I verily believe that I would have died for joy. But it was her unremitting aloofness which schooled me in patience, and taught me to find consolation.
>
> Ring of the Dove, 214

Again, the story evolves against a background of social and political disaster, in the course of which the author suffers imprisonment and exile. A civil war rages during the rule of Hishām al-Mu'ayyad (Hisham II). Córdoba is conquered by the Berbers, causing the poet again to leave his homeland for six years. It is during this time that the object of his affections loses her beauty.

Many of the women described by Ibn Ḥazm are singing-girls. On the one hand such women were literally the property of their owners, bought and liable to be sold at any time. *The Epistle on Singing-Girls* by Abu Uthman Amr. B. Bahr a-Jahiz (776–869 CE) well describes the slave's reified status:

> Slaves are a variety of merchandise, subject to bargaining and chaffering over price; and both vendor and purchaser need to examine the piece of goods carefully.[99]

On the other hand, singing-girls were greatly appreciated for their skills. As Beeston points out, they had a special value: their training was long and expensive, so they represented a considerable capital investment on the part of the merchant who dealt in them. Although he might recoup his expenses by an outright sale to a wealthy client, in many cases the women stayed with him as a source of income, both from hiring them out as entertainers at parties and from 'more dubious practices.'[100]

'Dubious practices' refers to the girls' frequent amorous relations with 'customers' attending suppers and other entertainments, for which the owner took payment in cash or in kind, in effect as pimp.[101] It follows that such women

---

99 *The Epistle on Singing-Girls of Jahiz*, ed. and tr. A.F.L. Beeston (Warminster, Wilts.: Aris & Phillips Ltd., 1980), 24.
100 Beeston, 2.
101 Beeston, 58.

would be chosen for their beauty, and dressed, coiffed and perfumed well so as to enhance their physical attractions. Al Jahiz comments that,

> The degree of estimation whereby singing-girls fetch high prices is due to infatuation. If purchase [of them] were made on the same basis as ordinary slaves, not one of them would run up to more than the price of a commonplace slave. But most of those who bid high prices for a girl do so because of passion. Such a one may have been intending to seduce her, thinking this an easier way to satisfy his ardent desire; then this proves impossible for him, and he turns to a legitimate approach.[102]

This, the author adds, satirically, turns a potentially illicit affair into a lawful one: the carefulness of the owners and the strictness of the girls' seclusion force the frustrated lover into purchasing the girl and thereby legitimising his sexual relations with her.

This account suggests the girls are merely pawns in their owners' hands. But Ibn Ḥazm presents an alternative reality: one in which the women's own feelings are often brought into play. They may resist men's overtures, as in the 'Of Forgetting' anecdote narrated above, or drawn into love affairs in which their own passions are strongly engaged. Where Jahiz reifies his singing-girls, Ibn Ḥazm humanises them, albeit often critically, as when he accuses them of being untrustworthy (*Ring of the Dove,* 109). Many of his stories though tell of slaves deeply in love with their owners or other men. One whom he holds up as a model for fidelity (an extremely rare instance of fidelity, he remarks) is so devastated when her beloved master dies that she gives up singing, despite having had a fine voice. Furthermore, despite her being sold 'with [her late master's] estate' to a new owner, and being beaten by him for refusing him and all other men, she remains celibate until she too dies (155–56).

But the slave-girl is by no means always passive when it comes to the affairs of her own heart. One modest young woman, tired of nurturing a passion for the 'son of a noble household', and even – on the advice of a wise older woman – sending him her own verses hinting at her feelings for him, without receiving a response, takes drastic action. One night, after she has been speaking with him tête-a-tête, she suddenly kisses him on the mouth and then abruptly leaves, 'coquettishly swaying'. This at last awakens in the startled young man a reciprocal passion. Overcoming his many fears and sleepless nights, he finally

---

102   Beeston, 27.

responds to her and the two find love which continues 'many moons', until eventually separation breaks 'the cords of their perfect union' (121–22).

Thus, the beautiful slave and especially the singing-girl, has a curious, ambiguous position in her society: she is 'owned', yet she is valued; she is liable to be sold at any time, yet she can withhold her 'services' and her affections; she is loved, but can also love and can control and manipulate her situation; she is socially liminal, yet central to many transactions and many men's affections.

However, the slave-girl's saleability is shown by Ibn Ḥazm to be a major hazard, potentially frustrating both the women and their lovers. Many of the stories tell of love affairs destroyed through the sale of the girl, with terrible consequences for one or both the lovers – as shown for example in the story told above about the woman presented as a model for fidelity.

In another story, a man believes a slander concerning his slave-girl and sells her. She falls into a decline and dies of love and grief (221). Two men in a different story turn mad when their respective slave-girls are sold – by a brother in one instance and by the man's mother in the other; both men end up in chains. One is later killed during the Berber invasion (200–01). Yet another man, an Andalusi, sells his slave girl to a Berber because he is short of money, but realises only belatedly how much he loves her. He searches out the new owner and pleads with him to sell her back, but the latter refuses and the lover grows desperate. At last, he appeals to the Berber king who, in a trial foreshadowing that in Bertolt Brecht's *The Caucasian Chalk Circle*, establishes that the former owner loves the girl more and restores her to him (227–29).

Love for a slave and the slavery of love are inextricably connected in a paradoxical nexus throughout Ibn Ḥazm's work. A singing-girl improperly addressed by a young man whom she loves threatens to denounce him. But when afterwards she performs at a function where he is present, in her song she challenges him, 'Let me thy ransom be!/Embrace me lawfully/I would not give my charms/Into licentious arms' (66–67). Love has ensnared them: only a lawful relationship will pay the ransom and free them both.

Another trope reverses the convention of captive as weak victim of the captor:

> The captive glowers,
> The captor cowers
> The slain assails,
> The slayer pales.
> *Ring of the Dove*, 127

In this stanza, the lover who has ensnared another is himself made weak, while the one trapped is the one empowered.

The love of a slave may make a man a slave, his emotions captive and tormented, whether through love unrequited or a lover departed. In another poem Ibn Ḥazm sings of separation from the beloved, when she dies:

> Love ravished me
> Her slave to be
> She chose to part,
> And slew my heart.
> Love came a guest
> Within my breast;
> My soul was spread;
> Love banqueted.
> *Ring of the Dove*, 177

Love, which was at first invited in (as 'a guest'), then enslaves the lover and ends up devouring his soul upon the beloved's death. The poet's imprisonment is only ameliorated when at night he is visited by the phantom of his dead lover, reviving memories of her smile and their sweet embraces when she was alive. The woman's name is Nu'm, which may be a homophonic play on words, as 'N[a]um' is the Arabic word for sleep, calling into question the woman's very existence: was she ever a real person, or only encountered in a dream?

But the slave woman's own vulnerability is starkly highlighted in a number of Ibn Ḥazm's tales. She could fall in love with an exploitative man, like one early Don Juan, Abu 'Amir, who looks on women as objects to be vanquished and then discarded when his desire turns to revulsion and aversion. Jahiz comments, regarding such a situation, '... the conquest of the loved one tends to hasten the dissolution of the passion'.[103] Many of Abu 'Amir's victims, hastily sold to the first available buyer after he has possessed them, have died of a broken heart (142–44).

Worse, a girl could lose her life simply by choosing to sing the wrong song:

> A certain poet in Cordova composed a love-poem in which he celebrated the charms of Subh, the mother of al-Mu'aiyad (God have mercy on his soul!). A slave brought before al-Mansur Muhammad Ibn Abi 'Amin

---

103   Beeston, 30.

with a view to his purchasing her, chose this very song to sing to him: he promptly ordered her to be executed.

Ring of the Dove, 80

The reason for the wrath of al-Mansur lies in the family background, which was presumably unknown to the hapless slave girl. Al-Mu'ayyad is better known as the Umayyad Caliph Hisham II (976–1013 CE) of Córdoba, whose father died when he was only eleven years old. His mother Subh, also known as Sobeya, was a Basque of Christian origin, from Navarro, who was taken as captive to Córdoba where she became a concubine and then favourite wife of the Caliph al-Hakam II [Figure 1.6].[104] However, his sexuality is unclear and he may have been homosexual, with a preference for boys. He obviously needed to produce an heir and it is said Subh dressed as a 'ghulam' [young boy] in men's clothes and took the masculine pseudonym Ja'far, so as to appeal to him.[105] An alternative view is that he was simply an excessively doting father, rashly appointing his young son as his heir, instead of a more mature relative.[106] On the death of her husband, Subh became regent for the boy. She appointed the Chief Minister, Muhammad ibn Abi 'Amir (938–1002), as her aide. He took control and effectively ruled Córdoba as Caliph (although he never assumed the title) with Subh as his mistress. He renamed himself 'al-Mansur' (he is known in the West as 'Almanzor') meaning 'victorious', a reference to the many battles he won against Christians.[107]

Which aspect of the story it was that so angered al-Mansur is not spelled out, but it is clear the girl's choice of subject was at best an unfortunate one, with possibly scandalous aspects as well as uncomfortable political implications. The story quoted by Ibn Ḥazm also illustrates savagely the uncertainty and ambiguity of the singing slave's position: on the one hand, she was admired and adored by poets and even rulers; on the other, she was liable to be put to death on a whim, at a moment's notice – although, as already noted, she was not alone in this vulnerability: in a society wholly lacking any independent institutions, where all justice resided in the ruler and what he chose to mete

---

104   Richard Fletcher, *Moorish Spain*, 1992 (repr. London: Phoenix Press, 2001), 73.
105   Evariste Lévi-Provençal, *España musulmana hasta la caída del Califato de Córdoba (711–1031 de J.C.)* (Madrid: Espasa-Calpe, 1957), 447–8; Louis Crompton, *Homosexuality and Civilisation* (Cambridge, MA: Harvard University Press, 2003),166–67; *Encyclopedia of Medieval Iberia*, ed. Michael Gerli (New York: Routledge, 2003), 398–99.
106   Pascual de Gayangos y Arce, *The History Of The Mohammedan Dynasties In Spain*, Vol II (London: Routledge Curzon, 2002), 176–77.
107   Fletcher, 73; Juan Lalaguna, *A Traveller's History of Spain* (Gloucestershire: Windrush Press, 1990), 312.

FIGURE 1.6 Monument to al-Hakam II in Córdoba (Spain)
PHOTOGRAPH BY THE AUTHOR

out, any individual, whether poet, prince, politician or mystic divine could be dispatched at any time without warning: summarily beheaded or perhaps tortured to death.

Even the ruler himself was not immune to sudden reversals of fortune: the history of Islamic lands is replete with examples of rulers being assassinated to make way for another claimant to the throne. Then that usurping ruler would himself become susceptible in turn. There is, however, something particularly poignant in the image of the singing-girl, whose whole life was devoted to pleasing powerful men and whose only 'weapons' were her voice, her charms and, perhaps, her wits, being utterly at their mercy.

Despite his many accounts of suffering through love, Ibn Ḥazm's view is a positive one: love, including that between free men and slave women, is an essential part of the natural order. Reflecting the Platonic notion of men and women as two halves of a single soul, he argues that lovers are naturally drawn to one another:

> I hold that it [love] is a conjunction between scattered parts of souls that have become divided in this physical universe … an affinity of their vital

> forces in the supernal world ... and a close approximation in the manner of their constitution.
>
> *Ring of the Dove*, 23

In a passage which evokes Plato more directly, he continues,

> My theory is further proved by the fact that you will never find two persons in love with one another without there being some likeness and agreement of natural attributes between them. ... The more numerous the resemblances, the greater will be their congeneity and the firmer their affection.
>
> *Ring of the Dove*, 26–27

8 Yusuf and Zulaikha

The Biblical story of Joseph and Potiphar's wife is also told in the Qur'an (Surah 12), which follows the Biblical version fairly closely, although details have been changed. In both Genesis and the Qur'an, the wife attempts to seduce Joseph with devastating consequences, including a long spell of imprisonment for Joseph. In both works, Joseph's history has a book devoted to it, but the focus in both is on his turbulent life and career, relationship with his father and brothers, enslavement, imprisonment and subsequent rise to the heights of Egyptian society. The episode with Potiphar's wife occupies a relatively small space and she is never named.

But the intrigue in which a woman falls in love with a young man beholden to her husband has a long and separate history traversing many cultures, including an ancient Egyptian fable (possible source for, or descendant of, the Biblical story), a Buddhist homily and versions in Chinese and Japanese. Yohannan also cites as relevant to this motif the *Hippolytus* of Euripides and various versions of the *Phaedra/Phèdre* story, including the ancient Greek original, Racine's in French and modern adaptations.[108] The legend of Joseph and Potiphar's wife has also been adapted as a romance in various Arab and Persian versions known as *Yusuf and Zulaikha*. One is a 10th-century poem which may or may not be by Firdausi, the author of Persia's most famous epic, the *Shahnameh*; the other, and most famous, is by the Sufi mystic Jami (1414–92

---

[108] Cf. *Joseph and Potiphar's Wife in World Literature: An Anthology of the Story of the Chaste Youth and the Lustful Stepmother*, ed. John D. Yohannan (New York: McClelland & Stewart, Ltd., 1968).

CE), incorporated in his *Haft Awrang* ('Seven Thrones') which converts the ancient myth into an allegory of the soul's yearning for God and names Yusuf's lover as Zulaikha.

8.1   *Jami's* Yusuf and Zulaikha

In this narrative, chronologically faithful to its source, Islam plays no part but it is, nevertheless, a romance between people from different cultural and religious backgrounds and is included here for its interest in that regard, and the fact that it is a product of a Muslim society. Yusuf himself is clearly defined as a 'Hebrew', rendering Zulaikha's feelings for him as very specifically love for an ethnic 'other'. Her husband's impotence, implied in the Qur'an and more expressly stated in some traditions, is hinted at by Jami although he never mentions it unequivocally.

In Jami's narrative, Zulaikha is transformed from an archetype of a lustful and scheming woman into a passionate but also pure and innocent heroine. The French-Turkish writer Elif Shafak comments, 'As wicked as Zulaikha might be in the eyes of the conservative Muslims, she was considered in a completely different way by the Sufis. For the Sufi mystic, Zulaikha simply represented someone purely and madly in love. Nothing more and nothing less'.[109]

In all versions of the Joseph/Yusuf story the male protagonist is a slave in Egypt. In the Bible, he is a Hebrew, whereas the Qur'an explicitly rejects the idea that his family were Jews (2: 132–141). But in both, Joseph is the best-loved son of the monotheist patriarch Jacob, betrayed by his wicked brothers and sold into slavery in a foreign, pagan land. In both the traditional stories, Joseph first encounters Potiphar's wife in his master's household. But in Jami's version, our introduction to him as readers is when Zulaikha sees his face in a dream, long before she comes to know him.[110] She is a young girl of incomparable beauty, growing up in 'distant Barbary'. Into her sleep comes the vision of a young man of similarly superlative beauty, to whose image she is instantly enslaved (12). The description of his appearance encompasses the book's central theme: captivity and the struggle to be free. Her soul becomes 'captive to

---

109   Elif Shafak, 'Women Writers, Islam, and the Ghost of Zulaikha', in *Words Without Borders*, Internet Magazine site by Sonnet Media, December 2005: https://wordswithoutborders.org/read/article/2005-12/women-writers-islam-and-the-ghost-of-zulaikha/ [accessed 3/8/2016].

110   My quotations throughout are from David Pendlebury's translation, *Yusuf and Zulaikha: An Allegorical Romance by Hakim Nuruddin Abdurrahman Jami* (London: The Octagon Press, 1980).

every perfumed hair on [his] head', and she is thenceforth in thrall to a consuming passion which never leaves her.

During Zulaikha's recurring dreams of the young man she is informed that her beloved is the Grand Vizier of Egypt and, failing to understand that the dream is a prophecy and not an indication of Yusuf's current status, she now convinces her father to marry her to the Vizier. The union is arranged and Zulaikha discovers too late that her betrothed is not the man of her dreams. She goes through with the ceremony however, being persuaded that it is her fate to marry him and without the marriage she will never meet the true object of her desire.

From here on the story roughly follows that of the Qur'an, elaborating on many of its details, such as a scene in which Zulaikha's women, who have been cutting fruit, slash their hands in confusion and shock at witnessing Yusuf's beauty; but altering some and also introducing many scenes of its own, such as one in which Zulaikha, tormented by frustrated longing, determines to acquire the slave for herself. At the slave auction, she bids for him in person, paying for the purchase with her own priceless pearls. Achieving her aim, she has 'escaped at last from the fetters of affliction' (53), but her freedom is temporary, as Yusuf steadfastly and repeatedly rejects her amorous advances, generating torments which constitute emotional slavery anew. Only after many years, during which she is widowed and becomes impoverished, ugly, old, and blind, while Yusuf is finally elevated to his prophesied position of Grand Vizier, does she find relief from her pain. Even metaphorically, their roles have been reversed: earlier, when Yusuf was in prison, Zulaikha had seen him as a bird in a cage, and worried about whether he had been tamed (104). In her impoverished misery, she herself becomes like a bird singing a doleful song, her whole world a 'cramped cage' (116). Seeing her so humbled, Yusuf takes pity on her and is filled with love. At last, she and Yusuf are united, his prayers effect a return of her youth and beauty and they are married. Eventually, after many happy and fruitful years together, they die: first he, then she.

Yusuf's symbolic attributes shift, he is a chameleon: at one time 'a perfect jewel'; then superhuman, 'not moulded, like Adam, from earth and water, but a holy angel come down from the heavens' (94); he is repeatedly depicted as a rose: 'a rose without a thorn' (95–96 and passim), or 'prostrated ... [on] the ground ... like a tender rose-twig' in prayer (104–05); he is like a wild bird that needs to be cooped up in a cage (94); a jug of wine whose intoxicating qualities affect each woman differently (94), a shining sun (97); he is compared with Jesus Christ when, dressed in crude homespun cloth with iron fetters round his neck, he is paraded through the streets riding an ass; immediately afterwards he is like an angel (100). On yet another occasion Yusuf is described as 'light upon light', a direct quotation from the Qur'an (Sura 24), where the words refer to God himself. And yet he is a man, at times tempted by Zulaikha against his moral principles and often anxious and confused by Zulaikha's advances: he likens himself to a wisp of dry cotton, and her to a blazing fire which could consume him at any time (80). He is not actually superhuman: his function, as Pendlebury points out, is 'to point to the superhuman beauty of the Deity' (155).

Jami's *Yusuf and Zulaikha* is an extravagant re-fashioning of the Biblical and Qur'anic drama into an allegorical romance. The Sufi author uses the narrative as a vehicle for his poetic and mystic philosophy. But the book exists on two parallel planes: that of a passionate romance and as a parable of the anguished search of the soul for God. Earthly love prepares the human for the love of the Divine.

As a romance, the story is framed by hyperbolic language in the extreme manner of a fairy-tale: Zulaikha's bridal entourage is 'a thousand slave girls'; they are not merely charming but 'graceful, rosy-cheeked, blossom-bosomed dolls ... fresh as morning flowers'; and her pages are not just youths but 'a thousand ... flirtatious heart-ravishers'. The horses are not just fast and graceful but 'swifter than the ball struck by the mallet ... Their movement as smooth as a stream flowing over grass'. The camels are 'rivalling the wind in fleetness of foot', yet 'sober as ascetics, patiently bearing their burden like saints (29). In wooing Yusuf, Zulaikha places her 'entire fortune' at his disposal' (76).

Beauty and sensuality pervade the narrative. Yusuf is not merely handsome, but 'like a moon ... like the sun at the height of its glory and splendour. He stood out from the throng like a torch; and before his beauty the beauty of the other vanished, like starlight extinguished by the light of the rising sun' (9).

Zulaikha is the most beautiful woman in the world. She builds a sumptuous palace to entice Yusuf, where each room is covered with painted images of herself and Yusuf amorously embracing. Even in her garden, the branches of the trees are 'entwined in impudent embraces' (71) and she sends a hundred 'pretty-breasted maidens' to Yusuf, hoping one of them will seduce him and she can then perform a 'bed-trick', secretly taking the girl's place. The scene of Yusuf and Zulaikha's eventual consummation is as erotic as any in literature; like the heroine of any Victorian melodrama, Zulaikha swoons before Yusuf has even touched her! To him she appears like a houri of paradise. The pair become like

> roses blown together by the morning breeze, one tightly furled, the other now unfurling: the rosebud sinks out of sight into the blossoming bloom. (127)

The couple's love-making is couched in sensual metaphors invoking paradise: Zulaikha tells her bridegroom that she has kept her 'pearl' of virginity for him. Thus his 'diamond' can pierce it for the first time. The pearl is a traditional symbol of purity and truth, as well as great wealth (as previously noted, Zulaikha had sold her priceless pearls to pay for Yusuf) and sacred power. In Islamic theology it often stands as an emblem of that which is ardently desired and difficult to attain.[111] The 12–13th century Persian Sufi mystic Farid al-Din Attar depicted pearls as symbols of ultimate desire. He repeatedly uses the story of Joseph (Yusuf) in this regard. In a poem entitled 'Majnun and Leili', Majnun is shown endlessly searching for 'the pearl' that is Leili and his search is compared with that of Jacob, seeking Joseph through eternity. A poem specifically about Joseph depicts him as a pearl, avidly desired by an old crone who wishes to purchase him. She is told his price is beyond her reach but she responds,

> The heart that does not strive can never gain
> The endless kingdom's gates and lives in vain;
> It was pure aspiration made a king
> Set fire to all he owned – to everything –
> And when his goods had vanished without trace
> A thousand kingdoms sprang up in their place.
> When noble aspiration seized his mind,
> He left the world's corrupted wealth behind –
> Can one who craves the sun be satisfied
> With petty ignorance? Is this his guide? [112]

In other words, it is worthwhile to aspire to such an aim which, the syntax tells us, equates to true knowledge, even if one is never able to attain it.

Slave status, both literal and metaphorical, shifts subtly from one to another. At first, both Yusuf and Zulaikha are free in every sense. But she becomes psychologically captive as soon as she dreams of Yusuf: she is 'enslaved by his image' (12) even though she retains her free-born status and wealth. Repeatedly, she proclaims to him her sense of being enslaved to him, while he, embarrassed, insists on his lowly rank as being literally 'owned' by her and wanting only to

---

[111] The Qur'an tells us that those admitted to paradise will be adorned with pearls (22:23 and 35:33), while the handsome boys who will wait on them are themselves compared with virgin pearls (52:24).
[112] Farid ud-Din Attar, *The Conference of the Birds,* tr. Afham Darbandi and Dick Davis (London: Penguin, 1984).

serve her, in a chaste and honest way (e.g. on 69). Later Yusuf is imprisoned and literally fettered at Zulaikha's command, but he remains emotionally and spiritually free, possessed by none but God. His charismatic sense of freedom is contagious: he converts another girl who has fallen in love with him to the worship of God, thus liberating her from her carnal passion; he also converts the women whom Zulaikha had sent to seduce him. And his cheerful presence turns even the prison into a 'rose-garden'. In contrast, his absence makes Zulaikha's dwelling 'darker than a dungeon', or like a garden stripped of roses with only the thorns left to torment the nightingale (101).

Only toward the end, when they are married, Yusuf begins to adore Zulaikha and becomes enchanted with her. In one episode their roles are explicitly reversed: Zulaikha, confused by his sudden overwhelming love, attempts to slip from his grasp. He seizes the hem of her dress and tears it down the back – as she once ripped his garment; she tells him this has made them 'partners in crime ... on an equal footing' but they are actually far from equal. Yusuf has become wealthy and powerful, while Zulaikha is now far below him socially, and whatever wealth she possesses comes from him. The wheel of fortune has turned and Yusuf has taken command of his fate and of his and Zulaikha's lives together. He can adore her all he will, but he is still in charge and, consequently, the slave imagery has now disappeared. Only at the very end, when Yusuf dies, Zulaikha's sense of enslavement returns: she becomes 'captive of [her] own sore-wounded heart' (132), and she too dies soon afterwards.

David Pendlebury denies that one should read Jami's portrayal of Zulaikha and her 'excesses' as 'simply another characteristic example of the misogyny of a male-dominated culture' or that her behaviour should be considered specifically feminine (172). He says it represents that which is in all of us and the allegory is thus free of gender discrimination. But I believe that implicit in this version of the story, as in its predecessors, is a judgment that Zulaikha's passion for a slave is inappropriate – as well as being disturbingly extreme. The role reversal whereby Zulaikha gives way emotionally to one who is her hierarchical inferior contributes to the sense that all is not as it should be: the social world has been turned upside down. When Yusuf takes charge, order is at last restored and the lovers are now 'free' to adore one another in the time-honoured fashion.

Allegorically, *Yusuf and Zulaikha* traces the journey of an individual and of the soul, escaping from the self to a condition of selflessness, 'freed ... from all worldly commerce' (57). This is achieved through immersion of the self into that of the divine, but also through earthly love: 'Happy is he who is able to escape from the self and ... lives only for love', says the author, referring as much to the profane love of his protagonists as to the sacred love of God. In this sense it is not only Zulaikha who finds contentment in loving Yusuf selflessly, but Yusuf must also love her in order to achieve the perfect state. The book ends with the words, 'lucky the lover who breathes his last with the aroma of union in his nostrils'. Here, earthly and divine loves are conflated into a single image of true fulfilment. But the lovers' happiness, lasting over many years, inevitably reaches its end with their deaths.

Yusuf and Zulaikha is an entertaining variation on the traditional religious versions of the story of Yusuf/Joseph and his 'owner's' wife which completely exonerates the woman and illustrates the power of fate in determining human affairs. In its depiction of the role reversal occurring between its protagonists, the work anticipates many of the stories that will follow. Both Muslim and Christian cultures treat the subservience of the male to the female as unnatural and undesirable: a necessarily temporary state where it occurs. In Muslim literature, the slave is almost invariably female (*Yusuf and Zulaikha* is exceptional in making the man the slave, although Zulaikha is 'enslaved' by love). But this does not negate the woman's power to determine the course of events and, in the literature, she is repeatedly shown taking the initiative in order to obtain her ends. These forthright women are almost invariably non-Muslim when the story begins, but like their counterparts in Christian literature, later, they must convert to the dominant religion in order to restore the 'proper order'.

CHAPTER 2

Mediaeval Christian Romances – Cultural Borrowings

> Thus every lover is the slave of Love … [he]
> Despising fame and great authority,
> Forgot his kin, his parents, and his country,
> Even denied his faith for a girl's love …
> The one-time foe was seen the slave of love.
> *Digenes Akrites*, Book III

∴

> O God, what a noble baron, if only he were a Christian!
> *Chanson de Roland*, BURGESS ed., line 3164

∴

One important means whereby customs and tastes could be transmitted from one culture to another was through the capture and transfer of slaves from their homelands to the realms of their captors. A.R. Nykl describes 'an incessant flow of ideas up and beyond the Pyrenees' during the reign in al-Andalus of the Umayyad Caliph Abd-al-Raḥmān III (912–61 CE), himself the son of a Muslim prince (Muhammad) and a Frankish slave (Maria).[1] Montefiore has spoken about human populations' 'hybridity', engendered by successive contacts, including both trade and conquests, followed by intermarriage or rape, producing ethnically and culturally mixed children.[2] Because of the substantial amount of intermarriage that occurred between the early Muslim conquerors and the Christian Goths, the two peoples on either side of the Pyrenees were

---

1 Nykl, 4. Cf. also Dwight Reynolds, 'Music', in *The Literature of Al-Andalus*, ed. Maria Rosa Menocal, Raymond Scheindlin and Michael Sells (Cambridge: Cambridge University Press, 2000), 70.
2 Simon Sebag Montefiore, speaking on BBC Radio 4's *Start the Week*, 'Power Play and Family Dynamics', on 10th October 2022.

racially akin, Nykl records, and consequently 'pre-disposed to feel and respond to impressions in a similar manner'. With each attack and counter-attack, prisoners were captured and enslaved, contributing to a 'thorough familiarity' of each side with the other's 'ways and tastes'.[3] Thus, wherever Muslims and Christians met, essences of each culture seeped into that of the 'other', even when they were officially at war.

Chief among such regions were Islamic Spain and the Maghreb, where Muslims and Christians perpetually rubbed shoulders, as well as in the eastern Mediterranean. Literature of those regions features characters belonging to the culture and faith of the 'other'. In Sicily too, the Norman court of Frederick II (ruled 1215–1250 CE) was thoroughly Arabised, even though Sicily had ceased to be an Arab possession almost two centuries previously (in 1071). The king wore a crown of Byzantine design but his robes were embroidered with Arabic. He spoke Arabic fluently and drew to his court 'literati and intellectuals from throughout the world', including many Muslims and Jews from both Al-Andalus and the Middle East.[4]

In Andalusia the very languages (Arabic and Romance – the Latin-based language of the Mozarabs, that is Christians living under Muslim rule in Spain) were penetrated by vocabulary and linguistic forms borrowed from the other.[5] The cross-cultural influence did not only concern the transmission from Arab to Christian of classical learning relating to science, philosophy, medicine and other productions of 'high culture', but went in both directions and extended to popular culture. Stories and poems featuring Muslims and Christians with a mixed-faith love interest, thrived in the border lands, where the two faiths were most likely to encounter one another. We saw examples of this in the Arab language in Chapter 1. But in Christian literature too, Muslim characters appear frequently.

•••

An early instance of such cultural mingling is shown in the *Disciplina Clericalis* [*the Education of the Clerk*], a compilation of stories and poems composed in Latin in the early 12th century CE by the Jewish convert to Christianity, Petrus

---

3   Nykl, 4–5.
4   Maria Rosa Menocal, *The Arabic Role in Medieval Literary History: a Forgotten Heritage* (Philadelphia: University of Pennsylvania Press, 1987), 61.
5   Cf. Consuelo Lopez-Morillas, 'Language', in *The Literature of Al-Andalus*, ed. Maria Rosa Menocal, Raymond Scheindlin and Michael Sells (Cambridge: Cambridge University Press, 2000), 31–59.

Alfonsi. Born in the then Islamic Spanish city of Huesca, Alfonsi moved to England and then France, and is noted as an intermediary between eastern and western cultures. Described as 'Oriental', his work is the first complete collection of its kind known in the western world; its origin is presumed to be Arabic.[6] Its stories and verses are written in the Arab manner: a number of them concern Arabs explicitly and are placed in Middle Eastern settings, including Baghdad and Egypt. The collection includes fables and parables, as well as humorous and even bawdy tales prefiguring those of Boccaccio and Chaucer; some have echoes of *One Thousand and One Nights*. Alfonsi gives no indication as to his own sources, but his work provides evidence of copious cross-cultural borrowing and transmission. Its popularity is attested to by the many manuscripts which appeared between the 12th and 16th centuries, sixty-three in all, and they were translated early on from their original Latin into languages including French, German, Icelandic, Italian, Spanish and English. Fourteen of the tales were printed by William Caxton.[7]

Bilinguality of a work is another product of a hybrid society. For example, many songs composed in Islamic Spain were in two languages: the Andalusi poetic form known as the *Muwashsha*, mostly dating from the Almoravid and Almohad *Taifa* periods (11th-12th centuries CE), is in Arabic. However, the concluding section, usually composed as though spoken by a woman, in contrast to the masculine *Muwashsha,* and known as the *kharja* (a word derived from the Arabic *kharaja*, meaning exit), is very often in Romance. An overwhelming number of *kharjas* are erotic, or panegyric.[8] Some express longing for a lover and sorrow at his absence, or appeal for his return.[9]

Kharjas are also typically characterised by descriptions of beautiful gardens: in one of these, Zwartjes says, 'the garden has a symbolic function as the garden of love, whose fruit the lovers enjoy'.[10] Gardens, evoking the original Paradise Garden, are frequent settings for love scenes in such poetry as well

---

6 Charles Burnett, 'Learned Knowledge of Arabic Poetry, Rhymed Prose, and Didactic Verse, from Petrus Alfonsi to Petrarch', in *Poetry and Philosophy in the Middle Ages: A Festschrift for Peter Dronke,* ed. John Marenbon (Leiden, Boston and Cologne: Brill, 2001), 35.

7 *Peter Alphonse's* Disciplina Clericalis *(English Translation), from the Fifteenth Century Worcester Cathedral Manuscript F 172*, ed. William Henry Hulme, Cleveland, Ohio: *Western Reserve University Bulletin*, Vol. xxii, No. 3 (May 1919) 7–8: https://ia601200.us.archive.org/34/items/cu31924026493514/cu31924026493514.pdf [accessed 17/8/2016].

8 Otto Zwartjes, *Love Songs from Al-Andalus: History, Structure and Meaning of the Kharja* (Leiden, New York and Cologne: Brill Publishing Co., 1997), 190.

9 Leo Spitzer, 'The Mozarabic Lyric and Theodor Frings' Theories', *Comparative Literature*, Vol. IV (Winter 1952), No. 1, 1–22, 8–11.

10 Zwartjes, 224.

as in prose narratives, as we shall discover (see also Appendix 2). In another poem, the speaker considers himself as a slave of his lady[11] and there is a specific reference to the love of a Christian woman. In a *kharja*, the lover says he can only love a Christian with an interpreter.[12] In general, interfaith romances and specifically those between Muslims and Christians, thrive in the liminal areas where these cultures met and were exchanged, on the frontiers between Christendom and Islam.

One striking instance of such cross-cultural fertilisation is shown in an anecdote, which is often quoted:

> Ben Hayán cuenta la anécdota de un conquistador de Barbastro en 1064, que hace grandes demonstraciones de interés y complacencia escuchando el canto de su cautiva mora, como si comprendiese los versos cantados, de los cuales sin duda, no se alcanzaría a penas nada.[13]

> [Ibn Hayān relates an anecdote about a conqueror of Barbastro [site of a devastating siege and Christian victory over the Muslims in Northern Spain] in 1064, who showed great interest and pleasure in listening to the song of his captive female Moor, as if he understood the verses she sang, when he doubtless understood hardly anything].

1   Arab Origins of the Idea of Courtly Love

Many Christians enjoyed listening to Arab music and it influenced the songs of the first troubadours in Aquitaine and Provence, an area also known as Occitania. According to Nykl, the troubadours would have heard and copied Islamic music.[14] Strong links between Arab culture and that of courtly love songs and poems composed by Christians have also been argued. Spitzer points to echoes of the *kharja* in mediaeval German *Frauenlieder* [women's songs], sung by the Minnesingers, and Spanish and Portuguese *cantigas de amor* [love songs] or *cantigas de amigo* ['songs of the beloved'], a type of mediaeval lyric poetry usually in the voice of a woman, sung by the troubadours, as well as Old French *refrains*.[15] He cites a theory that the Mozarabic *kharjas* represent

---

11   Zwartjes, 193.
12   Zwartjes, 200.
13   Quoted by Nykl, 406, N. 39.
14   Nykl, 380.
15   Spitzer, 16–18.

a 'primavera temprana de la lírica europea' [an early Spring of the European lyric].[16] Boase asserts that courtly love was either imported into the south of France from Muslim Spain, or was strongly influenced by the culture, poetry and philosophy of the Arabs. He adds that,

> the institution and ideal of chivalry was introduced into Europe from Moorish Spain or from the Middle East, together with prose romances, through cultural, commercial and military contacts, and as a consequence of the Crusades.
>
> The music to which the European troubadours set their songs was Arabic in inspiration [as were] *Rhyme and poetic forms* ... and Provence learnt the art from Moorish Spain.

Even the verb *trobar*, 'to compose poetry' derives from the Arab *tarab*, 'music', 'song', or from the root *taraba*, 'to strike' (as in striking out a rhythm), and the Arabic word for minstrel or troubadour was *tarrabi*.[17]

Among themes the Christians borrowed from Muslims were new notions of romantic love, the love of slaves and the idea of love as slavery. Boase lists dozens of features shared by Hispano-Arabic and mediaeval European poetry, including using a masculine form of respectful address to a woman (*midons*, rather than *madomna*), similar *dramatis personae*, many aspects of courtly love itself, including the elevation of the lady into an object of worship and the poet's submission to her capricious tyranny.[18]

Ibn Ḥazm's *Tawq al-ḥamāma* [*The Ring of the Dove*] is cited as a prime source for theories of courtly love, along with Ibn Dawud's *Kitab al-Zahra* [The Book of the Flower, a 9th century anthology of verses on the subject of love] and the *Risala fi l-'Ishq* [Treatise on Love] by the 10th-11th century CE philosopher Avicenna [Ibn Sina].[19] Menocal also describes Ibn Ḥazm as the Andalusian counterpart of Andreas Capellanus, author of *De Amore,* a 'rule book of courtly love'[20] and she relates his 'inquiry into the nature of love' to the mediaeval Christian romance, *Aucassin et Nicolette*.[21]

---

16 Quoted by Spitzer, 18.
17 Roger Boase, *The Origin and Meaning of Courtly Love: a Critical Study of European Scholarship* (Manchester: Manchester University Press, 1977), 62.
18 Boase, 63.
19 Boase, 62–63. And cf. Menocal, *The Arabic Role*,151.
20 Menocal, *The Arabic Role*,151.
21 Menocal, The *Arabic Role*, 110; 144.

Some, such as Maribel Fierro, have questioned the idea of a direct link between Ibn Ḥazm's work and that of the troubadours – arguing that the *Tawq al-ḥamāma* was relatively unknown before the 20th century and survived via only a single manuscript in Arabic.[22] Yet she herself acknowledges that,

> A work can have a major intellectual impact without enjoying a particularly wide circulation as a material object. This was the case, for example, of Ibn Ḥazm's legal works, both on casuistry (al-Muḥallà, of which some ten manuscripts have survived) and on uṣūl (AL-IḤKĀM [principles of Islamic Jurisprudence], three manuscripts).[23]

Bearing in mind that two disparate ideas may be 'polygenetic', as Giffen calls it, i.e. having common origins rather than directly causal links (for example, both the *Tawq al-ḥamāma* and courtly love theories have some antecedents in Greek popular literature), Giffen remarks that, with regard to courtly love,

> There remains a large body of evidence strongly suggestive of Arab influence at a number of points, though some supposed connections have proven wrong, and not all scholars familiar with the evidence accept that anything much is proven.[24]

Giffen then goes on to list numerous 'courtly elements' in Ibn Ḥazm's work. These include love's power to reform the lover and make him 'more generous, brave, noble, elegant and well-spoken', while amending his faults; its creating an 'insatiable desire and an exquisite anguish'; the concept of love as a malady leading to the loss of appetite, wasting, pallor, sleeplessness, melancholy, emotional extremes, obsession, and possibly madness – all leading even to death; the necessity of secrecy and the dangers of jealousy; the role of the spy, the slanderer and the trusted confidant or messenger; the lover's humility and submissiveness before the beloved, reflecting a kind of worship; a tendency to address the beloved with the masculine 'my lord' – sayyidi, or 'my master',

---

22 Maribel Fierro, 'The Bestsellers of al-Andalus', in *Artistic and Cultural Dialogues of the Late Medieval Mediterranean: Mediterranean Perspectives,* ed. María Marcos Cobaleda, (Cham, Switzerland: Springer International Publishing: Imprint: Palgrave Macmillan, 2021), 31–56, 36.

23 Fierro, 35.

24 Lois A. Giffen, 'Ibn Ḥazm and the Tawq al-ḥamāma', in *The Legacy of Muslim Spain*, ed. Salma Khadra Jayyusi (Leiden, New York and Cologne: E.J. Brill, 1994), 435. Cf. also Lois A. Giffen, *Theory of Profane Love among the Arabs: The Development of the Genre* (New York, London and Leiden: Brill, 1971), esp. 23–25.

mawlaya. The troubadours also adopted the habit of addressing the lady as midons, 'my lord', rather than madomna, 'my lady'.[25]

Numerous other scholars, including some in the Arab and Muslim world, have seen connections between the *Tawq al-ḥamāma* and courtly love literature.[26] Parallels between *Tawq al-ḥamāma* and Middle and New High German *Minnelehre*, as well as in the poems of Guillaume IX (1071–1127), the first troubadour of Provence, have also been drawn by Charles Barrack; he detects other Arab influences in the lyrics of Bernard de Ventadour of Provence.[27]

The earliest troubadour whose work survives was the poet prince Guillaume the VII of Poitiers and IX of Aquitaine (1071–1126 CE), whose father Guillaume VIII of Aquitaine, had participated in the siege of Barbastro referred to above and who must have spent his formative years in a household that included Andalusi singing girls whom he probably came to possess upon his father's death.[28] Guillaume IX combined in himself a love of warfare (he participated in and also led several crusades) and of women, as well as secular courtly culture.[29] It was a culture condemned by the clergy as effeminate, but which was to have far-reaching influence.[30]

Guillaume's songs are said to be the first in the *lengua romana*.[31] Several are quite bawdy, celebrating the poet's own sexuality and referring crudely to women, as well as to sex itself. But in Song No. 8 (45–47) he refers to himself as having surrendered to his beloved, being her vassal and being bound to her.[32] In Song 5/C he quotes words uttered to two married women whom he is attempting to seduce, to persuade them that he is a mute and can therefore be trusted not to make their affair public (49, lines 10–12). The words are

---

25   Giffen, 'Ibn Ḥazm', 436–37. Numerous other scholars, including some in the Arab world, also point out that Ibn Ḥazm's beloved may not always be female (Ibid, 433).
26   Cf. e.g. Abdulla al-Dabbagh, 'The Oriental Sources of Courtly Love', *International Journal of Arabic-English Studies*, Vol. 3 No. 1 (2002), 21–32. https://doi.org/10.33806/ijaes2000.3.1.2 [accessed 25/2//2024]; Nazan Yıldız, 'A Bird after Love: Ibn Ḥazm's *The Ring of the Dove (Tawq al-ḥamāmah)* and the Roots of Courtly Love', *Academic Journal of Interdisciplinary Studies* 2, 8 (October, 2013), 491–98. Doi:10.5901/ajis.2013.v2n8p493 [accessed 25/2/2024].
27   Charles M. Barrack, 'Motifs of Love', 173–200.
28   Boase, 465–66, Reynolds, 'Music', 71.
29   *The Poetry of William VII, Count of Poitiers, IX Dule of Aquitaine,* ed. and tr. Gerald A. Bond (New York and London: Garland Publishing, 1982), xli-lviii.
30   Bond, xlviii. Guillaume's own colourful life included abducting the Viscountess Dangerose (Dangerosa), wife of one of his vassals, and then installing her as his mistress in his palace while his own wife was absent: an episode which brought him into direct conflict with the church.
31   Nykl, 373.
32   Page references are to Bond's edition, cited above.

'Tarrababart, Marrabsbelioriben, Saramahart'. Bond glosses these as meaningless 'pseudo-Arabic' (84) but, as we have already discussed, and as Menocal points out in a different context, the word *tar[r]aba* is an Arabic word, meaning 'to sing',[33] or to strike etc. In Song No 4 (15), the poet speaks about loving a woman he has never seen, in a manner recalling Ibn Ḥazm's 'Of Falling in Love through a Description'. Boase cites a lost song, *Cantar de la Mora Zoraida*, in which the Spanish King Alfonso VI falls in love with a Muslim princess, sight unseen, responding to her repute. The woman in question was Zaida, daughter of the defeated king of Seville, Muhammad al- Mu'tamid ibn Abbād.[34] Alfonso married Zaida, who converted to Christianity and was renamed Isabella.

2 *Digenes Akrites*: Product of a Muslim-Christian Frontier[35]

Cross-cultural influences were not restricted to Islamic Spain or Sicily, but were also a feature of life on the Arabo-Christian frontiers of the Near East, manifest in popular literature featuring individuals from both sides, warring but also sparring erotically.[36] One of the earliest Christian treatments of romance between Christians and Muslims is the Byzantine epic, *Digenes Akrites*, or *Digenis Akritas*, etc. (the spelling is inconsistent), often seen as an analogue to the epic *Sīrat Dhāt al-Himma* and similarly set in a frontier territory in what is now eastern Turkey (in or near Armenia). The story is thought to be based in part on historic events of the late 8th and early 9th centuries, close in time to that of several *Nights* tales, for example, those featuring fictionalised actions of the real-life Caliph Hārūn al-Rashīd (763 or 766–809 CE).

Digenes Akrites may have been composed in the 10th or 11th century CE or even earlier and further developed in the 12th century. Different versions appeared in various towns of Europe and the eastern Mediterranean, including Istanbul and Trebizond (present-day Turkey), Andros and Chios (Greece),

---

33 Maria Rosa Menocal, *The Arabic Role in Medieval Literary History*, ix.
34 Boase, 69.
35 Sometimes spelled Akritas. I have chosen to stick with Akrites. The name and title of the epic have been given assorted spellings by modern editors, and it has been translated variously, e.g. by Mavrogordato, literally if somewhat clumsily, as 'Twyborn the Borderer': *Digenes Akrites*, ed. with an introduction, translation and commentary by John Mavrogordato (London: Oxford University Press, 1956, repr. 1970); or, alternatively, as 'The Two-Blood Border Lord': *Digenis Akritas: The Two-Blood Border Lord*, ed. Denison B. Hull (Athens, Ohio: Ohio University Press, 1972).
36 We have seen evidence of this comingling of Muslim and Christian protagonists at the end of the preceding chapter, particularly in the epic *Sīrat Dhát-al-Himma*.

Madrid, also known as the 'Escorial' version (Spain), Grottaferatta (Italy), Oxford and Moscow (this and the Escorial version are incomplete). It has been translated into several other languages beside its original Greek.[37]

The events of *Digenes Akrites* are situated on what was for many years an important frontier between the Byzantine Empire and the Islamic world, straddling parts of Armenia and extending to the banks of the Euphrates. This area experienced constant conflict, not only between Muslims and Christians but, as in mediaeval Spain, alliances often straddled religious lines: Christians fought against other Christians with the aid of Muslims and vice versa. Some of these cross–frontier alliances were the result of coercion, the stronger party forcing the weaker into a condition of vassalage; others were for mutual gain. The battles were for territory, influence and booty including slaves.[38]

Digenes Akrites mixes epic fiction with references to actual people and events, and popular lyrics with classical elements and quotations from the Old and New Testaments. It is thought to have borrowed from Homer, as well as Hellenistic antecedents, including Achilles Tatius and Heliodorus;[39] with qualities similar to some of those in *Sīrat Dhát al-Himma*,[40] as well as being influenced by, or even parallel to some *Thousand-and-One-Nights* stories.[41] Persian elements have also been detected in the work.[42]

---

[37] I have worked primarily with two versions, both comprising parallel texts in Greek and in English: the 'Grottaferrata', a long poem which the editor John Mavrogordato believed to be the story's earliest iteration, dating back to the 14th century; and, for comparison and contrast, the incomplete, 'Escorial' version, believed to be from the mid- or late-15th century, formed of five separate but linked poems: *Digenes Akrites: New Approaches to Byzantine Heroic Poetry*, ed. Roderick Beaton and David Ricks (Aldershot: King's College London, 1993). I have chosen to quote substantially from Mavrogordato's text, despite its often-stilted language, as it is close to being literally correct, in contrast to some later, freer translations.

[38] Cf. e.g., Warren Treadgold, *A History of the Byzantine State and Society* (Stanford, Calif: Stanford University Press, 1997), esp. 476–82 and passim; and Steven Runciman, *The Emperor Romanus Lecapenus and his Reign: A Study of Tenth-Century Byzantium* (Cambridge: Cambridge University Press, 1963), esp. 120, and Chapter Vll, passim.

[39] Beaton and Ricks eds., 83, line 719 and note to lines 710–19; and re. the work of Heliodorus and Achilles Tatius, Mavrogordato, ed., xiv-xv, xviii, and lxxx.

[40] Cf. Marius Canard, 'Les principaux personages du roman de chevalerie arabe *Dāt al-Himma wa-l-Bāttal*', *Arabica, Journal of Arabic and Islamic studies*, No. 8, 158–173, 170.

[41] Cf. e.g.Vassilios Christides, 'Arabic Influence on the Akritic Cycle', *Byzantion* 49 (1979), 97 ff. 5. Cf. also, Christides, 'An Arabo-Byzantine Novel *'Umar al-Nu'mān* Compared with *Digenēs Akritas*', *Byzantion* 32 (1962), 549–604.

[42] Christopher Livanos, 'A Case Study in Byzantine Dragon-Slaying: Digenes and the Serpent', *Journal of Oral Tradition*, 26/1 (2011): 125–144, 126, 130, 131, 133, 134, 138, 139, and 140.

The story celebrates the mixing of faith and blood. Its hero Digenes Akrites is the product of a union between an Arab emir and the daughter of a (Christian) Greek general whom he had captured in a raid across the Byzantine frontier. The Emir Mousour, who is prince of Syria, converts from Islam to Christianity so as to win permission from his beloved's family to wed their daughter, Eirene. Their son bears in his name the record of his origins and an allusion to his way of life: Digenes, meaning [of] two races and Akrites, denoting 'a man of the borders';[43] in this case he becomes a warden of the frontier Marches, occupying exactly the same role as his female counterpart Dhát al-Himma in the *Sīrat Dhát al-Himma*.

Emir Mousour tells his prospective in-laws his father had died when he was still a baby and his mother had then given him to his 'Arab kinsmen' who brought him up 'in faith of Mohamet' [sic]. Subsequently, he was made ruler of Syria and conquered many lands, both Greek and Muslim (Grottaferrata 19–20), suggesting an ambiguity over his parents' actual religion. Interestingly for our purposes, Mousour's father Chrysoherpes has been identified with the historical figure of Chrysocheir, a leader of the Paulician heretics and hence a Christian, who rebelled against Byzantium and fought alongside Muslims before being defeated in the 870s C.E. (Grottaferrata XXXI–II). If he was indeed a Christian, this would render all the more remarkable his mother's decision willingly to hand Mousour over to Arab relatives, presumably to be raised as a Muslim. Christian origins would make him, like his son, a man of a hybrid nature. However, Chrysocheir may also have been a prototype for the Muslim Yanis, in *Sīrat Dhát al-Himma*, providing a further link between these epics of Christian and Muslim provenance, respectively. Alternative possibilities have been offered in the *Historical Dictionary of Byzantium* under the heading *Digenes Akritas*, where Mousour is identified with Omar of Muslim Melitene (in present-day Turkey, one-time capital of Armenia), allied to the Paulicians; and by Mavrogordato and Hull, who suggest another emir of Melitene, Omar's grandson (identified by Hull as Abu Hafs), as a possible original for the father of Digenes Akrites.

Melitene was strategically placed on the upper Euphrates, at the crossing of vital trade routes and hence, 'one of the crucial points of contention between the Byzantine and Muslim empires', and 'one of the most important strongholds of the Muslim-Byzantine frontier'. It changed hands repeatedly and was, alternatively, a seat of Armenian, Byzantine, Muslim and Tartar power.[44]

---

43   Beaton and Ricks eds., 11.
44   Melitzki, 142.

But if Abu Hafs converted to Christianity, it was not for love but because the Melitenians were forced into negotiation by the besieging Byzantine general John Kourkouas.[45] A condition of the peace treaty was that the Melitenian troops, said to be 12,000 horsemen, should join forces with the Byzantines, after which most of them converted to Christianity. Abu Hafs died not long afterwards, putting his death between 928 and 934 CE. The final capitulation of Melitene, and hasty conversion of most of its people (in order to avoid deportation, when the city was 'cleansed' of its non-Christians), also occurred in 934.[46] The 'conversion for love' aspect of the plot represents an example of the author's readiness to distort history in order to foreground the theme of romance across frontiers.

Such identifications of important characters in *Digenes Akrites* with historic personages living on the Arab/Byzantine frontier enhance the evident liminality of the individuals and locations and the works in which they are found. Both history and fiction emphasise the porosity of boundaries, geographical and theological, and the fluidity of religious beliefs and affiliations, with shifts to the religion of the victors being – then as at other times in history – symbolic manifestations of military defeat.

Digenes Akrites, the product of this 'happy union of Roman and Arab' (Grottaferrata xxxii) soon displays exceptional heroic prowess in hunting and athletics. He imitates his father by carrying off the daughter of a Greek general, albeit with her connivance: Digenes's courtship of Evdokia culminates with her jumping from her window onto his horse, to be married. Afterwards, the couple take to a nomadic life with Digenes hunting robbers and other miscreants and undertaking feats of valour.

But Digenes's other relationships show him in a less than heroic light. He ostensibly rescues a young woman convert from Islam to Christianity, Aissé, who had been abandoned in the desert by her Christian lover, Eudoxius. Aissé had freed her lover from captivity in hopes of marrying him and together they had fled with the family valuables, even though her mother lay dying. Their elopement represents the third account of, as Mavrogordato puts it, 'the major theme of the poem, that of a runaway marriage between an Arabian and a Greek' (xlvii). Aissé tells Digenes she had been 'by desire enslaved' and, longing for union with her lover, had been baptised into Christianity (Grottaferrata v, lines 2398–400). They had made love along the way. But then Digenes himself

---

45   Cf. e.g. Runciman, *The Emperor Romanus Lecapenus*, 141–42; Treadgold, 480–81; and Mark Whittow, *The Making of Byzantium, 600–1025* (Basingstoke: Macmillan, 1996), 317.
46   Mavrogordato ed., lxxiii-iv; Hull ed., xl-xli, xliv, and xlvi-vii.

rapes her, before being overcome by remorse, confiding his guilt even to strangers, as if looking to them for redemption:

> this wondrous and noble Borderer,
> Who was enriched by all the gifts of God,
> Within a little making vain his youth
> Fell heedlessly into adultery's sin.
> And afterwards being penitent for this
> To those who met him he would tell his fault
> Not for the sake of boasting but of penitence'.
> GROTTAFERRATA V, lines 2183–90

This story, which does not appear in the Escorial version, shows us several kinds of betrayal, with guilt heaped upon guilt and mounting shame. First, there is Aissé's guilt in following her own desires and stealing away as her mother lies dying. Second is Aissé's and her lover's theft of goods from the parental home. Third is the guilt she feels over becoming 'enslaved' to desire and giving up her virginity before marriage. Fourth is Eudoxius's betrayal of her, leaving her potentially to die in a barren wilderness. Finally, there is Digenes's double guilt in taking advantage of a woman already betrayed, as well as his own adultery. The critic W. Ker found the morality of the epic unsettling and described Digenes's rape of Aissé and subsequent repentance as 'filthy'.[47] This is an account of mixed-faith romance which veers towards tragedy and sheds a malign light on its supposed 'hero'.

Digenes's next sexual encounter is even darker, with echoes of Arab stories, such as that of 'Umar ibn al-Nu'mān and the story of Ali and Miriam, discussed in the last chapter. As with the story of Aissé, the perpetrator of a crime is once again the 'hero' himself rather than, as in "Umar ibn al-Nu'mān', his father and then a brutal slave. The seductive Amazonian woman suffers – even to the point of death in the Grottaferrata version, giving it as bitter an outcome as that in "Umar ibn al-Nu'mān', and unlike that of the resourceful, and successful Miriam. Digenes fights a beautiful warrior woman called Maximo (Maximou in the Escorial version, implying she is of Byzantine heritage) and overpowers her. She begs for mercy and tells him she has been saving her virginity for the man who will defeat her. She strips off her armour, calls out to him, 'Hail Master mine', declares 'I am your slave indeed by war's fortune' (Grottaferrata VI,

---

47   W. Ker, *The Dark Ages,* 1904 (repr. London: Thomas Nelson and sons Ltd, 1955), 345.

lines 3248–50) and kisses his hand. Desire rises up in him as before, but once again he experiences guilt and berates himself,

> And when the fire of lust in me was kindled
> I knew not who I was, I was all burning.
> Then I tried all means to escape from sin,
> And I would reason thus myself accusing:
> Demon, why love you all things that are foreign?
> GROTTAFERRATA VI, lines 3251–55

In the full knowledge that what he is doing is wrong, Digenes gives in to temptation and deflowers Maximo. Then, like Eudoxius before him, he casts off the woman he has just seduced and who is now in love with him. Later, he will compound his perfidy by lying to his wife about the encounter until, on his deathbed, he tells her the truth at last (Grottaferrata VIII, lines 3655–57).

In most versions of the saga, Digenes returns to his wife, ignoring Maximo's pleas for him to stay. However, in the 'Grottaferrata' version, having returned home, Digenes then has second thoughts. On the next day, 'boiling over in much rage', he sets out 'as if for the chase' (VI, 3299) and kills Maximo, as he would a hunted animal. He says that he 'slew her ruthlessly' because of her adultery – even though the adultery had in fact been his own since she had previously been a virgin and was unmarried. Here is a clear case of a man who, ashamed of his own lusts, kills the woman who had aroused them. In a sense, he is trying to kill his own feeling of wrongdoing and destroying the one person who could give his guilt away. In addition, since Maximo has repeatedly been extolled for her superlative beauty, he removes the temptation of her once and for all; for him to again be faithful to his wife and free from the appeal of sexual transgression, the cause of that temptation must sacrifice her life.

It is notable, given the work's celebration of mixed-faith unions, that Digenes should admonish himself for loving 'all things that are foreign' (lines 3254–55 quoted above). But in the language of this epic and, as we see in many other such works, love between mixed-faith 'others' can only be approved by the conversion of one member of the couple to the religion of the other so that the two former 'others' end up as theologically 'the same'. Here, as the relationship is adulterous and the woman is soon to die, there will be no conversion and hence no 'unification' in faith terms.

In the 'Escorial' version, both the character of Maximou and the circumstances of her sexual congress with Digenes are treated very differently from those of Grottaferrata. In 'Escorial', when Maximou abases herself before the 'hero', kissing his shoe and telling him, 'you alone have vanquished me, and may not other vanquish me' (Escorial line 1566), there is no sense that she is naively innocent. Moreover, Digenes here justifies his adultery and removes any apparent obligation to Maximou by branding her a 'strumpet' (line 1518) and a 'whore' (line 1578): 'if you are bent on fornication, then I shall do it to you' (line 1574).

The last part of Digenes's recounting of the episode in 'Escorial' dwells on Maximou having been 'shamed', 'lost her valour' [lines 1597–98], and suffered 'disgrace' (1599). In addition, he is completely open with his wife concerning his affair with Maximou, at which she laughs and rewards him with 'kiss upon kiss' (Escorial, lines 1593–4), so there can be no sense of guilt or betrayal in relation to her either, at least in the text's own terms. The rape of Aissé, the seduction and killing of Maximou and Digenes's lying to his wife in the 'Grottaferrata' version add a harsh realism to what is in essence a mythical epic with fairy-tale qualities. These grim passages inscribe the brutality of warfare and qualify the character of a man who, though hailed as a peerless warrior and hero by his contemporaries, is morally deeply flawed. This version lends its protagonist a dark, psychologically guilt-ridden aspect.

Both versions of the epic end however with Digenes enjoying married life and building a wonderful palace and garden on the banks of the Euphrates, a site traditionally associated with the Garden of Eden and described as a 'paradise', (Grottaferrata line 3321; Escorial line 1626). Even though this is a Christian work, while the *Nights* stories derive from Muslim cultures, we see a similar absence of poetic justice: a hero committing terrible crimes, emerging unscathed and eventually dying a natural death, honoured by illustrious mourners; his wife, distraught at the thought of living without him, has marginally predeceased him and lies dead at his side (Grottaferrata VIII, lines 3740 ff; Escorial lines 1864–65).

As for the 'mixed-faith romance' motif which permeates the epic, it is generally shown in a positive light, but only because it is in each case afforded the sanction of conversion to Christianity by the Muslim concerned. When Digenes reproaches himself as 'Demon' for his love of foreign women and earlier speaks of a 'wrong and lawless union' (like that between Aissé and Eudoxius), the effect is ironic, since he is himself the product of a mixed-faith and mixed-ethnic union brought about in the context of a similar elopement, attested to in his very name. But in all of the unions, religious conversion has unified the lovers: Digenes's father converted to Christianity in order to marry Eirene; Digenes himself, though born of a technically exogamous union, is brought up as a Christian and marries a Christian woman, and Aissé has also converted to Christianity in order to marry Eudoxius.

Digenes Akrites offers us mirror-image resolutions to the problems of exogamy previously presented in Arab works. Whereas the Arab solution is conversion to Islam, the Byzantine answer is conversion to Christianity. In each case, the captivity of either the man or the woman is crucial: the catalyst for bringing the lovers together. The author of the Grottaferrata version makes the etymological connection, speaking of Digenes's father, but with words that apply to other characters in this and many other works:

> Thus every lover is the slave of Love,[48]
> For he is as a judge tormenting hearts
> Of who keep not rightly the roads of love;
> Straightly he aims his bolts and shoots at hearts,
> And stands with fire to enflame consideration.
> Whoever has him can no more escape,
> One of the famous even or very rich,
> For he uprising quickly catches him …
> Thus happening that wonderful Emir,
> Despising fame and great authority,
> Forgot his kin, his parents, and his country,
> Even denied his faith for a girl's love,
> One indeed truly fair and very noble,
> The one-time foe was seen the slave of love.
>
> GROTTAFERRATA, Book III, lines 638–51

These patterns of captivity and enslavement, literal and metaphorical, fused with religious conversion for love will be discovered repeatedly in works covered by this book.

3   Two Mediaeval French/Middle English Romances

Floire et Blanchefleur and *Aucassin et Nicolette* were originally written in French, then translated into Middle English, as well as several other languages. *Floire et Blanchefleur* is thought to be from the 12th century – possibly between 1155–1170 and originating in the Loire region, while the Provençal *Aucassin et Nicolette* is from a later period, probably in the 13th century. Both have been

---

48   Mavrogordato's translation from the Greek, Ουτως δουλος πας ο ευρών του ερωτος υπαρχει (Book III, line 1 in his Greek text).

reissued many times since their composition by unknown authors. The two works have common features, including illicit love across religious boundaries and between slave and free, enslavement also resulting from forbidden love and travels in search of a captive lover. But there are also significant differences in theme, style, and other aspects. Let us explore each in turn.

3.1　*Floire et Blanchefleur*

Two versions of this text survive in the original French and four texts in English, all of them incomplete copies or revisions of one or more older manuscripts, now lost.[49]

According to this story, Floire is the son of a Muslim king of Spain. His father Felix wages war against a Christian band in Galicia, who are on a pilgrimage journey to Santiago de Compostela. Felix captures the widowed daughter of a Christian knight killed in the battle. Returning home, he gives the woman to his queen, to serve her, and they become friends. Some months later, both women give birth on the same day: the Christian woman to a daughter, and the Muslim queen to a son. The babies are given names echoing the day of their births: Palm Sunday, which is also celebrated as a festival of flowers. The girl is called Blanchefleur, the boy Floire. Their names in English: Blancheflour and Floris respectively, occur in the English-language versions but are sometimes used there interchangeably with the French. I have stuck with the French Blanchefleur and Floire for consistency, except when using direct quotations with alternative spellings.

The children are brought up together and treated similarly in every respect, except that, as the text emphasises, they are nursed separately:

> Save only for the suckling, they
> Took food and drink in the same way.
> They slept together in one bed,
> Together drank, together fed.
> 　　HUBERT ed, lines 187–190, 28

---

[49]　The first two, known as Cambridge Ms. Gg. 4.27.2, and Cotton Vittelius D. iii respectively, were written in the 13th century. Another text, the Auchinleck Ms, dates from the first half of the 14th century; and one called Egerton Ms. 2862 is from the 15th century. The texts vary as to details, but agree, more or less, regarding the plot. The narratives all take the form of rhymed couplets, both in French and in their Middle English translations. I have quoted primarily from a modern translation from the French, that of Merton Jerome Hubert, *The Romance of* Floire and Blanchefleur: *A French Idyllic Poem of the Twelfth Century, translated into English Verse*, ed. M.J. Hubert, (Chapel Hill, North Carolina: North Carolina University Press, 1966). All textual references are to this edition, unless otherwise stated.

The fact that they are not suckled by the same woman is significant for, according to many traditions, such suckling, even if the children are not related, would make them effectively siblings, rendering any romantic attachment between them incestuous.[50] This obviously cannot be allowed to happen, as the boy and girl will later marry.[51] The children play together and, at the boy's insistence, are educated together. Deep love grows between them, at first based on childhood friendship, which turns to passion as they mature [Figure 2.1]. The king is alarmed by their growing affections: he wants the boy to marry in his own class and faith, not tie himself to the daughter of a Christian slave. Floire is sent away to stay with an aunt in Mountargis in central France, in hopes that he will meet other young girls and forget Blanchefleur.

Floire pines so much for his beloved that he neither eats nor drinks. The worried chamberlain alerts the king, who proposes to his wife that they have Blanchefleur killed, but she suggests instead that the girl be sold into slavery. She is sold to a burgess for twenty gold marks and a priceless gold cup, which is ornamented with wrought scenes from Greek mythology and topped by a huge gem (a carbuncle). The burgess travels to Cairo (called Babylon in the story), selling her on to the Emir, who contemplates marrying her one day. She is placed in his harem, in a high tower. Meanwhile, the king orders a grave to be dug with two lines on it:

> The beautiful Blanchefleur lies here,
> She whom Floris loved and held so dear.
> HUBERT ed., lines 652–53, 41

Floire returns and is led to her supposed grave, bearing this epitaph. He draws a knife, intending to stab himself. His mother prevents him and persuades the king it is better to tell the boy the truth. Floire vows to find Blanchefleur and is now given money, horses and men, as well as a magic ring to protect him from

---

50   It is believed that the 17th century poet and dramatist, Aphra Behn, was the daughter of a wet nurse, who also suckled one Col. Thomas Culpeper or Colepeper. Henceforth, according to Janet Todd, he considered her as his foster-sister, even though they were in no other way related. Cf. Janet M. Todd, *the Secret Life of Aphra Behn* (London: Andre Deutsch, 1996), 13.

51   However, in a 14th century Spanish version of the story, the *Crónica de Flores y Blancafor*, the children have the same wet-nurse, Blancaflor's mother Berta. Moreover, Flores's later inclination to convert to Christianity is associated with his having been suckled by a Christian woman whose milk was a vital conduit of the faith. Cf. Patricia Grieve, 'Floire and Blancheflor' *and the European Romance* (Cambridge: Cambridge University Press, 1997), 26 and 97, 30n, 46n, 96–98, 143, 62, 162, 162n, and 178.

danger. He also takes the precious cup which was part of Blanchefleur's sale price, so he will be able to buy her back.

Floire travels in search of Blanchefleur, obtaining news of sightings of her as he goes; eventually he arrives in Babylon. There a burgess called variously Dayre, Darys, Daris, or Darie (probably all variations of Darius) tells Floire that Blanchefleur is sequestered in a gigantic stone tower, together with more than forty other maidens and guarded by eunuchs, with a fierce warden at the gate. Like Shahriyar, in *One Thousand and One Nights,* the Emir constantly takes new wives and Blanchefleur is forecast to be next. With the guard's help, Floire is concealed in a basket of flowers that is to be brought to Blanchefleur's chamber.

By mistake, the basket is conveyed to Claris, Blanchefleur's confidante, who takes him to Blanchefleur. She brings the couple a bed, promising not to betray them. Blanchefleur remains clasped in Floire's arms until the Emir, searching for her, discovers them together [Figure 2.2]. Enraged, he summons his barons to decide their fate. A fire is prepared so as to execute them, whereupon each lover pleads for the other's life and offers to die first. The Emir is so moved by the lovers' loyalty to one another, his own love for Blanchefleur, and the

FIGURE 2.1 Floris en Blancefloer, produced by the Dutch engraver, printer and translator Jan van Doesborch, ca. 1517. Image in the public domain
SOURCE: HTTPS://COMMONS.WIKIME
DIA.ORG/WIKI/FILE:FLORIS_ENDE_BLANCEFLOER
_LG_68.JPG

weeping of the onlookers at the prospective killing of the beautiful young pair, that he relents and forgives them.

The Emir has the couple married in church [sic] and takes Claris as his queen. On hearing that his father is dead, Floire returns with Blanchefleur to Spain, where they are crowned king and queen and Floire converts to Christianity. Early on, in a brief preliminary summary of the plot, the text explains that,

> Floire was baptised and became
> Christian to please Blanchefleur his dame
> HUBERT ed., lines 21–22, 23

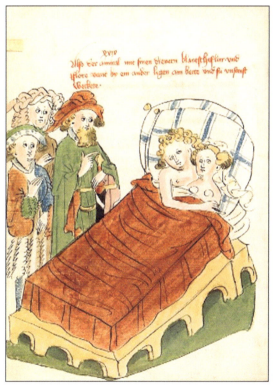

FIGURE 2.2 Flore and Blanscheflur discovered in bed together, illustration by Konrad Fleck, Hagenau, Workshop of Diebold Lauber, around 1442–1444. Image in the public domain
SOURCE: HEIDELBERG UNIVERSITY LIBRARY, COD. PAL. GERM. 362, DOI PAGE / CITATION LINK: HTTPS://DOI.ORG/10.11588/DIGLIT.2212#0354

This is surprising: one might expect him to convert out of deep conviction, rather than to satisfy his beloved. But the wording is no accident. When the episode is related in more detail at the end, the text's author reiterates that,

> He had decided, for the sake
> Of Blanchefleur, his loved one, to take
> The Christian way of life
>
> HUBERT ed, lines 3008–10, 110

At this point Floire, until now a man of humane qualities, suddenly displays a convert's zeal, forcing all those around him to convert; those who refuse are 'beheaded, burned or flayed' (line 3023, 110). The author in no way censures such cruelty, for the killings are dismissed in the single line just quoted and the story concludes with happiness and good fortune for Floire and his beloved – and for her mother, who becomes a duchess when Floire marries her off to one of the peers. The penultimate line, 'May God vouchsafe us all His glory' (3039, 111), while expressing a hope and being a prayer rather than a statement of fact, suggests nevertheless that God is likely to approve of all that has gone before.

3.2   *Spiritual Kinship of Muslim and Christian*

Throughout the narrative, the author stresses the similarities between the Muslim Floire and Christian Blanchefleur, and their spiritual kinship, despite the differences in their religion and culture. Physically, they resemble one another closely and being born on the same day means that, according to astrological theories then becoming current, they possess similar characters and personality traits. The mid-12th century saw a series of translations of Arabic astrological texts into Latin, such as the *Kitāb al-mudkhal al-kabīr* (in English the *Introduction to Astrology*) of Abū Ma'shar al-Balkhī (787–886 CE), the best-known astrologer of the Middle Ages and an important conduit for the revival of Aristotelian thought in Europe.[52]

Abu Ma'shar's works map out attributes of the signs of the zodiac and their influence on terrestrial phenomena, including human beings.[53] He spells out how zodiac 'houses' determine a man's possessions, family, wealth, libido and

---

[52] Abu Ma'shar al-Balkhī's work was translated by John of Seville in 1133, and again, less literally and abridged, by Herman of Carinthia in 1140 CE. His shortened version, the *Kitāb mukhtaṣar al-mudkhal*, or *Abbreviation of the Introduction*, was translated by Adelard of Bath (ca. 1080–1152) in the early 12th century.

[53] *Abu Ma'sar: the Abbreviation of the Introduction to Astrology*, ed. and tr. Charles Burnett, Keiji Yamamoto and Michio Yano (Leiden and other locations: E.J. Brill, 1994), 2–3.

offspring, wives and marriage, travels, sufferings and hardships,[54] demonstrating thoroughly the importance attached to astrological factors at the time. One of the earliest of Adelard of Bath's works, the *De Eodem et Diverso*, (*On Sameness and Diversity*) conflates astrology and astronomy, personifying the latter as a radiant woman whose,

> science describes the whole form of the world, the courses of the planets, the number and size of their orbits, the position of the signs; she traces parallels and colures, and measures with sure hand the twelve divisions of the zodiac ... If a man acquire this science of astronomy, he will obtain knowledge, not only of the present condition of the world, but of the past and future as well. For the beings of the superior world ... are the principle and cause of the inferior world here below.[55]

Thus, the stars and planets influence every aspect of a human being and his or her life. Floire and Blanchefleur will share similar characteristics and a common fate:

Being born on *Palm Sunday* – one of the holiest days in the Christian calendar as the start of Holy Week, suggests the lovers would have been doubly blessed from their birth. The mediaeval church frowned on astrology but eventually came to an accommodation with it. St. Augustine (354–430 CE) had already argued for an influence of the stars over human bodies.[56] Subsequently, Aristotle's doctrine of the Prime Mover, endowing the heavens with motion which they in turn impart to the lower spheres, including the earth, came to be fitted into a Christian scheme of the universe.[57] In the case of our text therefore, there need be no contradiction between the idea of the stars affecting the lovers' lives and their births being on a sacred day in the Christian calendar. The association of the lovers' birth date with Jesus's ride into Jerusalem on Palm Sunday, referred to as 'triumphal' in two of the gospels (St. Matthew and St. Luke in the King James version) and routinely so by the church, suggests that the idea of triumph adheres to both the children.

The likelihood is that the lovers are born in the month of April, *under the sign of Aries*, a sign traditionally associated with energy, enthusiasm, adventurousness, leadership and courage. Both lovers show all these characteristics

---

54   Abu Ma'sar, *Abbreviation,* sections 109–120, in Burnett et al, 105.
55   Quoted by Theodore Otto Wedel, *The Mediaeval Attitude Toward Astrology, Particularly in England,* 1920 (repr. Newhaven, Conn: Yale University Press, 1968), 49–50.
56   Wedel, *Mediaeval Attitude,* 65.
57   Wedel, 63.

in the course of the story. April was also, in the mediaeval period, associated with spring and planting, enjoying the countryside or picking flowers.[58] Palm Sunday too was associated with flowers, in addition to the palm fronds which were laid down in the streets of Jerusalem to greet Jesus's entry.[59] Hence the flower names which are given to both lovers.

However, the lovers' births on Palm Sunday could also have darker associations, according to an Anglican priest to whom I spoke about the poem. The Rev. Canon Frances Ward, Dean of St Edmundsbury in the Diocese of St Edmundsbury and Ipswich, suggested that because Palm Sunday preceded the crucifixion by just five days, events on the Sunday might be infused with a sense of foreboding of death.[60] But in addition, it holds promise of resurrection. Early in the narrative, Blanchefleur is alleged to have died: has died as far as her lover is concerned, but is then 'resurrected'. In several of Shakespeare's plays the supposed deaths of female characters, followed by the eventual revelation that they are actually alive, embody themes of regeneration in a cycle of 'prosperity, destruction, and renewed prosperity'. Tillyard sees the 'complex material of the prose romance [as] ... congenial' to Shakespeare's needs.[61]

The theme is Christian, but also pre-Christian: in a discussion of the supposed Christianity of *The Winter's Tale,* Pafford cites additional and parallel associations between Shakespeare's character of Perdita and the Greek classical figure of Persephone (or Proserpina); and also between Hermione and Demeter (or Ceres), seeing in them all mythologies of spring returning to the earth.[62] Such a 'tragic-comedy' as *The Winter's Tale* and its Greek antecedents (such as Chariton's *Chaereas and Callirhoe*) is *Floire et Blanchefleur,* a tale of reversal of fortune with a symbolic death, and renewal ending in general prosperity and personal happiness.

---

58   Cf. Bridget Ann Henisch, *The Medieval Calendar Year* (University Park, Pa: Pennsylvania State Univ. Press, 1999); J.C. Webster, *The Labors of the Months in Antique and Mediaeval Art to the End of the Twelfth Century* (Princeton: Princeton University Press, 1938).
59   The State of Florida received its name when, on March 27, 1513 (Easter Sunday), Manuel Ponce de Leon first sighted the land and named it in honour of the great feast. The term Pascua Florida, which in Spain originally just meant Palm Sunday, was later also applied to the whole festive season of Easter Week. Cf. the 'History of Palm Sunday' on the *CatholicCulture* website: http://www.catholicculture.org/culture/library/view.cfm?rec num=105 [accessed 31/1/2017].
60   Conversation in Cambridge on 15th March 2012.
61   *Shakespeare's Last Plays'*, ed. E.M.W. Tillyard (London and Toronto: Chatto and Windus, 1938, repr. 1954), 40.
62   *The Winter's Tale,* ed. J.H. Pafford, 1922 (repr. Bungay, Suffolk: Methuen for the Arden Shakespeare series, 1972), xiii.

Flower emblems recur throughout the narrative. Blanchefleur means white flower, which associates her with the Virgin Mary, while statues of the lovers mounted on the tomb prepared for Blanchefleur remind us of the meaning of her name: Floire's is holding out to Blanchefleur's image a 'gold white lily' (line 573, 39). When Blanchefleur is captured, she is taken to a garden on the Euphrates, called the 'Stream of Paradise' (line 1767, 74); the Bible (Genesis 2: 14–15) locates the Garden of Eden precisely between four rivers, one of which is the Euphrates. The garden blooms throughout the year (lines 1780–81, 74) as does a wonderful tree called the Tree of Love. But here again is a symbolic association with death. Blanchefleur's incarceration, in a paradisiaical setting, implies another type of death: her being withdrawn from human society, while her freeing represents a return to a full life. The Emir has devised a complex means of establishing who is to be his next bride: candidates must walk under the Tree of Love and the girl on whom its blossoms fall is selected. The Emir uses witchcraft to make the blooms land on the woman he favours. Before Floire interrupts the plan, Blanchefleur is to be his next chosen bride. Finally, in an almost comic scene, Floire is conveyed to the harem where Blanchefleur is held, concealed in a basket of flowers (lines 2080 ff., 83 ff).

Several times in the narrative, *similarities in both the lovers' physiques and behaviour* prove key to Floire's locating of Blanchefleur. At the first inn where Floire lodges in his pursuit of Blanchefleur, the hostess challenges Floire, relating his behaviour to that of a girl who had stayed at the inn, called Blancheflour:

> She resembled you
> So much. Upon my faith it's true.
> She might be the same age. You are
> In face and features similar.
> She too ate not, but, lost in dreams,
> Was mourning for her friend, it seems.
> His name was Floire, she said
>
> lines 1097–1104, 54–55

The girl was on her way to Babylon to be sold to the Emir, who was willing to pay twice what had previously been paid for her. At another inn on Floire's route, in Bauduc, the host makes a similar observation, confirming the girl's destination (lines 1271–86, 59–60).

A third time Floire obtains news of Blanchefleur when a ferryman who is to take him across an inlet to a chateau called Montfelix compares the youth with a lovely girl whom he has recently seen, so closely resembling him that the ferryman thinks they may be related:

> the reason for my query
> Was that you looked dismal and dreary,
> And one who looked exactly so
> I saw, not half a year ago:
> It was a young girl, similarly downcast.
> You look like her, my faith, 'tis true.
> I know not if she's kin to you'.
> > lines 1349–1356, 62

The Middle English version of these texts similarly introduces the idea of a possible kinship between the lovers. The inn-keeper's wife tells Floire he has been preceded by a maid called Blancheflour and comments,

> Thou are like hire of alle thyng
> Bothe of semblaunt [resemblance] and murnyng [mourning].[63]

Hubert remarks on the 'happy series of coincidences that combine to guide the questing Floire so conveniently and accurately in his search for his lost sweetheart' (18). But I would assert that these events are part of an authorial intent, to underline the lovers' inherent physical and spiritual connection, even to the extent of blurring gender differences. For example, during an episode in the harem tower, the Emir's chamberlain mistakes Floire for a girl. Floire has been smuggled into Blanchefleur's room and has been sleeping with her in her bed. The chamberlain, sent to check up on Blanchefleur's whereabouts, sees the two together and supposes the boy to be Claris, or Clarice, Blanchefleur's great friend:

> Through the glass pane he could descry
> The bed, and saw 'twas occupied.
> He had the impression that he eyed
> Both Claris and lovely Blanchefleur.
> And why should other thought occur
> To him? For there was not a trace
> Of beard or mustache on Floire's face.
> In all the tower there was in truth
> No maiden fairer than this youth.
> > lines 2379–87, 91–2

---

63   *Five Middle English Narratives,* Robert D. Stevick (Indianapolis: Bobbs Merrill, 1967), lines 411–12, 113.

This incident is omitted from the Middle English version, as the critic A.B. Taylor has remarked. But in a footnote, he says it is impossible to judge how far this and another omission are due to the original English author, and how far to imperfect memorising by minstrels on whom his text is based.[64] Finally, the lovers' fates are merged entirely when Floire too is captured and both the lovers are threatened with death.

3.3   Possible Sources of Floire et Blanchefleur

Speculation about the sources for *Floire et Blanchefleur* has focussed largely on classical and ancient literature. For example, Apuleius's story of Cupid and Psyche in *The Golden Ass* and the Biblical *Book of Esther*, have both been put forward as candidates (Hubert, 20), as has *Apollonius of Tyre*.[65] Floire's voyage across the water recalls Orpheus's crossing of the river Styx as he attempts to rescue Eurydice from the underworld. Floire's journey to Montfelix – Mountain of Happiness, again implying Paradise? – will have a happier outcome than Orpheus's, but the episode hints once again at the sense in which Floire is, metaphorically, bringing his beloved back from a kind of death.

Mediaeval texts such as the *Roman d'Eneas*, ca. 1155, have also been cited,[66] as have some German myths.[67] It has also been suggested that a Spanish version may have preceded the French.[68] But some scholars, such as du Méril, find Byzantine antecedents for the piece.[69] Key factors in *Floire et Blanchefleur* are suggestive of such forerunners: for example, the supposed death followed by captivity and sale into slavery of Blanchefleur and her lover's eventually successful search for her, recall scenes from the ancient Greek novellas *Chaereas and Callirhoe*, the *Aethiopica* of Heliodorus and the *Ephesiaca,* or *The Tale of Anthia and Habrocomes,* attributed to Xenophon of Ephesus, in

---

64   Introduction to *Floris and Blanchflour: A Middle English Romance,* ed. A.B. Taylor (Oxford: Clarendon Press, 1927), 21.
65   Gédéon Huet, 'Sur l'origine de *Floire et Blanchefleur*', *Romania* (July 1899) No. 111, 348–359, 349.
66   A. Adams, 'Destiny, Love and the Cultivation of Suspense: the "Roman d'Eneas" and Aimon de Varennes' "Florimont"', *Reading Medieval Studies,* V (1979), 57–70, 63.
67   Taylor ed., 12.
68   Grieve suggests the original of *Floire et Blanchefleur* is likely to have been Spanish rather than French. She argues that the *Crónica de Flores y Blancaflor* was likely based on an earlier Spanish text, now lost, and may have been composed as a political allegory recalling the marriage in 1269 CE of the Spanish prince Fernando de la Cerda, son of Alfonso el Sabio, to the French princess Blanche, daughter of Louis IX, a descendant of Charlemagne. Cf. Grieve, '*Floire and Blancheflor*', 28, 34, and Part I passim.
69   Quoted by Taylor ed., 12.

which repeated sales into slavery of both the main protagonists, followed by their new 'owners' lusting after them and Habrocomes's ultimately successful search for Anthia, serve to drive the plot through many vicissitudes to its happy conclusion.

Persuasive arguments have also been made for *One Thousand and One Nights* as a source for *Floire et Blanchfleur*. Huet and Price cite common details, including the description of the harem interior, the setting in a polygamous society, the procurement of a beautiful slave by merchants, Blanchefleur's incarceration in a guarded tower, the numbers of rooms in the tower (140, each inhabited by a young woman shut off from the outside world), and the girls' daily morning service to the Emir. All these features recall tales from the *Nights*, such as: *Beder and Gianhare, Noureddin and the Beautiful Slave, The Ebony Horse*, as well as the story of *Shemselnihar* [Shams al-Nahar] and *The Awakened Sleeper* as contained in the Burton edition of 1885.[70] Other elements noted include the jealousy of the Emir which, though less fierce, resembles that of the *Nights*'s sultan Shahriar, and his determination that he alone shall possess his wife; the sale of Blanchefleur by the king and his construction of a magnificent tomb for her; Floire's passing himself off as a merchant and managing to penetrate the harem at risk to his life, as well as the search for a beloved slave.[71]

Floire's disguise and his girlish appearance may also owe something to the *Nights* story of the Prince Taj al-Muluk, who poses as a merchant and then as a slave-girl, in order to enter the private quarters of his beloved Princess Dunya and consummate their love. Discovered, he is about to be executed when he is saved by the arrival of his father's army and the subsequent revelation that he is himself of royal blood.[72] In addition, the theme of young men in love with slave girls belonging to the Caliph is a recurrent one in the *Nights,* as we have seen. A notable example of this, with a plotline largely identical to that of *Floire and Blanchefleur* is the *Nights* story of *Neameh and Noam*. In this tale, a girl slave and a boy are brought up together, form a tight bond of love and

---

[70] Pierre-Daniel Huet, *A Treatise of Romances and their Original. By Monsieur Huet. Translated out of French* (London: Heyrick, 1672), 349 ff. The authors of the *Arabian Nights Encyclopedia* also speculate on a possible *Nights* source for *Floire and Blancheflor*: Vol. 2, 551.

[71] Gédéon Huet, 'Sur l'origine', 349–357; J. Price, '*Floire et Blancheflor*: the Magic and Mechanics of Love', *Reading Medieval Studies*, VIII (1982), 12–33.

[72] 'The Tale of Taj al-Muluk; the Lover and the Loved', is inserted into the story of 'Umar ibn al-Nu'umān. It is told by the latter's vizier Dandan in order to comfort Daw al-Makān after his brother Sharkān's violent death.

are married, but by trickery she is taken away from him. He pursues her and, disguised as a girl, finds her in the Caliph's harem; they are reunited through the bounty of the Caliph.[73]

Price remarks that 'For courtly romance the key note of the idea of Islam is less the figure of the militant Saracen as chivalric enemy than the luxurious sensualism of the Islamic paradise'.[74] Hubert observes that *Floire et Blanchefleur* displays none of the hostility seen in the *chansons de geste*, where Islam had been viewed as the enemy and Saracens had regularly been depicted as savage, brutal, treacherous and menacing. In *Floire et Blanchefleur* on the contrary, the Saracens 'are neither better nor worse than the Christians'; in fact, Floire's father consults his wife on important decisions, unlike the traditional Muslim tyrant and the queen too is shown in a kindly light (Hubert, 17), although selling Blanchefleur into slavery is certainly open to criticism, from a modern perspective at least.

But in my view Floire's actions in butchering Muslim recusants, after he becomes a Christian, are far more inhumane than anything he did when a Muslim. As a youth, and as a lover, he is feminised (viz. his being mistaken for a girl by the chamberlain in the harem tower). Once he ascends to the throne, he adopts stereotypically masculine qualities in ways distasteful to modern sensibilities, if not perhaps to those of his contemporaries, given the martial culture of his own day. However, the most important aspect of the story, to my mind, is that the physical resemblances and spiritual kinship of the lovers: one Muslim, one Christian, far outweigh any differences due to their different faiths and cultural origins, a subject to which I will return.[75]

3.4   *Aucassin et Nicolette*

As with *Floire et Blanchefleur*, this story begins with the sale and enslavement of a woman. Here though, the setting is a Christian court: that of Count Garin de Biaucaire (Beaucaire in the English version) in Provence and the form is the unusual *chantefable*, each chapter consisting of a section of verse ('chanter', to sing), followed by a passage of prose ('fabler', to speak) which elaborates

---

73   *The Thousand and One Nights, or, the Arabian Nights' Entertainments*, ed. Edward Lane (Boston: De Wolfe, Fiske, 1800), 366 ff: https://archive.org/details/thousandonenightool ane/mode/2up [accessed 1/7/2024].

74   Price, '*Floire et Blanchefloir*', 15–16.

75   *Floire et blanchefleur* had descendants in many languages in addition to the Middle English and Spanish, including Middle High German, Old Norse, Old Swedish, Icelandic, Middle Dutch, Greek and Italian, the last including Boccaccio's *Il Filocolo*, although some of the Scandinavian versions may have come directly from Spain, rather than France, via the Vikings' frequent contact with Moorish Spain. Cf. Grieve, 'Floire et Blancheflor', 36–37.

on the verse, as well as advancing the story. The verse has assonance rather than rhyme which, as Roger Pensom points out in his critical edition of the piece, relates it to epic and lyric poetry of the period, as composed by Northern French imitators of the troubadours of Provence.[76] The linking of the work is apposite, as Provence like Spain but unlike northern France, had had direct experience of Muslim rule and thus, like other regions ruled by Muslims or contiguous to their lands, had come under Islamic cultural influence.[77]

The backdrop to the story is that Nicolette has been kidnapped from her, as yet unknown but presumably Muslim, native land by Arab traders who have sold her to the wealthy Viscount of Beaucaire. He has adopted her, had her baptised and brought her up as one of his own. Count Garin, governor of Beaucaire, has an only son, Aucassin, who is fair and gifted and who has fallen in love with Nicolette [Figure 2.3]. But his parents want him to marry a woman of suitable high status – not a bought woman of 'Saracen' birth. Meanwhile, the land is being attacked by the forces of Count Bougars de Valence. Count Garin repeatedly exhorts his son to lead his men into battle, but Aucassin is so besotted with Nicolette that he refuses to leave her side.

The infuriated Count orders the Viscount, his vassal, to dispose of her. He seals her away in a tower at the top of his palace. Aucassin, distraught at Nicolette's disappearance, agrees to fight on condition that after the battle the lovers will be allowed to meet, exchange a few words, and kiss. At first Aucassin fights aimlessly, but eventually he rallies, defeats the enemy and captures Count Bougar de Valence. But Garin reneges on his word and denies Aucassin access to Nicolette – at which point Aucassin makes Bougar swear he will spend the rest of his life harming his (Aucassin's) father! Garin then locks him up too, in a deep dungeon. Aucassin sinks into despair and resigns himself to dying in prison.

Nicolette determines to break free and using towels tied together, she clambers out of her tower window and down to the garden. Warned by the watchman that she is still at risk, she struggles over a palace wall and runs into the nearby forest. There, she entrusts some shepherds to take a message to

---

76 Roger Pensom, *Aucassin et Nicolette: the Poetry of Gender and Growing Up in the French Middle Ages* (Bern and other locations: Peter Lang AG,1999), 16–17.

77 Although Charles Martel defeated the Saracens at Tours in 732, the Arabs remained a powerful force in the Provençal coastal area long afterwards. Provençal cities rebelling against French rule called for help from the Arabs in 737, and the latter were not finally driven out of the region until 973 CE. Cf. Edouard Baratier, 'Entre Francs et Arabes', *Histoire de la Provence*, ed. Baratier (Toulouse: Editions Privat, 1990).

MEDIAEVAL CHRISTIAN ROMANCES – CULTURAL BORROWINGS

FIGURE 2.3 Aucassin and Nicolette, oil on canvas painting by Marianne Stokes (1855–1927). Image in the public domain
SOURCE: HTTPS://COMMONS.WIKIMEDIA.ORG/WIKI/FILE:MARIANNE_STOKES_AUCASSIN_AND_NICOLETTE.JPG

Aucassin. She builds a small hut, decorated with her signature lily flowers and waits for him to arrive.

Released at last from confinement, Aucassin too makes his way to the forest where, after various encounters, he finds Nicolette and together the lovers ride toward the sea and manage to board a merchant ship. A storm drives them to the topsy-turvy land of Torelore, where the queen is away fighting a war, while the king is indisposed, expecting a baby. Aucassin attacks the king, forcing him to promise never again to allow men to give birth and to accompany him to the battlefield, where the weapons consist of food: crab apples, cheeses, eggs and mushrooms.

Having established that the opponent is a genuine enemy, Aucassin lashes out with his sword, killing and wounding many men, to which the king objects. The citizens of Torelore urge the king to banish Aucassin and marry Nicolette to his son. At this point, a *deus ex machina* in the form of a Muslim force lands, besieges and then sacks the castle, finally kidnapping the lovers. They are thrown into different vessels.

Another tempest drives Aucassin's ship back to Beaucaire where, owing to his parents' deaths, he is crowned ruler. Meanwhile, Nicolette is taken to Carthage, home of her captors, and brought before the king, who turns out to be her own father. Seeing him and his palace and the countryside reminds her that this was once her home. She is warmly received, but laments privately that she is among 'savages' [i.e. non-Christians]. Discovering that the powerful barons intend to marry her off to a Muslim king, Nicolette slips away by night, disguises herself as a dark-skinned (male) minstrel and boards a ship bound for Provence. Arriving in Beaucaire, she maintains her disguise and addresses the court. Gradually she reveals her true identity. The lovers are reunited, marry and live happy lives thereafter.

...

Aucassin et Nicolette has often been described as a parody of the mediaeval knightly epic and it is tempting to see it as, among other things, an ironic comment on *chansons de geste,* such as the *Chanson de Roland,* or on *Floire et Blanchefleur.* Albert Pauphilet, for example, sees *Aucassin et Nicolette* as satirising current literary themes of war, adventure and romance, while Robert Harden describes the work as satirising "'the vapid plots and equally vapid personages of the idyllic novel'," and sees Aucassin as an anti-hero.[78] Martin finds in Aucassin echoes of Lancelot in Chrétien de Troyes's *Le Chevalier de la charrette,* while Omer Jodogne comments that Aucassin is "'un fou au pays des sages'", but Martin sees the work as a parody of the pastoral.[79] In the protagonists' very names lies a paradox: that of the Frenchman Aucassin could be understood as a contraction of what his contemporaries would have recognised as an Arab name, al-Qasim or al-Kassim, meaning 'one who distributes', while the quintessentially French name, Nicolette, belongs to a woman from a Muslim land. I think of *Aucassin et Nicolette* not only as mocking specific works, but holding up mediaeval social customs for ridicule.

---

78 Quoted by June Hall Martin, *Love's Fools: Aucassin, Troilus, Calisto and the Parody of the Courtly Lover* (London: Tamesis Books Ltd., 1972), 23–36.
79 Martin, *Love's Fools,* 27.

From the outset, the mediaeval conventions of warfare are derided: in Aucassin's initial woeful, lovelorn, military (non)-performance; in his furious exacting of a promise from the captive Bougar de Valence to harm his father – the opposite of the usual enforced declaration of fealty; and, most extremely, in the topsy-turvy arrangements in Torelore, where women fight and men produce children, as well as the use of food as weaponry. Using food as weapons in battle is documented in a later mediaeval text – although the context suggests a ceremonial practice. Ibn Battuta describes an occasion orchestrated by the man he describes as the ruler of China, 'the great amir Qurtay' [probably a contraction of Quaratay, a Turkish title, given to the commander by Turkish troops].[80] After a banquet in the Amir's palace, Ibn Battuta and other guests are taken onto a ship, where they are entertained with songs in Chinese, Arabic and Persian, followed by a brilliant mock skirmish:

> On this canal there was assembled a large crowd in ships with brightly-coloured sails and silk awnings, and their ships too were admirably painted. They began a mimic battle and bombarded each other with oranges and lemons.[81]

Indeed, by adopting a militant stance in Torelore, engaging in more conventional warfare, Aucassin is himself succumbing to the principle of topsy-turvy, since his normal disposition is peaceful and, above all, passive.[82]

The phenomenon of women as fighters is part of a wider picture of women acting out the roles of men, like the many Amazonian women of Arab fiction (Chapter 1), and may point to an Arab source.[83] The contrast between Aucassin's relative passivity and Nicolette's proactivity is striking. The imbalance between the lovers is even seen in the conditions of their imprisonment: he in an underground dungeon, literally and metaphorically cast down, while she is up in the highest tower. While he despairs, she plans. When he resigns himself to life – and death – in prison, she determines to escape. Finally, while he, having

---

80   Cf. *The Travels of ibn Battuta AD 1325–1354*, ed. H.A.R. Gibb (London: George Routledge & Sons Ltd., 1929), 372, Note 25.
81   Gibb ed., *Travels*, 296.
82   From Ibn Battuta, also, comes an expression of astonishment at finding the town of Iznik (in present-day Turkey) being governed by a woman, one of the consorts of the Sultan (Gibb ed., 451–54).
83   Cf. Kruk, *Warrior Women*. After the death of the Prophet Muhammad, one of his widows – previously his favourite wife, A'isha bint Abi Bakr – led troops to fight her rival for power, the Prophet's cousin and son-in-law Ali ibn Abi Talib. The so-called 'Battle of the Camel' took place at Basra in 656 CE.

returned home, waits and mourns, Nicolette seeks him out. Their eventual happiness is entirely due to her resourcefulness. If all were left to Aucassin, they might both have died, or she might have been killed and he been forced to marry a princess from some neighbouring kingdom.

3.5 Floire et Blanchefleur *and* Aucassin et Nicolette: *Analyses*

Despite their differences, the lovers *Aucassin et Nicolette* like Floire and Blanchfleur are remarkably similar, and their likeness is emphasised throughout. For example, Aucassin is described as follows:

> Biax estoit et gens et grans et bien tailliés de ganbes et de piés et de cors et de bras ; il avoit les caviax blons et menus recercelés et les ex vairs et rians et le face clere et traitice et le nes haut et bien assis.
>
> [He was fair and slim, tall and well fashioned in legs and feet and body and arms. His hair was golden and in little curls; and his eyes were blue-grey and laughing; and his face was bright and oval; and his nose high and well-set.]
>
> II, 9–12

Nicolette is described in almost identical terms:

> Ele avoit les caviaus blons et menus recercelés, et les ex vairs et rians, et le face traitice, et le nes haut et bien assis.
>
> [Her hair was golden and in little curls, and her eyes blue-grey and laughing, and her face oval, and her nose high and well-set.]
>
> XII, 17–19; 21–23[84]

In between and following these lines, the descriptions diverge with the focus being on Aucassin's qualities of character, while the additional lines about Nicolette stress her distinctive femininity and her beautiful, and sexually attractive, figure.

---

84 All quotations are taken from http://www.umilta.net/aucassin.html, a parallel text, in Middle French and English, with the translation into English provided by Julia Bolton Holloway [accessed 8/9/2016].

3.6 Ethno-Cultural Kinship

As with Floire and Blanchefleur, such striking similarities serve to underline and symbolise the innate spiritual kinship of Aucassin and Nicolette, even though they are initially of different religions and ostensibly of different ethnic origins. Sharon Kinoshita describes the 'uncanny physical resemblance between [Floire and Blanchefleur] – one a Saracen prince, the other a Christian slave' – as 'an allegory for the intense interconnection between medieval Islamic and Latin Christian cultures'.[85] She relates this to a 'reterritorialization of the medieval Mediterranean: formerly cast as the space of *translation* – the historical migration of political and cultural hegemony from Greece to Rome to France … remapped as a space of commerce and interconfessional exchange'.[86]

Nicolette is the picture of a European woman, despite being the daughter of a North African king. The depiction of her is conventional, but many Muslims of both sexes throughout the Islamic world and in many periods, had fair or light colouring because of the widespread inter-marriage between Arabs and other peoples in the lands they conquered, or with whom they traded. In particular, many slaves owned by Muslims had been taken from European nations and vice versa.

Women slaves were automatically available in various working capacities, such as menial and domestic servants, but also as concubines and sometimes even as potential wives and mothers of Muslim men, including rulers. As already noted, Haroun al-Rashid had a slave mother and another slave, one of his wives, became mother to his heir. The Ottoman sultan Suleiman I ('the Magnificent') married a Ukrainian woman slave, Hürrem (also known as Roxelana or Roxolana) noted for her fair colouring [Figure 2.4].[87] The union seems to have been one of marital bliss, at least on his side: for Hürrem's sake the Sultan became monogamous, eschewing sex with all the many other women available to him.[88] The couple exchanged love letters whenever they were parted; hers, stilted at first, became ever more expressive as her skills in the Turkish language increased.[89] Hürrem was the first of a series of

---

85 Sharon Kinoshita, *Medieval Boundaries: Rethinking Difference in Old French Literature* (Philadelphia: University of Pennsylvania Press, 2006), 10.
86 Kinoshita, 10.
87 *Roxolana in European Literature, History and Culture*, ed. Galina I. Yermolenko (Farnham, Surrey, and Burlington, Vermont, USA: Ashgate Publishing Ltd., 2010), 4.
88 Leslie Peirce, *The Imperial Harem: Women and Sovereignty in the Ottoman Empire* (New York: Oxford University Press, 1993), 59–60. Cf. also, Leslie Peirce, *Empress of the East: How a Slave Girl became Queen of the Ottoman Empire* (New York: Basic Books, 2017).
89 Peirce, *The Imperial Harem*, 63.

FIGURE 2.4   Hürrem Sultan – Roxelana, 'La Sultana Rossa', painted by Tiziano Vecelli or Vecellio (Titian) ca 1550. Image in the public domain
SOURCE: HTTPS://EN.WIKIPEDIA.ORG/WIKI/ROXELANA#/MEDIA/FILE:TIZIAN_123.JPG

powerful foreign, formerly slave women, known as the 'Sultanate of Women' (ca. 1533–1656).[90]

The children of mixed unions such as those just mentioned might themselves be light-coloured. Yahya ibn Tamim (d. 1116 CE), ruler of Ifriqya, an area of North Africa which included Carthage [comprising what is today Tunisia, Tripolitania (western Libya) and the Constantinois (eastern Algeria, where Nicolette originated]), had a slave for a mother.[91] Ibn Tamim is described by Ibn al-Athir (1160–1233 CE) as 'handsome, blue-eyed, and rather tall'. The

---

90   Peirce, *The Imperial Harem,* 55.
91   *Ibn Khallikan's Biographical Dictionary,* 4 vols., Vol. IV, tr. William MacGuckin de Slane in 1871 (repr. New York: Cosimo Classics, 2010), 96. Tunis, where Carthage is situated, was an

Berber leader of the Almohads (later to conquer al-Andalus) Muhammad ibn Tumart, arriving at Tinmal (or Tinmel) in the Atlas Mountains at the start of his campaign for power, observed many fair-haired and blue-eyed children. He was told that Ibn Tamim had a large number of Frankish (Christian) and other Christian Mamelukes (slave warriors) in his service, whose colouring was predominantly fair. Expressing horror, the puritanical Ibn Tumart ordered his followers to trap and kill all the Mamelukes, which they did.[92]

In Al-andalus similar patterns prevailed. Abd ar-Rahman I, founder of the Umayyad Dynasty in Spain, was blond; Hisham I (ruled 788–796 CE) had very white skin and reddish hair; Abd Allah ibn Muhammad (ruled 888–912) had white skin, blue eyes, and blond hair.[93]

Abd-ar-Raḥmān III, who proclaimed himself Caliph of Córdoba in 929 CE, had a Christian mother and a Christian paternal grandmother [Figure 2.5].[94] He too is described as blue-eyed with 'hair so light he died [sic] it black out of embarrassment' over his northerly appearance. He is said to have spoken the Christian language Romance, rather than Arabic.[95] Caliph al-Hakam al-Mustansir (961–976) had reddish hair; Caliph Hisham II (976–1013) was blond, with blue eyes and a reddish beard. Indeed, the practice of having children with Spanish Christian women probably began immediately after the Muslim conquest of Spain, when 'Abd al-'Azīz, son of the Arab commander Mūsā bin Nuṣair, married Egilo (or Egilona), widow of the last Visigothic king, Rodrigo.[96]

The 10th–11th century Andalusi polymath Ibn Ḥazm, who may himself have been of European Christian origin (although his family claimed Persian

---

important centre for piracy and the slave trade, which had burgeoned during the early 12th century (See Chapter 3).

92 *The Chronicle of Ibn al-Athir for the Crusading Period from al-Kamil fi-l ta'rikh, The Years 491–541/1097–1146, the Coming of the Franks and the Muslim Response*, (Part I of III), tr. D.S. Richards (Aldershot, Hants and Burlington, Vermont: Ashgate Publishing Co., 2006), 218.

93 Darío Fernández-Morera, *The Myth of the Andalusian Paradise: Muslims, Christians and Jews under Islamic Rule in Medieval Spain*, 2016 (repr. Wilmington, Delaware: ISI Books, 2017), 162.

94 *Kitāb al-bayān al-mughrib fī ākhbār mulūk al-andalus wa'l-maghrib* (*Book of the Amazing Story of the History of the Kings of al-Andalus and Maghreb*) (1312), 3 vols., tr. Francisco Fernández y González (Granada: Francisco Ventura y Sabatel, 1860), Vol. 1.

95 Mark R. Williams, *The Story of Spain*, 1990 (repr. Mijas-Pueblo, Malaga, Spain: Santana Books, 2009), 59.

96 Joaquín Vallvé Bermejo, *Al-Andalus: sociedad e instituciones*, Madrid: Real Academia de la Historia, (1999) 41, quoted in Fernández-Morera, *Myth of the Andalusian Paradise*, 162.

FIGURE 2.5 Bust of Abd-ar-Raḥmān III, displayed in a restaurant in Córdoba – formerly a 16th century palace
PHOTOGRAPH BY THE AUTHOR

descent),[97] speaks of his preference for fair-haired women, adding that his tastes are shared by many rulers of al-Andalus, perhaps partly because of their own colouring, due to their maternal ancestry:

> All the Caliphs of the Banu Marwan (God have mercy on their souls!), and especially the sons of al-Nasir, were without variation or exception disposed by nature to prefer blondes. I have myself seen them, and known others who had seen their forebears, from the days of al-Nasir's reign down to the present day; every one of them has been fair-haired, taking after their mothers, so that this has become a hereditary trait with them.

---

97 Fernández-Morera, 161. That he claimed Persian descent (as well as the possibility of his having Iberian Christian origins in Manta Lisham [west of Sevilla]) is mentioned in the *Encyclopedia Britannica* online, under the entry for Ibn Ḥazm authored by J.W. Fiegenbaum: https://www.britannica.com/biography/Ibn-Hazm, [accessed 27/2/2024].

He continues,

> As for al-Nasir and al-Hakam al-Mustansir (may God be pleased with them!), I have been informed by my late father, the vizier, as well as by others, that both of them were blond and blue-eyed. The same is true of Hisham al-Mu'aiyad, Muhammad al-Mahdi, and 'Abd al-Rahman al-Murtada (may God be merciful to them all!); I saw them myself many times, and had the honour of being received by them, and I remarked that they all had fair hair and blue eyes. Their sons, their brothers, and all their near kinsmen possessed the self-same characteristics.[98]

3.7 Comparisons

Similarities between *Floire et Blanchefleur* and *Aucassin et Nicolette* abound, despite the century which separates them. Both sets of lovers are uncannily alike; in both stories a girl has been brought into an aristocratic court as a captive: that of the Muslim girl in a Christian court mirrors the status of the Christian in the Muslim court. In both stories the girl has been raised with favour which has not, however, obscured the precariousness of her situation due to her origins and her vulnerability as a woman and as a slave or former slave. Both works centre on love between the formerly captive woman and the son of the ruler, one Christian, the other Muslim (or in the case of Nicolette a Muslim converted to Christianity), transcending the boundaries of religion, status and national origin. Sources in *One Thousand and One Nights* have been assigned to both works.[99]

But in some ways the situation at the centre of *Aucassin et Nicolette* is a reversal of that in *Floire et Blanchefleur*. Blanchefleur is the passive victim of, at first, captive status and then actual slave/concubine status within the Emir's harem. Floire is the active character, risking his life to discover Blanchefleur's whereabouts. In *Aucassin et Nicolette* however, the roles are completely reversed: the girl is the intrepid one, planning and initiating escape plans for them both. In this story there is a blurring of gender lines, as well as ethno-religious ones.

However, one aspect is common as well as critical to each story, in both it is the Muslim (in Nicolette's case the former Muslim) seeking the Christian. Figuratively it might be said the Muslim is seeking the true (Christian) faith, which is embodied in the beloved 'other'. Only religious differences at first separate two similar individuals whose destiny is to unite and be as one, when the

---

[98] Arberry, tr. and ed., *The Ring of the Dove*, 61–62.
[99] M. Fauriel, quoted by Walter Pater in 'Two Early French Stories' (1872) in *The Renaissance: Studies in Art and Poetry*, ed. Pater (Berkeley, Los Angeles and London: University of California Press) 1893, 12.

Muslim's conversion to Christianity makes possible and confirms their union. Given all their echoes from the East, it could be said that *Floire et Blanchefleur,* along with *Aucassin et Nicolette,* constitute bridging works between Islamic and Christian romantic literature.

4   The Charlemagne Narrative Tradition

4.1   *The* Chanson de Roland/Song of Roland

The 11th century *Chanson de Roland* is thought to be the oldest surviving French literary text, and the first *chanson de geste* [epic poem celebrating the heroic exploits of historic or legendary figures]. It became widely known across Europe, including England, and was translated into several languages. The context is that of a struggle between the Frankish King Charlemagne and the Muslim King Marsile in Spain. The poem is a compendium of tales in which individual lives are played out against a background of warfare between Muslims and Christians, with relationships being created across religious and cultural lines.[100]

In the *Chanson de Roland,* the Franks have taken all Spain except for the city of Saragossa, which remains in Muslim hands. Although they have the advantage, the Franks are tricked by King Marsile into retreating from Spain, in exchange for what they believe will be peace. On their way back to France, having been betrayed by Ganelon, one of their own men, the Franks are ambushed in the narrow pass at Roncevalles (also known as Roncevaux), attacked from the rear and defeated [Figure 2.6]. The eponymous Roland, who is one of the French King's twelve peers, as well as his nephew and favourite, and who had vainly warned Charlemagne against Marsile's duplicity, dies fighting, as a hero and martyr. The episode is based on the actual Battle of Roncevaux in 778

---

[100]   A 'song about Roland' is believed to have been sung to William of Normandy's soldiers during their invasion of England, as they prepared for the battle of Hastings in 1066. (Cf. William of Malmesbury, *History of the Kings of England,* 3.1.) The oldest surviving copy of the text is the Anglo-Norman so-called 'Oxford manuscript', also known as 'Digby 23', dated between 1140 and 1170, now held at the Bodleian Library. Chaucer, in his *Book of the Duchess* (1368?) refers to the treachery of 'the false Genelloun', and the friendship between Roland and Oliver, another important figure in the *Chanson de Roland* (quoted by Phillipa Hardman, 'Roland in England: Contextualising the Middle English *Song of Roland*, in *Medieval Romance, Medieval Contexts,* ed. Rhiannon Purdie and Michael Cichon [Cambridge: D.S. Brewer, 2011], 94). I have worked primarily with a modern translation of one of the French originals, because of its treatment of religious themes: *The Song of Roland,* tr.and ed. Glyn Burgess (London: Penguin Books, 1990).

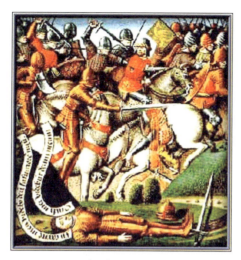

FIGURE 2.6   Battle of Roncevaux Pass in 778 CE, 15th century anonymous painting. Image in the public domain
SOURCE: HTTPS://COMM ONS.WIKIMEDIA.ORG/WIKI/FILE: BATALLA.RONCESVALLES.JPG

CE but, historically, the Franks' enemies on that occasion were Basques, not Muslims, and while Charlemagne was a historic figure, that of Marsile is an invention. The *Chanson de Roland's* substitution of Muslims for Basques foregrounds the more important of the Franks' conflicts at that time and the clash of religions forms an important motif of the piece.

4.2   *The Character of Baligant*

A significant character in the *Chanson de Roland* is Baligant, the Muslim Emir of Babylon, who comes to the aid of Marsile, his stricken vassal. In an epic poem structured symmetrically to balance character with character and episode with episode, Baligant is Muslim counterpart to the venerable Christian Charlemagne. He is represented as being almost Charlemagne's equal in strength, skill and good looks, and matching him in years. In contrast to Baligant, the Christian Ganelon (stepfather to Roland) is villainous, betraying the Franks to Marsile, resulting in the rout at Roncevaux. He is ultimately executed as a traitor. In one version, the fragmentary late 15th-century Middle English text, the *Song of Roland,* Ganelon gets the soldiers drunk and they end up in bed with Muslim women, a sin which contributes to their subsequent deaths.[101] Baligant, however, is noble and courageous, and he grieves for Marsile's anguish, suffering with him (Burgess, tr. and ed, lines 2835–39). He goes into battle lavishly costumed with saffron-coloured garments and a shield adorned with gold and crystal. His physique indicates a man of sexual potency, despite his advanced years, as well as wealth and strength, an attractive figure:

> His crotch is very large
> And he has slender hips and broad ribs;
> His chest is large and handsomely formed,
> His shoulders are broad and his face is very fair,
> His look is fierce and his hair curly.
> It was as white as flowers in summer;
> O God, what a noble baron, if only he were a Christian!
> BURGESS ed., lines 3157–64

Later Baligant is described as 'learned in his faith/And fierce and arrogant in battle' (lines 3174–75), as well as 'a man of great wisdom' (line 3279). He admires Charlemagne's courage and terms him a man of 'honourable deeds' (lines 3180–81). He brings hope to Marsile and his men but is finally overwhelmed by Charlemagne's forces and dies valiantly. In the schematic formula of the *Chanson de Roland,* Baligant is a pagan and his defeat by a Christian is inevitable. The *Chanson*'s author is utterly ignorant of Islam, representing it as the worship of idols and several gods of whom [the Prophet] Muhammad is supposed to be one. In this he conforms with his contemporaries.[102]

Baligant goes into battle carrying the standard of the Prophet. But at one point, he 'begins to realise/That he [i.e. Baligant himself] is wrong and Charlemagne is right' (*Chanson,* lines 3553–54). Later however, Charlemagne urges Baligant to convert to Christianity, but Baligant refuses scornfully. The latter, though, makes no attempt to convert Charlemagne to Islam – in accordance with the precepts of the Qur'an, which dictate that 'there shall be no coercion in religion'; Charlemagne should only submit politically, acknowledging himself as Baligant's vassal. He will then be allowed to rule as a fiefdom the land he was trying to take from the Muslims (lines 3589–3601). From a modern perspective, Baligant's is the more moderate stance. But according to the values of the period, Charlemagne stands firm for Christ. Uncompromisingly, he will allow his adversary nothing short of conversion or death. In the event,

---

101 Hardman, *Roland in England,* 99–100.
102 Comfort, 30–31.

with the help of the Angel Gabriel, Charlemagne prevails. Baligant's demise comes close to the end of the poem and forms a climax within it. Afterwards, the already severely wounded Marsile loses the will to live and succumbs also.

4.3   The Character of Bramimonde

In the account of the Muslim queen of Zaragoza, Bramimonde, the themes with which this work is concerned are more literally foreshadowed: capture and enslavement, and the conversion of a highborn Muslim – usually a woman – to Christianity. Bramimonde, wife and then widow of the villainous King Marsile, is noble, if misguided. Early on in the story she is represented as a fervent adherent to Islam. But when Marsile is desperately wounded, his right hand severed by Roland in the battle, she begins to doubt her faith. Lamenting loudly, she does not speak when the Muslim fighters curse their gods, finally destroying them (lines 2580–91). Later the people of Saragossa weep for the loss of Marsile's son Jurfaleu the Blond, beheaded by Roland, as well as for Marsile's own injuries. They too abuse their gods and smash their images. Now Bramimonde joins in the reproaches, but still her reprimands fall short of outright rejection:

> O Saragossa, how you have been deprived this day
> Of the noble king who held you in his power!
> Our gods have committed a grave crime
> In failing him this morning in battle.
>   Lines 2598–2601

Later, having lost her faith completely, she cries despairingly:

> These gods of ours have abandoned the fight;
> At Rencesvals [Roncevalles] their powers deserted them;
> They allowed their knights to be slain
> And they let down my own lord in battle …
>
> What will become of me, miserable wretch?
> O, woe is me that I have no-one to kill me.
>   lines 2715–18; 2722–23

One last time Bramimonde appeals to the Prophet, from the top of her tower in Saragossa, to which she has climbed:

> Help us, Muhammad!

> O noble king, now our men are vanquished;
> The Emir is slain with such great shame'
>> lines 3641–43

Bramimonde's anguish causes Marsile to die of grief. Bramimonde's surrender of her towers completes Charlemagne's conquest of the city and of Spain. Here the protective and commanding image of the tower suggests strength, which Bramimonde relinquishes to the victor. Elsewhere, as noted particularly with regard to *Floire et Blanchefleur* and *Aucassin et Nicolette*, women are locked in towers, underlining their weakness.[103] Charlemagne and his men demolish the 'statues and idols' in the mosques and synagogues [sic] and hang, burn, or otherwise put to death all who stand in their path, while more than a hundred thousand individuals are baptised in the Christian faith. The queen is made an exception: Charlemagne wishes her to be converted 'through love' (line 3674). His intentions for her, the text adds, are 'entirely good' (line 3681).

Bramimonde is now a prisoner and is brought back to France. Her conversion to Christianity, in the last two *laisses* [stanzas] of the poem, almost completes it. But even though Charlemagne links this event to love rather than compulsion, the text infers otherwise. The emperor [Charlemagne] addresses the bishops of France,

> In my house there is a noble captive;
> She has heard so many sermons and parables
> That, wishing to believe in God, she seeks Christianity.
> Baptize her, so that God may have her soul ...
> [at Aix] they baptize the Queen of Spain.
>
> They found for her the name of Juliana;
> She is a Christian, convinced of the truth ...

However, the sting is in the tail:

> When the emperor has completed his justice
> And appeased his great anger,
> He has Bramimonde christened.
>> lines 3978–90.

---

[103] See my Appendix 1 for a more detailed discussion of the tower in mediaeval literature.

The text makes clear Bramimonde's powerlessness in the matter; she has no choice. The last line relating to her, *He has Bramimonde christened* [*'En Bramidonie ad chrestientet mise'* in the original] uses passive verb forms to describe the process. Furthermore, even though Bramimonde is said to be seeking Christianity, she only *wishes* to believe in [the Christian] God [*Creire voelt Deu*] and it is never stated that she does, or ever will. In later texts including the Anglo-French romances, as will be seen repeatedly, the conversion is voluntary and, in many cases, has already taken place well before the end of the narrative, sometimes even before its beginning, but not here.

Bramimonde's conversion is essential to the *Chanson's* aims. As Brault says,

> The surrender of Saragossa by Bramimonde, which represents, at the level of the plot, the culmination of Charlemagne's expedition to Spain, succeeds at the same time in expressing, on a metaphorical level, the idea of spiritual conquest, a simple variation of the theme of conversion.[104]

Kahf, quoting Brault, adds that Bramimonde 'must be emptied of her Saracen content' and must be converted, not only to Christianity, but to the passive European style of femininity as well.[105] But Bramimonde is not married off to one of Charlemagne's knights; as Kahf says, she is not given any sexual attention, in contrast to the 'scopophilic', i.e. voyeuristic, treatment of the Christian Aude, fiancée to Roland. Kahf relates this to Bramimonde's pagan identity:

> Because Bramimonde is not Christian, the qualities of earlier 'not-Christian' 'tort' women accrue to her. And nearly every 'tort' woman in medieval texts, from Eve, Jezebel and Delilah, to Semiramis and Cleopatra, is transgressively sexual.[106]

But in fact, Bramimonde is not even transgressively sexual; she is not really sexual at all.

However, she does take the initiative in a number of scenes, as when she presents Ganelon with precious jewels for his wife after he arrives to offer his services to Marsile; and when she surrenders Saragossa to Charlemagne as the head of the Muslim forces, indicating her importance and power. Kahf

---

104 *The Song of Roland*, tr. and ed. Gerard J. Brault (University Park, Pa.: Pennsylvania State University Press, 1978), 2 vols., Vol. 2, 313.
105 Mohja Kahf, *Western Representations*, 30.
106 Kahf, 26.

describes her as a 'forward' woman,[107] and in this she foreshadows Nicolette, in the work which includes the latter's name. However, Bramimonde's main function in the story is to convert to Christianity, relinquish her assets and hand them over to the Franks. As Britton points out, she illustrates 'one of the primary desires of romance: to transform and then incorporate that which is different but desirable'.[108]

∴

The *Chanson de Roland* is the original for a large number of texts dealing with the '*matière de France*', stories of Charlemagne and his grandfather Charles Martel, Frankish rulers who repeatedly confronted Muslim forces and checked their advance into Europe, even though the original epic distorts history, by inserting Muslims in place of Basques at Roncevaux. The reality differed in another way: historically, Charlemagne repeatedly joined forces with Muslim armies as part of the centuries-long shifting pattern of alliances in Spain, which saw Muslims often appealing to Christians for aid against other Muslim enemies, and sometimes vice versa. As Comfort notes, although the struggle between the Christians and Saracens [Muslims] is 'the great epic topic of the Middle Ages', the epic poems and ballads of Spain and France,

> reflect a period in the relations of Christians and Moors when the two peoples were forced to live in close proximity and in mutual commerce with each other. Political expediency was of more weight than considerations of religion in determining their relations.[109]

According to another epic tradition, Charlemagne was even related to Marsile by marriage, having taken Marsile's sister Galienne as his wife following a childhood at the court of another Muslim king.[110]

Being a *chanson de geste* (song about heroic deeds) and, unlike most of the works surveyed for this book, the poem's emphasis is always on warfare, rather than love, the battle scenes and slaughter are reported in great (and in my view distastefully repetitive) detail. But those who fight and die are individualised on both sides: they are named and often described with considerable

---

107 Kahf, 27.
108 Dennis A. Britton, *Becoming Christian: Race, Reformation and Early Modern English Romance* (New York: Fordham University Press, 2014), 22.
109 Comfort, 23–48, 26.
110 Comfort, 35.

particularity. The reactions to their deaths are human: triumph or grief, according to the identity and allegiance of the man or woman reacting. The grief is frequently extremely moving: the *Chanson* does not gloss over the suffering incurred in warfare and the mutual anguish at the loss of so many young, vigorous and talented men. Despite his victory, Charlemagne cries out in the penultimate lines of the poem, 'God ... how wearisome my life is'; then he weeps and tugs his white beard (Lines 4000–01).

5   Other Charlemagne Texts

5.1   *Rouland and Vernagu*

A number of other texts survive, derivatives of the original *Chanson,* with strong focus on religious conversion of the Muslim 'other'. The achievement of total control of Spain by the Franks, such as that accomplished by Charlemagne in the *Chanson de Roland*, is also a recurring motif and a product and symbol of wish-fulfilment contrary to historic reality in other Charlemagne texts. For example, Charlemagne also conquers all of Spain in *Rouland and Vernagu* (1330 CE?).[111] On a par with territorial conquest is victory in the battle for souls. In *Rouland and Vernagu* the eponymous pair debate religious ideology, with Muslim Vernagu questioning the Christian doctrines of the Holy Trinity and the virgin birth. He cannot believe that God can be manifest in three forms and still be One; that God, in one of those forms could become a human, be born of another human being, and a virgin at that, and that he could die and rise again.

To a non-Christian, such questions seem quite logical, and even Christian theologians have wrestled with them, at times rending the church. But Roland answers Vernagu eloquently and persuasively enough to make him understand (lines 671–787) – though not to embrace Christianity – before killing the Muslim, with God's help. In his death throes Vernagu begs for assistance from his own gods: Mahound [Muhammad], Iubiter [Jupiter] and Apolin (Apollo), the 'unholy trinity' which many mediaeval Christians ascribed to the Muslim faith. His pleas are of course in vain.

5.2   *Turpin's History of Charles*

In *Turpin's History of Charles*, Roland conducts a religious debate on similar lines to those of his debate with Vernagu, in this case with the 'Saracen' giant

---

111   Sidney J.H. Herrtage, ed., *The English Charlemagne Romances,* Part VI, *With the Fragments of* Roland and Vernagu *and* Otuel, 1882 (repr. London, New York and Toronto: Published for the Early English Text Society by Oxford University Press, 1969), lines 185–274.

Ferragus.[112] Having heard him through, Ferragus tells the Christian they should fight for the glory of their respective faiths:

> 'Tali igitur pacto', inquit Ferracutus, 'tecum pugnabo; quod si vera est haec fides quam asseris, ego victus sim; et si mendax est, tu victus sis; et sit genti victae iugiter opprobrium, victoribus autem laus et decuis in aeuum.
>
> HERRTAGE ed., XXII–XXIII

> ['Let us make a pact then', said Ferragus, 'I will fight with you, and if your faith is true, as you have asserted, I will be overcome; and if it is false, you will be overcome; and may the vanquished people be perpetually disgraced, but the victors be praised and honoured for ever'.]

After a brief fight, Roland kills Ferragus, again with God's aid, and making use of information rashly confided to him earlier by the seemingly invincible giant, namely that, just as Achilles was vulnerable only in his heel, Ferragus can only be killed via a wound to the navel. This mortal stroke is duly administered by Roland. It is a triumph of Christianity – and superior guile!

5.3 *Otuel*

In *Otuel* (1330 CE?), Roland is more successful in his efforts at conversion. The anti-hero Otuel is presented as a 'Saracen' counterpart to Roland, although he is a king's son, whereas Roland himself is only a king's nephew; but he is fearless and, like Roland, a superb fighter. He is the right-hand man to the Muslim ruler Garsie, as Roland is to Charlemagne. He strides into Charlemagne's court and challenges the Frankish king, in Garsie's name, to convert to Islam. Uproar breaks out, with various knights trying to kill Otuel. But Roland protects him, following which Otuel challenges him to a duel. Roland entreats Otuel to convert to Christianity, offering him the hand of the king's daughter Belecent as a bribe. Otuel adamantly refuses to abandon his Muslim faith. But at the height of their battle, and after each has inflicted wounds on the other, a white dove lands on Otuel's head and he instantly agrees to convert. Charlemagne at once affirms the offer of Belecent in marriage.

Thereafter, Otuel becomes the Christians' staunchest ally, killing many Muslims including former friends. His only nod to his past is that, when

---

112   Herrtage, Extract from *Turpin's History of Charles*, xix-xxii.

Garsie is finally captured, Otuel manages to persuade the Christians to spare the Muslim king's life. But the humbled Garsie is forced to pay homage to Charlemagne. Otuel, meanwhile, is made an earl and will presumably marry Belecent, once the fighting is over; the manuscript is incomplete, but this is strongly implied in the extant material. Having converted to Christianity and having proved a loyal and brilliant fighter in the Christian cause, Otuel is and will continue to be treated exactly like any other Christian nobleman. Belecent herself is not consulted on the matter of her marriage, and is only ever referred to in the third person.

6   The Character of Floripas in Medieval French and English Literature

The motif of a powerful Muslim woman allying herself with Christians has antecedents in Byzantine literature and in the character of Bramimonde in the *Chanson de Roland*, although in the latter's case, the alliance is involuntary and she is more or less asexual. But in several other Christian romances concerning the trials and victories of Charlemagne and his men, the Muslim woman is an eroticised figure who acts on her own initiative and her deeds are critical to the resolution of the action. Such a one is Floripas. She is a central, recurring, Amazonian figure in Northern European literature of the Middle Ages, a 'warrior woman of Islam',[113] and an analogue to some of the Christian women in Muslim literature, such as Miriam the Sashmaker and the tragic Abriza. In Christian literature the woman's fiery character, at first uncompromisingly Muslim, and then – once she has converted – resolutely Christian, was fascinating to mediaeval readers and audiences. Her interstitial role between the two worlds, Christian and Muslim, make her central to the narrative in whichever work she appears.

6.1   Fierabras *and* Sir Ferumbras

In *Fierabras* Floripas, daughter of the Muslim ruler Balan and sister to the giant Fierabras [Figure 2.7], who have been fighting the Christian forces of Charlemagne, falls in love with the Frankish knight Guy de Bourgogne, and for his sake defects to the Christian side. She rescues him and four of his companions who have been captured by the Muslim forces. Eventually, Fierabras is defeated and he too converts to Christianity. Two versions of *Fierabras* still

---

113   Cf. Kruk, *Warrior Women*, 201.

exist, one originally written in French ca. 1170, the other in Provençal and then translated into other languages. Both are thought to be based on a lost French original. Another version of the story was called *Balan*. Two early versions appeared in England, probably in the late 14th century: *Sir Ferumbras*, based on *Fierabras*, and *The Romance of the Sowdone* [Sultan] *of Babylone and of Ferumbras his Sone who Conquered Rome*, based on *Balan*. There have been many other versions.[114]

Like their antecedent *Chanson de Roland*, and unlike *Floire et Blanchefleur* and *Aucassin et Nicolette* which are both 'true romances' in the modern sense, these *chansons de geste* are full of bloodthirsty accounts of fighting, maiming and killing. Apart from this, they differ substantially as to episode and incident, and also with regard to the personalities involved. What they all have in common, however, is the character of Floripas: she and her initiatives are the only constant factors in the stories I have mentioned, although the treatments of her character vary from one to another.

It is intriguing that Floripas shares with Blanchefleur (and of course with Floire) a floral name, and one also associated with Easter. Her brother Ferumbras is given a similarly flowery name once he is baptised: 'Florens' in *Sir Ferumbas*, 'Floreyn' in *The Sowdone of Babylone* and Floren in *Charles the Grete*, although he also continues to be known as 'Ferumbras' or 'Fierabras' in all three stories.[115] The name Floripas is thought to be an equivalent of 'passe-fleur' which, as Herrtage translates it, means wood anemone (Herrtage ed, *Sir Ferumbras*, xviii); in at least one instance, Floripas is associated with the peach-blossom, 'flour-de-peskier' (*Sir Ferumbras*, xviii, note 2).

---

114   *The Romance of the Sowdone* [Sultan] *of Babylone and of Ferumbras his Sone who Conquered Rome. English Charlemagne Romances,* Part v, ed. Sidney J.H. Herrtage, 1882, (repr. London, New York and Toronto: Published for the Early English Text Society by Oxford University Press, 1969). Another version of *Fierabras* was translated and published by William Caxton, as the *Lyf of the Noble and Crysten Prince, Charles the Grete*, in 1485; and *Sir Ferumbras* became particularly popular in Spain where, after being translated by Nicolás de Piemonte, it was published in 1528 as the *Historia del Emperador Carlo Magno y delos doze pares de Francia & dela cruda batalla que ouo Oliveros con Fierabras, Rey de Alexandria, hijo del grande almirante Balan* [*History of the Emperor Charles the Great and of the twelve peers of France and of the brutal battle between Oliver and Fierabras, King of Alexandria, son of the great Admiral Balan*]. Cervantes was indebted to this work for details of *Don Quixote*, as was Pedro Calderón de la Barca in his play, *La Puente de Mantible* [*the Bridge of Mantible*] (1627–30). All foreign and domestic publishing details are from *Sir Ferumbras*,, ed. Sidney J. Herrtage, 1879, repr. for the Early English Text Society (London, New York and Toronto: Oxford University Press, 1966), v-xx.

115   *Sir Ferumbras*, lines 1087–89; *The Sowdone of Babylone*, lines 1480–84; *Charles the Grete*, 85, lines 11–14.

FIGURE 2.7 The giant Fierabras. Engraving from the 1497 edition of Jehan Bagnyon's *Roman de Fierabras le Géant* (P. Maréchal et B. Chaussard, Lyon), BNF RES-Y2-993. Image in the public domain
SOURCE: HTTPS://EN.WIKIPEDIA.ORG/WIKI/FIERABRAS

But the name also suggests the passion-flower [Passiflora], and as with the name Blanchefleur, the Passion, and by extension, Easter time. In addition, one of Floripas's attendants is 'the kynges doytre of Floyre' and two others are named Clarymounde and Floraunce, respectively (*Sir Ferumbras*, Herrtage ed., lines 334–35). Is it just coincidence that these recall names in *Floire et Blanchefleur*: Clarice or Claris, Blanchefleur's friend in the harem, as well as Floire and Blanchefleur themselves? Such details form a connection between stories that are otherwise quite disparate.

In character, Floripas is utterly unlike Blanchefleur. Akin to Nicolette, but more ruthless, she is resourceful and essential to the resolution of the action. Both women are also portrayed as beautiful and gentle. Nicolette is lovingly and intimately described by Aucassin, yearning for her when they are separated:

> Nicolette so gent, so sweet
> Fair the faring of thy feet
> Fair thy laughter, sweet thy speech
> Fair our playing each with each
> Fair thy clasping, fair thy kiss.
> MASON ed, 7

Floripas too is described as 'a maide fair and swet' [*Sir Ferumbras*, line 1201] and a 'maide fair and gente' [line 1204]. However, she is also tough and bellicose, making her ferocious as an opponent, especially in furtherance of her love interest. Floripas instructs the Christian knights how to find and kill the Muslims. When some of the Christians are captured, she goes to the dungeon where they are being held [Figure 2.8]. Refused entry, she murders the jailer, Britamoun, by knocking out his brains with her staff (lines 1250–51). Later she lures her uncooperative governess Maragounde [or Marigounde] to a window overlooking the sea and orders her attendant to push her into the water to drown (lines 1360–73). Thus, in a single scene she removes all obstacles to her aims – which are to rescue the Frankish knights and marry Guy de Bourgogne. With the pitiless zeal of the convert, Floripas is also merciless in her treatment of her father. Balan refuses to be baptised and, whereas her brother pleads with the Frankish Emperor for him to be given another chance, Floripas dismisses his appeals and remonstrates with the Emperor,

> Wy tariest thou so longe wyth that man,
> that hath the and thyne agreued?
> Al is for noyt ... ye ne bringeth him neuere to youre purpos.
> Lines 5819–22

> [Why do you waste so much time with that man,
> Who has wronged you and yours?
> It is all for nothing ... you will never bring him to your purpose.]

Balan remains obdurate and is beheaded at the king's command.

What are we to make of Floripas? Herrtage describes her as 'handsome but certainly undutiful' to her father, and as 'an exceedingly strong-minded young lady, determined to have her own way, whatever the cost may be.' (xvii). At other times, he says, her 'naturally soft disposition ... shows itself' and he adds, grudgingly, 'we cannot help admiring the daring of the woman who is never at a loss for an expedient, and who always effects her purpose, though without the slightest consideration as to the means adopted' (xvii). Evidence that Floripas has a naturally soft disposition is strikingly lacking in this tale however, except toward the end of the poem once her goals are achieved. Furthermore, to say that she is an 'undutiful' daughter is euphemistic at the least. The inference is that she is fierce and violent in relation to the Saracens against whom she has turned so vehemently, and meek and eventually 'womanly' toward the Christians whose cause she has joined, and finally as a Christian wife. In many ways, like Miriam the Sashmaker in the Muslim story, Floripas resembles the Greek sorceress Medea, who killed her brother and scattered his body parts in order to delay her father's pursuit of her and her lover Jason; the difference of course is that Medea remains violent to the last, while both Miriam and Floripas are 'tamed'.

At the end of *Sir Ferumbras*, Floripas strips off naked in order to be baptised, precipitating another rapturous description of her beauty by the narrator:

> Hyr skyn was as whyt so
> the melkis fom, fairer was non on molde:
> Wyth eyene graye, and browes bent, And yealwe traces, and fayre
>   y-trent,
> Ech her semede of gold.
> Hure vysage was fair & tretys, Hure body iantil and pure fetys,
> & semblych of stature.
> In al the werld ne miyt be non fayrer wymman of flesch and bon,
> Than was that creature ...
>   lines 5879–86

> [Her skin was as white as milk foam, there was none fairer in the world:
> With eyes gray, and brows bowed, and fair tresses, beautifully curled/
>   plaited,
> each hair seemed [to be made] of gold.
> Her face was fair and slender, her body gentle and perfectly
>   proportioned,
> and handsome her stature.
> In all the world there was no fairer woman of flesh and bone
> than was that creature ...]

Floripas is baptised. Charlemagne then orders Guy de Bourgogne to marry her, which he has previously agreed to do, 'gladlych' (*Sir Ferumbras,* line 5875). She and Guy are crowned, Spain is divided between Guy and Ferumbras and each then rules over his part. Floripas has one other important role in the narrative: to return to the Christians the sacred relics which Ferumbras had stolen from Jerusalem and carried off to his father Balan.

6.2   *The Sowdone of Babylone*

Floripas's actions in *The Sowdone of Babylone* are similar to those in *Sir Ferumbras*, although there are some additional incidents which are absent from *Sir Ferumbras,* such as one concerning a magic girdle, and another in which Floripas gives the knights some of her father's riches to hurl at the Muslims as a distraction during battle. The character of Floripas's father, here the 'Sowdone' (Sultan) of the title, is embellished and made more evil – as when he repeatedly curses his daughter and when he tries to force her to watch her lover Guy de Bourgogne's execution (lines 2639–45). By contrast, her character is somewhat softened: for example, despite his hostility towards her, Floripas welcomes her father 'Wiith right gode cher' when he is brought as a captive to Charles, but he again curses her (lines 3127–32).

In many other respects the two stories are comparable. In *The Sowdone of Babylone,* Floripas kills the jailer and the governess in ways similar to those in *Sir Ferumbras*. She gives succour to the Frankish prisoners whom she has rescued, and to whom, as in *Sir Ferumbras*, she gives shelter in her tower chamber. This is a neat reversal of the usual fairy-tale trope, echoed in *Floire et Blanchefleur,* of the maiden incarcerated in a tower from which she is rescued by a man. Furthermore, the manner of the knights' liberation: the letting down of a rope from Floripas's apartments with which she and her maidens draw the knights up (*Sir Ferumbras,* lines 1647–51), seems a very deliberate twist on the folk tale motif of the knight drawn up by a rope. Here the knights are drawn up for their own salvation, not that of the girl.

One important aspect of *Sir Ferumbras,* missing from *The Sowdone of Babyone,* is the opulence of Floripas's apartments. These are sumptuously adorned with precious stones, gold and silver gilt, richly embroidered cloth, and the like (*Sir Ferumbras,* lines 1323–41), recalling many descriptions of a harem, including details of the one in *Floire et Blanchefleur,* such as the silk sheets and gold basin used by Blanchefleur. This again is a twist on a convention, for the harem is built to confine women in luxury intended as much for the male owner's pleasure as that of the women, whereas here it is for Floripas alone. Similarly, the fifteen maidens who surround Floripas are not fellow-wives or concubines of a man, but attendants on herself, a princess, there to do her bidding, not a man's.

FIGURE 2.8 Floripas listens outside the prison. Image taken from f. 94 of *Roman de Brut*, a verse epitome (begins imperfectly) with continuation to *Edward III; Destruction de Rome; Fierabras*. Written in French. Image in the public domain
SOURCE: BRITISH LIBRARY, HTTPS://PICRYL.COM/MEDIA/FLORIPAS-LISTENS-OUTSIDE-OF-THE-PRISON-FROM-BL-EG-3028-F-94-29FF98

6.3 *Charles the Grete*

A late mediaeval work giving another account of Charlemagne and his knights is *Charles* [Charlemagne] *the Grete* [Great] (1485), translated into early modern English and printed by William Caxton. The work is divided into three books; however this discussion will be restricted to Book II as it is the only one in which a woman has a prominent position. Despite being ostensibly based on *Fierabras*, *Charles the Grete* is substantially different from both *Sir Ferumbras* and *The Sowdone of Babylone*, although many of their aspects and incidents exist here too and are much elaborated upon. Caxton introduces *Charles the Grete* as giving models of behaviour to show people reading it how to live.[116]

Of all the works considered so far, this is the most overtly religious, mapping a meta-struggle for spiritual, no less than geographical dominion. Each side appeals to its deity or deities for help at critical times, especially in the context of the narrative's copious number of battles. As in earlier works, the Muslims are depicted worshipping an olio of supposed Islamic and Greek gods in the forms of idols. When the Christian God or Jesus Christ is invoked by the Franks, the suppliants are invariably successful; at times God performs miracles to save them, such as sending a magical white hart to conduct one of the knights across a rushing river to safety (157, lines 29–158, line 14). But the Muslims' appeals to their gods invariably fail. In one scene, the Franks use the idols as weapons, hurling them from a tower into the ranks of the besieging Muslims (182, lines 11–18). At times of extreme frustration, such as when the Muslim ruler the 'admyral' Ballant [Balan] hears of the capture of the bridge and fortified town of Mantryble by the Christians, he too smashes his idols (178, lines 1–10). But at the end, as in *Sir Ferumbras*, he refuses to convert to Christianity even on pain of death, which is then duly administered (195–97).

From a modern perspective, the Franks are callous in forcing a choice between conversion and death: 'Thenne the batoylle took an ende; and he that wold not be conuerted was incontynent put to deth' (194, lines 12–14). Fierabras converts at the point of a sword and only after he has been severely wounded (77, line 9–78, line 8), whereas the Muslims, as we have seen, imposed no such choices. But, like Charlemagne in the *Chanson de Roland*, *Charles the Grete* is uncompromising in demonstrating the triumph of the 'good' [Christian] religion over the 'evil' [Muslim] faith.

---

116   *The Lyf of the Noble and Crysten Prynce Charles the Grete*, translated from the French by William Caxton and printed by him in 1485, ed. Sidney J.H. Herrtage, (London, New York and Toronto: published for the Early English Text Society, Oxford University Press, 1880, repr. 1967), 1.

At the heart of *Charles the Grete* are the two converts, Florypes, or Floripes or Floripas and her gigantic brother Fierabras, both children of the villainous Ballant. Floripas's presence is enormously expanded in a work whose episodic prose style, developed characters, and what we would now call 'human interest', recall those of Sir Thomas Malory's *Morte d'Arthur*, published in the same year (1485) also by William Caxton. Although the subject material of *Charles the Grete* is drawn from the *chansons de geste* and specifically the 'Matter of France' account of Charlemagne's battles with Muslim forces in France and Spain, Caxton refers to Book II, with which we are concerned, as being translated from an old French romance, whereas Books I and III are taken from historical material (Postscript to *Charles the Grete*, 251).

While in *Sir Ferumbras* and *The Sowdone of Babylon* the love story remains a relatively minor element, in *Charles the Grete*, as in the *Morte d'Arthur*, romantic love is the motivating force for much of the action. The character of Floripas is developed to make her into a complex woman and the love story between her and Guy de Bourgogne is greatly amplified here. Floripas's role as comforter and solver of problems is also much enhanced as compared with the two earlier works. The depictions of her person and her chamber are also more elaborate than in the previous works. The initial description of Floripas's beauty takes up 39 prose lines (all of 90 and lines 1–4 on 91), as compared with just a few words in *Sir Ferumbras*, while the description of her naked when she is baptised at the end of *Charles the Grete* takes up twenty sensuous and in places lubricious lines (198, lines 6–26), compared with the eight lines of verse in *Sir Ferumbras*.

Floripas's courtly manners are emphasised: she is described as '*cortoys florypes, notwithstondying that she was not crystened, had so grete noblesse & so grete compassion.*' (92, lines 25–6). But her courtesy is inconsistent, for in volunteering to save the knights from her father, her motive is purely for the love of Guy de Bourgogne, whom she has seen in Rome winning a joust against her cousin Lucafer. She is ready to convert to Christianity, but *only* if she can be sure to have Guy for a husband. The knights readily agree but, as in *Sir Ferumbras*, Guy is reluctant and at first says he will only marry her if the Emperor [Charlemagne] will give her to him. At this, Floripas swears 'by her god mahommet' that if he will not marry her she will have them all hanged. Roland presses Guy, who then agrees to take her as his wife. At this, Floripas kisses Guy and promises to convert to Christianity (115, lines 6–31). Later in the narrative, Floripas wavers, turning back to her old religion and enjoining the knights to convert to it, but is again persuaded to give up her gods and accept Christianity (125, line 9–126, line 24) on the knights' assurance that they will help to rescue Guy, or see him avenged (130, line 11–131, line 5).

Just as the love-interest between Floripas and Guy is enhanced, so too are other elements of the plot, to which some dramatic and prurient factors have been added. These include the attempted rape of Floripas by Lucafer, to whom she was to have been forcibly married, and an assault by another Muslim called Marpyn [Marvin]. Guy hears her cries and cuts the man down with his sword (123, lines 1–29). It is after the smashing of the idols episode that Guy begins to develop feelings for his bride-to-be, as he becomes increasingly protective, several times rescuing *her* from disaster. We are witnessing the beginning of a role reversal and rebalancing of power back to the 'norm', with the man now in the ascendant. Elsewhere, Guy kisses Floripas passionately (143, lines 3–5) and Floripas adopts a conventional womanly role when, from a window, she watches Guy fighting, The scene resembles a mediaeval joust, where the beloved but physically inactive woman encourages her man to win (137, lines 29–34).

But as in the other stories in which she appears, Floripas is otherwise proactive rather than passive. She repeatedly provides practical, psychological and magical succour to the beleaguered knights. When Guy is captured, she threatens to surrender the castle if he is not rescued (130, lines 24–131, line 5); she brings out the sacred crown of Jesus from among the relics of the Crucifixion to raise their courage (134, line 29–135-line 31); and when the castle is set alight by a Muslim enchanter, Floripas's knowledge of magic allows her to concoct an anti-incendiary to put out the fire (141, lines 27–142, line 13) – again like the sorceress Medea, who used her knowledge of magic and potions at first to win her lover, then to dispatch her rival. When the Franks have run out of ammunition, Floripas gives them her father's gold pieces to use as missiles, which causes the Muslims to fight among themselves for the spoils (142, lines 23–143, line 14); in this the gold is likened to the idols with which the knights also assault their attackers later (182, lines 11–18).

At last, Floripas has her reward for her conversion and steadfast support for the Frankish and Christian cause when she is baptised and married to her lover, Guy de Bourgogne [Figure 2.9], and they are crowned king and queen of Spain, jointly to rule with Fierabras (198, line 1–199, line 5). Finally, she hands the relics over to Charlemagne (199, lines 21–28). Nevertheless, Floripas is invariably central to the action, where her warrior spirit and role as a quasi-mascot to the Franks ensures their survival. As protector and comforter of men in trouble, and of captives, she also has aspects of the Virgin Mary.[117] As guardian of the sacred relics, Floripas evokes the Knights Templar, who escorted Christian

---

117   See Chapter III for a fuller discussion of the Virgin Mary's function as protector of captives.

pilgrims to Jerusalem and, according to legend, carried sacred relics away from that city after the Crusades. But, as in her other stories, she can also be brutal.

Floripas is a woman of powerful contradictions, with an iron will, as the narrator asserts:

> But it is grete scyence for to eschewe the wylle of a woman, whan by effecte she putteth hyr entente to a thynge, that her hert directly draweth, and taketh no regarde to the ende of her entente but onely that she may achyeue hyr enterprise and determynacyon. Florypes retched on noo thynge but that she myzt haue tydynges certeyn of guy of bourgoyne, to whom she had gyuen hyr hert, and was contente to be crystened for the loue of hym.
> 114, lines 6–14

> [But it is great folly to disregard the will of a woman, when she sets her intention to something that her heart desires, and takes no regard to the consequences, but only that she succeed in her enterprise and aim. Floripas thought of nothing except that she might have certain news of Guy de Bourgogne, to whom she had given her heart, and was content to be Christened for the love of him.]

All her actions flow from her determination to win Guy and she threatens to revert to her pagan religion until eventually, like the Biblical patriarch Abraham or the prophet Muhammad at Mecca, Guy smashes her idols physically and metaphorically. Floripas is at last truly converted and begins to pray to the Christian God (126, lines 4–24).

As in all the works considered for this book, captivity is the situation and status which makes possible a connection between Christian and Muslim as lovers, rather than as enemies. The function of the tower, so often in myth and literature (including the two romances discussed above) the locus of a woman's incarceration, here unites men and woman in confinement, as well as providing a place of refuge. In other respects, the kinship between Muslim and Christian, so obvious in Provençal romances, is at first missing from the *chansons de geste*. But, especially in *Charles the Grete*, attachments grow in the nexus of battle, in the close confines of the tower and through common cause. The Christian ethos brooks no difference however and the Muslim, here misrepresented as a pagan, must convert or die. Conversion is the goal, the justification, and the climax of the story.

...

Floripas's white skin and the light colouring of other Muslim women foregrounded in Christian literature have been the subject of considerable scholarly attention, some of it condemnatory. Stephen Lake queries, rhetorically, 'why would Floripas have snow-white skin and golden hair?'.[118] But phenotypic fairness is an essential feature of beloved Saracen women in mediaeval Christian literature including, besides Floripas, Nicolette, Orable in *La prise d'Orange*,[119] and other forthright Muslim heroines. Derek Brewer points to whiteness as being part of the mediaeval aesthetic, tracing its origin to the 12th century CE: the ideal woman was blonde, white, rosy, slender, with perfect white teeth, eyes like stars, etc.[120] Kim Hall speaks of 'fashion' in ideals of beauty working to circumscribe women.[121]

All these women will convert to Christianity, but are in essence already Christian from the start of each narrative. As Jerome Cohen argues, 'their embrace of their new religion is more a declaration of what they always already were';[122] their whiteness is a signifier of their predisposition to convert. Cord Whitaker speaks of 'rhetorical shimmer', i.e. something that simultaneously is and is not, as in a late 15th century romance, *The Turk and Sir Gawain*, in which the Turk is theologically and physically converted to Christianity when he changes both his faith and his shape, to be incorporated into King Arthur's court as one of its knights. In appearance he is 'like a Turk', but not quite Turkish and even before his conversion he already understands and adheres to certain Christian practices.[123] His religious identity 'shimmers like sunlight on a calm sea', Whitaker adds. 'The Turk is ethnically and phenotypically the same. The Turk is not Christian. The Turk is Christian'. Like the Turk, I suggest,

---

118 Stephen Lake, review of Michael Newth's translation of *Fierabras* and *Floripas*, Italica Press, in 2016: http://www.italicapress.com/index331.html [accessed 22/5/2023].

119 Numerous editions of this work are available. Cf. for example, the parallel text, *La Prise d'Orange. Chanson de geste (fin XII e – début XIII e siècle)*, ed. and tr. Claude Lachet, Champion Classiques, Moyen Âge, 31 (Paris: Champion, 2010). A modern English-language version is *An Old French Trilogy: Texts from the William of Orange Cycle*, ed. and tr. Catherine M. Jones, William W. Kibler and Logan E. Whalen (Gainsville, Fla.: University Press of Florida, 2020).

120 Derek S. Brewer, 'The Ideal of Feminine Beauty in Medieval Literature', *Modern Language Review*, 50, (1955), 1–40, 31, https://www.jstor.org/stable/3718320 [accessed 19/2/2023].

121 Kim F. Hall, *Things of Darkness: Economies of Race and Gender in Early Modern England* (Ithaca and London: Cornell University Press, 1995), 8.

122 Jeffrey Jerome Cohen, 'On Saracen Enjoyment: Some Fantasies of Race in Late Medieval France and England', *Journal of Medieval and Early Modern Studies*, 31:1 (Winter 2001), 113–46.

123 Cord J. Whitaker, *Black Metaphors: How Modern Racism Evolved from Medieval Race-Thinking* (Philadelphia: University of Pennsylvania Press, 2019), 18–19. Whitaker notes

Floripas and her sisters, with their pale skin, conformity to European aesthetic ideals and predisposition to convert to Christianity, shimmer: they are, and yet are not Christians.[124] Britton elucidates an 'eroticized whiteness that allowed for the imagining of sameness where difference had been'. The women's white skin in these stories not only makes them desirable sexual partners, but also signals that after conversion and marriage they can become members of and then reproduce an aristocratic race.[125]

In contrast, I have already spoken about the relative absence of alterity due to common origins, intermarriage and the continuing physical proximity of Muslim and Christian. That Muslim women could be light-skinned is no fantastic invention or anachronism: as Epstein records, 'Saracens came in black, white and every shade in between'.[126] So closely did Muslims and Christians (as well as Jews) resemble one another that it required an edict from the church, forcing a difference in dress on non-Christians (Muslims and Jews) to visually set them apart in a vain attempt to discourage marriage across faith – or former faith – lines. The Fourth Lateran Council in 1215 decreed the sartorial markers in order 'to prevent inadvertent sexual miscegenation between individuals not differentiated by sight into racial-religious kinds'.[127]

Regarding cultural and religious factors, Sahner observes that, where Muslims and Christians first rubbed shoulders in the early years of Islam, 'it was not always clear where the practice of one faith ended and the other one began'. Theological uncertainty was compounded in turn by deep social and cultural similarities between the two populations, especially as the ranks of the Muslim community swelled with converts from non-Arab, non-Muslim backgrounds. Sahner likens this process to what he calls, 'the muddy shift from paganism to Christianity centuries before'.[128] Menocal, writing about *Aucassin et Nicolette*, states that most writing on the Middle Ages 'obscures the extent to

---

that the term 'Turk' had by the 15th century overtaken the terms 'Saracen' and 'Moor', to denote a Muslim.
124   Whitaker, *Black Metaphors*, 15.
125   D.A. Britton, 'From the Knight's Tale to the Two Noble Kinsmen: Rethinking Race, Class and Whiteness in Romance', *Postmedieval, Suppl. Making Race Matter in the Middle Ages*, 6 (1) (2015), 64–78, https://www.proquest.com/docview/1672981752 [accessed 19/5/2023].
126   Epstein, *Speaking of Slavery*, 185.
127   Geraldine Heng, *The Invention of Race in the European Middle Ages* (Cambridge: Cambridge University Press, 2018), 80.
128   Christian Sahner, 'Swimming against the Current: Muslim Conversion to Christianity in the Early Islamic Period', in *Journal of the American Oriental Society* (2016) 265–284, 267: https://www.academia.edu/28388644/_2016_Swimming_against_the_Current _Muslim_Conversion_to_Christianity_in_the_Early_Islamic_Period [accessed 13/5/2023].

FIGURE 2.9   A mediaeval wedding (The Marriage of Louis de Blois and Marie de France in 1360): Master of the Getty Froissart (Flemish, active about 1475–1485), Bruges, Belgium, about 1480–1483, Tempera colours, gold leaf, gold paint, and ink on parchment
CREDIT: ALAMY

which what we label – and thus distance ourselves from – "Arabic" or "Oriental" was functionally and contextually no more alien or foreign or distant than the baptised and flawlessly assimilated Nicolette'.[129]

---

129   Maria Rosa Menocal, 'Self and Other in *Aucassin et Nicolette*', *Romanic Review* 80, (1989), 497–511, 503.

Some authors have criticised the masculinised and murderous behaviour of Muslim women such as Floripas, suggesting it would have repelled mediaeval audiences. De Weever, for instance, refers to her 'immoral acts';[130] and Millar-Heggie, quoting de Weever, records that out of 21 Muslim princesses in French literature of the period, 17 will betray their fathers and countries. This means their identity must be erased so they can be incorporated into the framework of the text. Mediaeval courtesy books, she adds, prescribed modesty and obedience for all women, rules which Floripas and her literary sisters clearly defy.[131] However, just as with the militance of Christian heroines in Muslim texts discussed in Chapter 1, nowhere in these accounts is there any censure of the women: they act in good causes (Islam and Christianity respectively) which obviates any suggestion of wrongdoing. In a seminal and much-quoted essay, Warren says categorically that these 'resourceful infidel princesses ... compelled the unqualified admiration of the romancers of Christian France'.[132] Ewoldt remarks that the romances make clear that everything the Saracen princess does – including murder, betrayal, scheming plots – is done out of love for and loyalty to her knight; she may be perceived as a threat, but is more dangerous to her own people than to the Crusaders.[133] Whatever else they represent, I consider that the European aspects of Floripas, like those of Nicolette and the other mediaeval Muslim heroines, denote their spiritual kinship with their Frankish men, whom they love, rescue from captivity and almost certain death, for whom they fight and change faith, and with whom they will live and die.

Finally, how true to history are these tales of enamoured Saracen princesses who marry Franks and convert to Christianity? Noblewomen throughout history have been used as bargaining chips in political negotiations, with their own preferences being ignored in the games of power. A woman would be 'given' to or 'exchanged' with a former adversary, military ally or trade partner by the men in her family; both de Weever and Heng point to intermarriage between

---

130   Jacqueline de Weever, *Sheba's Daughters: Whitening and Demonizing the Saracen Woman in Medieval French Epic* (New York and London: Garland Publishing, Inc., 1998), 41.
131   Bonnie Millar-Heggie, 'The Performance of Masculinity and Femininity: Gender Transgression in The Sowdone of Babylone', *Mirator* (*Lokakuu/Oktober/October 2004*) 1–14, 6–7.
132   F.M. Warren, 'The Enamoured Moslem Princess in Orderic Vital and the French Epic', *PMLA*, Vol. 29, No. 3 (1914), 341–358, 358.
133   Amanda M. Ewoldt, *Conversion and Crusade: The Image of the Saracen in Middle English Romance* (University of Louisiana at Lafayette, ProQuest Dissertations Publishing, 2018): https://www.proquest.com/docview/2206784524/D51EE944BF664B25PQ/1?sourcetype=Dissertations%20&%20Theses [accessed 26/2/2023], 81–82.

Muslims and Christians being common before the Reconquista,[134] although Heng states that while many Christian noblewomen married Muslims, there is little historical basis for the reverse process – Muslim women marrying Christian men.[135]

No doubt love might sometimes follow such unions, but it was in no way inevitable and huge numbers of women must have suffered within painful forced marriages and concubinages. Spanish folklore tells of a Muslim king who gives his sister to a Christian captive, in recompense for having killed the man's sons. The woman (called a *morica* – Moor), as Mirrer interprets her, is a stand-in for Muslim Spain, which the Christians desire totally to possess. In several versions of the story, she cooperates willingly, but in at least one, the *Primera crónica general* of 1344, she has to be threatened with beheading to force her capitulation. Following this, the Christian rapes her. In another account, the *Romance de la morilla burlada* [ballad of the deceived young Moorish woman] set on a Muslim-Christian frontier of Spain, the *morilla* is tricked into allowing into her home a Christian man, who goes on to rape her.[136] The 'Floripas trope', according to which a Muslim woman would fight for and win her choice of Christian man, must have been vanishingly rare. Equally unlikely is the Muslim princess's betrayal of her people: 'Neither history nor chronicle records any [such] instances', according to de Weever.[137]

7   The King of Tars

One final mediaeval work deserves mention here as a conversion romance, but one whose emphasis is almost entirely on religion and also on race, or rather skin colour, rather than on romantic love; here skin colour and religion are inextricably linked and the colour acts as a signifier of faith, as well as moral virtue: hence black (skin) = Muslim = bad, while white (skin) = Christian = good.[138]

---

134 De Weever, 41; Heng, 140.
135 Heng, 141.
136 Louise Mirrer, *Women, Jews and Muslims in the Texts of Reconquest Castile* (Ann Arbor: University of Michigan Press, 1996), 17–30.
137 De Weever, 151.
138 Cf. *The King of Tars*, ed. John H. Chandler, Robbins Library Digital Projects: University of Rochester, 2015: https://d.lib.rochester.edu/teams/text/chandler-the-king-of-tars [accessed 16/07/2024]. The on-line text is based on Chandler's book on the same subject: *The King of Tars*, ed. Chandler (Kalamazoo, Michigan: Medieval Institute Publications, 2015), itself based on the so-called 'Auchinleck' Manuscript, of 1330 or earlier, according to the editor.

The heroine of *The King of Tars,* a Christian princess with a pure white and rosy skin, marries the dark-skinned Muslim 'Soudan' (Sultan) of Damascus, not for love, but in order to restore peace after the enraged Sultan, his offer of marriage to the princess having been rejected, has attacked and routed the Christians, killing thousands.

As in other mediaeval Christian texts, the Sultan worships a hodgepodge of 'heathen' deities. He forces his wife to accept his religion, but secretly she remains a Christian. Their first offspring is born as a dead, limbless and shapeless lump of flesh, for which the Sultan blames his wife, accusing her of an insincere conversion. She challenges him to ask his gods for help. But finding his religion useless in vivifying or altering the dead infant, the Sultan smashes the idols in the temple and reluctantly agrees to allow a Christian priest to try. A captive priest baptises the lump, which is immediately transformed into a beautiful living child. The Sultan then accepts baptism for himself, at which his skin turns from black to white! His wife persuades him to baptise all in his land. This precipitates a holy war with the now fervently Christian Sultan fighting alongside the king of Tars against his own people. The Christians are victorious and most of the vanquished 'Saracens' are converted, while those who refuse conversion are beheaded.

The motif of skin colour being associated with faith recalls the *Nights* story discussed above: *The Man from Upper Egypt and his Frankish Wife*; the echo is strengthened by its setting – like that of the *Nights* tale – in Damascus. The assignations of skin colour are the same in both works: red and white for the Christian and dark for the Muslim. But only in the Christian tale is the skin colour transformed with a change of religion. In the *Nights* story the woman's colour stays the same after she has converted to Islam, and her children remain 'Christian' in colouring.

Modern editor John Chandler finds the Christian poem's 'casualness about … religious cleansing' disturbing, in that it 'echoes the desire of some crusaders to reclaim the Holy Land solely for Christians as well as the expulsion of the Jews from England by Edward I in 1290'. But this is a polemical work whose purpose, as Chandler also points out, was to celebrate the power of Christianity'.[139] Accordingly, its focus is on religion much more than on love. Indeed, although the Sultan falls in love with the Princess and at one point asks her advice 'for the love thou hast to me' (Line 830), nowhere does she herself state that she loves him, even after his conversion. She refers to the love her father and her husband have for her, but not to any love of her own.

---

139   Footnote to lines 1225–29.

Thomas Hahn points out that to a mediaeval European audience, colour was a surface trait indicating an inner essence and therefore mutable if that essence was changed. Thus, religious conversion, representing a change of heart and soul could alter an individual's appearance in the way we have seen in *The King of Tars*. Hahn cites another instance in which conversion to Christianity changes a man's hue from dark to white: the *Cursor Mundi* (ca. 1325). Here King David finds three rods blessed by Moses. Their miraculous power cures illness and converts the skins of four Muslims who were "'black and blue as lead ... horribly shaped ... repulsive ... and loathsome'", to milky white with red colour, "'and all their appearance was made new'".[140]

Another aspect of *The King of Tars* is reminiscent of some of the *Nights* tales discussed above in that the agent of change is the woman, here the Princess, daughter of the King: she takes the initiative to go to Damascus and marry the Sultan, convincing her reluctant parents that this is the only way to stop the bloodshed and relieve the suffering of her people (although this is belied by the final religious war, which also takes place at her instigation). She is, in addition, the means whereby her child is cured and her husband converted. Although the text repeatedly refers to her as 'hende' (gracious, courteous, pleasant, or gentle in the sense that she is a gentlewoman), she is in fact a robust, self-possessed woman who determines her own fate, deceiving (with regard to religion) when she feels justified and finally controlling her powerful husband.

But, as Geraldine Heng indicates, the Sultan and his blackness are products of the author's fantasy and powers of invention. In reality, when the Princess of Tars arrived in Damascus, she would have found in the Sultan 'not a "loathly" black man *in situ* who needed to be Christianised, but a fair, once-Christian Caucasian who had been Islamised. His change of religion brought war not against Muslims. but against Christians and in fact prevented Christians from ever possessing the Holy Land again'.[141]

∙ ∙ ∙

The treatments of Islam in all these versions of the Charlemagne story, as with other mediaeval Christian depictions of the faith, constitute absurd caricatures by authors who either know nothing about it or deliberately falsify

---

140   Quoted by Thomas G, Hahn, 'The Difference the Middle Ages Makes: Color and Race before the Modern World', *Journal of Medieval and Early Modern Studies* 31.1 (2001) 1–37, 14.
141   Heng, 150.

Muslim beliefs. As in the *Chanson de Roland*, 'Mahound' [Muhammad] is represented as a god, rather than a prophet, who is worshipped by the Muslims and repeatedly appealed to for help in times of need. *The Sowdone of Babylon* refers to the Muslims' worship of (plural) 'goddes' [gods] several times, e.g. in lines 309 and 2105, where one of the gods is named as 'Apolyne' [Apollo]. In lines 427–50, the Muslim Estragot is killed and his soul is taken by Mahounde 'And broght ... to his blis' (lines 447–48).

8 Boccaccio and His Successors

The story of *Floire et Blanchefleur* continued to have resonance in the literature of several countries. Boccaccio worked the themes of *Floire et Blanchefleur* into an epic-length novel, *Il filocolo* (1335–36), that is said to be the first prose novel in Italian literature. He used the story as a vehicle to incorporate philosophical digressions and various sub-narratives.

In Boccaccio's *Decameron*, in the seventh story of the second day, Alatiel, a princess of unparalleled beauty, daughter of the Sultan of Babylon, is sent to marry the (Christian) king of Garbo (Algarve). Her ship is wrecked, the male crew are all drowned trying to escape and she and her women are rescued where the ship has beached, on the coast of Majorca. She then falls into the hands of a succession of Christian and Muslim aristocrats in various lands, each of whom becomes obsessed with her and several commit murder in order to obtain her.

This story is said to be influenced by Greek romances as well as Arab tales, and one in particular: the *Ephesiaca* or *Anthea and Habrocomes*, by Xenophon of Ephesus.[142] Shakespeare, using similar 'Greek' themes in *Pericles, Prince of Tyre* (1607 or 1608), has his virtuous and beautiful heroine Marina sold into a brothel after being shipwrecked and then kidnapped by pirates. But he insists that she retains her virginity, against all the odds. However, unlike Marina and her predecessors, Alatiel gives in to her seducers' advances with little hesitation and much good grace and, after a short period of grieving for each preceding lover, enjoys amorous dalliances and contentment with successive admirers. Finally, she is recognised by a visitor who happens to serve in her father's court and is brought home. With his help, she constructs an elaborate edifice of lies

---

[142] For this observation I am much indebted to the late Shakespearian scholar, Leo Salingar, who drew my attention to the parallels between the stories, and the genres.

to conceal her loss of virginity and is eventually married to the King of Algarve for whom she had been intended all along.

> And thus she, who had lain perhaps ten thousand times with eight different men, went to bed with him as if a virgin and made him think she was one. And thereafter she lived with him happily as Queen. Hence the saying: A kissed mouth loses no savour, but is renewed like the moon.[143]

Boccaccio's scandalous tale is clearly a parody of the *Ephesiaca* and all stories in its vein. Its raucous comedy resides precisely in knowledge of how it alters its originals, as it is in the disjunction between its heroine's beauty – which is traditionally conflated with virtue – and her extreme lack of it. Her lustful enjoyment of 'sin' almost places the work in a category of pornography. But Boccaccio's attitudes towards Islam are generally shown to be favourable as, according to Matar, he 'refused the racist invective of his correspondent Petrarch about Arabs and Muslims, and approached the "Saracens" through an entirely non-religious perspective'.[144]

The 'Matter of France' formed the basis for a number of other works in Italian, including Mateo Maria Boiardo's romance, *Orlando Innamorato* (*Orlando in Love*) believed to be from the 1460s. It tells of Orlando (Roland)'s anguished love for the pagan Princess Angelica of Cathay, for whom he competes with his cousin Rinaldo who also loves her. But the epic poem was left unfinished at the author's death. In the early sixteenth century Lodovico Ariosto took up the story, naming his version *Orlando Furioso* – meaning Orlando driven mad: he is crazed by his unrequited love for Angelica and the discovery that she loves another man.

Although these books, like their original *Chanson de Roland,* map the wars between Charlemagne and the Muslims, they are both in the form of chivalric romances. Their emphasis is entirely on the love affairs of the warriors, including that between the apparently Muslim knight, Ruggiero (son of a Christian father and Muslim mother, who had been brought up as a Muslim) and Rinaldo's sister Bradamante. At one point in the later work Ruggiero is temporarily enamoured of Angelica. Following complications and digressions, involving sea voyages, monsters, a trip to the moon, magic love potions and episodes

---

143 Richard Aldington, tr., *The Decameron of Boccaccio*, 1957 (repr. Aylesbury, Bucks: Hazell Watson and Viney Ltd., 1972), 2 vols., Vol. I, 122.
144 Nabil Matar, 'Christians in the *Arabian Nights*', in The Arabian Nights *in Historical Context: Between East and West*, ed. Saree Makdisi and Fecicity Nussbaum (Oxford: Oxford University Press, 2008), 138.

of captivity, Ruggiero is baptised and married to Bradamante. Orlando's story fades into the background as Angelica marries the Muslim Medoro, and Orlando, his wits now restored, is reconciled to her loss. As with the original *Chanson de Roland*, the author makes his heroes ancestors of a great family. In this case it is Ruggiero and Bradamante from whom are descended the d'Estes of Ferrara, representing the fusion through marriage of Christianity and Islam. It is interesting to consider whether the d'Estes, Ariosto's patrons, would be flattered by being assigned such forbears.

The Orlando romances had great influence on subsequent European literature. Some of the characters and other elements were adopted by writers including Torquato Tasso, whose *La Gerusalemme Liberata* (*Jerusalem Delivered*, 1581) has three strong Muslim women (two warriors and a sorceress) falling in love with Christians and converting to Christianity. One of the characters, Clorinda, is modelled on Ariosto's Bradamante but the circumstances of her birth are taken from Heliodorus's *Aethiopica*.[145] Other elements are used by Spanish writers including Luis Barahona de Soto and Lope de Vega, in the late sixteenth and early seventeenth centuries respectively, and by the sixteenth-century English writer, Robert Greene.

---

145   An episode in which the maddened Orlando comes upon a tree in whose bark are engraved the names of Angelica and Medoro is later taken up by the sixteenth century English writer Robert Greene: see Chapter 4.

CHAPTER 3

The Lived Experience of Slavery in North Africa and the Mediterranean – Development of the Mediterranean Slave Trade

From the end of the 15th century onwards, the slave trade in the Mediterranean grew rapidly to become a vastly greater enterprise. This was due to several factors, but especially the expulsion from Spain of the Muslims and crypto-Muslims, creating an exiled group of people who were both knowledgeable about the ways of Christians, and burning with resentment over their forced departure from their native land. After the conquest of Granada (the last Muslim outpost) in 1492 by the armies of the devout Christian monarchs Ferdinand and Isabella, large numbers of Spanish Muslims were ejected from their homeland or fled to North Africa. All those remaining went through apparent conversions to Christianity. But just over a century later, between 1608 and 1612, all the former Muslims (Moriscos) who could be identified and who had not already integrated imperceptibly into the Christian population, were evicted from Spain, thus further swelling the numbers of angry exiles on the Barbary Coast, especially Algiers [Figure 3.1].

In addition, as María Antonia Garcés has pointed out, not content with extirpating Islam from within Spain's frontiers as best they could, the Spanish monarchs extended their crusade to North Africa, conquering Mers-el-Kebir (1505), Oran (1509), and Bijayah and Tripoli (1510).[1] Algiers, taken by the Spaniards in 1509, was recaptured by the renegade corsair brothers Aruj (Oruç) and Kheir ad-Din (Hayreddin) Barbarossa [Figure 3.2]. Hayreddin succeeded Oruç as ruler in 1517 and, after briefly losing and then regaining the city-state once more, formally invited the Sultan Suleiman 'the Magnificent' to accept sovereignty over Algiers and to annexe it to the Ottoman Empire in 1529. By the later 16th century all of North Africa, with the exception of Morocco which had its own Sultan or king, was ruled by Ottoman Turkey: each state had its regent who governed under Turkish hegemony, although the relationship was often an uneasy one and the power balance shifted several times. Once in North Africa, the Spanish exiles found an existing slaving enterprise in which they

---

[1] María Antonia Garcés, 'Introduction' to *An Early Modern Dialogue with Islam: Antonio de Sosa's Topography of Algiers* (1612), tr. into English by Diana de Armas Wilson, ed. María Antonia Garcés (Notre Dame, Indiana: University of Notre Dame, 2011), 27–28.

FIGURE 3.1 Map of Algiers, 1602, engraving by Giovanni Orlandi (active 1590-ca 1613)
CREDIT: BRIDGEMAN IMAGES

could participate and many did this with alacrity, often having specific, as well as general, old scores to settle.

Rulers of the 'Barbary' states (Algiers, Tunis, Tripoli, and Morocco), resentful at the loss of their enclaves to Spain, exploited the exiles' bitterness toward Christendom in general and their former homeland in particular to expand the numbers of corsairs in the Mediterranean. Their activities contributed to an increasingly lucrative business, with Spain as the main target of attacks. Both Oruç (known as Oruç Reis, and also Baba Oruç) and, following him, Hayreddin personally assisted many Mudejars (people who had been living openly as Muslims in Christian parts of Spain before their forced conversion or expulsion) and Moriscos to emigrate from Spain to the Maghreb. In addition, by capturing Spanish ships they succeeded in liberating African Muslim galley-slaves. With these acts, they assured themselves of a following both loyal to them and knowledgeable about Spain.[2]

These men engaged on a massive scale in what the historian Robert C. Davis has termed 'faith slavery' – the capture and enslavement of Christians, which was justified not only on economic grounds but specifically because of their

---
2 Simon Sebag Montefiore, *Titans of History* (London: Quercus, 2012), 196–97.

FIGURE 3.2   The Barbarossa brothers, Aruj (Oruç) (died 1518) and Kheir-ad-Din (Hayreddin) (died 1546), engraving, Dutch school, 17th century
CREDIT: BRIDGEMAN IMAGES

religion.[3] One group of expellees established itself in the Moroccan town of Salé, becoming notorious for their ruthless efficiency in snaring European captives; in England they were known as the 'Salé Rovers', corrupted to 'Sallee Rovers'. They were feared but also mocked, and their exploits became proverbial. With regard to Spain, Moriscos (now re-named 'Moors' by the Spaniards) had vital geographic knowledge of the terrain which they could use to capture vessels, but also to raid and carry off the inhabitants of whole towns and villages, at times venturing quite far inland,[4] although Friedman argues that far

---

3 Robert C. Davis, *Holy War and Human Bondage: Tales of Christian-Muslim Slavery in the Early Modern Mediterranean* (Santa Barbara, Calif., Denver, Colorado, and Oxford UK: ABC-CLIO) 2009, VII–VIII; Davis, *Christian Slaves, Muslim Masters: White Slavery in the Mediterranean, the Barbary Coast, and Italy, 1500–1800*, 2003 (repr. Basingstoke, Hants., and New York: Palgrave Macmillan, 2004), xxv.

4 Ellen Friedman, *Spanish Captives in North Africa in the Early Modern Age* (Madison: University of Wisconsin Press, 1983), 14.

more captives were acquired through coastal raids than via military or naval engagements, and one-fifth of all those taken were captured on land.[5] The Moriscos' local knowledge aided them in pointing out which areas were least defended and potentially the most profitable; and in ferreting out terrified villagers trying to hide from their attackers.

Indeed the fear that Moriscos, supposedly converted to Christianity, had privately remained loyal to Islam and had been secretly helping the marauding North Africans, had been an important factor in their deportation from Spain.[6] Considered a fifth column by many 'Old' Christians, these 'New Christians' had been subject to increasing suspicions, until eventually the clamour for the Moriscos' expulsion achieved its aim.[7] On the high seas and in North Africa, the Moriscos could again openly practise their religion as well as assuaging their thirst for vengeance. As late as 1728–29 it was said that '"Spanish slaves especially dread falling into the hands of a Tagarine [i.e. someone from Aragon: also used as a generic name for the former Moriscos], or Morisco Patron ... who still remember the Injuries done to their Fore-Fathers ... they being, generally, the worst Masters they can have, on Account of those old Grudges'".[8]

Conversely, the slaves' treatment by Muslim-born citizens tended to be more benign: 'those lucky to fall into the hands of a true Muslim or natural Turk suffer only insofar as they have lost their liberty', wrote the French nobleman de Fercourt, who was captured together with the dramatist Jean-François Regnard in 1678. Those true Muslims, he added, would offer comfort and encouragement to their slaves, rather than the cruelties often meted out by renegades.[9] Other former captives endorsed this view. Writing about his experiences after his return home, the former slave the Rev. Olafur Egilsson said,

> The Turkish [his generic term for Muslim-born men and women] ... are quiet and well-tempered in their manner – if it is possible to describe them like that. But the ones who have once been Christians and have

---

5 Friedman, 4.
6 Friedman, 11.
7 Cf. Andrew Wheatcroft, *Infidels: A History of the Conflict between Christendom and Islam*, 2003 (repr. London: Penguin Books, 2004), 153–154; Friedman, xxiii-iv.
8 Joseph Morgan, *A Compleat History of the Piratical States of Barbary*, 1728, (repr. London: R. Griffiths,1750), 487; also cited by Davis, *Holy War*, 170.
9 Claude Auxcousteaux de Fercourt, *Relations de l'esclavage des sieurs de Fercourt et Regnard, pris sur mer par les corsairs d'Alger 1678–79*, quoted by Gillian Weiss, *Captives and Corsairs: France and Slavery in the Early Modern Mediterranean* (Stanford, Calif.: Stanford University Press, 2011), 68.

forsaken their religion, although they dress like the Turkish, are by far the worst of people, and cruelly brutal to Christians.[10]

Not only Spain, but also other Christian countries were subject to the corsairs' attentions, especially those friendly to Spain. The main sufferers, apart from the Spaniards, were the Catholic Italians and French, but patterns of enslavement varied in relation to shifting political alliances so that a peace treaty between two nations might mean a cessation, or lessening, of captive-taking between the signatories and vice versa. Thus, because the Protestant Queen Elizabeth I of England was at war with Spain, and friendly to Morocco and to the Ottoman Sultan, the North African corsairs were less likely to kidnap and enslave English people.[11] But from 1603, when James I signed a treaty with Spain, Britons were systematically added to the number of targets for capture. The corsairs even made their way as far north as Iceland: in 1627, four hundred individuals (including the Rev. Olafur Egilsson, quoted above) were carried off to Algiers, where most of those who survived the terrible journey and the harsh conditions of captivity in a strange land with a burningly hot climate, remained permanently.

Their story is still remembered in Iceland today and the magnificent Hallgrimskirkja church in Reykjavik (consecrated in 1986) commemorates a poet and iconoclastic priest, Hallgrimur Petursson, whose task it was to re-educate and re-Christianise those few captives who were ransomed and able to return home. Among the captives whom Hallgrimur instructed was Guðriður Simonardottir, sixteen years his senior, with whom he fell in love. Guðríður was already married and their affair caused a great scandal, especially when it became obvious that she was carrying Hallgrimur's child. After this, he left the seminary where he was still studying and the couple lived in poverty. Later it emerged that Guðríður's husband had died and she and Hallgrímur married

---

10   Ólafur Egilsson, *Reisubók Séra Ólafs Egilssonar*, 1969, tr. and ed., as *The Travels of the Reverend Ólafur Egilsson: Captured by Pirates in 1627*, by Karl Smári Hreinsson and Adam Nichols (Keflavik, Iceland: Saga Akademia ehf, 2011), 27.
11   Elizabethan England's various alliances with Muslim lands, especially the Ottoman Porte and Morocco, are detailed by Jerry Brotton, in *This Orient Isle: Elizabethan England and the Islamic World*, 2003, repr. UK and seven other countries (Allen Lane, an imprint of Penguin Random House UK, 2016). Cf. also works by Nabil Matar, including *Islam in Britain, 1558–1685* (Cambridge: Cambridge University Press, 1998); *Turks, Moors and Englishmen in the Age of Discovery* (New York: Columbia University Press) 1999); and *Britain and Barbary, 1589–1689*, Gainsville (Florida: University Press of Florida) 2005; also *Piracy, Slavery and Redemption: Barbary Captivity Narratives from Early Modern England*, ed. Daniel J. Vitkus (New York and Chichester: Columbia University Press, 2001).

promptly. He eventually became famous for his preaching and his poetry including many hymns.[12]

• • •

Piracy had a quadruple benefit for the raider states: it was a way of harrying their opponents and obtaining revenge for perceived former injustices; there was rich booty to be plundered from the ships and towns; the slaves could be put to useful work by their captors; and some could be ransomed back to their home countries, often for large sums. Clissold notes that 'once the sword was sheathed, the freeing of captives, or their ransoming, was regarded by Islam as a pious work'.[13] It is evident that, unlike most conditions of slavery in the New World, the state of slavery in Muslim countries was not always an immutable one: slaves who had been captured in war could be freed, depending on their status and access to funds, by ransom, or by treaty; they could buy their freedom or they could be liberated through the defeat of their masters in further warfare.[14] A few also managed to escape. Slaves could attain positions of great power, rising to become the favourites of a ruler or, as in the cases of the Mamelukes in Egypt and janissaries in Turkey, privileged troops and, eventually, even rulers.

Various attempts were made by Christian countries to put a stop to the capture and enslavement of their peoples: for example, the French savagely bombarded Algiers in 1682 and again in 1683, hoping to compel the corsair state to leave French citizens alone. Great damage and much suffering were caused to the town and its residents and, overwhelmed by the assault, the then ruler Baba-Hassan hastily freed several hundred French Christians. This unpopular move resulted in Baba-Hassan's assassination, but the following year the Algerians did sign a peace treaty with France. The French achieved a similar result, with similar means, in Tripoli three years later. War between France and

---

12 The story is told, with the focus on Guðriður, in Steinunn Johannesdottir, *Reisubok Guðriður* (Guðriður's Journey) (Reykjavik: Mál og menning, 2001); and, briefly, in a pamphlet published and sold by the Hallgrimskirkja Church.
13 Clissold, 7.
14 Even transatlantic slavery was not invariably for life: the story of Olaudah Equiano, for example, attests to the possibility of a slave buying his or her freedom: Cf. Olaudah Equiano, *The Interesting Narrative of Olaudah Equiano, or Gustavus Vassa, the African* (1789), in which he describes the horrors of the slavery he experienced, and his eventual buying of his own freedom. But such occurrences were rare, whereas in the Mediterranean, the ransoming of captives was routine, as will be shown.

Algeria broke out again in the following century however, and the slave trade then resumed.[15]

Muslim corsairs did not operate exclusively from North Africa, nor was their focus confined to Western Europe: a vigorous trade on behalf of the Sultan in Istanbul involved raids into Eastern Europe, particularly Poland, Russia and the Ukraine, buying and capturing slaves to be brought back to various parts of the Ottoman Empire. As is well known, the very term 'slave' derives from the Slavic origins of many such people. Indeed, it has been calculated that the Ottoman slave trade may have outnumbered that of Barbary by a factor of two to one or even more: Istanbul's imports of East European slaves via the Black Sea alone may have accounted for around 2.5 million slaves between 1450 and 1700.[16] By contrast, Robert Davis has calculated an approximate total slave population in the Barbary states of between one and 1.25 million between 1530 and 1780 (a slightly later but similar time-scale to that quoted for the Ottomans).[17] But the Sultan also periodically received Europeans and others who had initially been taken as slaves to North Africa, and who were then given or sold to him for his own purposes. Those shipped from Barbary to the Levant were far less likely ever to regain their freedom. It was therefore, a fate much feared.

Slave labour played a vital role in the rising prosperity of several Barbary states, becoming integral and essential to their economies and ways of life.[18] One calculation is that slave labour was responsible for fifty per cent of the production of Algiers, in particular; and corsairing is said to have been its chief – or even only – industry, with up to 35,000 Europeans in bondage at any one time.[19] Another estimate suggests that by the mid-17th century, up to forty per cent of the city's 100,000 inhabitants were enslaved Europeans.[20] This trade continued well into the 19th century.[21]

---

15   Cf. Adrian Tinniswood, *Pirates of Barbary: Corsairs, Conquests and Captivity in the Seventeenth Century Mediterranean* (London: Jonathan Cape, 2010), 240–41, and 68.
16   Cf. William G. Clarence-Smith and David Eltis, 'White Servitude', *The Cambridge World History of Slavery*, ed. David Eltis and Stanley L. Engerman (Cambridge: Cambridge University Press, 2011), 3 vols., Vol. 3, AD 1420–AD 1804, 145.
17   Cf. Davis, *Christian Slaves, Muslim Masters,* 45, and quoted by Clarence-Smith and Eltis, 153.
18   Friedman, *Spanish Captives,* 3.
19   Davis, *Holy War,* 38; Friedman, 76.
20   Clissold, quoting Emanuel D'Aranda, 53.
21   Davis, *Christian Slaves, Muslim Masters,* 45.

1   The Lived Experience of Slavery

Having arrived in the Barbary States, slaves were employed in every conceivable activity and walk of life. They constructed ships, buildings, harbours and roads, fought in the rulers' armies, and worked in crafts, trades and professions including medicine and surgery, carpentry and silver-smithing, as well as in domestic service as cooks, cleaners, child-carers and gardeners. The worst fates were those of galley-slaves, serving as oarsman in the brutal conditions of the pirate ships, as well as in construction projects and mines where labourers were treated with equal harshness and often little mercy. Some unfortunates toiled in the galleys during the summer and in construction at other times of year. The death rate in both these spheres was very high, although some slaves somehow survived to labour in the galleys for decades. Ottoman galley-slaves were marked out by their shaven heads and wore an iron ring on one foot as a symbol of their captivity.[22] The nature of domestic duties, on the other hand, depended on the temperament and inclinations of the slave's owner but could be relatively easy, especially in a small household, and if the owner took a liking to a slave. Peter Parish says,

> slavery rested upon a basic contradiction: Its guiding principle was that slaves were property, but its everyday practice demonstrated the impossibility of living up to, or down to, that denial of the slave's humanity. The master learned to treat his slaves both as property and as men and women; the slaves learned how to express and affirm their humanity even while they were constrained in much of their lives to accept their status as chattel.[23]

A captive's fate would therefore depend on his or her age, sex, state of health, skills, access to funds, and just plain luck. A well-connected male might be spared the worst rigours of forced labour, while he waited to be ransomed: some could even live well, perhaps from loans raised against the anticipated sum. A man with poorer prospects but a valuable skill, an artisan for example, might be used productively for projects such as tailoring or furniture-making. Entering into a household, a woman could become anything from a

---

22   David Abulafia, *The Great Sea: A Human History of the Mediterranean*, 2011 (repr. London and other locations: Penguin Books, 2012), 426.
23   Peter J. Parish, *Slavery: History and Historians* (New York and Other Locations: Harper and Row, 1989), 1. Parish's context here is slavery in the American South, but his assessment could equally apply to many instances of North African slavery.

concubine to her master to the personal attendant of his wife, daughter, or any other woman in the home; less frequently, she might become her master's wife. Some young boys found favour with older men and, as in ancient Greece, became their catamites: many records speak of widespread homosexuality which, although forbidden by Islam, was never effectively suppressed.

Sexual relations between Muslim men and Christian captive women were considered normal and inevitable, the practice being sanctioned, as we saw in Chapter 1, by the Qur'an and some Hadith. Gordon even states that the most common and enduring purpose for acquiring slaves in the Arab world was to exploit them for sexual purposes. A slave owner 'had fairly complete access to his female slaves and kept for his own kinship group the children he sired with them. These women were nothing less than sexual objects'.[24] Gordon adds that white – i.e., European and Central Asian – women were far more highly valued as slaves than women of Africa or other parts of Asia.[25] But this was also a feature of the Christian slave trade, as Epstein points out.[26] Of course, genuine affection could develop on both sides.

References to unions between Muslim men and Christian women abound, in historical documents as well as literature, often with significant consequences. The feared and celebrated corsair Hayreddin Barbarossa, who became ruler of Algiers and admiral of the Ottoman navy, had a Turkish father and a Greek Orthodox Christian mother, whom his father had captured before marrying her.[27] This gave him a knowledge and understanding of Christian culture, while the Muslim faith which he and his older brother Oruç professed allowed them to cultivate valuable connections in the Ottoman world. He is said to have spoken Greek and understood the basics of the Christian faith.[28]

In contrast to the liberty in Islamic countries of Muslim men to mate with non-Muslim women, sexual relations between Christian men and Muslim women were strictly forbidden in these societies, as already noted, with harsh penalties prescribed for offenders of both sexes.[29] The only exception to this

---

24   Gordon, 79.
25   Gordon, 81–82.
26   Epstein, *Speaking of Slavery*, 21, 59, 64, and 106.
27   H.T. Norris, *Islam in the Balkans: Religion and Society between Europe and the Arab world* (London: Hurst Publishing, 1993), 201; Tijana Krstić, *Contested Conversions to Islam, Narratives of Religious Change in the Early Modern Ottoman Empire* (Stanford, Calif: Stanford University Press, 2011), 65.
28   Krstić, 67.
29   Yusuf al-Qaradawi, *The Lawful and the Prohibited in Islam; al-halal wal-haram fil Islam*, tr. by Kamal El-Helbawy, M. Moinuddin Siddiqui and Syed Shukry (London: Shourouk International (UK) Ltd., 1985), 184–86. Mixed-faith lovers Zulpha and Ferdinand violated this rule, and suffered accordingly (see below).

was if the man concerned had already converted to Islam or, possibly, would agree to do so.

2 Conversion and Religious Practice

In North Africa, as in other times and places, many captives found it expedient to convert to Islam. Conversion could mean an easing of their sufferings: only Christians could be used as galley-slaves, for example.[30] Conversion also increased a slave's chances of gaining manumission, made it possible for him to inherit from his master and, above all, paved the way to rising through the system. It has been estimated that one half or even more of the leading (and sometimes most feared) corsair captains were renegades of European origin.[31] The theologian and missionary Pierre Dan, writing in the 1630s, calculated there were 9,500 renegades in Algiers alone and perhaps 14,000 in the Maghreb as a whole.[32] In addition, some of the rulers' most important advisers were renegades, for unlike Christianity, Islam did not hinder their advancement.[33] Nor were the renegades only former captives: many had joined the Muslim cause voluntarily. Abulafia states,

> Muslim naval power was based on the exercise of piracy. It was this that made service in Muslim fleets palatable to the Greeks, Copts, Berbers and Spaniards who undoubtedly manned the ships. [34]

The 16th century traveller Nicolas de Nicolay went so far as to say that most of the 'Turkes' of Algiers were European converts, and he was far less charitable about the fruits of their excursions than some modern-day historians, including Parish, quoted above:

> The most part of the Turkes of Alger, whether they be of the kings household or the Gallies, are Christians renied [renegades], or Mahumetised, of al Nations, but most of them, Spaniards, Italians, and of Prouence, of the Ilands and Coastes of the Sea Mediterane, giuen all to whoredome,

---

30 Clissold, 4.
31 Robert C. Davis, Holy War, 25, 49.
32 Cited by Davis, *Holy War,* 49.
33 Clissold, 86.
34 Abulafia, *The Great Sea,* 249. He was writing about an earlier period in the history of the Mediterranean, but the point he makes is also applicable to much later periods.

sodometrie, theft, and all other most detestable vices, lyuing onely of routings, spoyles, & pilling [pillaging] at the Seas, and the Ilande, being about them: and with their practick art bryng dayly too Alger a number of pore Christians, which they sell vnto the Moores, and other merchauntes of Barbarie for slaues, who afterwarde transport them and sell them where they thinke good, or els beating them miserably with staues, doo imploy and constraine them too woorke in the fields, and in all other vile and abject occupations and seruitude almost intolerable.[35]

Apostasy effectively committed the former Europeans to life-long residence in Barbary, as it was in Christian as in Muslim countries considered a capital crime, which put renegades at risk of execution should they ever return home. Once converted, they could attain positions of great wealth and power, and many of the leading corsairs and even rulers of the Barbary States were renegade Christians, like the Barbarossa brothers; others were men such as the Dutch-born Jan Janszoon, who after his enslavement by Algerian pirates converted to Islam and became known as Murad Rei's, eventually rising to control the independent republic of Salé. The Englishman Samson Rowlie was seized in 1577, castrated and forcibly converted to Islam, but under the name Hassan Aga rose to become the Chief Eunuch and Treasurer of Algiers.[36] Some indeed converted for specifically economic reasons: as Daniel Vitkus puts it, 'many Christians "turned Turk", converting to Islam in order to enjoy the privileges of belonging to the Islamic community'[37] and in time many came to have their own slaves. Even those renegades who remained slaves acquired greater freedom following their conversion.

Evidence regarding the Muslim authorities' attitude to slaves' religious conversion is mixed. Conversion was often discouraged as it diminished the value of the slaves who, as apostatisers and heretics, could no longer be ransomed, as well as reducing the potential scope of their labour because Muslims, even if they remained slaves, could not be put to the hardest tasks.[38] On the other

---

35   Nicolas de Nicolay, *The Nauigation, peregrinations and voyages, made Into Turkie by Nicholas de Nicolay Dauphinois, Lord of Arfeuile, Chamberlaine and Geographer ordinarie to the King of Fraunce: conteining sundry singularities which the Author hath there seene and obserued* ... (London: Thomas Dawson, 1585), tr. 'out of the French [into English]' by T. Washington the younger (repr. Amsterdam: Theatrum Orbis Terrarum Ltd., and New York: Da Capo Press, 1968), 8.
36   Brotton, *This Orient Isle,* 141, and illustration on a page between 240 and 241.
37   Daniel Vitkus, *Turning Turk: English Theater and the Multicultural Mediterranean, 1570–1630* (New York and Basingstoke, Hampshire, England: Palgrave Macmillan, 2003), 31.
38   Friedman, *Spanish Captives,* 88–89.

hand, many slaves were pressurised or even compelled to convert, as we have seen with Samson Rowlie and as was the case with Thomas Pellow, an English boy taken by force to Morocco and, according to his own testimony, to which we shall return, tortured until he agreed to convert. It may be that his extreme youth was a factor in this (he was only eleven when he was captured), and his master felt he could be better moulded to the society as a Muslim. However, Pellow mentions numerous other slaves who converted under duress.[39] Children were generally expected to convert and many were coerced into doing so. Women too were usually required to convert to Islam, especially if they became concubines.[40]

Unlike their Christian counterparts in Europe, the Muslim states provided opportunities for those slaves who remained Christians to practise their faith. Chapels were established for Christian worship and priests were offered guarantees of safety (not always honoured) if they would come to the Barbary States to conduct services on a regular basis. It was thought this would not only help to dissuade slaves from conversion to Islam, but they would be more docile and less likely to rebel if they were permitted their own form of worship. Some contemporary accounts tell of elaborate masses and religious processions being held at Easter and on other special occasions in the Christian calendar.

The Ottoman-sponsored trade in Christian slaves diminished substantially during the later 17th century, as both sides concentrated on more pressing internal problems. However, the enslavement of Christians by Muslim corsairs of the Barbary Coast continued unabated; indeed the corsairs now had free reign for expansion of their activities, as sailors formerly obliged to serve in Sublime Porte armadas were no longer required to do so and could focus their full attentions on corsairing.[41] It is this enslavement of Christians by Muslims around which much of the literature of slavery, romance, and love for the 'other' developed during the European Renaissance period, although, as noted, it had its antecedents in literature of the Islamic world, and Christian writing of the Middle Ages.

---

39 Cf. Thomas Pellow, *The history of the long captivity and adventures of Thomas Pellow, in South Barbary: giving an account of his being taken by two Sallee Rovers ... in which is introduced a particular account of the manners and customs of the Moors ... together with a description of the cities, towns, and publick buildings in those kingdoms / written by himself,* 2nd ed. (London: Printed for R. Goadey and sold by W. Owen, 1740 [?]), 15–16.
40 Pellow, 24.
41 Friedman, *Spanish Captives*, xxiii; 7.

3 Personal Narratives of Enslavement

Although several of the earliest slave narratives are by Spaniards, men and women of various nationalities also contributed to this very specialised type of travel writing. Their accounts are in French, Italian, English, some Scandinavian languages, and others. The genre survived well into the 19th century, along with the institution of Barbary Coast slavery itself. The narratives which follow represent a small cross-section of the numerous surviving personal accounts of slavery written by men of different nationalities in various languages. My aim is to demonstrate the practices and conditions of slavery, as witnessed and interpreted by those who experienced them first-hand. Some slaves wrote letters home pleading to be ransomed. These reports emphasise the victims' sufferings, the better to persuade their relatives and other compatriots to donate the often huge sums needed to free them. Other accounts were embellished for dramatic effect: in his captivity narrative Joseph Pitts cites a proverb which acknowledges that not everything reported about the experience of slavery is strictly factual; he says, 'travelers [sic] must be allowed to what stories they please: its better believe what he saith than to go and seek out the truth out of it'.[42]

Some captors deliberately piled on the agony, forcing their slaves into the most harrowing kinds of work for which they may have been quite unsuited, or tormenting them in other ways so they would write home more feelingly and raise larger sums. This was especially so in the case of captives whom the master believed to be high in the social hierarchy at home – wealthy or privileged or both. Captives with this sort of background went to some lengths to conceal their origins, but might at any time be betrayed by their compatriots.[43] On the other hand, a fine line would be drawn between violently 'persuading' rich or well-connected captives to pressure their countrymen for ransom money, and harming them enough to kill them. As we shall see later in relation to Miguel Cervantes, where a large ransom could be expected, harsh treatment could be mitigated even if the captive might be thought to deserve it: if, for instance he were caught trying to escape.

---

42 Joseph Pitts, *A True and Faithful Account of the Religion and manners of the Mohammetans, with an Account of the Author's Being Taken Captive*, in *Piracy, Slavery, and Redemption: Barbary Captivity Narratives from Early Modern England*, ed. Daniel J. Vitkus (New York: Columbia University Press, 2001), 222.
43 Davis, *Christian Slaves*, 50–53.

3.1 Father Jeronimo Gracián

Some of the earliest written narratives were by captive priests, whose literacy enabled them to write eloquently about their own experiences, and those of others which they witnessed, or which were confided to them. Such was the fate of the Spanish Carmelite priest Father Jeronimo Gracián, source of much contemporary information about North Africa and its institutions. Born in Valladolid in 1545, Gracián was ordained after studying at the University of Alcalá and became a friend and confessor of St. Teresa of Ávila. He was a leader of her ascetic reform movement, the so-called 'Carmelitas descalzos' (shoeless Carmelites), who walked barefoot as an aspect and symbol of their simplicity and devotion to God. He wrote a number of treatises on mysticism and on St. Teresa's work. Like Teresa herself, he fell into disfavour with some of the Catholic authorities and was, for a time, persecuted by the Inquisition. While returning from a fruitless attempt to rehabilitate himself in Rome, Father Gracián was captured by corsairs near Sicily. They stripped him of his habit, rifled his few possessions, and cleaned their muskets with a manuscript he had just completed on Mystical Theology.[44]

Fr. Gracián was taken to Tunis, where he was held from 1593–95. The role of a priest, whether enslaved or free, was to minister to the spiritual needs of Christian slaves, raise their morale and also to try to dissuade them from converting to Islam. His experiences, together with his observations on the lives of slaves and the workings of the slave state, are recorded in writings including the *Tratado de la Redención de Cautivos* (Treatise on the Redemption of Captives), 1595; *La Peregrinación de Anastasio* (The Pilgrimage of Anastasio),[45] completed in 1613 but not published until 1905; and the *Crónica de cautiverio y de la misión* (Chronicle of Captivity and Mission), published in 1942. In addition to describing the episodes of his incarceration in Tunis, the *Peregrinación de Anastasio* contains substantial autobiographical details about Gracián's religious life before and after that period.

---

44 Clissold, 1–2.
45 *Peregrinación de Anastasio: Diálogos de las persecuciones, trabajos, tribulaciones y cruces que ha padecido el Padre Fray Gerónimo Gracián de la Madre de Dios, desde que tomó el hábito de Carmelita Descalzo hasta el ano 1613 y de muchos consuelo y misericordias de nuestro Señor que ha recibido. Pónese su manera de proceder en lo espiritual con algunas luces que acerca de sus sucesos tuvieron la beata madre Theresa de Jesus y algunas otras siervas de Dios que se los pronosticaron. Dirigidos a sus hermanos el Padre fray Lorenzo de la Madre de Dios, y las Madres María de San Joseph, Isabel de Jesús y Juliana de la Madre de Dios, de la Orden de Nuestra Señora del Carmen de los Descalzos,* Burgos: 'El Monte Carmelo' (1905). The dialogue is between Anastasio, i.e., Gracián, and a questioner called Cirilo.

Many prisoners would be confined within a bagnio or baño, a prison so-named because the originals of such spaces had once been bath-houses. Fr. Gracián describes it as an underground dungeon, where at night 600 slaves were packed together in tiers. He himself was so heavily fettered he could barely climb out of his bunk to celebrate mass.[46] His fellow prisoners came to Gracián for advice and support. In his own words, he

> reproved them, comforted them when they had been thrashed, tended them when sick, reconciled their quarrels, and when any of them was in danger of having his ears and nose cropped [as a punishment], bribed the judges with money readily contributed by the Christians ... I kept their earnings for them, so that they might not gamble them away ... served as an oracle with regard to thefts, for if a Moor had had something stolen by a Christian, he would seek my help in recovering it.[47]

The temptation for a Christian slave to convert to Islam was ever-present. Priests not only strove to prevent this happening, but endeavoured to persuade renegades to revert to Christianity and be reconciled with the church, if possible, to save their souls from eternal damnation. Since apostasy from Islam was a capital offence in Muslim states, only the threat of perpetual suffering in a hell gruesomely depicted by the church was likely to induce a convert to renounce Islam and suffer a painful execution, unless he was first rescued and allowed by the Christian authorities to return to the faith. Gracián relates that, while taking Arabic lessons from a renegade called Mami, he convinced the man to relinquish Islam and resume his Christian name, Alonso de la Cruz, which he had to do in front of both Christian and Muslim witnesses. That night the two men were ordered into the presence of several Muslim men, who struck off their chains. Certain they were about to die (the usual punishment for such offences was death at the stake, with the victim unfettered), the men discovered that, instead, they were only to be loaded with even heavier chains: Gracián because the ruling Bey was convinced the priest would command a substantial ransom and de la Cruz because he could now be sent to the galleys, while as a Muslim he had been exempt from such wretchedness.[48]

Every slave hoped eventually to be ransomed and sent home. But the ransom negotiations were often tortuous and protracted, as well as being fraught with corruption and broken promises. Father Gracián describes how the process

---

46   Gracián, 56.
47   Gracián, 94, quoted by Clissold, 62.
48   Clissold, 92–93.

THE LIVED EXPERIENCE OF SLAVERY IN NORTH AFRICA   163

could be prolonged and frustrated, with ransom money sent by families often being appropriated by unscrupulous intermediaries. Increasing desperation, as time dragged on and the captive heard nothing more about his release, could often induce him to convert to Islam.[49] Gracián was himself eventually ransomed, with the help of a Jew whom he had previously assisted, and who arranged for him to go into hiding until he could leave Tunis for fear the Bey would renege on the deal.[50]

Ransoming captives became a major operation, with religious orders having this as their primary intent. A Roman Catholic order, the 'Redemption of the Captives', also known as 'Our Lady of Ransom', the 'Order of the Blessed Virgin Mary of Mercy', (or the 'Order of Merced', 'O. Merc', 'Mercedarians', the 'Order of Captives', or the 'Order of Our Lady of Ransom') was established in 1218 by St Peter Nolasco in Barcelona. Its function was to ransom impoverished Christians (slaves) held in Muslim hands, especially along the frontier that the Crown of Aragon shared with Muslim Al-Andalus in Spain. Other associations were founded in France, Italy and elsewhere in Europe during the 12th and 13th centuries as institutions of charitable works. But the primary objective was to rescue the captives' souls, for fear they might convert to Islam.[51] The Orders raised enormous sums in order to buy back the captives and this helped turn the kidnapping and ransoming of Christians into such a profitable business.[52]

Slaves' own accounts are supported by secondary sources such as advertisements in newspapers appealing for donations, as when the inhabitants of whole villages in Devon and Cornwall were abducted and carried off to Barbary from the 1620s onwards.[53] The most famous such case was when in 1631 pirates raided Baltimore in County Cork, on the west coast of Ireland, carrying 108 residents back to Barbary as slaves. The episode is described as the largest single attack by Barbary pirates on England or Ireland. The villagers' subsequent fate in North Africa is imagined in a poem by the 19th century Irish poet Thomas Osborne Davis:

---

49   Gracián, 168, cited by Clissold, 105.
50   Gracián, 110–15, cited by Clissold, 106–07.
51   *Encyclopedia of Catholic Devotions and Practices*, ed. Ann Ball (Huntingdon, Indiana: Our Sunday Visitor, Inc., 2003), 525; Peter J. Chandlery, *Mary's Praise on Every Tongue: A Record of Homage Paid to Our Blessed Lady* (London: Manresa Press, 1910), 181.
52   Muslim and Jewish communities also set aside funds for ransoming their co-religionists. Cf. Abulafia, *The Great Sea*, 346.
53   Frederick C. Leiner, *The End of Barbary Terror, America's 1815 War against the Pirates of North Africa* (Oxford: Oxford University Press, 2006), 13.

Oh, some must tug the galley's oar, and some must tend the steed;
This boy will bear a Scheik's chibouk,[54] and that a Bey's jerreed.[55]
And some are in the caravan to Mecca's sandy dells.
The maid that Bandon gallant sought is chosen for the Dey:[56]
She's safe – she's dead – she stabb'd in the midst of his Serai!
And when to die a death of fire that noble maid they bore,
She only smiled, O'Driscoll's child; she thought of Baltimore.[57]

3.2 *Diego Galán*

Diego Galán was captured off the coast of North Africa, within sight of the then Spanish garrison town of Oran, in 1589, and taken to Algiers. His ultimate destination was Istanbul, but in his account of his captivity he gives a vivid description of the slave market in Algiers and of his sale.[58] First, as was customary, the new slaves were offered to the Pasha, as he was entitled to take the best of them for himself. The rest were then brought to market to be sold. A 'Turk' grasped Galán by the arm and took him along with the other slaves and, calling out his wares, put Galán and the rest on display. Galán became the object of curious questions from potential buyers as to whether he had any ailments, disabilities or other failings. His teeth were examined, and: 'yo consideraba que lo propio se hace en España cuando venden un jumento' [I felt they behaved as they would in Spain when selling an ass].[59] The slaves were not given a moment before they had to walk, followed by the crowd, anxious to see which seemed the best fitted for work.

An elderly Christian approached Galán, and asked him in a friendly tone whether he had eaten. On hearing he was hungry, the Christian brought him a doughnut (buñuelo) and some cooked meat, which the captive and his companions ate, giving thanks for such an act of charity in the midst of their misfortune. After three days, a renegade arrived and asked Galán where he was from; Galán answered from Toledo. The renegade said he was also from Toledo and identified locations there. He asked Galán if he should buy him, to which Galán replied that it was up to him. The renegade put down three hundred and fifty doblas. About a dozen of the slaves were then brought before the Pasha.

---

54 Chibouk: a long-stemmed type of tobacco pipe used in Ottoman territories.
55 Bey: a ruler or high official in Central Asia or the Middle East; Jerreed or Jerid: a blunt javelin used in mock fights in Ottoman lands.
56 Bandon: a town in County Cork; Dey: a regent of Ottoman Algiers.
57 From Thomas Osborne Davis, 'The Sack of Baltimore', in *The Ballad Poetry of Ireland*, 39th ed., ed. Charles Gavan Duffy (Dublin and London: James Duffy, 1866), 213–15.
58 *El Cautiverio y Trabajos de Diego Galán, Natural de Consuegra y Vecino de Toledo* (ca. 1589) (repr. Madrid: La Sociedad de Bibliofilos Espanoles, 1913).
59 *El Cautiverio*, 11.

Two men from Granada: Luis, known as Mustafa, and another called Ferrat, now urged the slaves to become Muslims.

The Pasha then asked Galán if he would convert to Islam, to which Galán replied, 'no sir'. With furious rage, the Pasha asked him, 'why not, Dog?' He replied, 'my parents were Christians, and in my family there have been no Moors, and I don't want to tarnish their blood with such a stain'. The man cursed Galán and tried to entice him by turns. But no amount of threats, blows and galley slavery, or attempts to bribe him with offers of freedom and luxury, could induce him to renounce his faith. Galán explains that God protected him and an angel stood by him and opened his eyes to the dishonour he would bring to his family.

Galán was then made to wash clothes in the palace, clean the house and perform other domestic tasks, all of which he bore with patience, hoping one day to regain his liberty. The renegades came and confessed to Galán that their conversions were only exterior: inside they were still Christian and hoped one day to go back to a Christian land. Galán urged them to return to the fold and then prayed earnestly for his own freedom.

In the Pasha's bagnio, Galán found most of his fellow-captives, about 550, of many nationalities. Spaniards were placed with other Spaniards, Italians with other Italians, and so on. The Italians, in order to relieve their distress, put on a play, a farce about St Catherine of Siena, with which they amused themselves all day. The Spaniards, overcome with envy at the Italians' enjoyment, caused a commotion which resulted in many of the captives being lynched. Finally, the Pasha handed six of the rest to a mob. All were tortured and murdered in terrible ways, which Galán details.[60] Only one man was spared: Dr Joan Blanco, who was in the process of being ransomed for three thousand ducats, which was, as the author comments, a 'cantidad que le valió la vida' [sum which his life was worth].[61]

In a happier vein, Galán describes a sumptuous feast consumed during an overland journey which he took with his master and his companions, in 1592. The meal, eaten at a campsite but off fine brocade cloths, included stews, veal, various kinds of poultry, bread made with figs, a dish containing honey and dates, more than forty whole roast sheep, cooked goats, huge containers of couscous, another delicacy called 'bacina', and pastries.[62] The variety of dishes

---

60 *El Cautiverio*, 22–23.
61 *El Cautiverio*, 22. Juan Blanco de Paz was a Dominican priest, born ca. 1538, in Montemolín. He was held captive in Algiers from 1577–1592, and got to know Cervantes during his captivity. Cf. Francisco Rodriguez Marín, *El Doctor Juan Blanco de Paz* (Madrid: Revista de Arch, 1916).
62 *El Cautiverio*, 29.

and quantities of meat consumed testify to the wealth of Galán's master and, by extension, of Algiers itself, as well as to the Algerians' catholic tastes in food.

3.3 Fra Diego de Haedo/Dr Antonio de Sosa

Another early report on life and conditions in a Barbary slave state is the *Topografía e historia general de Argel*, published in Spanish in 1612. Included in the history are three dialogues: De Captividad (On Captivity); De los Martyres (On the Martyrs); and De los Maraboutes (On the Marabouts). On its flyleaf Fra Diego de Haedo is named as author, 'dirigida al [directed by the] Ilustissimo Senor Don Diego de Haedo Arcobispo, Presidente, y Capitan General del Reyno de Sicilia' [Fra Diego de Haedo's uncle]. All three dialogues involve the persona of Doctor Sosa, a captive in Algiers, and are set in a prison where he is incarcerated. He is visited in turn by friends with whom he discusses captivity as well as Christian 'martyrs'; and he debates matters of philosophy and religion with the son-in-law of Sosa's owner, and son of two renegades, who addresses Sosa as 'papaz', meaning [Christian] 'pastor'.

Ellen Friedman describes Haedo as a Benedictine monk who was captured and enslaved by Algerian corsairs from 1579–82. His narrative, she says, is 'one of the most reliable eyewitness accounts of Algerian society in the late 16th century'.[63] He died ca. 1612. For the best part of four centuries the attribution of the work to Haedo remained unquestioned. As recently as 2004 Robert C. Davis quoted various statistics contained in the Topografía as being those of Haedo.[64] But in the last few years Maria Antonia Garcés has argued persuasively that the work is in fact by the Iberian priest Antonio de Sosa, (whose name is hinted at in the dialogues), saying this has been known since the 1970s.[65] In another of her works, Garcés resolves the conundrum by simply attributing the account to De Sosa, whom she describes as a cleric in the Portuguese Order of St John of Malta.[66]

---

63 Ellen Friedman, *Spanish Captives*, 172, n. 14.
64 Robert C. Davis, *Christian Slaves, Muslim Masters*, 23, 35, 79.
65 Maria Antonia Garcés ed., *An Early Modern Dialogue with Islam*, 67–78.
66 Maria Antonia Garcés, *Cervantes in Algiers: A Captive's Tale* (Nashville, Tennessee: Vanderbilt Press) 2002, repr. 2005, 11. And cf. María Antonia Garcés, 'Captivity in Cervantes', *The Oxford Handbook of Cervantes*, ed. Aaron M. Kahn (Oxford: Oxford University Press, 2021), 51–84. De Sosa died in 1587, the King in 1598, Haedo the Elder in 1608, and it remains unclear why the book was only published in 1612. But see also Daniel Heisenberg, 'Cervantes, autor de la *Topografía e historia general de Argel* publicada por Diego de Haedo', *Cervantes: Bulletin of the Cervantes Society of America*, Vol. XVI, No. 1 (Spring, 1966), 32–53 where, as its title suggests, Eisenberg argues that Cervantes was the true author of the *Topografía*.

Whoever the author was, the *Topografía* is an important source of information about living conditions in Algiers, for both slaves and free people, as well as the involvement of Spanish Moriscos in attacks on the Spanish mainland. One such raid was on Alicante in 1582, prior to which the Algerian corsair Hasan Pasha had forewarned some local Moriscos of his coming. The author alleges that many of the Moriscos helped the corsairs to sack the city, and then some two thousand of them embarked with their possessions in the Algerian galleys.[67] In another such incident Moriscos of Almenara were accused of collaborating with Algerian corsairs in an attack on the village of Chilches in 1583, for which fifteen who failed to escape suffered exemplary punishment.[68]

Haedo/de Sosa speaks of the unhappy situation in which the captives live, 'el más cruel … y el más inhumano y desdichado que en el mundo ha avido' [the cruellest and most inhumane and miserable which have existed in the world].[69] The worst conditions are suffered by galley slaves, rowing day and night, whether the wind be favourable or not, and whose only food and drink is breadcrumbs, two or three dirty and often rotten biscuits and a little watered-down vinegar. Some galley slaves died of thirst. The treatment of slaves could be brutal in other ways, as in their having their noses and ears bitten off by their masters, either for some minor infraction or simply due to sadism.[70]

Yet the priest's observations about Algiers are by no means wholly negative, and he was able to distinguish between the sordidly miserable lives of the humblest of slaves, and those of the free population and some luckier slaves. He praises both the Barbarossa brothers, describing Oruç as 'a most valiant and enterprising commander'.[71] He speaks of Algiers as being governed 'in all peace and justice', and Kheir ad-Din as welcoming ships and merchants of all races,[72] while also praising his son Hassan as being 'eminent for many singular virtues' and the equal of his father in 'fine qualities and Princely Qualifications'. Of another ruler, Djafer Aga, the author pronounces, 'Never did anyone make the least complaint of his administration. Nor has anyone yet remarked him to be

---

67 Maestro fray Diego de Haedo, *Topografía, e Historia General de Argel, Repartida en Cinco Tratados, do Severan Casos Estranos, muertes espantosas, y tormentos exquisitos, que conviene se entiendan en la Christiandad: con mucha doctrina, y elegancia curiosa*, Valladolid: Diego Fernandez de Cordova y Oviedo, MDCXII (1612), 89.
68 Friedman, *Spanish Captives*, 11.
69 *Topografía*, 98.
70 *Topografía*, 117.
71 Quoted by Sir Godfrey Fisher, *Barbary Legend: War, Trade, and Piracy in North Africa 1415–1830* (Oxford: Clarendon Press, 1957), 44, 46.
72 Fisher, 61n.

FIGURE 3.3 Portrait of Emmanuel d'Aranda (anonymous artist, Brugge? 1642): collection Musea Brugge Groeningemuseum. Image in the public domain
SOURCE: HTTPS://COMMONS.WIKIMEDIA.ORG/WIKI/FILE:PORTRET_VAN_EMMANUEL_DE_ARANDA,_1642,_GROENINGEMUSEUM,_0040769000_(CROPPED).JPG

addicted to any vice whatever'. Another ruler, Shaaban, governed Algiers 'with general Applause and Satisfaction ... very gay and jovial ... he was to all mankind exceedingly affable and well-behaved'.[73]

3.4 *Emanuel (Emmanuel) d'Aranda*

Emanuel d'Aranda, though born in Flanders (Bruges or Dunkirk) in 1602, was from a Spanish family and spent part of his youth in Spain [Figure 3.3]. He was travelling back from Spain on an English ship when it was seized near the mouth of the English Channel. He spent a little more than a year as a slave

---

73 Fisher, 85–87.

in Algiers, before being ransomed. His account of his captivity was published in French as *Relation de la captivité et liberté du sieur Emanuel d'Aranda, jadis esclave à Alger, ou se trouvent plusieurs particularités de l'Afrique, dignes de remarque* (1656), and then into English by John Davies as *The History of Algiers and it's* [sic] *Slavery* in 1666. In it d'Aranda narrates the events of both his own and his fellow-slaves' captivity. I quote from the English translation.[74]

The first part of d'Aranda's narrative outlines the circumstances of his capture and eventual release, when he is exchanged, together with his two companions and after many obstacles are overcome, for some Muslims held captive in Flanders. The second part consists of anecdotes: of cruelty, cozening, sadness and loss, but also of great kindnesses – especially among the slaves, but also from others, and unexpected displays of a kind of 'honour' among the freemen of Algiers. Thus it is, for example, in the case of d'Aranda's 'patron' (as he calls his master) Alli Pegelin, the captain of the galleys, a man otherwise ruthless and completely mercenary. But, once he has negotiated a price for a captive's redemption, he stands by it, even if he later learns – as happens in one instance – that the slave could have afforded far more. D'Aranda cites a Genoese merchant who negotiates with Alli Pegelin for his own release and that of his nine-year-old daughter. They agree a figure of 6,000 Patacoons, at which another Genoese slave tells Pegelin that the merchant could afford four times as much. But Pegelin stands by the bargain, at which d'Aranda comments that 'This shews that Turks and Infidels keep their words, to the shame of Christians who many times take occasion to break theirs' [67–68]. In another incident, Pegelin teaches a lesson to a zealous Muslim who pleads to be allowed to kill a Christian for the sake of the faith. He hopes to attack his victim by stealth, but Pegelin directs him to the biggest and strongest of the Christian slaves, who is forewarned of the impending assault and is able to ward it off. Pegelin then lectures the frustrated would-be-killer, saying that it is no piety, and by no means compliant with the Qur'an, to kill a man who cannot defend himself (256–57).

While there are numerous mentions of brutality in d'Aranda's narrative, he does not dwell on them, perhaps because he was early on exempted from the harshest work, for which his physique was clearly unsuited. Having failed miserably at tasks including operating a wheel for grinding wheat flour and heaving heavy sacks of wheat up long flights of stairs, he was able to bribe his

---

74   Emanuel d'Aranda, *The History of Algiers and it's* [sic] *slavery with many remarkable peculiarities of Africk | written by the Sieur Emanuel D'Aranda, sometime a slave there; English'd by John Davies* (London: Printed for John Starkey, 1666). All references are to this edition unless otherwise stated.

overseer to give him lighter work and was therefore not exposed to the cruellest treatment. In addition, he was enslaved together with two countrymen, one M. Caloen and an M.R. Saldens, and these three helped to keep up each other's spirits. Finally, his captivity proved to be relatively short, so that he was able to recover from his ordeal fairly quickly after his release.

D'Aranda's purpose, it seems, was to both inform and entertain his readers with an account of a culture that was mostly alien to them, and to narrate episodes (50 in all) concerning his own and others' experiences in Algiers. Like numerous observers, he depicts a society in which everything and everyone has a price and can be bought. This, paradoxically perhaps, makes for a curiously egalitarian social structure. There is a 'natural order' over which Turks preside at the top, while Arabs, Berbers, renegades, Jews and slaves occupy various levels below. But anyone, of no matter how low a birth or station, slaves included, may become rich and may rise up the social hierarchy (the reverse is also true, of course). The key to advancement is converting to Islam: hence the number of renegades, from the top down. Those particularly prone to conversion include poor men, who have little hope of ever being ransomed; women, who are under particular pressure as the prospective or actual sexual partners of Muslims; and children, who are expected to integrate into the society. Among other 'renegades' are criminals of differing social classes on the run from regimes in their native lands.

D'Aranda discusses conversion in various contexts as, for example, when he mentions two slaves who wanted to convert but were not allowed to as this would diminish their value as prospective galley-slaves (128–29). Another man who wanted to 'turn Turk' is forbidden to do so by Alli Pegelin, so the slave changes into clothes characteristically worn by Muslims, shaves his head and calls himself Mustapha. Pegelin has him beaten until he admits to his original name and religion. D'Aranda notes wryly that Pegelin 'cudgell'd a Christian into his Christianity, which he would have renounc'd' (173–74). Most of the ruler's twelve thousand soldiers are 'Renegadoes', although d'Aranda comments contemptuously that they are actually 'dissolute persons, without religion or Conscience, fugitives out of Christendom and Turkey for the enormity of their crimes' (102).

In a different vein, a young Christian boy who has been bribed and 'debauch'd' by a Portuguese renegade sues to change his religion, despite having been promised redemption from his slavery. The Pasha is not pleased, for he would have preferred the ransom money to having another convert, but the presence of some 'Turks of quality' lead him to smother his feelings and the boy is duly converted to Islam (132–33). On the other hand, a woman who has been given as a gift to the Pasha's wife proves such an excellent needlewoman that her mistress presses her to convert. The slave refusing, the mistress has her severely beaten, stripped and forced to wear Muslim clothing. She accepts the clothes, but only, as she says, to cover her nakedness; however, she still stands firm in her Christian faith (120–21).

In another anecdote, two French slaves pretend to convert to Islam and make great shows of their supposed religious devotion, berating their countrymen who offer the 'converts' pork or wine, and frequenting the mosques assiduously in order to gain the Muslims' trust. By these means they manage to obtain control of a trading ship, get the Muslim crew-members off the vessel, rescue some other Christians who are waiting nearby by prior arrangement, and put to sea, loudly mocking the Muslims left on shore. After a while they arrive safely in a Christian country (268).

The readiness of slaves to convert to their masters' religion can prove inconvenient in the opposite direction. D'Aranda and his two friends, Caloen and Saldens, are finally about to be exchanged for five Muslims held in Flanders, but the negotiations are threatened when it transpires that one of the five in Flanders has converted to Christianity. D'Aranda and the other Christians realise that if his conversion becomes widely known, the Christian authorities will prevent his leaving, and their own departure from Algiers will then be vetoed from the other side. They are uncertain what to do, on the one hand feeling it would be morally wrong to let the convert leave a Christian country and return to a Muslim one, but of course also longing to be free, so they take counsel from a wise older Christian. With his help the problem is quietly resolved by the convert being challenged as to whether he would rather remain in Christendom or go back to his home country. He opts for returning home where, presumably, his conversion will be kept secret and in due course forgotten (69–70).

Life in the 'bagnios' could be very grim, but also had its lighter side. D'Aranda describes the baths pejoratively as like 'Babylon' [Babel] because of the profusion of nationalities and tongues spoken – twenty-two languages in his one alone – and the miseries suffered there (216–17). These languages are in addition to the Spanish- and Italian-based 'lingua franca' which masters use in order to control their slaves. But d'Aranda is also able to talk freely to other slaves about their lives and home countries, as a form of diversion and entertainment (158). As Christian worship is permitted, there are chapels with attendant clergy, of various denominations: captivity narratives comment repeatedly on the comfort they derive from being able to practise their own religion, and dAranda's is no exception. Captives are allowed to celebrate religious feast-days and holidays. One of the prisons has a theatre where plays are put on – for instance, a Spanish comedy 'tolerably well written', on the story of

Belisarius (a victorious general in the army of the Emperor Justinian, who was the subject of Byzantine and later literature).[75] Taverns in the baths are run by slaves, some of whom grow quite wealthy as a consequence, and on the day of the Belisarius play slaves are standing around drinking and smoking in anticipation of the entertainment.[76] Other leisure pursuits enjoyed by Christian slaves involve Muslim women, but I will discuss this aspect later, in a separate section on women and the harem.

3.5   Jacques Philippe Laugier de Tassy/John Morgan

Jacques Philippe Laugier de Tassy's *Histoire du royaume d'Alger* (1724) was written in French and varies from the narratives we've considered so far in that the author was not himself a slave, but the French Consul to Algiers. It is, however, a first-hand account of life in a Barbary state for both slaves and free individuals. Its interest lies particularly in its measured and relatively broader approach to its subject, in contrast to so many of the other first-hand narratives which concentrate on depicting the horrors experienced by slaves. It was translated into several other languages including English, the latter by the historian John Morgan.[77] In this discussion I shall quote from the French and English versions consecutively, in aid of clarity for the English-speaking reader and to enable comparisons, as there are significant differences between them.

Of Laugier de Tassy little is now known except that he claims to have been imprisoned in Spain in 1706 and his appointment as consul to Algiers lasted for fewer than six months in 1718.[78] The date followed closely on the publication of the twelfth and final volume of Antoine Galland's celebrated *Les mille et une nuits* (*One Thousand and One Nights*) (1704–17), an early exemplar of and stimulus to the cultural vogue for Orientalism which was to extend through France and the rest of Europe; Laugier de Tassy's own work appeared in 1724.

---

75   In contrast to the Italian theatricals, whose terrible fate was described by Galán (see above), the Spaniards seem to have suffered no repercussions from performing their own play.

76   D'Aranda, *History of Algiers*, 260.

77   Laugier de Tassy's work was translated into Spanish as *Historia del Reyno de Argel, con el estado presente de su govierno, de sus fuerzas de Tierra, y Mar, de sus Rentas, Policia, Justicia, Politica, y Comercio*, appearing in 1732; and into English, 'with some additions', by John Morgan, appearing as *A compleat history of the piratical states of Barbary, viz. Algiers, Tunis, Tripoli, and Morocco: containing the origin, revolutions, and present state of these kingdoms, their forces, revenues, policy, and commerce* (London: printed for the author by J. Bettenham, 1728–1729). It was reprinted several times over the following years.

78   Jacques Philipe Laugier de Tassy, *Histoire du Royaume d'Alger, Avec l'Etat présent de son Gouvernement, de ses Forces de Terre et de Mer, de ses Revenus, Police, Justice, Politique et Commerce*, ed. Noël Laveau and André Nouschi (Paris: Éditions Loysel, 1992), 11.

About Joseph Morgan even less is now known: he flourished between 1707 and 1739, according to the *Dictionary of National Biography*, and wrote a number of books on North Africa and Islam. His version of de Tassy's work, *The History of Algiers*, appeared in 1728–29.

Laugier de Tassy's preface bears the stamp of those Enlightenment values which were likewise spreading across Europe, as when he condemns what he describes as the prejudice against Islam and insists that slaves in Barbary, as well as those who represent them, exaggerate their sufferings. He seizes the opportunity to take a swipe at his Spanish ecclesiastical forebears who wrote about Barbary as though from direct knowledge, even though they had never been there; and who promoted false images of life and the treatment of slaves in North African states:

> Les préjugés de la plupart des Chrétiens sont si terribles contre les Turcs et les autres Mahométans, qu'ils n'ont point d'expressions assez fortes pour faire voir le mépris et l'horreur qu'ils ont. C'est souvent sur la foi de quelques moines espagnols, qui débitent mille fables, pour faire valoir les services qu'ils rendent au public en allant dans la Barbarie, faire le rachat des esclaves, ou sur des contes supposés que font de prétendus esclaves qui courent le monde en geusant, avec des châines qu'ils n'ont jamais portées en Afrique, mais qui se servent adroitement de quelque certificat des religieux de la rédemption des captifs, qu'un véritable esclave racheté leur aura donné ou vendu.[79]

> [Prejudice against the Turks, and all other Mahometans, is so firmly rooted in the Breast of most Christians that they seem to want Words to express the bitterness of their hearts. They are so often instigated to this by some Spanish Monks, who spread a thousand Falsities in order to inhance the merit of their Voyages into Barbary for the Redemption of Slaves. Sometimes this Hatred is augmented by the false Relations of pretended Slaves, who beg round the Country, with Chains about them, which they never wore in Africa. And in order the better to conceal their Fraud, produce a Certificate from the Fathers of the Redemption, which they have either begged or bought of some real Slave who has been ransomed].[80]

---

79   Laugier de Tassy, *Histoire du Royaume d'Alger*, 10.
80   Morgan, *Compleat history*, iv-v.

De Tassy continues,

> Mais je suis persuadé que si ces même personnes pouvaient converser, sans le savoir avec les Mahométans qui n'eussent point le turban, et qui fussent habillés à la manière des Chrétiens, ils trouvèraient en eux ce qu'on trouve dans les autre peuples. Mais s'ils avaient le turban, cela suffirait pour les faire opinionâtrer dans leur préventions.[81]

> [Yet I am persuaded that were such Persons to converse unknowingly with Mahometans in Christian Dress, they would look upon them to be just such Creatures as themselves, having the same Faculties and Dispositions; but did they wear a Turban, that alone would be abundantly sufficient to eclipse all the beauties of their Deportment].[82]

3.5.1   Laugier de Tassy – Interior Stories
3.5.1.1   *Aruch and Zaphira*

His ameliorating remarks notwithstanding, the picture of this world which Laugier de Tassy paints for us has some starkly unpleasant features. Included in his 'history' are salacious accounts of sexual and romantic intrigues, at least one of which reads like a contemporary French epistolary novel, inspired perhaps by the notorious story of the English King Richard III and Lady Anne (widow of Edward, Prince of Wales), as depicted by Shakespeare. It tells of the unbridled passion of the corsair king Oruç (he calls him Aruch) Barbarossa for an Arab princess, Zaphira. In pursuit of her, he murders her husband, Prince Selim Eutemi, and then bombards her with letters imploring her to marry him. Her growing fear and loathing of him are reflected in her supposed replies to his letters, the texts of which are reproduced in full. Eventually, after a failed attempt to stab her would-be lover, who is by now determined to rape her if nothing else will win her, she takes poison and dies.[83]

3.5.1.2   *Zulpha and Ferdinand*

Another tragic anecdote chronicling a love-triangle concerns a Turkish officer, Hagi Seremeth Effendi, who has been shockingly disfigured in an accident. In 1680 he marries a beautiful young woman called Zulpha, who is so repelled by him that she falls ill. She recovers, but the sexual incompatibility between

---

81   de Tassy, 10.
82   Morgan, *Compleat History*, v.
83   de Tassy, 22–31; Morgan, 10–23.

the ageing and corpulent man and the slight, thirteen-year-old girl means the marriage cannot be consummated. During Seremeth's temporary absence, she embarks on a rapturous affair with a handsome young slave much favoured by her husband, a Portuguese Jew masquerading as a Christian. But, betrayed by Seremeth's jealous wives, the lovers are discovered, tried in court, and put to death. The revelation that Ferdinand is really a Jew, in a country where, Laugier de Tassy has told us, Jews are particularly reviled, has made his crime even worse than if he had genuinely been a Christian.[84] Seremeth, distraught at the losses of the two people he had loved most, brutally slaughters the wives and servant responsible for their downfall, before escaping.[85] To his translation of Laugier de Tassy's account, Morgan adds a moral which is absent from the source, 'Thus every precipitate Passion often proves its own Destruction' (162).

Much in the story of Zulpha and Ferdinand recalls the Persian Yussuf and Zulaikha. It deviates from the earlier work however in that the slave reciprocates the woman's passion from the outset, leading to an illicit and ultimately deadly affair. The court hearings and subsequent deaths of the two lovers belong to a quite different fictional world from that of Joseph and Zulaikha: more like the tragic sphere of some stories in *One Thousand and One Nights*.

In this supposedly 'factual' work we see combined many of the seeds and elements of romantic fiction which have already come to dominate writing about slavery in the context of relations between Muslims and Christians. Here, however, instead of religious conversion leading to a happy ending, an attempt at conversion (of Ferdinand) is thwarted, its failure leading to tragedy. In a story told by Christians, there cannot be a happy conversion to Islam. If Ferdinand had been genuinely Christian (instead of only passing for a Christian), the story might have ended well with the lovers escaping to a Christian country and Zulpha embracing Christianity. Furthermore, this account demonstrates that the image of the charming and desirable Muslim woman can pervade the 'factual' as much as the openly fictional accounts of life in Islamic lands. Frequently, she is already secretly a Christian or else has yearnings in that direction which can only be fulfilled when she is united with a Christian man. Figuratively, she is a land waiting to be conquered and her religious conversion represents a victory for Christendom which confirms and validates its victory by military means.

∙ ∙ ∙

---

[84] de Tassy, 55–57; Morgan, *Compleat History*, 60–63.
[85] This account is summarised from Laugier de Tassy, *Histoire du royaume d'Alger*, 108–22; Morgan, *Compleat History*, 139–62.

Laugier de Tassy indulges in some other horrific accounts of torture and gruesome forms of execution in Algiers. For example, he describes the punishment meted out to an Algerian who had insulted the English consul on the Mole (the narrow causeway linking Algiers with an outlying peninsula on which stood a fortress and other defences). The Algerian, whom the author assumes to have been drunk, jostled and then struck the diplomat, pushing him over. The ruling Dey condemned the offender to two thousand, two hundred Bastinadoes, that is, beatings on the soles of the feet for which a special contraption called a 'falaca' was used which upended the victim as it hoisted his feet in the air, more readily exposing them to the blows. After one thousand blows, the man's feet dropped off. As he was close to death, and as the Dey was determined to extend his suffering so as to avoid similar such incidents in the future, the condemned man was sent back to prison without any succour. The next day he received the remaining twelve hundred blows on his buttocks, whereupon he lost the power of speech and his senses, according to Morgan (Laugier de Tassy says he could not breathe). He remained in prison, alone and without any relief until he died, Laugier de Tassy adds, of hunger and thirst.[86]

Descriptions of the bastinado punishment appear frequently in Barbary slave narratives, as do visual depictions of its implementation. The slave priest Fr. Pierre Dan included several images of the punishment in his work;[87] others either used his pictures, or added images of their own. Tortures and painful forms of execution as carried out by 'Orientals' fascinated Europeans, reinforcing a common view of Islamic countries as nations of savages. Dan was especially scathing in his condemnation of Islam in general, and Algerians in particular. At the same time, it is worth recalling how brutal were tortures and several forms of execution in European states: the burning of 'heretics', suspected witches and others, in Spain and elsewhere and the hanging, drawing and quartering reserved for convicted traitors in England and other countries being just two examples.

Laugier de Tassy alludes to such parallels in his concluding remarks. Listing the principal charges levied by Europeans against the Barbary States, he defends Islamic nations by comparing practices in their countries with those of Europeans. He considers their supposed savagery as following the dictates

---

86   de Tassy, 71–72; Morgan, *Compleat History,* 85–87.
87   Pierre Dan, *Histoire de barbarie et de ses corsairs* (*History of Barbary and its Corsairs,* 1637), e.g., has some horrific illustrations of tortures, as does the frontispiece of a play, *The Empress of Morocco* by Elkanah Settle, acted at the Dorset Garden Theatre in London (1673), which shows victims suspended in various obviously agonising postures, and body parts strewn among spikes on the ground.

of nature, comparing it with the guile of Europeans. As to the 'Turks" practices of killing, plundering and enslaving travellers, he relates this to their previous maltreatment by Christians. Regarding the assassinations of rulers, Laugier de Tassy accepts this as a frequent occurrence in Algiers, but points out how often the histories of European nations furnish similar instances. To illustrate the savagery of fellow-Europeans, he offers several examples, among them the barbarous treatment of two Dutchmen at the Hague. The brothers Jean (Johan) and Cornelis de Witt who, notwithstanding years of service to their country, one as 'Grand Pensionary' [effectively the political ruler], the other as burgomaster, were later blamed for a military defeat and were tortured, massacred, and horribly mutilated by a lynch mob, who finally ate their flesh.[88]

As for the Algerians' alleged cruelty toward their slaves, Laugier de Tassy maintains that slaves are only punished for misdeeds and crimes, and compares their treatment by their rulers and masters favourably with that meted out by Spain to the native people of Peru, or to the Algerians when Spain conquered Oran. Referring to his own imprisonment in Spain in 1706, Laugier de Tassy adds, 'j'ai été traité avec tant d'inhumanité et de rigueur, que je préférais dix ans d'ésclavage à Alger à un an de prison en Espagne' ['I was used with such Hardships and Cruelty, when a Prisoner of War among the Spaniards, that I would sooner be ten Years a Slave at Algiers than one a Prisoner in Spain'].[89] Many further arguments are adduced in defence of the Algerians and their practices, including their religion – praised for its toleration – and their forbearance in general; their alleged abhorrence of vice and low levels of crime; and other factors that compare favourably with those of Europeans.

4   Morgan's Additions and Comparisons with de Tassy's Account

To Laugier de Tassy's exposition of Algiers, Morgan adds three further sections of his own: one on Tunis, one on Tripoli, and one on Fez and Morocco. Although he has faithfully translated Laugier de Tassy's praise of Algiers, Morgan offers a far less sympathetic view of his subjects. His discussion of Tunis focuses on the murderous rivalries of its ruling families and includes a very different perspective on the Algerians from that of Laugier de Tassy: he accuses them of systematic brutality towards the Tunisians, even though they were supposed

---

88   de Tassy, 183–89; Morgan, *Compleat History*, 248–58. Johan de Witt controlled the Netherlands political system from 1650 to shortly before his death in 1672. The lynching is depicted in Alexandre Dumas's *The Black Tulip* written in 1850.

89   de Tassy, 194; Morgan, *Compleat History*, 266.

to be their allies (289–91). His account is not wholly negative, as he praises the country's 'happy' climate from which the plague has long been absent, and the fertility of its soil (298). But its people are lazy and careless, and a quality which Laugier de Tassy had lauded, namely the Algerians' supposed fidelity to nature, Morgan finds abhorrent. In general, he says, they 'study neither Elegance nor Improvement', and are happy to leave tasks like hunting to the Christians, as long as a 'Moor' is always present to share in the spoils. The religious toleration Laugier de Tassy found among the Muslims of Algiers is entirely absent from Morgan's settings: for example, his Tunisian Christians stick together for protection in a country where they are 'so much despised and insulted' (300–01).

By contrast to Laugier de Tassy, in his account of the Algerians' attempts to re-take Ceuta and Oran, Morgan once again writes admiringly about the Spaniards, who emerge victorious, despite being heavily outnumbered. Their leader the Marquis de Santa Cruz is singled out for praise, for his nobility and many virtues. He is represented fighting courageously and dying 'in the Flower of his Age', when he is captured and then treacherously slaughtered by his enemies (338–344). Morgan explains that he has dwelt on this episode so as to remedy an omission from the section on Algiers (344). Nowhere does he acknowledge how contradictory is his view of the Spaniards, and indeed the Algerians, to that of his earlier source, Laugier de Tassy.

Tripoli comes in for even worse treatment by Morgan: in his brief description he finds it 'poor and despicable' with 'mean, low and dark' houses in streets 'narrow, dirty, and irregular', its inhabitants 'wretched ... [and] reduced to the utmost Misery by Taxes, and all kind of Oppressions'. It is a state whose principal riches derive from piracy (313–16). In most respects it is much like Tunis, and therefore not worth a separate elaboration (316).

In his chapter on the history of the kingdoms of Fez and Morocco, Morgan offers his readers a repellent account of multiple murders committed in the course of political intrigues. He dwells on the corruption of its rulers, and one in particular: Muley Hamet Deby, who was so dissolute that his father the Emperor nominated him his successor, so his own misdeeds would seem like virtues by comparison (326). The story abounds with strangling, blinding, people being nailed alive to doors, and other atrocities. Muley Hamet Deby's half-brother Abdalla, who succeeded him, is no better than his predecessor, choosing to kill for pleasure, preferably with his own hands (344).

Deviating from his catalogue of horrors, Morgan describes a pleasant landscape, well provided with raw materials which, with more industrious inhabitants and better rulers, would make it very productive. But, he continues, no trade can flourish under a government so 'despotick, oppressive and rapacious' (356). The people too are lewd, intemperate, and lazy, the women – valued for fatness, cram themselves with food: their dining habits are 'unseemly', their 'Mahometan' religion founded by an 'Imposter' (360–61).

According to Morgan, the lives of slaves of Fez and other parts of Morocco are the most wretched of all in Barbary. At daybreak they are roused with blows, the work they are forced to carry out is hard and 'filthy', consisting in providing materials for the emperor's 'extravagant' buildings: quarrying limestone, stamping earth mixed with lime and water to make building blocks, hauling large baskets of earth, driving waggons pulled by bulls and horses, and guarding the cattle by night on pain of death should the animals come to any harm. Some slaves cut, cement and erect marble pillars, or make gunpowder and small arms; some tend horses and sweep the stables, others grind with hand-mills or inspect water-works and aqueducts. All this labour is carried out in the cruellest and harshest of conditions: the slaves must work with one hand while they eat their 'coarse Morsel of Bread' with the other. Most terrible is that human beings are harnessed to carts along with mules and asses. Slaves live in dungeons to which the only access is by being lowered on a rope ladder. They are allowed just one fragment of black barley bread and a 'pittance' of oil per day. Desperate slaves sometimes leap from the high walls to search for a few wild onions. The pathetic beings are dressed only in coarse wool.

Morgan, like many others writing on slavery in Islamic states, dismisses the idea that labouring for the ruler might be considered an honour: on the contrary, work for the Dey, Bey, or Sultan, can be the harshest and most dangerous of all. Slaves of the state are liable to be victims of sudden and violent attacks by the ruler, often resulting in their deaths. The slaves' only relief from such misery is that they are allowed to make and consume brandy. Any attempt to escape is likely to result in torture, and death.[90] Nowhere in Morgan's account is there any defence of the slavers or suggestion, as with Laugier de Tassy, that tales of the slaves' sufferings might be exaggerated.

Morgan's concluding remarks are consistent with those quoted above, being unrelenting in their condemnation of the 'Barbary Dominions', which he summarises as being tyrannical, their rulers rapacious, their people neglectful of their lands, and of commerce and the sciences, remaining ignorant and poor. As fighters they are no match for the Europeans. His final paragraph speaks of the 'Enormities and Miseries of the Barbary Dominions' and their 'Irregularities and Evils'. The moral he adduces is that 'as Honesty is the best policy in private life, so is the public Repose, and Prosperity of a State, inseparably connected with the Virtue of its Members' (367–8). The message is clear: the individual

---

90   These paragraphs are summarised from Morgan, *Compleat History*, 363–66.

vices of Barbary citizens create abusive and oppressive governments and a wretched life for all.

∙ ∙ ∙

I have dwelt on these two works by de Tassy and Morgan at some length, partly because of the light they shed on how differently two writers can respond to similar material. In addition, I believe they illustrate many of the features we shall find in contemporary and subsequent fiction, as well as the fascination exerted by aspects of the 'Orient', no matter whether the writer be sympathetic to his subject like Laugier de Tassy, or hostile as with Morgan. It is remarkable that Morgan has faithfully translated Laugier de Tassy's words, including all of his 'enlightened' comments defending Islam and Muslim people. And yet in the concluding chapters, the ones he himself has added, we discover a quite contrary attitude which is presumably Morgan's own. He can find nothing good to say about his North Africans, not even those of Algiers whom he (translating Laugier de Tassy) had previously praised. It makes for a strangely fissured work.

We have in these two narratives a great deal of romantic material presented to the reader as fact: romance clothed as history. Each writer is seduced by what he sees as some exotic elements of Barbary, and here also are some typical ingredients of European 'Orientalist' literature: attributions to Muslims of religious excess, cruelty and arbitrary punishments, as well as love between slaves and free people, across religious and cultural boundaries. But Laugier de Tassy is fascinated and thrilled by some of these features, whereas Morgan is clearly appalled by all of them. Finally, these two accounts demonstrate two important and parallel impulses in 18th century European thought: on the one hand, the Enlightenment, expressing admiration and exhorting tolerance for people from different societies and faiths; on the other hand, by stressing his subjects' baseness and unfitness to rule, Morgan implicitly justifies colonialism, which will supply that fair and efficient government for which the lands and people he describes must be crying out.

5   Miguel de Cervantes

In the process of transition from 'fact' to fiction Cervantes is a pivotal figure [Figure 3.4.]. He was captured by pirates and carried off to North Africa, where he remained enslaved for five painful years. Cervantes fought against Muslims repeatedly: against the rebellious Granadine Moriscos in 1568; at Lepanto,

FIGURE 3.4 Statue of Cervantes by Joan Vancell Puigcercós, 1892, in Madrid
SOURCE: LUIS GARCÍA, CC BY-SA 2.0. IMAGE IN THE PUBLIC DOMAIN. HTTPS://COMMONS.WIKIMEDIA.ORG /WIKI / FILE:CERVANTES_(J._VANCELL)_MADRID _ 01.JPG

where he was wounded and lost the use of his left arm, in 1571; and at Tunis, under Don Juan of Austria in 1573–74. He was finally bested by his opponents and taken to Algiers in 1575, while on a return journey to Spain from Italy. His experiences as a captive are chronicled in the narrative by de Sosa, with whom he became close friends during his time in Algiers.

During the rest of his life as a writer, Cervantes dwelt obsessively on captivity themes and every variation on the topic was grist to his mill. But he himself supplied little autobiographical information outside of what can be hypothesised from his fiction, and no first-hand account of his captivity at all. So much of what is now known about this period of his life is due to de Sosa and to the patient reconstruction of 18th and 19th century Spanish scholars using contemporary correspondence and other documents. In addition, building upon their research, more concise biographies have been produced by successors such as James Fitzmaurice-Kelly and Jean Canavaggio. It is to them that I have referred in establishing the bare facts of Cervantes's captivity which, in summary, are as follows:[91]

After fighting at Tunis, Cervantes travels to Italy, where he serves as a soldier under the Duke of Sessa y Terranova. Ambitious for promotion, or perhaps hoping to obtain compensation for his injuries, Cervantes is granted leave to return to Spain, armed with letters of recommendation from both Don Juan of Austria and the Duke of Sessa. In early September 1575 he departs from Naples, together with his brother Rodrigo, heading for Barcelona aboard the galley, El Sol. On the 26th September, having been blown off course by stormy weather, the ship is attacked by corsairs headed by an Albanian renegade known as Arnaut or Arnaute Mami. After some hours of fruitless resistance, during which the captain and several others are killed, the Spanish survivors are captured and taken to Algiers. Once there, Cervantes becomes a slave of Arnaut's deputy, a Greek renegade known as Dali Mami. He is handcuffed, chained, and put in a dungeon. The letters of recommendation found on him obviously gave his captors hope of receiving a great ransom, as for five years both his desperate family and the interlocutors sent to negotiate his release were unable to raise the huge sum demanded.

Little is known of Cervantes's day-to-day life in Algiers, except that he spent much of his time closely confined and that he had already begun to write while still a slave. But that he made four attempts to escape – one in each of the years 1576–79, and barely managed to avoid being killed when his plans were discovered – is well documented. The first attempt in January 1576 was aborted because the Muslim engaged to lead him and some other slaves to safety in Oran, then under Spanish control, deserted them and the group was obliged

---

91   James Fitzmaurice-Kelly, *Miguel de Cervantes Saavedra: A Memoir* (London and Other Locations: Oxford University Press) 1913, 28–55; Jean Canavaggio, *Cervantes* (1986), tr. from the French by J.R. Jones (New York and London: W. W. Norton & Company, repr. 1990), 73–96.

to return to Algiers; Cervantes was now more closely watched than before. Early in 1577 Cervantes tried again. His brother, on whom a much lower price had been set, had by now been liberated and the brothers agreed secretly that Rodrigo would send a frigate, which would rescue Cervantes and his companions. A Navarrese gardener called Juan was enlisted to the cause and helped Cervantes dig a cave into which, gradually in twos and threes, a total of some fourteen or fifteen captives were concealed. Cervantes somehow managed to smuggle food to them, with the help of a Spaniard nicknamed 'El Dorador' (the gilder) and eventually after some months he joined them. However, as they were about to escape, 'El Dorador', whether through fear or hope of gain, or both, betrayed the conspirators and they were brought before Hassan Pasha, Dey of Algiers. Cervantes immediately claimed responsibility for the whole affair, seeking to absolve his co-conspirators. But this was not enough to save Juan, who was condemned to be hung up by one foot until he suffocated, while Cervantes himself was taken prisoner by the Dey and kept in close confinement, handcuffed and chained once again.

Cervantes's third escape attempt involved sending a letter to Martín de Córdoba, commander of the garrison at Oran, appealing for help. However, the messenger was caught before even reaching Oran and, sentenced to impalement, died stoically. Cervantes himself was this time sentenced to two thousand lashes: a death sentence had it been carried out, but for reasons unknown today it was not, and he survived. For his last escape attempt, Cervantes enlisted the help of a Granadine renegade called Girón, or otherwise Abderrahman. The pair hired two Venetian traders in Algiers to secrete sixty prisoners on board their vessel. But again, the group were betrayed: this time by another Spaniard, one Dr Juan Blanco de Paz, again for reasons unknown. One of the traders, by now terrified, offered to ransom Cervantes himself, but in vain. Cervantes was again threatened with death but somehow evaded it and the other conspirators seem also to have survived.

How and why Cervantes managed to avoid being severely tortured or killed despite all his failed escape attempts, and the brutal executions of individuals less responsible for those attempts than he, remains a mystery. It is generally assumed that he owed his survival to the letters of credit he carried from two highly prestigious men, and his captors' consequent and continuing hope of obtaining a hefty ransom. Fitzmaurice-Kelly speculates, moreover, that Cervantes's courage when threatened with torture and death may also have played a part in persuading Hassan to spare him following his second attempt, as well as his 'gallant effrontery' and the intercession of an influential renegade, when his last plot was exposed.[92] Canavaggio alludes to some speculations that a homosexual attraction or even an affair between Cervantes and Hassan could have protected the Spaniard.[93]

Finally, in 1580 two Trinitarian monks, Fray Juan Gil and Antonio de la Bella, reached Algiers and began negotiations to free some slaves. After months of bargaining, and ransoming many 'lesser' captives, Juan Gil succeeded in buying back Cervantes [Figure 3.5] at a cost of 500 gold escudos – equivalent to tens of thousands of pounds in today's currency – just in time: Hassan's tenure as Dey of Algiers was coming to an end and he was about to depart for Istanbul, taking Cervantes with him. Had this happened, the Spaniard might never have been rescued, as the ransoming of captives in the Eastern Mediterranean was far more difficult than in the Maghreb, especially if they had the misfortune to land in the Sultan's galleys,[94] for, 'to be transferred to Constantinople or other cities of the Ottoman Empire supposed a perpetual imprisonment'.[95] The money for Cervantes's release was raised via contributions from his parents, together with donations by Spanish traders in Algiers and funds allocated for the purpose by the Trinitarians.

Juan Blanco de Paz, perhaps fearful of being labelled a traitor by Cervantes, was now attempting to blacken the writer's name. In response, Cervantes asked the Trinitarian monk Fray Juan Gil to hold an inquiry and gather testimonies which would exonerate him. All concerned, including Fray Juan Gil himself, spoke highly of Cervantes's character, praising his courage, kindness and personal charm. It is thanks to these statements that much of the factual knowledge about Cervantes's captivity is now available. After this, the ransomed man was free to go and by the end of 1580 he was back in Madrid. At some time in the early 1580s he began to write in earnest. Although Cervantes's fiction is clearly and substantially informed by his lived experiences,[96] it is here, rather than in any autobiographical narrative, that he deals with the subjects of captivity and romance, repeatedly re-working these themes in numerous novels and plays; for this reason, his writing belongs to the next chapter.

---

[92] Fitzmaurice-Kelly, 39 and 43–44, respectively.

[93] Canavaggio, *Cervantes*, 93–94.

[94] Davis, *Christian Slaves, Muslim Masters*, 20, 78, 80. And cf. Géza Pálffy, 'Ransom Slavery Along the Ottoman-Hungarian Frontier in the Sixteenth and Seventeenth Centuries', in *Ransom Slavery Along the Ottoman Borders: (Early Fifteenth – Early Eighteenth Centuries)*, ed. Géza Dávid and Pál Fodor (Leiden: Koninklijke Brill, 2007), 44–45.

[95] Garcés, *Cervantes in Algiers*, 108.

[96] Cf. e.g., Friedman, *Spanish Captives*, xxvii, 58, 71, 73, etc., where she quotes various fictions of Cervantes for factual 'evidence' of North African slaves' lives and living conditions.

FIGURE 3.5   Miguel de Cervantes Saved by the Fathers of the Redemption, 1580, colour engraving, French school
CREDIT: BRIDGEMAN IMAGES

6   Women Slaves and the Harem

Europeans were both horrified and fascinated by the idea of women being enslaved. Even though the reality was that many, if not most women slaves would probably end up in domestic roles, the favoured trope was that of the white woman in the harem: captive, but living a life of idleness devoted to self-beautification and pleasing men. Non-European women living in harems were also subjects of intense appeal, servicing the fantasies of both European men and women. There was, moreover, an absorbing interest in Islam, the forbidden 'other' religion, and in the idea of encounters between Muslim men and Christian women, as well as vice versa.

Gordon claims that concubinage and the harem made women 'the focal point' of the slave trade'.[97] On the other hand since, unlike Christianity, Islam officially sanctioned polygamy and had no prohibition on men marrying their slaves, and since no jointure or bride price was payable for such a marriage, it could be ultimately to a man's financial advantage to marry his slave; as we have seen, many men did so. Some of the great rulers of Islam such as Haroun

---

97   Gordon, 91.

al-Rashid and Suleiman 'the Magnificent' also married such women because they had no families nearby to challenge the monarch's power.

Islamic law protected the status of concubines and in the royal harems some gained influence even surpassing that of wives. Since much of their power was wielded through their sons, especially if one of these acceded to the throne, fierce rivalries and intrigues were often conducted among and between the women.[98] Guarding the harem were eunuchs, and Western readers were fascinated almost as much by them as by the ideas of forbidden sex. On the one hand were the supposedly highly sexualised encounters between men and women of different colours, faiths and nationalities; on the other hand, was the ambiguity of unsexed men forced to witness sexual encounters and possibly – one might conjecture – longing for such encounters themselves, despite their castrated status, perceived as peculiarly titillating.

The taste for literature with these preoccupations was fuelled by fantasies and imagination which were also fed, to some extent, by the accounts of people who had personally witnessed life in Muslim lands, had knowledge of one or more harems, or who had been in close contact with Muslim women. But information from women who had themselves experienced captivity is sparse: Baepler says that 'while many of the North African regencies captured Western women, none of these captives appear to have written a narrative that has survived'. All supposedly personal accounts of life as a harem slave have turned out to be fiction.[99] And so we must look to accounts by other witnesses for more information.

One of the more interesting accounts of sexual relations between men and women in a Muslim land is by the Flemish captive Emanuel d'Aranda, whose *Relation de la captivité et liberté du sieur E. d'Aranda* ... Englished by John Davies as the *History of Algiers and it's* [sic] *slavery* ... has already been discussed. However, his narrative, supposedly based on his real-life observations, is a far cry from European literary fantasies of Christian men converting Muslim women and bringing them back to Christian countries: more often the reverse occurs. According to d'Aranda, Muslim women are drawn to Christian male captives and 'will take any occasion to fall into discourse with the Christians'.[100] Although Muslim women go veiled in the streets, and would never show their faces to a Muslim man, they reveal themselves in front of their Christian slaves, arguing that Christians are reputed to be blind [to

---

98   Gordon, 88.
99   Baepler, 147.
100 D'Aranda, 37.

such sights]. D'Aranda remarks on the strangeness of this behaviour, but says it is necessary because of the 'lewd inclinations' of the women, who will find a hundred ways to circumvent their fathers' and husbands' restrictions so as to get out of the house. Their destinations are the bathhouses, as well as holy men, with a pretence of piety not unknown in Christian lands. But, he adds, without giving any corroborative detail, 'they prostitute themselves ... to all they meet, though they be common Rogues, Sodomites, and the meanest sort of people'.[101]

Care has to be taken to prevent the women's husbands becoming jealous, which can have disastrous consequences. D'Aranda tells of a Portuguese man whom he nicknames 'Dom Oenophilo' (lover of wine) who falls in love with his 'patroness' (his master's wife). Plied with drink by two other slaves one day, he begins to woo his mistress but is interrupted by her husband, who beats him. The drunken suitor retaliates, at which the doubly incensed husband reports the slave to the Pasha and he is offered the 'choice' of conversion, or being burnt alive. On refusing to convert, he is condemned to death. But the Pasha, now being in charge of Dom Oeonophilo's fate, and minding his own interests, decides to pardon him, and takes the slave for himself instead.

Two other examples are given of mixed-faith relations, but here they come to fruition. In one instance, a Christian slave called 'Joseph' is captured together with his wife 'Vipra'. By chance, Joseph gets into conversation with some free Christians and is able to escape with them and make his way to his own country. Meanwhile, the discovery of his mule still standing on the shore causes his fellow-slaves to assume he has been kidnapped or killed. Once home, Joseph sells all his goods in order to raise the ransom money to free his wife, and writes to her and his former master offering the sum which had previously been demanded for the two of them. Vipra, however, is far from thrilled with the prospect of being ransomed, for she has since fallen in love with a renegade called Assan (presumably Hassan) and refuses to leave. Her master is uncomfortable: he would have liked to receive the money and let her go. But she has now converted to Islam and the master's wife convinces him that it is better for the Prophet Muhammad if she remains a convert. In addition if, in spite of this, her master sends her away he may be accused of favouring the Christians. The narrator D'Aranda, who has been kept abreast of the developments, tells Vipra he is unhappy with her decision. But she explains, 'A Turkish Garment will become me as well as a Spanish petticoat', whereupon she leaves the house to take up life in Algiers with her 'Gallant'.[102]

---

101   D'Aranda, 151.
102   D'Aranda, 188–192.

The other account of love between Christian and Muslim is more sinister and offers an additional perspective, informed by a claim that many 'Turkish' men's predilection for 'abhominable love' (presumably homosexuality) drives their frustrated wives to turn to their Christian slaves for consolation. The women make the slaves an offer: if they will renounce their religion, the women will marry them and make them master of the house. Many of the men being 'ordinary seamen' and poor in their own countries find these enticements from a 'handsome woman' irresistible, preferring 'temporal' to 'eternal' happiness. The wives then slowly poison their husbands and, after a few months, marry their renegade slaves. Curiously, no great inquiry is made into the crimes. D'Aranda cites this pattern as one example of the frequent use of poison in Barbary.[103]

In the cases cited above, where religious conversion occurs, it is from Christianity to Islam rather than the other way around and, contrary to the tropes of European romance, the Christians, far from taking their Muslim lovers to Christendom, remain in the Muslim land as converts. In many instances, this was no doubt a matter of free choice, but if the lovers were caught the man would, as we have seen in the case of Dom Oenophilo, be offered 'Hobson's Choice' between converting to Islam and marrying the woman, or death.[104] I have not yet come across a real-life account in any captivity narrative of a Muslim, whether man or woman, converting to Christianity and departing with a Christian lover. That occurrence is reserved for fiction.

7   Thomas Pellow

Within two years of each other, in the first quarter of the 18th century, two English nationals, one quite unwillingly, the other voluntarily, travelled to Muslim lands and there observed women's (and men's) lives at first-hand, recording and communicating their experiences and impressions in writing to their fellow-countrymen. The unwilling observer was a sailor, Thomas Pellow, who in 1716 boarded a ship bound for Genoa, was captured at sea and sold into slavery in Morocco, together with the rest of his ship's crew and the crews of two companion ships.[105] He was just eleven years old.

---

103   D'Aranda, 163–164.
104   Bartolomé Benassar and Lucile Benassar, *Les chrétiens d'Allah: L'histoire extraordinaire des renégats, XVI et XVII siècle* (Paris: Perrin, 1989), 384; cited by Garcés, *Cervantes in Algiers,* 169.
105   The account of Pellow's life which follows is substantially taken from Giles Milton, *White Gold: The Extraordinary Story of Thomas Pellow and North Africa's One Million European Slaves* (London: Hodder and Stoughton, 2004).

Pellow is one of the few slaves to have left an account of his own relationships with women in a Muslim state, and indeed his marriage to a Muslim woman. He is also one of a very few to have written and spoken openly about his own apostasy. Under extreme duress, which included desperate overwork, starvation, beatings and other forms of torture administered by a savage master determined to make the boy 'turn Turk', Pellow converted to Islam. He describes the events leading to his decision and excuses it as follows:

> I was, through my severe scourging, and such hard Fare, every Day in Expectation of its being my last; and happy, no Doubt, had I been, had it so happened: I should certainly then have dy'd a Martyr, and probably thereby gained a glorious Crown in the Kingdom of Heaven; but the ALMIGHTY did not then see it fit: My Tortures were now exceedingly encreased, burning my Flesh off my Bones by Fire; which the Tyrant did, by frequent Repetitions, after a most cruel Manner; insomuch, that through my so very acute Pains, I was at last constrained to submit, calling upon God to forgive me, who knows that I never gave the Consent of my Heart, though I seemingly yielded, by holding up my Finger.[106]

Pellow's narrative gives a rare and deep insight into the life of a European convert to Islam in a North African slave state. His focus is on the experiences of men, including himself and, as we have seen, women appear only sketchily and only in relation to men. Following Pellow, his modern biographer Giles Milton repeatedly emphasises the pressure European captives were under to convert to Islam,[107] despite some contrary pressures on them to remain Christian so as not to jeopardise their chances of being ransomed.

After his conversion Pellow was taught to speak and write Arabic and how to behave in the presence of the Sultan. He was then promoted to the trusted but exceptionally precarious post of imperial guard in the garden of the Sultan, Moulay Ismail, noted for his vicious and capricious ways. As an example, the Sultan had all male and female black people in his realm rounded up, both slaves and free men, including those previously enslaved who had been freed,

---

[106] This simple act was apparently deemed sufficient to display a willingness to convert to Islam. Cf. Thomas Pellow, *The history of the long captivity and adventures of Thomas Pellow, in South Barbary: giving an account of his being taken by two Sallee Rovers ... in which is introduced a particular account of the manners and customs of the Moors ... together with a description of the cities, towns, and publick buildings in those kingdoms / written by himself,* 2nd ed. (London: Printed for R. Goadey and sold by W. Owen, 1740 [?]), 15–16.

[107] Milton, *White Gold.*

known as '*Haratin*', whom he re-enslaved and forcibly conscripted – ignoring their protests and attempts to escape, as well as the misgivings of several *ulama* (religious scholars and interpreters of Sharia law).[108] 'No black person was spared ... the colour of the skin was reason enough for a person to be enslaved ...'[109]

For Pellow, one of the greatest risks in serving the Sultan lay in accidentally encountering one of his wives, as the emperor had decreed an absolute prohibition on any man, apart from his eunuchs, seeing the harem women. When any of them left the palace compound, the eunuchs walked ahead and fired weapons to warn any man in the vicinity to take cover. Yet, in an episode recalling early scenes from the story of Yusuf and Zulaikha or from *One Thousand and One Nights* Pellow, still only fifteen years old, is by chance glimpsed in the garden by the Sultan's favourite wife Halima el-Aziza. Taking a liking to the youth, she prevails upon her spouse to allow Pellow to serve her and her favourite son, Moulay Zidan, then about eight years old; Pellow is also appointed chief porter in the Sultan's harem. Now his position becomes even more risky. Having survived a test of his loyalty by the Sultan, Pellow finds that:

> The Queen ... being extreamly amorous, and the Emperour no less jealous of her ... made my Condition very dangerous, and might, through some unforeseen Accident, (let my Behaviour be never so innocent,) happen to prove of very bad Consequence to me, therefore I thought it highly prudent to keep a very strict Guard upon all my Actions.[110]

Unlike his fictional counterparts, Pellow apparently succeeds in both warding off the queen's advances and continuing to retain the Sultan's trust, but he is always in fear of 'her Poison, or his Sword', and so he begs her to help him find other work. This leads to his appointment as the Sultan's own servant. This new position is hardly more secure however, because of the Sultan's brutal and unstable nature, coupled with his absolute power. Many instances are given of his penchant for torturing and killing those around him at whim, sometimes believing gossip imparted to him by a victim's malicious rivals. Even his 'Grandees' never knew from one day to the next how he would treat them, for they could be 'to-day hugged, kissed and preferred, tomorrow stript,

---

108 Chouki El Hamel, 'Blacks and Slavery in Morocco: the Question of the Haratin at the End of the Seventeenth Century', in *Diasporic Africa: A Reader*, ed. Michael A. Gomez (New York: New York University Press, 2006), 177–199, 190–94.
109 El Hamel, 191.
110 Pellow, *The history of the long captivity*, 24.

robbed and beaten' (148) and the Sultan killed savagely, arbitrarily and, not infrequently, personally.

When Pellow's sexual experience and marriage do eventually take place, the circumstances are far from romantic and not of his choosing. An aspect of Moulay Ismail's power is displayed through his periodic matchmaking sessions, when he forces his slaves to marry spouses of his choice, pairing hundreds at a time. His preference is to match blacks to whites, so as to produce mixed-race offspring who, he believes, will prove most loyal and reliable. The Sultan tries at first to marry Pellow to one of his black women slaves, then to a woman of mixed race. Pellow resists both these efforts and appeals to the Sultan to match him to a woman 'of my own Colour'; the ruler then whimsically offers him a woman with dark hands and feet. However, once she is unveiled, she turns out to be pale-skinned, her hands and feet having been coloured with henna, and the pair are summarily married by the Sultan.

Pellow is welcomed by his bride's large and, as it turns out, influential family. The next day the couple are given a wedding certificate and some money, and three days of feasting and celebration ensue, although the Qur'anic ban on alcohol is strictly adhered to. Pellow goes on to specify the elaborate make-up and paint with which Moroccan brides generally adorn themselves, and the rituals surrounding the first night (including conveying the bride's stained underwear to her relatives to prove she had been a virgin prior to the marriage), but says nothing about his own wedding night. A few days after the marriage, Pellow is sent on a mission to subdue rebels in the south of the country, accompanied for the first part of the journey by his wife and six hundred other newly-married couples, as well as other individuals who are settled into a garrison (70–77).

Pellow never mentions his wife's name and says little about her, but it is evident that he becomes very fond of her and of the two children they have together. Time spent with them obviously provides him (and the reader) with some relief from a life otherwise fraught with danger and drenched in blood, in chaotic and despotic lands fractured by plotting, intrigues, and war. One anecdote serves to demonstrate the affection and humour that Pellow and his wife clearly share: returning to his garrison after many months of fighting, Pellow is greeted by his wife and says he 'entered very merrily with my Girl', neglecting to ask her about the child she had been carrying before his departure. When he finally remembers to ask her, she plays a trick on him, telling him that she had given birth to a daughter, but that this child had been taken from her. Pellow becomes enraged, whereupon 'the cunning Gypsy', as he calls her, orders that the child be brought to him, explaining that the 'Thief' who took the baby from her was the midwife. Pellow responds by being 'not a little pleased with the

Joke, laughing and embracing the Child very heartily'. Later he comments that the returnees and their families lived 'very comfortably together' (105–06) and elsewhere he speaks of the deep attachment that developed between himself and his daughter who, when he would come home wounded from a battle, would rush to greet him, clasping him round the neck, pitying his plight, and begging him to take her and her mother to England (190).

Pellow's thoughts are never far from the hope of escape and he makes some abortive attempts at it. But the question of what should happen to his wife and daughter should he succeed in this aim is resolved when he receives news that both have died within three days of one another (his baby son, 'a brave Boy', having died previously, aged just ten months), an event Pellow describes as like 'a Dash of Water ... thrown into our Wine' (134).

Pellow gives no details whatsoever as to how these tragedies happened, which is strange considering that in the course of his narrative he recounts a great many other deaths in elaborate and often shocking detail. The news of his own wife's and daughter's deaths is brought to Pellow in hospital where he is recovering from an injury, the local carrier of the tidings expressing regret at being the bearer of bad news, especially to one so recently wounded. Pellow comments wryly in the text that the man was 'One of Job's Comforters indeed!', but adds that,

> I thought them to be by far better off than they could have been in this troublesome World, especially that Part of it; and I was really very glad that they were delivered out of it, and therefore it gave me very little Uneasiness.
> 180–81

And although afterwards he often reflects upon their loss, at the same time the fact that they, following his tutelage, 'had died in the Knowledge, and ... Belief in Christ' comforts him. as well as facilitating his escape plans, there being nothing now to bind him to Barbary, nor any other person to worry about in planning his flight (190). Indeed, he feels he has no excuse not to try to escape, which he eventually achieves.

Apart from his wife, only one other woman is spoken of at any length and she is actually named: Madam Luna, a Jewish woman of Morocco, who happens to be on board the vessel in which Pellow finally makes his getaway, when its Irish captain, fearing betrayal by the Muslims with whom he has been trading, decides quite suddenly to set sail. Lady Luna is described as a 21-year-old widow, pleasant, once she has overcome her fear at unexpectedly finding herself in the Europeans' power, and having a 'Bright beauty [which] was to all of us a very sufficient Cordial'. She is in due course set free, when they land in Gibraltar (374). As to the lives of women slaves in Morocco generally, their sufferings are not mentioned; they do not seem to have been as readily tortured and killed as the men, but neither can their lives, in the Meknes which Pellow depicts, have been very happy. Milton emphasises the particular stresses that women were under as sex objects, prey to the lusts and aberrations of their male 'owners': Moulay Ismail is said to have had particularly perverted tastes.[111] It is a society built on fear in which no man or woman, no matter how high or low their status, can rest easily and without fear of destruction.

In a region where violence and oppression were commonplace, Morocco seems to have been the most brutal of all and, among sadistic and authoritarian rulers, Moulay Ismail appears to have been unsurpassed. Pellow himself only survives for so many years by joining in the general slaughter, hoping at every turn that the next body to be tortured, torn and flung aside won't be his own. The only good thing Pellow has to say about the Sultan is that, by means of his excessive religiosity (or at least the trappings of it) and the force of his personality, allied with the unpredictable brutality, he was able to subdue his unruly nation, so that under his reign roads which had been infested with robbers became completely safe; after his death civil war erupts and brigands once again roam the landscape.[112]

8   Lady Mary Wortley Montagu

A picture of a very different kind is given by an English contemporary of Pellow's, who witnessed a Muslim society at first hand and was able to give an account of the lives of Muslim women. Unlike most men, Lady Mary Wortley Montagu was, because of her sex, allowed to visit the harem and was thus able to observe and describe the appearances and lives of the slave concubines and wives; she was indeed the first Englishwoman, and possibly the first European, to do so. The setting was not Barbary but Turkey; however, as the terms 'Moor' and 'Turk' were conflated in both the European mind and its literature, and given the widespread hostility to Islam and its territories, her

---

[111]   Milton, 6; 223.
[112]   Moulay Ismail is succeeded by several of his sons in turn, each of whom rules only briefly and dies a violent death. Most appear to have been just as cruel and arbitrary as their father, but they lacked his power to intimidate, and thus control their countrymen, and so their reigns were all beset by civil strife.

account is remarkable for the tolerance and freedom from negative bias which it expresses.

Lady Mary went to Istanbul with her husband, who was sent as Ambassador Extraordinary to the Ottoman Court in 1716. Her experiences there are chronicled in a series of letters to her sister, as well as to friends and acquaintances in England.[113] Her descriptions of women's lives entirely gainsay western stereotypes of the closeted Muslim woman, restricted from most of what in the West is seen as normal activity: in effect enslaved to men. Furthermore, at a time when much of public debate in England on and off the stage focussed on liberty and its absence in the lives of Englishwomen,[114] Lady Mary compares her countrywomen's situation unfavourably with that of women in Turkey. Nor, she explains ironically, and with a humour based on paradox to confound conventional and linguistic expectations, are Turkish women as chaste as Westerners might think:

> Turkish ladies don't commit one sin less for not being Christians … 'Tis very easy to see that they have more liberty than we have, no woman, of what rank so ever being permitted to go in the streets without two muslins, one that covers her face all but her eyes and another that hides the whole dress of her head, and hangs half way down her back and their shapes are wholly concealed by a thing they call a ferace [a long dark robe covering a woman's other clothing] which no woman of any sort appears without. … You may guess then how effectually this disguises them, that there is no distinguishing the great lady from her slave and 'tis impossible for the most jealous husband to know his wife when he meets her, and no man dare either touch or follow a woman in the street.[115]

Lady Mary's tone here is that of the arch sophisticate, refusing to simplify her analysis of another culture but instead engaging with it on its own terms in the enlightened manner of her age; and whereas such absolute coverage of a woman's face and body might to a Western observer imply repression and restriction, she interprets it as promoting liberty. She goes on to narrate the

---

113   *Lady Mary Wortley Montagu: Turkish Embassy Letters*, ed. Malcolm Jack (London: William Pickering, 1993).
114   The subject of women's 'slavery' to men, especially in marriage, arises repeatedly in Restoration comedies, and in pamphlet debates about marriage. Cf. Eva Simmons, *'Virtue Intire: the Comedies of Aphra Behn"* (Ph.D. thesis, Royal Holloway College, University of London, 1990) available on-line, e.g., at https://www.grafiati.com/en/literature-selections/aphra/dissertation/ [accessed 8/10/2018].
115   *Turkish Embassy Letters*, 71. Page numbers relate to this.

ease with which Turkish women exploit their concealment in order to carry on love affairs with their 'gallants'. It is a world like that of Restoration comedy but where burqas take the place of masks and assignations are made in Jews' shops rather than in theatres or public parks.

Nor have these women anything to fear from their husbands, for unlike most gently-bred Englishwomen 'those ladies that are rich [have] all their money in their own hands, which they take with them upon a divorce with an addition which he is obliged to give them: Upon the whole', Lady Mary adds, 'I look upon Turkish women as the only free people in the Empire' (72). Later Lady Mary relates the amusement with which a Turkish woman regards what she perceives as the restrictions placed on English women, relative to her own freedom. Her manner anticipates Goldsmith's ironic observations on the English as seen from a Chinese person's point of view in *A Citizen of the World* (1760), which similarly frustrates western stereotypes.

Lady Mary's references to the harem and the institution of slavery challenge, and at the same time sustain, standard western ideas of it. Of Turkish slave markets she says, writing to her friend Lady Bristol,

> I know you'll expect I should say something particular of [the slave market], and you'll imagine me half a Turk when I don't speak of it with the same horror other Christians have done before me, but I cannot forbear applauding the humanity of the Turks to those creatures. They are never ill used and their slavery is in my opinion no worse than servitude all over the world. 'Tis true they have no wages, but they give them yearly clothes to a higher value than our salaries to any ordinary servant. But you'll object men buy women with an eye to evil. In my opinion they are bought and sold as publicly and more infamously in all our Christian great cities (130).

With this defence Lady Mary, as she herself acknowledges, is setting herself iconoclastically against prevailing western notions of Turkish slavery as brutal and depraved. But her favourable account of her visit to a harem in Adrianople, in which she praises her hostess and the setting, while consistent with the passage quoted above in its approval of Turkish customs and conventions also, perhaps unwittingly, legitimises and gives substance to western Orientalism.

The picture she paints could easily have emerged from the pages of Galland and *One Thousand and One Nights*: the harem door is guarded by black eunuchs; beyond it are rows of beautiful young girls dressed in damask ornamented with silver brocade; there is a gilded pavilion shaded by perfumed trees and shrubs, with a white marble fountain located in one corner and an intricately patterned, gilded ceiling. Then, at last, seated on a richly carpeted and cushioned dais, is seen the lady of the house: Fatima, a woman whose lovely eyes, perfect complexion and graceful figure Lady Mary now describes in detail. Hers is a beauty which 'effaced everything I have seen … that has been called lovely either in England or Germany and must own that I never saw anything so gloriously beautiful, nor can I recollect a face that would have been taken notice of near hers' [89]. Added to that the 'Kabiya's lady', as Lady Mary calls her, is blessed with grace and charm which could rival that of any European queen.

As with her natural assets, Fatima's dress is favourably depicted in elaborate and fine detail: she wears a costume of gold and silver, pink, green and white, richly jewelled and hung all around by her fine black hair. She is surrounded by girls as lovely as 'ancient nymphs' who play stringed instruments and dance in a manner one assumes to be highly seductive, for Lady Mary alludes to them suggestively as [raising] 'certain ideas' which 'the coldest and most rigid prude on earth could not have looked upon … without thinking of something not to be spoke of' (90)!

In its hyperbolic and ecstatic language, this passage too is replete with the lavish imagery offered by Galland and others in their descriptions of Arab women's quarters, thus endorsing western ideas of Islamic lands as realms of luxury and decadence, at once enviable and distasteful. However, Lady Mary appears unaware that her writing might have this effect: the unambiguously approving attitudes she expresses toward the way of life she witnesses in the upper echelons of Turkish society, and her narrative style, harmonise with her view of pleasure as the apogee of human experience, more to be valued than any other.[116]

9   Lived Experience and Literature: Some Concluding Remarks

The ransoms paid by Christian individuals and nations on behalf of their incarcerated countrymen and women ensured the survival of the North African slave trade for centuries. These activities, while rescuing captives from suffering and bringing them home, on the other hand provided a reliable source of income for the slave states which made the continuance of their activities well worthwhile. This is a conundrum which, even today, gives rise

---

[116]   Cf. Lady Mary's observations on the values of pleasure, and the enjoyment of the senses, e.g. on 134 and 142 of the *Turkish Embassy Letters*.

to painful debates regarding hostage-taking: whether the captives' representatives should accede to the kidnappers' demands in order to provide victims with relief and a return home – even though this will likely encourage more of the same, or sacrifice the hostages in hopes of putting a stop to the practice. In the 16th and later centuries however, redemptions of European slaves became routine – although, as previously noted, many slaves were never ransomed and lived out their lives in the new environment.

Religion played an important part in the process: one clear motive for bringing captives home was to prevent them apostatising under duress, or simply to improve their lives and prospects – as we have seen. Vigorous fund-raising activities of the Catholic redemption orders attest to the importance of this motive in the eyes of the church. In addition, many of the personal testimonies concerning life in the slave states were compiled by holy men – as we have also seen. We cannot be certain how accurate they were, as narrators could have had various reasons for embroidering them with lurid detail.

It is evident that these reports provided rich source material for fiction – especially when, as with Miguel de Cervantes and Jean-François Regnard, the authors had direct lived experience of incarceration. Already within the 'factual' accounts of returning captives are embedded stories and anecdotes, such as descriptions of theatre performances in the bagnios and the tales of Aruch and Zaphira, Zulpha and Ferdinand, which read like fiction. The horrors, the sexual activity and the glamour relating to wealth that captives and other travellers to Muslim countries observed or imagined fed nicely into slavery and romance literature – whether written to be read, or to be performed on stage. Ultimately, the public taste created by such material would develop into the Orientalism that was to sweep Europe.

CHAPTER 4

Slavery and Romance in 16th–17th Century Novels and Plays of Spain

Matarme bien podrás … que en tu poder me tienes, mas no podrá vencerme, sino quien una vez me venció.

[You can kill me … for you have me in your power, but only the one who has already defeated me can conquer me.]
  El Abencerraje

∴

te libré; y tú me venciste y cautivaste: ¿con qué armas peleaste, que tan presto me venciste?

[I delivered you from thraldom, and in return you have made me your prisoner. What [weapons] magic spell hath given your arms success?]
  Las Guerras civiles de Granada

∴

As we have seen, love affairs between male slaves and women in Barbary states were relatively rare, and where they occurred it was the man who converted – to Islam – and not the woman to Christianity. Their life together would be lived in the Muslim state, not a Christian one. Yet in defiance of lived experience and true-life narratives, Christian authors in the sixteenth and, more particularly, seventeenth centuries turned episodes of captivity and enslavement into dramatic incidents, illustrating and romanticising the twists of fate, almost invariably concluding with the conversion of Muslims to Christianity. In so doing, they devised a genre which came to be known as the 'Moorish' novel or play, although it clearly has antecedents in the Byzantine novellas which we encountered in Chapter 1. Indeed, themes of slavery and captivity became essential to literature set in 'Moorish' or 'Turkish' surroundings. Friedman notes (quoting Albert Mas) that when the 'infidel' is the subject of Spanish Golden Age literature, the captive is central to the plot, while Hegyi observes that the genre of '*turqueries*' is always linked with the theme of captivity,[1] an observation I would extend equally to settings in Muslim Spain and North Africa. For most Spaniards, as well as many other Europeans, the association of Muslims and slavery/captivity was inescapable.

Moreover, although Christians held large numbers of slaves, even in Granada, and including North Africans and Spanish Moriscos,[2] Christian writers focused almost exclusively on the enslavement of their own kind by Muslims. And where a reciprocal love interest occurs between Christians and Muslims, the Muslim is usually female and the Christian male, allowing for plot resolutions in which both Christians and males prevail. A stock variation involves Muslims falling in love with unresponsive captive Christians and attempting to impose their unwelcome attentions on the captives. In this situation the Muslims (and the objects of their affections) may be of either sex. Generally speaking, where a Muslim's advances are rejected by a Christian, the Christian's love for another Christian is usually a factor, as will be shown.

1   A Shared Culture in Spain

Throughout Spain, before and after the conquest of Granada – the last Muslim frontier – by the Christians, the cultures of Muslims and Christians had merged. Long years of '*convivencia*', however imperfect and frequently interrupted by bouts of strife, had created a common culture and the influence began early. The 9th-century Cordovan poet and theologian, Paul Alvarus, complained bitterly that the Mozarabs (Christians living under Islam) had been so indoctrinated by the dominant culture that they knew more Arabic than Latin and in many other ways lived like Muslims, forgetting their own faith:

---

1   Friedman, *Spanish Captives,* xxvi. Her reference is to Albert Mas, *Les Turcs dans la littérature espagnole du siècle d'or,* 2 vols. (Paris: Centre de Recherches Hispaniques, 1967), Vol. 1, 357–58; Ottmar Hegyi, *Cervantes and the Turks: Historical Reality Versus Literary fiction in* 'La gran sultana' *and* 'El amante liberal', Newark, Del.: Juan de la Cuesta, 1992, 195.

2   Cf., for example, Aurelia Martin-Casares, *La esclavitud en la Granada del siglo XVI: Genero, raza y religion* (Granada: Universidad de Granada y Diputacion Provincial de Granada, 2000). Samuel Chew discusses Christian enslavement of Muslims, as well as other Christians (especially Catholics enslaving Protestants and vice versa) at some length in *The Crescent and the Rose*: *Islam and England During the Renaissance* (New York: Oxford University Press, 1937), 341–45, and Chapter 8, *passim.*

> Our Christian men, with their elegant airs and fluent speech, are showy in their dress, and are famed for the learning of the gentiles [i.e. Muslims]; intoxicated with Arab eloquence they greedily devour and zealously discuss the books of the Chaldeans [i.e. Muslims again], and make them known by praising them with every flourish of rhetoric, knowing nothing of the beauty of the Church's literature and looking down with contempt on the streams of the Church that flow forth from Paradise; alas! ...
>
> They can even make better poems, every line ending with the same letter, which display high flights of beauty and more skill in handling metre than the gentiles themselves possess.[3]

So influential were such views that a group of Christians went on to seek martyrdom by deliberately maligning the Muslim faith and the prophet Muhammad: between 850 and 859 C.E. some fifty Christians were executed as a consequence.

But the influence went both ways. Bertrand and Petrie state that during the course of the 11th century, 'the Arabs became almost completely Hispanicised, their fanaticism waned, and they appeared to be won over to the ideal of luxurious and intellectual life'.[4] Wasserstein more cautiously points to a common identity among Andalusia's various social groups through 'a process of conversion' to Islam,[5] which reached its peak during the time of the chancellor and effective ruler of Andalusia, al-Mansur (c. 938–1002), although many divisions remained. Large numbers of Andalusis were classed as *muwalladun*, converts from other religions, chiefly Christianity.[6] Deferrari points out that 'an appreciation of the vast numbers of Christians who became Mohammedans, and of Mohammedans who became Christians is essential to a full understanding of the influence constantly and naturally exerted between the two faiths, in spite

---

3   Quoted by William Montgomery Watt and Pierre Cachia, *A History of Islamic Spain* (Edinburgh: Edinburgh University Press, 1965), 47.

4   Louis Bertrand and Sir Charles Petrie, *The history of Spain / Part I: From the Visigoths to the death of Philip II,* by Louis Bertrand; *Part II: From the death of Philip II to 1945,* by Sir Charles Petrie [the French translated by Warre B. Wells] (London: Dawsons of Pall Mall, 1969), Part I, 99.

5   David Wasserstein, *The Rise and Fall of the Party-Kings: Politics and Society in Islamic Spain 1002–1086* (Princeton: Princeton University Press, 1985), 56.

6   Estimates of how many Christians converted to Islam vary: some put the percentage as high as 50 or even 80 per cent. For a discussion citing sources for various calculations, cf. Sedef Dönmez, *Conversions In Umayyad Emirate of Al-Andalus* (London: School of African and Oriental Studies, MA Thesis in Turkish Studies, date not given), 3–6: https://www.academia.edu/9508173/Conversions_In_Umayyad_Emirate_of_Al_Andalus [accessed 1/3/2024].

of their underlying prejudices'.[7] Carrasco-Urgoiti elaborates on how Christians and Muslims of al-Andalus before the conquest of Granada had shared cultural tastes and practices – including architecture, dress, music, art and leisure activities such as jousting – to such an extent that after the conquest, 'Ethnic differences were not strong enough to clearly differentiate the Morisco community from the Old Christians'.[8] We have already considered (Chapter 2) the blurring of ethnic distinctions in lands where Muslims and Christians met, because of interbreeding and intermarriage. But in Spain even language boundaries could be obscured: as Stern points out,

> It is now generally admitted that both vulgar Arabic and the Romance dialect [derived from Latin and akin to Spanish] were employed by the Christians of Muslim Spain and by the Muslims of the country alike … As the Reconquest advanced, [this] Mozarabic dialect gradually receded in the face of dialects of the Christian conquerors.[9]

Wasserstein states that during the Taifa period, 'bilingualism seems to have been the norm', seeing the bilingual and specifically Andalusi poetic form known as the *muwashsha,* discussed above, as an exemplar.[10]

Before reviewing works foregrounding culturally mixed relationships in Spain, I want to consider two novellas featuring Muslims in love with one another because of their influence on subsequent literature. *El Abencerraje,* also known as *La historia del Abencerraje y la hermosa Jarifa*; and *Ozmín y Daraja,* also known as *La historia de Ozmín y Daraja* are noted for their sympathetic treatments of Muslim characters. This characteristic has come to be known as *morofilia* or *maurophilia* (love of or sympathy for 'Moors'), at a time when Muslims were often being demonised by others, in literature as in life, and there were already moves to expel them from Spain altogether.

The immediate inspiration for 'Moorish' texts lies in events which occurred in southern Spain, especially Granada (al-Andalus), around 1492, the year of the region's final re-conquest by the Catholic monarchs Ferdinand and Isabella [Figure 4.1]. However, it was another seventy years before the texts themselves

---

7   Harry A. Deferrari, *the Sentimental Moor in Spanish Literature Before 1600* (Philadelphia: University of Pennsylvania Press, 1927),12.
8   Carrasco-Urgoiti, *Moorish Novel,* 31.
9   Samuel Miklos Stern, *Hispano-Arabic Strophic Poetry* (Oxford: Oxford University Press, 1974), 150.
10 Wasserstein, 186–87. Cf. also Roger Wright, *Late Latin and Early Romance in Spain and Carolingian France* (Liverpool: Francis Cairns, 1982).

FIGURE 4.1　Muhammad XII's family in the Alhambra moments after the fall of Granada in 1492, painting by Manuel Gómez-Moreno González, c. 1880: Salida de la familia de Boabdil de la Granada [The Family of Boabdil leaving Granada]. Image in the public Domain
SOURCE: HTTPS://COMMONS.WIKIMEDIA.ORG/WIKI/FILE:SALIDA_DE_LA _FAMILIA_DE_BOABDIL_DE_LA_ALHAMBRA.JPG

began to appear: they are by definition backward-looking, quasi-historical and idealising. In these works, the lives and characters of Moriscos are glamourised and relations between them and Christians romanticised.

1.1　*El Abencerraje*

According to Carrasco-Urgoiti, the first coherent source of what became the 'Moorish' novel, play, etc. was the anonymous text, *El Abencerraje*, published in three versions between 1561 and 1565,[11] although it is thought to have been composed at least ten years before that, in 1551 or even earlier.[12] The piece is

---

11　This date is mentioned by Carrasco-Urgoiti, in *The Moorish novel*, 1976. But the work was ready for printing in 1551, according to Barker. Cf., Lope de Vega, *El remedio en la desdicha*, ed. J.W. Barker (Cambridge: Cambridge University Press, 1951), xii.
12　Marcelino Menéndez y Pelayo, *Orígenes de la novela* (Madrid: Bailly-Ballière é hijos, 1905–15), I, CCCLXXVI, ff., quoted by Deferrari, 38–39.

set some time before 1492 and represents a nostalgic look back to when there still was an Islamic Spain.

Here the love interest is between two Muslims, one of whom, the knight Abindarráez, is captured by Christian nobles roaming in search of adventure. Abindarráez belongs to the once powerful Abencerraje clan, most of whom have been massacred by the ruler of Granada, incited to hatred by a rival clan. He has been travelling to visit his beloved, Jarifa, who has been taken by her father to Coín, and is overcome by despair at the thought of failing to keep his rendezvous. Touched by his story, the knight leading the Christian group, the powerful governor of Álora and Antequera Rodrigo de Narváez, allows him to leave so as to make his visit, on condition that he return at the end of three days.[13] Abindarráez goes to Coín and consummates his love with Jarifa, but insists on keeping his word to Rodrigo as a matter of honour. She decides to accompany him there and pleads for mercy from his captors. Rodrigo is so overcome that he receives the couple with honours, grants them their freedom and even intercedes on their behalf with Jarifa's father who has opposed their match.

Although to a modern sensibility the Christian knights in the early part of this text have some repellently brutal qualities, the author of *El Abencerraje* appears to find no disgrace in their actions: rather he stresses the nobility of all the characters, the two male protagonists' courage and physical strength and their moral parity. For, despite their differences of race and religion, the men share a code of honour and generosity of spirit, and the Muslims, like the Christians, idealise gallantry. Abindarráez fights off five men and is only, finally, vanquished by Rodrigo de Narváez himself, and after having been weakened by his wounds.

The language of *El Abencerraje* is suffused with images of captivity which conflate the physical with the spiritual in the chivalric mode. Abindarráez tells his captor that in Granada, before its fall to the Christians,

> no se tenía por Abencerraje el que no servía dama, ni se tenía por dama la que no tenía Abencerraje por servidor.

---

13   The manner in which this condition is imposed recalls ways in which heroes are often subjected to tests in fairy tales, and the outcome is similarly gratifying, proving that virtue will always be rewarded.

[One who served no lady was not considered an Abencerraje, nor was she who had no Abencerraje as a suitor [servant] considered a lady].[14]

He merges the idea of ardour for his beloved Jarifa with physical confinement, referring to himself as Jarifa's captive and telling Narváez that,

> Matarme bien podrás ... que en tu poder me tienes, mas no podrá vencerme, sino quien una vez me venció'.
>
> [You can kill me ... for you have me in your power, but only the one who has already defeated me can conquer me'].[15]

Later he confesses to Jarifa that her prisoner (i.e. himself) is also prisoner of the governor of Álora. Jarifa too plays with these metaphors, describing herself as Abindarráez's captive.

Like the Abencerrajes, Narváez, it transpires, has served a lady, but he has given her up on learning that her husband had praised him highly. In this act too he has shown his capacity for generosity as well as through his courteous intercession with the (Muslim) king of Granada, obtaining pardon for the lovers who have married secretly, without parental consent. Finally, Jarifa's father insists they should reward Narváez's generosity with gifts and money. Abindarráez writes to Narváez, pointing out what he (Abindarráez) sees as a paradox in the governor's gesture:

> Si piensas, Rodrigo de Narváez, que con darme libertad en tu castillo, para venirme al mío, me dexaste libre, engañaste, que cuando libertaste mi cuerpo, prendiste mi coraçón; las buenas obras, prisiones son de los nobles coraçones.
>
> If you think, Rodrigo de Narváez, that in giving me freedom in your castle, to come to mine, you left me free, you are in error: for when you liberated my person, you took my heart captive. Good deeds are prisons of noble hearts.[16]

---

14   *El Abencerraje*, by Antonio de Villegas, 1565. I have worked with and quoted from a modern bilingual version (Spanish and English): *El Abencerraje, a Collaboration of Francisco López Estrada and John Esteng Keller* (tr.) (Chapel Hill, N.C.: The University of North Carolina Press, 1964), 52–53.
15   *El Abencerraje*, 48–49.
16   *El Abencerraje*, 80–81.

The letter then proceeds to say that its author can only express his indebtedness through gifts, including money. The governor passes the money on to Jarifa as recompense for her gracing him by visiting his castle. Thus are sealed bonds of friendship 'que les duró toda la vida' – 'which lasted them all their lives'.

This uniting of Christians and Muslims through commonly-held values is a trope that will be employed repeatedly by writers on 'Moorish' themes. Whereas in later accounts of the relations between Muslim and Christian what is often emphasised is *difference* between the two, here in *El Abencerraje* the focus is on similarity and spiritual kinship, as it had been in mediaeval texts considered previously. And this is so, despite the fact that the Muslim lovers retain their faith throughout. As Barbara Fuchs puts it, '"The Abencerraje" is striking for its sympathy for Moors qua Moors, with no intimation whatsoever that these are Christians in the making or future converts'.[17] But although *El Abencerraje* has no love affair between a Muslim and a Christian, one of its most important relationships is between Abindarráez and his captor, Rodrigo de Narváez, which lies at the heart of the narrative and is so powerful as to be almost homo-erotic. Their relationship dictates the course of their story and its outcome. Unusually, no pressure is placed on the Muslims to convert to Christianity and they are able to maintain their close friendship with Narváez despite the differences in their religions.

1.2   *Pérez de Hita*, **Guerras civiles de Granada (Civil Wars of Granada)**

Within a few years, new stories on 'Moorish' themes emerged with captivity and slavery as essential elements. But whereas *El Abencerraje* is set at some indeterminate time during the long period of intermittent clashes between Christians and Muslims, before the collapse of Granada, Ginés Pérez de Hita's *Las Guerras civiles de Granada* (*The Civil Wars of Granada*), Part I, chronicles the period immediately before the fall and the fall itself. It is mostly set inside, or just outside, the walls of Granada and was published in Spanish in 1595, in Paris in 1606, translated into French two years later (and abridged by the novelist Mlle de la Roche in 1683) and then translated into English by Thomas Rodd in 1801. Part II, which deals with the Alpujarra Rebellion of the Muslims, was published in Spain in 1619. I have concentrated on Part I as being the better-known, more fabulously fictionalised and influential of the two.

---

17   The Abencerraje *and* Ozmin and Daraja: *Two Seventeenth-Century Novellas from Spain*, ed. and tr. Barbara Fuchs, Larissa Brewer-Carter and Aaron J. Ilika (Philadelphia: University of Pennsylvania Press, 2014), 13.

The author, Pérez de Hita, claims to have received the book from a Jew who had it from a Moor, who in turn heard the stories 'from the Sultana herself' and the book is a hybrid of indistinguishably mingled 'fact' and fiction, presented as fact, typical for its time. It has always been assumed that this claim for cross-cultural literary transfer was in fact a conceit of the Spanish author, devised to add colour and authenticity to his account. But I see no reason automatically to deny his assertion with regard to at least one of the transfers: given the merging of peoples and cultures in early modern Spain, it may just as well be true, or partly true.[18] Indeed, Thomas Rodd gives the name 'Abenhamin' as author, along with that of Ginés Pérez de Hita as 'translator from the Arabic' on the flyleaf of his edition. Moreover, it is widely believed that the text offers a reasonably accurate picture of life in Granada in the years leading up to its fall.[19]

Many other details supplied within the narrative reinforce the supposed connections between the book and its author(s). For example, the name of a Christian captive, slave to Granada's queen, who is to play a crucial role in the story, is given as Esperanza de Hita, suggesting a link with the author/translator Ginés Pérez de Hita and by implication further legitimising his account because of his being possibly related to one of the (albeit minor) protagonists. Similarly, the name of the putative author Abenhamin makes a brief appearance among the cast of players in *Las Guerras civiles*, and many more details link known real-life individuals with those in the books. Seniff refers to *Las Guerras civiles* as 'a key work in the crystallization of the image of the Spanish Moor' for an array of literary figures, and as seminal in fostering the ideas of Rousseau and others about the 'noble savage', and 'the sentimental hero nurtured in the Romantic imagination in the 19th century'.[20]

Las guerras civiles depicts a society that is liminal in every sense: it is on the political boundaries dividing Spain between Christian and Muslim, and subject to all the tensions of that geographic positioning. Cross-border raids constitute a way of life, with individuals from each community routinely captured by its rivals; it is also on a religious boundary in the sense that conversions are frequent, with former Christians (Mozarabs) who had converted to Islam

---

18   A possibility which is persuasively argued for with regard to at least one of the ballads incorporated into the text, by Şizen Yiacoup, *Frontier Memory: Cultural Conflict and Exchange in the Romancero fronterizo* (London: Modern Humanities Research Association, Texts & Dissertations Series, Volume 87 [2013]) 110, and again on 121.

19   Cf. Dennis Seniff, Review of *Las Guerras civiles de Granada, primera parte*, ed. Shasta M. Bryant, *South Atlantic Review*, Vol. 48, No. 4 (Nov., 1983), 85–89, 87.

20   Seniff, 'Review', 85.

living within its borders, while many Muslims (Mudejars) and former Muslims converted to Christianity (Moriscos) live on the other side. It is on a historic and cultural frontier: the way of life is essentially mediaeval, but is on the verge of destruction, its members about to be forced into exile by a Catholic society more unified than the Muslim, as well as relentlessly militaristic and bent on conquest.

The community portrayed by Pérez de Hita is sybaritic: many of the scenes he describes are of lavish banquets, as well as jousting, with knights flaunting their ladies' colours in the mediaeval fashion. The contests are often *juegos de cañas* – combat with light canes or reeds, rather than weapons – or *juegos de sortijas*, games of rings, the emphasis in both being wholly on skill rather than on the contestant's capacity to wound his opponent. Elegantly-dressed women watch their lovers' and admirers' progress from high windows.

But the Muslims had for centuries been internally split, one kingdom often allying with Christians against another and dependant on Christian mercenaries for their survival. This contributed substantially to their ultimate downfall. Bertrand and Petrie state that,

> These Musulman kinglings [of Southern Spain], softened by all the charms of the climate, lost their warrior virtues. So did their Arab and African soldiers. More and more, in order to defend themselves, they were obliged to appeal to Christian auxiliaries. [21]

Granada itself became divided from within between two clans or factions: the Zegries and the Abencerrajes whose rift, as noted above, will contribute to the city-state's destruction.

The form of the narrative is a series of romantic episodes, featuring different – and sometimes re-appearing – individuals as protagonists within each. They chronicle life during the last days of Granada and its capitulation. Slavery and captivity images and events are crucial to many individual stories, and to the entirety of *Las guerras civiles*. From the beginning, Granada is represented as a captive of Africa that must be freed. Captivity is a state that could overwhelm an individual at any time: before an important battle (the Battle of the Alporchones), the Muslims seize a Christian called Quiñonero. He tells them – in one of the many poems illustrating the piece:

---

21   Bertrand and Petrie, *History of Spain,* 99.

Que la guerra es condición,
que hoy soy tuyo, y ya confío
mañana podrás ser mío,
y sujeto a mi prisión.[22]

[Such the chance of fickle war is,
Such the fortune of the brave,
Tomorrow you may be my captive,
Tho' to-day I bow your slave].[23]

True to the prophecy, his captor is later taken prisoner and killed for a display of arrogance.

Confinement episodes are not only incidental hazards of life in the region, but also critical in determining the fate of Granada. A (Zegrie?) woman called Zayda is locked up by her parents to prevent her seeing her lover, the Abencerraje Zayde. This leads by degrees to the ultimately internecine conflict between the Zegries and the Abencerrajes, the enmity of the King Boabdil to the Abencerrajes and the latter offering their support to the Christians. The Abencerrajes befriend captive Christians and visit them in prison; they are accused by a Zegrie of giving them alms. Love and captivity are here present too: a Muslim knight called Reduan frees a Muslim lady called Haxa/Haja from the Christians. He becomes 'a willing captive' to (her) charms:

> te libré; y tú me venciste y cautivaste: ¿con qué armas peleaste, que tan presto me venciste? Pero ¿para qué lo pregunto, pues eres semejanza y cifra de la hermosura, dotada en discreción, bravo donaire, brío y gentileza? Éstas son las armas con que peleaste conmigo. No hallaste en mí resistencia, porque de mis potencias estabas apoderada; tu siervo soy, y tú mi señora y mi bien.[24]

---

22 Ginés Pérez de Hita, *Guerras civiles de Granada*, Tomo I (Madrid: D. Leon Amarita, 1833), reissued Gutenberg online, 2022; https://www.gutenberg.org/cache/epub/67631/pg67631-images.html [accessed 25/4/2024],11.

23 *The Civil Wars of Granada; and the History of the Factions of the Zegries and Abencerrajes, Two Noble Families of that City, to the Final Conquest by Ferdinand and Isabella, Translated from the Arabic of Abenhamin, a Native of Granada, by Gines Perez de Hita, and from the Spanish by Thomas Rodd* (London: Printed for Thomas Ostell, No 3 Ave Maria Lane, 1803), 10.

24 *Guerras civiles de Granada*, 215.

[I delivered you from thraldom, and in return you have made me your prisoner. What magic spell hath given your arms success? But why do I enquire? You are the Goddess Beauty's Self, armed with every virtue, with every grace and gentleness, and modesty. These are the arms you wield, arms which no power can withstand, and to which all nature gladly yields a willing sacrifice. Reduan is your slave, you are his conqueror].[25]

Reduan and Haxa are of the same religion – like the lovers in *El Abencerraje*. But toward the end of the book, the themes of captivity and of love across religious boundaries merge and become central, as the vicious Zegries accuse the queen of adultery with one of the Abencerrajes, and the king locks up his wife in Alhambra's Tower of Comares. He tricks many of the leading Abencerraje nobles into entering the palace, where thirty-six of them are seized and beheaded, one by one, until an Abencerraje page alerts the others in time for some to save themselves [see Figure 4.2].

Many of the victims convert to Christianity as they die. The survivors retaliate with mass slaughter in the palace; they are meanwhile negotiating with the Christian King Ferdinand to be allowed to defect to him, with a freed Christian acting as messenger. Later they are banished from the kingdom and convert en masse, taking the Christians' part against Granada. Boabdil's queen now faces a desperate choice: to accept conviction for adultery and be burnt at the stake, to commit suicide, or to clear herself, which she can only do by means of four knights going into battle with her accusers and winning, on her behalf. Despairing, the queen resolves to kill herself, but her life is saved by the Christian slave Esperanza, whom she frees and who advises her and converts her to Christianity, persuading her to put her faith in the Virgin Mary. From then on, the queen's life becomes inextricably linked with Christians. She engages Christian champions, who include Manuel Ponce de Leon (a historical aristocrat), and they disguise themselves as 'Turks' to enter the gates of the kingdom. In an elaborately drawn-out combat scene, they overcome the queen's accusers. She now plays a crucial political role in the defeat of the Muslim kingdom – helping to organise mass baptisms and urging the Christians to attack.

At the end, Boabdil is forced to flee, weeping for the loss of his kingdom as he rides, thereby famously suffering the contempt of his mother for his weakness. The queen is baptised as Doña Isabella of Granada and marries a wealthy Christian nobleman. She will become an important figure in later

---

25   *Civil Wars of Granada*, 192.

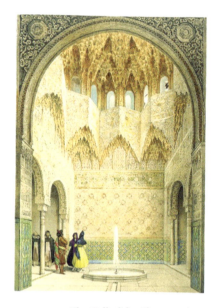

FIGURE 4.2 The Hall of the Abencerrajes, Alhambra, Granada, where according to tradition 30 members of the Abencerrage clan were murdered. Painting by Leon Auguste Asselineau (1808–89)
CREDIT: THE STAPLETON COLLECTION/ BRIDGEMAN IMAGES

literature. The conversion of the Abencerrajes, the 'good' people of Granada, to Christianity also appears logical and natural and represents a moral and spiritual fulfilment, which henceforth will give shape and meaning to their lives. The facts of their defeat and loss of autonomy as a people are glossed over: they had, in any case, been persecuted by their king. Where Boabdil had been corruptible, weak, unstable and unjust, the new Christian ruler will be righteous, steadfast and strong. Boabdil's bad judgment in killing so many Abencerrajes, incurring the survivors' implacable enmity, is decisive in bringing about his downfall, as these knights had represented the flower of Muslim Granada and will be staunch defenders of its erstwhile enemies and of Christendom.

Some traditions also point to Muslim rulers' intemperate desires for their Christian slave women as being integral to their defeat. Boabdil's father, Abu l-Hasan Ali, also known as Muley-Hacén, fell in love with his slave, the Christian Isabel de Solís (fl. late 15th century), who had been captured and sold to the king. At first Isabel, herself the daughter of a Castilian nobleman and an Andalusi Muslim captive, was Muley-Hacén's concubine. But then the besotted ruler married her, casting aside his previous wife, Aixa, in favour of Isabel, renamed Zoraya or Zoraida. Both these incidents have been identified as causes of the catastrophic Muslim defeat in 1492, since they precipitated a civil war in which the spurned queens played critical roles in opposition to the kings. The divided Muslims then became easy prey to the Christians.[26] Some other instances are recorded of love and marriage between Christian noblemen and Muslim women, for example, that of King Alfonso VI of Castile and Zaida of Seville, reputedly the daughter of the Muslim ruler Al-Mu'tamid. With the fall of Seville to the Almoravids she is said to have fled and sought refuge with Alfonso, who made her his mistress and then his wife. She converted to Christianity and took the name of Isabel.[27]

The impact of the *Guerras civiles* was immense on the literature first of Spain, and then of other European countries. Ballads about the events, many of which are included in the *Guerras civiles*, contributed to their romanticisation, lending them imaginative force. One in particular, quoted by Pérez de Hita (33–34), has the monotonous rhythm of a dirge – both in Spanish and in English – which gives it a hypnotic appeal similar to that of *The Ancient Mariner*:

Mataste los Bencerajes	King you slew th'Abencerrajes
Que eran la flor de Granada	Of our city slew the flow'r
Cogiste los tornadizos	Runagates of famed Cordova
De Córdoba la nombrada	Chusing these in evil hour.
!Ay de mi Alhama!'	Alas! Alas! Alhama.
Por eso mereces, rey	And you merit fierce chastisement
Una pena muy doblada	Double loss and double pain;
Que te perdas tu y el reino	Not Granada, not your kingdom

---

26 Carrasco-Urgoiti, *Moorish Novel*, 27–28.
27 Cf. Ramón Menéndez Pidal, *Reliquias de la poesía épica española* (Madrid: Espasa Calpe, 1951), xliv, quoted in Carrasco-Urgoiti, *Moorish Novel*, 41.

Y aquí se pierda Granada	Not your life shall long remain.
¡Ay de mi Alhama![28]	Alas! Alas! Alhama.[29]

The ballad was translated many years later by Lord Byron as, 'Woe is Me, Alhama'.

Poignant images of the last bright days of Granada, the destruction of a civilisation and effective extinction of a people – at least as they had existed for hundreds of years, portraits of the last Andalusi King Boabdil, 'el rey chico' [the little king] turning back from his flight to gaze for the last time on Granada and lament, like Orpheus, on what he has lost – had a potent attraction for Christians. But more significantly for the argument here, the story of the captive queen fighting for her life and turning to knights from a rival religion for help, gripped the imagination of later writers – particularly, as we shall see, in France. That almost all the principal Muslims in the story ended up as Christians made it somehow 'safe' to sympathise with, and even admire them.

2   Changing Fortunes of the Moriscos

The conquest of Granada by the Christians in 1492 represented the culmination of a process begun, arguably, in the 11th century, when the papacy, seeking to expand its influence, became directly involved in the Spanish Christians' conflict with the Muslims. In 1063, after the assassination of Ramiro I of Aragon by a Muslim, Pope Alexander II offered indulgences to soldiers who would fight the Muslims in the peninsula, encouraging combatants from other European countries to join those in Spain. Other papal initiatives against the Muslims were undertaken in the years that followed including, at the end of the century, forbidding Spanish Christians to join the Crusade in the holy land.[30]

In 1085 Fernando, the king of Leon addressed the Toledano population, informing them that it was the Christians' intention to take back all of Spain,

---

28   *Guerras civiles de Granada,* ed. Shasta M. Bryant (Newark, Delaware: Juan de la Cuesta, 1982), 253–54. I have here cited Bryant's version, as the text varies considerably between editions, and some lack the haunting, traditional ballad line, '¡Ay de mi Alhama!', which I believe adds such power to this version.
29   *Civil Wars of Granada,* 334.
30   Wasserstein, 268–70.

which had been and remained Christian by right and to force the Muslims across the Straits of Gibraltar to Morocco.[31] This statement of intent, 'the first explicit and complete formulation in the Arabic sources of the Christian project of conquest',[32] followed by the taking of Toledo by Fernando's son Alfonso VI of Castile in the same year, filled the Muslim population with 'fear and despair', according to contemporary chroniclers, as it seemed to them a 'complete reversal of forces in the relationship between Muslims and Christians'.[33] Both Christians and Muslims saw it as a portent of what might follow, although the process of re-conquest dragged on over the next four centuries.

When Granada finally capitulated in 1492, the Catholic authorities including the monarchs were confronted with what they saw as an urgent task: to convert the surviving Muslims and bring them safely into the Christian fold. 'New Christian' 'Moriscos', as they were now known, played a crucial role in aiding 'Old Christian' clerics in this task, using their knowledge of the Qur'an and the Islamic faith so as directly to communicate with their erstwhile co-religionists.[34] Men such as Juan Andrés, a convert from Xàtiva, assisted by Juan Gabriel, a convert from Aragon and a former *alfaquí* (Islamic religious authority) translated the Qur'an for these purposes and schooled the Christian clerics in how to preach to Muslims. Extracts and arguments from the Qur'an were quoted, sometimes in order directly to refute them, in sermons and documents known as *antialcoranes*. At other times they were used to maintain that the Qur'an was in sympathy with Christianity, but superseded by it.[35] Both the Arabic language and Arab musical instruments were employed during a paradoxical flurry of interlingual and intercultural exchange – although this was not destined to last:

> [Archbishop] Talavera's campaign also included intense linguistic activity, whereby the people of Granada were taught Spanish while the clergy learned Arabic. To this end Talavera brought the printing press to the city, and he commissioned and had printed an Arabic-Spanish glossary

---

31 Alejandro García-Sanjuán, 'Replication and Fragmentation, The Taifa Kingdoms', *The Routledge Handbook of Muslim Iberia*, ed. Maribel Fierro, (London and New York: Routledge, 2020), 64–88, 79–80.
32 García-Sanjuán, 79.
33 García-Sanjuán, 81, 83.
34 Cf. Mercedes García-Arenal, Ryan Szpiech, and Katarzyna K. Starczewska, 'The Perennial Importance of Mary's Virginity and Jesus's Divinity: Qur'ānic Quotations in Iberian Polemics after the Conquest of Granada (1492)', in *Journal of Qur'anic Studies* 20, no. 3 (2018): 51–80.
35 'Perennial Importance', 60–61.

and an Arabic catechism written in the Latin alphabet, i.e, in phonological transcription.[36]

A key element of the process was a focus on the Virgin Mary (as well as on Jesus), to whom it was thought Muslims could relate because of her significant presence in the Qur'an, and the respect in which she was held by Muslims. In Spain in particular, Mary had become associated with 'miracles of conversion' from the 13th century onwards. After 1492, portable religious images of Mary were produced 'on a semi-industrial scale' and extracts from the Qur'an which allude to Mary were cited in sermons.[37] This chapter shows how Muslim converts to Christianity, notably the heroines of Cervantes as well as the queen of Granada (above), cling to idealisations of the Virgin Mary and even identify with her.

Sadly, the Christians' evangelising project did not terminate hostilities between themselves and the Moriscos. At least two bitter and protracted battles ensued between rebellious 'Moriscos' and the Spanish authorities: the 'Rebellion of the Alpujarras', in 1499–1501 and the 'War of the Alpujarras', 1568–71, both precipitated by the Christians' continuing and often oppressive attempts to compel the Muslims to assimilate. The rebels, divided and disorganised, lost both encounters and were savagely suppressed. During the 16th century, tens of thousands were dispersed to other parts of Spain or expelled from the country (many went to North Africa: see Chapter 3).

The remaining Moriscos were viewed with increasing suspicion by populace and government alike, because of the past revolts, and fears that they represented a fifth column plotting to aid the forces of the Ottoman Turks, who constituted a very real threat to Spain. Christians were cognisant that many Muslim refugees from earlier expulsions had joined the corsairs of North Africa and were even leading raids on Spanish ships and towns. Mutual resentments, together with mounting repression of the Moriscos during the 1590s and early 1600s would culminate in their final expulsion over the period 1609–14.[38]

By the end of the 16th century, Spain was in a period of transition and considerable apprehension. The piously Catholic King Philip II had just died (September 1598), to be succeeded by his son Philip III who was even more

---

36   'Perennial Importance', 58.
37   'Perennial Importance' 57–58.
38   Benjamin Ehlers, *Between Christians and Moriscos: Juan de Ribera and Religious Reform* (Baltimore, Maryland, USA: The Johns Hopkins University Press, 2006), 20–22 and *passim*. Cf. also, Matthew Carr, *Blood and Faith: The Purging of Muslim Spain* (London: Hurst, 2009); and Carrasco-Urgoiti, *The Moorish Novel*, 30.

anti-Muslim than his father. Already in 1582, the Archbishop of Valencia, Juan de Ribera, had urged that the Moriscos be eliminated from Spain. For thirteen years since his appointment at Valencia (1569) Ribera, encouraged by the king, had worked consistently to achieve full conversion of the Moriscos, pressing them to live as devout Catholics. Now he had become convinced that these efforts, as well as those of the Inquisition, were futile: the 'leniency' on the one hand, and the threats, tortures and burnings on the other, had failed alike. He wrote to the Grand Inquisitor Gaspar de Quiroga y Vela, referring to the Moriscos as 'enemies' and urging Quiroga to use his influence with the king to promote their wholesale expulsion. Ribera followed this up with a direct appeal to the king and then a series of further letters to the same effect.[39]

Others among Ribera's contemporaries had alternative solutions, no more humane than his, including plans for a massacre of the entire Morisco people; castrating Morisco men and sterilising the women; expelling the people to non-Muslim parts of Africa (so Spain could not be accused of allowing them to become infidels); or sending males over sixteen to the galleys and confiscating the children to raise them as Christians. Another suggestion was branding all Moriscos on the face for easy identification; there was even a proposal to send all adult male Moriscos on a forced migration to the Indies, where they would be made to work in the mines, or to other uninhabited parts of the New World.[40]

Yet, alongside this hostile agitation, contrary forces were at work, binding Muslims and Christians together and reminding them of their kinship as fellow-countrymen over almost a millennium. Childers tells of a mock 'Moros y Cristianos' battle (a 'zuiza') staged by Moriscos in Manzanares, in which they 'captured' some Christians and then 'ransomed' them to raise money to regild the altarpiece of the Virgin Mary in the church. The author gives this as evidence: (a) that Moriscos could participate in community life by playing their own ancestors in support of a local cause; (b) of how the figure of the Virgin Mary, revered by both Muslims and Christians, could symbolically link the two communities together; and (c) that, at the height of deliberations about ethnic cleansing, Christian populations could still appreciate festivities organised by Moriscos.[41] It all came to an end when some local busybody informed the

---

39 Ehlers, 103–04.
40 Cf. *Tratado acerca de los moriscos de España*, ed. J. Gil Sanjuán (Málaga: Algaraza, 1997), esp. 31–40; Henry Charles Lea, *The Moriscos of Spain; their Conversion and Expulsions* (Philadelphia: Lea Brothers and Co., 1901), 296–98; Wheatcroft, 152–55.
41 William Childers, 'Manzanares 1600: Moriscos from Granada Organize a Festival of "Moors and Christians"', in *The Conversos and Moriscos in Late Medieval Spain and Beyond*, ed. Kevin Ingram (Leiden: Brill, 2009), 287–309.

authorities in Madrid that Moriscos were being allowed to carry weapons, in defiance of an edict forbidding this.[42]

King Philip II had his own reasons for not heeding the advice of those who would expel the Moriscos. Many of the nobility relied on Moriscos to work as farmers, muleteers and artisans on their lands, and a faction led by the Marquis of Denia warned of disastrous economic consequences if thousands of Spain's most productive workers were exiled all at once. They backed this appeal with a hefty donation of one hundred thousand libras from the Valencian nobility, 'ostensibly for the "peace and security of the realm"'. In addition, the king's policy had lately been changing. With the Netherlands in revolt against Spain, and preparations underway for Spain to attack England, Philip now favoured rapprochement with the Ottoman Turks, a strategy which would preclude expelling Spain's Muslims.[43]

Then, with a new king on the throne, Ribera published the *Catechismo para Instruccion de los Nuevamente Convertidos de Moros* (Catechism for the Instruction of the Newly Converted Moors) in the form of a dialogue between a Christian cleric and a North African Muslim desirous of becoming a Christian. This work had been contemplated as early as 1587, but was held back due largely to a protracted debate as to which language it should be published in: Latin, Spanish, or even Arabic. In the event it was printed in Spanish and its publication in 1599 was a prelude to a new, wider, and ultimately successful clerical and lay campaign to persuade Philip III to reverse his father's policy and eject the Moriscos from Spain. The work directly attacked the Muslim faith, the Qur'an and the Prophet Muhammad reflecting, Ehlers says, 'a fundamental disdain for Islam that impeded any willingness to engage the Moriscos in a truly reciprocal dialogue'.[44]

All the more extraordinary then, that in the same year and in such an inflamed atmosphere, a work as sympathetic to the Moriscos as *Ozmín y Daraja* should appear.[45] But in context, it is not surprising that both of its protagonists are converted to Christianity, nor that religious conversion should be central to so much subsequent fiction involving Muslims.

2.1 *Ozmín y Daraja*

La Historia de Ozmín y Daraja (*The Loves of Osmin and Daraxa*), was included as a romantic novelette in the otherwise picaresque tale of the rogue, *Guzmán de*

---

42   Childers, 'Manzanares', 289.
43   Ehlers, 106–112.
44   Ehlers, 123.
45   Cf. Fuchs, et al, *The Abencerraje* and *Ozmin and Daraja*, 15.

FIGURE 4.3 Mateo Alemán Oil on canvas, by Manual Cabral y Aguado-Bejarano (1827–1891), Gallery of the University of Seville. Image in the public domain
SOURCE: HTTPS:// COMMONS.WIKIME DIA.ORG/WIKI/FILE:MATEO_A LEM%C3%A1N_%C3%B3LEO.JPG

Alfarache (1599, translated into English in 1623) by Mateo Alemán [Figure 4.3]. Like the author of *El Abencerraje,* Alemán is believed to have been from a *converso* family (i.e. previously Jewish).[46] Such hybrid origins could help to explain the writer's appeals for sympathy and understanding for the defeated Muslims. But by the time *Guzmán de Alfarache* and its interior story of *Ozmín y Daraja* were written, a great deal had changed since the days of *El Abencerraje*.

Ozmín y Daraja deals briefly with the last period of Muslim-Christian warfare and the actual conquest of al-Andalus, but most of it is set immediately after the conquest, when the Catholics are finally in control and beginning to mould the formerly Muslim society to suit Christian values. Disguise, performance, and duality form integral themes. Like *El Abencerraje,* on which it may have been based[47] (and unlike *Las Guerras civiles*), *Ozmín y Daraja* charts a

---

46 Fuchs et al, *The Abencerraje,* 9.
47 *El Abencerraje* is cited as a possible source for *Ozmín y Daraja*, along with Heliodorus's *Aethiopica*. Cf. Judith A. Whitenack, 'The alma diferente of Mateo Aleman's "Ozmín y

single love affair, disrupted by war and captivity. And, like *El Abencerraje*, it deals with two people of the same religion (Muslim) who encounter Christians through the captivity of one of them.

The lovers of *Ozmín y Daraja*, who are from Granada and Baza, respectively, are separated when Daraja is captured by forces of the Catholic monarchs Ferdinand and Isabella and held for ransom. Ozmín assumes a variety of disguises in order to gain access to his beloved, while Daraja becomes complicit in concealing the true nature of their relationship right until the end. Their marriage takes place only after their mutual conversion to Christianity, a process which Whitenack interprets as occurring under extreme coercion.[48] Daraja chooses to remain with the soon-to-be-converted, but essentially Muslim, Ozmín despite having had numerous wealthy and well-established Christian suitors.

The author Alemán uses fairy-tale superlatives to describe his high-born lovers, both related to kings, as well as to one another: Daraja is connected through her mother to the king of Baza, whereas *Ozmín* is a cousin of that king's nephew, Boabdil [the famous 'Little King'], of Granada. Daraja possesses 'una de las más perfectas y peregrine hermosura que en otra se había visto'[49] ['one of the most perfect and rare beauties ever seen']; although she is not yet seventeen years of age, she has discretion, seriousness ['gravedad'], mature wisdom, and grace. *Ozmín* matches her in being rich, gallant, modest and above all, brave. Furthermore, unlike the lovers of *El Abencerraje*, who plan to marry in secret, Ozmín and Daraja have been promised to one another by their parents, to cement the families' tight bonds of friendship. Their betrothal is also in keeping with Islamic traditional custom, to marry cousins to one another and it accords with their own feelings, as they have loved one another since childhood. All this was disrupted by war and Daraja's capture.

Yet, once again the kindred similarities between the lovers and the Christians are emphasised, their affinities manifest across religious and cultural lines. Both lovers speak fluent Spanish: Daraja could pass for an 'Old Christian' (as opposed to the recently converted 'New Christians'). This is a factor which, it is strongly implied, helps bind her to the affections of King Ferdinand and Queen Isabella, to whom she is first assigned:

Daraja''', *Romance Quarterly* 38, No. 1 (1991), 59–73; and Michel Cavillac, *Picaros y mercaderes en el Guzmán de Alfarache* (Granada: Universidad de Granada, 1994), 443.

48 Whitenack, 65.
49 Mateo Alemán, *Historia de Ozmín y Daraja*, from the series, *10 grandes clásicos de la literatura española* (Madrid: Libros de Autor, 1994), 9.

El rey la estimó en mucho pareciéndole de gran precio. Luego la envió a la reina su mujer, que no la tuvo en menos y, recibiéndola alegremente, así por su merecimiento como por ser principal descendiente de reyes, hija de un caballero tan honrado como por ver si pudiera ser parte que la entregara la ciudad sin más daños ni peleas, procuró hacerle todo buen tratamiento, regalándola de la manera, y con ventajas, que a otras de las más cercanas a su persona'.[50]

[The King thought highly of her as she seemed very precious (i.e. she was valuable as a person). And so, he sent her to his wife the Queen, who valued her no less, receiving her gladly, as much for her merits as for her being descended from kings, daughter of a most honourable knight, as for the possibility that she might deliver up the city without more damage or fighting, and (the Queen) treated her in a manner, and with advantages, not given to others].

The queen dresses Daraja in her own Castillian clothes, heightening the impression of her 'Spanishness' so successfully that Ozmín almost fails to recognise her when they meet again. Thereafter she is sent to live in the household of a Spanish nobleman whose daughter, Doña Elvira de Guzman, becomes her constant companion. Ozmín is, for his part so fluent in Spanish that it is 'como si en el riñon de Castilla se criara y hubiera nacido en ella' [as if he had been born and raised in the very heart of Castille]. Only in private the lovers speak fluent Arabic: it is their 'secret' means of communication. Later in the story Ozmín is able to pass himself off as a Spanish nobleman, 'Don Rodrigo de Padilla' and in that persona to forge a firm friendship with a Spanish captain who had at first suspected him.

Daraja too enters into the spirit of deception. Having been observed in close and potentially dangerous conversation with the 'gardener' 'Ambrosio' (Ozmín in another of his disguises), she invents a history in which 'Ambrosio' was a nobly-born Christian captive who had been her husband's close friend. In a twist of dramatic irony, Ozmín tells a Christian nobleman how much he wishes that Daraja would follow his own faith, to which the author adds wryly, 'No mintió el moro palabra en cuanto dijo, si hubiera sido entendido.' [the Moor did not lie in what he said, if only his true meaning could have been understood]. Truth and fiction become more and more inextricably intertwined. Those around the lovers are inflexibly tied to one culture, but the couple are

---

50   Alemán, *Ozmín y Daraja,* 9–10.

hybrids with protean capacities for slipping between cultures and roles, and using these skills to survive.

As with *El Abencerraje* there are no love affairs across religio-cultural boundaries, but the intimate friendships traverse these: between Daraja and the queen, and then between Daraja and Doña Elvira. *Ozmín* appears to befriend several of the noble Spaniards, but his repeated deceptions call those friendships into question. The wider impulse of the work appears, however, to advocate 'leniency' rather than harshness as the best method of converting Moriscos. It suggests that kindness and persuasion, not persecution and punishment, will be the means to bring Moriscos safely into the arms of the mother church.

There has been some discussion about the apparent disjunction between the romance of *Ozmín* and Daraja, and the picaresque framing tale of a penniless young man who cheats and steals his way through Spain. But dissimulation lies at the heart of the romance too, only the elevated tone of the narrator appears to justify the lovers' means in order to secure worthy ends: conversion to Christianity and matrimony. Moreover, Ozmín's wanderings and changes of identity in search of an income – as well as to be near to Daraja – mirror in miniature Guzmán's journeys in search of his fortune. Barbara Fuchs comments that,

> Although the tale [of *Ozmín* and Daraja], with its incomparable and noble protagonists, certainly reflects the idealizing tradition of maurophilia, it also betrays certain picaresque affinities. Ozmín's serial disguises, episodic adventures, and menial positions cannot help but recall those of a *pícaro*, and both he and Daraja ably trick their masters … in order to achieve their own goals.

But, Fuchs adds, just as the novella is 'tarnished' by *Guzmán*'s traces of the picaresque, so is the latter enriched by the novella's instances of resourcefulness and 'self-fashioning'.[51]

Another subplot of *Guzmán de Alfarache* also links the framing narrative with the romance: Guzmán's father is captured by pirates and taken as a slave to Algiers. In order to better his circumstances he converts to Islam and marries a rich Moorish woman whom he proceeds to cheat out of her house, money and jewels, before leaving her destitute. Thereafter, he reverts to his former faith. That this act is as hypocritical and opportunistic as his previous actions

---

51   Fuchs, Introduction to *The Abencerraje and Ozmin and Daraja*, 17.

Alemán underlines with the words, 'reduciéndose a la fe de Jesucristo arrepentido y lloroso' [reducing himself to the faith of Jesus Christ repentantly and tearfully'].[52] Alemán leaves open whether it is he himself as author or his character who considers the re-conversion a 'reduction', and in what that reduction consists. Either way, this anti-heroic episode reverses and mocks the themes of nobility, wealth, love, marriage, captivity and religious conversion which animate *Ozmín y Daraja*, at the same time as it connects the two narratives.

3   Cervantes: 'Moorish' Themes, in Prose Fiction and on the Spanish Stage

With Miguel de Cervantes we come to fiction with overtly 'Moorish' themes, both drama and non-dramatic prose. Much of it is set in North Africa or Istanbul, and in the dramatist's own era, the late sixteenth and early seventeenth centuries. The Moriscos having now ostensibly converted to Christianity, or left Spain altogether, the only way in which openly practising Muslims and Spanish Christians were likely to come into close contact was through the institution of slavery, with members of one religion being enslaved by the other.

Although they still have much in common with their 'Moorish' predecessors, these plays and novels are very different: gone are the courtly and chivalrous niceties of the earlier works, replaced by a much harsher reality. Cervantes's work is informed by his personal experience of slavery in Algiers. As we have seen, he had been captured by Muslim corsairs in 1575 while returning home from a period in Naples. He spent five harrowing years in Algiers, while his family tried desperately to ransom him, and he several times came close to death after four abortive attempts to escape. Apart from the accounts of these episodes by others who knew him, little is known about his real life in Algiers, but he drew on those experiences to authenticate fictional backgrounds while creating plots, ranging from the all-too grimly realistic to the fantastically embellished, fed from the romance tradition.

Cervantes re-worked these themes in numerous novels and plays, as if he were attempting not only to confine his painful experiences, to 'imprison' them in the fictional realm, as it were, thus diluting their potency, but then, as *deus ex machina*, to define the nature and outcome of those experiences according to his own desires. Projecting all experience onto third person characters further assists the processes of control and distancing: the reader/theatregoer

---

52   Alemán, *Guzmán de Alfarache*, 1641, 5–6.

may become entirely immersed in the world of the slave, even experience it vicariously, but the author remains aloof; in the end, he is able to place the text on the table and walk away.

María Antonia Garcés relates Cervantes's constant return to the topic of captivity to Freud's theses on obsessive-compulsive behaviour and trauma and Lacanian notions of '"Tuché and Automaton" [Chance and Spontaneity]', which compel the victim persistently to re-enact an otherwise 'unassimilated' traumatic event through dreams and other manifestations.[53] Garcés rightly focuses in her work on the horrific aspects of Cervantes's experiences and discusses at some length the concept of 'spiritual death' in relation to captivity:[54] the captive's legal status is that of a '"dead body"' and he experiences his total loss of liberty as nothingness 'as if he did not exist in the world'.[55] In this extreme state of despair, the traumatised captive may experience a psychological 'splitting', she says, a fragmentation of the ego in which a 'double' is created, the '"traumatized self",' who is put in charge of the experience which the subject cannot bear to experience directly, but which exists alongside the other self without being integrated into it.[56] This splitting may later help the survivor of such a trauma to testify to his terrible experiences, as Cervantes did in *El trato de Argel*. Garcés identifies the character Saavedra, who appears in no fewer than three of Cervantes's works, as the author's alter ego, an ideal ego and 'second identity that speaks of his [Cervantes's] traumatic experience in Algiers'.[57]

But what fascinates me is how his works also ameliorate these episodes by romanticising them and giving most of his stories a 'happy ending' within the romantic and Orientalist literary traditions: all of his tales contain a 'love interest', a central pair of lovers who are typically brought together at the end. In this way Cervantes remains within established literary conventions, even while breaking new ground as a writer; one of Cervantes's biographers and four modern editors, among others, state that he set a literary precedent as his plays 'inaugurate a kind of theatrical mini-genre, the Barbary or Turkish

---

53   Garcés, Introduction to *Cervantes in Algiers*, 6–10.
54   Garcés, *Cervantes in Algiers*, 148–77.
55   Sosa, II, 119, cited by Garcés, *Cervantes in Algiers*, 149.
56   Cathy Caruth, 'An Interview with Robert Jay Lifton, in *Trauma: Explorations in Memory*, ed. Cathy Caruth (Baltimore: Johns Hopkins University Press, 1995), 128–47, esp. 137; and Robert Jay Lifton, *The Broken Connection: On Death and the Continuity of Life* (New York: Basic Books, 1983), 163–78, cited by Garcés, 174.
57   Garcés, *Cervantes in Algiers*, 194–95. Cervantes had adopted and incorporated the name Saavedra into his own name some years after his return from Algiers, and his illegitimate daughter Isabel used it as her only surname until her marriage in 1606.

captivity play, which he himself perfected and enriched'.[58] I am particularly interested in how his stories, involving true love between Spaniards harassed by unwelcome attentions from amorous Muslims (their captors), could later be transformed into stories of love between Muslims (or former Muslims) and Christians.

Most importantly, Cervantes saw in his painful experiences of captivity rich source-material for spellbinding fiction or dramatic performance: even the horror could provide entertainment, just as in England Jacobean tragedy traded on terror and suffering. Furthermore, he understood the possibilities inherent in his material for eroticising slavery and cross-cultural connections. As Fuchs and Illika point out, Cervantes's 'combination of historical specificity and romance fancy was quickly imitated' in England and elsewhere.[59] Whether it was cathartic for Cervantes or not, he was dispassionate enough to hope that staging his (and his characters') experiences in captivity could be lucrative. According to his own testimony his plays, probably including his early treatment of North African slavery, *El Trato de Argel* (1582?) achieved at least modest success: 'todas ellas recitaron sin que se le ofreciese ofrenda de pepinas ni de otra cosa arrojadiza; corrieron su carrera sin silbos, gritas, ni barahúndas' [all of them (his plays) were represented without their being offered offerings of cucumbers or other throwing weapons; they ran their course without whistling, yelling, or pandemonium].[60]

Among the works which encompass captivity and slavery themes are comedies including *El trato de Argel*,[61] *Los baños de Argel*, *El Gallardo español* [The Spanish Gallant] and *La gran sultana* [The Great Sultana]; as well as several novels or novelettes including *La historia del cautivo* [the Captive's Tale] (a short story framed within *Don Quixote*); *La Galatea*, *La Española Inglesa* [the English Spanish Girl], *Persilea,* and *El amante liberal* [the Liberal Lover]. That

---

58   Cf. *Obras completas de Miguel de Cervantes Saavedra,* 3 vols., ed. Sevilla Arroyo and Antonio Rey Hazas (Alcala de Henares: Allianza/ Centro de Estudios Cervantinos, 1995), 3 vols., Vol. 2, xi, quoted in Garcés, *Cervantes in Algiers,* 129; and 'The Bagnios of Algiers' *and* 'The Great Sultana': *Two Plays of Captivity* [*by*] *Miguel de Cervantes,* ed. and tr. Barbara Fuchs and Aaron J. Ilika (Philadelphia: University of Pennsylvania Press, 2010), xiii. Cf. also Fuchs and Ilika, eds., *Two* Plays, xxvii.
59   Fuchs and Ilika, 'The Bagnios of Algiers' *and* 'The Great Sultana', xxvii.
60   Cervantes, *Ocho Comedias,* 1614, quoted and translated by Garcés, *Cervantes in Algiers,* 129.
61   The word 'trato' is almost untranslatable into English, as its meaning varies so much, according to its context. Some common translations are, 'matter', 'commerce', 'manner', and 'treatment'; Google Translate offers the variant 'deal'; and the title has even been translated as *Life in Algiers.* I have chosen to use only the original Spanish title of the play, so as to avoid having to restrict its meaning.

Cervantes drew not only on his personal experience, but on the existing corpus of Andalusi Spanish tales is evidenced by a scene in Don Quixote in which the knight, being wounded in his first sortie, imagines himself as Abindarráez on the field. Another scene in Don Quixote (Part 1, Chapter 47) references Fierabras, the Saracen [Muslim] giant who converts to Christianity and whose story we encountered earlier (Chapter 3). According to Villanueva, the text of Fierabras became very popular reading matter in 16th century Spain, with a prose version of the poem, composed by Nicolas de Piamonte, appearing in Seville in 1525.[62]

4 Cervantes's Works

4.1 El trato de Argel[63]

El trato de Argel is Cervantes's first venture into creating literature with a 'Moorish' theme and appeared within a few years of his return from captivity in 1580, probably about 1582. Little is known of its early performance history and it was not published until 1784. The play opens with a protracted soliloquy by Aurelio, a Christian who has been seized by pirates at sea and brought to Algiers as a slave, bemoaning his captive state and longing for death. He briefly mentions Silvia, from whom he has been parted and for whom he yearns. He does not know that she has also been captured and is living close to him in Algiers. The play has a symmetrical structure in that Silvia is loved by the Algerian King Yzuf (Yussuf), who is Aurelio's master, while Aurelio is courted by Sylvia's mistress, Zahara or Zara. But these mixed-faith and transcultural attachments are both aborted as both Christians resist the Muslims' advances, each one suggesting that for a Christian and a Muslim to love one another is improper. Both master and mistress appeal to their Christian slaves to intercede with the beloved but obdurate Christian on their behalf. Indeed, it is through this mechanism that the lovers meet.

Numerous details of the plot authenticate the setting: for example, one scene shows the slave market in the *zoco*, or square of Algiers, where members of a Christian family are separated and auctioned off individually. One of the

---

[62] Francisco Marquez Villanueva, *Fuentes literarias cervantinas* (Madrid: Gredos, 1973), 135.
[63] In the discussion which follows I have worked with two versions of the play: Miguel de Cervantes, *Obras Completas* (Madrid: Editorial Castalia, 1999), 827–850; and the work's translation into English, included in *The voyage to Parnassus; Numāntia, a tragedy; the commerce of Algiers / by Cervantes; translated from the Spanish by Gordon Willoughby James Gyll* (London: A Murray, 1870), 221–288. All subsequent references are to one or other of these texts.

family's young boys is required to show his teeth, to prove that he is healthy, before being sold. Also apparently credible are the boy's subsequent rapid conversion, under duress; his rejection of his older brother (still Christian) who tries to embrace him; the change of his name from the Spanish Juan to Muslim Soliman; the shedding of his shabby clothes for the rich brocade garments of a 'Turk', with a turban; and, finally, his new taste for North African food. Two historic figures appear in the text: Mamí, an Algerian, whose name is similar to that of Cervantes's own captor, the renegade Dali Mami and Saavedra, a minor figure whose name is also that of the author himself. But Cervantes makes the same (deliberate?) mistake as his mediaeval predecessors by suggesting in several places that the Muslims worship and pray to the Prophet Muhammad, rather than to God.

El trato de Argel is written in a heroic style with lengthy speeches and lamentations, and the personification of two abstract entities, Occasion and Necessity, in the manner of a Morality play. They are conjured up by Fátima, a sorceress and friend of Zahara, to tempt Aurelio to accept Zahara's advances and convert to her faith. He repeats many of their lines verbatim, or nearly so, and one can imagine them being spoken by an actor in a dazed monotone, suggesting that the characters are externalisations of his interior psychological impulses and that he is temporarily hypnotised by temptation. But at the end of the scene, he recovers his resolve to remain a Christian.

Repeatedly in *El trato de Argel,* Cervantes plays with the slaver-enslaved paradox. The power relations between Aurelio and Zahara are transformed by her unrequited feeling for him: as a free and wealthy Muslim woman living in a Muslim land, she ought to have dominion over Aurelio the foreign slave. But loving him as she does, she relinquishes all her advantage. This fact is not lost on Aurelio, who reproaches her for her inappropriate passion, reminding her of his servile status. She replies, 'El amor todo lo iguala' (828, line 115) [love maketh all alike] [1, 225]. In fact, love has converted her into a metaphorical slave to him, reversing the equilibrium between them. She confides in Silvia that she had witnessed the capture by pirates of a Spanish galley and saw:

> un cristiano que allí perdió la dulce
> y amada libertad, para quitarla
> a quien quiere rendirse a su rendido.

> [... a Christian who there lost his sweet
> and beloved liberty, only to take it
> from her who would surrender to her slave.]
> *El trato de Argel* II, 1259–61

Again, responding to Zahara's passion, Aurelio asks her, '¿Cómo queréis que yo entienda de amor en esta cadena?' (828, lines 157–58) 'how would you that I understood/In this chain aught of love?' [I, 226]. She offers to remove his chains if he will only love her, but he resists, saying that in losing his bonds he would be risking a greater servitude which would bind his soul: 'Quitando al cuerpo este hierro, cairé en otro mayor hierro, que al alma fatigue más' (828, lines 166–68). In other words, by keeping his physical chains, he retains his morally superior status as well as his spiritual freedom.

Izuf is similarly humbled by his unrequited passion for Silvia. His love, he laments, 'me ha hecho esclavo de mi esclava' (836, line 1085), ['is making me a slave for a slave maid'] (III, 1, 253). But like her Christian lover, Aurelio, Silvia maintains her dignity and refuses Izuf. She tells Zahara, to whom Izuf has given her, 'vuestra soy, señora mia' (837, line 1121), 'I am yours, my lady', and describes herself as 'Casada soy y doncella' (837, line 1131) 'Married I am [because she is promised to Aurelio], yet in the virgin state' (III, 1, 254). She belongs to no man but Aurelio, her only other 'owner' being another woman. Thus do both Christians retain the upper hand in relation to those who love them, psychologically reducing their 'owners' to the status of their slaves. However, the respect with which each Christian addresses his own master or mistress lends dignity to characters who might otherwise, because of their symbolic subjection to slaves, appear ridiculous.

The use of Muslim characters in the drama has given rise to a genre typing: the *comedias de moros y cristianos* which, as Carrasco-Urgoiti puts it, 'derived much of its appeal from a colorful portrayal of Moorish-Christian confrontation, and it emphasised the affinities and contrasts among the knights who on both sides of the frontier were supposed to have embodied the spirit of chivalry'.[64] But *El trato de Argel* is comic only in the sense that the main male protagonist, Aurelio, is freed at the end; most of the play's action is sombre and one could describe it as a tragicomedy. The implication is that Silvia also gains her freedom, although her absence from the last scene is puzzling. The play concludes with Aurelio rendering a hymn of thanks for his deliverance, and plea for pardon of his failings to the Virgin Mary. But given this is a work of fiction, the lack of a lovers' reunion and mutual rejoicing at the end leaves it curiously unfinished.

This play rewards lovers of the same religion and where love occurs across religious boundaries, it is castigated and thwarted. But the character of Zahara is painted in sympathetic colours: she is described as young, wealthy,

---

64 Carrasco-Urgoiti, *The Moorish Novel*, 138.

nobly-born, and very beautiful, and one scene between her and Silvia has the two women exchanging confidences about their respective loves (who are, of course, unknown to them at the start of the scene, one and the same man). Zahara is genuinely interested in Silvia, notwithstanding the latter's servile status: she is portrayed simply as a woman desperately in love and the atmosphere of the scene is intimate, as between equals and friends. At one point, she even offers to reject 'Mahomet', so as to serve love (and Aurelio) instead (829, lines 229–32; I, 228).

It is a short imaginative step to allowing the man whom the Muslim woman loves to love her in return, despite their religious differences, and for her then to convert to Christianity. This is indeed what happens in Cervantes's novella, *La Historia del cautivo,* and his later play, *Los baños de Argel,* in both of which the beautiful and amorous Algerian woman is re-shaped from being the author of sexual advances which the captive rejects, to being a much-loved woman and object of his desire, whom he goes on to marry.

4.2   *La Historia del cautivo/The Story of the Captive*

La Historia del cautivo is an early and vivid account which, like *Ozmín y Daraja,* is a self-contained, digressive story framed by a much longer work, in this case *Don Quixote Part 1.* The first part of *Don Quixote* was published in 1605, however Cervantes's biographer Jean Canavaggio, still widely considered a leading authority on the dramatist, and a modern editor, Donald McCrory, both believe *La Historia del cautivo* was written fourteen or fifteen years earlier, placing it much closer in time to the presumed composition of *El Trato de Argel.*[65]

La Historia del cautivo incorporates several features which we have seen in the mediaeval literature and which will also be common to many stories that will follow. They include love between a captive Christian man and a Muslim woman who is also, in her way, captive to a wealthy male (here it is her father, but in other stories it may also be a husband, etc), to her society, and to her religion. She appears, as though confined, at the top of a high building; in some stories this may take the form of a tower. She makes contact with the Christian by means of discreet signs, which he at first does not understand. They meet in a charming garden: in some stories, the captive is the gardener. The captive is befriended by the powerful Muslim to whom the woman is subject: in some stories the captive becomes the man's favourite. Finally, the heroine's conversion to Christianity is a standard outcome.

---

[65]   Canavaggio, *Cervantes*; *The Captive's Tale* (*La historia del cautivo*), ed. and tr. Donald McCrory (Warminster, England: Aris and Phillips, 1994), 51–52.

The hero, Ruy Pérez de Viedma, walking out one day on the roof of the house in which he is jailed, catches sight of a cane with a white handkerchief attached to one end being lowered from a high window opposite. It transpires the handkerchief contains gold and belongs to the daughter of a wealthy Muslim citizen, Zoraida, who had been secretly converted in childhood by a Christian woman slave of her father's, and as a consequence is determined to embrace Christianity publicly. Having fallen in love with Ruy Pérez from a distance, she also sees him as her means of 'escape' to a Christian land where she can live openly as a Christian. Gallantly, having learned (without first seeing her) of the woman's incomparable beauty, the Captive agrees to find a way of escape for them both and then to marry her. The account that ensues is essentially an adventure story in which the lovers manage to abscond amidst great dangers, during which they are forced to take Zoraida's father hostage, then abandon him on a distant shore. Renegades play an essential role in their flight. Eventually the lovers achieve their desires and are married.

La Historia del cautivo demonstrates the power of religion – and specifically, Christianity – that can drive a woman to desert her homeland, culture and people to join forces with a virtually unknown man and travel to a foreign country where she will live for the rest of her days. Once there, she must cast aside her Algerian Muslim past, including the garments she is still wearing when we first encounter her (*Don Quixote*, Chapter 37), as well as the customs and habits of thought formerly connected with Algiers. This however is her own free choice.

The character of Zoraida is illuminated by her dedication to the Virgin Mary, with whom she becomes associated. She repeatedly refers to the Virgin as 'Lela Marien'[66] and is herself addressed at one point as 'Lela Zoraida', but she corrects the speaker, telling him henceforth to call her María, the name she has chosen for herself.[67] When she and the now-freed Ruy Pérez arrive in Spain, she rides on a donkey, just as the Virgin Mary is said to have travelled, accompanied by Joseph on their way to Egypt. Just like their Biblical forbears, they find there is no room at the inn (they are then offered accommodation by one of *Don Quixote*'s other characters, Dorotea).

---

66   From the Arabic 'Lalla', equivalent to doña or señora, in the sense of 'lady', according to a textbook on Cervantes: *The Cervantes Encyclopedia*, ed. Howard Mancing (Westport, Connecticut, USA: Greenwood Press, 2004), 428.

67   Lela Zoraida is the name Ruy Pérez uses to address her when she and the captive first arrive at the inn of Juan Palomeque. Mancing points out that 'Lela Marien' and variants such as 'Lela Maria' are used in several other works of Cervantes, notably *Persiles and Sigismunda*, *Los baños de Argel*, and *La gran sultana*: Mancing ed., *Cervantes Encyclopedia*, 428.

These verbal and visual scriptural echoes, together with Zoraida's purity and fidelity to the Virgin Mary, as well as to the Captive and their mutual faith, make her an emblem of the Virgin. Garcés states that she is 'transformed into the very incarnation of the Virgin when the Captive calls her '*señora de nuestra libertad*' (lady of our liberty), which 'evokes one of the titles given to Mary as the protector of captives held by the Turks: "Nuestra Señora de la Libertad."'[68] McCrory finds an antecedent to Zoraida in the character of Floripas, whose name evokes not only flowers but also Easter, and who frees her father's Christian captives, rejects and betrays her father and her Saracen (Muslim) society, and converts to Christianity for the love of a Christian (see Chapter 2).[69] The association is strengthened if we consider that Zoraida and Zara/Zahra (variant names of the captive Don Lope's beloved in *Los Baños de Argel*) all derive from the Arabic 'zahra', meaning 'flower', just as Floripas's name evokes the Latin 'flores'.

As for the Muslim women's betrayals of their fathers, Sean di Renzo justifies Zoraida and by implication Floripas and the other mediaeval heroines who do as they do. Their behaviour, he says is fully in concord with the teachings of the Catholic church:

> the theology at the time does not see a grave sin in the actions of Zoraida. The Tridentine Catechism expounds on the meaning of 'Honor your father and mother' to include both the duty of parents to raise their children in the knowledge and practice of the faith and the duty of everyone to respect any legitimate civil authority. No Church official would claim that the Spanish Reconquest was a violation of Divine Law, since the Spanish fighters were freeing land from what Christians viewed as an illegitimate authority. Zoraida, then, was performing the same liberation 'por la religion verdadera, la verdadera libertad'. [70]

He adds,

> Christians are the only people who can expect to inherit eternal life (II, 8). God, then, would not mandate obedience to that which would lead one to hell, and therefore Zoraida must be able to free herself in order to save her soul. Church Father Saint Jerome says that 'the only loyalty in such cases [involving that which is contrary to God] is to be cruel',

---

68 Garcés, *Cervantes in Algiers*, 215.
69 McCrory, *The Captive's Tale*, 56.
70 Sean di Renzo, 'From Darkness into Light: The Baptism of Zoraida and the Council of Trent', *Romance Notes* 46:1 (2005), 3–11, 8.

and he cites Christ's commandment that 'if a man hate not his father and mother he cannot be my disciple' to extend the obedience of the Fourth Commandment to the God who 'is in the truest sense our Father' (Catechism; cf. Lk. 14: 26, Dt. 32: 6). Therefore, Zoraida is in fact breaking no commandment when she forsakes her biological father for the one whom Jesus taught his people to call 'Father' (Mt. 6:9).[71]

Trachtman also contrasts Zoraida with her forbears in mediaeval literature and Spanish *romances fronterizos* in that, whereas for them profane love leads to Christianity, Zoraida's conversion to the true faith is through spiritual love alone, her love for the captive being secondary.[72]

These comparisons infer differences in motivation between the late mediaeval writers and those of the Golden Age. The former wrote in a pre-Inquisition era, before the conquest of Granada by the Catholics, when the conflict between Christians and Muslims in Spain was essentially a competition for land, rather than ideology. Christian soldiers of fortune might fight together with Islamic armies, or vice versa, as in the case of El Cid who fought as a mercenary, now with Christian armies, now with Muslims against Christians, until finally he threw in his lot with the Christians to wrest Valencia from the Muslims, thereby winning the status of national hero of Spain.[73]

Mediaeval authors sought, among other aims to present entertaining tales of love with an intriguing ('Oriental') twist, to which motifs of love for a liminal 'other' lent an additional *frisson*. By contrast, Cervantes lived in an age obsessed by questions of faith as well as ethnic purity and driven to try to extirpate all manifestations of other religions and cultures in futile attempts to effect a 'cleansing of the blood' [*limpieza de sangre*]. The conversion of a Muslim to Christianity, if genuine, represented a triumph of the Christian faith over its rival, a victory in a bitter ideological struggle for what we might now call 'hearts and minds', as well as a political gain. A Muslim sincerely converted to Christianity was an enemy transformed into an ally who would never betray Spain to her Muslim adversaries south or east of the Mediterranean. In addition, her children and grandchildren would, in all probability, be raised

---

71   Di Renzo, 8.
72   Sadie Edith Trachtman, *Cervantes's Women of Literary Tradition* (New York: Instituto de las Españas en los Estados Unidos, 1932), 42.
73   Cf. Richard Fletcher, *The Quest for El Cid* (London: Hutchinson, 1989). El Cid's numerous shifts of allegiance are omitted from the famous *El cantar de mio Cid* (*The Song of the Cid*), which represents him as simply a Christian hero.

as devout Christians. On the other hand, a convert who may well marry into 'Old Christian' society introduces a problematic element of 'racial impurity'. Discussing a different but related branch of Spanish literature, Yiacoup points out the tensions that existed 'between desire and conflict', as she puts it, complicating any attempt at reductionist criticism of such texts. Yiacoup's subject is the frontier ballads of mediaeval Spain, including some included in the *Guerras civiles de Granada* discussed above. But her analysis is applicable to many other 'Moorish' texts.[74]

In this context it is important to note that, like the lovers in *Ozmín y Daraja*, and despite her devout Christianity, Zoraida remains culturally hybrid. The Captive's first encounter with Zoraida is when he sees her hand emerging from a high window: the hand is described as 'muy blanca' (very white) (82–83). He at first thinks Zoraida must be a renegade Christian 'a quien de ordinario suelen tomar por legítimas mujeres sus mesmos amos, y aun lo tienen a ventura, porque las estiman en más que las de su nación'. ('whom their masters ordinarily take as their wives and are glad to do so because they value them more highly than the women of their own nation': *The Captive's Tale*, 82–83). Zoraida's mother is not mentioned in the text, but the editor of *The Captive's Tale*, Donald McCrory, confirms that the real-life father of Zoraida, Agi Morato, had 'married the daughter of a Spanish woman' (83, Note 47).[75] In addition, Agi Morato, like so many prominent members of North African society, is a renegade from Europe: in this case Ragusa, a maritime republic on the Dalmatian coast (now Dubrovnik) which was officially Roman Catholic, but had Orthodox Christian, Muslim and Jewish minorities.[76]

In other words, Zoraida is 'ethnically' European and her eventual marriage to the Captive Ruy Pérez will be a union between 'ethnically' similar individuals. But she is only partly European, in that her father is a Muslim convert from a hybrid European state and one whose title Agi (Hajji) indicates that he has made the pilgrimage to Mecca, meaning that he is committed to his adopted

---

74   Şizen Yiacoup, *Frontier Memory: Cultural Conflict and Exchange in the Romancero fronterizo*, London: Modern Humanities Research Association, Texts & Dissertations Series, Vol. 87 (2013) 12.

75   See also, Jaime Oliver Asín, 'La hija de Agi Morato en la obra de Cervantes', *Boletín de la real academia española*, Madrid, XXVII (October 1947-April 1948), 245–339, 254–55. Regarding Agi Morato's wife, in relation to *Los Baños de Argel*, Asín cites evidence that Agi Morato's mother-in-law was a Mallorcan, captured in 1529.

76   Ragusa was repeatedly fought over, and came under the influence of various European powers but was, in Cervantes's time, an Ottoman protectorate. This helped it to retain its independence, while at the same time, its position straddling east and west, its shifting allegiances, and its religious minority groups, gave it a certain 'hybridity' of its own.

religion.[77] When Zoraida is first introduced into the story, she is ornamented with bracelets in the 'Moorish' style (82–83) and speaks only Arabic (88–89). Later we learn she has a smattering of the *lingua franca* of the region, a bastard mixture of Spanish, Italian, Portuguese and Arabic in which the European captives and the North African and Turkish-speaking citizens of Algiers all communicate (98–99). However, even after she has arrived in Spain, Zoraida continues to wear Algerian dress. Garcés, in an essay called 'Zoraida's Veil', is preoccupied with Zoraida's silence when she and the Captive arrive at the inn where Don Quixote and Sancho are lodged, as well as her ambiguity as a would-be Christian concealed behind a Muslim veil and adorned with 'Moorish *ajorcas* (bracelets)'. Garcés sees Zoraida as a 'cryptic' and cross-cultural 'sign' which confuses the character of Dorotea, observing her, and which:

> fluctuates between history and fiction, between the Spanish and the Arab cultures, between the Castilian and the Arabic languages, between the socio-economic language of power and the unspoken language of desire, in the indeterminacy which is best expressed by Dorotea's question to the Captive: '¿esta senora, es cristiana o mora?' [is this lady Christian or Moor?].[78]

Thus, although she will no longer be living as a Muslim, Zoraida still brings into her husband's life a flavour of the exotic 'other', which is yet the 'same' a perpetual reminder of the life he lived in the land of cultural and religious 'others'. It was a life of bitter hardship, but its association with Zoraida must also sweeten his memories of it and, in retrospect, ameliorate his whole sense of his life in Algiers.

When Zoraida and the Captive enter the inn, Ruy Pérez is described as wearing a blue cassock, shoes and hat. Sean di Renzo, quoting Joaquín Casalduero, observes that this colour symbolises 'purity and infiniteness'. Di Renzo then alludes to its 'aquatic connotations', saying that it 'prefigures and underscores the desired baptism of the captive's companion and the purity and eternal life she will inherit as a result'.[79] More specifically however, blue is the colour most often associated with the Virgin Mary, as depicted in centuries of western art. The Captive's blue costume to me suggests his congruence and compatibility with Zoraida and their shared commitment to the same ideal: that of the Virgin.

---

77 Cf. Canavaggio, *Cervantes*, 88; Oliver Asín, 'La hija', 252.
78 María Garcia Garcés, Zoraida's Veil: the Other Scene of the Captive's Tale', in *Revista de estudios hispánicos* 23 (1989), 65–98, 69.
79 di Renzo, 4.

La Historia del cautivo is linked thematically to both *El trato de Argel* and to *Los Baños de Argel*. But it is in other ways too suggestive of theatrical performance as, for example, when the captive Rui Pérez, winding up his autobiographical narrative, says of it, '...si es agradable y peregrina júzguenlo vuestros buenos entendimientos.' ['Whether it is pleasing and strange may your better judgment decide']. One is reminded of dramatic epilogues, when a character who has appeared in a play steps forward at the end of the action, sometimes onto an apron stage, to appeal to the audience to signal their approval (typically by clapping their hands) before they leave.[80]

4.3 Los Baños de Argel [*The Dungeons of Algiers*]

The play text of *Los Baños de Argel* was published in 1615, immediately after the expulsion of the last Muslims from Spain, but was probably written some years before that.[81] Whereas *La Historia del cautivo* begins *in medias res*, or even, so to speak, *ex post res*, with the captives having already escaped from Algiers and arrived safely in Spain, telling their story in retrospect, the action of *Los Baños de Argel* is chronological. It begins with a raid by Muslims and renegades on a Spanish coastal village, from which the residents are snatched, forced into waiting Algerine boats and thence taken in chains to Algiers. Significantly, the man in charge, the renegade villain Yzuf, tells how he was born and raised in the village where the incursion is taking place and, hence, knows his way around. Later he acknowledges that two of the captives are his own young nephews, while their abducted father is Yzuf's brother.

---

80   This device was popular in English drama of the period: e.g., at the end of Shakespeare's *Twelfth Night*, when Feste the clown assures his audience of the actors' intent to please; and in the closing lines of *The Tempest*, where Prospero appeals to his audience to 'set him free' by applauding the play.

81   *Los Baños de Argel* may have been written around 1607–08, or possibly even earlier in the 1600s, but in 1615 it was included among a group of Cervantes's plays, *Ocho comedias y ocho entremeses*. There is some dispute as to whether it was written before or after *La Historia del cautivo*; Fuchs and Ilika give a possible date of between 1601–05 for the play, which might put it before the novella (Cf., Fuchs and Ilika, 'The Bagnios of Algiers' *and* 'The Great Sultana', xxii); but Canavaggio states that *La Historia del cautivo* was already being written in 1590, which might place it before the play, although it was revised for inclusion in *Don Quixote*, Part I, in 1605: Cf. *Los Baños de Argel*, ed. Jean Canavaggio (Madrid: Taurus, 1984), 13. The editor of *The Captive's Tale*, Donald McCrory, believes the two Algerian captivity plays, *El Trato de Argel* and *Los Baños de Argel*, as well as the novella, were all written quite close to one another, chronologically (McCrory, *The Captive's Tale*, 49). I have placed my discussion of *Los Baños de Argel* after that on *La Historia del cautivo*, purely on the basis of their relative publication dates.

This play borrows elements from both *El trato de Argel* and *La historia del cautivo,* as well as Lope de Vega's play, *Los cautivos de Argel* (1599), which was itself inspired by Cervantes's *El trato de Argel.* In *Los baños de Argel*, as in *El trato de Argel,* two Christian captives, here named Don Fernando and Costanza are loved by two Muslims, Halima and her husband, the Algerian captain Caurali, respectively. Caurali tries to enlist the help of Don Fernando to further his suit. But, as in *El trato de Argel,* the besotted slave owner is unaware that his slave Don Fernando and the object of his affection Costanza had previously been betrothed to one another. As in *El trato de Argel* also, it is the captor's efforts to woo his beloved that restores the Christian couple to one another. At the same time Caurali's wife, Halima, falls in love with Don Fernando, whom she encounters just after she has confided in Costanza her sense of being subjugated to her husband: 'Sólo por estar sujeta/a mi esposo, estoy de suerte/que el corazón se me aprieta' (Act II) which Fuchs and Ilika translate as 'I am oppressed simply by being tied to my husband' (II, 31). But when Fernando is presented to her by her husband, she remarks 'Ahora esclavo recibo/que será señor después.' ['I take as captive one who will be my master...']. Ironically then, her new-found passion will lead her metaphorically from one form of enslavement to another.

But as in *La Historia del cautivo*, there is also a reciprocal and ultimately successful love affair between a captive Christian man, Don Lope, and a Muslim woman, Zahara or Zara. This is the same name as that of the rejected Muslim woman in *El Trato de Argel*, further emphasising the connections between the plays and the deliberate reversal, whereby a beautiful Muslim woman is at first disdained, but finally loved by a Christian captive. The heroine is the daughter of a rich man (again Agi Morato) and is betrothed to the heir to the throne of Morocco, Muley Maluco, whom she does not love. As in the novella, she has been schooled by a Christian slave woman and has a burning desire to become a Christian herself; the governess-slave, Juanita Rentería, now dead, is extolled for her matchless virtue by the renegade Hazén:

> Ella fue una gran matrona,
> archivo de cristiandad,
> de las cautivas corona;
> no quedó en esta ciudad
> otra tan buena persona.[82]

---

[82] This and subsequent quotations are taken from an online edition of the play, based on its original version: *Los Baños de Argel, en Ocho Comedias y Ocho Entremeses nuevas*

[She was a great matron,
a paragon of Christianity,
queen of the captives,
there's no one as good in this city now].[83]

Also, as with Zoraida in *La historia del cautivo,* Zara makes herself known to the Christian by lowering a cane, to which is attached a bundle: a tied-up handkerchief containing gold. The whiteness of the handkerchief which Zara dangles from her window matches her light-skinned ethnicity as well as her spotless character. The timing of the bundle's first appearance is significant: it occurs immediately after Don Lope and another captive called Vivanco have witnessed a dying captive being savagely beaten by the (Algerian) warden. Just as Vivanco is despairing in the face of such brutality, the remedy appears like a gift from a merciful God or from the Virgin Mary with whom Zara/Zoraida is associated. The metaphor of Zara as an emissary from God and emblem of the Virgin Mary is extended in the passages which follow. Don Lope observes that among the coins is a doblón (doubloon) 'que parece necesario paternóster del rosario' ['that's like the Our Father to this rosary'].[84] He also exclaims, '¿Qué maná del cielo es ésta? ¿Qué Abacuc nos vino a dar en nuestra prisión la cesta deste que es más que manjar?' ['What manna from heaven is this? What Habbakuk has come to our prison to give us this basket filled with something better than food?'].[85]

The second appearance of the cane with its attached bundle of money is once again glossed as a gift from divine providence, this time by Vivanco. An accompanying note is immediately understood by the captives, unlike the Arabic-language note in *La Historia del cautivo,* which required translation by a trusted renegade. This implies it is written either in the Algerian *lingua franca* or, more likely, in Spanish, the underlying suggestion being that Zara has learned the language from her Christian governess.

nunca representados, compuesta por Miguel de Cervantes Saavedra (Madrid: Viuda de Alonso Martín, 1615), ed. in electronic form by Vern G. Williamsen ,1997 (Act I); with electronic versions of Acts II and III by Vern G. Williamsen and J.T. Abraham, 2002. This version: http://cervantes.dh.tamu.edu/english/ctxt/comedias/banarg.html [accessed 21/4/2024] will take the reader to all three.

83 Fuchs and Ilika, *Bagnios*, 16.
84 In their English-language edition of the play Fuchs and Ilika point out that rosaries are often organised into 'decades' of ten beads representing 'Hail Marys' and a larger bead for the 'Our Father' (Cf. Fuchs and Ilika, 12, Note 17).
85 The English-language editors gloss this with a reminder that, according to the Latin Vulgate Bible, Habbakuk brought bread to Daniel in the lion's den (Fuchs and Ilika, eds., 13, Note 18).

That Zara clearly understands the mercenary nature of the society in which she and the captives live is demonstrated by her sending them money, before even informing them of her name or the nature of her business. She is in fact wooing Don Lope with her gold to gain his attention and to enable him and the others to ransom themselves, or bribe someone to help them escape. As before, the captives are starkly reminded of the dangers inherent in trying to flee. A Christian appears with bloody rags covering the sides of his head: he has had his ears cut off as a punishment for repeatedly trying to escape. These rags, evidence of savagery, may be contrasted to the immaculate handkerchiefs used by the heavenly Marian figure Zara for her gifts of gold.

Like Halima, Don Lope experiences his love for 'the other' as a kind of slavery:

> De cautividad sacaste
> el cuerpo que rescataste
> con tu liberalidad;
> pero más con tu beldad
> al alma yerros echaste.
>
> [Your generosity freed the body
> that you rescued from captivity;
> but your beauty
> has bound my soul in irons].[86]

In the final act, Don Lope tells Zara that 'soy, señora, un tu esclavo que te adora' ('I am a slave who adores you, mistress'), using the term 'esclavo' (slave) in both the metaphysical Petrarchan sense and the literal one. Later in the scene, and in an even greater extravagance of self-abasement, Don Lope tells Zara,

> vesme aquí a tus pies postrado,
> más tu esclavo y más rendido
> que cuando estaba aherrojado;
> por ti ganado y perdido,
> preso y libre en un estado'.
>
> [see me here prostrate at your feet,
> all the more your slave and more vanquished

---

[86] Act II. Fuchs and Ilika, *Bagnios,* 55.

than when I lay in chains;
lost and won by you, at once
imprisoned and free.] [87]

Because Zara is receptive to his love, Don Lope's enslavement, in contrast to Halima's, is a good one; it is also temporary, for his bride-to-be can soon be expected to obey him. His subjugate passion is acceptable, moreover, because he is a Christian man wooing a formerly Muslim woman who has already converted to Christianity and will in due course live in Catholic Spain. But Zara, meanwhile, acts to re-balance the power relations between them and protect herself from his passion, by steering her worshipper away from his secular desire back toward religion. She is the zealous convert, so devoted to her new faith that she tells him, 'soy tuya, no por ti, sino por Cristo' ('I am all yours, not for you but for Christ'). Her love for Christ, above all men, will arm her in her future marriage so that whatever Don Lope may feel or become, she will not be 'a slave to love'. As the more practical of the two, she reminds Don Lope that they must hasten to escape and not waste time making love as he would wish. Don Lope tells her he will leave the next day, but promises to return for her.

Paradoxically, therefore, while Don Lope exchanges the chains of a captive for the new chains of love, his beloved Zara will rid herself of the shackles she experienced as a woman by boldly creating a means of escape from her culture through her initiative towards a Christian, and by worshipping a 'higher cause' than a mortal man. Just as some women have historically escaped the bonds of marriage by taking holy vows, so too Zara finds refuge in religion, although she rejects outright celibacy. Her marriage to Don Lope will satisfy the demands of stage comedy for a happy marital ending; but by positioning Christ between herself and her husband, Zara is freeing herself from his potentially possessive grasp and the masculine authority with which he might otherwise rule her. Her last words in the play are when she tells Don Lope 'Ya no Zara, sino María me llamo' ['I am] Zara no more, I am María now'], emphasising her spiritual as well as semantic kinship with the Virgin.

As to Fernando and Costanza, there is dramatic irony in the relations between them and the Muslims who love them. Seeking reassurance that in wooing Don Lope she has made a sound choice, Zara asks Fernando whether in Spain people keep their promises and are loyal, even to their enemies; Fernando assures her they do:

---

87   Act III, Fuchs and Ilika, *Bagnios,* 86.

ZAHARA:	... dime, cristiano ¿en tu tierra hay quien prometa y no cumpla?
D. [FERNANDO]:	Algún villano.
ZAHARA:	¿Aunque dé en parte secreta su fe, su palabra y mano?
D. [FERNANDO]:	Aunque sólo sean testigos los cielos, que son amigos de descubrir la verdad.
ZAHARA:	¿Y guardan esa lealtad con los que son enemigos?
D. [FERNANDO]:	Con todos; que la promesa del hidalgo o caballero es deuda líquida expresa, y ser siempre verdadero el bien nacido profesa.

[ZARA:	... tell me, Christian, in your land is there anyone who makes a promise and does not keep it?
FERNANDO:	Perhaps some villain.
ZARA:	Even if he gives his faith, his word, and his hand in secret?
FERNANDO:	Even if the only witnesses are the heavens, which often reveal the truth.
ZARA:	And are they loyal to their enemies?
FERNANDO:	To everyone; for the promise of the noble or gentleman is a proven debt, and a well-born man pledges always to be true].[88]

Yet soon afterwards, both Fernando and Costanza are shown betraying their words to their captors – arguably their 'enemies' – by several times disobeying and lying to them. For example, when the Muslim couple find the Christians embracing, they do not hesitate to deceive their captors, pretending (during one of the play's several comic exchanges) that they are 'collecting embraces' to pass on to the two Muslims. In the context of gulling their captors, Costanza

---

[88] Act II; tr., Fuchs and Ilika, *Bagnios*, 36.

does at one point acknowledge that 'tarde se alza una afrenta', which the English-language editors translate as, 'dishonor shows up at the eleventh hour'. The editors/translators comment that although all editions of the text have Costanza speak this line, they believe it would make more sense spoken by Halima.[89] But I think Costanza is quietly admitting (possibly as an aside) that she and Fernando are committing perjury, however justified their actions may be considered in context.

The play ends with a tense, dramatic scene in which the Christians (including Zara) make their escape from Agi Morato's garden. The Muslims in love with Christians are fooled yet again by Fernando's ambiguously-worded reassurance. He and Costanza leave Halima behind, unaware that she is losing the man she loves. But, as in the novella, the two Muslim captors in love with Christians (here, Cauralí and Halima) are portrayed relatively sympathetically, in contrast to individuals such as the brutal Cadí and the foolish and bullying Christian Sacristán (Sexton) (*pace* McKendrick, who finds these two much less sympathetic than their forbears in *El trato de Argel*).[90] Inserted into the drama (and missing from the novella) is a comical and musical 'play within a play', which is put on by prisoners for entertainment and attended by both captives and captors. The preparations for the performance open Act III, but it is ended abruptly when news of a 'real-life' massacre of Christian captives interrupts the scene, quite suddenly converting the atmosphere from farcical comedy to sorrow. Fernando comments that 'siempre en tragedia acaban/las comedias de cautivos' ['captive plays always end in tragedy'].

∴

There are other significant differences between novella and play. For example, the novella's kidnapping and abandonment of Agi Morato on a distant shore is entirely missing from *Los Baños de Argel*, freeing the character of Zara from any possible taint of betrayal or cruelty toward a devoted father. In the play, her character has been sharpened to make her tougher and more resourceful than her counterpart in the novella. In one scene of the drama, she pretends to have been stung by a wasp as a pretext for lifting her veil so that Don Lope will see her beauty. Her feelings for Don Lope are ambiguous: for example, in

---

89 *Bagnios*, 61, Note 27.
90 McKendrick refers to Cervantes's attitudes toward the two as seeming 'paradoxically to have hardened with the passage of time'. Cf. Melveena McKendrick, 'Writings for the Stage', in *The Cambridge Companion to Cervantes*, ed. Anthony J. Cascardi (Cambridge: Cambridge University Press, 2002), 131–59, 140.

the novella, while Zoraida is no less devoted to the Virgin Mary than Zara, she is seen putting her arm affectionately round the captive's neck and walking alongside him with her arm still round him. When the captive kisses her hand, she does not withdraw it or admonish him. By contrast in the play however, Zara twice rejects Don Lope's attempts to kiss her hands and feet, citing her devotion to Christ and the urgency of their plans as excuses. She makes Don Lope swear his devotion and loyalty to her several times, but nowhere does she tell him she loves him. Finally, renegades, so important to the action of *La Historia del cautivo*, play minor roles in the drama.

Notably, all three of the main Muslims in the play were real historic figures of whom Cervantes would have known, and perhaps known personally. In real life, Agi Morato was indeed a wealthy, respected and well-connected Algerian, also known as Haci Murâd, whose beautiful daughter Zahara was educated by a Christian woman, Juana de Rentería, and who felt sympathy for the Christian captives and concern for their welfare.[91] Like her fictional character, she was indeed engaged to Muley Maluco (also known as 'Abd-al-Malik), sometime king of Morocco, but she also went on to marry him. He died in battle in 1578, at which she married another prominent Muslim, a renegade called Hassan Basha (or Pasha) Veneziano (one of the Captive's 'owners' in *La historia del cautivo*), who was governor-general, or 'King' of Algiers. She left Algiers in 1580 (the year of Cervantes's release from captivity), but her destination was Istanbul, not Spain,[92] and she never converted to Christianity. As we have seen, all events referred to above occurred during the time of Cervantes's captivity in Algiers (1575–80). The questions therefore arise: why did he, almost certainly knowing the girl's real history,[93] alter it so radically as to bring together the (formerly) Muslim woman and the Christian man, contradicting actual events? And why did he revise the materials he had gathered together for *El trato de Argel* to develop a play and a novella in which the love between Muslim (or former Muslim) and Christian is reciprocal, leading to marriage, rather than taking the form of unwelcome advances by Muslims to Christians?

Various theories have been put forward to explain Cervantes's choice of characters. Critics commonly quote the author himself describing his work as 'verdad e historia' ('truth and [hi]story'), that is to say, a free mingling of fact and fiction. Asín refers to it as a kind of mythmaking, born of wishful thinking.[94] In addition, Asín points out that some wives and daughters of prominent

---

91   Asín, 287–88.
92   Asín, 320.
93   Asín, 276, 281, and passim.
94   Asín, 287–89.

renegades in Ottoman lands were Christians in secret, making it plausible that Agi Morato's daughter, educated by a Christian slave, would be devoted to the Virgin Mary, would desire to be baptised in a Christian land, and would fix her aspirations on a (Christian) captive.[95] In this sense, although the romantic part of her story is clearly Cervantes's invention, it is grounded in factual circumstances. However, the choice of a Muslim woman, raised in a Muslim land as an emblem of the Virgin Mary is remarkable, even if she is secretly a Christian. In the drama, the Spanish captive and friend to Don Lope, Vivanco, pronounces that Zara is 'en obras cristiana, aunque en moro cuerpo mora' ('Christian in deeds even if moored in a Moorish body').[96] She is truly trans-cultural, a hybrid individual whose transfer to Christian society will enrich both it and herself.

The technique of merging fact and fiction suited Cervantes's literary purpose: to employ the names of real personages to enact his fictional schemes, lending his stories additional verisimilitude: what Asín calls, 'la técnica literaria de Cervantes ... de trabar lo fingido con lo real' ['Cervantes's literary technique of ... yoking together the artificial and the real'].[97] But, given that the captives in all three of the works discussed above may be understood as representing (to some degree at least) alter egos of their author, could it also be that the real-life Cervantes was indeed attracted to Agi Morato's daughter, whose name was Zahara? As noted above, Zahara was temporarily widowed when her first husband died in 1578. Could Cervantes at that time (or at any time) have had some kind of erotic relationship with Agi Morato's daughter in real life, a possibility to which Michael McGaha alludes?[98] Alternatively, Zahara's solicitude for the captives may have encouraged in Cervantes a fantasy of loving her; maybe quietly engaging in such wishful thinking helped him to withstand the rigours of his servitude and allay the despair he must have felt at the successive failures of his escape attempts.

In two of the three works cited (*La Historia del cautivo* and *Los Baños de Argel*), escape attempts are successful: further evidence, one might suspect, of past frustrated longings being converted into more palatable fictional and theatrical 'reality' in the present, since none of Cervantes's own real-life attempts to escape from Algiers succeeded, and he was only freed after being

---

95 Asín, 337.
96 Act II, Fuchs and Ilika, *Bagnios*, 51.
97 Asín, 196.
98 Michael McGaha, Review of Maria Antonia Garcés' *Cervantes in Algiers: a Captive's Tale*, *Cervantes: Bulletin of the Cervantes Society of America*, 23.2 (2003): 437–442, 440–41.

ransomed.[99] In the absence of any reliable verification of the author's frame of mind and motivations, speculation falls into the realm of intentional fallacy. But how else to explain Cervantes's re-engineering of the lives of such (in their own land) well-known people, several of whom (Agi Morato, Abd-al-Malik and Hassan Veneziano, for example) had diplomatic dealings with Spain?

At the end of the play *El trato de Argel* the male Christian protagonist Aurelio, having resisted the advances of the Muslim Zahara, is freed and can return to Spain. The inference is that his original, Christian lover, Silvia, will go with him and that once home, they will marry. But in taking the Muslim/Christian woman Zoraida/Zahara/Zara along, the male protagonists of *La historia del cautivo* and *Los baños de Argel* are carrying with them a memento of their traumatic experiences, events now transformed in retrospect by love and by religious conversion of the Muslim beloved which has also empowered the former captives. It is this which allows the male protagonist – and perhaps the author – to reinvent, or reinterpret the past, as an episode in which he has triumphed over adversity, conquering not only his own despair but also a woman of Algiers and, by extension, Algiers itself. The process is a healing one, aiding the re-fusing of the former captive's split parts and enabling him to reintegrate into his own society.

4.4　*El Amante Liberal* [*The Generous – or Liberal – Lover*]

El Amante liberal returns us to the world of Muslim corsairs and love between Muslim and Christian, although the main action takes place in Turkish-occupied Cyprus, rather than in North Africa. One of the *Novelas ejemplares* published in 1613, this tale begins *in medias res* with a Christian captive called Ricardo lamenting the fate which led to his and some other characters' kidnapping by Turkish corsairs from a garden in Sicily. Ricardo then narrates, as a flashback, the events which led up to this unhappy occurrence. The pattern in some ancient Greek novels of pirates carrying off individuals, thereby impeding the resolution of a love story, has already been mentioned. In his Preface to the *Novelas exemplares*, Cervantes testifies to his familiarity with the genre by referring to the Byzantine Heliodorus, author of the *Aethiopica*, with regard to his own work.

Cervantes here revisits the theme of an eroticised female 'other' who is in fact the 'same' as oneself, by virtue of having been born of Christian parents in a Christian land. Halima's 'otherness' as the would-be adulterous wife of the

---

[99]　In *El Trato de Argel*, the earliest of the three works under discussion, and the one closest in time to Cervantes's own freeing, the Captive is ransomed, as was Cervantes himself.

Muslim Cadí is erased when she moves back to a Christian country and reconverts to her native religion. But in the end Cervantes chooses to ally his hero with his longed-for and virginal lover Leonisa, who has remained Christian throughout the text, rather than with the renegade Halima. However, Halima is dignified through her reconversion and by her union with the reluctant renegade Mahmoud, consistently portrayed as a virtuous and faithful friend to the hero, so close as to be addressed by Ricardo as 'hermano' ['brother'] (154).

Hybrid identity issues permeate this work, with clothes functioning as complex and ambiguous signifiers. In Cyprus Leonisa appears richly dressed in Turkish costume, in which she is offered for sale. The clothes are described in exquisite detail: her dress is of green satin, liberally embroidered with gold and pearls, which also adorn her hair, wrists and ankles. The gold bracelets on her arms are just visible through the teasingly diaphanous silk of her sleeves. Initially, Leonisa is shown with a mask of crimson taffeta, which she removes to display the dazzling loveliness of her face. So bewitching does she appear that her would-be buyer (the Cadí) demands that the garments be included in her price, while her current 'owner' insists on being paid half as much again for them. Eventually, that price too is paid.

When, finally, the lovers are united and about to land in Sicily, Ricardo insists that Leonisa put on the beautiful Turkish costume once more. He too dons Turkish clothing, as do Mahmoud, Halima, and the members of their ship's crew, and in this fashion, they return home, briefly terrifying the people waiting on the shore to greet them. The implication is that Turkish trappings have become for the Christians part of a complex new identity: the wearers are, so to speak, 'performing' another religion and nationality, and proclaiming their 'foreignness' to their witnesses. The effect is to destabilise the widely-held ideal of '*limpieza de sangre*' [purity of blood]. As Fuchs expresses it:

> in Cervantes's texts ... depictions of characters who effectively perform another gender or another religion challenge the attempt to identify and categorize 'proper' Spanish subjects ... Even as Spain becomes increasingly intolerant of ethnic and religious difference within its population, these literary scenes of passing suggest the impossibility of drawing rigid boundaries between often indistinguishable subjects.[100]

Furthermore, this episode, as well as other 'multiple scenes of cross-cultural transvestism in "El amante liberal"', according to Fuchs, 'drive home the fluidity

---

[100] Barbara Fuchs, *Passing for Spain: Cervantes and the Fictions of Identity* (Chicago: Univ. of Illinois Press, 2003), 3.

between Christianity and Islam in the eastern Mediterranean'.[101] Regarding Leonisa in particular, it is clear that Turkish clothing shows her at her best: she is more beautiful dressed 'a la turque' than in western dress. But the resolution to the plot marries Old Christian to Old Christian and reformed renegade with reformed renegade, rather than bringing lovers together across any ethno-cultural divide.

4.5 La Gran Sultana [The Great Sultana] Doña Catalina de Oviedo (Published 1615)[102]

In this play we are transported to Turkey itself, although as Manuel Duran points out, it draws heavily on Cervantes's memories of Algiers.[103] Cervantes had never been to Turkey: as previously noted, he was ransomed from captivity just in time to prevent being transferred from Algiers to Istanbul, possibly on the very day of his intended departure.

In *La gran sultana,* Cervantes revisits his technique of mingling fact and fiction and using themes of 'exogamous' love (lasting devotion between people from different faith and social backgrounds), here Muslim and Christian, to devise a drama based on real-life circumstances, located in the eastern Mediterranean. The factual basis of the play is the marriage between the Sultan Amurates, or Murad III (1546–95) and a Venetian or possibly Albanian Christian woman slave called Safije (Sophie) [Figure 4.4].[104]

Safije, presented to Murad at the age of thirteen, became his chief consort and advisor and later '*Valide Sultan*' (mother of the sultan, or queen mother), which was a powerful position in its own right. Several times in *La gran sultana* the Sultan is referred to or addressed directly as Amurates, although his beloved Catalina, the gran sultana of the title, has a different name from the woman on whom she is modelled.

The historic Murad III was himself the son of a slave of Venetian Christian origin who, brought to the harem of Selim II, rose to become a Sultana (Nurbanu Sultan) and dominated both her husband and her son.[105] Murad's grandfather too, Suleiman ('the Magnificent': 1520–66), married his slave from what is now Ukraine. Alexandra Lisowska, better known as Roxelana, who also became known as '*Hürrem Sultan*' ('Sultan's joy'); and both Murad's son and

---

101   Fuchs, *Passing for Spain*, 76.
102   I have worked with the Fuchs and Illika edition of *Bagnios* and *La gran sultana*, noted above.
103   Manuel Duran, *Cervantes* (Boston USA: Twayne Publishers, 1974), 45.
104   Fuchs and Ilika, eds., *Bagnios*, XXV–VI.
105   Chew, *Crescent and Rose*, 494.

FIGURE 4.4 Safiye Sultan, also known as Valide Sultan (1550–1618), artist unknown. Image in the public domain
SOURCE: HTTPS://COMM ONS.WIKIMEDIA.ORG/WIKI/FILE: SAFIYE_SULTAN_L.JPG

grandson married Christian slaves. These women were all required to convert to Islam, but what is remarkable about Cervantes's play is that the eponymous heroine is allowed to retain her Christian faith throughout. The literary pairing of a Muslim man and Christian woman is also unusual in Christian literature: the Muslim (or at least nominally Muslim) character is most often female, who must convert to Christianity before the end of the story.

The reader/playgoer's first introduction to the Sultan is a glamourising reference to him in Act I, spoken by the renegade Roberto, as 'mancebo de buen talle,/y que, de gravedad y bizarría,/la fama, con razón,/puede loalle' ('a good-looking young man, justly famed for his poise and elegance'),[106] making him physically suitable to be consort to a beautiful heroine in a romantic comedy. In reality, contemporary portraits of Murad III show him as a heavily bearded and grim-faced individual, although not actually unattractive, and he is sometimes shown wearing a tall turban almost twice the height of his head.

---

106   Fuchs and Ilika, *Bagnios*, 102.

Amurates's closeness in age to Catalina is again highlighted in Act III, when the captive Madrigal sings a ballad narrating the history of Catalina's capture and placement in the harem. He recites that she was only ten years old at the time, while the Sultan was also 'mozo entonces' ('a young lad at that time').

A more sanguine perspective on the Sultan as a man capable of ruthless violence and arbitrary behaviour is subsequently revealed: when Catalina asks her protector, the eunuch Rustán, whether the 'Gran Señor' is a cruel man, Rustán responds, 'Nombre de blando le dan;/pero, en efecto, es tirano' ('They call him gentle, but he's really a tyrant').[107] And when Rustán later owns up to having concealed the girl for her safety, the Sultan justifies the eunuch's assessment of him by threatening him with death by fire if she does not live up to his description of her. When, at last, he has the lovely captive before him, the Sultan threatens both eunuchs with impalement, or worse, for being too mean in their praise of her (as well as, in Rustán's case, for having hidden her). Only when Catalina pleads for their lives does he relent, even offering to free the other captives in the dungeons.

Returning to their initial encounter, the Sultan announces thar he will marry Catalina, declaring her to be ruler of his world and of himself: he has, in effect, become a slave to his slave and does not care whether she is Muslim or Christian. Catalina counters this by insisting that she will never leave her Christian faith. Bluntly and somewhat crudely she berates him, arguing against the possibility of a mixed-faith marriage:

> ¿Dónde, señor, se habrá visto
> que asistan dos en un lecho,
> que el uno tenga en el pecho
> a Mahoma, el otro a Cristo?
> Mal tus deseos se miden
> con tu supremo valor,
> pues no junta bien Amor
> dos que las leyes dividen.
>
> [Where, my lord, has anyone seen
> two in a bed, one who holds
> Mohammed in his heart, and the other Christ?
> Your desires do not measure up
> to your supreme valor,

---

107 Fuchs and Ilika, *Bagnios,* 107.

for Love cannot bring together
two people divided by their faiths]. [108]

The Sultan's answer is surprising: he declares Catalina to be his present and future equal, complicating this notion by suddenly kneeling at her feet and saying that he is humbled there, while she is raised high. She asks for, and is granted, three days' grace before reaching any decision. Act I ends with her prayer to God for support.

Like the heroine converts Zoraida and Zahra of *The Captive's Tale* and *The Baños of Algiers* respectively, Catalina is associated as a figure of piety with the Virgin Mary to whom she also prays and to whom the Muslim Sultan similarly refers as 'Lela Marien' [Arabic for Lady Mary]. The link between Catalina and those other heroines is reinforced later in Act III when one of the captives relates how she resisted attempts to change her name to Zoraida. While there is no question of his ever converting to Christianity, the Sultan expresses respect for the Virgin Mary, describing her as sacred to Muslims as well as Christians.

The Sultan's enslavement to Catalina is referred to repeatedly in the play in various contexts and by different people. Rustán describes him as being ruled by Catalina (Fuchs and Ilika *Bagnios*, 145), while the Sultan himself sees his subjection as entirely reasonable, explaining to the eunuch Mamí,

> el Amor, cuyas hazañas alabo
> tendiéndome por su esclavo
> no me deja ser señor
>
> [... love has taken possession of me,
> has me as his slave
> and does not allow me to rule]
> FUCHS AND ILIKA, *Bagnios*, 153

Again in the course of his narrative song before the Sultan in Act III, Madrigal refers to Catalina as having defeated and overcome the ruler, treading on the 'indomable' ('indomitable') neck of the Ottoman lion. Later in the scene another musician theatrically adopting the Sultan's persona sings how he would rather be Catalina's slave than command a thousand empires, while Catalina herself literally dances to the same tune.

---

108   Fuchs and Ilika, *Bagnios*, 118.

As to the Sultan's declared subjugation to his slave mistress, Paul Lewis-Smith points out the incongruity of his stance: '[Cervantes] presents the Sultan as *gran señor*, an institutional role whose salient properties, exceptional majesty and worldly authority, radically contrast with the Sultan's servitude as a lover'.[109] My own assessment is that the text shows the Sultan's subjection to be entirely notional and therefore also readily adjustable or even reversible, for when, toward the end, he announces that he is freeing all the captives and Catalina kneels at his feet in gratitude, he tells her to rise, making it quite clear that the general liberation does not include her. He uses the spurious and paradoxical argument that since she commands him as if she were Allah, he cannot allow her to leave (*Bagnios*, 157). Significantly, she does not respond. We can imagine her heart sinking with her dawning realisation that she will never be able to leave, so that even to request freedom would be futile and probably dangerous. If the Sultan were really subject to her command and striving to please her, his best means would be to free her and allow her to go home to her own people, unlikely though this would have been in reality.[110] But he places his own gratification above her needs, indulging an erotic fantasy of his own submission and couching his decision in exaggerated, mock Neo-Platonic terms [... love ... has me as his slave ...], all the while maintaining absolute authority.

The power balance between the Sultan and Catalina may be contrasted to that between the lovers in the mediaeval *Aucassin et Nicolette* (Chapter 2). In the earlier work, the (Muslim) woman's supremacy over her lover is inevitable given her superior courage and ingenuity, as well as being an aspect of life in the topsy-turvy lands in which the poem is set. In *La gran sultana* the Sultan's 'enslavement' to Catalina is an imaginative fiction of his own making: qualified and, when tested, shown to be false.

Catalina's own feelings for the Sultan are unclear, as is the point at which she and the Sultan are married and their union consummated. Initially, she repeatedly resists his advances on the stated grounds that she will not relinquish her Christian faith, while he insists he will not require this of her anyway. In the final act, when her union with the Sultan is confirmed, she has changed from Turkish dress into 'Spanish' clothes and has clearly not apostatised. But

---

109 Paul Lewis-Smith, 'La gran sultana doña Catalina de Oviedo: A Cervantine Practical Joke', *Modern Language Studies* 17 (1981), 68–82: https://doi.org/10.1093/fmls/XVII.1.68 [accessed 10/4/2017].

110 Hegyi points out that, in reality, no women were ever freed from a sultan's harem, still less so in the case of a woman who had attained the status of a *kadin*, or official concubine (Hegyi, *Cervantes*, 204).

earlier, when her captive father challenges her for being lax in opposing the Sultan, she defends herself, calling the Sultan 'descreído, ministro de mi tormento' ('unbeliever, minister of my torment') and saying she had not 'pacifico' (peacefully) submitted but had repeatedly resolved to kill herself, rather than give in to the Sultan's demands. However, finding that her scorn had made him even more zealous she had, reluctantly and anxiously, given in to him in order to preserve her 'nombre de cristiana' ['name of a Christian']. She makes no mention of having any feeling for the Sultan other than disdain (145–46).

Only toward the end when the Cadí is urging the Sultan to take other mistresses so as to ensure the succession, does Catalina reveal that she is already three months pregnant, presumably with a prospective male heir. Then she reproaches the Sultan for having only 'tibio amor' ('lukewarm love') for her and professing to love him, she challenges him to dismiss the other women:

> Échalas de ti, señor,
> y del serrallo al momento:
> que bien merece mi amor
> que me des este contento
> y asegures mi temor.
> Todos mis placeres fundo
> en pensar no harás segundo
> yerro en semejante cosa.
>
> [Cast them away from you, my lord,
> and from the seraglio this minute:
> for my love well deserves
> that you grant me this satisfaction
> and reassure my fears.
> All my pleasure depends
> on believing that you won't make another
> such mistake].[111]

But, given her confession to her father it remains uncertain just how genuine is Catalina's profession of love and on what her pleasure is truly based, other than the hopes of freedom from persecution and fear of her rivals, as well as the unpredictability of her husband.

---

111   Fuchs and Ilika, *Bagnios*, 165.

How Cervantes acquired his apparent knowledge of the Ottoman court is unclear. Mas suggests possible oral sources, for example, talk among the captives of Algiers regarding Sultan Murad III's love affair with his wife.[112] Hegyi also cites an abundance of contemporary Italian writing by former slaves of the Turks and others.[113] Catalina's uncompromising Christianity, which leads her to proclaim that she would rather die a martyr's death than give up her faith is dismissed by many critics as inconceivable in reality. In response, Hegyi points to the historic presence of Christian women in the Sultan's harem and the Sultan's own religious toleration to argue for possible verisimilitude in her staunch adherence to her faith. He even speculates that Murad III, under the influence of his Christian mother, may himself have been secretly baptised, and was, in any case, very likely to have been sympathetic to Christians.[114] The atmosphere in Constantinople [sic], he adds, was 'considerably more tolerant' than that in North Africa.[115]

∴

A half comical, half ironic parallel to the love of the Sultan for Catalina is presented in scenes involving the captive Madrigal, whom Fuchs and Ilika describe as an 'authorial figure', in other words another alter ego for Cervantes himself.[116] Madrigal has in his *persona* aspects of the *gracioso* (comic) and *pícaro* (rascal or rogue) characters from Spanish literary tradition as he relentlessly mocks and deceives those around him and, through cunning, extricates himself from numerous potentially lethal (to him) situations.

In a more serious vein, Madrigal declares himself to be in love with an Arab woman, to whom he feels so bound 'con nuevo cautiverio y nuevas leyes, ['in a new captivity and new laws']'[117] that twice he rejects the opportunity to obtain his liberty and leave Turkey. Lottman points out that 'In Madrigal's cross-cultural love-making, he resembles both Catalina and the sultan'. But his 'freedom and mobility throughout the cultures of Islam, Judaism, and Christianity'

---

112   Albert Mas, *Les Turcs,* Vol. I, 342 and 349; Hegyi, *Cervantes and the Turks,* 23 and 34–35.
113   Hegyi, 27–31.
114   Hegyi, 66–74.
115   Hegyi, 78.
116   Fuchs and Ilika, *Bagnios,* xxv. And cf. McKendrick, '…the creative jester within the play [Madrigal] is after all the creating jester outside it [Cervantes himself]',142.
117   Fuchs and Ilika, *Bagnios,* 112.

contrast radically with our initial image of Doña Catalina, who is compared to 'a rose in a walled garden',[118] defined by her confinement as a slave.

Found out in their 'crime', Madrigal and his lover are separated: she to be imprisoned and he to face death, unless he will convert to Islam and marry her. He firmly rejects this option, declaring that apostasy and marriage are 'dos muertes' [two deaths] so that paradoxically by adhering to his religion, he retains more freedom, even if facing death. But Madrigal reveals that he has no intention of dying and proceeds to extricate himself from his predicament through trickery and disguises, persuading the gullible Cadí (judge) that he understands the languages of birds and animals and can teach the Sultan's elephant to speak Turkish. Several episodes of high comedy ensue before Madrigal gains his freedom.[119]

Scenes involving Madrigal function almost like *entremeses*, farcical interludes, which lighten the otherwise predominantly sombre and intense main action. One episode features some musicians who join Madrigal and Rustán in preparing a musical entertainment to be performed before the Sultan and Catalina. Their jocular banter is punctuated with expressions of fear at the torture which the Sultan could inflict upon them if they put a foot wrong. A seemingly casual exchange in which the Sultan asks Madrigal to identify his and the other captives' skills ends on a note of bleak realism. Telling the Sultan he is a town crier and the other captives include a musician and a tailor, Madrigal asks the ruler whether he would prefer a smith, shipbuilder, or an expert in gunpowder or artillery. The Turk responds that he would value and reward such skills above all others, to which Madrigal replies knowingly, 'Bueno;/en humo se nos fuera la esperanza/de tener libertad' ['Well, and there would go our hopes of freedom']. This reflects the practical reality which meant that any captive known to possess skills which could be useful to their Muslim masters in warfare, or for their endless construction projects, would never be allowed to leave.[120]

∙∙∙

---

[118] Maryrica Ortiz Lottman, '*La gran sultana*: Transformations in Secret Speech', *Revista Cervantes* Vol. XVI, No. 1 (Spring 1996), 74–90, 76.

[119] Hegyi notes that, after his initial declaration of his love for the anonymous Arab woman, Madrigal shows no further concern for her, and speculates that the pardon given to him may not have been extended to her (Hegyi, 57–58).

[120] Cf. Canavaggio, *Cervantes*, 80.

The play ends with general rejoicing and Madrigal, now finally liberated, boasting of his plans to become a poet on his return to Spain, one of his first prospective topics being to tell the story of the superlative Christian Sultana Catalina de Oviedo. Lewis-Smith interprets this as evidence that the entire play is in fact Madrigal's fictional creation and a practical joke played by Cervantes on the audience.[121] But of all the Muslim-Christian relationships featured in Cervantes's works, and indeed all those we have considered so far, this relationship is the most complicated, ambiguous and troubling, with the male lover's supposed subjection to the woman shown to be a flamboyant expression of artistic licence rather than reflecting any kind of truth, while the woman's feelings are unclear, and her actions probably dictated as much by duress and expediency as by any genuine sentiment of love. In the context of Christian literature she remains, moreover, a paradoxical figure: Christian wife to a Muslim Sultan who rules over Muslim lands, while she reverts to wearing her Christian clothes.

Although history shows that marriages between Ottoman sultans and Christian women could succeed, it was usually within the framework of the woman converting to Islam. Cervantes, writing in early 17th-century Spain just before the final expulsion of the Moriscos,[122] would hardly be likely to advocate such a conversion, no matter how enlightened or 'maurophile' he may have been otherwise. A number of critics including Hegyi have praised the supposed toleration of Cervantes's Sultan and the openness of the society he rules, as well as Cervantes's own liberality as author. In the 21st century, we are increasingly accustomed to seeing mixed-faith and mixed-race marriages. However, I believe that Cervantes's insistence on the woman's retaining her Christian faith does not constitute a 'happy ending', but rather an awkward resolution to a thorny dilemma. In addition, the reasons she gives her father for accepting the Sultan's advances suggest an ending which is for her pragmatic, but far from 'happy'.

5   Other Cervantine Texts

Cervantes returned repeatedly to the topics of captivity, religious difference, and Christian interactions with Muslims. Some of his other works incorporating captivity themes are set in non-Muslim lands: *El Celoso extremeño*

---

[121]   Lewis-Smith, '*La gran sultana*', 71.
[122]   Although not published until 1615, among the *Ocho Comedias*, *La gran sultana* is generally thought to have been written no later than 1608.

(*The Jealous Extremaduran*) for example takes place in Seville, where the Extremaduran of the title locks up his young wife in an attempt (vain, as it transpires) to ensure her fidelity and to keep her from harm; however, religion plays no part in this tale.

Religious difference is important to *La Española inglesa* (*The English Spanish Girl*) which is set partly in Protestant England, to which the young Spanish girl of the title, Isabela, has been brought following her capture in battle. But the principal religious tension here is between Protestants and Catholics, including a number of English Catholics as well as Spanish, rather than between Christian and Muslim although, true to his preoccupations with Muslims and captivity, Cervantes interrupts his narrative by having his hero, Ricaredo, captured at sea and taken to Algiers. From there he is ransomed and returns in captive's clothing only just in time to prevent his heartbroken mistress from taking the veil.

In this work a metaphor of slavery echoes the actual confinement experienced by both protagonists. In a twist recalling the Persian story, *Yusuf and Zulaikha*, Ricaredo reaffirms his love for Isabela when she is temporarily deprived of *her* beauty after being poisoned by a jealous woman at court, on the grounds that he can still love her virtue. Isabela offers herself to Ricaredo as his slave when he declares his enduring love for her, despite the loss of her beauty. Just as Zulaikha is restored to beauty by the grace of God and through the love of Yusuf, so too does Isabela, loved by Ricaredo and recovering from her toxic ordeal, fully regain her beauty – though without the stated help of Providence. The resolution of Cervantes's story pairs 'like' with 'like' in that Isabela, being Spanish, is Catholic, while Ricaredo, though English, is from a recusant family and the couple end up living in Catholic Spain.

5.1   El Gallardo Español [the Gallant Spaniard], *Published 1615*

This play was published among the *Ocho comedias y entremeses;* in it, Cervantes returns to the subject of love of a Muslim for a Christian, but the couple are not brought together at the end.[123] The play is situated in the *presidio* of Oran, a Spanish outpost of North Africa, which he himself had visited after his release from captivity in Algiers. The action takes place as the fortress is being besieged by Muslim forces (based on an historic assault in 1563) and the play, whose title refers to the suggestively named 'hero' Fernando de Saavedra, is ideologically

---

123   Line references are to the online edition, https://www.cervantesvirtual.com/obra-visor/el-gallardo-espanol--0/html/ [accessed 21/4/2024].

situated somewhere between the courtly traditions of mediaeval Christian chivalry and the Muslim code of honour.

Fernando is admired by two women: the Muslim Arlaxa and the Christian Doña Margarita, who disguises herself as a man in order to search for him. Neither woman has ever met him and only know of him through his reputation as a valiant soldier. Arlaxa is in turn loved by the Muslim Alimuzel, who describes her as 'una reina de la hermosura' [queen of beauty], to whom he is a humble slave (I, line 165). Overwhelmed with curiosity about don Fernando and desiring to see him, Arlaxa urges Alimuzel to challenge him to a duel. But Fernando's superior captain, Don Alonso de Córdoba, forbids him to take part, seeing it as pointless and risky, and reminding him that his individual desires must be subordinated to the military cause and the king.

Fernando defies the order, defects to the Muslim side under a false name and, to Arlaxa's astonishment, asks to be treated as her Christian captive. He even dresses as a Muslim and promises Arlaxa his protection, should her camp be attacked by Christians. As Anne Fastrup points out, at this point he evidently prefers a position as Arlaxa's slave to remaining Don Alonso's subject.[124] He is joined there by Doña Margarita, who has followed him in her masculine disguise and contrived also to be enslaved by Arlaxa. Don Fernando takes the Muslim side in battle and even prepares an attack on his fellow-Christians. But at last, quite precipitously, he reverts to his true identity and fights with the Christians in order to defeat the North Africans and the Turks, thereby earning forgiveness from his superiors for his previous misdemeanours.

Don Fernando's allegiances, motivations, and his sense of identity have all been scrutinised by critics. William Stapp, for example, considers him changeable and inconstant, preoccupied only with appearances, while Hughes sees his defection and the acts surrounding it as 'a case of misplaced honour', finding the character selfish and petulant. Casalduero, on the other hand, assesses him as a quintessential Spanish hero, while Minni Sawney, following Edward Friedman, views Don Fernando's actions as a search for his individuality in the face of a controlling and conforming system; she describes the soldier as cosmopolitan.[125]

---

124   Anne Fastrup, 'Cross-cultural Movement in the Name of Honour: Renegades, Honour and State in Miguel de Cervantes's Barbary Plays', *Bulletin of Spanish Studies: Hispanic Studies and Researches on Spain, Portugal and Latin America*, Vol. 89, Issue 3 (2012), 347–67, 353.
125   William A. Stapp, '*El gallardo español*: La fama como arbitrio de la realidad', *Anales Cervantinos* 17 (1978), 123–36, 129; Gethin Hughes, '*El gallardo español*: A Case of Misplaced Honour', *Bulletin of the Cervantes Society of America* 13.1 (1993), 65–75; Joaquin Casalduero, *Sentido y forma del teatro de* Cervantes (Madrid: Aguilar, 1951), 33; Minni Sawhney, 'Cervantes's Cosmopolitan *El Gallardo Español* During an Earlier Clash of Civilisations',

Questions of identity and true loyalties pervade the play. Encountering him in battle the Christian Guzman confronts Don Fernando, asking him, '¿sois ya de Cristo enemigo?' ['Are you now an enemy of Christ?], although Don Fernando assures him he is not, 'Ni de versa, ni burlando' ['neither in reality nor in jest'] (II, 652–53). And yet, he becomes confused as to where his real honour lies: as Fastrup puts it, 'Desiring to maintain his reputation and pursue recognition among the Moors, Saavedra has at this point incorporated so much "Moorishness" that he is no longer able to distinguish between his two identities'.[126] While in the Muslim camp Fernando befriends Alimuzel and the promised duel between them never actually takes place. But when at the end Fernando's commitment to the Christian side is clear, Alimuzel reproaches him, calling him 'amigo enemigo' [friend/enemy] (III, 645) and tells him that he is neither true Moor nor true Christian, but 'moro fingido/y cristiano mal cristiano' ['a feigned/false Moor and a bad Christian'] (III, 678–79).

And so, finally, Muslim is united with Muslim (Arlaxa and Alimuzel) and Christian with Christian (Doña Margarita and Don Fernando), restoring the social order. It is as though Don Fernando moved to the brink of transmutation, to be merged into the world of the 'other' and possibly union with a Muslim woman, but then stepped back to the safer, familiar world of Christian society. Like his protagonist, Cervantes has, it seems, thought better of mingling the two faith-cultures in favour of a more conventional outcome in which each character unites with a member of his or her own culture, rejecting the lure of hybridity. But the play humanises and validates its 'Moorish' characters and, to a degree, their cause. And interestingly, as Hughes points out, neither of the principal Muslims is required to convert to Christianity.[127]

6   Summary

Let us now reconsider Cervantes's output in the context of his younger and older contemporaries. The first of the works to offer portraits of Muslims as participants in matters of romantic love was *El Abencerraje* (1561). Here, as we have seen, the idealised lovers are both Muslim and they are eventually united

---

in *Theatralia: El teatro de Miguel de Cervantes ante el IV Centenario*, ed. Jesús G. Maestro (Vigo, Spain: Mirabel Editorial S.L. and Vanderbilt University, 2003), 167–175; Edward H. Friedman, *The Unifying Concept: Approaches to the Structure of Cervantes's 'Comedias'* (York, S.C.: Spanish Literature Publications Company, 1981).

126   Fastrup, 354.
127   Hughes, '*El gallardo español*, 74.

with one another; the Christian knight Rodrigo de Narváez, by interrupting the progress of their love, is an enabler and essential participant in the plot concerning them, but he is not involved romantically with Jarifa. Cervantes in *El trato de Argel* (ca. 1582) first brings into play the idea of Muslims in love with Christians, but these feelings are not reciprocated and so no union across religio-cultural boundaries is possible.

It is in *La historia del cautivo* (1589 or 1590?) that the idea of love across these margins is introduced, together with the conversion of the formerly Muslim woman to Christianity, followed by Pérez de Hita's *Las guerras civiles de Granada* (1595), where the Andalusi queen converts to Christianity and marries a Christian knight. In *Ozmín y Daraja* (1599) the lovers convert from Islam to Christianity but are married to each other and neither one to an 'Old Christian'. It is Cervantes who, once again, unites lovers across religio-cultural boundaries in *Los baños de Argel* (1607–08? Printed 1615). Again, however, the woman has already converted before the play begins and it is as a Christian that she marries her Spanish lover. Finally, *La gran sultana* (1615) breaks new ground in bringing together a Muslim man and a Christian woman who retains her faith at the end: it is thus a true 'mixed marriage' resolution, although, as I have suggested, it may not be a happy one as far as the woman is concerned.

We do not know for certain when *La historia del cautivo* was written or – if the conjectured date of ca. 1590 is correct – how widely it was known before being published as part of *Don Quixote* in 1605. But it is clear that it is in his later work that Cervantes unites lovers from disparate backgrounds. Most striking are the ways in which *La historia del cautivo* and *Los baños de Argel* reorganise the setting and much of the material of *El trato de Argel* in service now of uniting the captive hero with an Algerian woman, rather than a woman of his own country. Thus whereas the overtures of the Algerian woman of *El trato* were deeply unwelcome to the hero, with much of the action concerning his avoiding and outwitting her, in the two later works the woman's approaches are not only welcome but much desired.

Given the historical events that have intervened between publication of the first of these works and the two later ones: the growing suspicion and fear of Moriscos in Spain, leading to their expulsion from 1609 onwards, Cervantes has made his two later heroines Christian from the outset. They remain however women of another culture and country to that of the hero. The texts inscribe not only their subjects' attraction for one another across cultural lines, the powerful and erotic 'lure of the other', but also their spiritual kinship, overriding their differences. Moreover, even where the protagonists marry into their own culture and faith, the texts delineate the extent to which what Yiacoub calls 'cultural exchange' has taken place: for example in the 'Moorishness' of

Fernando, in *El Gallardo español*, and the cross-dressing into 'Turkish' costume of the Christian lovers returning home in *El amante liberal*.[128] The further away Cervantes is from the original defeat of the Muslims in 1492, the more willing he is, it seems, to create love affairs across religio-cultural boundaries.

Both these models of Cervantes: the 'like with like' pattern and the 'like with converted (or about to convert, or as in *La gran sultana* not converted) other' resonated with future generations of writers who adopted one or other of these patterns, just as Cervantes himself had borrowed from earlier writers. Above all, the twin ideas of captivity and romantic attraction between lovers of different faith backgrounds, especially Muslim and Christian, proved irresistible to generations of writers and readers into the 21st century.

•••

7 Cervantes's Literary Heir: Lope de Vega

Following Cervantes, all the major Golden Age dramatists of Spain, but especially Felix Lope de Vega, used 'Moorish' settings in plays such as *El cerco de Santa Fe* (1587?-98?) and *El remedio en la desdicha* (published 1624 but probably written much earlier, around 1596), based on *El Abencerraje*, as well as the novel, *La desdicha por la honra* (1624). Lope de Vega's *Los cautivos de Argel* (ca. 1598) is based on Cervantes's *El trato de Argel* and its plot is virtually identical to that of the earlier play, with lovers now entitled Leonardo and Marcela, both of whom are also loved by Muslim captors. In *La envidia de la nobleza*, Lope de Vega focussed on the hatred and rivalry between the Zegries and the Abencerrajes in Nasrid Granada. *La mejor luna Africana*, written by a total of nine authors including Pedro Calderón de la Barca, uses the trial of the Granadine queen as its theme. Muslims who convert to Christianity are a recurring feature of these works.

Lope's *La remedia en la desdicha* [*The Remedy for Misfortune*] is especially pertinent to our purposes in that it takes a minor element of the original Abencerraje story, Rodrigo de Narváez's love for a married woman, which had only been hinted at through hearsay in the original, and develops it as an integral part of the play, a plotline which parallels the matter of Abindarráez and Jarifa. And whereas in the original by Villegas and others the object of Narváez's love is a Christian, here the beloved woman is a beautiful 'Morisca', a native of Coín, called Alara. Narváez asks a recently captured Muslim called

---

128 Yiacoub, *Frontier Memory*, introduction, and passim.

Arráez to write to her in Arabic on his behalf. The letter is taken to her by the bilingual soldier Nuño, who also dresses as a Muslim in order to enter the city. Alara, recognising her husband's handwriting, hastens to ransom him.

Eventually, Narváez learns that the woman he loves and who by now loves him, is married to Arráez, who has been agonising over her welfare without realising that he has been writing to his own wife on behalf of a would-be lover, and risks being the architect of his own cuckoldry. Narváez generously frees Arráez and gives up his attempts on Alara, much to her regret. She reproaches him,

> ¡Que me deprecies ansi!
> ¡Oh riguroso cristiano!

> [How in this way do you diminish me,
>   Oh stern Christian!]

On discovering that Narváez has been his rival, Arráez misinterprets the situation and at first attempts to kill the alcaide [governor], and is then intent on murdering his wife when Narváez and Nuño arrive in time to save her. Narváez takes the husband away, leaving Alara alone with neither husband nor lover. But by then she has converted to Christianity, leaving open the possibility that she and Narváez will get together, although this is not stated.

In Lope's treatment we see an aspect of 'morofilia' or 'maurofilia' at work, in the sympathetic portrayals of Arráez and Alara in early scenes of the play, written at a time (ca. 1596) when discussions about expelling the Muslims from Spain were well underway. But these representations of the two Moriscos are tempered by Alara's subsequent willingness to cuckold her husband and the latter's descent into violence. The only character to emerge unscathed from the bitter triangle is Narváez, who nobly resists the strong temptation to sin and takes control of a tortured situation in order to resolve it in a manner which is presented to the audience as ethical. The ending of this particular plot-line is anti-romantic in that no two lovers are brought together. It functions in contrast and counterpoint to the love between Abindarráez and Jarifa, two members of the same faith and cultural background who are married at the end of the earlier source work. The suggestion here, contrary to the stance adopted several times by Cervantes, is that the best and only reasonable matches are those made by people with common cultural origins, rather than across any barriers of culture, language, or faith.

∙∙∙

CHAPTER 5

Slavery and Romance in 16th–17th Century England and France

> Tout mon repos vient de ma peine
> Et l'Amour m'a bien fait choisir;
> Car si je n'avais point de chaîne,
> Mon cœur n'aurait point de plaisir.
>
> [All my respite comes from my pain
> And Love has made me choose;
> For if I had no more chains,
> My heart would have no more pleasure].
> Almahide, liv. III, 1431
>
> I wonnot love you, give me back my heart.
> But give it as you had it, fierce and brave:
> It was not made to be a womans slave ...
> Restore its freedom to my fetter'd will.
> JOHN DRYDEN, The Conquest of Granada, 341–358

1 'Moorish' and 'Turkish' Themes in 16th–17th Century England

Tragic themes concerning the love of a Christian woman for a Muslim man abound in English texts of the Elizabethan and Jacobean periods. I will mention a few to provide context and contrast to the comedies and tragi-comedies which are the main focus of this book. The most famous instance is in Shakespeare's *Othello, or, the Moor of Venice* (1604), whose tormented protagonist may or may not have been a Muslim: his religion has been a matter of dispute, but the designation 'Moor' points to a possible Muslim past.[1] Whether Muslim

---

1   Thomas Rymer (1693) and Charles Gildon (1694) both argued that Othello was a Muslim, although Samuel Chew questions this in *The Crescent and the Rose*, 521, N. 2; Robert West says that Othello is Christian: Robert H. West, 'The Christianness of Othello', *Shakespeare Quarterly*, Vol. 15, No. 4 (1964), 333–343. Cf. also Mohamed Ibrahim Hassan Elaskary, *The Image of Moors in the Writings of Four Elizabethan Dramatists: Peele, Dekker, Heywood and*

or Christian, convert or not, the noble general retains much of the 'Moorish' 'other' in his personification, and the notion that tragedy ensues from the mixing of cultures as well as races is implicit in the play, even though the character who most forcefully alludes to this is the arch-villain Iago. Shakespeare's *Titus Andronicus* (1594) is set in pre-Christian times, but features cross-cultural love, or rather lust, between the 'white' queen of the Goths, Tamora and Aaron the Moor, who incarnates the spirit of evil in a revenge play saturated with blood.

More unequivocally Muslim are the male protagonists who appear in many variations on a theme purporting to be drawn from Turkish history, the story of Mahomet and Irene, regarding the 15th century Ottoman Sultan Mehmed II, conqueror of Constantinople, who abandons all affairs of state when he falls deeply in love with a Greek Christian captive named Irene (sometimes called Hyren, or Hyrenee etc). So besotted is he that in some versions of the story a rebellion is threatened. As the 17th century English writer Richard Knolles puts it, '*Mars* slept in *Venus* lap' when Mahomet became 'distraught with the sweet but poisoned potions of love' and his janissaries [palace guards] plotted to overthrow him and set up one of his sons in his stead.[2]

Eventually, a boyhood friend, Mustapha, warns the Sultan that he risks losing his realm to the hostile forces massing against him. Knolles purports to quote Mustapha, '*What auaileth it you to have won* CONSTANTINOPLE, *and to have lost your selfe? Shake off the golden fetters wherein the wilie Greeke hath so fast bound you*".[3] The Sultan decides to prove he can overcome his infatuation. He first 'has his pleasure' of Irene, as Samuel Chew puts it, then commands her to be brought to him dressed in her finest clothes and jewels. Finally, within view of all his nobility, he strikes off the woman's head and begins preparations for a new round of warfare.[4]

Shakespeare (Ph.D. Dissertation for the University of Exeter, submitted April 2008): https://core.ac.uk/download/pdf/12827241.pdf [accessed 17/5/2024], 146 and N. 517. Matar states that Othello was a convert to Christianity from Islam: cf. Nabil Matar, *Islam in Britain 1558–1685* (Cambridge: Cambridge University Press,1998), 130. Vitkus suggests that Othello 'turns Turk' metaphorically, when he betrays his love and traduces the Christian state of Venice, becoming contaminated by 'Turkish' qualities of violence, cruelty and thirst for vengeance, rather than 'Christian charity' (*Three Turk Plays from Early Modern England,* ed. Daniel Vitkus [New York: Columbia University Press, 2000]), 2.

2   Richard Knolles, *The generall historie of the Turkes from the first beginning of that nation to the rising of the Othoman familie: with all the notable expeditions of the Christian princes against them. Together with the liues and conquests of the Othoman kings and emperours faithfullie collected out of the- best histories, both auntient and moderne, and digested into one continuat historie vntill this present yeare 1603* (London: Adam Islip, printer, 1603), 350–51.

3   Knolles, 352.

4   Chew, 479–90.

The story of Mahomet and Irene was told in William Paynter's *Palace of Pleasure* (1566) and several Elizabethan dramas, now lost, as well as being referred to in numerous other works such as *The Merry Conceited Jests of George Peele* (1607) and Jonson, Marston and Chapman's *Eastward Ho!* (1605). Successive treatments alter the names of the Sultan and his beloved, as well as the setting and details of the plot, in a tradition continuing well into the 18th century and beyond.[5] In all these narratives, individual variations notwithstanding, the lady ends up dead, usually by her lover's hand.[6] Significantly, the story of the Sultan and Irene survived to become, in very much altered form, the matter of at least one comedy in the Restoration period: the anonymous and unperformed *Irena: a Tragedy* (1664) which has, its subtitle notwithstanding, a felicitous outcome.

Numerous tragic tales are also built around the story of Suleiman 'the Magnificent' and Rukhselana, or Roxelana, renamed Ḥürrem Sulṭān.[7] Most of these turn on the couple's shared responsibility for the death of the Sultan's son Mustapha, whose murder the Russian Roxelana instigates so as to make her own son the successor.[8] Other tragedies featuring doomed love between male Muslims and female Christians include Thomas Kyd's *The Tragedy of Soliman and Perseda* (1590), where Sultan Soliman's violent passion for the Christian captive Perseda leads to both their deaths and that of Perseda's real love Erastus; Marlowe's *Lust's Dominion* (1600?), involving the love of the Spanish queen for Eleazar the Moor; and a Restoration tragedy based on it, Aphra Behn's *Abdelazar; Or, the Moor's Revenge* (1676). As D'Amico puts it, during this period,

> The Moor as villain becomes a convenient locus for those darkly subversive forces that threaten European society from within but that can be projected onto the outsider. The destructive forces of lust and violence are thus distanced by being identified with a cultural, religious, or racial source of evil perceived as the inversion of European norms.[9]

---

5 Examples include Thomas Goffe's *The Courageous Turk* (1618), in which the besotted Sultan is named Amurath, his lovely Greek slave is Eumorphe, and the counsellor advocating her despatch is the Sultan's tutor, Lala Shahin.
6 Chew; Vitkus, *Piracy, Slavery and Redemption*, passim.
7 Chew maintains that the name 'Roxolana' simply means 'the Russian' in Turkish, and that her real name was Rosa (498).
8 Chew, 497–503.
9 Jack d'Amico, *The Moor in English Renaissance Drama* (Tampa, Florida: University of South Florida Press, 1991), 2.

If the cross-cultural and cross-faith love is one-sided, e.g. a Muslim man or woman loving (or at any rate wooing) a Christian who does not reciprocate his or her feelings, the result may be comic instead of tragic, as for example in Shakespeare's *The Merchant of Venice* (1600), where Portia ridicules the Prince of Morocco's attempt to win her; and Thomas Heywood's *The Fair Maid of the West,* Parts I (1604?) and II (date unknown, both parts published 1631). In the latter, the Barbary King Mullisheg and Queen Tota fall in love with Christian captives Bess and Spencer, respectively, unaware that (like the captive couple in Cervantes's *El trato de Argel*) they are secretly in love with one another. By means of a bed-trick staged by courtiers, the royal pair end up sleeping with each other rather than with the desired captives, who are eventually allowed to leave and marry.

2 Tragicomedy

It is in the Jacobean and early Caroline periods that romantic tragicomedy really comes into its own and the pairing of Christian with Muslim 'other' is, once again, made possible and acceptable through the Muslim's conversion to Christianity. The themes and settings of Muslim-Christian conflict, as well as of captivity, lend themselves to the tragicomic mode for, to battle with Muslim opponents, let alone to be captured, meant dangers to life (the potentially tragic element). But in tragicomedy, the action centres on the loves of the dominant characters, rather than their successes or failures in war or politics. The 'comic' part of tragicomedy is the averting of death to a hero or heroine. As one of its chief proponents John Fletcher famously described it, the genre

> is not so called in respect of mirth and killing, but in respect it wants deaths, which is inough to make it no tragedie, yet brings some neere it, which is inough to make it no comedie.[10]

Given the gloom and unrelenting violence of Jacobean tragedy and the worldly cynicism of much of the period's city comedy, tragicomic romance must have come as a relief to audiences and readers: diverting fantasy in which, calamitous aspects of the plot notwithstanding, all ends well. Tragicomedy 'escapes from the tyranny of Jacobean incertitude' and is 'bound neither by the weight

---

10   John Fletcher, *Address to the Reader,* prefixed to the first edition of *The Faithful Shepherdess,* 1609, quoted in Una Ellis Fermor, *The Jacobean Drama: An Interpretation,* 1936, repr. (London: Methuen & Co., 1977), 203–04.

and horror which oppresses the tragedy nor by the compensatory pragmatism which binds the comedy to realistic portraiture'.[11] It is thus freed to allow idealised, even mythical characters to be presented in glamorous and often exotic locations.

Tragicomedy also, like tragedy and unlike Jacobean city comedy, foregrounds rulers and other high-born individuals whose lives are played out against a vivid tapestry of historical or quasi-historical events. We may be returned to the fantastic world of French and English mediaeval romance of *Floire et Blanchefleure* and its successors, or stories in the *Chanson de Roland* tradition. The settings may be more or less contemporary – or indeed timeless, but far away. Shakespeare's late plays, influenced by Fletcher and his collaborator Beaumont among others, are located in distant times or places and are infused with the tragic-comic spirit of reconciliation and redemption.

2.1   Robert Greene (1558–1592)

As Una Ellis-Fermor points out, elements of the tragi-comic genre are already present in some earlier Elizabethan dramatists, notably Robert Greene. Greene, himself influenced by his friend Christopher Marlowe, especially the latter's *Tamburlaine* (1587 or 1588), was a prolific writer, publishing more than twenty-five prose works as well as poetry, including several plays, in his short life. He is considered one of England's first professional authors and wrote for some of the leading actors of his day, including Edward Alleyn who played Orlando and was also the original Tamburlaine. Greene twice conceived plots which paired a Christian man with a Muslim woman and ended in their marriages. Yet in neither play is there even a hint of the woman's conversion to Christianity. Given Greene's university education and the long tradition requiring religious conversion before such a story could end, this was clearly deliberate, especially since the source works for both of Greene's 'Muslim–Christian' plays conclude with just such conversions.

2.2   Greene's Orlando Furioso (1589? Printed 1594)

In *The History of Orlando Furioso* Greene takes his audience back to the 'Matter of France' in a play based specifically on Ludovico Ariosto's epic poem, an early version of which was published in 1516, although it was not completed until 1532. Ariosto's work is often thought of as a parody of the chivalric legends of Charlemagne and his favourite knight, Roland/Orlando. It centres on the Christian Orlando's unrequited love for the pagan princess Angelica, which

---

11   Ellis-Fermor, *The Jacobean Drama*, 201.

FIGURE 5.1 Angelica Carving Medoro's Name on a Tree, fresco by Giovanni Battista Tiepolo (1757). Image in the public domain
SOURCE: FILE:GIOVANNI BATTISTA TIEPOLO - ANGELICA CARVING MEDORO'S NAME ON A TREE - WGA22341.JPG - WIKIMEDIA COMMONS

drives him mad. Eventually, she falls in love with the Muslim, Medoro, and marries him. In one episode, made famous by the artist Giovanni Battista Tiepolo, Angelica carves Medoro's name on a tree [Figure 5.1].[12] Orlando is restored to sanity by his cousin, Astolpho. The poem was translated into English by John Harington in 1591, supposedly at the behest of Queen Elizabeth I.[13]

12 A similar device is used in Shakespeare's much better-known but later play, *As You Like it* (1599?), when Orlando carves some verses onto trees in the Forest of Arden.
13 Miranda Johnson-Haddad, 'Englishing Ariosto: "Orlando Furioso" at the Court of Elizabeth I', *Comparative Literature Studies*, Vol. 31, No. 4 (1994), 323–350, 326.

The play's setting is the on-going conflict between Christianity and Islam. A secondary plot involves the love between a Christian female warrior Bradamante and the Muslim Ruggiero. Bradamante insists Ruggiero convert to Christianity before she will marry him, which he eventually does, and they are united. The couple were said to be ancestors of both Boiardo's and Ariosto's patrons of the noble House of d'Este, making their Christian faith all the more imperative to their descendants, as well as the chroniclers of their lives. Another character, the Muslim knight Brandimarte, becomes Orlando's friend and is baptised into Christianity.

Ariosto's work is steeped in matters of religion and, as with its mediaeval forerunner the *Chanson de Roland* (discussed in Chapter 2), conversions to Christianity are essential elements; in the *Chanson de Roland*, in addition, the Muslim queen of Saragossa Bramimonde, at first a devout Muslim, is converted to Christianity by Charlemagne when her husband's city falls to the Frankish army. Yet Greene has deliberately chosen to marry his Orlando to Angelica without any suggestion that she will convert to Christianity, while the Bradamante/ Ruggiero plot is omitted altogether, as are the conversions of Brandimarte and Bramimonde: Brandimarte appears in Greene, but is given very different functions from those of his predecessor.[14]

Greene's *Orlando Furioso* turns Ariosto's work on its head by having Angelica reciprocate Orlando's love. His madness, and the tragic elements of the plot, arise when the villainous Sacrepant schemes to persuade Orlando of Angelica's infidelity. With the aid of accomplices, Sacrepant convinces the knight that she is in love with Medor (now a relatively minor character). The episode of the initials carved on a tree is reversed so that it is not Angelica who engraves them but the spurned Sacrepant, who works to whip up Orlando's jealousy in revenge. Another tragic feature occurs when the twelve 'Peers of France', supported by Angelica's father, Marsilius, vow to kill her for her supposed lust and betrayal. She is saved at the eleventh hour when the truth is uncovered. As Sanders points out, echoing Fletcher, 'the default mode of tragicomedy [is] the halted violent act, the swerve from the darkest action into reconciliation' and in this aspect Greene's play is a true ancestor of decades of Jacobean and Caroline tragi-comedies.[15] One might add however, that the halting of the violent act need not offer reprieve to villains: Angelica's fidelity is confirmed when

---

[14] He is a relatively minor character, dubbed 'King of the Isles', one of the unsuccessful suitors to Angelica; he is eventually killed by Orlando.

[15] Julie Sanders, *Cambridge Introduction to Early Modern Drama 1576–1642* (Cambridge: Cambridge University Press, 2014),189.

Orlando fights and mortally wounds Sacrepant, extracting a confession from the dying man.

In Greene's treatment, *Orlando Furioso* exemplifies a tragicomic type condemned by Sir Philip Sidney as "'mongrel tragicomedy', by which he means plays which injudiciously mix kings and clowns and "match hornpipes and funerals'".[16] Two clowns disguise themselves several times, providing not only comic relief but requisite ingredients of the main plot, as when one of them, dressed as a shepherd, pretends to have witnessed the infidelity of Orlando's beloved Angelica. In other scenes they taunt the maddened Orlando.

Disguises are a key feature of the play: Orlando pretends to be a mercenary soldier in order to find out the truth regarding Angelica. Angelica disguises herself for self-protection when her father, persuaded that she has played false with Orlando, exiles her from the kingdom. Even Marsilius and his ally Mandricard, king of Mexico, conceal their identity. Greene was fascinated by gulling and deception, authoring a series of pamphlets on 'Coney-catching': Elizabethan slang for thieving confidence-trickery. In this play nothing and no-one are what they seem and alliances span nationality and creed. The plot's structure is like that of an onion, with skins of misinformation being peeled away successively in a continuous revelatory process.

Angelica's character is radically altered from that of her namesake in Ariosto: Greene makes her an emblem of womanly fidelity and stoicism, a victim wrongly accused, and precursor of the suffering heroines of later 'she-tragedy', although in early scenes she is allowed to choose her own husband. Each of her several suitors sets out his case, ending with 'I love, my Lord; let that suffice for me'. But Orlando ends his appeal with the words, 'I love, my Lord; Angelica her selfe shall speak for me' and she chooses him [Act I, scene 1, 169–70].[17] When Sacrepant declares his love to her once more, becoming angry when she refuses him, she replies calmly and in a conciliatory voice,

> Let not, my Lord, deniall breed offence;
> Loue doth allow her fauours but to one,
> Nor can there sit within the sacred shrine
> Of Venus, more than one installed heart.

---

16   Quoted in Jacqueline Pearson, *Tragedy and Tragicomedy in the Plays of John Webster* (Manchester: Manchester University Press, 1980),13.

17   References are to *Robert Greene*, ed. Thomas H. Dickinson (London: T. Fisher Unwin, 1909, and New York: Charles Scribner's Sons) n.d., xxxiv.

> Orlando is the Gentleman I loue,
> And more then he can not injoy my loue.[18]

With these words she underscores her autonomy. However, when she is matched with Orlando at the end, even though she does not convert to Christianity, her secondary status as a wife will be reinforced as Orlando announces their imminent move from 'Africa', where the action takes place, to France. Thus, she loses her position of relative independence, as the daughter of an enlightened father in a land ruled by her family, to the country of a foreigner, always dependent upon her husband.

The confirmation of male hegemony marks Greene out as a conservative with regard to gender roles. However, the absence of religion from the play, notwithstanding its centrality in the sources, underscores Greene's iconoclasm: his perspective is rare indeed. Angelica's father Marsilius, the 'Emperor of Africa', is clearly a Muslim (his near-name-sake antecedents Marsile, king of Saragossa, in the *Chanson de Roland* and Marsilio, king of Spain, in Ariosto's *Orlando Furioso* are Muslims) which means Angelica must be Muslim too.

Greene's reasons for such changes are unclear, as are his true attitudes to religion; in fact, he doesn't appear to have adhered to any single point of view or faith.[19] He was in the same literary and social coterie as Christopher Marlowe, whom he criticised yet admired and copied. Marlowe had a reputation as an atheist, which Greene condemned by inference in the Preface to his pamphlet, *Perimedes*. Greene refers to Marlowe as 'daring God out of heaven with that Atheist Tamburlaine, or blaspheming with the mad priest of the Sun'.[20] Yet he too was accused of atheism, a charge substantiated in some of his own works, at least according to his 19th century editor, Alexander Dyce.[21] Dyce goes on to cite a fictional dialogue in which Greene is quoted as having no fear of God or hell-fire and determination to live for the day without any thought of the consequences.[22]

---

18 Quoted from Robert Greene, *Orlando Furioso*, in *The Life and Complete Works in Prose and Verse of Robert Greene, MA., in Fifteen Volumes*, ed. Alexander B. Grosart, 1881–86 (reissued New York: Russell and Russell, 1964), vol. XIII, 139.

19 A tradition that Greene was for a time a minister of the church is now generally discredited (Dickinson, *Robert Greene*, xxiii).

20 Quoted in Dickinson, ed., *Robert Greene*, xxxiv. Dickinson comments that it was Marlowe himself who was the atheist, and not Tamburlaine.

21 *The Dramatic and Poetical Works of Robert Greene and George Peele, with Memoirs of the Authors and Notes*, ed. Rev. Alexander Dyce (London: Routledge, Warne and Routledge, 1861), 29–30.

22 J. Payne Collier's *The Poetical Decameron* (Edinburgh, 1820), quoted by Dyce, *Dramatic and Poetical Works of Robert Greene and George Peele,* 30 Note.

At the end of his life, Greene was full of remorse for his self-confessed dissolute life. In *The Repentance*, he says he 'seemed as one of no religion, but rather as a mere Atheist, contemning the holy precepts vttered by any learned preacher ... a mere reprobate ... one wipt out of the booke of life'.[23] One commentator on Greene, Nicholas Storojenko, saw a seemingly irreconcilable contradiction between the author's life and his works: his life being that of a 'sensualist and cynic', while his writings were 'ideally pure and edifying'.[24] Whatever the truth, he must surely have been less than a devout Christian when he wrote *Orlando Furioso*, suggesting a greater consistency between his work and his life than Storojenko supposed. If there were any doubt remaining, it would surely be dispelled by a study of the play most influenced by the arch-atheist, Christopher Marlowe.[25]

2.3 Greene's The Comicall Historie of Alphonsus, King of Aragon (1599)

This play too ends without the religious conversion of its Muslim heroine, Iphigina. It concerns the life and love of the eponymous Alphonsus, rightful heir to the throne of Aragon, whose grandfather was murdered and dispossessed of his lands by his younger brother, while his father Carinus was forced into exile, along with Alphonsus. As in *The History of Orlando Furioso*, Greene has drawn on some mediaeval 'matter' and adapted it for his own purposes. Here the source is quasi-historical, rather than literary: two real-life figures have been put forward as possible originals for the character of Alphonsus: Alfonso I, king of Navarre (1073–1134) and, more plausibly, Alfonso V, king of Aragon and Naples (1385–1458).

In the play Alphonsus vows to regain the throne and his rights. To that end he attacks the usurper's son and reigning King Flaminius, killing him. Alphonsus also aspires to wear the crown of Constantinople, overcoming Amurack, the 'great Turk'. Amurack dreams of defeat by Alphonsus and berates the god 'Mahound', also referred to as Mahomet: he sees the god as complicit in his

---

23   Quoted by Lori Humphrey Newcomb, 'A Looking Glass for Readers: Cheap Print and the Senses of Repentance', in *Writing Robert Greene: Essays on England's First Notorious Writer*, ed. Kirk Melnikoff and Edward Gieskes (Aldershot, Hants., and Burlington, Vermont: Ashgate Publishing Co., 2008), 133–56, 138.

24   *Robert Greene: His Life and Works, A Critical Investigation by Nicholas Storojenko*, tr. E.A.R. Hodgetts, ed. Alexander B. Grosart, first published Moscow, 1878 (this edition published in New York: Russell and Russell, 1881–6), 15 vols, Vol I, 60.

25   Resemblances between Marlowe's plays, particularly *Tamburlaine*, and *Alphonsus King of Aragon* have been well summarised in *Christian-Muslim Relations. A Bibliographical History*, ed. David Thomas and John A. Chesworth, Vol. 6. *Western Europe* (1500–1600) (Leiden/Boston: Brill, 2014), 835. Top of Form.

[Amurack's] capture, 'his Princely feete in irons clapt/Which erst the proudest kings were forst to kisse', and swears that, henceforth, he and all his people will instead follow 'Ioue' [Jove], who will help him 'scape' his 'bondage' [Act III, 370, lines 1007–1011]. Amurack also 'sees' that Alphonsus will love his daughter Iphigena and prepares himself mentally to welcome Alphonsus as his son-in-law [Act III, 371, lines 1030–35].

Amurack's wife, Fausta, overhearing his dreaming soliloquy is convinced he will offer his daughter to the enemy. Mother and daughter then threaten to attack Amurack with an army of Amazons and he banishes them. A theatrical spectacle ensues in which a brazen head is brought on stage, representing Mahound/Mahomet and shooting 'flakes of fire'. As Venus has foretold, Mahound urges the Turks to march against Alphonsus. Alphonsus approaches, leading a grand procession with the heads of three of his slain enemies perched at the corners of a canopy over his own head and addresses Amurack as 'Pagan dog' [IV, 394, line 1595] and just 'Pagan' [395, line 1619]. In a fight, Amurack and his forces are routed and flee, pursued by Alphonsus and his men.

Act V begins with Venus predicting Amurack's utter defeat and his subsequent imprisonment by Alphonsus, until Amurack's daughter, by marrying the victor, achieves her father's release. Iphigina mourns her father's betrayal by the 'Gods'. Fausta vows to vanquish Alphonsus with her Amazons and it is his turn to flee. Iphigina catches up with him and challenges him:

> How now *Alphonsus*! you which neuer yet
> Could meet your equall in the feates of armes,
> How haps it now that in such sudden sort
> You flie the presence of a sillie maide? ...
>
> Or do you else disdaine to fight with me,
> For staining of your high nobilitie?
> Act V, 399, lines 1733–41

Unconsciously echoing the Arab Sharkān, Alphonus responds that while he would not shy away from any battle, on this occasion love has halted him.

Iphigina reproaches him, 'we came to fight, and not to loue ..'. (line 1761). Alphonsus tells her that if she will only agree to marry him, she shall be queen of all the world. She rejects him haughtily, whereat he threatens to make her his concubine. They fight and Iphigina flees, pursued by Alphonsus, who then takes her, her mother and all their soldiers prisoner. After many appeals by mother and daughter, Carinus tells Alphonsus to forget the rejections and pursue his suit: 'What, know you not that Castles are not wonne/At first assault, and women are not wooed/When first their suters profer loue to them?' (v, 409, lines 1986 ff). Carinus then turns to Iphigina and reassures her that her pardon is as good as granted, if she will only agree to marry his son.

Iphigina complies and Alphonsus now gladly accepts her capitulation, agreeing wholeheartedly to marry her, while Fausta too gives her consent. Amurack consoles himself with the thought that Alphonsus is 'sonne vnto a King' and so worthy of his daughter's love. [v, 413, lines 2077–78]. Her dowry will be 'the Turkish Emperie' (line 2085–86). The play ends with Venus and the Muses announcing a festival proclaimed by 'Jupiter', before Venus is raised up in a spectacle recalling Medea's being drawn up in a chariot in the Greek *Medea*, but in happier circumstances!

Marlowe's influence on *Alphonsus, King of Aragon* is seen in Greene's copious use of bombastic and overblown rhetoric which points forward to the language of Restoration tragedy; here the context is tragi-comic, within the terms set out by Fletcher: i.e. an important character is threatened with death, which is then averted. Alphonsus's courtship of Iphigina, as well as numerous other actions of his, recall aspects of Marlowe's *Tamburlaine*.[26] Also, like Tamburlaine, Alphonsus rises from relative obscurity 'solely through the greatness of his spirit and exceptional heroism; as with Tamburlaine, in a fit of rage and senseless pride he even dares Mahomet'.[27]

Religion is intrinsic to the action, but the perspective and treatment of it are certainly unorthodox. The scene in which a brazen head speaks for the Muslim prophet could not be staged today without risking grave offence. Greene's use of the name 'Mahomet' in that form, as well as 'Mahound', and portrayal of him as a petulant, unreliable and deluded – or else deliberately deceptive – god, who is at first worshipped and later rejected by his followers, taps into much mediaeval material.

However, the alternative to Islam proffered by Greene is not Christianity, but rather magic, and a hotchpotch of quasi-Roman or Greek polytheistic elements. The Roman god Venus prophesies and dictates events and other characters deriving from classical mythology, including Jupiter/Jove and Medea, influence the action. Jupiter and Jove were sometimes used on the 16th- and 17th-century English stage to stand in for the Christian God, for fear of blaspheming.[28] But, combined with the Greek/Roman features of this play, any relation to Christianity, such as that confidently proclaimed by Storojenko,

---

26　Charles W. Crupi, *Robert Greene* (Boston: Twayne Publishers, 1986), 101–02.
27　Storojenko, *Robert Greene*, 175.
28　For example, the unfortunate steward Malvolio thanks Jove for his supposed good fortune in *Twelfth Night*.

must be purely suppositious as nowhere in Greene's play is it actually mentioned.[29] In fact, Alphonsus twice refers respectfully to 'the God Mars' [Act v, line 1845, 403; and line 1851,404] and to the power of 'the gods' (1941, 407), as well as to that of Fortune and the Fates. As for religious conversion, the sole instance of it in the play is that of Amurack, discarding his worship of 'Mahound/Mahomet' in favour of following the Roman god Jove.

And yet, there is a clear cultural difference between Iphigina, ostensibly Muslim daughter of the 'Great Turk' Amurack, and Alphonsus of Aragon, a region in Christian Spain. In fact, the basis for marriage between the two is questionable: Iphigina plainly accepts Alphonsus under duress, having been threatened by him with forced concubinage, or death. Not long before, she had responded to his extravagant proposal of marriage with disdain, claiming to hate him (Act v, lines 1774–79, 401). It is only after Iphigina, Fausta and the Amazons have been defeated by Alphonsus in battle that the two women heed the counsel of the enchantress Medea and agree to the match between Iphigina and Alphonsus.

The scene in which Iphigina challenges and then fights Alphonsus is striking in its originality on the English stage, as is her later 'wooing' of Alphonsus, but it recalls the Muslim women warriors' wooing in mediaeval Christian epics and romances and Amazonian Christian women confronting men in literature from the Muslim world, as well as looking forward to Restoration actresses' 'breeches' roles. The world of the play is divided between the realms of Mars and Venus: the first acts being dominated by warfare and the reversal of Alphonsus's status from dispossessed outcast to omnipotent ruler; the last act by the wars of love and the victory of Venus over Mars. Iphigina implicitly condemns Alphonsus's aggression as having delayed their union:

> *Cupid* cannot enter in the brest
> Where *Mars* before had took possession.
>
> That was no time to talke of *Venus* games
> When all our fellows were pressed in the warres.
>   v, 410–11, lines 2029–32

The military conflicts being ended, peace and matrimonial harmony can reign.

But the play's ostensibly happy outcome is overshadowed by the circumstances in which Iphigina has first yielded to, and then courted Alphonsus. Her

---

29   Storojenko, *Robert Greene*, 175.

apparent change of heart, in response to Medea's counsel, occurs when she, her parents and two kings who are also enemies of Alphonsus, appear on stage 'bounde' with their hands tied behind them (v, 1790–92, 401). The spectacle of a beautiful young woman, trussed and helpless, pleading with her captor and 'wooing' him, may have provided the audience with an erotic charge. But the nature of Iphigina's compliance is questionable. Is she feigning love to restore her and her parents' liberty, and possibly save their lives? Or does she now genuinely love the man who has spurned her? Alphonsus's agreement to marry her seems more in keeping with his own actual will, but he too must be cajoled by his father, whom he deeply loves and will not disobey. The play's outcome in marriage, though superficially satisfying comedy's need for a 'happy ending', leaves questions regarding the coercion on both sides and especially with regard to the bride.

Religious questions also linger: how is it that Greene, knowing the literary tradition as he obviously did, demonstrated by his reworking of Ariosto's *Orlando Furioso*, once again refrains from having his heroine convert to Christianity? The absence of a conversion here would seem to reinforce contemporary claims that Greene was at best little concerned with religion and perhaps even espoused atheism, to which he himself confessed.

2.4   Philip Massinger, The Renegado (*Licensed 1624, Published 1630*)

With *The Renegado* we are back in North Africa, in this case Tunis, in a play principally inspired by Cervantes's *Los Baños de Argel* (*The Prisons of Algiers*) and *La historia del cautivo* (*The Captive's Tale*).[30] Massinger is best-known for his contemporary city comedies such as *A New Way to Pay Old Debts* and *A City Madam*, in which he is noted for his satirical force, social realism and intricate plotting. But he also wrote plays inspired by historic events and set around the Mediterranean. *The Renegado* played at the Cockpit Theatre in 1624, remained in the repertory and was revived after the Restoration.

The drama both exploits and plays with ideas and images of slavery throughout the action: at first literally, its main Christian characters being physically enslaved to the rulers of Istanbul and Tunis; then metaphorically, as both of the Muslims in love with Christians feel their authority ebbing away from them, making them 'slaves to love'; and finally, in relation to religion. *The Renegado* has many aspects of a romantic comedy, but there is an unrelenting religious didacticism at its heart – the very spirit which was so conspicuously

---

30   Chew discusses the play's links to *Los Baños de Argel*: *Crescent and Rose*, 534; he also cites Theodore Heckmann, *Massinger's* The Renegado *und seine Spanischen Quellen* (Halle: C.A. Kaemmerer & Co., 1905).

absent from Greene's plays. It employs multiple lexical inversions to contrast Christianity and Islam. Vitelli is the play's key protagonist but the Renegado himself is Antonio Grimaldi, a pirate converted to Islam and a relatively minor character – but essential to the plot.

The Renegado opens with an exchange between Vitelli, 'a gentleman of Venice' and Gazet, his servant, posing as Vitelli's apprentice. Vitelli has come to Tunis disguised as a merchant so he can search unhindered for his missing sister Paulina. His shop offers crystal, porcelain, and paintings purporting to be portraits of famous noblewomen, but which in reality are pictures of Venetian courtesans and bawds. This is a play dominated by metaphors of the marketplace, emphasising that in this part of the world nothing exists which does not have a price, including humans peddled as slaves.

The play is also replete with puns and sly references to sexual commerce and trade. For example, in the opening scene, Vitelli and Gazet's 'wares' are described with several joking puns relating to lost virginity and a woman's sexual parts and later ones confusing circumcision with castration. In one scene, when Vitelli is filled with remorse for acceding to the advances of the Ottoman Sultan Amurath's beautiful niece, Donusa, he reproaches her, again using the language of commerce 'At what an overvalue I have purchased/The wanton treasure of your virgin bounties' [3.5. lines 41–42] and returning treasure she had given him: 'now I do deliver back the price/And salary of your lust' [3.5. lines 48–49]. Religion may also be traded and matters of conversion and apostasy are central elements driving the plot. Intertwined tropes of literal and metaphorical slavery also abound, layering the action with multiple ironies.

From a Jesuit priest called Francisco, Vitelli learns that Paulina has been abducted by the renegade Grimaldi and sold as a slave to the Turkish Viceroy of Tunis, Asambeg, who is infatuated with her and determined to 'conquer her virtue', as the play's editor Michael Neill puts it (3).[31] She has thus far been able to resist his onslaughts, protected by a powerful relic which the priest has given her. Gazet proclaims his willingness to profess the beliefs of whichever country he finds himself in. Vitelli challenges him as to whether, being in Tunis, he is now ready to 'turn Turk'. Gazet balks at this, joking that he is not willing to undergo circumcision, a process he mistakes for castration. Francisco appears, informing the Venetians of the arrival of the Pasha of Aleppo, Mustapha, come to claim the Turkish Sultan's niece, Donusa, as his bride.

---

31 All references to this play, unless otherwise stated, are from the Arden Early Modern Drama edition of Philip Massinger, *The Renegado,* ed. Michael Neill (London: Methuen Drama, A & C Black Publishers Ltd., 2010).

Enter Donusa with her servant Manto and the formerly English slave and eunuch, Carazie, discussing the Pasha (Asambeg)'s infatuation with his new captive (Paulina). Donusa contrasts the supposed freedom of Englishwomen with the relative seclusion of her own countrywomen. But the play also expresses a view widely held by Europeans that Islam had an 'indulgent attitude toward pleasures of the flesh' [Neill ed. 103, FN to lines 49–50]. And when Donusa receives the suitor, Mustapha, she cites a custom permitting the female members of the Sultan's family to behead a husband if he fails to please them [1.2, lines 89–97]. For this, Massinger may have drawn on a report by his near-contemporary, George Sandys, who tells us that the daughters, sisters and aunts of the 'Grand Signior' [Sultan],

> have the *Bassas* [pashas, or noblemen] given to them for their husbands: the *Sultan* saying thus, '*Here, sister, I give thee this man to thy slaue* [slave], *together with this dagger, that if hee please thee not, thou maiest kill him*'. Their husbands come not to them vntill they be called: if but for speech onely, their shooes which they put off at the doore, are their suffered to remain: but if it is to lie with them, they are laid out ouer the bed by an Eunuch: a signe for them to approach, who creeps vnto them at the beds feet.[32]

In this sense, the royal women are far freer than ordinary Turkish women or indeed European princesses and queens, in accordance with the reports of Lady Mary Wortley Montagu (Chapter 3).

Strolling in the marketplace, Donusa falls into conversation with Vitelli, whose witty and learned presentation of his wares impresses and intrigues her. Suddenly, in an action reminiscent of Cervantes's Zara in *Los Baños de Argel*, she pulls off her veil, revealing a face of such matchless beauty that Vitelli, overwhelmed, backs away. But Donusa finds a pretext to summon him to the palace. She anticipates Vitelli's arrival in an agony of yearning but also self-reproach: she has lost her vaunted freedom and become a slave to love – and desire:

> What magic hath transformed me from myself?
> Where is my virgin pride? How have I lost

---

32   George Sandys, *A Relation of a Journey Begun An. Dom. 1610, containing a description of the Turkish Empire, of Aegypt, of the Holy Land, of the Remote parts of Italy, and Islands adioyning*, 3rd ed. (London: Printed [by Thomas Cotes] for Ro: Allot, 1627), 74–75. Quoted by Neill in a footnote to his edition of *The Renegado*, 107.

My boasted freedom? What new fire burns up
My scorched entrails? What unknown desires
Invade and take possession of my soul ...?
>   2.1. lines 23–27

Both the plot device and the sentiments just described recall those in the tale of Shams al-Nahar and the merchant Ali ibn Bakkar in *One Thousand and One Nights* (Chapter 1).

Although no firm evidence exists for the *Nights* tales being known in Europe before Galland's translations (1704–17), individual stories are believed to have found their way to Europe well before then.[33] In both *The Renegado* and the *Nights* story of Shams al-Nahar, an ordinary man is suddenly thrust into the lavish world of a despotic Muslim ruler's palace, through a chance meeting with a beautiful woman in a merchant's shop. Both narratives exploit the peril inherent in such illicit trysts and incursions; in *The Renegado*, there is the added titillation that Vitelli and Donusa belong to different faiths and cultures, a fact to which he himself draws attention, noting that he is in a 'forbidden place/Where Christian ne'er yet trod' (2.4, lines 32–33).

In the *Nights*, as we saw in Chapter 1, the desired woman Shams al-Nahar is literally a slave, a concubine of the Caliph Haroun al-Rashid, who loves and is loved illicitly but chastely by a young man, Nur al-Din Ali ibn-Bakkar. By the end, both lovers have died, heartbroken by their enforced separation. This story has been identified as the most detailed exploration of pathological love sickness among several tales examining this theme in *One Thousand and One Nights*.[34] However, Donusa in *The Renegado* has no intention of wasting away, nor does she mean her tryst with the supposed merchant Vitelli to be chaste; she decides to accept her destiny:

Oh, my fate!
But there is no resisting: I obey thee,

---

33 See Chapter 2. There has also been considerable speculation regarding the sources of the Sly plot in Shakespeare's *The Taming of the Shrew*. Some scholars have noted the resemblance between this tale, in which Sly, in a dream, imagines himself to be a king, and a story with a similar plotline in *One Thousand and One Nights*. There are also echoes of Calderón de la Barca's play *La vida es sueño* ('Life Is a Dream'), 1636, in which a young man reigns briefly as a prince, before being drugged and locked up so that he believes his experiences were only elements in a dream.

34 Daniel E Beaumont, *Slave of Desire: Sex, Love, and Death in the 1001 Nights* (Madison, New Jersey: Fairleigh Dickinson University Press, 2002), 74.

> Imperious god of love, and willingly
> Put mine own fetters on to grace thy triumph.
>> 2.1. lines 37–40

When Vitelli arrives in the palace, he is taken to a richly adorned room, a setting which he, like Ali ibn Bakkar compares with Paradise (2.4. lines 5–9).

In the course of an elaborately formal conversation, Donusa gives Vitelli bags of gold and jewels, recalling the actions of Cervantes's heroines. Finally, she seduces him with amorous touches and kisses to which Vitelli succumbs: 'Though the Devil/stood by and roared, I follow! Now I find/That virtue's but a word and no sure guard,/If set upon by beauty and reward' (2.4. lines 134–37). Later, Donusa refers explicitly to having 'forfeited' the name of 'virgin' (3.1. lines 7–8). In a different sort of play, an occurrence of this kind could lead to appalling bloodshed and tragedy. But this is a tragic-comedy and, perhaps surprisingly, no-one is punished for such surrenders to lust.

The scene now shifts to Assambeg, Viceroy of Tunis, who is in his own right a slave to love – paradoxically snared by the woman he sought to enslave. Getting ready to visit Paulina, he takes out a gilt key, then laments,

> Why should I hug
> So near my heart what leads me to my prison,
> Where she that is enthralled commands her keeper
> And robs me of the fierceness I was born with?
>> 2.5, lines 104–07

Paulina rejects him scornfully, but in an inadvertently ironic nod to her religion, he refers to her as 'sweet saint' (2.5. line 164). Numerous linguistic echoes of the scene which passed between Vitelli and Donusa explicitly contrast the two situations. In both scenes it is the Muslim and not the Christian who is enslaved by love and lust, the technically 'free' person who is psychologically imprisoned, not the vulnerable Christian. Paulina is effectively a slave, while even though Vitelli is not technically a slave, he is constrained as all foreigners are, and will soon be physically imprisoned. Asambeg speaks of his vow to await Paulina's 'free consent' until she 'grace me with [another] name … [that of] Your husband' (2.5. lines 154–57). Paulina's dismissal of him contrasts with Vitelli's willing acceptance of Donusa's overtures. Donusa refers to her hope that Vitelli will be 'mine by a nearer name' – that of husband (2.4. line 52); Vitelli finds Donusa's 'soft touch' (2.4. line 18) irresistibly alluring, while

Asambeg trembles at Paulina's 'softness' and feels himself unmanned by it, not least because of her steadfast rejections of his advances.[35]

Vitelli likens Donusa's name to 'a potent charm ... [which]/Hath brought me safe to this forbidden place' (2.4. lines 29–32) and which will eventually unite them in marriage, reversing the role of the magic charm which Paulina wears to help ward off Asambeg. Significantly, as in Cervantes's works, the successful courtship in *The Renegado* is initiated by a woman wooing a man, rather than the other way round. And in both authors' works it is the Muslim woman wooing the Christian man, who responds to her advances with reciprocal passion.

The perceived imbalance between woman and man, and between Muslim and Christian, is 'righted' by degrees, at first when Donusa kneels before Vitelli (3.5. line 71) pleading with him to love her, but she and the guilt-ridden Vitelli are discovered by Asambeg and imprisoned in the 'Black Tower'.[36] Vitelli then achieves noble stature through his courageous endurance of torture (4.2. lines 45–52) while Donusa is further humbled, reduced from greatness to a penitent pleading for her life. But then she too rises to the occasion with a stirring speech, denouncing the hypocrisy of her tormentors:

> To tame their lusts
> There's no religious bit: let her be fair
> And pleasing to the eye, though Persian, Moor,
> Idolatress, Turk or Christian, you are privileged
> And freely may enjoy her. At this instant
> I know, unjust man, thou hast in thy power
> A lovely Christian virgin: thy offence
> Equal, if not transcending, mine, why then –
> We being both guilty – dost thou not descend
> From that usurped tribunal and with me
> Walk hand in hand to death?
>
> 4.2. lines 133–43

---

35 The idea of a gentle touch is again invoked in Act IV (4.1. lines 92–96) when the now deeply penitent renegade Grimaldi imagines himself being whipped for his crimes and thinks the 'stripes' of the iron whip would be like gentle touches, correcting him and bringing him redemption.

36 Historically, there was a notorious Black Tower – not in Tunis, but in Constantinople/Istanbul, built ca. 1100. Prisoners incarcerated there would supposedly never leave alive. Cf. https://www.hürriyetdailynews.com/underground-cells-ottoman-dungeons-22155 [accessed 22/4/2024].

This defiant, even feminist speech, defined by the editor Michael Neill as 'probably calculated to appeal to the increasingly influential female audience in Jacobean theatres',[37] restores the moral balance between Donusa and Vitelli as well as between her and her captors. Then, in an attempt to escape from her dilemma, she cites a law according to which she should be permitted to try to convert Vitelli to Islam and which, if she were successful, would allow her to marry him. This is granted and she is freed.

Donusa pleads with Vitelli to accept Islam, imagining Christianity as a kind of slavery or a demanding mistress, using the language of servitude and liberation:

> My suit is
> That you would quit your shoulders of a burden,
> Under whose ponderous weight you wilfully
> Have too long groaned, to cast those fetters off
> With which, with your own hands, you chain your freedom.
> Forsake a severe – nay imperious – mistress,
> Whose service does exact perpetual cares,
> Watchings and troubles; and give entertainment
> To one that courts you, whose least favours are
> Variety and choice of all delights
> Mankind is capable of.
>
> 4.3. lines 74–83

Neill's gloss points out that the language of courtly love is here inverted, since conventionally it was the lady who accepted a lover's service (4.3. Footnote to line 8). In this scene Donusa is urging Vitelli to accept service (from her) rather than give it to his faith. Vitelli rails against the Prophet Muhammad, quoting from some contemporary anti-Islamic texts and exhorting Donusa to face up to the prospect of death. In that instant, Donusa understands that only by embracing his religion can she hope to win back Vitelli's love. And so the would-be converter is herself converted to lately-scorned Christianity and abases herself to Vitelli: 'I came here to take you,/But I perceive a yielding in myself/To be your prisoner' (4.3. 147–49). She spits at the name 'Mahomet' and then both she and Vitelli are sentenced to death.

As the lovers prepare for both marriage and death, Vitelli 'baptises' Donusa by throwing water in her face and she, repurposing the metaphor she had

---

[37] Neill ed, *The Renegado,* Footnote to lines 127 ff.

used earlier regarding Christianity, proclaims herself 'freed from the cruellest of prisons –/Blind ignorance and misbelief,' in other words, Islam. Paulina, watching, now feigns her own conversion to Islam and claims she is ready to marry Asambeg in order to buy (as a favour from the joyfully astonished man) another day of life for the condemned couple and the use of Donusa as her personal 'slave'.

This ploy allows the Christians to escape to a ship that has secretly been readied for them by the priest Francisco, its Turkish crew having been clapped under hatches, as in Cervantes's *La historia del cautivo*. Brother and sister are finally reunited, as are all the other Christian and formerly Christian characters, including the eunuch, Carazie, and the repentant former renegade Grimaldi, a Christian once more (unlike his penitent original in Cervantes's work, who dies a martyr's death). The play ends on a sombre yet triumphant note: the Viceroy Asambeg, being apprised of the deception and the escape of all prisoners including his beloved Paulina, rants in impotent rage.

Throughout, Massinger intertwines images of slavery with literal scenes of captivity and multiple ironic reversals. Thematically, the Christians progress from physical captivity, or the threat of it, to physical freedom, while Donusa progresses from spiritual enslavement to moral and religious freedom. Within the terms of the play and the mores of the period, balance has been restored. But viewed from a modern perspective, Donusa's authority as niece to the Sultan, with the promise of dominion over any future husband, drains away once she is converted: she has become completely subservient to the Christian Vitelli on four levels: as a lover overwhelmed by passion; as a wife controlled by a husband; in moving to a strange land, where she will live as a foreigner, speaking an alien tongue; and finally as a convert from a religion in which she was powerful, to one which (her claim to new freedom notwithstanding) will reinforce her submission to the male-dominated world of Christianity.

The only woman to emerge from the drama independent and unscathed is Paulina, who has maintained her chastity throughout, thwarting her would-be seducer; and who has organised a plot which was instrumental to all the Christian characters' escapes, albeit through the questionable tactic of feigning conversion to Islam. At the end of the play, she is free, Christian and subservient to no man. Only once is the play's atmosphere of mounting religious fervour moderated, when it is gently mocked by the Boatswain of the Christians' ship: he complains, 'This religion/Will keep us slaves and beggars', to which the Ship's Master replies, 'The fiend prompts me/To change my copy', meaning he is tempted to convert to Islam (5.2. lines 19–21). But this is a moment of light relief in an increasingly earnest play, inspired by and in many ways modelled on, two works of Cervantes.

However, the incidence of pre-marital sex in Massinger seems like a riposte to Cervantes, whose heroine Zoraida, identified with St Mary as we saw in Chapter 4, remains virginal until her marriage. In another context, Donusa's loss of her virginity before marriage would render her 'damaged goods'. But Vitelli justifies marrying her, telling the priest Francisco that he had courted her 'with sacred and religious zeal' (95.1. lines 19–22). Vitelli's account appears somewhat disingenuous – as the first courting and winning were all done by her, and religion only came into their affair belatedly. But the point is that neither of *The Renegado*'s sexual 'culprits' (Vitelli and Donusa) is punished for their 'sins' of passion. They are, on the contrary, rewarded with freedom, marriage and the promise of Christian salvation. In this sense, the play is relatively liberal for its time.

Despite its transitions from comic banter to sombre matters of life and death, Massinger's *The Renegado* is skilfully unified in representing the dual seductions of Islam: sexual, because of the beauty and blandishments of its women and social and religious, because in a society where preferment and sometimes even survival depend on a person's Muslim faith, the appeal of apostasy could prove irresistible. There are in fact two 'renegades' in the play: Vitelli, transiently spurning an ideal of chastity and Grimaldi, temporarily deserting his faith. Two types of repentance then follow these temptations: Vitelli's, for succumbing to sexual enticement and Grimaldi's, for embracing the 'false religion', Islam. The central unifying figure is the priest Francisco, who brings both men back from the brink, as well as helping to rescue all the Christians from Barbary. A third kind of relationship to Islam is shown in Paulina's feigned conversion: a mask which she adopts and as quickly discards, with no compunction about her deception.

Commercial elements are ubiquitous in this play, for example, Gazet refers to Donusa as Vitelli's 'she-customer' (4.1. line 143), and mercantile factors are present even in matters of religion: Grimaldi, seeking pardon for his past apostasy and other misdeeds, is told by Francisco that he may 'Purchase it/ By zealous undertakings.' (4.1. lines 86–87). *The Renegado* is chronologically interstitial, informed by themes and settings, such as captivity in North Africa and religious conversion, dating back to the previous century. But its bawdiness, both implicit and explicit, looks forward to comedies of the Restoration period. Revived in 1662, this play was among the first to be performed after the theatres re-opened, following the long closures of the Commonwealth period. Among several changes, however, the play's inherent Catholicism, suggested by elements such as the noble character of the Jesuit Francisco and the many references to sacraments, relics, magic charms, etc., is watered down in the later version to negate the play's 'potential for arousing sectarian controversy'.[38] By contrast, some salacious elements such as Vitelli's anticipation of pleasure with Donusa are enhanced.

3   Growth of 'Moorish' and Muslim Themes in France during the 17th Century

France's fascination with Islamic lands and culture took a new turn in the 16th century when, as Philip Mansel has shown, the French looked to the Ottomans for support against the Holy Roman Empire and even gave military advice to the Sultan.[39] France allied with the Ottoman ruler of Algiers, Kheir-ad-Din, who sent an envoy to France in 1535 and spent time there himself in 1544, while a Parisian diplomat and writer, Guillaume Postel, was sent with a French delegation to Istanbul in the following year, and again in 1547.[40] Already well-versed in Hebrew, Postel learned Arabic, including the dialects of Syria, Egypt, and Morocco, as well as Turkish and Persian.[41] Described by McCabe as 'the first Orientalist',[42] Postel developed a passion for reading Arabic texts.[43] In the mid- to late-sixteenth century influential men including ambassadors and their entourages, as well as independent travellers wrote about their travels. Men such as Postel, Nicolas de Nicolay, the diplomat Jacques Gassot, and the priest Jerome Maurand compiled detailed accounts of their experiences in Turkey and other Muslim lands. As a result, 'thanks to books and politics, the Ottoman Empire became more familiar in France than in most of Christian Europe'.[44]

---

38   Neill, ed., *The Renegado*, 62.
39   Philip Mansel, 'The French Renaissance in Search of the Ottoman Empire', *Re-Orienting the Renaissance: Cultural Exchanges with the East*, ed. Gerald MacLean (Basingstoke, Hants., and New York: Palgrave Macmillan, 2005), 96–107, 97 and passim. See also, Ina Baghdiantz McCabe, *Orientalism in Early Modern France: Eurasian Trade, Exoticism, and the Ancien Regime* (Oxford and New York: Berg Publishing, 2008), Chapter 2, passim.
40   McCabe, *Orientalism*, 37–43. The alliance between Kheir ad-Din and France was not an unmitigated success, nor did it inhibit the corsair ruler's expansionist aims: in 1543, the Algerian Turks occupied Toulon, from which they took many individuals captive, and they besieged Nice. According to McCabe, this was done with the connivance of the French king Francis I for his own political reasons, but it produced a backlash from the French population.
41   McCabe, 40.
42   McCabe, Chapter 1, passim.
43   McCabe, 44.
44   Mansel, 105. See also McCabe, 48 ff.

In the first decade of the seventeenth century, Spanish fiction emerged as a new influence on French literature and through it 'Moorish' themes swept across France. The *Guerras civiles de Granada* of Pérez de Hita, the story of *El Abencerraje* and other works became well-known, both in their original language and in translation. Voiture, sent as ambassador to Madrid in 1632, disliked the city and the court of Phillip IV and lamented that the old civilisation was gone forever. However, he consoled himself by reading Spanish works including the *Guerras civiles*.[45] The authors known as the *précieuses* knew and admired the *Guerras civiles* and drew inspiration from it. D'Urfé's seminal *l'Astreé* is an imitation of one of the books in which the story of *El Abencerraje* was included by Montemayor, and numerous other novels in this period drew on Spanish and 'Moorish' themes, many of them influenced by works of Cervantes.[46] Spanish grammars and dictionaries proliferated in France to the extent that Cervantes himself remarked that, 'En Francia, ni varón ni muger deja de aprender la lengua castellana' [In France neither man nor woman leaves off learning the Castilian language].[47]

A taste for the Orient took hold in France, in travel writing as more widely in the literature and in French culture generally. The Qur'an was translated into French by André du Ryer in 1647 (and thence into English, by Alexander Ross, two years later). Coffee, first tasted by Frenchmen in Egypt, Turkey, or Persia, became popular in upper-class France. Louis XIV indulged a taste for the consumption of silk, cotton cloth, spices, tea, china, gems, flowers and other imports. He thereby propagated knowledge of these foreign luxuries, helping to 'give rise to a new discourse about the "Orient" which in turn shaped ideas about science, economy and politics.'[48]

Coetaneously with these developments, the 17th century also saw a rapid growth in the transatlantic slave trade. With it came a rising awareness among the public of slave-trading nations that Afro-diasporans were becoming part of the fabric of everyday life, not only on remote plantations, but also in their own countries. This is reflected on the English stage, as well as in poetry. In

---

45   Jean Cazenave, 'Le roman hispano-mauresque en France', *Revue de littérature comparée*, 5e annee (Paris, 1925), 594–640, 603.
46   Cf. Esther J. Crooks, *The Influence of Cervantes in France in the Seventeenth Century* (Baltimore: Johns Hopkins Press, and London: Oxford University Press, 1931).
47   Quoted by Paul Patrick Rogers, 'Spanish Influence on the Literature of France', *Hispania*, Vol. 9, No. 4 (Oct., 1926), 205–235, 209: https://www.jstor.org/stable/331608 [accessed 25/4/2024].
48   From an abstract summarising McCabe's book on the Bloomsbury Publishing website: https://www.bloomsbury.com/uk/orientalism-in-early-modern-france-9781845203740/ [accessed 14/6/2023].

the court of King James I, for example, *The Masque of Blackness* (1605) and the masque of *The Gypsies Metamorphosed* (1621) were performed in blackface by aristocrats, including the queen in the case of the former.

In France, stage plays specifically related black slaves to themes of romantic love. An early instance of this is *Lo Schiavetto* (*the Little Slave*, 1613) brought to Paris by a troupe of Italian players at the request of the Italian-born Queen Marie de Medici, in which the abandoned heroine Florinda disguises herself as a black male slave in order to hunt down and kill her faithless lover. The plot fails and the lovers are reunited.[49] The frontispiece for the printed edition of the play depicts Florinda in blackface and a slave collar, rendering her in the words of Ndiaye, quoting Emily Wilbourne, "'the material embodiment of a literary figure: the slave to love.'"[50]

Enslavement to love is even more disturbingly represented from a modern perspective in a ballet, *The Happy Shipwreck* (*Ballet du naufrage heureux*) (1626), in which black-face characters announce they are 'burning with love' for the ladies in the audience, before being literally burned by an alchemist, ostensibly to beautify their ugliness. And in the *Boutade des Mores esclave d'amour délivré par Bacchus* (1609) the 'Mores', again addressing the female spectators, conclude, 'We are overjoyed and we love our shackles when we have the honor to wear them for you'.

Ndiaye comments that such black-face scenarios resolved any contradictions between old ideals of liberty for all and colonial realities of the burgeoning slave trade, by circulating fantasies of consensual enslavement.[51] However, in the French and English works with which I am primarily concerned, lovers of both sexes and diverse nations are ethnically similar; the slave, literally and metaphorically, is often also the hero or heroine and many of the settings, as in the plays of Spain, are in Islamic lands. The trope and concept of the 'slave to love' have become embedded in European literature accompanied by heightened linguistic usage. In the works reviewed in this chapter, as elsewhere in this book, the 'slave' is typically European, not black, and frequently a man.

---

49 Noémie Ndiaye, 'A Brief Herstory of Baroque Black-Up: Cosmetic Blackness, Gender, and Sexuality', in Ndiaye, *Scripts of Blackness: Early Modern Performance Culture and the Making of Race*, 83–136. (University of Pennsylvania Press, 2022): https://doi.org/10.2307/j.ctv2gz3zr2.5 [accessed 4/02/2023], 87–88.
50 Ndiaye, 88.
51 Ndiaye, 91–96.

3.1 Almahide

Almahide, ou, la reine esclave (1660–63), by Georges and/or Madeleine de Scudéry (today generally attributed to Madeleine) is considered to be the first important 'Moorish' novel in France. The author took the *Guerras civiles* as the main source for this enormously long work, dubbed a 'roman de la grande haleine' [literally, 'novel of the great breath' – i.e. a long-winded novel!] consisting of 6,523 pages. But she also drew on her knowledge of Greek novels for inspiration, especially *Theagenes and Chariclea* as well as *L'Astrée* and the pseudo-Greek *Theagenes et Charide*.[52]

The captive Muslim Queen Almahide's fate is pivotal to the novel. In each of the work's five stories at least one person is captured. The stories' narrator is a slave, a Christian in Granada, who relates his tales to another captive. In addition, Almahide has earlier been abducted by Turkish corsairs, destined to be sold and sent to the Sultan's harem where she is trapped in a forced, loveless marriage. She is rescued by the Spanish nobleman Manuel Ponce de León and taken as a slave to Spain, but is returned to Granada, by now in love with her saviour. This plot-line is entirely missing from the original by Pérez de Hita. The close erotic association between love, captivity and pain is spelled out by Almahide:

> Tout mon repos vient de ma peine
> Et l'Amour m'a bien fait choisir;
> Car si je n'avais point de chaîne,
> Mon coeur n'aurait point de plaisir.
> *Almahide*, liv. III, 1431

> [All my respite comes from my pain
> And Love has made me choose;
> For if I had no more chains,
> My heart would have no more pleasure].

---

52 Nicole Aronson, *The Life of Mademoiselle de Scudéry*, tr. Stuart R. Aronson (Boston: Twayne Publishing, 1978), 23. In 1599 was published the supposed translation from the Greek, *Du vray et parfait amour, escrit en grec, par Athénagoras, philosophe athénien, contenant les amours honestes de Theagenes et de Charide*, actually a heroic novel authored by Martin Fumée. Cf. Günter Berger, 'Legitimation und Modell: Die "Aithiopika" als Prototyp des Französischen heroisch-gallant Romans', *Antike und Abenland*, Vol 30 (2) (1984), 177.

Manuel Ponce de León, whose surname belonged to a historic aristocratic family,[53] and who, in the *Guerras civiles* became one of the queen's champions in the battle to clear her name, is portrayed in *Almahide* not only as her rescuer but also her slave and lover. In Pérez de Hita he was never a slave and the *Guerras civiles* left unresolved the question of whether the Christian nobleman the queen later married was Ponce de León or someone else. Here also are echoes of mediaeval courtly romance, where a man is subject to a woman and exists to serve her needs. Love relations between Muslim women and Christian men occur in several of the sub-plots too.

Whereas in Spanish literature love plays a major part but exists within a larger political framework, in *Almahide* and other French novels love is ever to the fore: indeed, one might say it is not only the point and purpose of the work, but of existence itself. The French novel employs an exaggeratedly formal, elaborate language occasionally echoing that of its source, but it is more often the product of its own author. The slavery motif has become a trope of *preciosité*, as well as a vehicle for discussions of correct behaviour and form. Schweitzer states that French novels of the period of *Almahide* were recognised as 'mirrors of polite society and as hand-books of etiquette' for people at court, as well as being both 'moral' and reflecting contemporary society.[54]

Almahide remained uncompleted by de Scudéry and had little success in its original, rambling form.[55] It was, however, translated into English in 1677 and used by Dryden as a source for his *The Conquest of Granada* (1670–71) (see below).

4   Some Other 'Moorish' and 'Turkish' Themes in French

Almahide drew on other French novels and plays, for example la Calprenède's *Cléopâtre* (1648) and *Faramond* (1661). In *Cléopâtre*, the use of slavery images as metaphors for love recur:

---

53   The Ponce de Leon family holds a special significance in the history of the Christian *reconquista* of Islamic Spain, in that one of their number, Rodrigo, led the expedition resulting in the capture of Alhama (1482), which marked the beginning of the Christians' final push to wrest all the remaining Andalusi territory from the Muslims. Cf. Yiacoup, *Frontier Memory,* 119. Another Ponce de Leon, Juan, joined Columbus in his second excursion to America in 1493, and later became the first governor of Puerto Rico.

54   Jerome W. Schweitzer, *Georges de Scudéry's* Almahide: *Authorship, Analysis, Sources and Structure* (Baltimore: Johns Hopkins University Press, 1939), 61.

55   Schweitzer, 23–27.

> il ne pouuoit rendre les armes qu'à Menalippe, & il ne pouuvoit vivre qu'esclave de Menalippe.[56]

[He could not but yield, nor live, but slave to *Menalippa*].[57]

And,

> Alcimedo laissa sa liberté aux pieds de la diuine Menalippe, & se chargea de ces glorieuses chaisnes qu'il veut porter au tombeau.

[Alcimedon left his liberty at the feet of the divine Menalippa and charged himself with these glorious chains which he will carry to his Tomb].[58]

In Mme de Villedieu's *Les galanteries grenadines* (1678), Ponce de León disguises himself as a Turkish slave to gain entry to the Muslim queen's court, and Mme de Gomes' *Histoire de la conquête de Grenade* (1723) ends with three 'Moorish'-Spanish marriages and the conversion of the three Muslim women concerned. A passionate meeting in the gardens of the Generalife (summer palace, adjacent to Alhambra), interrupted by a duel, forms the centrepiece of this tale. These authors too referred back directly to Pérez de Hita's *Guerras civiles de Granada* for their material.[59]

4.1 Zaïde/Zayde

In 1669 appeared the first volume of *Zaïde, histoire espagnole*, ostensibly by one M. de Segrais but in fact by Mme. de La Fayette. This story, which has been described as a Heliodoran romance,[60] concerns the passion between an

---

56 Gaultier de Coste, seigneur de La Calprenède, *Cleopatre*, Dediee a Monseignevr le Prince, Hvictesme Partie [Part VIII]. Paris, Chez Antoine de Sommaville, a Palais, en la Gallerie des Merciers, á l'Escu de France, MDCLIII (1653), 286.
57 Gaultier de Coste, seigneur de La Calprenède, *Hymen's præludia, or Loves master-peice being that so much admired romance, intituled Cleopatra: in twelve parts / written originally in the French, and now elegantly rendred into English by Robert Loveday* (London: Printed by W.R. and J.R., 1674), in twelve parts: https://archive.org/details/bim_early-english-books-1641-1700_hymens-praeludia-_la-calprende-gaultier-_1659 [accessed 17/5/2024], Part VIII, 'The History Of Alcamenes and Menalippa', 129.
58 French version, 307; *Hymen's præludia*, 126 [i.e. 132, as the pages are misnumbered].
59 Schweitzer, 27–28.
60 Ellen R. Welch, *A Taste for the Foreign: Worldly Knowledge and Literary Pleasure in Early Modern French Fiction* (Newark: University of Delaware Press, 2011), xxiii.

ostensibly Muslim princess (Zaïde) and a Spanish Christian nobleman named Consalve. The novel is in two parts and is set in 9th-century Spain, against the backdrop of the continuing wars between Muslims and Christians during the reign of the Spanish King Alfonso III. The narrative incorporates reports of several victories won by Christians over Muslims, which accords with historic accounts of Alfonso's success in wresting territory back from Muslims and one – essential to the plot – won by Muslims over Christians.

Zaïde draws on the *Guerras civiles de Granada* for some of its material. The novel's structure involves frequent authorial shifts between third-person narratives, accounts related by one of the characters telling other people's stories; first person narratives, in which individuals tell their own stories to others; and letters which are by definition in the first person, exploring characters' own motives and feelings. The settings are on several military frontiers, but love affairs are always central to proceedings. and in the thoughts not only of the main protagonists, but even those not directly concerned – such as the prince, later King, Garcie. Scenes of warfare are hurriedly sketched in, so that the author can return to her intercalated romantic plots, told largely through a series of flashbacks. A distinguishing feature of the novel is how Mme de Lafayette foregrounds the problem of language barriers between lovers of different nations, so often glossed over in other mixed-faith romances. Most of the misunderstandings at the heart of this story are engendered by the hero and heroine's inability to communicate verbally with one another. Only when each learns the other's language are revelations, as well as resolutions, made possible.

Consalve, renamed Gonsalvo in the English-language version, is the only son of Count Nugnez Fernando, Governor of Castile, a 'grandeur [d'] esprit' i.e. a great landowner with a great spirit. Consalve is similarly well-endowed, a man 'd'une beauté extraordinaire.' [of extraordinary beauty], an ideal hero of whom the author says,

> ne voyait rien dans toute l'Espagne qu'on luit put comparer: et son esprit et sa personne avaient quelque chose de si admirable, qu'il semblait que le ciel l'eut formé d'une manière différente du reste des hommes.

> [(there was) none who cou'd in the least be compar'd with him in the whole Kingdom; and there was something so admirable in his Wit and

Person that he seem'd to be form'd in, a Manner different from the rest of Men.]'[61]

The story begins when Consalve, heartbroken after suffering a rejection in love, determines to leave his home in Léon (León) and go into seclusion. Using a pseudonym, he finds refuge in north-eastern Spain at the home of a stranger, Alphonse Ximénès, who had sought out a retreat after also experiencing misfortune, and the two develop a strong friendship.

Early one morning in late Autumn, Consalve is walking by the seashore after a violent storm. He comes upon a richly clothed woman lying insensible on the sand close to the wreck of a sloop. He and Alphonse carry her to the house where Consalve keeps a vigil by her bedside. He remarks on her radiant beauty and also 'la blancheur de sa gorge'/'the whiteness of her neck' (French, 30, English, 12). In the morning when she wakes, she reveals exquisitely fine, large black eyes. Against his declared intention to shun women and remain solitary, Consalve falls in love with her.

Consalve believes the woman's clothes mark her as an 'étrangère', with 'quelque chose de ceux des Maures'/'of foreign parts' and wearing clothes resembling 'Moorish' habit (French, 31, English, 14). but she then begins to speak in a tongue which, despite knowing Arabic and Italian, in addition to Spanish, Consalve does not understand and she does not comprehend any of his languages. Alphonse brings in a woman wearing similar 'Moorish' dress; the two women recognise each other and embrace, the shipwrecked stranger making clear her name is Zaïde/Zayde, while the other woman's name is Félime/Felima: she too has been washed up on the shore and rescued by fishermen. Both appear to be 'd'un rang au dessus du commun'/'of a superior Rank'. Walking to the beach, Zaïde weeps and mentions Tunis several times, which Consalve interprets as meaning she is mourning the loss of a lover and he becomes desperately jealous for the first time in his life. Consalve confides in Alphonse, admitting his true name. The next part of the story is wholly taken up with Consalve's previous history and the cause of his flight from Léon.

---

[61] Mme. de Lafayette, *Zaïde, Histoire espagnole,* ed. Janine Anseaume Kreiter (Paris: Librairie A.-G. Nizet, 1982), 26. An English translation, by P. Porter, appeared in 1678, but I have worked from a later edition: *A Select Collection of Novels, in Six Volumes, Written by the most celebrated authors in several languages, many of which never appear'd in English before, all new translated from the originals, by several eminent hands,* ed. S. Croxall (London: printed for J. Watts; and sold by W. Mears, J. Brotherton and W. Meadows, W. Chetwood, J. Lacy, 1722), 6 vols., Vol. 1 (which includes *Zayde*), 4. All subsequent references will be to these two volumes.

It takes most of the book for Zaïde and Consalve to confess their true feelings to one another: for much of the time they are divided by their lack of a common language, which will give rise to many misconstructions. A key feature of this novel, as with so many tragicomic works, is the miraculous accidents and unfortunate misunderstandings, each of which serves to advance the plot. In the course of the narrative the lovers suffer an enforced separation, during which each learns the other's language: she studies Spanish while he, by chance, discovers her language is Greek. Consalve goes in search of Zaïde. In Tortosa, he glimpses her and learns that she and her companions are 'des personnes considérable parmi les Maures'/'People of Distinction ... among the Moors', looking for a vessel to take them to their homeland (91,127).

In Part II the scene shifts to Muslim-controlled Talavera, on the Muslim-Christian frontier. Consalve has joined King Garcie to fight against the Muslims, and his forces take over the town. Consalve rescues a man who turns out to be Zulema, nephew to the Caliph Osman, a man famed for his courage and dignity and also, unknown to Consalve, Zaïde's father. Consalve then enters the fortress, discovering in it a lavishly ornamented apartment in which are reclining a number of 'Arabian ladies', whom he and his men take captive. Sitting apart from the rest and weeping on a couch is Zaïde, magnificently dressed and looking more beautiful than ever, despite her unhappiness (99, 143). Zaïde speaks to Consalve in Spanish, while he addresses her in Greek and so they are at last able to communicate with one another fully. But now the incessant warfare and the delicacy of the lovers will act like the former language barrier, to separate and confuse them. Consalve reflects on his lucky encounter, 'dans un lieu dont il était le maître'/'in a Place of which he was [now] master' (101, 147) and Zaïde is now his captive. But his anguish is renewed when he learns that Zaïde has a long-term suitor, Alamir, prince of Tarsus, whom he assumes she loves and who is on his way to Talavera.

The Muslims in the story are portrayed ambivalently: sometimes with empathy, but at others, with disgust. For example, following another battle Gonsalve, victorious and surrounding the Muslim infantry on all sides, is so moved to think that 'such brave men' might perish, that he spares their lives, and they in turn express their highest admiration for him. But later, the Muslims are accused of having unparalleled inhumanity and of committing 'tant de cruautés'/'many Barbarities' (109, 162). By chance, Consalve saves the life of a Muslim who turns out to be his rival in love for Zaïde, Alamir. They fight a duel in which both are wounded, Consalve slightly but Alamir most seriously. King Garcie determines to execute Alamir in revenge for a murdered Christian prince, but Consalve intervenes to save his opponent's life a second time.

Félime, who first spoke to Zaïde on the shoreline, reveals that she and Zaïde are cousins. Their fathers, Zulema and Osmin respectively, had lived in Cyprus. Prior to this, their grandfather had been exiled from North Africa; the brothers Zulema and Osmin had married two Cypriot Christian sisters, who were allowed to raise their daughters as Christians. In a parallel but interconnected plot, Félime reveals that she had fallen in love with Alamir, but he only cares for Zaïde. She, however is determined only to marry a Christian. Zaïde rejects Alamir, who dies of his wounds and from a broken heart. Twenty-four hours later, Félime too expires: dying, like her beloved, from a broken heart.

Peace is concluded between the warring Muslims and Christians and all the loose ends of the plot are now tied. Zulema discloses that he intends to convert to Christianity, which seemed to him the only true faith when he married Zaïde's mother, but he was deterred by its 'austerité'/'austerity' and delayed his conversion (162, 260). In Africa he was further deflected, enjoying the 'délices' and 'corruption'/'pleasures' and 'Dissoluteness of Manners' of Islam. The wedding of Zaïde and Consalve is celebrated in hybrid fashion, 'avec toute la galanterie des Maures, et toute la politesse d'éspagne'/'with all the Gallantry of the *Moors*, and all the Politeness of *Spain*' (164, 263).

•••

Mme de Lafayette's novel has many of the classic trappings of its genre, as well as some original features. *Zaïde*'s eponymous heroine is a true hybrid: half European, half 'Moorish', as attested by her combination of white skin and large black eyes. Consalve's sister Hermenesilde is described in similarly mixed, but complementary terms, as having black hair and blue eyes. Zaïde has been Christian all her life but was brought up among Muslims as well as Christians.

The author's emphasis on the importance of a shared language is significant, for with language comes culture. Mme de Lafayette insists that true communication must be intellectual, as well as physical. That each learns the other's language gives them an essential equality missing from other 'Moorish' novels and plays, although it is only when Zaïde is captured by Consalve that their difficulties can begin to be resolved and their love brought to fruition.

Faiths are mingled in the background to the novel, as well as in its primary narrative. The prince of Fez, to whom Zaïde is temporarily promised by her father, is himself hybrid, in that his mother was a Christian captive and he and the hero are revealed to be first cousins, despite being raised in different religions. The close family relationship and a physical resemblance between Consalve and the prince of Fez suggest a wider similarity between Christians and Muslims and their fused history. The commingling of cultures is re-inscribed in the description of a portrait in which Consalve wears African costume, this detail serving further to confuse the identity of the sitter and complicate the novel's outcome. Finally, the merging of cultures is symbolised even in the duplexity of the wedding celebration.

The timing of the novel and the setting for the heroine's upbringing are both significant, in relation to the hybridity of its theme and its characters. In 688 CE the Arab Caliph Abd-al-Malik ibn Marwan and the Byzantine Emperor Justinian II reached an agreement to rule Cyprus jointly, administering the island as a condominium (a territory shared between two or more sovereign powers) and dividing the taxes they collected. The island was de-militarised and neither empire claimed it as a possession. Despite the constant warfare between Christians and Muslims around the Mediterranean, this unprecedented concord lasted (with brief interruptions) for almost three hundred years, ending in 965 CE.[62] Thus during the reign of Alfonso III (848–910 CE), the period in which *Zaïde* is set, the land in which she was raised was both Muslim and Christian. This territorial and political fusion underpins the larger motifs of the book and the dual influences to which Zaïde and her cousin Félime are subject. And so, as Consalve's wife living in a Christian land, Zaïde will need to adapt far less and be less disadvantaged than so many of the other Muslim-to-Christian women converts we have been studying.

But the contrast between Zaïde's story and that of her tragic cousin Félime underscores the essential message: in a work of Christian provenance with religious conversion themes at its heart, the heroine Zaïde achieves happiness in marrying a man of her own faith – Christianity, to which her father Zulema has also converted, erasing differences within the family. Félime pines for a man of a faith different from her own, a Muslim. Had he reciprocated her affections, she would presumably have been required to convert to Islam and this cannot be allowed to happen. The pattern is consistent with that in other works: where the hero is of the dominant religion and the heroine the 'other', happiness may ensue. When these factors are reversed, tragedy is most often the outcome.

4.2　Jean-François Regnard, La Provençale (*Published Posthumously in 1731*)

Almost a century after Cervantes was captured and taken as a slave to Algiers, a similar fate befell the wealthy young Frenchman and future author

---

62　Romilly Jenkins, *Byzantium: The Imperial Centuries AD 610-1071* (London: Weidenfeld and Nicolson, 1966), 50 ff.

Jean-François Regnard. Like his Spanish predecessor, Regnard drew on his personal experiences as a Barbary captive to create a compelling piece of literature. While Cervantes made no attempt to pass off any of his plays or novels as true histories, Regnard's prose work, *La Provençale*, straddles the boundary between historical fact and fiction and is generally taken to be autobiographical, despite its novelistic structure and grandiloquent tone. Regnard assures his readers that he is telling them nothing but the unvarnished truth. The writing is greatly embroidered, however: Regnard's editor Edmon Pilon, discussing the book in the context of French Orientalism, asks, rhetorically,

> est-ce-qu'e Regnard, lui-même amoureux et lui-même captif, n'a pas transformé et forcé tout cela au point qu'a bien des passages de ce charmant livre la fiction apparaît, tant elle est embellie, purement romanesque? [63]
>
> [... Has Regnard, himself in love, and himself a captive, not transformed and embellished {his subject} to the extent that many passages of this charming book appear to be purely fictional?]

And yet, again unlike Cervantes and counter to the practice of so many of his contemporaries, Regnard eschews romance between Christian and Muslim: while several Muslims in the story harbour obsessive desires for the two main Christian protagonists, these prove to be vain, and the essential amour of this novel (and its core theme) is the passionate love of the author's alter-ego Zelmis for the 'Provençale' of the title, Elvire de Prade.

Where fact and fiction merge is in Regnard's account of the protagonists' capture by pirates at sea, many aspects of which were later independently corroborated by Regnard's friend and fellow-voyager, Claude aux Cousteaux de Fercourt (Pilon, Preface to *La Provençale*, 35–40). Examples include the pirates' playing a cat and mouse game while in pursuit of a European ship, by several times changing the flags on their vessels (to French, then Spanish, then Dutch, Venetian and Maltese) so as to confuse their intended victims, before finally hoisting a flag of 'Barbary' and, after a fierce skirmish, seizing the surviving Europeans in their true roles as corsairs and then hauling them back to Algiers (88–91), exactly as in Fercourt's description (Pilon ed., 38–39).

---

63   Jean-François Regnard, *La Provençale, suivie de la Satire Contre les Maris, Textes accompagnés d'une Préface sur Regnard et la littérature barbaresque*, ed. Edmond Pilon (Paris: Édition Bossard) 1920, 33. All future references to *La Provençale* or to the *Satire Contre les Maris* are to this edition, unless otherwise stated.

Regnard starts by describing a visit to Bologna, where he falls in love with Elvire, as does his hero Zelmis. Regnard introduces his persona as narrator because, being such a close friend of Zelmis, 'pour me flatter qu'il ne m'a rien caché de tout ce qui lui est arrivé, et assez persuadé de sa bonne foi pour vous assurer qu'il n'entre rien de fabuleux dans ce que je vais vous dire'. [that I flatter myself that he has hidden nothing from me of anything that has happened to him, and ... can assure you that there is nothing untrue in what I am about to tell you'] (62–63). As for Elvire, Regnard describes her as a woman 'd'une beauté extraordinaire' (64). Zelmis's attachment to Elvire is reciprocated, but she is already married to a M. Prade and has a strong sense of duty which prevents her betraying him, which will ultimately determine the outcome of the romance. Continuing his journey, in September 1678 Regnard/Zelmis finds himself on the same English ship bound for Marseilles as the Prades, which they had boarded at Genoa. Their vessel is followed for some distance and then suddenly overtaken by two pirate ships [Figure 5.2].

FIGURE 5.2   An Algerian Ship off a Barbary Port, oil painting by the 17th century Flemish marine artist, Andries van Eertvelt
CREDIT: NATIONAL MARITIME MUSEUM, GREENWICH, LONDON, PALMER COLLECTION. ACQUIRED WITH THE ASSISTANCE OF H.M. TREASURY, THE CAIRD FUND, THE ART FUND, THE PILGRIM TRUST AND THE SOCIETY FOR NAUTICAL RESEARCH MACPHERSON FUND. HTTPS://WWW.RMG.CO.UK/COLLECTIONS/OBJECTS/RMGC-OBJECT-12243

Arriving in Algiers, Zelmis becomes the property of a cruel master called Achmet Thalem, a Tagarine (a Muslim from Aragon who, like other Muslims, was evicted from Spain). Zelmis wrests various privileges from Thalem by assuring him that a great ransom is in store for him and he is able thus to wander about the town unhindered, exercising his profession as a painter (94). Elvire meanwhile has fallen into the hands of the Dey, Baba-Hassan, who has instantly become besotted with her. This ruler is based on a real man of that name, possibly a renegade, and probably the same one who in 1683 was murdered by his own side after attempting to appease the French, who were bombarding Algiers, by releasing hundreds of French slaves (see Chapter 3).[64] Despite the fact that Baba-Hassan is his rival in love, Regnard describes him admiringly as:

> Ce prince … était doux, civil et généreux, au delà de tous ceux de sa nation. Il n'avait rien de barbare que le nom; et la nature avait pris plaisir à former en Afrique un naturel aussi rich qu'elle eut pu faire en Europe. (93).

> [This prince … was gentle, civil, and generous, above all others of his nation. He had nothing barbarous about him except the name; and nature had delighted in forming in Africa a natural form as rich as she might have done in Europe.]

Baba-Hassan tells Elvire that he will make her servitude as light as possible (93) and he sets out to win her love. This throws Zelmis into paroxysms of emotion which are spelled out in painful detail and include love, jealousy, fear, joy, sadness, misery and more, all experienced simultaneously (96).

The readers (always addressed by Regnard in the feminine, as 'mesdames') are told what they too must be feeling, including alarm. But he reassures them that they have no cause for such sentiments, as Baba-Hassan 'possède toutes les qualités d'un parfait honnête home, n'a pas moins de respect que de tendresse pour elle.' (97) [possesses all the qualities of a perfectly honest (or honourable) man, whose respect for her was no less than his tenderness (or affection) for her …].

In the harem, Elvire goes native, being dressed like other women there in a costume which is sensually depicted as rendering her almost naked, her dark tresses bound with a scarf the colour of fire, falling over her dazzlingly white

---

64   Cf. *Martin's History of France*, ed. and tr. Mary Louise Booth, 2 vols., Vol. 1: *the Age of Louis XIV*, by Henri Martin (Boston: Walker, Wise and Co., 1865), 522; Tinniswood, 240.

shoulders (100). Zelmis is engaged by the Dey to paint her and so is able frequently to visit her: he is then happy to be a slave, so that he can serve her. He succeeds in freeing her and they board a ship bound for the Balearic Islands, at which he is suffused with joy, although Elvire mourns because her husband has not also been saved! However, their freedom is short-lived as in the midst of a thick fog they are intercepted by a Berber brigantine and brought back to Algiers. Fearing the worst, they are confronted by Baba-Hassan but he welcomes Elvire back and in elevated formal language, as if he were himself a Frenchman, declares his love for her:

> je m'étais imaginé que l'amour que j'ai tâché de vous faire paraître en adoucirait les peines. Vous fuyez, cependant, madame, mon amour n'a pu vous arrêter; ... Bien loin de faire aller sur vos pas, je m'estimais heureux de n'avoir plus devant les yeux une personne si belle et si sévère; et je suis au désespoir que votre vue, si contraire à mon repos, renoue des liens que votre éloignement aurait rompus.
> 110–111

> [I had imagined that the love I have tried to show you would soften the pain (of being confined). You fled, however, madam, my love could not stop you ... Far from following in your footsteps, I considered myself lucky to no longer have before my eyes a person so beautiful and so severe; and I am in despair that the sight of you, so contrary to my repose, renews the ties that your distance would have broken.]

She, however, responds in equally flowery language, that she cannot love him.

Now follows a Muslim-Christian anti-romance: Zelmis becomes the object of infatuation of two of Achmet Thalem's harem women, Immona and Fatma [sic]. Calling him to her room, Immona appears stretched out, almost naked on a magnificent Turkish rug like some odalisque painted by Ingres or Matisse. Zelmis describes Immona as 'Cette belle Africaine' (114) and would have been tempted by her, but for his love of Elvire. Rejected by Zelmis, Immona finds her love has turned to hate. In a twist on the Joseph/Potiphar's wife theme, she tells Achmet Thalem that Zelmis has been having an affair with Fatma and almost succeeds in having them both killed. This time, Zelmis is saved by the intervention of the French consul, who persuades Achmet that he will receive a rich ransom for Zelmis and this causes the Algerian to withdraw his complaint. The Consul then proceeds to ransom both Zelmis and Elvire, who informs Zelmis that her husband is dead.

A happy ending would now seem to be in store. The liberated lovers return to Arles and a rapturous welcome from Elvire's family. Just before their wedding is due to take place however, two religious men appear, followed by a miserable-looking individual who turns out to be none other than Elvire's husband Prade: not dead, but ransomed by the holy men. In his attempts to win Elvire's love, Baba-Hassan had paid to get Prade away from Algiers, so he could woo his wife unhindered: he it was who had spread the rumour of Prade's death. But when the Dey realised he had no hope of winning Elvire, he encouraged the ransomers to work on Prade's behalf and then release him. Once again, as when Elvire was in the Dey's harem, multiple feelings of joy, astonishment, fear, spite, and chagrin are mingled among the assembled congregation. Elvire dutifully returns to her spouse and sends Zelmis away, to travel the world in an attempt to relieve his overwhelming sadness. Eventually Prade does indeed die and Zelmis returns to France, anticipating at last to achieve his dream. But Elvire now enters a convent and the tale ends with Zelmis still hoping, by some miracle, to win her one day.

∴

In this novel based on his own life experiences, Regnard has inserted two mixed-faith and mixed-culture infatuations. But these are both one-sided: Muslims loving Christians vainly, their feelings unreciprocated. Yet neither of the Muslim would-be lovers is unappealing. The Dey, Baba-Hassan, is depicted as honourable and kind as well as being extremely powerful, while Immona is dangerous, but also alluring. Immona's attempt at revenge is due partly to her being thwarted, and partly trying to cover herself, in fear of her master. Overwhelmingly, considering its basis in real events, this is a fantastic Oriental tale with many of the trappings of pure fiction and the structure of an 'escape from Barbary' narrative, with a sombre concluding twist. As with Cervantes, the author has romanticised, even glamourised what must in reality have been quite a terrifying experience, and so contributed to the fast-expanding body of European Orientalist literature.

5   The 'Moorish' or 'Turkish' Text in England after the Restoration

We have seen how English authors of the 16th and early 17th centuries looked back to the *Chanson de Roland* and its descendants for source material, as well as to Spain, and the works of Cervantes in particular. However, after the Restoration of Charles II to the English throne, writers turned to more recent treatments of 'Moorish' and Islamic themes, often mediated through French literary sensibilities. These were more in tune with the manners and mores of the period in both countries: such works were linguistically marked by a mixture of elegance and bombast, with a focus on form and fancy, baroque and rhetorical.

As we have also seen, a number of very influential French authors took slavery as an essential element of their narratives and exploited its potential for eroticism and extravagance. By the 17th century, slavery had become firmly associated with the perceived excesses of Islam, in France and in England: in the popular mind Turkish rule and, by extension, that in Islamic lands generally, was signified by despotism and cruelty, but also opulence and indulgence. In short, the seraglio and all its trappings offered a world in which readers and audiences could escape from their daily existence and, by identifying with various master and slave characters, psychologically play at being powerful or overpowered.

Imported directly from the Spanish, or via the French, these stories held a peculiar resonance for several late 17th century English playwrights, in particular, John Dryden and Aphra Behn. After the Restoration, the theatre and the royal court were as close to one another as at any time in English history. King Charles II personally oversaw the reopening of the theatres in 1660, issuing charters for just two establishments: one to Sir Thomas Killigrew for the Theatre Royal (King's Theatre) and the other to Sir William D'Avenant for what became the Duke's Theatre. He also took a personal interest in performances. As Ward puts it,

> the primary object of the London stage, when re-established with the monarchy, was to please the king, his court and its surroundings and, inasmuch as, in that court, many besides the king himself had acquired a familiarity with the French stage and its literature ... French influence upon the English drama in the restoration age was, almost as a matter of course, both strong and enduring.[65]

With D'Urfé's *l'Astreé* began a 'literary reaction towards a refinement of sentiment and expression which had been incompatible with the turbulence

---

65 *The Cambridge History of English Literature*, ed. A.W. Ward and A.R. Waller (Cambridge: Cambridge University Press, 1908–16), 14 vols., Vol. VIII: The Age of Dryden, 1912, 12–13. The first chapter, which is only on Dryden (and in which this quotation falls), is by Ward alone.

of a long epoch of civil war'.[66] In addition to D'Urfé, French writers popular in England included Madeleine de Scudéry and Madame de La Fayette. Not only was La Fayette's *Zaïde, histoire espagnole* popular, but her historical novel *La Princesse de Clèves* had even more success both in France and in England, although it was not published until 1678. These works were characterised in part by elaborate formality of tone, 'heightened' and often sentimental language, obsession with romantic love, and foregrounding idealised lovers torn between love and honor and engaged in acts of heroic self-sacrifice. Such features transferred well to a stage which aimed to please a king and his court, and appropriate acting styles were developed, involving deliberate speaking patterns, gestures, and facial expressions 'in a curious mixture of flamboyance and decorum'.[67]

An early post-Restoration play is the anonymous *Irena, a Tragedy* (1664) which revisits the story of the Sultan and Irene, but which, as Chew points out, is only superficially tragic: a minor character is substituted for the heroine and killed, while she herself enjoys a happy ending, not with the Sultan, who finds another woman to pair off with, but with her former true lover.[68] This structural symmetry is characteristic of the period, as is the ameliorating of a work's tragic source material in order to achieve the 'happy ending'. One of the most famous (or notorious) instances of this practice is Nahum Tate's revision of Shakespeare's *King Lear*, which Tate found so unbearable that he altered the conclusion to preserve the lives of Cordelia and even Lear himself: at the end Cordelia marries Edgar, while Lear regains his throne. This version, written in 1681, remained the standard for theatre performances until well into the 19th century.

Another survivor of the Sultan/Irene theme, but genuinely tragic, is Charles Goring's much later *Irene, or the Fair Greek* (1708). Here Irene is typical of numerous heroines in 'She-Tragedy' dramas of the period, so-called because they feature a suffering and usually powerless, or recently disempowered, heroine at the centre.[69] Irene is forced into a relationship with the Sultan, despite having previously been betrothed to Aratus, captive prince of Corinth. Compelled to become Mahomet's concubine, she breaks off her engagement

---

66   Ward and Waller, *Cambridge History*, 14.
67   Eva Simmons, 'Restoration and 18th-century Drama', in *Augustan Literature: A Guide to Restoration and Eighteenth Century Literature: 1660–1789*, ed. Eva Simmons, one of a series of *Bloomsbury Guides to English Literature* (London: Bloomsbury Publishing Ltd., 1994), 45.
68   Chew, 490, Note 1.
69   Other examples include Thomas Otway's *The Orphan* (1680), John Banks's *Virtue Betrayed, or, Anna Bullen* (1682), Thomas Southerne's *The Fatal Marriage* (1694), and Nicholas

with Aratus, who fights with Mahomet and is killed. The play ends with Irene being placed on the throne and then stabbed by Mahomet, who justifies the murder because Irene had not reciprocated his passion, while his interfering mother, Valide, is confined to her apartments for life. Genest damns the play as 'an indifferent T[ragedy]'; Chew dismisses it entirely.[70] Finally, the theme was appropriated by Dr. Johnson in his neo-classical tragedy, *Irene*, produced in 1749 by the actor–manager David Garrick, who was also a friend and former pupil of Johnson's.[71] It had a successful (for the period) nine-day run, before disappearing from the stage.[72] The appeal of all such plays is well summarised in the Epilogue to the anonymous bloody play *Selimus* (1594):[73]

> If this first part, Gentles, do you like well,
> The second part shall greater murthers tell.

5.1 *John Dryden:* Almanzor and Almahide, Or, The Conquest of Granada

Dryden (named England's first poet laureate in 1668) was a dominant figure in Restoration England, a literary polymath, whose works included savage satires, such as *MacFlecknoe* (1682), *The Medal* (1687) and the political *Absolom and Achipotel* (1681), as well as literary criticism, translations, and numerous plays. Among these were the comedy, *The Wild Gallant* (1663), the tragicomedy *Marriage a La Mode* (1672), and the heroic tragedies *Aurenge-Zebe* (1675) and *All for Love* (1677), based on Shakespeare's *Anthony and Cleopatra*.

Dryden took up Muslim-Christian themes with happier outcomes in two plays, *Almanzor and Almahide, Or, The Conquest of Granada, Parts I and II*, performed and published in the early 1670s (1670–73). These were relentlessly mocked by a number of his contemporaries but contain some beautiful

---

Rowe's The *Fair Penitent* (1703), and *Lady Jane Grey* (1715). Rowe was actually the first to use the term 'she-tragedy', in 1714.

[70] John Genest, *Some Account of the English Stage*, x vols., London, 1832, Vol. ii, 396–97; Chew, 490, N. 1. Cf. also Allardyce Nicoll, *A History of Early Eighteenth Century English Drama 1700–1750* (Cambridge: The University Press, 1929), 80.

[71] Chew; and D.N. Smith, 'Johnson's *Irene*', in *Essays and Studies by Members of the English Association* xiv (1929), 35–53.

[72] Samuel Johnson, *Poems*, ed. E.L. McAdam, with George Milne (New Haven, Conn: Yale University Press, 1964), 110.

[73] *The First Part of the Tragical reigne of Selimus, sometime Emperour of the Turkes, and grandfather of him that now reigneth. Wherein is showne how hee most unnaturally raised warres against his owne father Bajazet, and prevailing therein, in the end caused him to be poisoned: Also with the murthering of his two Brethren Corcut and Acomat.*

poetry.[74] Both the names of Dryden's characters and his plot lines draw heavily on *El Abencerrage* and *Las Guerras civiles,* as well as de Scudéry's *Almahide*. Dryden's purpose, as his famous essay, *Of Heroique Plays* prefixed to Part I makes clear, was to demonstrate the actions of idealised characters in plays 'whose themes', Ward says, 'like those of heroic poetry and fiction in general, are the "emprises" and conflicts of absorbing human passions – love, jealousy and honour – all raised to a transnormal height and expressed with a transnormal intensity'.[75]

Here Dryden's particular ideal is Almanzor, in love with Almahide [Figure 5.3], said to be betrothed to Boabdelin [Figure 5.4], although she is identified as 'Queen' from the outset, and they refer to one another as husband and wife. *The Conquest of Granada* dramatises the period before Granada's fall as a series of conflicts between individuals as well as rival groups within the doomed city. The besieging Christian camp of Ferdinand and Isabella is also depicted on stage and the action shifts from one to the other. Although most of the play's scenes are set in Muslim Granada, Dryden's account reveals an intense interweaving of Muslim and Christian lives, culminating in the disclosure that the eponymous Almanzor is in fact Christian-born, the lost son of the Catholic Duke of Arcos. As a child, he had been captured by pirates and brought up as a Muslim in North Africa. This historically plausible scenario allows him to function as a 'Noble Moor', apparently Muslim. But the conclusion in which Almahide converts to Christianity makes, once again, for a union between Christians, tracing the pattern we have witnessed repeatedly in stories with a 'happy' ending (or, as in this case, at least nominally happy): Christian-born man marries Muslim woman who converts to his faith.

Scenes of capture and enslavement, literal and metaphorical, abound in both plays and in diverse plot lines – transforming a sometime grim reality into scenes of Romanesque and fantastic adventure. Almanzor, fighting with the Zegry clan in an early scene, captures Queen Almahide from the rival Abencerrages. She is both terrified by and attracted to him. But in unveiling her face, she instantly enslaves *him* while remaining both physically and psychologically his captive. In this pivotal scene, the smooth flow of Dryden's heroic

---

74   George Villiers, 2nd Duke of Buckingham, was among the first to ridicule Dryden's *The Conquest of Granada* in his *The Rehearsal* (performed in 1671 and published the following year). This devastating satire did more than anything to put paid to the genre of Restoration tragedy, and especially heroic tragedy. Another assault on Dryden's play came from Henry Fielding, in his *Tragedy of Tragedies, or the Life and Death of Tom Thumb the Great* (1730).

75   Ward, *Cambridge History*, 22.

couplets is ruptured and the lines are fragmented to register the emotional disorientation of the characters, in heightened language typical of the genre:

ALMAH: [*Angrily*] I know I am your Captive, Sir.
ALMANZ: You are – You shall – And I can scarce forbear –
ALMAH: Alas!
ALMANZ: 'Tis all in vain; it will not do:
   I cannot now a seeming anger show:
   My Tongue against my heart no aid affords,
   For Love still rises up and chokes my words.
ALMAH: In half this time a tempest would be still.
ALMANZ: 'Tis you have rais'd that tempest in my will,
   I wonnot love you, give me back my heart.
   But give it as you had it, fierce and brave:
   It was not made to be a woman's slave ...
   Restore its freedom to my fetter'd will.
   Act III, I, Lines 341–358

The ending of Part II, although technically a 'happy' one, is actually ambiguous. After the conquest of Granada, Almahide – by now a Christian – is ordered by the victorious Catholic queen to marry Almanzor. Isabella invokes triple powers to force the union: as queen, as conqueror, and in her self-styled role as surrogate parent to Almahide. Almahide is ambivalent: she remains loyal to her now-dead 'husband's' memory and, although she loves Almanzor, she fears the power of his demanding passion, describing him as a 'greedy Cormorant', devouring 'all my life can give you ...'. (I, V, i, 454–55). The one concession Isabella makes is to allow Almahide a year of mourning before her marriage. At the end of the play, the couple's arranged marriage remains unconsummated.

In *The Conquest of Granada,* the patterns of enslavement are reversed, with Almahide's powers of 'command', and her earlier ability to 'enslave' a man shown to be worthless in the face of stronger political, military and masculine powers. In another play, *Amphitryon* (1690), Dryden has his character Jupiter confirm the temporary and illusory nature of a man's submission to his mistress:

   I gave women beauty, to subdue the strong,
   A mighty Empire, but it lasts not long,
   I gave them pride, to make mankind their slave,
   But in exchange, to men I flattery gave.

FIGURE 5.3 Portrait of an Unknown Woman, traditionally identified as Nell Gwyn (1650–1687), playing the original Almahide in Dryden's *Almanzor and Almahide,* Workshop of Sir Peter Lely. Image in the public domain
SOURCE: HTTPS://COMMONS.WIKIMEDIA.ORG/WIKI/FILE:STUDIO_OF_LELY_-_UNKNOWN_WOMAN,_FORMERLY_KNOWN_AS_NELL_GWYN_-_NPG.JPG

Th'offending lover, when he lowest lies
Submits, to conquer; and but kneels, to rise.
   III, I, 74

5.2   *The Fair One of Tunis*

The Fair One of Tunis, Or, The Generous Mistress: A New Piece of Gallantry (1674), attributed to Charles Cotton, is a translation from the French of a novel called *L'Amoureux Africain, ou, nouvelle galanterie,* by Gabriel de Brémond. Elements of the story strongly recall Cervantes and also Pérez de Hita, although the borrowings are diffuse. But the subject matter which effectively trumps all other considerations is love in its various forms. The setting is subordinate and

FIGURE 5.4 Edward Kynaston (c. 1640–1712), The first Boabdil in *Almanzor and Almahide, or, The Conquest of Granada*, by John Dryden. Image in the public domain
SOURCE: HTTPS://WWW.WIKIDATA.ORG/WIKI/Q1857298

chosen because of its perceived exoticism and potential for allowing indulgence in Oriental fantasies. However, the narrative also binds together pain, pleasure, suffering and beauty in a complex nexus, which at times tips over into sadomasochism.

Like de Brémond and Regnard, Cotton claims authenticity for his story which is, he says 'really a true History', except for some details of the ending. The English author, like his original, dissociates himself from any didactic or naturalistic intent, choosing instead to make as his chief and even only aim 'to entertain the amorous with a new piece of Gallantry.[76] The account which follows traces the fortunes of its French hero Albirond who, forced to flee his homeland after committing some unspecified faux pas (possibly taking part in

---

76 Charles Cotton, *The Fair One of Tunis, Or, The Generous Mistress: A New Piece of Gallantry* (London: Henry Brome, 1674), 4–5.

a duel), lands in Tunis. Here he becomes a favourite of its ruler, the Beglerbeg [Bey of Beys]. Unlike Cervantine heroes, Albirond is not a slave but he is away from his own country and in an alien culture. The woman with whom he falls in love, the Beglerbeg's favourite wife, is effectively a captive in his harem, to whose isolation and inaccessibility high up in a tower numerous references are made.

Albirond first becomes aware of the Beglerbeg's wife while walking in the ruler's gardens, loudly mourning a lost love. From a high window of the seraglio, a beautiful woman sings to him in Spanish (a language he knows well), responding to his laments. She sends down an arrow with a message on it, challenging him to reply. Despite his fervent promises to himself to remain loyal to his beloved Urania, he is soon beguiled by this newcomer's incomparable beauty, set off by her 'exquisite' clothing and 'infinite number' of priceless jewels, glimpsed through the window. He discovers she is the Sultana – 'la Sultane' in the French; in the English translation she is almost always referred to as the 'Sultaness' even though her actual name is 'Kahekma'.

Albirond's encounters with the Sultaness grow ever more amorous each time they meet. At times he climbs up to her window by means of a rope which she lets down to him. At last, he is alone with her in her bedchamber, but at the critical moment when he is about to make love to her, her husband is heard approaching and the panic-stricken lover is forced to hide in her toilet. When the couple resume their embraces, Albirond is still frozen with fear, rendering him completely impotent, much to the frustration of the Sultaness who taunts him with his shortcoming. This episode provides a rare comic interlude in the work. It is not until the next evening that the eager lover is offered another opportunity to acquit himself in the bedroom, a feat he then accomplishes successfully – and repeatedly.

As in the *Guerras civiles* and its descendant, *Almahide*, the Muslim heroine is attended by a virtuous Christian who influences her mistress profoundly. Trapped on one occasion in his lover's quarters, Albirond is left alone with this slave, Isabella, who informs him she is from Valencia in Spain. Her account of her former life is a digressive 'story within a story' but occupies more than a third of the entire narrative. Hers is a memoir of intrigue, incorporating rivalry between two of her suitors and the animosity of her brother and then her father towards the man of her choice. The formality of the exchanges related between Isabella and her beloved Don Pedro contrasts strikingly with the sexual intimacies enjoyed by Albirond and the Muslim Sultaness, so salaciously described by the author as to border on pornography. The Spaniards' emotions are expressed initially through a long epistolary exchange, ornamented with flowery language in which they declare their love. They elope but become separated; she is captured by pirates and sold into slavery, hence her present predicament. At the end of Isabella's long narrative, the two stories coalesce as Don Pedro, following his beloved to Tunis, has contrived to get himself sold as a slave to the Beglerbeg so as to be near her. Several misunderstandings ensue, exposing Don Pedro's obsessively jealous nature. This, however, does not in the least deter Isabella, and after a while the two Spanish lovers are reunited.

Cotton now returns to the main plot with the Sultaness attempting to persuade Albirond to convert to Islam and wait for the Beglerbeg to die, so they can be married. The Frenchman staunchly refuses, telling her he will never renounce his faith. He is also reluctant to betray the Beglerbeg after the latter's many kindnesses to him. Soon Albirond overcomes his scruples with regard to the Beglerbeg and, after some temporary setbacks, the four lovers succeed in escaping together and arrive in Spain. By now all obstacles to their loves have apparently been removed: the Beglerbeg is presumed dead and Isabella's family have either died or become reconciled to her marriage to Don Pedro. The Sultaness converts to Christianity and the two couples celebrate their marriages with feasts, tilts, bullfights, and juegos de caños: entertainments common to both Christian and Muslim cultures. Eventually, Albirond and the Sultaness make their way to France.

Several pages of *The Fair One of Tunis* are devoted to describing Albirond's first walks in the Sultan's garden, which is depicted as a verdant paradisiacal oasis, ever scented with orange and lemon blossoms. Remembering his first love, Urania, he composes elaborate and artificial stanzas which he engraves onto the trees, walls and even leaves of the garden. His pleasure in the garden is enhanced by his melancholy over his loss. In keeping with his French source, Cotton merges pleasure and pain so that while the pleasure induces pain, the pain itself also seems pleasurable. MacKendrick speaks of a context 'in which delight and pain are not readily distinguishable.'[77] The beautiful garden and the love-sick Frenchman become one:

> Every thing in this Garden already proclaim'd, and was full of *Albirond's* passion, the trees were all wrought with his Cyphers, and the walls, nay the very leaves that were not too tender to endure the Graver, were carv'd, and graven with verses, and several other amorous fancies.[78]

---

[77] Karmen MacKendrick, *Counterpleasures*, Albany (New York: State University of New York Press, 1999), 146.
[78] Cotton, *The Fair One of Tunis*, 13–14.

In keeping with the pleasure–pain paradox, Albirond seems to luxuriate in his own suffering. He refers to his 'wounds' multiple times in the novel: twenty-nine to be precise, eight of which are metaphorical, referring to the wounds of love, while the rest allude to injuries actually suffered in combat or through assault. Still mourning the loss of Urania, Albirond challenges the garden groves rhetorically, 'Can you not cure my hearts deep wound …?' (15). Then, abandoning her memory by degrees and replacing her instead with the Sultaness as his adored mistress, Albirond becomes 'our new wounded *Amoroso*' (33). He experiences the charms of the Sultaness as poison, mixed in with fruit and sweets she has thrown down to him:

> the sweets that had so charm'd him, were not those he had tasted in the Conserves, but they were the fair eyes of the beautiful *African,* that in poisoning, had enchanted his heart. (32)

But the Sultaness is also wounded by her love for Albirond: speaking through her faithful slave Isabella, she tells him, 'I find my heart enclin'd to lay open its deepest wounds to your view'(95). Nor is the pleasurable pain confined to the metaphorical but may also be literal. Able at last to embrace her Frenchman, albeit through the bars of a window which initially separates them the Sultaness, in kissing him, bites his lips so hard that the blood spurts 'in above twenty places' (68). This she follows by scratching him hard enough to tear his skin, all of which merely inflames both their desires. From this point, the encounter develops further with Albirond ready to match his mistress's ability to hurt:

> *Albirond* in revenge of this kindness recompenc'd himself with his hands for the loss of his bloud, and whilst the *Sultaness* carrest him after this bloudy manner, grop'd her all over, without any manner of respect, which she was so far from being angry at, that she took no notice at all of that action, no more than if she had not perceiv'd it (68–69).

Here we are deep into the territory of sadomasochism, with the Sultaness repeatedly inflicting pain on Albirond, which increases his sexual arousal. Jessica Benjamin reminds us that in erotic play, the roles of tormentor and tormented, of master and slave, do not necessarily follow normal patterns of masculine–feminine as they occur in the conventional social order. Even though in society men 'have everywhere dominated women':

it is apparent that the roles of master and slave are not intrinsically or exclusively male and female respectively; as the original 'masochist' of *Venus in Furs* (Leopold von Sacher-Masoch) reminds us, the opposite is often true: the actual practice of sado-masochism frequently reverses heterosexual patterns.[79]

The irony here is that the Sultaness inflicting pain is actually and at the same time the one who is restrained, confined within her apartments (behind bars), while Albirond, though technically a slave, is free to roam the gardens. He responds to his lover's attacks with assaults of his own, groping her all over 'without any manner of respect' in a sense imitating a characteristic of rape. The lovers are acting out and exchanging roles in the relationship of master and slave. Benjamin tells us that 'aggression, internalised as masochism, reappears as sadism. Through this internalisation comes the ability to play both roles in fantasy, to experience vicariously the other's part, and so enjoy the act of violation',[80] as well as, I would add, the act of being violated.

An essential part of the lovers' enjoyment is the thrill of transgression: engaging in that which is forbidden. A pleasurable sense of risk is embedded in the text: the Sultaness is married, the 'property' (as woman and as slave) of another man; and he is no ordinary man, but a ruler owning every resource for punishing any offence. Moreover, the Beglerbeg has befriended Albirond, favoured him and given him the run of his palace and gardens. The Frenchman's courtship of the Sultaness is therefore the most blatant betrayal, as well as placing them both in mortal jeopardy. However, it is these very factors which intensify the excitement: Isabella says, 'if Love had not its dangers, the pleasure would not have been half so great' (92). The danger is not just to the heart, but also the rest of the body.

As in *The Renegado* and other works we have considered, we witness a woman voluntarily accepting a life of subservience to her husband and his culture, although the Sultaness, unlike Donusa or Greene's heroines, is explicitly described as being among numerous 'fair slaves' in a 'prison' [i.e. the harem, 53]. However, in relation to Albirond, she initially has the upper hand. Early on Albirond is described as being in her thrall, 'ravisht with the delight of beholding so beautiful a person, and to such a degree, that, as if he had been charm'd, he had not once the power to open his mouth, to speak so much as one syllable to the fair *Sultaness*' (35); and she proudly warns him that

---

79   Jessica Benjamin, *The Bonds of Love: Psychoanalysis, Feminism, and the Problem of Domination* (London: Virago Press, 1990), 74.
80   Benjamin, *The Bonds of Love*, 69–70.

> I am one of those Conquerors who never restore the places I have taken by assault, and am of an humor to reduce all things to fire, and bloud, before I will consent to be depriv'd of what is once my own (39).

But when at last their love is consummated, their roles are palpably reversed; the narrator tells us:

> this is most certain that never Conqueror since the first practice of arms, came more puft with glory for the greatest victory he ever obtein'd, than *Albirond* came off from this amorous encounter (243).

Cotton (following de Brémond) explicitly connects metaphorical and literal slavery when speaking about the lovers' joyful anticipation of leaving Tunis, 'people escape very willingly out of servitude to go meet a Lover … although it be but to quit one slavery for another' (273–74). But with the escape, Albirond has gained control of his mistress, his emotions, and his life; only the Sultaness is, in effect, exchanging one literal form of slavery for another: in the battle of love, she has lost and Albirond has won. In future she will be triply subdued: as wife; as foreigner in a strange country, without the relative advantages of a Zaïde, obliged to learn and speak a strange language; and as woman in a patriarchal religion. It is a more palatable form of subjection than her last because entered into willingly and for love. Nevertheless, she has been re-subjugated. And, emblematically, despite the ornate language, exotic setting, and adventure trappings of the piece, it is another victory of Christianity over Islam.

⋯

Publication of this exotic and erotic tale coincided more or less precisely with the publishing of new accounts of actual North African slavery. Many of these narratives exhibited a certain bravado as they described the slave's inevitable bold and daring escape. But, as if perhaps to enhance the reader's admiration for the slave's courage, they made no bones about communicating, or exaggerating, the fears, hardships including near-starvation and tortures, and the general brutality, quite literally experienced by the enslaved European. The diarist Samuel Pepys in 1661 described hearing former captives relating how they [in Algiers], eat nothing but bread and water... are beat upon the soles of their feet and bellies at the Liberty of their *Padron* ... And theft there is counted no crime at all.[81]

Another shocking memoir, *The Adventures of (Mr T.S.) An English Merchant, Taken Prisoner by the Turks of Argier* appeared in 1670. This pulls no punches in describing the Turks' gruesome methods of torture and execution.[82] And Emmanuel d'Aranda's partly horrifying slavery narrative (see Chapter 3), was reprinted, both in French and in English, at least five times between 1657 and 1671. Given the timing of these novels, coincident to the appearance of such grim travellers' tales, there is an illogical paradox in the romanticisation and linguistic elevation of their themes, as well as the love stories at their heart. Only once in *The Fair One of Tunis* does the protagonist Albirond genuinely fear for his life when he anticipates that 'the least that could befall him, should he be taken ... [in the Sultaness's private quarters], was to be roasted, or fleed [flayed] alive, and that without appeal or any hopes of pardon' (86).

5.3 *Some Other Post-Restoration Texts in French and English*

One use to which the slave theme was put during this period was in political satire, including *Hattigé, ou les amours du roi de Tamaran* – also known as *La belle Turque* by Sébastien de Brémond (1671?), a Frenchman who lived for a time in England. His story was translated into English as *Hattigé: or the Amours of the King of Tamaran* (1680). *Hattigé* has been read as a satire on the extra-marital affairs of King Charles II, but I am more interested in it as a romance, rather than in its real-life politics. The action takes place largely in the Mediterranean, where the Maltese knights are at war with Muslim corsairs but are themselves pirates too. One of the knights takes pity on a Turkish noblewoman whom his forces have captured and enslaved. She offers to tell him about Tamaran, a country where 'Love at this day reigns more absolute than ever he did at Cyprus or Granada' and about its king, who like his subjects is 'wholly given up to love'.

The narrative which follows is a cynical and, at one point, scatological tale of seduction, partly incestuous intrigue and plotting, in a society depicted like an Ottoman court, with the harem concubine Hattigé at the centre. Back in the framing tale, the knight has himself become enslaved to 'the fair slave' and climbs up to her window to free her from her chains, but then takes his leave of

---

81 Quoted in Gerald MacLean and Nabil Matar, *Britain and the Islamic World 1558–1713* (Oxford: Oxford University Press, 2011) 143.
82 MacLean and Matar, 144–45.

her rather than marry her. The king of Tamaran was said to be a caricature of Charles II with Hattigé representing his mistress, the Duchess of Cleveland.[83] But the framing story is a conventional slave romance, employing the paradox of the free man enslaved to the slave.

In 1677, and following on from the success of his *L'amoureux Africain*, de Brémond published *l'heureux esclave,* many of whose details echo and repeat those of their predecessor. The book was immediately translated into English as *The Happy Slave* (1677)[84] and proved so popular in England that four editions had appeared by 1699. The title announces a work in which the subjects of captivity and slavery have been transformed from the traditional accounts of cruelty and misery, into material wholly preoccupied with romance. This is confirmed even in its introductory paragraph:

> AFRICK, for some Ages, hath past for a part of the World, where the People were no less Cruel and Savage than the Lions and Tygers that fill the Desarts of that Countrey: But since the discovery of Love there, it hath appear'd, that as Love grows in all Countreys, so *Barbary* it self hath nothing of Barbarous but the Name. To verifie this, I shall entertain you with a piece of Gallantry acted there, which may justifie what I affirm.[85]

The novel concerns a Roman aristocrat called Alexander, who is young, wealthy and good-looking, but disinclined to marry. He is captured at sea by Barbary corsairs and taken to Tunis. However, far from tormenting him, the 'gallant and generous' and equally attractive renegade into whose power he falls, the Bassa (Pasha) Mahomet, lodges his prize in a 'handsom Apartment'. There, wounds Alexander received in the course of being captured are tended and as he begins to recover, the Bassa seeks out his company and befriends him.

---

83 Cf. e.g. Rachel K. Carnell, 'Slipping from Secret History to Novel' (2015), English Faculty Publications, Cleveland State University, 78: https://engagedscholarship.csuohio.edu/cleng_facpub/78 [accessed 1/6/2023].

84 A previous book with the same title, *l'Heureux esclave*, by the physician, surgeon and explorer, Pierre-Martin de la Martinière (1634–76?), was published in Paris by Olivier de Varennes in 1674, but purports to be a factual and autobiographical captivity narrative, and appears to have no connection with the work of Sébastian de Brémond, unless, perhaps indirectly, as source material. Episodes chronicle attacks by corsairs on vessels of various countries, and the account dwells on the cruel punishments and tortures meted out to both Muslims and Christians for various offences, real or perceived.

85 *The Happy Slave, a Novel in three Parts compleat, translated from the French* [*l'Heureux esclave, by* Gabriel de Brémond – i.e. Sébastian Brémond] *by a Person of Quality* [i.e. P. Porter] (London: Printed for Gilbert Cownly, 1686), 1.

Each man tries to outdo the other in gallantry: Alexander confesses his wealth and offers a substantial ransom payment, while the Bassa assures him that all he wants is his captive's company and to indulge in such pleasures as hunting, walking and horse-racing. Soon the Bassa determines to find his slave a mistress. He chides the Italian for his reluctance, telling him that in his own country (Tunis) men follow the 'Law of Nature' before that of Islam, feeling themselves 'obliged to pay kind regard and affectionate tenderness to Female Beauty, and expect from it a return of complacency' (21), a sentiment which might in reality befit society in France, as well as North Africa. Here are echoes of the *Guerras civiles*, where embattled Granadines spend their time jousting and pursuing affairs of the heart, rather than minding those of the state (Chapter 4).

The woman the Bassa chooses for Alexander is a young Italian called Laura, slave to his wife, the Sultaness Alhie. But Laura informs Alexander that it is her mistress who, trapped in an arranged marriage, neglected by her husband, and having 'ever had a great inclination for Christians', yearns for a man like himself. Alexander is torn between desire and reason, which tells him not to engage with the wife of a man to whom he is so beholden, but passion triumphs. Forbidden at first to see the Sultaness, he eventually glimpses her, reclining in the classic odalisque posture on a bed of damask, her hair jet black and her skin snow white; her rich costume, adorned with gold, pearl and diamonds, recalls the seductive image of Elvire in the harem, in Regnard's *La Provençale*. They become lovers. As in the author's *L'Amoureux Africain*, the lovers' kisses are so passionate that they draw blood; this time it is her blood, an occurrence so satisfying to the Sultaness that she saves the blood in a handkerchief to show Laura. After many vicissitudes, deceptions and disguises, the lovers escape and eventually reach Italy. The Sultaness converts to Catholicism, and she and Alexander are married.

A parallel plot concerns the beautiful slave and favourite, Laura, who has been captured by pirates and brought to Tunis in the course of fleeing from her home in Naples. There she had been deceived and dishonoured by the Marquess Hippolito, whom she had loved and believed reciprocated her feelings. In Tunis complications ensue when the Bassa falls in love with her and vainly tries to seduce her. The Marquess returns to the story, now renamed Beyran, having reached North Africa, pretended to convert to Islam and become the favourite 'Aga' (officer of state) of the Dey. The two former lovers are reconciled and they too flee, eventually meeting up by accident with the shipwrecked Alexander and Sultaness. Multiple patterns are repeated in the novel, with desperate love triangles involving all the characters in Italy, and then again in Tunis. A third narrative reveals the mirror–like fate of a Muslim,

Assen, who had been slave to Laura's family in Italy and escaped. In between he had been the lover of Laura's stepmother. In Tunis he becomes a favourite of the Bassa, but then also the means to bring all the lovers together. He too converts to Christianity at the end.

Slavery is a dominant feature, as are slaves who become favourites across religious boundaries. All the main characters in the novel, apart from the Sultaness – Laura, Alexander, Assen and the Marquess/Beyran – are loved by masters who are of another religion. Conflicts between love and loyalty, and passion and reason also recur as plot devices in each of the love triangles. Finally, by means of disguise and dissembling, all complications are resolved but at the expense of the Muslim rulers – their favours notwithstanding. But faith-identity is revealed as fluid throughout and the lives of Muslims and Christians are intricately entwined right until the end, when the Christians separate themselves from the ruling Muslims and those Muslims travelling with them convert to become absorbed into Christian society.

5.4   *Aphra Behn/Thomas Southerne* Oroonoko

Whereas romantic literature involving slaves of black African (i.e. non-Muslim) origin evolved to take its place eventually in the Abolitionist debate, that involving slaves in Muslim lands remained predominantly entertaining. Aphra Behn's most famous novel *Oroonoko, Or, the Royal Slave* (published 1688) is about two Africans taken in slavery to an English-owned plantation.[86] The hero is an African prince, tricked into slavery by English traders and brought to the South American country Surinam. He is separated from his beloved wife Imoinda but meets up with her unexpectedly in Surinam, where she is also captive. Eventually he leads an abortive slave rebellion. He kills Imoinda to spare her a worse fate, but before he can commit suicide, he is caught and brutally put to death. Oroonoko is, throughout, portrayed as an embodiment of nobility and refinement.

The novel was reworked into a play by Thomas Southerne (1696) and, in this better-known form, was eventually used by the Abolitionist movement, although neither the novel nor the play is abolitionist in intent. Significantly, Southerne changed the character of Imoinda from black to white, making the love affair a mixed-race one and, as noted in relation to other works, underlining the spiritual and emotional kinship between two individuals across ethnic lines.

---

86   *Oroonoko* in *The Works of Aphra Behn* (6 vols), ed. Montague Summers (1915), Vol. v, available online: https://www.gutenberg.org/ebooks/author/9866 [accessed 24/4/2024].

Despite its focus on plantation slavery, Behn's story is obliquely and, perhaps unexpectedly, influenced by 'Moorish'/French predecessors. She had read *Hattigé* and other French novels and used them as sources for her plays; in *Oroonoko* the influence is more covert. *Oroonoko* is not a 'Moorish' novel, in the sense that none of the action takes place in a Muslim land. But, as Moira Ferguson among others has pointed out, in the first part of the book which is set in Oroonoko's home country, Coromantien in West Africa, the court that is described resembles an 'Oriental' one. The king rules as autocratically as any 'Oriental' despot. He has a harem, which Behn calls an 'Otan', a Turkish word, and he has many wives, concubines and eunuchs. The lavishness of the court, its gardens adorned with citrus groves, the banquets, balls, and love intrigues would all fit in with a 'Moorish' or 'Turkish' setting. Moira Ferguson detects in this part of the novel scenes which 'conjure up a picture of a Middle Eastern seraglio' that are possibly indebted to Dryden's Orientalist play, *Aureng-Zebe* (1676).[87] The world of Coromantien has also been likened to that of a European royal court with its mixture of luxury and scheming: the character Oroonoko has been interpreted as a personification of James II, who like Oroonoko himself, represented Behn's 'ideal masculine hero' and was betrayed – as Behn would have seen it – by those around him.[88]

The influence of the French novel is felt throughout the book, moreover, in the flowery language used to describe Oroonoko and Imoinda, and the extravagant courtesy with which he courts her. She is described as his 'conqueror'; his love is referred to as his 'Flame'. Oroonoko is ruled by the two principles pervasive in both French and English heroic literature of the period: love and honour: he holds 'refin'd Notions of true Honour, that absolute Generosity, and that Softness that was capable of the highest Passions of Love and Gallantry' (135). The world into which Oroonoko and Imoinda are brought as slaves, run by 'such notorious Villains as Newgate never transported' (200) and largely peopled by 'Rabble' and 'inhuman ... Justices' (208), is in crude contrast to the civilised land of Coromantien, where the lovers had lived in dignity and ease, before the king's vanity and cruelty ended their lives there.

• • •

---

87 Moira Ferguson, *Subject to Others: British Women Writers, 1670–1834* (New York and London: Routledge, 1992), 37.
88 Melinda S. Zook, 'The political poetry of Aphra Behn' in *Cambridge Companion to Aphra Behn*, ed. Janet Todd and Derek Hughes (Cambridge: Cambridge University Press, 2004), 46, 48, 60.

CHAPTER 6

The 18th Century Onwards

1   Galland and the Spread of Orientalism

The work of Antoine Galland at the end of the seventeenth century and especially in the early eighteenth century was critical in renewing Europe's fascination with the Orient. The first influential work bearing Galland's name was his *Bibliothèque orientale, ou dictionnaire universel contenant tout ce qui regarde la connoissance des peuples de l'Orient* ('Oriental Library'), a huge compendium of information about Islamic culture. It was begun by Barthélemy d'Herbelot de Molainville who died in 1695 leaving it unfinished and completed by Galland, being finally published in 1697. The alphabetically organised miscellany was reissued, with alterations and additions, several times and in various languages in the course of the eghteenth century. This was a major contribution to European knowledge about the Middle East, influencing the historian Edward Gibbon, who drew on it for his *Decline and Fall of the Roman Empire* (1776–88), as well as the poets Robert Southey and William Beckford, who 'plundered it' for their 'Oriental' fantasies, such as Beckford's Gothic *Vathek, an Arabian Tale or The History of the Caliph Vathek* (written in French, 1782; then translated into English by the Rev. Samuel Henley in 1786).[1]

Galland is best known for his hugely successful *Les mille et une nuits* (1704–17), the first parts of which were rapidly translated into English as *One Thousand and One Nights* (1706) [Figure 6.1]. These stories introduce Islamic fairy tales with their themes of magic, both benign and evil, into mainstream European literature through tales of love, mystery and adventure. Among French and English authors who drew on the *Nights* for inspiration were Chateaubriand, Stendahl, Coleridge, Byron, Thomas de Quincy, and Edgar Allan Poe. The *Nights* also inspired generations of librettists, composers, choreographers, painters and illustrators. Galland's work places him in the tradition of French diplomat-authors, such as Guillaume Postel and Jacques Gassot (See Chapter 5): he was for a time attached to the French Embassy at Istanbul and travelled to Syria and the Levant. He knew Arabic, Turkish, and Persian.

---

1 Nicholas Dew, *Orientalism in Louis XIV's France* (Oxford: Oxford University Press, 2009),170.

FIGURE 6.1   Illustration from *The Arabian Nights* by Dutch artist David Coster (1686–1752): Shahrazad tells her story to Shahryar, while her sister Dunyazad is listening. Image in the public domain
SOURCE: WIKIMEDIA COMMONS – HTTPS://EN.M.WIKIPEDIA.ORG/WIKI/FILE:DAVID-COSTER-MILLE-ET-UNE-NUIT.JPG

2   England

The taste for Orientalist trappings expanded in England, as in France. In the middle of the 17th century, trade with the Ottoman Empire already amounted to one-tenth of all English trade.[2] Imports of coffee led to the establishment of coffee-houses frequented by an eclectic group of people, including politicians and literati. And, as Charlotte Morgan has shown, writers of fiction 'were not slow to perceive the picturesque value of the Moorish setting'.[3] By the early 18th century, exotic 'Eastern' tropes had permeated English literature and culture. Daniel Defoe has his character Roxana performing a 'lascivious pseudo–Turkish dance', bejewelled and in 'Turkish dress' which leaves her breasts partly uncovered, introducing into the 'already luxurious court of Charles II [where part of the story is set] a note of near-Eastern luxury'.[4] A few generations later, the Regency court was often associated with the Turkish seraglio.[5] Such predilections were to become increasingly prevalent among the rich upper classes, many of whom adorned their homes with precious imports from the East, such as Oriental carpets; they ate food flavoured with nutmeg, cloves and other spices from the East and they had their portraits painted dressed in Oriental attire.

3   Continuation of Slavery and Romance Themes

The fusion between tropes of literal slavery and metaphorical slavery to love, in the Petrarchan sense, present in the literature from early on as we have seen, acquires added force in the 16th century. Cervantes is a towering figure in the literature of slavery and romance, not only because of his own substantial output, but for his effect on other European writers. Slavery and romance tales, many drawing on works of Cervantes as source material, were now well established in many European countries and the 'Moorish' novel was becoming quotidian fare for readers.

A closer look at Samuel Croxall's *A Select Collection of Novels and Histories* (1722), which includes *Zayde* (Chapter 5 above), is instructive in this respect [Figure 6.2]. Dedicated to Princess Anne, the *Collection* is noteworthy in that all the novels which comprise its six volumes are of foreign origin, mainly

---

2 Charles Issawi, 'The Ottoman Empire in the European Economy, 1600–1914. Some Observations and Many Questions', in *The Ottoman State and its Place in World History*, ed. Kemal H. Karpat (Leiden: E.J. Brill) 1974, 114.
3 Charlotte E. Morgan, *The Rise of the Novel of Manners: a Study of English Prose Fiction between 1600 and 1740* (New York: Columbia University Press) 1911, 37.
4 Maximilian E. Novak, *Daniel Defoe: Master of Fiction: his Life and Ideas* (Oxford: Oxford University Press) 2001, 621. Defoe's novel, *Roxana, or the Fortunate Mistress*, was published in 1724, but is set during the English Restoration period.
5 Novak, 621, Note 50.

French and Spanish, plus a few Italian. They include numerous 'Moorish' stories, among them, in addition to *Zayde,* translations of *Ozmín y Daraja* (now called Osmin and Daraxa); *The Happy Slave* from the French *l'Heureux esclave*; *Hattigé,* retitled *The Beautiful Turk*; Cervantes's *La historia del cautivo* (*The History of the Captive*) and several others of his *novelas exemplares* encompassing captivity themes, such as *The Liberal Lover* from his *El amante liberal* and *The English Spanish Lady,* translated from *La Española inglesa*.[6] By 1752 the *Collection* had been reprinted several times, with new stories being added to later editions, and new editions continuing to appear subsequently, testifying to its lasting popularity.

Preceding the *Collection* is an English translation of an essay by the French Jesuit priest, antiquary and scientist Pierre Daniel Huet, in the form of a scholarly letter to his friend, the French poet and novelist, Jean Regnaud de Segrais, *Traité de l'origine des romans,* first published in 1670. An English version came out just two years later.[7] The essay preceding the *Collection*, now named *Upon the Original of Romances,* traces the history of romance, from the ancient Egyptians, Arabs, Persians, Syrians, Greeks and Romans, down to Huet's own day. Early examples of romance he cites include Achilles Tatius's *Clitophon and Leucippe* and Heliodorus's ubiquitous *Aethiopica*. Arab works, he adds, employ for their effects, 'nothing ... but Metaphors ... Similitudes and Fictions'; even the Qur'an was thus embellished 'to the end that it might more easily be learnt, and not easily forgotten'.[8]

Huet adopts the Horatian ideal for fiction, arguing that romance should aim to educate as much as to entertain. In fact, its principal purpose should be didactic: to reform its readers by demonstrating the rewards of virtue and chastisement of vice. But, since 'the Mind of Man' naturally rebels against instruction, 'he must be sooth'd and deluded by the Baits of Pleasure, and the Author must temper the Severity of Precept by the Agreeableness of Example'

---

6 For more on English translations of Cervantes and the influence of his works in England, cf. *The Cervantean Heritage: Reception and Influence of Cervantes in Britain*, ed. J.A.G. Ardila (London: Modern Humanities Research and Maney Publishing, 2009).

7 Huet, *A Treatise of Romances*, 1672.

8 *Monsieur Huet's Letter to Monsieur de Segrais, Upon the Original of Romances,* prefixed to *A Select Collection of Novels in Six Volumes, Written by the Most Celebrated Authors in Several Languages, Many of which Never Appear'd in English Before; and all New Translated from the Originals, by Several Eminent Hands*, ed. Samuel Croxall (London: Printed for J. Watts, 1720), vii.

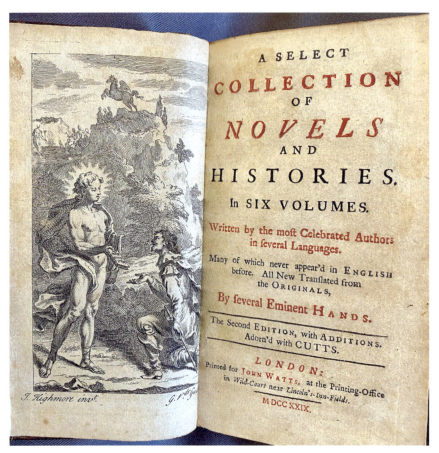

FIGURE 6.2 Flyleaves for Vol. 1 of the second edition (1729), of Samuel Croxall's *A Select Collection of Novels and Histories*
PHOTOGRAPH BY THE AUTHOR, REPRODUCED BY PERMISSION OF THE MASTER AND FELLOWS OF ST. JOHN'S COLLEGE, CAMBRIDGE

in order to achieve the necessary improvement.[9] In other words, moral teaching should be sugar-coated with adventure, romance, and drama.

The choice of contents for Croxall's Collection, as well as its favourable reception, demonstrate the extent to which translations of 'Oriental' slavery and romance stories such as *Ozmin y Daraja*, *Zaïde* and the rest were becoming part of mainstream fiction in England, as in France. In later editions, they

---

9 *A Select Collection of Novels and Histories,* ed. Samuel Croxall (London: Printed for John Watts, at the Printing Office in Wild-Court, near Lincolns-Inn-Fields, 1720, repr. 1729), 6 vols., Vol. I, ii.

mingled happily with English historical narratives such as *The History of Lady Jane Grey, the History of Jane Shore, The Loves of Henry II* [of England] *and Fair Rosamond,* and a prose version of the *Unhappy Favourite* (*The Unhappy Favourite: Or, the Fall of Robert, Earl of Essex*), earlier conceived as a stage play of that name by John Banks (1681) which was itself inspired by a novel: *The Secret History of the most Renowned Queen Elizabeth and the Earl of Essex* (1680).[10]

By 1769 the Collection had expanded to include not only several new novels added to each volume, but a seventh volume containing five supplementary novels, some tragic (like *The Unhappy Favourite*) and some happy in outcome, some continental, and some English in origin.[11] As Michael Gamer points out, Croxall is offering fiction that can be considered as typical (exemplary), but also, 'as the term "select" affirms, Croxall claims to have assembled only the finest specimens of their kind ... In this sense, *A Select Collection of Novels* does everything in its power to claim an elite status for its assembled contents ... The aim here is to raise the prestige of the novels contained therein.'[12]

Thus the 'slavery and romance' novels are identified as being of the highest order and worthy of providing instruction as well as entertainment.

4 Slavery and Romance in the 18th Century Theatre

4.1 George Colman the Younger

By now anything to do with pirates, slaves, 'Turks' or 'Moors' signalled passion and romance and these themes offered rich sustenance for the theatre, often sentimentalised, and reflecting ideals of the Enlightenment and current notions of the 'Noble Savage'. The popular playwright George Colman the Younger chose Cervantes's *La historia del cautivo* (*the History of the Captive*), as well as his two Algerian plays *El trato de argel* and *Los baños de argel,* as sources for his three-act musical drama *The Mountaineers* (1793), whose primary themes had by now become stock material.

---

10 Cf. David Wykes, 'The Barbinade and the She-Tragedy: on John Banks's *The Unhappy Favourite*', in *Augustan Essays in Honour of Irvin Ehrenpreis*, ed. Douglas Lane Patey and Timothy Keegan (Newark: University of Delaware Press and London and Toronto: Associated University Presses, 1985), 79.
11 *A Select Collection of Novels,* 7 vols. (Dublin: James Hoey Jr., 1769–72).
12 Michael Gamer, 'Assimilating the Novel: Reviews and Collections', in *English and British Fiction, 1750–1820*, ed. Peter Garside and Karen O'Brien, Vol II of the *Oxford History of the Novel in English*, 12 vols. (Oxford: Oxford University Press, 2015), 542.

The Mountaineers features three sets of lovers: the enslaved Spaniard Virolet and his 'Moorish' beloved Zorayda who wants to convert to Christianity; Virolet's sister Floranthe and her lover Octavian (their story is a sub-plot based on Cervantes's *Story of Cardenio and Lucinda*, interpolated, like *The History of the Captive*, into *Don Quixote*); and Sadi, a 'Moorish' slave-guard who converts from Islam to Christianity, and the servant Agnes, his Christian mistress. *The Mountaineers*, possibly one of 'the most outstanding successes of the 18th century',[13] featured two members of the celebrated Kemble family among its cast: Elizabeth (nee Satchell) who played Zorayda, and John Philip Kemble as Octavian. In the early 19th century Octavian was played by the great reforming actor Edmund Kean.[14]

Set in al-Andalus during the Siege of Granada, the play dramatises the escapes of the various captives and eventual uniting of the appropriate lovers. Details of the Virolet/Zorayda plot follow that of Cervantes's *La historia del cautivo* and *Los baños de argel*. Dubbed a melodrama by the theatre historian Allardyce Nicoll, the play is raised from banality, he also suggests, by, among other factors, the absence of a true villain, and softening of the harsher element of predecessors. These include threats of death by a candidate for the role of villain, Zorayda's father Bulcazin Muley, who then relents.[15] This turn of events accords with the 'sentimentalising' tendencies of many eighteenth century English plays to ameliorate characters and situations borrowed from earlier sources so as to avoid outright villainy, tragedy, etc. Bulcazin achieves a measure of reform at the end, although he does not attain full redemption as he does not convert to Christianity. In keeping with the colonial period in which it was written, the play is replete with overtly racist metaphors and repeated associations of Muslim-ness with dark skin.

The Muslim ban on alcohol is also mocked and there is gung-ho English nationalism too, but abolitionist sentiments are expressed by Zorayda (1, ii, 15). Despite its racist elements, the play also exhibits a kind of egalitarianism, or perhaps rather a sympathy for and identification with the lower classes. Other plays of George Colman the Younger connect him with mixed-faith and mixed-race motifs: in *A Turk and No Turk* (1785) for example, a young Englishman assumes the guise of a wealthy Turk in order to win the approval of his beloved's rich parents. The deception is only revealed at the wedding ceremony.

---

13   Allardyce Nicoll, *A History of English Drama 1660–1900* (Cambridge: Cambridge University Press, 1952), 6 vols, Vol. III, 104.
14   Cf. *The British Drama: A Collection of the Most Esteemed Tragedies, Comedies, Operas, and Farces, in the English Language. In Two Volumes* (London: Jones & Co., 1824), Vol. 1, 69.
15   Nicoll, *History of English Drama*, Vol. III, 123.

The opera *Inkle and Yarico* (1787) also has instances of love across racial boundaries, although religion plays no part in the action and the 'others' of the story are not Muslim. Colman's work offers a comic twist on what was initially recounted as a tragedy. The story of Inkle and Yarico was first published by Richard Ligon in his *A True & Exact History of the Island of Barbadoes*, 1657. From there it was redacted by the essayist and editor Richard Steele in his *Spectator Magazine*,[16] and then re-told numerous times before George Colman the Younger adapted it for the theatre.

The original story tells how an English merchant named Thomas Inkle, voyaging to the West Indies is shipwrecked on the coast of America together with his companions, and rescued by an American Indian maiden, Yarico, who loves him. He betrays her by selling her into slavery: the name of Inkle became a byword for perfidy. In Colman's softened version however, Inkle reverses his plan to sell Yarico and marries her instead. As in *The Mountaineers*, Colman devises a parallel but lower-class mixed-race couple who also marry at the end. In fact, the working-class Englishman Trudge demonstrates his moral edge over the well-born Inkle and exposes the latter's greed when he declares that he would never sell his beloved (who has the absurd name of Wowski). The opera, staged at the Haymarket Theatre like other dramas by Colman, was performed 96 times. Peter Tasch describes it as Colman's first great success.[17]

In *Inkle and Yarico*, as in *The Mountaineers*, we see a class-consciousness fed by growing inequality in 18th century England. Lindert, citing Malthus and Ricardo, traces a growth in income disparity between 1740 and 1810, not only in England but also other parts of Western Europe.[18] Other factors include the Abolitionist movement building a consensus against slavery. At the same time however, the experience of colonialism had sharpened race-consciousness and racism in England. Nandini Bhattachariya has ably demonstrated the extent to which race language and motifs dominate Colman's *Inkle and Yarico* and has analysed the subtleties of distinction between Yarico's 'red' skin and the 'black' skin of other characters including Wowski. These make Yarico an acceptable mate for an upper-class Englishman (despite his moral failings), while Wowski is more appropriately wedded to a lower-class man. Bhattachariya states,

---

16   *The Spectator*, No. 11, 13th March 1711.
17   *The Plays of George Colman the Younger*, ed. Peter A. Tasch (New York and London: Garland Publishing, 1981), xvii.
18   Cf. e.g. Peter H. Lindert, 'When did inequality rise in Britain and America?' *Journal of Income Distribution* 9 (2000) 11–25. esp. 12, 19, 21, and passim.

> Eighteenth-century racial theory would suggest that the Amerindian being closer to the European ethnically, interracial sex between European and Amerindian was more acceptable than sex between European and African or black Caribs ...
>
> In Colman's *Inkle and Yarico* ... the language of late eighteenth-century racism encounters sentimental civilizational discourse emboldened by abolitionism, and empowered by the notion of a relative civilizational and racial affinity with the Amerindian. [19]

Even so, Bhattachariya notes, this play is far less preoccupied with race than many of its contemporaries, as it does not 'linger excessively on the "contrast" between Yarico's and Inkle's appearances'.[20] Furthermore, unlike the plays featuring Muslim characters, here religion is unimportant. Theatres in Colman's day were huge (his own theatre, the Haymarket, had a capacity of 1800; other theatres could seat more than 3,000 people) and his plays reflect the attitudes and tastes of the wider population.

5   Nineteenth Century

5.1   Ann Lemoine

The fall of Muslim Alhambra and related themes, including the enslavement of Europeans in North Africa, continued to invite fictional accounts varying from the romantic/sentimental to the tragic. In 1805 *The Beautiful African; Or, Love and Slavery*: *An Interesting Tale* by Ann Lemoine appeared in London with the caption on its cover that it was 'Sold by all the Booksellers in the United Kingdom'. Its ready availability and relatively modest price (four pence) reveal that it was aimed at a broad reading public, while the title also suggests that its author expected the association of love and slavery to win buyers and readers. Lemoine was a successful chapbook publisher and author, believed to be the first woman book publisher who specialised in issuing what we might now call potboilers.[21]

---

19   Nandini Bhattacharya, 'Family Jewels: George Colman's Inkle and Yarico and Connoisseurship', *Eighteenth-Century Studies* 34.2 (2001) 207–226, 209.

20   Bhattachariya, 209.

21   Roy Beardon-White, *How the Wind Sits; Or, the History of Henry and Ann Lemoine, Chapbook Writers and Publishers of the Late Eighteenth Century*, MA Thesis submitted to Southern Illinois University, 2005, published online in 2007, and now in paperback form (Morrisville, North Carolina: Lulu Press, 2017).

Lemoine's story is marked by acts of nobility and self-sacrifice on the part of key characters, including the Dey and the heroines: Muslim Zara and the Englishwoman Elvira who, dying toward the end of the novel, instructs her beloved Ernesto to marry Zara upon her death. After a suitable period of mourning, the pair comply and they spend the remainder of their days 'in mutual fondness and indulgencies'.

Piracy and enslavement motifs remained popular: among Lemoine's publications was a shortened adaptation of a novel by another remarkable author and businesswoman, Penelope Aubin, written in 1723, and one of several of Aubin's titles to use slavery as a theme; she also incorporated travels in the Ottoman Empire in a number of her books. Lemoine redacted Aubin's *The Life of Charlotta Du Pont, an English Lady: taken from her own memoirs: giving an account of how she was trepan'd by her stepmother to Virginia, how the ship was taken by some Madagascar pirates and retaken by a Spanish man of war … and, the history of some gentlemen and ladies she met withal in her travels, some of whom had been slaves in Barbary and others cast on shore by shipwreck* … and much more in this vein: the title acted effectively as a précis of and advertisement for the whole book. Lemoine altered and substantially abbreviated the title, as well as amending the book itself.

5.2   Lord Byron

'Oriental' settings, including Ottoman Turkey and Granada just before and after its conquest by Catholic forces, proved irresistible to novelists, poets and artists of the early 19th century. Byron in particular was attracted to the East, in which he travelled extensively, and to Orientalist themes, which he used partly as means to construct a critique of English society.[22] He led the way to a whole genre of writing with his series of tragic poems published under the general heading, *Turkish Tales*, including *The Giaour* (1812–13), a revenge tragedy about the love of a Christian (the Giaour)[23] for a slave woman called Leila, in a Muslim harem. She is killed on orders from her master, Hassan, and the Giaour then kills Hassan. Other poems in *Turkish Tales* include *The Bride of Abydos* (1813), which features another doomed love affair between a Turkish nobleman turned pirate and the ruler's daughter; and *The Corsair* (1814), in which a captive pirate-captain is visited by the chief slave of the Turkish Pasha's harem, who falls in love with him and rescues him. He then risks his life to save her, but

---

22   Seyed Mohammad Marandi, 'The Oriental World of Lord Byron and the Orientalism of Literary Scholars', *Critique: Critical Middle Eastern Studies*, 15:3 (2006), 317–337: http://dx.doi.org/10.1080/10669920600997191 [accessed 27/4/2016], 317–37, 318.

23   The Giaour is a Turkish word, originally derogatory, which means, simply, a Christian.

they do not marry. *The Corsair* was immensely popular, selling ten thousand copies in a single day and providing source material for works in several other media including a ballet, an opera, and a painting by the French Orientalist master Eugene Delacroix.

Set at the scene of an Ottoman massacre of Venetians, *The Siege of Corinth* (1816) tells of the love between the Venetian renegade Alp, now fighting for the Ottomans, and the daughter of the Venetian governor, Francesca. True to the pattern discussed above with regard to love between Muslim men and Christian women in Byron, the story of Alp and Francesca ends tragically. Other works of Byron, such as the farcical *Don Juan* (1821), contain 'Oriental' episodes, as do Thomas Moore's *Lalla Rookh*, Disraeli's novel *Tancred, or the New Crusade*, and Matthew Arnold's *Sohrab and Rustam*. In the fifth canto of *Don Juan* the hero is smuggled into a harem disguised as a woman, but temporarily resists the advances of the Sultana, proclaiming that love can only be enjoyed by the free.[24]

5.3   *François-René de Chateaubriand and Washington Irving*

In the hands of Chateaubriand, a story told against the backdrop of post-conquest Granada again gives rise to tragedy, precisely because religious conversion is now seen to be impossible.

His *Les aventures du dernier Abencerraje* (*The Last of the Abencerrajes*), written in 1810 and published in 1826, traces the development of a love affair between a brave and handsome Muslim, the Abencerraje Aben-Hamet, and a beautiful, noble Spanish woman, Doña Blanca, who is descended from Rodrigo Diaz de Vivar (El Cid). Forced to leave Spain with the rest of his clan, Aben-Hamet migrates to Tunis, where the Abencerrajes dwell among the ruins of Carthage. They cherish memories of Granada as of a lost Paradise and stories of this Eden and its downfall are retold through generations. When they pray, they turn not to Mecca but to Granada.

Aben-Hamet resolves to make a pilgrimage to his ancestral home in Spain, which he reaches after a long journey. There he meets Doña Blanca and the two share tender exchanges in idyllic landscapes of Alhambra and its surroundings, the lyrical descriptions of which evoke scenes from the *Nights*. Both lovers hope their shared passion will lead to marriage, but neither will convert to the other's religion.

Finally, Aben-Hamet is psychologically 'vanquished' because of his consuming love for Doña Blanca. But immutable history overwhelms the present,

---

24   For a discussion of this episode, Cf. Ruth Bernard Yeazell, *Harems of the Mind: Passages of Western Art and Literature* (New Haven and London: Yale University Press, 2000), 144–48.

making their union impossible. He is about to give in and convert to Christianity, when he learns that his lover is the granddaughter of El Cid, who had invaded Granada and killed Aben-Hamet's own grandfather.[25] Even though, being so in love with Doña Blanca, he is – figuratively speaking – forever her slave, Aben-Hamet declares that he,

> could not think without horror of the idea of uniting the blood of the persecutors to that of the persecuted. He thought he saw the shadow of his grandfather rise from the grave to condemn so unholy an alliance.[26]

And so, we see that his emotional enslavement only goes so far: the Muslim's psychological captivity is trumped by his sense of honour and loyalty to his family, thwarting his desires. All of the participants in this tragedy are impossibly noble. The two ruins of Alhambra and of Carthage are intimately associated at the end of the tragedy, as at the beginning: both evoking folk-memories of warfare and destruction, and images of loves, homes and peoples all lost.

In 1829, a few years after Chateaubriand's novel was published, Washington Irving returned to Alhambra, literally and metaphorically, in order to revive traditions surrounding the last days of the Nasrid kingdom of Granada. His *Tales of the Alhambra* is an anecdotal meditation on 'Moorish' themes in which legends, largely culled from Pérez de Hita, are woven through his very personal account of living within Alhambra's walls, with past and present closely intermingled. His narrative style shifts from intimate reports of his day-to-day encounters with local – often quite comic – figures, to piquant re-telling of the old stories and ruminations on the historic, philosophical and spiritual meaning of it all. His description of Alhambra as a place of enchantment and his vision of its Andalusi inhabitants as a glorious but doomed race is exactly of his period, according with the poetic accounts of Byron, Chateaubriand and other contemporaries.

∙ ∙ ∙

---

25   The chronology here is somewhat convoluted, in that El Cid lived in the 11th century (1043–99), and Granada was taken by the Catholics in the 15th century (1492), so El Cid could hardly have been Doña Blanca's grandfather, nor a contemporary of Aben-Hamet's grandfather. A little forbearance is called for on the part of the reader, and a willingness to turn a blind eye to the facts or, failing that, simply ignorance.
26   François-René de Chateaubriand, *Les Aventures du dernier Abencérage* (*The Last of the Abencerrajes*), was translated into English by A.S. Kline, published with Lithographs by Francisco Javier Parcerisa: *Poetry in Translation Series*: https://www.poetryintranslation.com/klineaschateaubriandabencerraje.php [accessed 29/4/ 2016], 71.

Lighter treatments of slavery and romance themes also prevailed, as in a musical, *Beautiful Haidée* (1863) by the prolific and popular dramatist, Henry James Byron. Here the once-feared Sallee Rovers have become subjects for farce:

> We pirates all haunt Sallee,
> We mercy never show;
> But in our pirate galley
> We spifflicate the foe;
> The joys of life we valley,
> And when on shore we go,
> Dance with the corps de ballet,
> On light fantastic toe.
> Yeo heave ho! what comical chaps are we:
> We're sanguinary ruffians,
> Yes, we're rovers of Sallee.[27]

The action takes place on a Greek Island in 'the Cyclades', but its cast are largely 'Moorish' pirates. The plot is conventional: the heroine Haidée is the daughter of a 'retired pirate' who is kept locked in her room (held 'chained' and 'captive') by her tyrannical father, but still manages to catch the eye of, and eventually marry, a dashing Englishman. The farce is full of truly terrible puns, one of the author's specialities, for which he was roundly condemned by the contemporary critic and author, William Archer. He accused Byron of committing 'word-torture' and fostering a taste for 'frivolous and puerile' work.[28]

6 Sadomasochism and Its Commercial Lure

The sadomasochistic potential inherent in the slave/master relationship, as well as the erotic associations of an 'Oriental' setting, lend themselves to deployment in pornographic literature, evincing what Masoch described as 'the mysterious affinity between cruelty and lust'.[29] It is but a short step from

---

27 Henry James Byron, *Beautiful Haidée; or, the Sea Nymph and the Sallee Rovers. A New and Original Whimsical Extravaganza. Founded on the poem of Don Juan, the Ballad of Lord Bateman, and the Legend of Lurline* (London: Thomas Hailes Lacy, 1863), Scene 2, 16.

28 William Archer, *English Dramatists of Today* (London: Sampson Low, Marston, Searle, & Rivington, 1882), 120, 121.

29 Quoted by Karmen Mackendrick, *Counterpleasures*, 62. And cf. Rana Kabbani, 'The *Arabian Nights* as an Orientalist Text', *Arabian Nights Encyclopedia*, Vol. 1, 25–29, 28–29.

the chained anguish of *Almahide* and the blood drawn by violent kisses in the novels of de Brémond, to sexually explicit writing, much of whose raison d'être and appeal lie in its depictions of pain and suffering in the service of erotica, especially when augmented by physical restraint. Whereas, one might argue, the love story at the heart of a novel by Cervantes works to alleviate the misery engendered by slavery and all its attendant cruelties, in these later novels it is the cruelty itself that is the point, the 'turn-on'.

Sadomasochistic elements are exploited to the full in the Victorian novel, *The Lustful Turk, or Lascivious Scenes from a Harem*, first published anonymously in 1828 by John Benjamin Brookes and reprinted by William Dugdale. For sixty-five years it was relatively unknown, but it achieved fame, or rather notoriety, when it was reprinted in 1893. The exposition consists largely of letters written by its heroine, Emily Barlow, to her friend Sylvia Carey. Captured by Muslim pirates in 1814, Emily is taken to the harem of the Dey of Algiers, Ali, who rapes her repeatedly. Her letters detail her growing enjoyment of the abuse and her sexual passion. Later the Dey contrives to bring Sylvia to his harem, with comparable responses from her. Several other European women are also raped, flogged, etc. in the harem, while Emily's maid Eliza is sent as a gift to the Bey of Tunis, whose capacity for violence and abuse is no less than that of the Dey. We are now 'in a context in which delight and pain are not readily distinguishable' from one another.[30] The novel ends with the Dey's castration by a disgruntled captive, offering a nod to poetic justice while at the same time heightening the story's sensationalism.

Among books inspired (if that is the word) by *The Lustful Turk* was the erotic novella, *A Night in a Moorish Harem*. This book, published under the pseudonym 'Lord George Herbert' in 1896, tells of a night spent by a shipwrecked British ship's captain in a Moroccan harem with nine concubines of various nationalities. Each of the women has a 'chapter' in which she relates her previous sexual history, followed by a brief account of the captain's intimacy with her in the 'present' of the narrative. These nine chapters are supplemented by an introductory section and four other parts in which the captain describes his own amours in the past for the entertainment and titillation of the harem women (and the reader): fourteen chapters in all. The accounts are graphic, lubricious and repetitive. In 1924 two New York booksellers were convicted for selling the book, but later prosecutions for the same 'offence' failed.

---

30   Mackendrick, *Counterpleasures* ,146.

7 Twentieth Century and Beyond

'Moorish' and 'Turkish' texts and their offshoots have survived into modern times. In the early 20th century James Elroy Flecker's *Hassan*, written around the time of the First World War and featuring the famous and evocative chant, 'The Golden Road to Samarkand' appeared; it was staged as recently as 2012.[31] This play, with incidental music by Frederick Delius, turns plot-lines we have seen in such works as *El trato de Argel* and *Il Seraglio* into tragedy. The Caliph of Baghdad (and of the *Nights*), Haroun al-Rashid, has a passion for an enslaved Christian woman, but she is in love with another man who has tried to rescue her from the harem and is now also captive. The Caliph offers her a stark choice: submit to him or die. She chooses death and the doomed lovers are allowed one night of passion before being horribly tortured to death. The play, much of whose language, style and imagery mimic those of Arabic writing, intricately links the phenomena of beauty and cruelty,[32] as well as love, suffering and death, and has been accused of containing unnecessary sadism.[33]

7.1 Gender Role Reversal and the Lure of the Desert: Genteel Heroines and Commanding Arab Heroes

Hollywood also exploited slavery/romance themes in films as, for example, in *The Sheik* [sic] (1921), starring Rudolph Valentino and Agnes Ayres [Figure 6.3]; and another silent film (now lost), based on *Hassan* but given a happy ending in which the lovers are united, *The Lady of the Harem* (1926).[34] *The Sheik* is based on a best-selling novel of the same name by the Anglo-American E.M. (Edith Maude) Hull (1919), who had herself visited Algeria and, like the author of *A Night in a Moorish Harem*, was influenced by *The Lustful Turk*.[35] With this book Hull appropriates the formerly masculine-authored fantasy of a woman

---

31 Performed by the Wellensian Consort and the Southbank Sinfonia, conducted by Neil Thomson, at the Cheltenham Festival, in July 2012.
32 C.E. Bosworth, *James Elroy Flecker, Poet, Diplomat, Orientalist*, a lecture delivered in the John Rylands Library, University of Manchester, on Wednesday, 10 December 1986, and published in the *Bulletin of the John Rylands University Library of Manchester*, 69: 2, 359–78, 377, and also on-line: https://www.manchesterhive.com/view/journals/bjrl/69/2/article-p359.xml [accessed 26/4/2024].
33 Dominick Head, *Cambridge Guide to English Literature*, in the entry for *Hassan* (Cambridge: Cambridge University Press, 2006), 491.
34 Such details as survive concerning *The Lady of the Harem*, including a brief synopsis of the plot and names of some members of the cast list, are given on a British Film Institute website, https://en.wikipedia.org/wiki/The_Lady_of_the_Harem [accessed on 1/3/2025].
35 E.M. (Edith Maude) Hull, *The Sheik* (1919, repr. London: Virago, 1996).

achieving sexual ecstasy through violent abuse and rape. Ahmed's repeated assaults and humbling of Diana situate the novel in a borderland of pornography, an aspect enhanced when the enslaved woman discovers she is in love with her captor and abuser.

The model employed in *The Sheik* and its successors subverts both the age-old trope of Christian man loving Muslim woman, resulting in the latter's conversion and its obverse, Muslim man loving Christian woman, leading to tragedy. These stories feature white women irresistibly drawn to Arab (or 'Arab') men, who capture and carry them away. The result is a quite altered dialectic in which, although the exotic man physically vanquishes the heroine, she then captivates *him* psychologically but also, tellingly, culturally, as he is drawn into accepting her social norms of monogamy, fidelity, and 'good manners'.

A later best-seller, *The Wilder Shores of Love* (1954) by Lesley Blanch, documented the lives of four real-life European women of the 19th century, who chose to 'leave behind the industrialised west for Arabia in search of romance and fulfillment'. These adventurers were 'Isabel Burton, the wife and travelling companion of the explorer Richard Burton; Jane Digby, who exchanged European society for an adventure in loving; Aimée Dubucq de Rivery, a Frenchwoman captured by pirates who became a member of the Turkish sultan's harem; and Isabelle Eberhardt, a Swiss woman who dressed as a man and lived among the Arabs of Algeria'.[36]

Hull followed *The Sheik* with several other novels on similar themes, including *The Shadow of the East*, *The Desert Healer*, and *The Sons of the Sheik*, and is credited with initiating a huge popular revival of the so-called 'desert romance'. The genre had previously been used by Victorian writers such as Robert Smythe Hichens and Kathlyn Rhodes, author of books including *The Lure of the Desert, The Desert Dreamers,* and *The Will of Allah*.

The film of *The Sheik* tones down some aspects of the novel, most notably omitting the Sheik's repeated rapes of its heroine Diana; in the film version his treatment of her is somewhat more gallant, if not less brusque. In the film, as in the novel, a love affair gradually develops between the Sheik and his captive, and at the end they passionately declare their feelings for one another. In the meantime, the Sheik has been revealed to be of western and Christian origin, the son of an English father and Spanish mother. And so, the dangerous love for the 'other' is made safe and acceptable when it turns out it is really love between two people who are culturally, and in terms of religious orientation,

---

36   The wording is from the website of the publisher Simon and Schuster: http://www.simon andschuster.com/books/The-Wilder-Shores-of-Love/Lesley-Blanch/9781439197349, [accessed 11/5/2018].

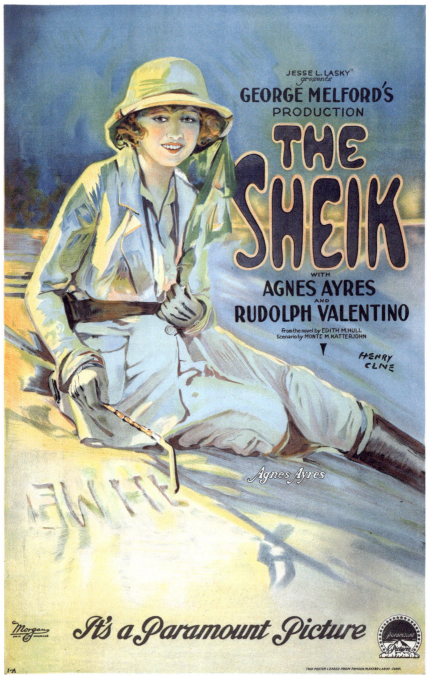

FIGURE 6.3 Poster for the film, *The Sheik*, 1921, showing Agnes Ayres, as Lady Diana Mayo
SOURCE: HENRY CLIVE, IMAGE IN THE PUBLIC DOMAIN. HTTPS://WIKIME
DIA.ORG/WIKIPEDIA/COMMONS/B/BC/THE_SHEIK_WITH_AGNES_AYRES_AN
D_RUDOLPH_VALENTINO%2C_MOVIE_POSTER%2C_1921.JPG

'the same' – although not before readers and audiences could enjoy the thrill and horror of being vicariously dominated by a powerful, handsome 'foreign' man (or perhaps identifying with his dominion).

Although the film baulks at suggesting actual rape, it shares with the novel the motif of a haughty woman made captive and humiliated by a more powerful male. This 'taming of a shrew', as it were, as well as the ruthlessly imposed transformation of a tough woman into a quivering submissive female, exploit the plot's inherently sadomasochistic and misogynistic nature, which may help to account for its huge success. The supposed 'taming' of the arrogant sheik by the heroine is a detail designed to appease the squeamish. As Hsu-Ming Teo puts it, [the Sheik] 'reverts to "civilized" standards of patriarchal European gender norms, presumably forsaking rape and promiscuity (though not necessarily his penchant for strangling evil Arab opponents when he deems this justified)'.[37]

This is fantasy fiction in the spirit of 'Orientalism', as defined by Edward Said, and true to the pattern (in Christian literature) that prohibits love between Muslim man and Christian woman or, where it exists on either side, one or both participants must be thwarted and possibly punished. Here the revelation of the man's 'true' Christian origins makes possible the happy ending. The book was enormously successful, being reprinted 50 times in 1921 alone and by 1965 it had sold close to two million hardback copies.[38] The book's sequel, *The Sons of the Sheik* (1925) and Valentino's performance in the film version of the novel in 1926 'brought a craze for all things romantically "Oriental" to its zenith in fashion and film'. Arabic fabrics, clothing, jewellery, cigarettes, cosmetics and design motifs proliferated, as did dozens of copycat films such as *Burning Sands* (1922), *The Tents of Allah* (1923), *The Arab* (1924), *Sahara Love* (1926), *and Love in the Desert* (1929).[39]

The later *Story of O* by 'Pauline Réage' (pseudonym of Anne Desclos), published in Paris in 1954, similarly depends for its effects on the debasement and humbling of its heroine and was also very successful. The eponymous O is a sexual slave who falls in love with successive tormentors and sees her redemption through them. The novel was printed with a preface by Desclos's lover Jean Paulhan, 'Le bonheur dans l'esclavage' ('Happiness in Slavery'). It is now considered a classic of sadomasochistic fiction.

---

37 Hsu-Ming Teo, https://www.jprstudies.org/2010/08/historicizing-the-sheik-comparisons-of-the-british-novel-and-the-american-film-by-hsu-ming-teo [accessed 18/5/2018].
38 Hsu-Ming Teo, *Desert Passions: Orientalism and Romance Novels* (Texas, USA: University of Texas Press, 2012), 1.
39 Teo, *Desert Passions*, 2.

Also in France, a less obviously brutal but no less successful series of thirteen novels set in the 17th century was published with the name of their heroine, Angélique, in each title. During the course of the stories, the heroine marries young and travels to the Mediterranean to search for her missing husband, thought dead but actually in hiding after being falsely accused of sorcery. In Book 4: *Angélique and the Sultan* [otherwise known as *Angélique in Barbary*] (1960) she is captured by pirates, sold into slavery, and taken to the harem of the king of Morocco, where she becomes his favourite. After many more adventures she and her husband are reunited and the series ends happily. The books, by Anne and Serge Golon, were published in the years 1957–85 and several were made into films during the 1960s. The last one, directed by Ariel Zeitoun, was made in 2013 and there were other spinoffs, including albums of music from the films and a video game series.

8 The 21st Century: Tables Turned

Captivity and romance stories involving Muslims and Christians are still being written today, but they tend to be set in the past, or in an indeterminate period, transformed into costume dramas and purple prose fiction. The books are mostly written by women, for a predominantly female readership. The novels tend to be quite formulaic, featuring heightened passions. and they are often salacious, earning themselves the soubriquet, 'bodice-rippers'. One item in this vein, which appropriated Aphra Behn's beguiling subtitle but for lascivious purposes, is American author Julia Fitzgerald's *The Royal Slave* (1978), a torrid tale set in the 18th century. It features a renegade pirate slave-trader, fittingly named 'Vincent de Sauvage' as its anti-hero, with whom the trafficked heroine Cassia falls madly in love, despite being sold by Vincent to the harem of 'the Grand Turk of Algiers'. A book-swap website describes the heroine of this book as 'hot-blooded and wildly passionate'. and its summary could stand for many such stories,

> Born to command men's passions, to be ruled by men's lusts, a harsh destiny made her a harem's prize! Cassia was an exquisite prize. Vincent Sauvage, legendary white-slave trader, bastard grandson of the French king, meant to take her, use her, and bestow her as a gift upon whom he pleased.[40]

---

40 Julia Fitzgerald, *The Royal Slave* (1978): http://www.paperbackswacom/Royal-Slave-Julia-Fitzgerald/book/1557850631/ [accessed 9/5/2018].

This is a variation on the mixed-faith romances in which the heroine falls for her 'master'. He renounces the slave trade and all other women to devote himself to Cassia. *The Royal Slave* is one of several Fitzgerald productions to include the word 'slave' in their title and slavery themes for their content, but it is said to be her most popular and has been reprinted a number of times.

More recently, the captivity and romance theme has become the subject for erotic and escapist fantasy novels on an industrial scale: the popular romantic fiction publisher, Mills and Boon, lists close to 300 books with the word 'sheik' or 'sheikh' in the title alone and there are dozens of women writing 'desert romance' books and their ilk in several English-speaking countries – although the largest numbers are in the United States. Book titles include *The Sheikh's Unexpected Wife,* and *The Sheik's Captive American,* both by Leslie North; *The Sheik's Missing Bride, The Sheik's Missing Love Child, The Sheik's Furious Bride,* and *The Sheik's Unfinished Business,* all by Elizabeth Lennox as well as numerous others in this vein.

Connie Mason is the best-selling American author of more than 60 historical romances and tales of 'passion and adventure', according to her website, including *The Pirate Prince* (2004), in which the English heroine, Willow, is 'Taken captive by a rakish pirate and sold into slavery ... [and] plunged into a dangerous game of seduction and power when two rivals vow to possess her'.[41] The setting is the Mediterranean during the 16th century and its hero is an Ottoman prince with an English mother. He eventually succeeds in capturing Willow's heart, as well as her body, and the two are united.

The Sheik and the Slave (2014) by another American author, Nicola Italia, has as its heroine Katharine Fairfax, youngest daughter of Lord Fairfax. She is kidnapped from her home in England and taken to Arabia, where she is sold to a wealthy sheikh. The Sheikh, Mohammed Aksam Al Sabid, is captivated by Katharine and pays a huge sum for her, intending her for his harem. She insists on returning home, but eventually she too falls in love with her captor. He disbands his harem to begin a new life with Katharine.

Samanthi Dissanayake, writing on the BBC News website, notes that the best-selling title of the June 2008 'Modern Romance' series was *Desert King, Pregnant Mistress* by Susan Stephens and 'at least one sheikh romance a month is published'. Quoting Dr. Joseph McAleer, author of *Passion's Fortune: The Story of Mills and Boon,* she adds, '"Exotic locations gave great scope to authors to be a bit racier. It is usually an English person going into the tropics to experience

---

41 Description on the Amazon website: https://www.amazon.com/Pirate-Prince-Leisure-Historical-Romance/dp/0843952342 [accessed 9/5/2018].

this different culture ... But they never lose their moral foundation. The heroines normally wind up reforming the sheikh'".[42]

Hsu-Ming Teo sees the harem historical romance novel as incorporating motifs developed in Victorian Orientalist pornography. But, paradoxically perhaps, she maintains that these plots in which the heroine submits to her Eastern captor/lover, allow her to '[achieve] her own liberty' and '[assert] her equality with him in a companionate marriage ... a variation of [Samuel Richardson's] *Pamela* ...'. She summarises,

> The harem or seraglio in all these stories is often a place where the Western virgin triumphs over the septic jealousies and vicious intrigues of competing concubines ... She either escapes the debauched sexual appetites and tyranny of the Muslim despot or brings him to his knees by virtue of her beauty, intelligence, uncompromising love of freedom, and vision of an egalitarian Western companionate marriage.[43]

9 Slavery and Romance in Entertainment of the East

In some Muslim countries, slavery and romance themes have become popular fare for films and television. In Turkey a lavish TV soap opera about Sultan Süleyman 'the Magnificent', focussing on his love for Hürrem Sultan, the East European slave girl who became sultana (Roxolana or Roxelana [see Chapter 4]), achieved tremendous success both at home and abroad. It was aired during prime time (with intervals) from 2011–14 and some or all of its 139 episodes were shown in more than fifty nations, including, in addition to Turkey, Iran and Israel, the United States and Japan (but not the UK), as well as numerous Balkan, Caucasian and Arab countries; it was reported to have an international audience of 200 million viewers. The series *Muhteşem Yüzyıl* (in English, 'The Magnificent Century'), written by Meral Okay and Yılmaz Şahin, featured a Spanish Princess, Isabella, who is kidnapped by Turkish pirates and sold to Süleyman, with whom she falls in love. But he views her as a tool he can use to bargain with European sovereigns. Isabella several times fails to escape, and is eventually freed.

At home the series caused controversy in two quite different camps: orthodox Muslims felt it was disrespectful to the Sultan, 'indecent' and hedonistic;

---

42 Samanthi Dissanayake, 'All because the lady loves a foreign accent', published 14th August 2008: http://news.bbc.co.uk/1/hi/magazine/7516672.stm [accessed 11/5/2018].
43 Teo, *Desert Passions*, 48–49.

Prime Minister Recep Tayyip Erdoğan also condemned it, as did religious authorities in several other countries. Conversely, some Turkish feminists argued that it reinforced misogynistic stereotypes and was demeaning to women. But it remained immensely popular with the viewing public in each of the nations where it was shown.

The Muslim-Christian erotic encounter relies for its excitement on a perception of the love object as 'other', and of his/her 'differentness', and 'exoticness' – whether in a Christian or a Muslim setting. Today, the settings of historical romances, tales of desert passion and the like, tend to be set far away in time or place, or both. But two 21st century stories originating in the Middle East were set in the recent past and in the present, respectively, and located close to home (see below: *Haret al-Yahud* and *Gader Haya*). Both demonstrate the powerful attraction of the religious/cultural 'other', even in modern times. But in neither of these stories is captivity a factor and neither one involves a Christian.

∙ ∙ ∙

10   Summary and Conclusion

It is both remarkable and significant that until the late 19th century in so much of European literature the love was between Christian and Muslim, rather than a Christian man 'rescuing' a Christian woman, although the latter model also exists, as noted above. But a strong element of the appeal lies precisely in the dangerous and transgressive nature of love for an 'other'. However, we have seen that traditionally, in Christian literature, when love occurs mutually between Muslim and Christian, it can achieve a happy ending only if the Muslim is female and the Christian male and provided the woman is at least willing or indeed eager to convert to Christianity. Conversely, in most Islamic literature such as some of the *One Thousand and One Nights* stories, the Christian woman must convert to Islam for a good ending to be possible.[44] The implicit assumption is that the man, as the stronger and more dominant of the two, is likely to prevail in matters of belief, as in other things, and so

---

44   As an exception, in *The Tale of King Umar ibn al-Nuʿuman and His Sons*, it seems inevitable that the Byzantine heroine will convert to Islam, but she is killed before that can happen, and the result, for her, is tragic.

his faith should accord with the established religion of the country where the lovers will live.

It follows, therefore, that if the love pattern is reversed, that is if love occurs mutually between a Christian woman and a Muslim man, the result in Christian literature is likely to be tragic, since a Christian woman cannot be shown happily converting to Islam. In Voltaire's *Zaïre* (1732), the eponymous heroine is a Christian who has been kidnapped as a child and raised as a slave in the palace of the Sultan of Jerusalem, Orosmane (Osman), with whom she falls in love, and he loves her. Their love is never consummated, however, due to a misunderstanding and the jealousy of the Sultan. He stabs Zaïre to death and then, on learning the truth about her fidelity, kills himself.[45]

Exceptions to this pattern are the mediaeval *Aucassin et Nicolette,* a satire in which everything, even including gender roles, is topsy-turvy and Cervantes' *La gran sultana* whose 'happy' ending is qualified and highly problematic. Another exception is represented in Ariosto's epic poem *Orlando Furioso,* whose denouement includes the conversion of two *male* Muslims, one so he can marry his female Christian lover. But if the Christian man converts to Islam for the love of a Muslim woman, the outcome will again be tragedy, as in Robert Daborne's play *A Christian Turn'd Turk* (1612), which fictionalises the career of a real-life Englishman turned Barbary pirate and convert, John Ward. Here he converts because of his love for the Muslim Voada, sister of the captain of the Janissaries, whom he then marries. The play ends with his suicide. In reality, there is no evidence that John Ward's conversion had anything to do with a woman. He had two wives; the second was a woman renegade whom he married *after* his conversion. He lived to the age of 70 and died a natural death.[46]

Many features of the French novel, including piracy and storms, can be traced back to classical Greek literature, while others, such as neo-platonic questions and answers about love in *Almahide,* refer back to Boccaccio.[47] I have shown how such themes migrate from culture to culture and from language to language. The theme of captivity also has a long literary ancestry. The idea of being trapped among alien forces can be a terrifying nightmare subject for a reader to imagine but, for a story-teller, supremely attractive, precisely because – among other elements – the situation is so unpredictable and offers such rich opportunities for surprise. One of the literary impulses in the theme of a hero and/or heroine enslaved is that primeval one of reversal of fortune.

---

45   Voltaire's play was translated into English by Aaron Hill and performed at Drury Lane in 1736.
46   Cf. Vitkus, ed., *Three Turk Plays,* 27–28.
47   Schweitzer, 49.

Myths, legends and fairy tales from ancient times onwards, foreground characters who, as children, were kidnapped or given away and raised by strangers. Typically, in Greek and later literature, well-born individuals are transported from their places of birth, brought up in poverty, and discover their true status much later. Shakespeare employed this scheme for the story of Perdita, the abandoned princess, in his *The Winter's Tale* and it is well-used by many other authors.

The potency of captivity and romance as a literary theme may speak to a reader's or spectator's feelings of hostility or alienation from their families and/or society which many individuals feel at some point in their lives, a sense of not being truly at home in the world into which they are born. It may express the need for a distinct identity, or for greater security within one's own community, leading to fantasies of being someone else – someone unrelated, perhaps, to parents who appear too strict, or too poor, or in other ways unsatisfactory; to explore other ways of being. Schweitzer also traces elements of a 'false identity' contributing to the theme's appeal.[48]

A notable feature of some of the texts is the forthright proactivity of the 'other' woman, who in Muslim texts is likely to be Christian (Abriza, Miriam the Girdle-Maker) and in Christian texts is Muslim (Nicolette, the Amazonian Floripas, Cervantes's Zoraida and Zara/Zahra, Massinger's Donusa, and even Zara in Lemoine's 19th-century *The Beautiful African*). These women take the initiative in shaping the romance, setting out to 'capture' and win the men whom they desire. For the man to take the lead would be far too dangerous, as well as an absolute breach of code: an unwelcome overture from him would almost certainly lead to his exposure and death. But according to an alternative code of courtesy, he cannot refuse a woman and in his enslaved state is unlikely to expose her to the master or ruler. Thus, the woman is temporarily powerful in relation to the man and shows him the path to freedom – as well as, in Cervantes and subsequent stories, financing the means. Again, by converting to his culture and religion, the woman relinquishes her power and accepts his and his peers' dominion.

As we have traced, texts in the 'Saracen'/'Moorish' romance tradition are firmly embedded in the mediaeval world of chivalry: knights and their ladies engaging in courtly romance. Violence is present, but the language of it is usually restrained and it acts as a background to the amours and passionate intrigues of the protagonists. Cervantes and Regnard, both of whom had personally experienced slavery, invoke a brutal realism in their narratives, but

---

48   Schweitzer, *Georges de Scudéry's* Almahide, 48.

their central love stories are conventionally romantic and retain courtly elements. By the later 17th century, the horrors of Muslim slavery are fantastic and devilish, where they are referred to at all, while the love stories are becoming formulaic. Here too literal and metaphorical slavery are often linguistically fused, while authors play with patterns of domination and subjection. In the 18th century the horrors recede into the background while the love element remains central, enhanced by Enlightenment motifs of noble self-sacrifice and courteous treatment of the 'other', by both Muslims and Christians.

10.1   *The 'Other' and the 'Same'/ 'Them' and 'Us'*
In the world depicted in European literature from the earliest mediaeval times onwards, religion denotes identity and culture, and a way of distinguishing 'them' from 'us' – oneself and one's co-religionists belonging to a familiar community offering refuge, support and security. Conversion involves a complete change of identity: converts were given new names and clothes, as well as a new community to call 'us'. And yet the absorption of these 'others' cannot help but introduce elements of hybridity into the new culture – reinforcing what was already there. The plot patterns are fraught with paradoxes: the (mostly Christian and mostly male) lover falls in love with an ostensibly Muslim woman, experiencing her as an exotic 'other', but also as a kindred spirit, a 'soulmate'. In this he is unconsciously identifying an underlying truth: for she can so often be almost literally 'the same' as him, in that so many Muslim women, especially the types of aristocratic women and women of the harem who populate these stories, had originally been Christian or were born of Christian mothers. Her conversion is therefore very often a reversion to the faith of her mother or other kinspeople.

Centuries of religious conversion and miscegenation, whether coerced or voluntary – due to rape, forced marriage, arranged marriage and/or marriage for love – resulted in peoples on politically opposed sides who were in most other respects already the same sort of people. They were ethnically similar, often looked and sounded similar (so they could easily, as we have seen in some mediaeval romances, 'pass' for one another), and had cultures and tastes in common.[49] In Spain in particular, before the expulsion of the Muslims (and Jews), Muslims and Christians shared a social space, together with Jews – their religious differences notwithstanding.[50] There were vibrant cross-cultural

---

49   Cf. Deferrari, passim, and especially 16–17, on similarities between Berbers and the people of Spain. Also, Pascual de Gayangos y Arce, *History of the Mohammedan Dynasties in Spain,* 2 vols. (London: Oriental Translation Fund, 1840–43).

50   De Lacy O'Leary, *Arabic Thought and its Place in History* (London: Trubner, 1922), 276.

links and encounters through trade and common tastes and cultural artefacts such as clothing, music, and architecture. That so many of the stories are set in borderlands, frontiers between Christendom and Islam, is no accident. Such regions produce liminal beings whose nature defies reduction.

The advent of Islamic orthodoxy, what we now call fundamentalism, together with the obsessive 'purification' policies of the Inquisition, served to harden attitudes and sever most of these cross-cultural ties. Henceforth, close encounters between Muslim and Christian took place mainly through one side capturing and enslaving members of the other, the resulting relationships being based on economic rather than cultural considerations and marked by mutual acts of brutality. These trends are reflected in Spanish literature and, following on from that, literature in France and England. Thus, in order for the romantic union to thrive, the apparent 'otherness' of the beloved must be erased and her kinship with the protagonist confirmed, through her conversion to his faith. But also, where a man woos and then marries a woman from a different faith (rather than physically overcoming her), each one is, on a deeper level, 'recovering' his or her own lost 'other', so as to recreate a whole being in the Platonic sense. However, for happiness to be possible, he must remain steadfast in his faith, withstanding any temptation to apostasy, so that lovers who had initially been 'other' to one another will eventually become 'the same' and able to share a romantic, same-faith future.

Apart from the personal ethnic and cultural ties which the stories reflect, love affairs between Christians and Muslims also affirm the kinship between the two communities and fulfil a need (in Spain at least and in other societies drawing on Spanish literature) to bridge the gap created by the Muslims' exclusion, an impulse so ably demonstrated and discussed by Barbara Fuchs.[51] Their absence created a void, which there was a longing to fill. But the predations of the Inquisition made it impossible to conceive of a union in which both parties were not of the same religion and, most preferably, both Christian.

In addition, when both man and woman are effectively slaves (he literally and she either literally, or in effect, being incarcerated in a harem which she cannot freely leave) they are 'the same' socially. Indeed, her social status as being either genetically related to Islamic nobility, or a consort who normally moves exclusively in aristocratic circles, may be technically superior to that of the man. However, when she converts to Christianity and moves to his home

---

51 Barbara Fuchs, 'In Memory of Moors: "Maurophilia" and National Identity in Early Modern Spain', *Journal for Early Modern Cultural Studies* Vol. 2, No. 1, A Special Issue on Representations of Islam and the East (Spring/Summer 2002), 109–125; and Fuchs, *Exotic Nation,* 2009.

territory, she will become subservient to him within his society. In this way the man can enjoy the exotic 'difference' of the woman, while merging her, safely subordinated, into his own culture.

The basis for the relationship between Muslim and Christian is ostensibly love and love alone. But the man's persuading the woman to convert, and to move to his social and religious realm (or her choosing to convert), represents a kind of political triumph as effective, in its way, as a military victory. To the extent that both Muslim and Christian societies treated women as chattel, the man is removing and annexing the property of the 'other' male, as surely as he would be in taking booty from a conquered town. The woman's twin acts of physical departure from her Christian or Muslim home, plus her religious conversion, represent double blows for Christianity against Islam, or vice versa, in the battle for territory and souls, as surely as are the male renegade's actions in joining forces with his erstwhile enemy: the conversion signals a protagonist's acceptance of their fate and absorption into the 'other's' society.

In Christian literature, such outcomes show that in the competition for proselytes between Christianity and Islam, the former has won, and the conversion of the nominally free woman to Christianity affirms her subjection both to the militarily superior culture and to the socially more powerful man. Enslavement of Christians and the rampant threat presented by Muslim corsairs to enslave more, destabilises Christian society, and the world of the captured individual is also overturned. His metaphorical 'capture' (through love) of a Muslim woman and her conversion to his religion and culture, while he himself regains his physical freedom, restore order and unity to his and his society's world. But these accompanying issues pertain subliminally; they are never spelled out in the texts, where the motivations are always inspired by pure love and faith alone; nor is the extent to which the man's world is enriched by subsuming within it the foreign and 'exotic' elements.

A number of critics have sought to apply post-colonial theory to the Spanish texts in particular. Anne Fastrup has cautioned against this approach. In a carefully-reasoned article, she compares the treatment of 'Moors' in Spain and by Spaniards elsewhere with that of the native peoples of America.[52] Her views are worth quoting at some length. In a discussion on Cervantes's *El Gallardo español,* she notes that,

> maurophilia should teach us to be careful when applying post-colonial theories to 15th- and 16th-century Spain and the Christianization of the

---

52   Fastrup, 347–67, 359.

Iberian Peninsula. The fact that Christians not only looked upon the Moors with a mixture of hate, fear and contempt, but also with admiration and wonder suggests that the Spanish Moors do not compare easily with colonized peoples like, for example, the American Indians ...

Furthermore, unlike indigenous people of the Americas, Spaniards saw the Muslims as members of a theocentric culture, worthy of admiration and of opposition in part for that very reason ... By basing the study of the Reconquista and its aftermath on post-colonial theory, one risks depicting the Christian conquest of al-Andalus as equal in kind to the Spanish intrusion in South America or the English and French conquests of 'Black Africa' ...

In fact, the Christian victory over the Moors is much more like the Roman 'colonization' of the Greeks, whose cultural supremacy the Romans could not but recognize, as is evident from their wholesale appropriation of Greek literature, philosophy and architecture. In much the same way, the Moors had created a culture on the Iberian Peninsula that, in almost all respects, was superior to that of Christians. [53]

Finally, many of the stories we have studied manifest a sense of the eroticism which love across boundaries can bring, as well as the *frisson* of being totally in another's power, or alternatively being all-powerful. The heightened language of mock-servitude in French and English romance re-enacts this potent situation, while stories in which men and women are captured at sea and then loved by alien captors or captives can evoke images of sexual bondage. Slavery and romance narratives invite identification of the reader with either the captors (sadistic identification) or the slave (masochistic identification). As Jessica Benjamin has shown, such master–slave relationships have kinship with religious impulses and the slave's submission to the master is like a kind of martyrdom. Analysing the sado-masochistic erotic novel, *The Story of O*, she writes:

> O's story, with its themes of devotion and transcendence, is suggestive of the surrender of saints. The torture and outrage to which she submits is a kind of martyrdom, seeming 'to her the very redemption of her sins.' O's great longing is to be *known*, and in this respect she is like any lover, for the secret of love is to be known as oneself. But her desire to be known is like that of the sinner who wants to be known by God.[54]

---

53   Fastrup, 359–60.
54   Jessica Benjamin, *The Bonds of Love*, 60; and see her Chapter 2: 'Master and Slave', passim.

One of the most remarkable aspects of slavery and romance fiction is the ways in which authors, starting from or incorporating the difficult and dangerous conditions of capture and enslavement, managed to spin romances based on fantasies of pure love. Most extraordinary to my mind is the case of Miguel de Cervantes who, having himself spent five years in captivity, placed his romantic stories and plays in just such settings. During his enslavement he must have experienced tremendous fear and witnessed some unspeakable horrors, as when people who had tried to help him escape were brutally executed. His repeated efforts to leave, despite the enormous risks, are testimony to the distress he must have felt as a slave in Algiers and his longing and determination to break free. It was his extraordinarily good fortune that, his plans being exposed, he was not himself tortured and put to death. And yet, employing this unpromising raw material, he devised love stories that have enthralled legions of readers and theatregoers and influenced other writers through four and a half subsequent centuries.

Today however, in western literature the Christian man/Muslim woman trope is inverted to: Christian woman/Muslim (or 'Muslim') man. But the moral purpose to 'reform' the 'other' and convert him/her to alternative cultural norms remains. Only in the world of romance, religion is no longer so important; instead ethics is the key, with the woman 'converting' the man to her moral code, rather than the other way round. Readers of the contemporary 'Desert (or "Sheikh") Romance' can be imaginatively transported to distant climes and enjoy a vicarious sense of drama, powerlessness and risk, while returning safely to a comfortably known sphere at the end. The woman's temporary helplessness makes her 'submission' to the erotic male morally justifiable and acceptable, while the subsequent 'conversion' of the 'savage' man to civility restores the power balance between the sexes. The couple's marriage establishes social order and harmony in the time-honoured fashion. However, with their roles now reversed, the woman is no longer required to remain, or become, submissive, unlike the converted female 'other' in the stories of earlier times.

11   Post Script: Two Tales of Mixed-Faith Romance in the 21st Century

11.1   *Haret al-Yahud [Jewish Quarter]*
The year 2015 was a bloody one in the Middle East. The so-called 'Arab Spring' of late 2010/early 2011, as well as the recrudescence of ancient divisions between Sunni and Shi'a Islam, had resulted in internal conflicts which were continuing in several Muslim states. In addition, Muslims were at war with Christians in

Afghanistan, Iraq, Syria and elsewhere. In the Eastern Mediterranean, Israeli Jews were fighting with Palestinians in Gaza. Arabs in various countries were also deeply hostile to Israel, and many were, by extension, antagonistic to Jews, while anti-Arab and anti-Muslim feeling was growing inside Israel.

Despite these factors, two works of fiction gripped the headlines and people's imaginations in two of the countries where arguably the conflict between Muslims and Jews reverberated as potently as had the centuries-long clash between Christianity and Islam. In Egypt, not long previously at enmity with Israel, a television serial called *Haret al-Yahud* (roughly translated as 'The Jewish Quarter') held audiences fascinated every day throughout the peak TV viewing time of Ramadan. The story began in the seminal year 1948, time of the establishment of the State of Israel, and told of a subsequent bitter war between Israel and the surrounding Arab nations (known to Arabs as the 'Nakba' – Catastrophe), which Israel won. But the centrepiece of the television serial was not the 1948 war, in which Egypt was an important player, but a love affair between a beautiful Jewish woman from the 'Haret al-Yahud' in Cairo, and a dashing Muslim Arab army officer.

The couple's passion is not rewarded, for in the end they part and she leaves to find solace and a life elsewhere. But what struck me in reading about it was the fact that such a story reached prime time television in an Arab state at all; and the huge following this piece had, sustained over thirty nights' (the nights of Ramadan's) transmission. In a newspaper of the Arab world it was described as 'the most talked-about' television "soap"' of the season'.[55] And the British newspaper, the *Financial Times*, noted that 'in a first for Egyptian media, where anti-Semitism is rampant, *Haret el-Yahud* [sic] offers an empathetic portrayal of the real-life Jewish community' in the 1940s.[56]

11.2 Gader Haya [Borderlife, *Initial English Translation, Later Changed to* All the Rivers]

Meanwhile, in Israel just a few months before, in 2014 – year of a particularly bitter clash between Israel and Gaza – a Jewish woman writer, Dorit Rabinyan, published a semi-autobiographical novel about a love affair between an Israeli

---

55   Hala Khalaf, 'Recapping this year's Ramadan soap operas', *The National: Arts and Life*, published in the UAE (United Arab Emirates) on 19th July 2015/Jumada al Ula 8, 1437: https://www.thenationalnews.com/arts/recapping-this-year-s-ramadan-soap-operas-1.5376, [accessed 16/2/2016].

56   Quoted from Roula Khalaf, 'Cairo Soap Opera Casts Islamists as the Bad Guys', *Financial Times*, published on the 1st July 2015: https://www.ft.com/content/2db617e8-1fd9-11e5-ab0f-6bb9974f25d0 [accessed online on 16/2/2016].

Jewish woman and a Palestinian man. This story, *Gader Haya* (translated into English as *Borderlife,* and then retranslated as *All the Rivers*), was highly praised by Israeli critics and educators, and gained international publicity when in 2015 it was banned from the curriculum in Israel's secondary schools. The UK's *Guardian* newspaper noted that 'Israel's Channel 2 TV reported that sales of the book have increased dramatically since the ban and its news anchor jokingly asked education minister Naftali Bennett if the author had thanked him'.[57] Many bookshops ran out of copies.

Here too, as in *Haret al-Yahud*, the story ends with the couple separating. But what, to me, is astonishing, is that such a book appeared at the height of hostilities between Israel and Palestinians, as well as the enormous stir it made, its popularity, and its positive reception in much of the Israeli press. These two works, *Haret al-Yahud* and *Gader Haya,* testify to the enduring appeal of 'the other' and escapist fantasies and longing, in times of conflict, to become romantically involved and 'at one' with someone from the other side.[58]

∴

---

[57] 'Novel about Jewish-Palestinian love affair is barred from Israeli curriculum', in *The Guardian* newspaper, 1st January 2016: https://www.theguardian.com/world/2016/jan/01/novel-about-jewish-palestinian-love-affair-is-barred-from-israeli-curriculum; and 'Israeli-Palestinian love story omitted from curriculum tops bestseller lists', *The Guardian* newspaper, 8th January 2016: https://www.theguardian.com/world/2016/jan/08/israeli-palestinian-love-story-excluded-curriculum-bestseller-gader-haya-borderlife#:~:text=Borderlife%2C%20published%20in%202014%2C%20is,the%20Israeli%2Doccupied%20West%20Bank [both accessed online on 16/2/2016]. As for reactions in the Arab world, most of the articles I have been able to locate focus primarily on the Israeli government's banning of the novel from school curricula, rather than on the story itself.

[58] For a fuller account of these two stories, *Haret al-Yahud* and *Gader Haya*, see Eva Simmons, *Love for the Other*: https://www.woolf.cam.ac.uk/blog/love-for-the-other.

Appendices

1 Recurring Symbols and Motifs

Certain themes and symbolic objects recur in the stories we have been studying, which are otherwise varied in nature and origin. Writing about *One Thousand and One Nights,* Robert Irwin notes,

> the reader's first impression is likely to be of the immense diversity of the stories … and of the free-flowing imagination, or imaginations, which shaped them. But after a while, the reader starts to notice things … In time, each story comes to resemble another story and the reader begins to recognize the patterns and permutations. Fantasy has its rules.[1]

Irwin's reflections are more widely applicable than purely to *One Thousand and One Nights,* but also apply to other slavery and romance stories.

1.1 The Tower

The tower is closely associated with danger: to a woman locked up in it and to any man attempting to access it. At worst it can presage total disaster. The seminal narrative of Spain's conquest by Muslims in the year 711 attributes its downfall to the excesses and follies of its Christian ruler, the last Visigothic king, Rodrigo. His unbridled sexual lust leads to his seduction or raping of Florinda, daughter of Count Julián who is the governor of the Christian enclave Ceuta in North Africa and hitherto Rodrigo's close ally.[2] The count's desire for vengeance causes him to ally with, encourage and assist the Muslims to conquer Spain. Meanwhile, Rodrigo's insatiable lust for knowledge leads him to smash through the myriad locks on the forbidden Tower of Hercules, inside which he finds a prediction of his and his nation's doom: by breaking into the prohibited space, he is symbolically re-enacting the rape, thus bringing about the fulfilment of the prediction, in effect invoking a curse. The story has been the subject of numerous literary texts.[3]

---

[1] Irwin, *Arabian Nights Companion,* 214.
[2] Accounts of the incident vary, some interpreting her as a seductress and placing responsibility for the transgression on her, while others have her taken by force and completely innocent in the affair.
[3] Cf. Israel Burshatin, 'The Moor in the Text: Metaphor, Emblem, and Silence', in *Critical Inquiry,* Vol. 12, No. 1 (Autumn 1985), 98–118, esp. 105–10. The legend is recounted in Don Quixote and was dramatised by William Rowley in *All's Lost by Lust* (1619). Sir Walter Scott, Walter Savage

The tower may also symbolise the phallus of an oppressive patriarch, functioning as an emblem of his power. It can pose a challenge to protagonists wishing to access goods or individuals incarcerated inside. In Ferdowsi's *Shahnameh* (ca 1000 CE), the hero Rostam is the product of marriage between Zal and Rudaba. In an effort to prevent the union, Rudaba's father locks her in a tower, but Zal is able to reach her when she unfurls her long hair. As we have seen in Chapter 3, Charlemagne's victory over the Muslims is symbolically completed when Bramimonde is forced out of her tower. The climbing of the tower thus also represents an assault by the hero on the rival male's masculinity. In addition, in stories such as *Floire et Blanchefleur* and others, the hero's reaching the top of the tower and the beloved woman incarcerated there allows them to scale the heights of passion. Figuratively, it brings them both nearer to Paradise. In *Aucassin et Nicolette* the reversal of circumstance – whereby the woman frees herself from the tower and then rescues the man, is part of its general topsy-turvy world.

But towers can also be imagined as columns for ascending into the unknown. In Islamic lands many mosques have tall, narrow tower-like minarets: from their summits, muezzins call the faithful to prayer and, by extension, to contemplation of the infinite. Minarets are often of extraordinary height, leading many visitors to want to ascend them: I myself observed a companion on a tour of Uzbekistan as he climbed every minaret where it was permitted. Gazing at such structures seemed like peering toward an elevated space, whose summit would offer otherwise inaccessible vistas to the viewer. Ascending these towers would then mean, figuratively, attaining greater knowledge: of the land, and of one's own capabilities and limitations.

Towers can also be associated with death, as in Central Asia, where some minarets were used for executions. Condemned men and women could be thrown down from the top to instant annihilation.[4] A particularly notorious one is the Kalyan Minaret in Bukhara, known until recent times as the 'Tower of Death' because of its frequent use for this purpose. From here, according to legend, an evil khan ordered that his wife should be hurled after she displeased him. Granted one last wish, she ordered that all her skirts and dresses be brought and she put them all on, one on top of another. When she was

---

Landor, and Robert Southey all took up the story, as did Washington Irving in his *Legends of the Conquest of Spain* (1835). More recently, Juan Goytisolo returned to the theme in *Count Julián* (1970), and in 2000 it found a new home in the West-End musical, *La Cava*.

4 In recent times the extremist Islamist group Daesh/Isis/Isil has been reported to have been executing homosexual men and other 'miscreants' by throwing them off high roofs or towers, or forcing them to jump to their deaths.

thrown from the tower, the wind lifted her skirts, turning them into parachutes so that she sailed safely to the ground. The astonished khan then lifted his decree against her.

In other parts of the world, people have been killed by acts of 'defenestration' i.e., being hurled out of high windows. We have already seen (in Chapter 3) how the Muslim Princess Floripas dispatches her difficult governess Maragounde, by heaving her out of a castle window into the sea. Such acts have been recorded, or are the subject of myths, throughout history, including the killing of the Biblical Queen Jezebel at Jezreel (2 *Kings*, 9.33); and King John was said to have been killed by his nephew, Arthur of Brittany, by defenestration from the castle at Rouen, France in 1203. In Prague in 1419 and again in 1618, several people were tossed from high buildings. Both incidents are said to have led to war: the first to the Hussite War and the second supposedly precipitating the Thirty Years War. Rarely, though, the tower may be a place of refuge as when, in several of the Anglo-French *chansons de geste*, Floripas shelters the Christian knights in the tower which is her domain and where she is powerful, removing the Franks from the dungeon depths and literally raising them up high.

To summarise, then: in the stories we have been considering, the climbing of the tower has associations with conquest as well as both knowledge and death. Taking the tower is a critical act in the hero's or heroes' process of conquering the tower's owner. But when the tower is climbed in secret it is a dangerous act: discovery by the male ruler or any of his servants will almost certainly lead to the climber's death; the very act of climbing is also perilous, as the climber could fall at any time. But a successful ascent will again bring knowledge about the incarcerated woman and ultimately sexual enlightenment, for both the man and the woman.

1.2   *The Garden*

The association of a garden setting with motifs of love and desire recur constantly in 'Turkish', 'Moorish' and *maurofile* literature, as it does in Islamic architecture. Harking back to the Old Testament, in which the very first love affair (between Adam and Eve) begins in the Garden of Eden; and the *Qur'an*, where Paradise is visualised as a realm in which loving spouses will be reunited (Sura 56: 34–37), and each male will have several *houris* assigned to him (Suras 44: 51–55, 52: 17–20 and 55: 70–74), important scenes in the stories we have been considering take place in garden settings.

The idea of the earthly garden as Paradise is prevalent in the literature and culture of Iran: the ancient Persian word for a walled garden being *paradeiza*, from which our word 'paradise' comes. In Persian tradition the precise details required to make a garden a 'Paradise Garden' are stipulated, such as water courses set perpendicularly to one another, creating quadrants of landscaped space; strongly perfumed flowers, including orange blossom and roses; and places of shade – especially pavilions. The garden was (and to many people remains) seemingly the nearest approximation to Paradise on earth.

If romantic love engages most of the senses (sight, sound, taste, touch and, possibly, the sense of smell), the garden similarly arouses the senses because of its visual beauty and the seductive perfumes of the plants. In Muslim Spain in particular, gardens were as significant for the design of grand homes as the houses themselves. This is evidenced in Islamic buildings: Alhambra, and especially the Summer Palace, the Generalife in Granada; Alcazar rebuilt by Mudejars in Seville; and many of the houses in Córdoba, whose walls encase the most gloriously vivid gardens, provide memorable examples.

Garden settings are pivotal in the plots of several mediaeval works we considered in Chapter 2. Moving on into the 16th century, some of the key encounters of the *Guerras civilises de Granada* take place in gardens. For example, a meeting of the lovers Lindaraja and Gazul is set,

> en un jardín muy florido,
> con amorosos regales
> siendo cada qual servido,
> Lindaraja, afficionada,
> una guirnalda ha texido
> de clavelinas y roses
> y de un alhaylí escogido
> Cercada de violetas,
> Flor que de amantes ha sido,
> Se la puso en la cabeça
> a Gazul ...[5]

> [Hand in hand they walk'd together
> In a garden full of flow'rs
> And in amorous converse sweetly
> Pass'd the love-devoted hours.

---

5   *Guerras Civiles de Granada*, 422.

> Breathing fondness, then a garland
> Of the choisest flowers she [Lindaraxa] wove;
> Pinks and roses, in the center
> Bloom'd a fine carnation-clove.][6]

And a garden is once more the location for a scene in which Abinhamad places a garland of roses on his own head after he has made love to the Queen (111–12).

In Cervantes too, the garden milieu is significant: a key scene of *El amante liberal* occurs in the garden of Cornelio, where the lovers are captured by pirates and taken to Algiers. Indeed, the garden is a reference point: firstly, underscoring the protagonists' shock at being wrested so violently from this seemingly safe and luxurious setting; and secondly, providing a poignant contrast between the seaside garden's cool and balmy beauty and the savage, overheated environment in which the protagonists are soon to find themselves as slaves in Algiers.

As we have seen, the garden setting is a favourite locale for French writers of the 17th century. As late as 1805, the lovers of *The Beautiful African*, the North African woman Zara, and the Englishman Ernesto, meet in a garden where he is employed as gardener. He is a slave, but with relative freedom to wander and to enjoy the beauty of his workplace.

So the garden functions in various ways: as a place where lovers may experience ecstasy – such as dead souls might be expected to feel on reaching Paradise; as a point of contrast for lovers catapulted from it into soul-destroying slavery, almost literally experiencing 'Paradise Lost' – except when, as in *The Beautiful African*, the setting becomes a 'Paradise Regained', where the lovers meet clandestinely; and, most of all, as pretext for interpolating bosky and flowery images to enhance the lyrical and escapist nature of the entertainment represented by many of the stories we have been considering.

1.3 Birds (Including Caged Birds)

The caged bird has been and remains today a symbol of the trapped and imprisoned human being, but birds are often also used as symbols of love. In recent literature, birds have tended to represent women but, historically, they could relate to either sex. In this sense they are fitting metaphors for the many slaves and captives discussed in this book. The bird symbol is important in the story of Yusuf and Zulaikha: Zulaikha sees Yusuf as a caged bird when he is

---

[6] *Civil Wars of Granada*, 395.

imprisoned and fears whether he is or can be tamed. Later, when their roles are reversed, she herself is represented as an unhappy bird.

Ibn Ḥazm's *Tawq al-ḥamāma (Ring – or Collar – of the Dove)* is a compendium of stories and observations about lovers in many different circumstances. The ringed or 'collared' dove is so-called because of the black and white ring markings on its neck. It is a species of bird which originated in North Africa and is also known as the 'Barbary Dove'. But it lives in many countries. It is often domesticated and is therefore a fitting metaphor for stories which include many confined (slave) women, and the men and women who become slaves to love. The relevance of the title *Tawq al-ḥamāma* is discussed by Nazan Yıldız:

> The title of the work is ... very significant as dove's necklace stands for the feathers around the neck of the doves and in the classical Arabic literature ... it symbolizes the chain of love which is worn around the neck till one's death. Moreover in, in the old African tribes, the dove's necklace symbolizes grandeur ...
>
> In modern times, it was found out that the doves have a specific ring around their necks called "manyetit" (magnetite) which works like a compass and helps the doves to find their ways ... the dover's [sic] neck refers to the compass of love in the Arabic literature.[7]

Birds were often symbols of love more generally, as with examples of mating pairs of doves or swans. Geoffrey Chaucer's poem *Parlement of Foules* [Fowls] (ca. 1380–90), describes a conference of birds that meet to choose their mates on St. Valentine's Day. The narrator falls asleep and dreams of a beautiful garden in which nature presides over a debate between three high-ranking eagles, all competing for the love of a beautiful female. The other birds then express their opinions. The work 'gently satirises the tradition of courtly love' and is thought to have commemorated the marriage of Richard II and Anne of Bohemia in 1382.[8]

---

[7] Nazan Yıldız, 'A Bird after Love: Ibn' Hazm's The Ring of the Dove (Tawq al- Ham?mah) and the Roots of Courtly Love (2013), *Academic Journal of Interdisciplinary Studies*, 2 (8), 491–97: https://www.richtmann.org/journal/index.php/ajis/article/view/763 [accessed 3/3/2024].

[8] *Encyclopedia Britannica: The Parlement of Foules*: https://www.britannica.com/topic/The-Parlement-of-Foules [accessed 4/3/2024]. Cf. also Michael J. Warren, *Birds in Medieval English Poetry: Metaphors, Realities, Transformations, Nature and Environment in the Middle Ages* (Woodbridge, UK: Boydell & Brewer, 2018).

Finally, with their ability to fly high, birds can also be symbols of freedom, may signify human spirituality and have been linked to the spirit world more generally, representing fate, dreams, prophecy and the future.[9] In Persian mystical literature, birds might represent the human soul 'rising towards a higher reality'.[10] The imagery of, first Yusuf, then Zulaikha as caged birds, suggests the imprisonment of their souls, for that time at least.

∙ ∙ ∙

---

9   Trinity College Library, Cambridge, *Treasures from the Collection*: Violet Sphinx, 'Bird iconography in a 13th-century English Bestiary', May 19, 2014: https://trinitycollegelibrarycambridge.wordpress.com/2014/05/19/bird-iconography/ [accessed 4/3/2024].

10 Irmawati Marwoto, 'Bird Symbolism in Persian Mysticism Poetry', *International Review of Humanities Studies*, Vo. 4, No. 2, article 13, https://scholarhub.ui.ac.id/irhs/vol4/iss2/13 [accessed 4/3/2024].

Bibliography

Primary Literature

Aldington, Richard, tr., *Decameron of Boccaccio, The* (1957, repr. Aylesbury, Bucks: Hazell Watson and Viney Ltd., 1972), Vol. I.

Alemán, Mateo, *Historia de Ozmín y Daraja,* from the series, *10 grandes clásicos de la literatura española* (Madrid: Libros de Autor, 1994).

Alemán, Mateo, *Vida y hechos del pícaro Guzman de Alfarache*, Primera Parte: Vida del pícaro Guzmán de Alfarache (1599); Segunda Parte: Atalaya de la vida humana, En Amberes (1604) (repr. Buenos Aires: Espasa-Calpe S.A., 1953).

Alphonse, Peter, *Disciplina Clericalis (English Translation), from the Fifteenth Century Worcester Cathedral Manuscript F 172,* Cleveland, ed. William Henry Hulme, Ohio: Western Reserve University Bulletin, Vol XXII, No. 3: May 1919, 7–8: https://ia601200.us.archive.org/34/items/cu31924026493514/cu31924026493514.pdf [accessed 17/8/2016].

Anonymous, *La Prise d'Orange,* Claude Lachet, ed. and tr. (Paris: Champion, 2010).

d'Aranda, Emanuel, *The History of Algiers and it's* [sic] *slavery with many remarkable peculiarities of Africk /written by the Sieur Emanuel D'Aranda, sometime a slave there; English'd by John Davies* (London: Printed for John Starkey, 1666).

Aucassin et Nicolette, an original mediaeval manuscript version reproduced in a parallel text, with the English translation provided by Julia Bolton Holloway: http://www.umilta.net/aucassin.html [accessed 27/2/2024].

Bagnyon, Jehan, *Historia del Emperador Carlo Magno y delos doze pares de Francia & dela cruda batalla que hubo Oliveros con Fierabrás, Rey de Alexandría, hijo del gran almirante Balan* [History of the Emperor Charles the Great and of the twelve peers of France and of the brutal battle between Oliver and Fierabras, King of Alexandria, son of the great Admiral Balan]., tr. Nicolás de Piamonte,1521 (repr. ed. Enrique Suárez Figaredo, Barcelona: Lemir 24, 2020).

Bond, Gerald A., ed. and tr. *Poetry of William VII, Count of Poitiers, IX Dule of Aquitaine, The* (New York and London: Garland Publishing, 1982).

Brault, Gerard J., tr. and ed., *Song of Roland, The,* 2 vols. (University Park, Pa.: Pennsylvania State University Press, 1978).

Brémond, Gabriel de [Sebastien], *The Happy Slave, a Novel in three Parts compleat, translated from the French* [*l'Heureux esclave,*] *by a Person of Quality* [i.e., P. Porter] (London: Printed for Gilbert Cownly, 1686).

British Drama, The: A Collection of the Most Esteemed Tragedies, Comedies, Operas, and Farces, in the English Language. In Two Volumes, ed. unknown (London: Jones & Co., 1824).

BIBLIOGRAPHY 353

Brown, Peter, ed., and tr. Balme, Maurice, *Menander: The Plays and Fragments*, 2001 (repr. Oxford and other locations: Oxford University Press [Oxford World's Classics]), 2002.

Burgess, Glyn, tr. and ed., *Song of Roland, The* (London: Penguin Books, 1990).

Burnett, Charles, Keiji Yamamoto and Michio Yano, eds. and trs., *Abu Ma'sar: the Abbreviation of the Introduction to Astrology* (Leiden and other locations: E.J. Brill, 1994).

Burton, Richard, tr., *Perfumed Garden of the Cheikh Nefzaoui: a Manual of Arab Erotology (XVI century), The,* Revised and Corrected , London and Benares: Cosmopoli, for the Kama Shastra Society of London and Benares, for private circulation only, 1886; digitized by the Internet Archive in 2010 with funding from Boston Public Library Library: https://en.wikisource.org/wiki/The_Perfumed_Garden [accessed 14/10/2016].

Burton, Captain Sir Richard F., tr., *The Book of the Thousand Nights and a Night: A Plain and Literal Translation of the Arabian Nights Entertainments*, 12 vols, 1885.

Byron, Henry James, *Beautiful Haidée; or, the Sea Nymph and the Sallee Rovers. A New and Original Whimsical Extravaganza. Founded on the poem of Don Juan, the Ballad of Lord Bateman, and the Legend of Lurline* (London: Thomas Hailes Lacy, 1863).

Casson, Lionel, tr. and ed. By, *Six Plays of Plautus* (Garden City, New York: Anchor Books, Doubleday and Co., 1963).

Caxton, William, tr. and ed., *Lyf of the Noble and Crysten Prince, Charles the Grete* (London: William Caxton, 1485).

Cervantes, Miguel de, *Los Baños de Argel*, ed. Jean Canavaggio (Madrid: Taurus, 1984).

Cervantes, Miguel de, *The Captive's Tale (La historia del cautivo)*, ed. and tr. Donald P. McCrory (Warminster, England: Aris and Phillips, 1994).

Cervantes, Miguel de, *Comedia famosa del Gallardo español*, online edition: https://www.cervantesvirtual.com/obra-visor/el-gallardo-espanol--0/html/ [accessed 26/3/2018].

Cervantes, Miguel de, *El Gallardo Español*: https://www.cervantesvirtual.com/obra-visor/el-gallardo-espanol--0/html/ [accessed 21/4/2024].

Cervantes, Miguel de, *Obras Completas*, ed. Florencio Sevilla Arroyo and Antonio Rey Hazas, 3 vols. (Madrid: Editorial Castalia, 1999).

Cervantes, Miguel de, *Ocho Comedias y ocho entremeses nuevos, nunca representada* (1614) (Madrid: Por la viuda de Alonso Martin. A costa de Iuan de Villaroel, 1615).

Cervantes, Miguel de, *Ocho Comedias*, ed. Vern G. Williamsen and J.T. Abraham, 2002: http://cervantes.dh.tamu.edu/english/ctxt/comedias/banarg.html [accessed 21/4/2024].

Cervantes, Miguel de, *The voyage to Parnassus; Numāntia, a tragedy; the commerce of Algiers / by Cervantes; tr. from the Spanish by Gordon Willoughby James Gyll* (London: A. Murray, 1870).

Chandler, John H. ed., *King of Tars* (Kalamazoo, Michigan: Medieval Institute Publications, 2015).

Chateaubriand, François-René de, *Les Aventures du dernier Abencérage* (*The Last of the Abencerrajes*), a tr. into English by A.S. Kline, published with Lithographs by Francisco Javier Parcerisa: Poetry in Translation Series: https://www.poetryintranslation.com/klineaschateaubriandabencerraje.php, [accessed 29/4/2016].

Colman, George, *The Plays of George Colman the Younger*, ed. Peter A. Tasch (New York and London: Garland Publishing, 1981).

Copley, Frank O. tr. and ed., *Comedies of Terence, The* (Indianapolis and New York: the Bobbs-Merrill Publishing Co., 1967).

Coste, Gaultier, seigneur de La Calprenède, *Cleopatre*, Dediee a Monseignevr le Prince, Hvictesme Partie [Part VIII]. Paris, Chez Antoine de Sommaville, a Palais, en la Gallerie des Merciers, á l'Escu de France, MDCLIII (1653).

Coste, Gaultier de, seigneur de La Calprenède, *Hymen's præludia, or Loves masterpeice being that so much admired romance, intituled Cleopatra: in twelve parts / written originally in the French, and now elegantly rendred into English by Robert Loveday* (London: Printed by W.R. and J.R., 1674), in twelve parts: https://archive.org/details/bim_early-english-books-1641-1700_hymens-praeludia-_la-calprende-gaultier-_1659 [accessed 17/5/2024].

Cotton, Charles, *The Fair One of Tunis, Or, The Generous Mistress: a New Piece of Gallantry* (London: Henry Brome, 1674).

'Coveras, Francisco de las' (i.e., Francisco de Quintana), *Experiencias de amor y fortuna*, tr. into English as *The History of Don Fenise* (London: Printed for Humphrey Moseley, and are to be sold at his shop, 1651).

Croxall, S[amuel], ed., *A Select Collection of Novels, in Six Volumes, Written by the most celebrated authors in several languages, many of which never appear'd in English before, all new translated from the originals, by several eminent hands*, 6 vols. (London: printed for J. Watts; and sold by W. Mears, J. Brotherton and W. Meadows, W. Chetwood, J. Lacy, 1722).

Dan, Pierre, *Histoire de Barbarie et des ses corsaires, des royaumes, et des villes d'Alger, de Tunis, de Salé, & de Tripoly : divisée en six livres, ou il est traitté de leur gouvernement, de leurs mœurs, de leurs cruautez, de leurs brigandages, de leurs sortileges, & de plusieurs autres particularitez remarquables; ensemble des grandes miseres et des cruels tourmens qu'endurent les chrestiens captifs parmy ces infideles / par Le R.P. Fr. Pierre Dan*. 1637 (repr. Paris: Chez Pierre Rocolet, 1649).

Davis, Thomas Osborne, 'The Sack of Baltimore', in Charles Gavan Duffy, ed., *The Ballad Poetry of Ireland*, 39th ed. (Dublin and London: James Duffy, 1866).

Dawood, N.J., ed. and tr., *Koran, The*, 1956 (repr. London, New York and other locations: Penguin Books [Penguin Classics], 1999).

Discourses of Epictetus, a series of extracts from the teachings of the Greek Stoic philosopher Epictetus, written down ca. 108 CE by the historian and philosopher Arrian of Nicomedia, who had studied with Epictetus: *Internet Classics Archive*: http: /classics.mit.edu/Epictetus/discourses.4.four.html [accessed 21/3/2018].

Dixon, Paul, tr., *Plautus,* in 5 volumes, Vol. II (London: William Heineman Ltd., and Cambridge, Mass: Harvard University Press, 1917, repr. 1965).

Dryden, John, *The Conquest of Granada by the Spaniards, in Two Parts,* performed 1670 and 1671 (London: Printed by T.N. for Henry Herringman, 1672).

Egilsson, Olafur, *Reisubok sera Olafs Egilssonar,* tr. and ed., as *The Travels of the Reverend Olafur Egilsson: Captured by Pirates in 1627,* by Karl Smari Hreinsson and Adam Nichols (Keflavik, Iceland: Saga Akademia ehf, 2011).

Equiano, Olaudah, *The Interesting Narrative of Olaudah Equiano, or Gustavus Vassa, the African* (1789), ed. Vincent Carretta (London: Penguin, 1995).

Fielding, Henry, *Tragedy of Tragedies, or the Life and Death of Tom Thumb the Great* (1730), repr. L.J. Morrissey, ed. (Edinburgh: Oliver & Boyd, 1970).

Fitzgerald, Julia, *The Royal Slave* (New York: Ballantine Books, 1978).

Fuchs, Barbara, Larissa Brewer-Carter and Aaron J. Ilika, eds. and trs, *"The Abencerraje" and "Ozmin and Daraja": Two Seventeenth-Century Novellas from Spain* (Philadelphia: University of Pennsylvania Press, 2014).

Fuchs, Barbara, and Aaron J. Ilika, eds. and trs, Cervantes, Miguel de, *'The Bagnios of Algiers' and 'The Great Sultana': Two Plays of Captivity [by] Miguel de Cervantes* (Philadelphia: University of Pennsylvania Press, 2010).

Fumée, Martin, *Du vray et parfait amour, escrit en grec, par Athénagoras, philosophe athénien, contenant les amours honestes de Theagenes et de Charide* (1599) (repr. Paris: D. Guillemot, 1612).

Galán, Diego de, *El Cautiverio y Trabajos de Diego Galán, Natural de Consuegra y Vecino de Toledo* (ca. 1589) (repr. Madrid: La Sociedad de Bibliofilos Espanoles, 1913).

Garcés, María Antonia, ed., *An Early Modern Dialogue with Islam: Antonio de Sosa's Topography of Algiers* (1612), tr. into English by Diana de Armas Wilson, Notre Dame (Indiana: University of Notre Dame, 2011).

Gibb, H.A.R., tr., *Travels of Ibn Baṭṭūṭa A.D. 1325–1354, The,* 4 vols., Vol. I. (published for the Hakluyt Society by Cambridge University Press, 1958).

Gibb, H.A.R., tr., *Travels of Ibn Baṭṭūṭa A.D. 1325–1354, The,* Vol. II. (published for the Hakluyt Society by Cambridge University Press, 1962).

Goffe, Thomas, *The Courageous Turk, or Amurath,* performed 1618, published posthumously, 1632 (repr. London: The British Library, 2010).

Gracián, Padre Fray Gerónimo de la Madre de Dios, *Peregrinación de Anastasio:Diálogos de las persecuciones, trabajos, tribulaciones y cruces que ha padecido el Padre Fray Gerónimo Gracián de la Madre de Dios, desde que tomó el hábito de Carmelita Descalzo hasta el año 1613 y de muchos consuelo y misericordias de nuestro Señor que ha recibido. Pónese su manera de proceder en lo espiritual con algunas luces que acerca de sus sucesos tuvieron la beata madre Theresa de Jesús y algunas otras siervas de Dios que se los pronosticaron. Dirigidos a sus hermanos el Padre fray Lorenzo de la Madre de Dios, y las Madres María de San Joseph, Isabel de Jesús y Juliana de la Madre de Dios, de la Orden de Nuestra Señora del Carmen de los Descalzos* (Burgos: 'El Monte Carmelo', 1905).

Greene, *The Dramatic and Poetical Works of Robert Greene and George Peele, with Memoirs of the Authors and Notes*, ed. Robert, Rev. Alexander Dyce (London: Routledge, Warne and Routledge, 1861).

Greene, Robert, *The Life and Complete Works in Prose and Verse of Robert Greene, MA., in Fifteen Volumes*, 1881–86, Alexander B. Grosart, ed. (reissued New York: Russell and Russell, 1964).

Greene, Robert, *Robert Greene,* ed. Thomas H. Dickinson (London: T. Fisher Unwin, 1909).

Greene, Robert? (or Thomas Lodge?), *Selimus,* or *The Tragedy of Selimus, Sometime Emperor of the Turks* (1594), ed. Alexander B. Grosart (London: J.M. Dent, 1898).

Haddawy, Husain, tr. and ed., *Arabian Nights, The, Based on the Text of the Fourteenth-Century Syrian Manuscript ed. by Muhsin Mahdi,* 1984 (repr. London: Everyman's Library, 1992).

Haedo, Maestro fray Diego de, *Topografía, e Historia General de Argel, Repartida en Cinco Tratados, do Severan Casos Estraños, muertes espantosas, y tormentos exquisitos, que conviene se entiendan en la Christiandad: con mucha doctrina, y elegancia curiosa* (Valladolid: Diego Fernandez de Cordova y Oviedo, MDCXII, 1612).

Ibn Ḥazm, Abū Muhammad 'Alī ibn Ahmad ibn Sa'īd, *The Ring of the Dove*, tr. and ed., A.J. Arberry (London: Luzac and Co., 1951).

Herrtage, Sidney J.H., ed., *English Charlemagne Romances, The,* 12 vols., Part VI, *With the Fragments of Roland and Vernagu and Otuel,* 1882 (repr., London, New York and Toronto: Published for the Early English Text Society by Oxford University Press, 1969).

Herrtage, Sidney J.H., ed., *Romance of the Sowdone* [Sultan] *of Babylone and of Ferumbras his Sone who Conquered Rome. English Charlemagne Romances, The,* Part V, 1882 (repr. London, New York and Toronto: Published for the Early English Text Society by Oxford University Press, 1969).

Herrtage, Sidney J.H., ed., *Sir Ferumbras,* 1879 (repr. for the Early English Text Society, London, New York and Toronto: Oxford University Press, 1966).

Hubert, Merton Jerome, ed., *Romance of* Floire and Blanchefleur, *The: A French Idyllic Poem of the Twelfth Century, translated into English Verse*, Chapel Hill, North Carolina: North Carolina University Press, 1966.

Huet, Pierre-Daniel, *A Treatise of Romances and their Original. Tr. out of French* (London: Printed by R. Battersby, for S. Heyrick, at Grays Inn Gate in Holborn, 1672).

BIBLIOGRAPHY 357

Hull, Denison B. ed., *Digenis Akrites: The Two-Blood Border Lord* (Athens, Ohio: Ohio University Press, 1972).

Hull, E.M. (Edith Maude), *The Sheik*, 1919 (repr. London: Virago, 1996).

Hürriyet Daily News: https://www.hürriyetdailynews.com/underground-cells-ottoman-dungeons-22155 [accessed 22/4/2024].

Ibn Idhari, *Kitāb al-bayān al-mughrib fī ākhbār mulūk al-andalus wa'l-maghrib* (*Book of the Amazing Story of the History of the Kings of al-Andalus and Maghreb*) (1312), 3 vols., tr. Francisco Fernández y González (Granada: Francisco Ventura y Sabatel, 1860), Vol. 1.

Jack, Malcolm, ed., Montagu, Lady Mary Wortley, *Turkish Embassy Letters* (London: William Pickering, 1993).

Jeffreys, Elizabeth, ed., *Digenis Akritis: The Grottaferrata and Escorial Versions* (Cambridge: Cambridge University Press, 1998).

Johnson, Samuel, *Poems*, ed. E.L. McAdam, with George Milne (New Haven, Conn.: Yale University Press, 1964).

Knolles, Richard, *The generall historie of the Turkes from the first beginning of that nation to the rising of the Othoman familie: with all the notable expeditions of the Christian princes against them. Together with the liues and conquests of the Othoman kings and emperours faithfullie collected out of the- best histories, both auntient and moderne, and digested into one continuat historie vntill this present yeare 1603* (London: Adam Islip, printer, 1603).

Lafayette, Mme. de, [Marie-Madeleine Pioche de La Vergne, Comtesse de La Fayette], *Zaïde, Histoire espagnole*, ed. Janine Anseaume Kreiter (Paris: Librairie A.-G. Nizet, 1982).

Lane, Edward, ed., *The Thousand and One Nights, or, the Arabian Nights' Entertainments* (Boston: De Wolfe, Fiske), 1800, https://archive.org/details/thousandonenightoolane/mode/2up [accessed 1/7/2024].

Laugier de Tassy, Jacques Philipe, *Histoire du Royaume d'Alger, Avec l'état présent de son gouvernement, de sesfForces de terre et de Mer, de ses Revenus, Police, Justice, Politique et Commerce,* ed. Noel Laveau and Andre Nouschi (Paris: Loysel, 1992).

Laugier de Tassy, Jacques Philippe, *Historia del Reyno de Argél, con el estado presente de su govierno, de sus fuerzas de tierra, y mar, de sus rentas, policía, justicia, politica, y comercio* (Madrid: en la Oficina de Pantaleón Aznar ..., se hallará en la Librería de Pasqual Lopez, 1733).

Lévi-Provençal, Évariste, *España musulmana hasta la caída del Califato de Córdoba (711–1031 de J.C.)* (Madrid: Espasa-Calpe, 1957).

Ligon, Richard, *A True & Exact History of the Island of Barbadoes* (London: Printed for Humphrey Moseley, 1657).

Lyons, M. C., ed., *Arabian Epic: Heroic and Oral Story-Telling*, 3 vols. (Cambridge: Cambridge University Press, 1995).

Lyons, M.C. and Ursula Lyons, trs and eds., *The Arabian Nights: Tales of 1,001 Nights*, 3 vols, 2008 (repr. London: Penguin, 2010).

Lyons, Malcolm C., tr. and ed., *Tales of the Marvellous and News of the Strange*, 2014 (repr. London: Penguin Classics, 2015).

MacGuckin, William, repr. tr., *Ibn Khallikan's Biographical Dictionary* [1256 to 1274], 4 vols., Vol. IV, 1871, de Slane (New York: Cosimo Classics, 2010).

Magidow, Melanie, ed. and translator, *The Tale of Princess Fatima, Warrior Woman: The Arabic Epic of Dhāt al-Himma* (London: Penguin Books, 2022).

Malmesbury, William of, *History of the Kings of England,* 1140–1170, tr. J.A. Giles (repr. CreateSpace Independent Publishing Platform [Amazon], 2016).

Martinière, Pierre-Martin de la, *l'Heureux esclave, ou Relation des aventures du sieur de La Martinière comme il fut pris par les corsaires de Barbarie et délivré, la manière de combat sur mer, de l'Afrique, et autre particularitez* (Paris: Olivier de Varennes, 1674).

Mason, Connie, *The Pirate Prince* (New York: Leisure Books, 2004).

Massinger, Philip, *The Renegado,* ed. Michael Neill (London: Methuen Drama, A & C Black Publishers Ltd., 2010).

Mavrogordato, John, ed. with an introduction, tr. and commentary by, *Digenes Akrite* (London: Oxford University Press, 1956, repr. 1970).

Morgan, Joseph, *A Compleat History of The Piratical States Of Barbary, Viz. Algiers, Tunis, Tripoli, And Morocco: Containing The Origin, Revolutions, And Present State Of These Kingdoms, Their Forces, Revenues, Policy, And Commerce* (London: J. Bettenham, 1728–1729, repr. 1750).

Nicolay, Nicolas de, *The Nauigation, peregrinations and voyages, made Into* Turkie by Nicholas de Nicolay Dauphinois, Lord of Arfeuile, Cham*berlaine and Geographer ordinarie to the* King of Fraunce: conteining sundry singularities which the Author hath there seene and obserued ... London: Thomas Dawson, 1585, tr. 'out of the French [into English]' by T. Washington the younger (repr. Amsterdam: Theatrum Orbis Terrarum Ltd., and New York: Da Capo Press, 1968).

Pellow, Thomas, *The history of the long captivity and adventures of Thomas Pellow, in South Barbary: giving an account of his being taken by two Sallee Rovers ... in which is introduced a particular account of the manners and customs of the Moors ... together with a description of the cities, towns, and publick buildings in those kingdoms/written by himself.* 2nd ed (London: Printed for R. Goadey and sold by W. Owen, 1740 (?).

Pendlebury, David, tr., *Yusuf and Zulaikha: An Allegorical Romance by Hakim Nuruddin Abdurrahman Jami* (London: The Octagon Press, 1980).

Pérez de Hita, Ginés, *Guerras civiles de Granada*, 2 vols., Tomo I, Madrid: D. Leon Amarita, 1833, reissued Gutenberg online, 2022: https://www.gutenberg.org/cache/epub/67631/pg67631-images.html [accessed 25/4/2024].

Pérez de Hita, Ginés, *The Civil Wars of Granada; and the History of the Factions of the Zegries and Abencerrajes, Two Noble Families of that City, to the Final Conquest by*

Ferdinand and Isabella, Translated from the Arabic of Abenhamin, a Native of Granada, by Ginés Pérez de Hita, and from the Spanish by Thomas Rodd (London: Printed for Thomas Ostell, No 3 Ave Maria Lane, 1803).

Pérez de Hita, Ginés, *Guerras Civiles de Granada* (2 vols), ed. Paula Blanchard-Demouge, Vol. I (Madrid: Bailly-Bailliere, 1913).

Pérez de Hita, Ginés, *Guerras civiles de Granada*, ed. Shasta M. Bryant (Newark, Delaware: Juan de la Cuesta, 1982).

Pitts, Joseph, *A True and Faithful Account of the Religion and manners of the Mohammetans, with an Account of the Author's Being Taken Captive*, in Daniel J. Vitkus (ed.), *Piracy, Slavery, and Redemption: Barbary Captivity Narratives from Early Modern England* (New York: Columbia University Press, 2001).

Réage, Pauline (pseudonym of Anne Desclos), *Story of O*, Paris: Jean-Jacques Pauvert, 1954, tr. Wenzell Baird Bryant and repr. In English (Paris: Olympia Press, 1965).

Reardon, B.P. ed., *Collected Ancient Greek Novels* (Berkeley, Los Angeles and London: University of California Press, 1989, repr. 2008).

Regnard, Jean-François, *La Provençale*, suivie de la *Satire Contre les Maris, Textes accompagnés d'une Préface* sur *Regnard et la littérature barbaresque*, ed. Edmond Pilon (Paris: Édition Bossard, 1731, repr. 1920).

Richards, D.S., tr. *Chronicle of Ibn al-Athir for the Crusading Period from al-Kamil fi-l ta'rikh, The Years 491–541/1097–1146, the Coming of the Franks and the Muslim Response, The* (Part I of III) (Aldershot, Hants and Burlington, Vermont: Ashgate Publishing Co., 2006).

Riley, Henry Thomas, ed., *Mercator, or The Merchant*, in *The Comedies of Plautus* (London: G. Bell and Sons, 1912).

Rosenthal, Frank tr. and ed., Ibn Khaldun, *Muqaddimah* (New York: Pantheon Books, 1958).

Sahih al-Bukhari, https://sunnah.com/bukhari:7263 [accessed 23/5/2024].

de Sélincourt, Aubrey, tr., *Herodotus, the Histories,* revised, with an introduction and notes by A.R. Burn (Harmondsworth, Middlesex: Penguin Classics, 1972).

Shakespeare, William, *Shakespeare's Last Plays*, ed. E.M.W. Tillyard (1938) (repr. London and Toronto: Chatto and Windus, 1954).

Steele, Richard, and Joseph Addison, *Spectator Magazine* (London: Addison and Steele), 1711–1712.

Stevick, Robert D. ed. *Five Middle English Narratives* (Indianapolis: Bobbs Merrill, 1967).

Summers, Montague ed., *Oroonoko* in *The Works of Aphra Behn* (6 vols) (1915), Volume V: https://www.gutenberg.org/ebooks/author/9866 [accessed 24/4/2024].

Taylor, A.B. ed., *Floris and Blancheflour: A Middle English Romance* (Oxford: Clarendon Press, 1927).

Vega, Lope de, *El remedio en la desdicha*, 1620, ed. J.W. Barker (Cambridge: Cambridge University Press, 1951).

Villegas, Antonio de, *El Abencerraje: la historia de Abindarráez y la hermosa Jarifa*, 1565, in *Antonio de Villegas' El Abencerraje, A Collaboration of Francisco López Estrada and John Esten Keller* (tr.) (Chapel Hill, N.C.: The University of North Carolina Press, 1964).

Villiers, George, 2nd Duke of Buckingham, *The* Rehearsal, performed 1671 (London: Printed for Thomas Dring, 1672).

Vitkus, Daniel, ed., *Three Turk Plays from Early Modern England* (New York, and Chichester, West Sussex: Columbia University Press, 2000).

Secondary Literature

Abulafia, David, *The Great Sea: A Human History of the Mediterranean*, 2011 (repr. London and other locations: Penguin Books, 2012).

Adams, A. 'Destiny, Love and the Cultivation of Suspense: the 'Roman d'Eneas' and Aimon de Varennes' "Florimont"', *Reading Medieval Studies*, V (1979), 57–70, 63.

Akbari, Suzanne Conklin, *Idols in the East* (Cornell, USA: Cornell University Press, 2009).

Ali, Adam, 'Slave, Queen, and Mother of Caliphs: the Story of Khayzuran': www.medievalists.net, 04, 2019 [accessed 9/5/2023].

Ali, Kecia, *Marriage and Slavery in Early Islam* (Cambridge, Mass. and London: Harvard University Press, 2010).

Ali, Kecia, *Sexual Ethics and Islam: Feminist Reflections on Qur'an, Hadith and Jurisprudence* (London: Oneworld Publications, 2015).

d'Amico, Jack, *The Moor in English Renaissance Drama* (Tampa, Florida: University of South Florida Press, 1991).

d'Amico, Jack, Catherine M. Jones, William W. Kibler and Logan E. Whalen, trs. and eds., *An Old French Trilogy: Texts from the William of Orange Cycle* (Gainsville, Fla.: University Press of Florida, 2020).

Arberry, A.J. ed, *Moorish Poetry: A Translation of* 'The Pennants', *an Anthology Compiled in 1243 by the Andalusian Ibn Sa'id* (Cambridge: Cambridge University Press, 1953).

Archer, William, *English Dramatists of Today* (London: Sampson Low, Marston, Searle, & Rivington, 1882).

Ardila, J.A.G., ed., *The Cervantean Heritage: Reception and Influence of Cervantes in Britain* (London: Modern Humanities Research and Maney Publishing, 2009).

Armstrong, Karen, *Muhammad: A Biography of the Prophet*, 1991 (repr. London: Phoenix Press, 2004).

Aronson, Nicole, *The Life of Mademoiselle de Scudéry*, tr. Stuart R. Aronson (Boston: Twayne Publishing, 1978).

Attar, Farid ud-Din, *The Conference of the Birds*, trs. Afham Darbandi and Dick Davis (London: Penguin, 1984).

Baepler, Paul, ed., *White Slaves, African Masters: American Barbary Captivity Narratives* (Chicago: University of Chicago Press, 1999).

Ball, Ann, ed., *Encyclopedia of Catholic Devotions and Practices* (Huntingdon, Indiana: Our Sunday Visitor, Inc., 2003).

Barrack, Charles M, 'Motifs of Love in the Early Courtly Lyrics of Moslem Spain and Hohenstaufen Germany: In Memory of Ernst Behler', *Monatshefte* 105: 2 (2013) 173–200.

Barton, Simon, 'Women on the Frontline', *History Today,* vol. 65, 1 January 2015.

BBC, 'Muhammad and Slavery', *Slavery in Islam,* published online, 7/9/2009: https://www.bbc.co.uk/religion/religions/islam/history/slavery_1.shtml [accessed 16/5/2024].

Beaton, Roderick and David Ricks (eds.). *Digenes Akrites: New Approaches to Byzantine Heroic Poetry* (Aldershot: King's College London, 1993).

Beardon-White, Roy, *How the Wind Sits; Or, the History of Henry and Ann Lemoine, Chapbook Writers and Publishers of the Late Eighteenth Century*, MA Thesis submitted to Southern Illinois University, 2005: DOI: 10.13140/RG.2.2.13854.95047 [accessed 20/5/2–24] .

Bearman, P, ed., *Encyclopedia of Islam, The*, 2nd edition, Brill Online: https://referenceworks.brillonline.com/browse/encyclopaedia-of-islam-2 [accessed 14/06/2022].

Beaumont, Daniel E., *Slave of Desire: Sex, Love, and Death in the 1001 Nights* (Madison, New Jersey: Fairleigh Dickinson University Press, 2002).

Beeston, A.F.L., ed. and tr., *The Epistle on Singing-Girls of Jahiz* (Warminster, Wilts.: Aris & Phillips Ltd., 1980).

Benassar, Bartolomé and Lucile Benassar, *Les chrétiens d'Allah: L'histoire extraordinaire des renégats, XVI et XVII siècle* (Paris: Perrin, 1989).

Benen-Wilson, Andrew, review of *The Abduction from the Seraglio,* Glyndebourne Festival Opera, Orchestra of the Age of Enlightenment Royal Albert Hall, 14 August 2015, *Early Music Reviews*: *Prom 39*, published on-line on the 18th August 2015: https://andrewbensonwilson.org/2015/08/18/prom-39-the-abduction-from-the-seraglio/ [accessed 29/4/2016].

Benjamin, Jessica, *The Bonds of Love: Psychoanalysis, Feminism, and the Problem of Domination* (London: Virago Press, 1990).

Berger, Günter, 'Legitimation und Modell: Die "Aithiopika" als Prototyp des Französischen heroisch-gallant roman', *Antike und Abenland*, Vol. 30 (2) (Jan 1, 1984).

Bertrand, Louis and Sir Charles Petrie, *The history of Spain / Part I: From the Visigoths to the death of Philip II*, by Louis Bertrand; *Part II: From the Death of Philip II to 1945,* by Sir Charles Petrie [the French tr. by Warre B. Wells] (London: Dawsons of Pall Mall, 1969).

Bhattacharya, Nandini , 'Family Jewels: George Colman's *Inkle and Yarico* and Connoisseurship', in *Eighteenth-Century Studies* 34.2 (2001).

Blanch, Lesley, *The Wilder Shores of* Love, London: John Murray, 1954, published online by Simon and Schuster: http://www.simonandschuster.com/books/The-Wilder-Shores-of-Love/Lesley-Blanch/9781439197349 [accessed 11/5/2018].

Boase, Roger, *The Origin and Meaning of Courtly Love: a Critical Study of European Scholarship* (Manchester: Manchester University Press, 1977).

Bond, Gerald A. ed. and tr., *The Poetry of William VII, Count of Poitiers, IX Dule of Aquitaine* (New York and London: Garland Publishing, 1982).

Booth, Mary Louise, tr. and ed. *Martin's History of France, Vol. 1: the Age of Louis XIV,* by Henri Martin (Boston: Walker, Wise and Co., 1865).

Bosworth, C.E., 'James Elroy Flecker, Poet, Diplomat, Orientalist', a lecture delivered in the John Rylands Library, University of Manchester, on Wednesday, 10th December 1986, and published in the *Bulletin of the John Rylands University Library of Manchester*, 69:2, 359–78, 377: https://www.manchesterhive.com/view/journals/bjrl/69/2/article-p359.xml [accessed 27/4/2023].

Brann, Ross, 'He Said, She Said: Reinscribing the Andalusi Arabic Love Lyric', *Studies in Arabic and Hebrew Letters: In Honor of Raymond P. Scheindlin*, ed. Jonathan P. Decter and Michael Chaim Rand (Piscataway, N.J.: Gorgias Press LLC, 2007).

Brewer, Derek S., 'The Ideal of Feminine Beauty in Medieval Literature, *Moden Language Review,* 50: Vols. XXXI–L. General Index (1955), 1–40: https://www.jstor.org/stable/3718320 [accessed 23/2/2023].

Britton, Dennis Austin, *Becoming Christian: Race, Reformation, and Early Modern English Romance* (New York: Fordham University Press, 2014).

Britton, D.A., (2015). 'From the knight's tale to the two noble kinsmen: Rethinking Race, Class and Whiteness in Romance. *Postmedieval, Suppl. Making Race Matter in the Middle Ages, 6* (1), 64–78. DOI: https://doi.org/10.1057/pmed.2015.3 [accessed 19/5/2023].

Brotton, Jerry, *This Orient Isle: Elizabethan England and the Islamic World,* 2003 (repr. London, UK and seven other countries: Allen Lane, an imprint of Penguin Random House UK 2016).

Burnett, Charles, 'Learned Knowledge of Arabic Poetry, Rhymed Prose, and Didactic Verse, from Petrus Alfonsi to Petrarch', John Marenbon, ed., *Poetry and Philosophy in the Middle Ages: A Festschrift for Peter Dronke* (Leiden, Boston and Cologne: Brill, 2001).

Burrows, Thomas and Eleanor Harding, 'The Triumph of Tim Nice But-Dim: Posh but Stupid Children End up Earning More Than the Poor-But-Gifted', *Daily Mail,* 26th July 2015, revised 27th July 2015: http://www.dailymail.co.uk/news/article-3174961/The-Triumph-Tim-Nice-Dim-Report-says-posh-stupid-children-end-earning-poor-gifted.html [accessed 18/6/2016].

Burshatin, Israel, 'The Moor in the Text: Metaphor, Emblem, and Silence', *Critical Inquiry* Vol. 12, No. 1, 'Race, Writing, and Difference' (Autumn, 1985), 98–118.

Canard, Marius, 'Les principaux personnages du roman de chevalerie arabe *"Dāt Al-Himma Wa-L-Battāl"*, Arabica, *Journal of Arabic and Islamic studies* (in French), No. 8, 158–173.

Canavaggio, Jean, *Cervantes,* tr. from the French by J.R. Jones (New York and London: W. R. Norton & Company, 1986, repr. 1990).

Carnell, Rachel K., 'Slipping from Secret History to Novel' (2015), English Faculty Publications, Cleveland State University, 78. https://engagedscholarship.csuohio.edu/cleng_facpub/78 [accessed 1/6/2023].

Carr, Matthew, *Blood and Faith: The Purging of Muslim Spain* (London: Hurst, 2009).

Carrasco-Urgoiti, María Soledad, *The Moorish Novel:* El Abencerraje *and* Pérez de Hita (Boston: Twayne Publishers, 1976).

Caruth, Cathy, 'An Interview with Robert Jay Lifton, in Cathy Caruth, ed., *Trauma: Explorations in Memory* (Baltimore: Johns Hopkins University Press, 1995).

Casalduero, Joaquin, *Sentido y forma del teatro de* Cervantes (Madrid: Aguilar, 1951).

Cavillac, Michel, *Pícaros y mercaderes en el Guzmán de Alfarache* (Granada, Spain: Universidad de Granada, 1994).

Cazenave, Jean, 'Le roman hispano-mauresque en France', *Revue de littérature comparée*, 5e année, Paris, 1925.

Chandlery, Peter J., *Mary's Praise on Every Tongue: A Record of Homage Paid to Our Blessed Lady* (London: Manresa, 1910).

Chew, Samuel Claggett, *The Crescent and the Rose: Islam and England During the Renaissance* (New York: Oxford University Press, 1937).

Childers, William, 'Manzanares 1600: Moriscos from Granada Organize a Festival of "Moors and Christians"', in Kevin Ingram, ed., *the Conversos and Moriscos in Late Medieval Spain and Beyond* (Leiden: Brill, 2009).

Christides, Vassilios, 'Arabic Influence on the Akritic Cycle', *Byzantion* 49 (1979), 94–109.

Christides, Vassilios, 'An Arabo-Byzantine Novel *'Umar al-Nu'mān* Compared with *Digenēs Akritas'*, *Byzantion* 32 (1962), 549–604.

Christie, Niall, (2012) 'Noble Betrayers of their Faith, Families and Folk: Some Non-Muslim Women in Mediaeval Arabic Popular Literature', *Folklore*, 123:1, 84–98, DOI: 10.1080/0015587X.2012.642988.

Clarence-Smith, William G., and David Eltis, 'White Servitude', David Eltis and Stanley L. Engerman, eds., *The Cambridge World History of Slavery*, 3 vols. (Cambridge: Cambridge University Press, 2011).

Clissold, Stephen, *The Barbary Slaves* (London: P. Elek, 1977).

Clot, André, *Haroun al-Rashid and the World of One Thousand and One Nights,* translated and edited by John Howe (London: Saqi, 1989).

Cohen, Jeffrey Jerome, 'On Saracen Enjoyment: Some Fantasies of Race in Late Medieval France and England', *Journal of Medieval and Early Modern Studies,* 31:1, Winter 2001.

Colley, Linda, *Captives: Britain, Empire and the World, 1600–1850* (London: Pimlico, 2003).

Comfort, William Wistar, 'The Saracens in Christian Poetry', *Dublin Review,* Vol. CXLIX, No. 298 (July and October 1911), 23–48.

'Coveras, Francisco de las' (i.e. Francisco de Quintana), *Experiencias de amor y fortuna*, tr. into English as *The History of Don Fenise*, 1651.

Crompton, Louis, *Homosexuality and Civilisation* (Cambridge, MA: Harvard University Press, 2003).

Crooks, Esther J., *The Influence of Cervantes in France in the Seventeenth Century* (Baltimore, London, Oxford and Paris: Johns Hopkins Press, Oxford University Press, 1931).

Crupi, Charles W., *Robert Greene* (Boston: Twayne Publishers, 1986).

Curta, Florin, *Borders, Barriers, and Ethnogenesis: Frontiers in Late Antiquity and the Middle Ages* (Turnhout, Belgium: Brepols, 2005).

Dabbagh, Abdulla al-, 'The Oriental Sources of Courtly Love', *International Journal of Arabic-English Studies*, Vol. 3 No. 1 (2002), 21–32. https://doi.org/10.33806/ijaes2 000.3.1.2 [accessed 25/2//2024].

Dadson, Trevor J., 'The Assimilation of Spain's Moriscos: Fiction or Reality?' *Journal of Levantine Studies*, Vol. 1, No. 2 (Winter 2011), 11–30.

Davis, Robert C., *Christian Slaves, Muslim Masters,* 2003 (repr. Basingstoke, Hants. and New York: Palgrave Macmillan, 2004).

Davis, Robert C., *Holy War and Human Bondage: Tales of Christian-Muslim Slavery in the Early-Modern Mediterranean* (Santa Barbara, Calif. and Other Locations: Praeger/ ABC-CLIO, 2009).

Decter, Jonathan P., *Iberian Jewish Literature: Between al-Andalus and Christian Europe* (Bloomington and Indianapolis: Indiana University Press, 2007).

Deferrari, Harry A., *The Sentimental Moor in Spanish Literature Before 1600* (Philadelphia: University of Pennsylvania Press, 1927).

Dew, Nicholas, *Orientalism in Louis XIV's France* (Oxford: Oxford University Press, 2009).

Dissanayake, Samanthi, 'All because the lady loves a foreign accent', published 14th August 2008, at http://news.bbc.co.uk/1/hi/magazine/7516672.stm, accessed on the 11th May 2018.

Dönmez, Sedef, *Conversions In Umayyad Emirate of Al-Andalus*, London: School of African and Oriental Studies, (MA Thesis in Turkish Studies) [date not given]: https://www.academia.edu/9508173/Conversions_In_Umayyad_Emirate_of_Al_Andalus [accessed 28/2/2024].

Duckworth, George E., *The Nature of Roman Comedy: a Study in Popular Entertainment* (Princeton, N.J.: Princeton University Press, 1971).

Duran, Manuel, *Cervantes* (Boston USA: Twayne Publishers, 1974).

Ehlers, Benjamin, *Between Christians and Moriscos: Juan de Ribera and Religious Reform* (Baltimore, Maryland, USA: The Johns Hopkins University Press, 2006).

Elaskary, Mohamed Ibrahim Hassan, *The Image of Moors in the Writings of Four Elizabethan Dramatists: Peele, Dekker, Heywood and Shakespeare*, Ph.D. Dissertation for the University of Exeter, submitted April, 2008: https://core.ac.uk/download/pdf/12827241.pdf [accessed 13/07/2024].

El-Cheikh, Nadia M., 'Describing the Other to Get at the Self: Byzantine Women in Arabic Sources (8th-11th Centuries)', *Journal of the Economic and Social History of the Orient*, Vol. 40, No. 2 (1997), 239–250.

Elerydl-Hibri, Tayeb, *Reinterpreting Islamic Historiography: Hārūn al-Rashīd and the Narrative of the Abbasid Caliphate* (Cambridge: Cambridge University Press, 1999).

El Hamel, Chouki, 'Blacks and Slavery in Morocco: the Question of the Haratin at the End of the Seventeenth Century', Michael A. Gomez, ed., *Diasporic Africa: A Reader* (New York: New York University Press, 2006, 177–199).

Ellis-Fermor, Una, *The Jacobean Drama: An Interpretation* (London, 1936, repr. London: Methuen & Co., 1977).

Eltis, David and Stanley L. Engerman, eds., *The Cambridge World History of Slavery* (3 vols.) (Cambridge: Cambridge University Press, 2011).

Encyclopedia Britannia: https://www.britannica.com/topic/Britannica-Online [accessed 13/07/2024].

Epstein, Steven A., *Speaking of Slavery* (Ithaca and London: Cornell University Press, 2001).

Esposito, John L., editor in chief, Oxford Dictionary of Islam, The (New York and Oxford: Oxford University Press, 2003).

Ewoldt, Amanda M, *Conversion and Crusade: The Image of the Saracen in Middle English Romance*, PhD dissertation for the University of Louisiana at Lafayette, 2018: ProQuest Dissertations Publishing: https://www.proquest.com/docview/2206784524?pq-origsite=gscholar&fromopenview=true [accessed 26/2/2023], 81–82.

Fastrup, Anne, 'Cross-cultural Movement in the Name of Honour: Renegades, Honour and State in Miguel de Cervantes's Barbary Plays', *Bulletin of Spanish Studies: Hispanic Studies and Researches on Spain, Portugal and Latin America*, Vol. 89, Issue 3 (2012), 347–67.

Feerick, Jean E., *Strangers in Blood: Relocating Race in the Renaissance* (Toronto, Buffalo and London: University of Toronto Press, 2010).

Ferguson, Moira, *Subject to Others: British Women Writers, 1670–1834* (New York and London: Routledge, 1992).

Fernández-Morera, Darío, *The Myth of the Andalusian Paradise: Muslims, Christians and Jews Under Islamic Rule in Medieval Spain*, 2016 (repr. Wilmington, Delaware: ISI Books, 2017).

Fierro, Maribel, 'The Bestsellers of al-Andalus', in María Marcos Cobaleda, ed., *Artistic and Cultural Dialogues of the Late Medieval Mediterranean: Mediterranean Perspectives* (Basingstoke, Hants.: Palgrave Macmillan, 2021), 31–56.

Finlay, George, *Greece under the Romans; a Historical View of the Condition of the Greek Nation, from the Time of its Conquest by the Romans until the Extinction of the Roman empire in the East, B.C. 146-A.D. 717,* 2nd ed. (Edinburgh: William Blackwood and Sons, 1857).

Finlay, George, *History of the Byzantine and Greek Empires, from DCCXVI to MCCCCLIII*, 1854, 2nd ed., 2 vols. (Edinburgh and London: William Blackwood and Sons, 1856).

Fisher, Godfrey, *Barbary Legend: War, Trade, and Piracy in North Africa 1415–1830* (Oxford: Clarendon Press, 1957).

Fitzmaurice-Kelly, James, *Miguel de Cervantes Saavedra: A Memoir* (London and Other Locations: Oxford University Press, 1913).

Fletcher, Richard, *Moorish Spain,* 1992 (repr. London: Phoenix Press, 2001).

Fletcher, Richard, *The Quest for El Cid* (London: Hutchinson, 1989).

Frakes, Jerrold C, ed., *Contextualizing the Muslim Other in Medieval Christian Discourse. (The New Middle Ages)* (New York: Palgrave Macmillan, 2011).

Friedman, Edward H., *The Unifying Concept: Approaches to the Structure of Cervantes's 'Comedias'* (York, S.C.: Spanish Literature Publications Company, 1981).

Friedman, Ellen, *Spanish Captives in North Africa in the Early Modern Age* (Madison: University of Wisconsin Press, 1983).

Frost, Peter, 'Fair Women, Dark Men: The Forgotten Roots of Colour Prejudice', *History of European Ideas,* Vol. 12, No. 5 (1990), 669–79.

Fuchs, Barbara, *Exotic Nation: Maurophilia and the Construction of Early Modern Spain* (Philadelphia, Pa.: University of Pennsylvania Press, 2009).

Fuchs, Barbara, 'In Memory of Moors: "Maurophilia" and National Identity in Early Modern Spain', *Journal for Early Modern Cultural Studies* Vol. 2, No. 1, A Special Issue on Representations of Islam and the East (Spring/Summer 2002), 109–125.

Fuchs, Barbara, *Passing for Spain: Cervantes and the Fictions of Identity* (Chicago: Univ. of Illinois Press, 2003).

Fuchs, Barbara, Larissa Brewer-Carter and Aaron J. Ilika, eds and translators, *'The Abencerraje' and 'Ozmin and Daraja': Two Seventeenth-Century Novellas from Spain* (Philadelphia: University of Pennsylvania Press, 2014).

Gamer, Michael, 'Assimilating the Novel: Reviews and Collections', Peter Garside and Karen O'Brien, eds., *English and British Fiction, 1750–1820*, Vol II of the *Oxford History of the Novel in English,* 12 vols. (Oxford: Oxford University Press, 2015).

Garcés, María Antonia, 'Captivity in Cervantes', in Aaron M. Kahn, ed., *The Oxford Handbook of Cervantes* (Oxford: Oxford University Press, 2021), 51–84.

Garcés, María Antonia, *Cervantes in Algiers: A Captive's Tale,* 2002 (repr. Nashville, Tennessee: Vanderbilt University Press, 2005).

Garcés, María Antonia, 'Zoraida's Veil: The Other Scene of the Captive's Tale', *Revista de estudios hispánicos* 23 (1989), 65–98.

García-Arenal, Mercedes, Ryan Szpiech, and Katarzyna K. Starczewska, 'The Perennial Importance of Mary's Virginity and Jesus's Divinity: Qurʾānic Quotations in Iberian Polemics after the Conquest of Granada (1492)', *Journal of Qurʾanic Studies* 20, no. 3 (2018): 51–80.

García-Sanjuán, Alejandro, 'Replication and Fragmentation, The Taifa Kingdoms', in Maribel Fierro, ed., *The Routledge Handbook of Muslim Iberia* (London and New York: Routledge, 2020), 64–88.

Gayangos y Arce, Pascual de, *History of the Mohammedan Dynasties in Spain*, 2 vols., London: Oriental Translation Fund, 1840–43 (repr. London: Routledge Curzon, 2002).

Gelder, Geert Jan van, 'Slave Girl Lost and Regained: Transformations of a Story', in Ulrich Marzolph, ed., *The Arabian Nights in Transnational Perspective* (Detroit, Michigan: Wayne State University Press, 2007), 65–82.

Gerli, Michael, ed., *Encyclopedia of Medieval Iberia* (New York: Routledge, 2003).

Genest, John, *Some Account of the English Stage: from the Restoration in 1660 to 1830. In ten volumes* (Bath: printed by H.E. Carrington, London: sold by T. Rodd, 1832).

Giffen, Lois A., 'Ibn Ḥazm and the Tawq Al-ḥamāma', Salma Khadra Jayyusi, ed., *The Legacy of Muslim Spain* (Leiden, New York and Cologne: E.J. Brill, 1994).

Giffen, Lois A., *Theory of Profane Love among the Arabs: The Development of the Genre* (New York, London and Leiden: Brill, 1971).

Gilli-Elewy, Hend, 'On the Provenance of Slaves in Mecca during the Time of the Prophet Muhammad', *International Journal of Middle East Studies* 49 (2017), 164–68: https://www.cambridge.org/core/journals/international-journal-of-middle-east-studies/article/on-the-provenance-of-slaves-in-mecca-during-the-time-of-the-prophet-muhammad/B11A052F86EF0061AD9DFE4C0EB4F5E0 [accessed 16/5/2024].

Glover, T.R., *The Ancient World*, 1935 (repr. Aylesbury and London: Penguin Books, 1948).

Goddard, Hugh, *A History of Christian-Muslim Relations* (Edinburgh: Edinburgh University Press, 2000).

Gordon, Murray, *Slavery in the Arab World*, 1987 (repr N.Y.: New Amsterdam Books, 1989).

Gould, Chester Nathan, 'The *friðþjófssaga*, an Oriental Tale', A.M. Sturtevant, ed., *Scandinavian Studies and Notes*, vol. VII, No. 8 (August 1923), 219–50.

Goytisolo, Juan, *Count Julián*, tr. Helen Lane (London: Serpent's Tail, 1989).

Grieve, Patricia, '*Floire and Blancheflor* and the European Romance (Cambridge: Cambridge University Press, 1997).

Grosart, Alexander B., ed., *Robert Greene: His Life and Works, A Critical Investigation by Nicholas Storojenko*, tr. E.A.R. Hodgetts, Moscow, 1878 (repr. New York: Russell and Russell, 15 vols, 1881–86).

Grunebaum, von, Gustave E. 'Greek Form Elements in the Arabian Nights', Dunning S. Wilson, ed., *Islam and Medieval Hellenism: Social and Cultural Perspectives* (London: Variorum Reprints, 1976).

Guardian Newspaper, The,: 'Novel about Jewish-Palestinian love affair is barred from Israeli curriculum', 1st January 2016: https://www.theguardian.com/world/2016/jan/01/novel-about-jewish-palestinian-love-affair-is-barred-from-israeli-curriculum [accessed 16/2/2016].

Guardian Newspaper, The, 'Israeli-Palestinian love story omitted from curriculum tops bestseller lists', 8th January 2016: https://www.theguardian.com/world/2016/jan/08/israeli-palestinian-love-story-excluded-curriculum [accessed 16/2/2016].

Hahn, Thomas G, in 'The Difference the Middle Ages Makes: Color and Race before the Modern World', *Journal of Medieval and Early Modern Studies* 31.1 (2001), 1–37.

Haleby, Omar, *El Ktab des lois secrètes de l'amour / d'après le Khôdja Omer Haleby, Abou Othmân;* traduction, mise en ordre et commentaires de Paul de Régla [Paris], 1838–1893.

Hall, Kim F., *Things of Darkness: Economies of Race and Gender in Early Modern England* (Ithaca and London: Cornell Universty Press, 1995).

Hardman, Phillipa, 'Roland in England: Contextualising the Middle English *Song of Roland*', Rhiannon Purdie and Michael Cichon, eds., *Medieval Romance, Medieval Contexts* (Cambridge: D.S. Brewer, 2011).

Head, Dominick, *Cambridge Guide to English Literature* (Cambridge: Cambridge University Press, 2006).

Heath, Peter, 'Romance as Genre in *'The Thousand and One Nights'*, *Journal of Arabic Literature* 18 (1987), repr. Ulrich Marzolph, ed., *The Arabian Nights Reader* (Detroit, Mich.: Wayne State University Press, 2006).

Heckmann, Theodore, *Massinger's* 'The Renegado' *und seine Spanischen Quellen* (Halle: C.A. Kaemmerer & Co., 1905).

Hegyi, Ottmar, *Cervantes and the Turks: Historical Reality Versus Literary fiction in* 'La gran sultana' *and* 'El amante liberal' (Newark, Del.: Juan de la Cuesta, 1992).

Henisch, Bridget Ann, *The Medieval Calendar Year* (University Park: Pennsylvania State Univ. Press, 1999).

Heng, Geraldine, *The Invention of Race in the European Middle Ages* (Cambridge: Cambridge University Press, 2018).

Hermes, Nizar F., 'The Byzantines in Medieval Arab Poetry: Abu Firas' *Al Rumiyyat* and the Poetic Responses of al-Qaffal and Ibn Ḥazm to Nicephore Phocas' *"Al-Qasida al-Arminiyya al-Malʻuna"* (The Armenian Cursed Ode)', *Byzantina Symmeikta,* 19.

Hermes, Nizar F., *The European Other in Medieval Arabic Literature and Culture: Ninth-Twelfth Century AD* (New York: Palgrave Macmillan, 2012).

Hermes, Nizar F., 'The Poetry of Frankish Enchantment: the Iffranjiyat of Ibn Qaysarani', *Middle Eastern Literature,* 20:3 (2017), 267–287: https://www.tandfonline.com/doi/full/10.1080/1475262X.2017.1385695 [accessed 2/05/2023].

Hershenzon, Daniel, *The Captive Sea: Slavery, Communication, and Commerce in Early Modern Spain* (Philadelphia: University of Pennsylvania Press, 2018).

BIBLIOGRAPHY 369

Holt, Andrew, *Medieval Masculinity and the Crusades: The Clerical Creation of a New Warrior Identity*, Ph.D. dissertation for the University of Florida, 2013, published online: https://ufdcimages.uflib.ufl.edu/UF/E0/04/53/51/00001/HOLT_A.pdf [accessed 25/2/2024].

Hopkins, Keith, *Conquerors and Slaves* (Cambridge: Cambridge University Press, 1978).

Huet, Gédéon, 'Sur l'origine de *Floire et Blanchefleur*', *Romania*, Vol. 28, No. 111 (July 1899), 348–359.

Hughes, Gethin, '*El gallardo español*: A Case of Misplaced Honour', *Bulletin of the Cervantes Society of America* 13.1 (1993), 65–75.

Ingram, Kevin, ed., *The Conversos and Moriscos in Late Medieval Spain and Beyond* (Leiden: Brill, 2009).

Irving, Washington, *Legends of the Conquest of Spain* (London: John Murray, 1835).

Irving, Washington, *Life of Mahomet* (London: Henry G. Bohn, 1850).

Irwin, Robert, *The Arabian Nights: a Companion*, 1994 (repr. London and other locations: Penguin Books Ltd., 1995).

Irwin, Robert, *The Dark Side of 'The Arabian Nights'* in https://www.criticalmuslim.io/the-dark-side-of-the-arabian-nights [accessed 16/4/2024].

Irwin, Robert, Introduction to *Tales of the Marvellous and News of the Strange*, tr. and ed. Malcolm C. Lyons, 2014 (repr. London: Penguin Classics, 2015).

Issawi, Charles, 'The Ottoman Empire in the European Economy, 1600–1914. Some Observations and Many Questions', Kemal H. Karpat, ed., *The Ottoman State and its Place in World History* (Leiden: E.J. Brill, 1974).

James, E.L., *Fifty Shades of Grey* (New York: Vintage Books, 2011).

Jayyusi, Salma Khadra, ed., *The Legacy of Muslim Spain* (Leiden, New York and Cologne: E.J. Brill, 1994).

Jenkins, Romilly, *Byzantium: The Imperial Centuries AD 610–1071* (London: Weidenfeld and Nicolson, 1966).

Johnson-Haddad, Miranda, 'Englishing Ariosto: "Orlando Furioso" at the Court of Elizabeth I', *Comparative Literature Studies*, 1994, Vol. 31, No. 4 (1994), 323–350.

Kabbani, Rana 'The Arabian Nights as an Orientalist Text', Ulrich Marzolph and Richard van Leeuwen, eds., with the collaboration of Hassan Wassouf, *The Arabian Nights Encyclopedia*, Santa Barbara, Calif.: ABC-CLIO Inc., 2 vols, Vol. I, 25–29.

Kabbani, Shaykh Muhammad Hisham and Laleh Bakhtiar, *Encyclopedia of Muhammad's Women Companions and the Traditions they Related* (Chicago, Illinois: Kazi Publications, inc., 1998).

Kahf, Mohja, *Western Representations of the Muslim Woman: from Termagant to Odalisque* (Austin, Texas: University of Texas Press, 1999).

Ker, W.P., *The Dark Ages* (London 1904 repr. London: Thomas Nelson and sons Ltd, 1955).

Khalaf, Hala, 'Recapping this year's Ramadan soap operas', *The National: Arts and Life*, published in the UAE (United Arab Emirates) on 19th July 2015/Jumada al Ula 8,

1437. https://www.thenationalnews.com/arts/recapping-this-year-s-ramadan-soap-operas-1.5376 [accessed 16/2/2016].

Khalaf, Roula, 'Cairo Soap Opera Casts Islamists as the Bad Guys', *FT* [*Financial Times*], published on 1st July 2015: https://www.ft.com/content/2db617e8-1fd9-11e5-ab0f-6bb9974f25d0 [accessed 30/6/2022].

Kinoshita, Sharon, *Medieval Boundaries: Rethinking Difference in Old French Literature* (Philadelphia: University of Pennsylvania Press, 2006).

Krstić, Tijana, *Contested Conversions: Narratives of Religious Change in the Early Modern Ottoman Empire* (Stanford, Calif.: Stanford University Press, 2011).

Kruk, Remke, *The Warrior Women of Islam: Female Empowerment in Arabic Popular Literature* (London and New York: I.B. Tauris, 2014).

Lake, Stephen, Review of Michael Newth's translation of *Fierabras* and *Floripas,* Italica Press, in 2016: http://www.italicapress.com/index331.html [accessed 22/5/2023].

Lalaguna, Juan, *A Traveller's History of Spain* (Gloucestershire: Windrush Press, 1990).

La Porta, Sergio, 'Conflicted Co-Existence: Christian-Muslim Interaction and Its Representation in Medieval Armenia', Jerold C. Frakes, ed., *Contextualizing the Muslim Other in Medieval Christian Discourse* (New York: Palgrave Macmillan, 2011).

Lea, Henry Charles, *The Moriscos of Spain; their Conversion and Expulsions* (Philadelphia: Lea Brothers and Co., 1901).

Leiner, Frederick C., *The End of Barbary Terror: America's 1815 War against the Pirates of North Africa* (Oxford: Oxford University Press, 2006).

Lewis, Bernard, tr. and ed., *Music of a Distant Drum: Classical Arabic, Persian, Turkish, and Hebrew Poems* (Princeton and Oxford: Princeton University Press, 2001).

Lewis, Bernard, *Race and Slavery in the Middle East: an Historical Enquiry* (New York and Oxford: Oxford University Press, 1990).

Lewis-Smith, Paul, 'La gran sultana doña Catalina de Oviedo: A Cervantine Practical Joke', *Modern Language Studies* 17 (1981), 68–82.

Lifton, Robert Jay, *The Broken Connection: On Death and the Continuity of Life* (New York: Basic Books, 1983).

Lindert, Peter H., 'When did inequality rise in Britain and America? *Journal of Income Distribution* 9, Issue 1 (May 2000) 11–25.

Lipking, Joanna, ed., *Oroonoko* (New York and London: w.w. Norton and Co [a Norton Critical Edition],1997).

Livanos, Christopher, 'A Case Study in Byzantine Dragon-Slaying: Digenes and the Serpent', *Journal of Oral Tradition*, 26/1 (2011): 125–144.

Loar, Christopher F., *Political Magic: British Fictions of Savagery and Sovereignty 1650–1750* (New York: Fordham University Press, 2014).

Lopez-Morillas, Consuelo, 'Language', in Maria Rosa Menocal, Raymond P. Scheindlin and Michael Sells, eds., *The Literature of Al-Andalus*, one volume of the series, the *Cambridge History of Arabic Literature* (Cambridge: Cambridge University Press, 2000).

Lottman, Maryrica Ortiz, '*La gran sultana*: Transformations in Secret Speech', *Revista Cervantes* Vol. XVI, No. 1 (Spring 1996), 74–90.

Lyons, Malcom C, *The Man of Wiles in Popular Arab Literature: a Study of a Medieval Arab Hero* (Edinburgh: Edinburgh University Press, 2012).

MacLean, Gerald, ed., *Re-Orienting the Renaissance: Cultural Exchanges with the East* (Basingstoke, Hants., and New York: Palgrave Macmillan, 2005).

MacLean, Gerald and Nabil Matar, *Britain and the Islamic World 1558–1713* (Oxford: Oxford University Press, 2011).

Maestro, Jesús G. ed., *Theatralia: El teatro de Miguel de Cervantes ante el IV Centenario* (Marbella, Spain, and Nashville, Tennessee: Mirabel Editorial S.L. and Vanderbilt University, 2003).

Makdisi, Saree and Felicity Nussbaum, eds., *The Arabian Nights in Historical Context: Between East and West* (Oxford: Oxford University Press, 2008).

Mancing, Howard, ed., *The Cervantes Encyclopedia* (Westport, Connecticut, USA: Greenwood Press, 2004).

Mansel, Philip, 'The French Renaissance in Search of the Ottoman Empire', Gerald MacLean, ed., *Re-Orienting the Renaissance: Cultural Exchanges with the East* (Basingstoke, Hants., and New York: Palgrave Macmillan, 2005).

Marandi, Sayyed Mohammad, 'The Oriental World of Lord Byron and the Orientalism of Literary Scholars', *Critique: Critical Middle Eastern Studies*, 15:3 (October 2006), 317–337, http://dx.doi.org/10.1080/10669920600997191 [accessed 27/4/ 2016].

Marenbon, John, ed., *Poetry and Philosophy in the Middle Ages: A Festschrift for Peter Dronke* (Leiden, Boston and Cologne: Brill. 2001).

Marín, Francisco Rodriguez, *El Doctor Juan Blanco de Paz* (Madrid: Tip. de la 'Revista de arch., bibl. y museos', 1916).

Martin-Casares, Aurelia, *La esclavitud en la Granada del siglo XVI: Género, raza y religion* (Granada: Universidad de Granada y Diputacion Provincial de Granada, 2000).

Martin, June Hall, *Love's Fools: Aucassin, Troilus, Calisto and the Parody of the Courtly Lover* (London: Tamesis Books Ltd., 1972).

Marwoto, Irmawati, 'Bird Symbolism In Persian Mysticism Poetry', *International Review of Humanities Studies*, Vo. 4, No. 2, article 13, https://scholarhub.ui.ac.id/irhs/vol4/iss2/13 [accessed 4/3/2024].

Marzolph, Ulrich, and Richard van Leeuwen, eds., with the collaboration of Hassan Wassouf, *The Arabian Nights Encyclopedia*, 2 vols. (Santa Barbara, Calif., Denver, Colorado, and Oxford: ABC-Clio Inc., 2004).

Marzolph, Ulrich, ed., *The Arabian Nights in Transnational Perspective* (Detroit, Michigan: Wayne State University Press, 2007).

Mas, Albert, *Les Turcs dans la literature espagnole du siècle d'or*, 2 vols. (Paris: Centre de Recherches Hispaniques, 1967).

Matar, Nabil, 'Arab Views of Europeans, 1578–1727', in Gerald MacLean, ed., *Re-Orienting the Renaissance: Cultural Exchanges with the East* (Basingstoke, Hants. and New York: Palgrave Macmillan, 2005).

Matar, Nabil, 'Christians in the *Arabian Nights*', Saree Makdisi and Fecicity Nussbaum, eds., The Arabian Nights *in Historical Context: Between East and West* (Oxford: Oxford University Press, 2008).

Matar, Nabil, *Islam in Britain, 1558–1685* (Cambridge: Cambridge University Press, 1998).

Matar, Nabil, *Turks, Moors and Englishmen in the Age of Discovery* (New York: Columbia University Press, 1999).

Matar, Nabil, *Britain and Barbary, 1589–1689* (Gainsville, Florida: University Press of Florida, 2005).

Maududi, Sayid Abul Ala, *Tafhim al-Qur'an – The Meaning of the Qur'an*, Section 1494: https://ia802301.us.archive.org/14/items/TheHolyQuranWithColorCodedEnglishTransliterationAndTranslationFaridBookDepot/quran-tafseer-maududi.pdf [accessed 10/11/2016].

MacKendrick, Karmen, *Counterpleasures* (Albany, New York: State University of New York Press, 1999).

McCabe, Ina Baghdiantz, *Orientalism in Early Modern France: Eurasian Trade, Exoticism, and the Ancien Regime* (Oxford and New York: Berg Publishing, 2008).

McCormick, Donald, *Erotic Literature: A Connoiseur's Guide* (New York: Continuum Publishing Co., 1992).

McGaha, Michael, Review of Maria Antonia Garcés' *Cervantes in Algiers: a Captive's Tale,* in *Cervantes: Bulletin of the Cervantes Society of America*, 23.2 (2003): 437–442.

McKendrick, Melveena, 'Writings for the Stage', Anthony J. Cascardi, ed., *The Cambridge Companion to Cervantes* (Cambridge: Cambridge University Press, 2002).

Melitzki, Dorothee, *The Matter of Araby in Medieval England* (New Haven and London: Yale University Press, 1977).

Menocal, Maria Rosa, *The Arabic Role in Medieval Literature: a Forgotten Heritage* (Philadelphia: University of Pennsylvania Press, 1987).

Menocal, Maria Rosa, *The Ornament of the World: How Muslims, Jews and Christians Created a Culture of Tolerance in Medieval Spain* (Boston, Mass. and London: Back Bay Books/Little, Brown and Co., 2002).

Menocal, Maria Rosa, 'Self and Other in *Aucassin et Nicolette*', *Romanic Review* 80 (1989), 497–511.

Menocal, Maria Rosa, *Shards of Love: Exile and the Origins of the Lyric* (Durham, North Carolina: Duke University Press, 1994).

Menocal, Maria Rosa, Raymond P. Scheindlin and Michael Sells, eds., *The Literature of Al-Andalus*, one volume of the series, the *Cambridge History of Arabic Literature* (Cambridge: Cambridge University Press, 2000).

Millar-Heggie, Bonnie, 'The Performance of Masculinity and Femininity: Gender Transgression in The Sowdone of Babylone', *Mirator Lokakuu/Oktober/October 2004*, 1–14.

Milton, Giles, *White Gold: the Extraordinary Story of Thomas Pellow and North Africa's One Million European Slaves* (London: Hodder and Stoughton, 2004).

Mirrer, Louise, *Women, Jews and Muslims in the Texts of Reconquest Castile* (Ann Arbor, Michigan: The University of Michigan Press, 1996).

Montefiore, Simon Sebag, BBC Radio 4 broadcast: *Start the Week,* 'Power Play and Family Dynamics', on 10th October 2022.

Montefiore, Simon Sebag, *Titans of History* (London: Quercus, 2012).

Montefiore, Simon Sebag, *The World: a Family History* (London: Weidenfeld and Nicholson, 2022).

Morgan, Charlotte E., *The Rise of the Novel of Manners: a Study of English Prose Fiction between 1600 and 1740*, New York: Columbia University Press, 1911.

Natarajan, Ambika, 'Sex and Marriage between Christians and Muslims during the Crusades', *Medieval Studies Research Blog*, August 7, 2020, repr. *Medieval Institute 14 September 2020*: https://medieval.nd.edu/news-events/news/from-the-medieval-studies-research-blog-sex-and-marriage-between-christians-and-muslims-during-the-crusades [accessed 20/5/2024].

Ndiaye, Noémie, *Scripts of Blackness: Early Modern Performance and the Making of Race,* ed. Geraldine Heng and Ayanna Thompson (Philadelphia: University of Pennsylvania Press, 2022).

Newcomb, Lori Humphrey, 'A Looking Glass for Readers: Cheap Print and the Senses of Repentance', Kirk Melnikoff and Edward Gieskes, eds., *Writing Robert Greene: Essays on England's First Notorious Writer* (Aldershot, Hants., and Burlington, Vermont: Ashgate Publishing Co., 2008).

Ng, Jeson, 'Women of the Crusades: the Constructedness of the Female Other 1100–1200', in *Al-Masāq, Journal of the Medieval Mediterranean*, 2019, https://www.tandfonline.com/doi/abs/10.1080/09503110.2019.1584453 [accessed 25/2/2023].

Nicoll, Allardyce, *A History of Early Eighteenth Century Drama, 1700–1750* (Cambridge: The University Press, 1929).

Nicoll, Allardyce, *A History of English Drama 1660–1900*, 6 vols. (Cambridge: Cambridge University Press, 1952).

Norris, H.T., *Islam in the Balkans: Religion and Society between Europe and the Arab World* (London: Hurst Publishing, 1993).

Novak, Maximilian E., *Daniel Defoe: Master of Fiction, his Life and Ideas* (Oxford: Oxford University Press, 2001).

Nykl, A.R., *Hispano-Arabic Poetry and its Relation to the Old Provençal Troubadours* (Baltimore: J. H. Furst and Co., 1946).

O'Leary, De Lacy, *Arabic Thought and its Place in History* (London: Trubner, 1922).

Oliver Asín, Jaime, 'La hija de Agi Morato en la obra de Cervantes', *Boletín de la real academia Española*, Madrid, XXVII (October 1947-April 1948), 245–339.

Pálffy, Géza, 'Ransom Slavery Along the Ottoman-Hungarian Frontier in the Sixteenth and Seventeenth Centuries', in Géza Dávid and Pál Fodor, eds., *Ransom Slavery Along the Ottoman Borders (Early Fifteenth – Early Eighteenth Centuries)* (Leiden: Koninklijke Brill, 2007).

Parish, Peter J., *Slavery: History and Historians* (New York and Other Locations: Harper and Row, 1989).

Pater, Walter, 'Two Early French Stories' (1872) in Pater ed., *The Renaissance: Studies in Art and Poetry* (Berkeley, Los Angeles and London: University of California Press, 1893).

Pearson, Jacqueline, *Tragedy and Tragicomedy in the Plays of John Webster* (Manchester: Manchester University Press, 1980).

Peirce, Leslie, *Empress of the East: How a Slave Girl became Queen of the Ottoman Empire* (New York: Basic Books, 2017).

Peirce, Leslie, *The Imperial Harem: Women and Sovereignty in the Ottoman Empire* (New York: Oxford University Press, 1993).

Peirce, Leslie, 'Writing Histories of Sexuality in the Middle East', *American Historical Review*, 114, 5 (December 2009), 1325–39.

Pensom, Roger, *Aucassin et Nicolette: the Poetry of Gender and Growing Up in the French Middle Ages* (Bern and other locations: Peter Lang AG 1999).

Perry, B. E., *The Ancient Romances: a Literary-Historical Account of their Origins* (Berkeley and Los Angeles, Calif.: University of California Press, 1967).

Phillips, William D., *Slavery in Medieval and Early Modern Iberia* (Philadelphia, Pa.: University of Pennsylvania Press, 2014).

Pidal, Ramón Menéndez, *Reliquias de la poesía épica española* (Madrid: Espasa Calpe, 1951).

Pomeroy, Sarah, *Goddesses, Whores, Wives and Slaves* (New York: Schocken Books, 1975).

Price, J. 'Floire et Blanchefloir: the Magic and Mechanics of Love', *Reading Medieval Studies*, VIII (1982), 12–33.

Purdie, Rhiannon, and Michael Cichon, eds., *Medieval Romance, Medieval Contexts* (Cambridge: D.S. Brewer, 2011).

Qaradawi, Yusuf al-, *The Lawful and the Prohibited in Islam; al-halal wal-haram fil Islam*, tr. Kamal El-Helbawy, M. Moinuddin Siddiqui and Syed Shukry (London: Shourouk International [UK] Ltd., 1985).

Rahmatullah, Muhammad, 'Slavery and Islam', *Islamic Literature,* Vol. XIII, No. 2, February, 1967, Lahore, Pakistan.

Ramsey, Lynne Tarte, *Christian, Saracen and Genre in Medieval French Literature* (New York and London: Routledge, 2001).

Renzo, Sean di, 'From Darkness into Light: The Baptism of Zoraida and the Council of Trent', *Romance Notes* 46:1 (2005), 3–11.

Reynolds, Dwight, 'Music', in Maria Rosa Menocal, Raymond P. Scheindlin and Michael Sells, eds., *The Literature of Al-Andalus* (Cambridge: Cambridge University Press, 2000).

Richlin, Amy, 'Talking to Slaves in the Plautine Audience', *Classical Antiquity*, Vol. 33, No. 1 (April 2014), 174–226.

Ridgeway, William, *The Early Age of Greece*, 1901 and 1931, 3 vols. (repr. Cambridge: Cambridge University Press, Vol. 1, 2014).

Rogers, Paul Patrick, 'Spanish Influence on the Literature of France', *Hispania*, Vol. 9, No. 4 (Oct., 1926), 205–235, https://www.jstor.org/stable/331608 [accessed 25/4/2024].

Rosser, John H., ed., *Historical Dictionary of Byzantium,*, 2001, 2nd ed. (Lanham, Toronto, and Plymouth, UK: Scarecrow Press, 2012).

Roxburgh, David J., ed., *Turks: A Journey of a Thousand Years, 600–1600,* London: Royal Academy of Arts, published to accompany the exhibition of the same name held 22 January–12 April 2005.

Rozen, Minna, *The Mediterranean in the Seventeenth Century: Captives, Pirates and Ransomers* (Palermo: Associazione no profit 'Mediterranea', 2016).

Runciman, Steven, *The Emperor Romanus Lecapenus and his Reign: A Study of Tenth-Century Byzantium* (Cambridge: Cambridge University Press, 1963).

Sahner, Christian C. 'Swimming against the Current: Muslim Conversion to Christianity in the Early Islamic Period' *Journal of the American Oriental Society*, vol. 136, no. 2, 2016, 265–84. *JSTOR*, https://doi.org/10.7817/jameroriesoci.136.2.265 [accessed 12/5/2023].

Said, Edward, *Orientalism* (New York: Pantheon Books, 1978).

Sanders, Julie, *Cambridge Introduction to Early Modern Drama 1576–1642* (Cambridge: Cambridge University Press, 2014).

Sandys, George, *A Relation of a Journey Begun An. Dom. 1610, containing a description of the Turkish Empire, of Aegypt, of the Holy Land, of the Remote parts of Italy, and Islands adioyning*, 3rd ed. (London, 1627).

Sanjuán, J. Gil, ed., *Tratado acerca de los moriscos de España* (Málaga: Algaraza, 1997).

Sawhney, Minni, 'Cervantes's Cosmopolitan *El Gallardo Español* During an Earlier Clash of Civilixations', in Jesús G. Maestro, ed., *Theatralia: El teatro de Miguel de Cervantes ante el IV Centenario* (Marbella, Spain, and Nashville, Tennessee: Mirabel Editorial S.L. and Vanderbilt University, 2003), 167–175.

Schweitzer, Jerome W., *Georges de Scudéry's Almahide: Authorship, Analysis, Sources and Structure,* Baltimore: Johns Hopkins University Press, 1939.

Seligman, Edwin, ed., *Encyclopaedia of the Social Sciences*, 15 vols., New York: The Macmillan Company, 1930–1935, Reissued 1937, transcribed by Andrew Chrucky, March 23, 2004, for http://www.ditext.com/moral/slavery.html [accessed 9/2/2016].

Seniff, Dennis P., Review of *Las Guerras civiles de Granada, primera parte*, ed. Shasta M. Bryant, *South Atlantic Review*, Vol. 48, No. 4 (Nov. 1983), 85–89.

Shafak, Elif, 'Women Writers, Islam, and the Ghost of Zulaikha', *Words Without Borders*, Internet Magazine site by Sonnet Media, December 2005: https://wordswithoutborders.org/read/article/2005-12/women-writers-islam-and-the-ghost-of-zulaikha/ [accessed 20/5/2024].

Shakespeare, William, *The Winter's Tale*, J.H.P. Pafford, ed. (North Yorks: Methuen for the Arden Shakespeare series, 1922, repr. Bungay, Suffolk, 1972).

Simmons, Eva, ed., *The Bloomsbury Guide to Augustan Literature: a Guide to Restoration and Eighteenth Century Literature 1660–1789* (London: Bloomsbury, 1994).

Simmons, Eva, ed., *Love for the Other*, https://www.woolf.cam.ac.uk/blog/love-for-the-other, 7th July 2016 [accessed 27/4/2024].

Simmons, Eva, 'Restoration and 18th-century Drama' in Eva Simmons, ed., *Augustan Literature: A Guide to Restoration and Eighteenth Century Literature: 1660–1789*, one of a series of *Bloomsbury Guides to English Literature*, London: Bloomsbury Publishing Ltd., 1994.

Simmons, Eva, 'Virtue Intire: the Comedies of Aphra Behn', Ph.D. thesis, London: Royal Holloway College, University of London, 1990.

Siyuti, Jala al-Din al-, *Kitab al-Izah fi-ilm bi-it-tamam wa al-kamal*, (*Book of Exposition, literally translated from the Arabic by an English Bohemian*), 1893 (repr. Paris, London and New York: Maison d'editions scientifiques, 1900).

Smith, D.N., 'Johnson's *Irene*', *Essays and Studies by Members of the English Association* xiv (Oxford: At the Clarendon Press, 1929).

Spitzer, Leo, 'The Mozarabic Lyric and Theodor Frings' Theories, *Comparative Literature*, Vol. IV (Winter 1952), No. 1, 1–22.

Stapp, William A., '*El gallardo español*: La fama como arbitrio de la realidad', *Anales Cervantinos* 17 (1978), 123–36.

Stern, Samuel Miklos, *Hispano-Arabic Strophic Poetry*, Oxford: Oxford University Press, 1974.

Suano, Marlene, 'The First Trading Empires: Prehistory to c. 1000 BC', David Abulafia, ed., *The Mediterranean in History*', 2003 (repr. London: Thames & Hudson, 2016).

Tavakoli-Targhi, Mohamad, *Refashioning Iran: Orientalism, Occidentalism and Historiography* (London: Palgrave Macmillan, 2001).

Thomas, David and John A. Chesworth, eds., *Christian-Muslim Relations: A Bibliographical History:* Vol. 6. *Western Europe (1500–1600)* (Leiden/Boston: Brill, 2014).

Tinniswood, Adrian, *Pirates of Barbary: Corsairs, Conquests and Captivity in the Seventeenth Century Mediterranean* (London: Jonathan Cape, 2010).

Teo, Hsu-Ming, *Desert Passions: Orientalism and Romance Novels* (Texas, USA: University of Texas Press, 2012).

Teo, Hsu-Ming, 'Historicizing The Sheik: Comparisons of the British Novel and the American Film', *Journal of Popular Romance Studies*, 4 August 2010, https://www.jpr studies.org/2010/08/historicizing-the-sheik-comparisons-of-the-british-novel-and-the-american-film-by-hsu-ming-teo/: [accessed 4/8/2010].

Todd, Janet, and Derek Hughes, eds., *Cambridge Companion to Aphra Behn* (Cambridge: Cambridge University Press, 2004).

Todd, Janet, *The Secret Life of Aphra Behn* (London: Andre Deutsch Ltd., 1996).

Trachtman, Sadie Edith, *Cervantes's Women of Literary Tradition* (New York: Instituto de las Españas en los Estados Unidos, 1932).

Treadgold, Warren, *A History of the Byzantine State and Society* (Stanford, Calif: Stanford University Press, 1997).

Trenkner, Sophie, *The Greek Novella in the Classical Period* (Cambridge: Cambridge University Press, 1958).

Valentine, Genevieve, review of the Lyons edition of Lyons, ed., *Tales of the Marvellous* ... for NPR (National Public Radio), on the 18th February 2015: https://www.npr.org /2015/02/18/385193561/tales-of-the-marvellous-is-indeed-very-strange [accessed 18/ 7/2023].

Villanueva, Francisco Marquez, *Fuentes literarias cervantinas* (Madrid: Gredos, 1973).

Vitkus, Daniel J., ed., *Piracy, Slavery and Redemption: Barbary Captivity Narratives from Early Modern England* (New York and Chichester: Columbia University Press, 2001).

Ward, A.W. and A.R. Waller, eds., *The Cambridge History of English Literature*, 14 vols. (Cambridge: Cambridge University Press, 1908–1916), Vol. VIII: *The Age of Dryden*, 1912.

Warner, Marina, *Stranger Magic: Charmed States and the* Arabian Nights (London: Chatto and Windus, 2011).

Webster, Thomas Bertram Lonsdale, *Studies in Later Greek Comedy* (Manchester: Manchester University Press, 1970).

Warren, F. M., 'The Enamoured Moslem Princess in Orderic Vital and the French Epic', *PMLA*, 1914, Vol. 29, No. 3 (1914), 341–358; also https://www.jstor.org/stable/456926 [accessed 18/5/2023].

Warren, Michael J., *Birds in Medieval English Poetry: Metaphors, Realities, Transformations, Nature and Environment in the Middle Ages* (Woodbridge, Suffolk: Boydell & Brewer, 2018).

Wasserstein, David, *The Rise and Fall of the Party-Kings: Politics and Society in Islamic Spain 1002–1086* (Princeton: Princeton University Press, 1985).

Watt, William Montgomery and Pierre Cachia, *A History of Islamic Spain* (Edinburgh: Edinburgh University Press, 1965).

Wedel, Theodore Otto *The Mediaeval Attitude Toward Astrology, Particularly in England*, 1920 (repr. Newhaven, Conn: Yale University Press, 1968).

Weever, Jacqueline de, *Sheba's Daughters; Whitening and Demonizing the Saracen Woman in Medieval French Epic* (New York and London: Garland Publishing, Inc., 1998).

Weiser, Fr. Francis X, 'History of Palm Sunday' on the *CatholicCulture* website: http://www.catholicculture.org/culture/library/view.cfm?recnum=105 [accessed 31/1/2017].

Weiss, Gillian, *Captives and Corsairs: France and Slavery in the Early Modern Mediterranean* (Stanford, Calif.: Stanford University Press, 2011).

Welch, Ellen R., *A Taste for the Foreign: Worldly Knowledge and Literary Pleasure in Early Modern French Fiction* (Newark: University of Delaware Press, 2011).

West, Robert H., 'The Christianness of Othello', *Shakespeare Quarterly*, Vol. 15, No. 4 (1964), 333–343.

Wheatcroft, Andrew, *Infidels: A History of the Conflict between Christendom and Islam* (London: Viking, 2003, repr. Penguin Books, 2004).

Whitaker, Cord J, *Black Metaphors: How Modern Racism Emerged from Medieval Race-thinking* (Philadelphia: University of Pennsylvania Press, 2019).

Whittow, Mark, *The Making of Byzantium, 600–1025* (Basingstoke: Macmillan, 1996).

Williams, Mark R., *The Story of Spain*, 1990 (repr. Mijas-Pueblo, Malaga, Spain: Santana Books, 2009).

Wiedemann, Thomas, ed., *Greek and Roman Slavery*, 1981 (repr. London and New York: Routledge, 1994).

Whitenack, Judith A., 'The alma diferente of Mateo Aleman's "Ozmín y Daraja"', *Romance Quarterly* 38, No. 1 (1991), 59–73.

Wright, Roger, *Late Latin and Early Romance in Spain and Carolingian France* (Liverpool: Francis Cairns, 1982).

Wykes, David, 'The Barbinade and the She-Tragedy: on John Banks's *The Unhappy Favourite*', Douglas Lane Patey and Timothy Keegan, eds., *Augustan Essays in Honour of Irvin Ehrenpreis* (Newark: University of Delaware Press and London and Toronto: Associated University Presses, 1985).

Yeazell, Ruth Bernard, *Harems of the Mind: Passages of Western Art and Literature* (New Haven and London: Yale University Press, 2000).

Yermolenko, Galina I., ed., *Roxolana in European Literature, History and Culture* (Farnham, Surrey, and Burlington, Vermont: Ashgate Publishing Ltd., 2010).

Yıldız, Nazan, 'A Bird after Love: Ibn' Hazm's *The Ring of the Dove* (*Tawq al-ḥamāmah*) and the Roots of Courtly Love', *Academic Journal of Interdisciplinary Studies* 2, 8 (October, 2013), 491–98. DOI: 10.5901/ajis.2013.v2n8p493 [accessed 3/3/2024].

Yiacoup, Şizen, *Frontier Memory: Cultural Conflict and Exchange in the Romancero fronterizo*, London: Modern Humanities Research Association, Texts & Dissertations Series, Vol. 87, 2013.

Yitzhak, Ronen, 'Muhammad's Jewish Wives: Rayhana bint Zayd and Safiya bint Huyayy in the Classic Islamic Tradition', *Journal of Religion & Society*, Vol. 9 (2007).

Yohannan, John D., ed., *Joseph and Potiphar's Wife in World Literature: an Anthology of the Story of the Chaste Youth and the Lustful Stepmother* (New York: McClelland & Stewart, Ltd.,1968).

Zook, Melinda S., 'The political poetry of Aphra Behn', in Janet Todd and Derek Hughes, eds., *Cambridge Companion to Aphra Behn* (Cambridge: Cambridge University Press, 2004).

Zwartjes, Otto, *Love Songs from Al-Andalus: History, Structure and Meaning of the Kharja* (Leiden, New York and Cologne: Brill Publishing Co., 1997).

Index

Abbasid dynasty 9, 29, 30, 37, 57
Abd Allah ibn Muhammad, ruler of al-Andalus 115
Abd ar-Rahman I (founder of the Umayyad Dynasty in Spain) 115
Abd-ar-Raḥmān III, (founder of the caliphate and first caliph of Córdoba) 115, 116
Abencerraje, el (Villegas) 8, 18, 20, 198, 201, 202–205, 209, 217, 218, 220, 257, 282
Abencerraje, Les aventures du dernier. See Chateaubriand
Abencerrajes (Granadine clan) 18, 20, 204, 207–211, 257, 324
Abriza (character in *The Tale of 'Umar ibn al-Nu'man...*) 40–47, 51, 127, 337
Abu Marra, devil 54
Abu Ma'shar al-Balkhi, astrologer 100, 101
Abulafia, David, *The Great Sea* 2, 4, 155, 157, 163
adornment / decoration 40, 78, 109, 120, 132, 191, 232, 243, 276, 311, 316
See also jewels, jewellery, embroidery
Aethiopica, The (Heliodorus) 11, 31, 32, 50, 105, 147, 217
Akbari, Suzanne Conklin, *Idols in the East* 26
Alemán, Mateo (*Ozmín y Daraja*) 217, 218, 219, 221
Alexandria 43, 46, 128
Alf Layla wa Layla (See *One Thousand and One* Nights)
Alfonso I, king of Navarre 268
Alfonso III, king of Asturias 287
Alfonso V, king of Aragón and Naples 268, 291
Alfonso VI, king of Castile 88, 211, 213
Algiers 5, 16, 18, 19, 148, 149, 152, 153, 156, 157, 164–172, 176–178, 180–184, 186, 187, 222, 224, 232, 233, 240, 241, 242, 244, 247, 250, 292, 342, 349
  Greek Literature, and 336
  Social structure 170
  French novel, and 285
Alhambra, The 21, 202, 209, 210, 286, 322, 324, 325, 348

Alicante 167
Almahide (de Scudéry) 20, 259, 284, 285, 304, 327, 336, 337
Almahide (Dryden). *See* Dryden, John
amazon, amazonian 53, 55, 92, 111, 127, 269, 271, 337. *See also* warrior women
Amoureux Africain, ou, Nouvelle Galanterie, l' (Gabriel de Brémond) 20, 310, 311
Andalucia 9, 18
Andalusia / al-Andalus / Andalusi 8, 9, 10, 14, 18, 22, 24, 29, 57–65, 70, 81–87, 115, 116, 163, 200–201, 211–212, 217, 224, 256, 285, 320, 325, 341
Antarah ibn Shaddad al-Absi/ *Antar and Abla* 30, 31
Apollonius of Tyre 32, 105
Aquitaine 84, 87
Arab, Arabs, Arabic 5–6, 8, 9–10, 12, 14, 17, 21, 25, 57, 59, 77, 90, 91, 95, 113, 140, 146, 156, 170, 174, 196, 213, 250–251, 289, 291, 334
  customs, culture 54, 62, 83, 207, 232
  family background 14, 90–91, 107
  language 13, 40, 82, 86, 100, 111, 115, 162, 189, 199, 201, 206, 213–214, 216, 219, 228, 229, 232, 235, 247, 258, 281, 288, 314
  literature 30–34, 39, 42, 50, 51, 55, 65, 75, 83, 84–88, 92, 111, 145, 314, 317, 328–332, 333, 334, 342–343, 350
  scholars 14, 87
  traders 108
Arab music (influence on European music) 84–5
Arabian Nights. *See* One Thousand and One Nights
Arabian Nights Encyclopedia, The 31, 39
Arabian Nights in Transnational Perspective, The (Ulrich Marzolph) 55
Aragón 151, 163, 212–3, 268, 270–1, 291
Arberry, A.J. (editor and translator) 60, 65, 117
Archer, William (theatre critic) 326
Aristophanes 10
Armenia, Armenian 2–4, 37, 40, 88–90
Armstrong, Karen 26
Arthur, king 15, 138. *See also* Morte d'Arthur

INDEX   381

Arthur of Brittany   347
astrology   31, 100, 101
Aucassin et Nicolette   15, 95, 107–117, 128, 248, 346

Baba-Hassan (ruler of Algiers)   153
Baba-Hassan (Dey of Algiers in Regnard's *La Provençale*)   294–296
Baepler, Paul, *White Slaves, African Masters:*   16, 186
Baghdad   39, 40–41, 47, 53, 57, 83, 328
Balearic Islands   295
Baltimore, Ireland   163–164
Barbarossa brothers (Oruç and Kheir ad-Din)   18, 148, 149, 150, 156, 158, 167
Barbarossa, Oruç, as character in Laugier de Tassy, *Aruch and Zaphira*   174
Barbary coast   148
Barbary states. *See* individual states: Algiers, Morocco, Tripoli, Tunis
Barcelona   163, 182
Beaumont, Daniel E.   275
Beautiful African, The; Or, Love and Slavery: An Interesting Tale. See Ann Lemoine
Behn, Aphra   7–8, 20, 97, 194, 261, 297, 312–313, 332
  Abdelazar; or The Moor's Revenge   261, 297
  Oroonoko   7, 20, 312–313
Benjamin, Jessica   306, 307, 341
Bible, the, biblical   12, 13, 24, 48, 74–75, 77, 103, 105, 137, 228, 347
Bijayah (North Africa)   148
birds, *See* Appendix 3   349–351
Blanch, Lesley *The Wilder Shores of Love*   329
Boccaccio, Giovanni   83, 107, 145, 146, 336
Bonds of Love, The: Psychoanalysis, Feminism, and the Problem of Domination (*See* Benjamin, Jessica)
Borders. *See* Islam, borders of with Christian lands
Bourgogne, Guy de (character in Mediaeval French literature)   127, 130–137
Bramimonde, queen (character in *La Chanson de Roland*)   121–124, 127, 265, 346
Brault, Gerard J.   123
Brecht, Bertolt   70

Brémond, Gabriel de   20, 302, 303, 308, 310, 327
Brémond, Sébastien   309
Brewer, Derek S. *The Ideal of Feminine Beauty in Medieval Literature*   138
Bride of Abydos, The (Byron)   20, 323
Brotton, Jerry, *This Orient Isle*   152, 158
Bukhārī, Abu Abd Allah Muhammad ibn Ismail ibn Ibrahim, al- al-Juʿfi   13
Burton, Captain Sir Richard F.   33, 39, 44, 45, 65, 106, 329
Byron, Lord George   20, 212, 314, 323–24, 325
Byron, Henry James (author of *Beautiful Haidée*)   326
Byzantine   82, 91, 95, 291
  empire   90
  epics   39, 88
  eunuchs   53
  frontier   89–90, 91
  literature   105, 127, 172, 198, 242
  wars with Arabs   57
  women   41, 52, 58, 92, 335

Cairo Genizah   14
Calprenède, La. *See* Coste, Gaultier, seigneur de la
Canavaggio, Jean (literary scholar)   182, 184, 227, 232
Cantar de la Mora Zoraida   88
Captivity   1, 3, 4, 5, 6, 11, 16, 17, 20, 23, 57, 62, 64, 75, 91, 95, 105, 141, 147, 152, 159, 160, 164, 166, 188, 208, 223, 250, 335
  Cervantes, and   182, 184, 223, 224, 240, 244, 252, 253, 342
  d'Aranda, Emanuel   169–171
  enduring appeal of   21
  erotic fantasy, and   333
  literary themes   20, 198, 199
  lived experience of   155
  orientalist and literary traditions   222
  passion, and   5, 236
  romance / romantic attraction, and   11, 20, 257, 310, 332–333, 337
  themes   11, 20, 221, 317, 336, 337
Carrasco-Urgoiti, María Soledad   8–10, 18, 201–202, 211, 226
Casalduero, Joaquin, *Sentido y forma del teatro de* Cervantes   232, 242

INDEX

Catholics/Catholicism 10, 18, 152, 161, 197, 199, 01, 207, 13, 218, 229, 231, 237, 252, 280, 311, 323, 325
   enslavement 11
   and Moriscos 215
   and Muslim society 217
   pre-inquisition 230
   See also ransom / ransoming
Cazenave, Jean, 'Le roman hispano-mauresque en France' 282
Cervantes, Miguel de 1, 3, 16, 19, 20, 48, 160, 180–185, 197, 214, 250, 255, 257, 280, 292, 296, 316, 338, 349
   alter ego in works of 222, 241, 250, 252, 253, 255
   influence on others 20, 257, 258, 272, 279, 282, 302, 316, 317, 319, 320
   personal captivity of 1, 16, 160, 165, 180–185, 197, 222–225, 240, 241, 242, 244, 252, 291, 296, 327, 337, 342
   Works:
      Amante Liberal, el [*The Generous – or Liberal – Lover*] 223, 242–243, 257, 317, 349
      Baños de Argel, los 19, 223, 227, 228, 229, 231, 233–242, 256, 272, 274, 319, 320
      Don Quixote 19, 223–224, 227–228, 232, 256, 320
      Gallardo Español, el 223, 253–255, 257, 340
      Española inglesa, la (The English Spanish Girl) 223, 253, 317
      Gran sultana doña Catalina de Oviedo, la (Cervantes) 19, 223, 244–252, 256, 257, 336
      Historia del cautivo, la (The Captive's Tale) 10, 19, 48, 223, 227–233, 241, 256, 272, 317, 319, 320, 337
      Novelas ejemplars (1613) *See* individual novel titles
      Numāntia, la, a tragedy 224
      Ocho Comedias y ocho entremeses (1614) *See* individual play titles
      Story of Cardenio and Lucinda, The 320
      Trato de Argel, el 19, 222, 223, 224–227, 233, 234, 239, 240, 242, 256, 257, 262, 319, 328, 337
      Voyage to Parnassus, The 224

Chaereas and Callirhoe (Chariton) 11, 32, 102, 105
chansons de geste 15, 107, 110, 118, 124, 128, 135, 137, 138, 347
Chanson de Roland 15, 26, 81, 105, 110, 118–128, 132–136, 144–146, 263, 265, 346
Charlemagne (King of Franks) 26, 105, 118–27, 131, 134, 135, 146, 147, 263, 265, 296
   joining with Muslim armies 124
   treatment of Islam in stories featuring 144
   wars with Muslims 135, 146, 346
Charles II 296, 297, 309, 310, 316
Charles the Grete 128, 134–137
Chateaubriand, François-René de, (*Les Aventures du dernier Abencérage – The Last of the Abencerrajes*) 20, 314, 324–325
Chaucer, Geoffrey 64, 83, 118, 350
Chew, Samuel Claggett, *The Crescent and the Rose* 199, 219, 29, 244
chivalry 42, 85, 226, 254, 337
   Saracen/Moorish romance, and 337
Christians, Christianity 2, 5–6, 36, 47, 80
   calendar 102, 159
   conversion to and from. *See* conversion, and Islam conversion
   as captives and slaves 7, 9, 13, 17, 28, 96, 98, 149, 153, 156, Chapter 3 passim, 206, 208, 209, 219, 224, 227, 228, 229, 234, 240, 242, 244–246, 254, 284, 304, 328–329, 332–335, 335–342
   knights 15, 121, 123, 126, 130, 132, 134–136, 138, 203, 207, 209–210, 212, 226, 309, 337, 347
   love and marriage with Muslims 8–9, 11, 15, 17–18, 19, 20, 26, 30, 37–38, 39, 40, 43, 48, 49–51, 88, 100–107, 107–112, 156, 175, 185–186, 187, 188, 199, 209, 211, 223, 227, 228, 229, 230, 234, 239, 242, 244–252, 253–256, 257–258, 259, 261, 262, 263–267, 272–281, 285, 286–291, 295–296, 299–302, 303–308, 311, 320, 323–325, 328
   love and marriage with other Christians 53, 58–59, 84, 90, 91, 96, 100–107, 126–127, 130, 135–142, 143, 145, 147, 199, 224, 227, 234, 237, 238, 242, 255
   military alliances with Muslims 89, 90, 91, 124, 207, 230

INDEX

Christians, Christianity (*cont.*)
  Muslim ignorance about   125
  Muslims with Christian mothers   63, 72, 90, 113–117, 156, 165, 240–241, 244
  'old' and 'new' Christians   151, 218, 231, 244
  profaning of   44–46, 270
  ransoming of   163, 184, 196
  shared culture and coexistence / kinship with Muslims   10, 15, 82, 84, 100–105, 112, 117–118, 124, 199–201, 202–205, 215–216, 218, 232, 243, 312
  taking captives / slaves   5–6, 108, 199, 203, 208, 218
  warfare between Christians and Muslims   11, 14, 15, 16, 39, 42, 60, 72, 84, 89, 118, 124, 126, 127, 205, 212–213, 217, 230, 254, 262, 287, 343
  See also Islam
Christie, Niall, 'Noble Betrayers of their Faith...'   52
Civil Wars of Granada, The. See Pérez de Hita
Cléopâtre. See Coste, Gaultier
Clissold, Stephen, *The Barbary Slaves*   6, 18, 153, 154, 157, 161–163
Clothes/costumes   41, 44, 52, 63, 72, 165, 170, 171, 195, 219, 225, 243, 248, 252, 260, 271, 288
Colman, George, the Younger (dramatist)   20, 319–320, 321, 322
  Inkle and Yarico   321, 322
  The Mountaineers   20, 319–320
Comfort, William Wistar, 'The Saracens in Christian Poetry',   15, 16, 120, 124
Comicall Historie of Alphonsus, King of Aragon, The (Robert Greene)   19, 268–272
Commerce, commercial, trade, traders   2, 4, 6, 14, 16, 22, 50, 79, 81, 84, 90, 108, 113, 124, 141, 154, 155, 178, 179, 184, 273, 280, 312, 315–316, 326–327
  See also Slave trade
Compleat History of The Piratical States Of Barbary. See Morgan
Conquest of Granada (event in 1492)   2, 18, 148, 199, 201, 213, 230
conversion, religious   2–6, 10–15, 17–19, 22, 24–28, 30, 39–44, 48–53, 55, 58, 79–80, 82, 88, 91–95, 97, 99–100, 117–127, 130, 134, 136–144, 147, 149, 151, 157–160, 162–163, 165, 170–172, 175–176, 187–189, 198, 200, 205–216, 218, 220–221, 227–231, 239–243, 245, 247, 251–252, 255–265, 267–268, 271–273, 278–280, 290–291, 300, 305, 311–312, 320, 325, 335–337
  apparent conversion   171
  appearance, and   142, 144
  change of identity, and   338
  Christendom, and   175
  forced   149
  literary theme   24
  Moriscos, and   215, 216
  North Africa and conversion   157, 158, 159, 165, 170
  symbol of masculine, military and cultural victory, as   11
  Virgin Mary, and   214
  See also Islam, conversion to, conversion from
Convivencia   199
Cordoba/Cordova   66, 71, 167, 199, 211
Corneille, Pierre   20
Corsair, The (Byron)   20, 323–324
Coste, Gaultier, seigneur de la Calprenède (*Cléopâtre*, *Faramond*)   286
Cotton, Charles *The Fair One of Tunis, Or, a New Piece of Gallantry*   302–308, 309
Courageous Turk, The, or Amurath   261
courtesans   60, 273
courtly love   24, 84–87, 110, 278, 350
'Coveras, Francisco de las' (i.e. Francisco de Quintana)   3
Cross-border raids   206
Croxall, Samuel, *Select Collection of Novels*   20, 288, 316–319
Cyprus   242, 243, 290, 291, 309

Dadson, Trevor J., 'The Assimilation of Spain's Moriscos...'   9
Damascus   42, 49, 50, 143, 144
Dan, Pierre   2, 157, 176
d'Aranda, Emanuel   168–172, 186–188
Davis, Robert C.
  Christian Slaves, Muslim Masters   1, 150, 154, 166, 184
  Holy War and Human Bondage   6, 150
Davis, Thomas Osborne (poet)   163
Dawood, N.J.   27

Deferrari, Harry A., *The Sentimental Moorin Spanish Literature Before 1600* 200, 201, 202, 338
Delacroix, Eugene 324
Desert Romance 329, 339, 342
   See also sheikh romance
Dhāt al-Himma/ Delhemma 50, 57–58
Digenes Akrites 14, 81, 88–95
diplomacy/diplomats 23, 176, 242, 281, 314
disguise 32, 46, 47, 53, 60, 106, 107, 110, 194, 209, 217, 219, 251, 254, 266, 273, 283, 311, 312, 324
Dryden, John 285, 297–299, 313
   Almanzor and Almahide or *The Conquest of Granada* 285, 287, 299–302
   Aureng-Zebe 313
D'Urfé, Honoré (*l'Astrée*) 282
Dyce, Rev. Robert Alexander 267

Early Modern Dialogue with Islam. See Sosa, de
Egilona (wife of the last Visigothic king and subsequently of Arab conqueror Mūsā bin Nuṣair) 9, 115
Egilsson, Olafur 151–152
Egypt, Egyptian 13, 30, 31, 44, 50–51, 53, 57, 74–80, 83, 143, 153, 228, 274, 281, 282, 317, 342–343
Ehlers, Benjamin, *Between Christians and Moriscos* 214–216
el Cid. See *Quest for el Cid*
Elizabeth 1, Queen of England 264, 319
Ellis-Fermor, Una, *The Jacobean Drama...*' 263
embroidery 82, 133, 243
   See also adornment
England 19, 20, 64, 82–83, 118, 128, 143, 150, 163 176, 192, 216, 259 260, 296–8, 309, 310, 333, 339
   imitation of Cervantes in 223
   matière de Bretagne 15, 135, 138, 347
   orientalism in 315–16
   racism in literature 32
English Charlemagne Romances. See Herrtage
English Dramatists of Today (See Archer, William)
epic poetry 14, 16, 39, 42, 52, 57, 58, 74, 88, 90–94, 108, 110, 118, 119, 124, 146, 263, 271, 336

Epistle on Singing-Girls of Jahiz, The (See Jahiz)
Epstein, Steven A., *Speaking of Slavery* 24, 25, 139, 156
Equiano, Olaudah 153
eunuchs 35, 53, 98, 158, 186, 190, 195, 246, 247, 274, 279, 313
Euphrates river 89, 90, 94, 103
Ewoldt, Amanda M, *Conversion and Crusade...* 141
executions 34, 60–1, 72, 98, 106, 119, 132, 158, 162, 176, 183, 200, 289, 309, 342, 346

Fair One of Tunis,The. See Cotton, Charles
Fastrup, Anne, 'Cross-cultural Movement in the Name of Honor...' 254, 255, 340, 341
Fatima. See *Princess Fatima*
Ferdinand, king of Aragon and of Spain 19, 148, 201, 208, 209, 218, 300.
   See also Isabella, queen of Castile and then of Spain
Fez (North Africa) 177, 178, 179, 290
Fierro, Maribel, 'The Bestsellers of al-Andalus' 86, 213
Fitzgerald, Julia(author) 332, 333
Fitzmaurice-Kelly, James, *Miguel de Cervantes Saavedra* 182, 183
Flanders 168, 169, 171
Fletcher, John (17th century dramatist) 262, 263, 265, 270
Fletcher, Richard (historian), *Moorish Spain* 72
Floire et Blanchefleur 10, 14, 42, 56, 95–107, 110, 112, 113, 117–118, 122, 128, 129, 132, 145, 263, 346
Floripas (character in the Charlemagne stories) 26, 59, 127–142, 229, 337, 347
Floris and Blanchefour. See *Floire et Blanchefleur*
Flowers 77, 109, 120, 128, 282, 348–9
   concealment, and 98, 102
   names, and 229
   Palm Sunday, and 96, 102
Frakes, Jerrold C *Contextualising the Muslim Other...* 3, 22

France 4, 19, 44, 57, 83, 85, 97, 108, 113, 118, 122, 141, 153, 163, 267, 281–296, 297, 298, 311, 332, 339, 347
   fascination with Islamic culture and literature in 281–282, 315, 318
   matière de / matter of 15, 19, 124, 135, 146, 263
   Moorish novel in 284
   Spanish fiction as influence 212, 282
   orient, and 172, 281–282, 318
   peers of 265
   stage plays in 283
Franks 37, 44, 51, 57, 115, 118, 119, 124–7, 130, 132, 134, 136, 141, 143, 265, 347
   Frankish women 38, 40, 43, 45, 50, 60
Frederick II (of Sicily) 82
French Christians. *See* Franks
Friedman, Ellen, *Spanish Captives in North Africa...* 6, 150, 151, 154, 158, 159, 166, 167, 184, 198, 199, 254
Frontiers 2, 8, 18, 38, 58, 84, 88, 148, 207, 226, 231 287, 289, 339
   ballads from 231
   romance across 91
Fuchs, Barbara 10, 205, 220, 223, 233, 235, 236, 243, 244, 250, 339
   Abencerraje', The, and 'Ozmin and Daraja...' 205, 220
   Exotic Nation: Maurophilia ... 10
   'In Memory of Moors: "Maurophilia"...' 339
   Passing for Spain: Cervantes and the Fictions of Identity 243

Galán, Diego 164–166, 172
Galland, Antoine 14, 20, 31, 39, 172, 195, 196, 275, 314
galley slaves
   Christian 155, 157, 162, 164, 165, 167, 169, 170, 184, 215
   Muslim 149
Garcés, María Antonia
   'Captivity in Cervantes' 2002, 166, 222, 223, 229, 232, 241
   Cervantes in Algiers: A Captive's Tale, 2002 166, 222, 224, 229, 241
   'Zoraida's Veil: The Other Scene of the Captive's Tale' 232

Gardens 286, 304, 307, 313, 348
   as settings for love scenes 83
   and *See* appendix 1.2
Gayangos y Arce, Pascual de, *History of the Mohammedan Dynasties in Spain* 72, 338
Generall historie of the Turkes. *See* Knolles
Genest, John, *Some Account of the English Stage...* 299
Genoa 188, 193, 293
genres
   Barbary captivity play
   'comedias de moros y cristianos'
   desert romance 329
   French 'Moorish' novel 290
   Greek and Arabic 32, 145, 242
   Moorish novel 198
   Restoration heroic drama 301
   Restoration tragedy 300
   Slave narratives 160
   tragicomedy 262–263
   'Turkish' tragic narrative (19th century) 323
   'turqueries' 199
Giaour, The (Byron) 20, 323
Giffen, Lois A. 86, 87
Gold Coast 7
Gordon, Murray, *Slavery in the Arab World* 6, 17, 28, 156, 185, 186
Gracián, Father Jeronimo 161–163
Granada 10, 18, 61, 148, 199, 203–215, 218, 257, 284, 300, 301, 309, 320, 323, 324, 325, 348
Greece / Greek 341
   individuals (including mythological) 90, 91, 102, 131, 134, 156, 182, 260, 261, 270, 298
   influence 31–32, 270, 336
   language 42, 89, 156, 289
   mythology 97
   novellas (also known as Byzantine romances) 8, 11, 24, 31–32, 51, 86, 102, 105, 145, 198, 242, 284, 336–337
      Aethiopica (Heliodorus) 11, 31, 32, 50, 105, 147, 217, 242, 317
      Anthia and Habrocomes, The Tale of, (Xenophon of Parnassus) 105, 106, 145

Greece / Greek (*cont.*)
   Chaereas and Callirrhoe
      (Chariton)   11, 32, 102, 105
   poetry   40
   Roman plays, and   24, 74
   See also Plautus and Menander
      (dramatists)
Greene, Robert (dramatist)
   Comicall Historie of Alphonsus, King of Aragon, The (Robert Greene)   19, 268–272
   Orlando Furioso (Greene)   19, 263–268, 272
Grunebaum, von, Gustave E. 'Greek Form Elements in the Arabian Nights'   31, 32
Guerras civiles de Granada. See Pérez de Hita, Ginés
Guillaume VII of Poitiers and IX of Aquitaine, prince and poet   87
Guillaume VIII, king of Aquitaine   87
Guillaume IX, poet   87
Guy de Bourgogne (character in Charlemagne romances)   127, 130, 132, 135, 136, 137

Haddawy, Husain   33
Haedo, Maestro fray Diego de   166–167
Hakam al-Mustansir, al-, caliph   115, 117
Hakam I, al-, emir   24, 62, 64
Hakam II, al-, caliph   72, 73
Haleby, Omar, *El Ktab des lois secrètes de l'amour*   65
Halevi, Yehuda (poet)   62
Hall, Kim F., *Things of Darkness*   138
Hamel, Chouki, el 'Blacks and Slavery in Morocco …'   190
Hammurabic Code   4
Harems   3, 7, 29, 62, 97, 103, 104, 106, 107, 117, 129, 132, 172, 190, 195, 244, 246, 248, 309, 311, 313, 323, 324, 327, 328, 329, 332, 333, 334
   Christian women, and   250, 284, 294, 295, 296, 304, 307
   conversion, and   338
   fiction, and   186
   Islamic Law, and   186
   Montagu, Lady Wortley, and   193–196
   women of foreign origin, and   29
   women slaves, and   185

Haroun al-Rashid, caliph of Baghdad and character in *One Thousand and One Nights*   29, 30, 34, 36, 37, 47, 48, 113, 185, 275, 328
Hassan, James Elroy Flecker   328
Hattigé   309–310, 313, 317
Hegyi, Ottmar, *Cervantes and the Turks…*   199, 250
Heng, Geraldine, *The Invention of Race in the European Middle Ages*   139, 141–142, 144
Hermes, Nizar F., 'The Byzantines in Medieval Arab Poetry…'   37
   European Other in Medieval Arabic Literature … , The   37
   'Poetry of Frankish Enchantment … The'   37, 38
Herrtage, Sidney J.H.   125, 126–130, 134
Hershenzon, Daniel, *The Captive Sea…*   6
   'Towards a Connected History of Bondage …'   6
Heureux esclave, (1674)   20, 310, 317
Hisham I, ruler of Córdoba   115
Hisham II, caliph of Córdoba   68, 115, 72
Histoire de Barbarie et de ses corsairs. See Pierre Dan
Histoire du Royaume d'Alger. See Tassy
Historia del Emperador Carlo Magno   128
History of the long captivity and adventures of Thomas Pellow. See Pellow
History of Don Fenise, The. See Coveras, Francisco de las
Homosexuality   25, 72, 156, 184, 188, 346
Hubert, Merton Jerome, ed.   104, 107
Huet, Gédéon, 'Sur l'origine de *Floire et Blanchefleur*'   105, 106
Huet, Pierre-Daniel, *A Treatise of Romances*   106, 317
Hull, Denison B.   90, 328–329
Hull, E.M. (Edith Maude)   21
Hürrem [Roxelana]   113–114, 244, 261, 334, 344
Hybrid / Hybridity   2, 3, 81, 83, 90, 217, 220, 231, 241, 243, 255, 290, 291, 338
Hymen's præludia, or Loves master-peice   286

Ibn ʿArabī (Andalusi scholar)   64
Ibn Ḥazm   65–74, 85–88, 115, 350

Ibn Khallikan (author of the *Biographical Dictionary* [1256 to 1274])   114
Ibn Qaysarani (poet)   37. *See also Ifranjiyyat*
Ibn Tashufin (Almoravid ruler)   64
Ibn Tumart, Muhammad (Almohad leader)   115
Ibn Zaidun (poet)   62
Iceland, Icelandic   83, 107, 152–153
identity   26, 38, 110, 123, 125, 138, 141, 200, 220, 222, 243, 254–255, 266, 291, 312, 337–8
Ifranjiyyat (Ibn Qaysarani)   37
Iliad, The   31
Inkle and Yarico   20, 321–322
Irving, Washington
  Legends of the Conquest of Spain   346
  Life of Mahomet   26
Isabella, queen of Castile and then of Spain   10, 19, 148, 201, 218, 300, 301
  See also Ferdinand, king of Aragon and of Spain
Islam
  architecture, and   347–348
  attitudes towards slavery of   3, 5, 12, 16, 17, 25–30, 153
  borders of with Christian lands   2, 4, 8, 14, 16, 57 58, 82, 84, 89, 90, 91, 142, 163, 199, 206, 244, 339
  Christian ignorance about   15, 120, 134, 144
  class, and   339
  conversion from, to Christianity   14, 26, 28, 90, 91, 95, 143, 144, 162, 198, 206, 256, 280, 340
  conversion to, from Christianity   2, 6, 13, 17, 39, 42, 43, 44, 48, 49, 50, 53, 55, 57, 58, 95, 120, 126, 143, 156–159, 161–163, 165, 170–171, 175, 187, 189, 198, 200, 220, 245, 251, 252, 273, 278, 279, 291, 305, 311, 320, 335, 336
  cross border raids, and   90, 206
  cultural and other connections with Christians and Christian societies   113, 118, 139, 147, 199, 230, 244, 250
  enemy to Christianity, as   107
  hostile attitudes towards / Christian campaigning against   148, 176–177, 179, 193, 196, 199, 213, 216, 265, 274, 280, 290, 297, 308
  influence of   108
  jurisprudence, and   86, 186
  literary themes, and   8, 13, 20, 75, 159, 175, 297
  positive attitudes (of Christians) towards   146, 173, 176, 180
  pre-Islamic era (the *Jahiliya*)   5, 30, 55
  race and   25, 26, 32, 142
  sexual relations, and   12, 24, 156
  Shahadah (Islamic creed) of   47, 55
  spread of   57
  true faith, as, and fidelity to   46, 48, 59, 121, 141, 151
  western preoccupation with   37, 185, 202–203, 281, 283, 297, 314
  See also Christianity
Istanbul   52, 88, 154, 164, 184, 194, 221, 240, 244, 272, 277, 281, 314
Italy   89, 150, 163, 181, 182, 274, 311–312

Jacobean comedy   262–265
  City Comedy   262
Jacobean Tragedy   223, 259, 262, 263
Jahiz, al-, Abu Uthnan Amr   68, 69, 71278
James I, king   152, 283
James II, king   313
Jami, Hakim Nuruddin Abdurrahman (*Yusuf and Zulaikha*)   74–80
Janszoon, Jan   158
Jerusalem   101, 102, 132, 137, 147, 336
Jesus Christ   47, 76, 101, 102, 134, 136, 214, 221, 230
Jewels, jewellery   44, 76, 123, 132, 196, 220, 243, 260, 276, 311, 316, 331
  See also adornment, embroidery
Jews, Judaism, Jewishness   14, 26, 62, 75, 82, 163, 139, 143, 163, 170, 175, 206, 217, 231, 338, 343, 344
Johnson, Samuel   299

Karmen, *Counterpleasures*   77, 305, 326, 327
Khayzuran bint Atta (slave and queen to Caliph al-Mahdi)   29–30
King of Tars, The   26, 50, 142–144
Kitab al-Zahra (The Book of the Flower, Ibn Dawud)   85
Knolles, Richard   260
Kruk, Remke, *The Warrior Women of Islam...*   15, 50, 51, 52, 111, 127

Kyd, Thomas, *The Tragedy of Soliman and Perseda* 261

Lafayette, Mme. de [Marie-Madeleine Pioche de La Vergne, Comtesse de La Fayette] 286, 287, 288, 290
   Princess de Clèves, la 298
   Zaïde, histoire espagnole 286–291
Lane, Edward 107
Laugier de Tassy, Jacques Philipe. *See* Tassy
Lemoine, Ann (novelist) 21, 322–323, 337, 349. *See also Beautiful African, The*
Les mille et une nuits, contes arabes traduites en français (Galland) 31, 172, 314
Leucippe and Clitophone 32, 317
Lewis, Bernard 12, 27, 59, 62, 64
   Music of a Distant Drum ... 59, 62, 64
   Race and Slavery in the Middle East 12, 27
L'heureux esclave 20, 310, 317
Ligon, Richard 321
Lope de Vega, Félix 147, 234, 257–258
Lustful Turk, The 327, 328
Lyons, Malcom C, *The Man of Wiles in Popular Arab Literature* 58
Lyons, M. C. and Lyons, Ursula 39, 52
   Tales of the Marvellous and News of the Strange [2014] 52–56
   See also One Thousand and One Nights

Madrid 89, 184, 216, 282
Mahdi, Caliph al- 29
Mahdi, Muhsin 33
Makdisi, Saree (and Felicity Nussbaum, eds.), 'The Arabian Nights *in Historical Context*...' 146
Malmesbury, William of (*History of the Kings of England*, 1140–1170) 118
Mamun, Caliph al- 30
Mansur (Muhammad ibn Abi 'Amir), al-, ruler 72, 200
Marlowe, Christopher 261, 263, 268, 270
   influence on Greene 267, 268, 270
   Lust's Dominion 261
   Tamburlaine 263, 270
Marriage 3, 9, 19, 25, 26, 28, 43, 49, 50, 53, 54, 55, 56, 58, 76, 91, 92, 101, 105, 124, 126, 127, 140, 142, 143, 147, 175, 185, 189, 191, 221, 231, 237, 240, 244, 246, 251, 256, 263, 271, 272, 277, 278, 280, 284, 286, 301, 305, 311, 324, 334, 338, 350

concept of slavery, and 7, 194
intermarriage 22, 30, 80, 113, 139, 141, 147, 201, 211, 252, 256
social order, and 342
Marsile, king (character in *La Chanson de Roland*) 118–124, 267
Martel, Charles 108, 124
Marzolph, Ulrich *Arabian Nights Reader* 9
Mas, Albert, *Les Turcs dans la literature espagnole ...* 198, 199, 250
Mascarenhas, João (Portuguese merchant) 1
Massinger, Philip, *The Renegado* 19, 272–281, 280, 307
   inspired by Cervantes 272, 307
   courtship in 277
   commercial elements 280
Matar, Nabil
   'Arab Views of Europeans ...' 6
   Britain and Barbary 1589–1689 152
   'Christians in the *Arabian Nights*' 146
   Islam in Britain, 1558–1685 152
   Turks, Moors and Englishmen in the Age of Discovery 152
Maududi, Sayid Abul Ala, *Tafhim al-Qur'an – The Meaning of the Qur'an* 28
McCabe, Ina Baghdiantz, *Orientalism in Early Modern France* 281, 282
Mecca 12, 29, 49, 127, 137, 164, 231, 324
   direction of prayer, and 324
   pilgrimage to 231
   Prophet Muhammad in 137
   slaves in 12
   slave market in 29
Mediterranean 2, 14, 58, 82, 88, 113, 157, 230, 244, 272, 309, 332, 333, 343
   corsairs, and 149
   piracy, and 4–5
   ransoming, and 184
   slave trade in 16, 23, 148, 153
   spread of Islam 57
   warfare, and 291, 309
Melitene. *See* Armenia
Melitzki, Dorothee, *The Matter of Araby in Medieval England* 8, 15, 90
Menander (Greek dramatist) 24
Menocal, Maria Rosa
   Arabic Role in Medieval Literature, The 82, 85, 88
   'Self and Other in *Aucassin et Nicolette*' 140

merchants   1, 44–5, 53, 68, 100, 109, 158, 167, 169, 273, 275, 322
Mers-el-Kebir   148
Miles Gloriosus (Plautus)   31
Milton, Giles, *White Gold: the Extraordinary Story of Thomas Pellow ...*   188, 189, 193
Miriam (character in the *Nights* story of Ali Nur al-Din and Miriam the Sashmaker)   43–48, 51, 56, 92, 127, 131, 337
'miscegenation'   3, 53, 139, 338
mixed faith romance   82, 92, 94, 187, 224, 296, 333, 342
  children, and   81, 114
  motifs, and   320
  parentage, and   2, 14
  relationships and unions, and   93, 191, 201, 246, 252, 256, 312, 321
  See also Christians and Christianity, Love and Marriage with Muslims
Montagu, Lady Mary Wortley   193–195, 274
Montefiore, Simon Sebag   22, 149
  Titans of History   149
  The World: a Family History   22
Moors/Moorish   124, 142, 150, 159, 165, 205, 216, 220, 241, 255, 289, 319, 256, 260, 288, 290, 313, 320, 326, 327, 328, Chapter 5 passim
  literary themes   7, 201, 205, 221, 224, 259–262, 281–286, 296–297, 316–317, 325, 348
  maurophilia   339–41
  novel   8, 10, 18–20, 198, 201, 211, 214, 226, 231, 284, 290, 313, 327
  poetry   60
  settings/style   257, 313, 316
  Spain   72, 85, 107
Morgan, John (or Joseph?)   17, 172–173
Moriscos   9, 16, 18, 148–151, 180, 191
  Cervantes, in   221, 252, 256, 258
  changing fortunes of   212–220
  conversion of   207
  corsairs, and   167
  romanticising of   202
Morocco   27, 155, 191, 327
Morte d'Arthur (Malory)   135
Mountaineers, The. *See* Colman, George the Younger
Mozarabs   82, 84, 199, 201, 206

Muhammad: A Biography of the Prophet   199. *See* Armstrong, Karen
Muhammad, Prophet. *See* Prophet Muhammad
Muley-Hacén (king of Granada)   18, 211
Muslim. *See* Islam
Muslim men and Christian women, relations between   19, 156, 244–252
Muslim recusants   107
Muslim Spain   85, 142, 199, 201, 348
Mu'tamid, al-, poet-king   63, 64, 211

Naples   182, 221, 268, 311
Nauigation, peregrinations and voyages, The, made Into Turkie. *See* Nicolay
Ndiaye, Noémie, *Scripts of Blackness*   283
Nicolay, Nicolas de (traveller)   157, 158, 281
Nicoll, Allardyce, *A History of Early Eighteenth Century Drama*   299
  A History of English Drama 1660–1900   320
Nykl, A.R., *Hispano-Arabic Poetry ...*   24, 61, 62, 63, 64, 81, 82, 84, 87

occidentalism   37–38
One Thousand and One Nights (*Alf Layla wa Layla*)   7, 8, 9, 13, 14, 19, 20, 29, 30–52, 53, 65, 83, 98, 106, 117, 172, 175, 190, 195, 275, 314, 335, 345
Oran   148, 164, 177, 178, 182, 183, 253
oriental   2, 7, 12, 14, 31, 37–39, 176, 222, 230, 281, 282, 292, 296, 313, 314, 319, 324, 331, 334
  literature   14, 83, 140, 180, 222, 230, 292, 296, 316–319, 324, 328, 331, 334
  people   12, 31, 176, 281, 282, 296, 313, 316, 324
  settings   2, 7, 37–39, 302–303, 313, 323, 326
orientalism   37–38, 172, 195, 197, 314–319, 331
Orlando Furioso (Ariosto)   265, 267, 272, 336
Orlando Furioso (Greene)   19, 263–268, 272
ornament, ornamentation   97, 232, 289, 304
Oroonoko: or, The Royal Slave (Behn)   7, 20, 312–313
Oroonoko (Southerne)   20, 312
Ottoman
  court   194, 250, 309

Ottoman (*cont.*)
  empire   16, 30, 148, 152, 154, 156, 159, 164, 184, 194, 214, 216, 231, 241, 247, 281, 315, 316, 323, 324
  sultans   19, 113, 152, 252, 260, 273, 277, 281
Ozmín y Daraja (Mateo Alemán)   18, 201, 216–221, 227, 231, 256, 317. *See also* Alemán, Mateo

pagan, paganism   48, 53, 54, 55, 75, 120, 123, 137, 139, 146, 263, 269
Paradise, garden of Eden   26, 35, 36, 48, 77, 78, 83, 94, 103, 105, 107, 200, 276, 324, 346, 347–349
Paris   283
Peele, George (dramatist)   259, 261, 267
Pegelin, Alli (character in D'Aranda's narrative)   169, 170
Peirce, Leslie   29, 113, 114
Pellow, Thomas   159, 188–193
Pepys, Samuel   308
Peregrinación de Anastasio:Diálogos el. See Gracián
Pérez de Hita, Ginés, author of *Las Guerras civiles de Granada*   10, 18, 198, 205–208, 211–212, 217, 231, 256, 282, 284–205, 286–287, 300, 302, 304, 311, 325, 348, 349
Persia, Persian   12–14, 30–31, 33, 38, 43–44, 59, 74, 78, 89, 111, 115, 175, 253, 277, 281, 282, 314, 317, 347, 351
Petursson, Hallgrimur   152
Phillips, William   5–6
Pidal, Ramón Menéndez, *Reliquias de la poesía épica española*   211
pilgrims, pilgrimages   44, 96, 137, 231, 324
Pilon, Edmond   292
pirates / piracy corsairs   1–8, 11, 16, 32, 44, 51, 145, 152, 153, 154, 155, 224, 225, 273, 292–293, 300, 305, 309, 311, 319, 323, 326, 327, 329, 332, 333, 334, 336, 349
  ancient times, in   4–5
  classical Greece, in   8, 11, 32, 145, 242, 336
  Istanbul / Turkish   154, 309, 323, 326, 329, 332, 334
  North Africa, and   1, 2, 6, 16, 152, Chapter 3 passim, 224, 225, 273, 292–293, 300, 305, 311, 309, 319, 327, 332, 336, 349
Plato, Platonic, neo-Platonic   10, 21, 73–74, 248, 336, 339

Plautus (Roman dramatist)   24, 31
poetic justice (and absence thereof)   51, 94, 327
pornography   146, 304, 326, 334
postcolonial theory   340–341
précieuses (17th century French women's literary grouping)   20, 282
Princess Fatima, Warrior Woman,The Tale of / The Arabic Epic of Dhāt al-Himma. See *Dhāt al-Himma/ Delhemma*   50, 57–59, 88, 89, 90
Prise d'Orange, la   138
Prophet Muhammad   9, 12, 25, 26, 28, 47, 52, 54, 55, 57, 111, 120, 121, 137, 187, 200, 216, 225, 270, 278
  Christian confusion over role of   120, 125, 137, 145, 225
  invocation of blessings on   27, 54, 55
  Shahada (Islamic Creed), and   47
  slavery and   9, 12, 13, 26, 28, 29
Provençale, La. See Regnard, Jean-François
Provence   84, 85, 87, 107–108, 110

Qaradawi, Yusuf, al-, *The Lawful and the Prohibited in Islam*   156
Quest for El Cid, The   230
Qur'an, The   12, 13, 24, 27–28, 35, 36, 44, 48, 56, 74, 75, 76, 77, 78, 120, 156, 169, 191, 213, 214, 216, 282, 317, 347

race, racism   9, 20, 25, 29, 30, 31, 50, 53, 54, 56, 138–140, 142–144, 191, 312, 321, 322
Racine, Jean   10, 74
ransoms, ransoming   5, 17, 54, 70, 152, 153, 158, 160, 162–163, 169, 170, 173, 182, 183–184, 187, 189, 196–197, 215, 218, 221, 236, 242, 244, 253, 258, 294–296, 311
  Mercedarian religious order (Order of Merced, Mercedarian)   163
  Trinitarian religious order (The Order of the Most Holy Trinity and of the Captives)   184–185
  Virgin Mary, Order of the (Redemption of the Captives, Our Lady of Ransom, Order of the Blessed Virgin Mary of Mercy, Order of Merced, O. Merc, Mercedarians, the Order of Captives, Order of Our Lady of Ransom)   163
Réage, Pauline (pseudonym of Anne Desclos)   331, 341

INDEX

Regnard, Jean-François   1, 3, 151, 197, 291–296, 311
Rehearsal, The [1671–2]. *See* Villiers
Remedio en la desdicha, el   (*See* Lope de Vega)
renegades   17–18, 149, 151, 157–158, 162, 164, 165–166, 170, 182, 184, 187, 188, 225, 231, 233, 234, 235, 240, 241, 244, 245, 254, 273, 277, 279, 280, 294, 310, 324, 332, 336, 340
Renegado, The. *See* Massinger, Philip
Restoration (period in English history and literature: 1660 onwards)   8, 19, 20, 194, 195, 261, 270, 271, 272, 280, Chapter 5 passim
Reykjavik   152
Ring of the Dove, The. *See* Ibn Hazm
Risalat al-Ghufran   26
Romance of the Sowdone [Sultan] *of Babylone and of Ferumbras his Sone who Conquered Rome*   128, 132, 134, 135, 145
Rome   47, 113, 128, 135, 161
Roncevalles/Roncevaux Pass, Battle of   118–119, 120, 124
Rowlie, Samson   158, 159
ruler poets   62–64

'Sack of Baltimore, The' (poem)   163–64
sadomasochism   8, 20, 303, 306–7, 326–7, 341
Said, Edward, *Orientalism*   37
Saladin, Salah ad-Din Yusuf ibn Ayyub   50, 51
Salé   150, 158
Sallee Rovers   150, 159, 326
'same' and 'other'   7–12, 14, 21–22, 25, 26, 39, 42, 51, 75, 82, 93, 117, 159, 218, 226, 232, 242, 291, 338–341, 329, 335, 337, 338–342, 344
Sandys, George, *A Relation of a Journey Begun An. Dom. 1610 ...*   274
Saracens   8, 15, 26, 107, 108, 113, 124–126, 131, 138–139, 141–143, 146, 224, 229, 337
   See also Muslim, Moors, Moorish
Saragossa   121, 123, 265
Scheindlin, Raymond P. and Michael Sells, eds., *The Literature of Al-Andalus*   81, 82
Schweitzer, Jerome W., *Georges de Scudéry's Almahide...*   285, 286, 336, 337

Scudéry, Georges and Madeleine   284–285, 298, 300, 337
seduction   58, 60, 69, 74, 77, 79, 87, 92–4, 145, 180, 196, 276, 279–280, 309, 311, 333, 345, 348
Select Collection of Novels and Histories, A   20, 288, 316–319
Selimus, or *The Tragedy of Selimus, Sometime Emperor of the Turks* (1594)   299
Seraglio, Il (Mozart)   35, 328
Seville   88, 211, 224, 253, 348
   Alcazar   348
   fall of to the Almoravids   211
   Zaida of Seville   211
sex, sexual
   commerce and trade, and   273
   intrigues   35, 74, 174, 186, 304, 309, 313, 334, 337
   slavery, and   4, 8, 22, 25, 26, 27, 28, 193, 197, 327, 331
   transgression   36, 93, 307, 345
Shafak, Elif   75
Shahnameh, The   346
Shahrazad (*One Thousand and One Nights*)   29, 31, 33, 315
Shahriyar (*One Thousand and One Nights*)   31, 32, 33–34, 53, 98, 106, 315
Shakespeare, William   8, 64, 102, 145, 174, 233, 259, 260, 262, 263, 264, 275, 298, 299, 337
   Anthony and Cleopatra   299
   As You Like It   264, 275
   King Lear   298
   Merchant of Venice, The   262
   Othello   259
   Pericles, Prince of Tyre   145
   Romeo and Juliet   64
   Taming of the Shrew, The   275
   Titus Andronicus   260
   Twelfth Night   233
   Winter's Tale, The   102, 337
Sheherazade (ballet)   33
Sheik, The (E.M. Hull novel)   21, 328–329
Sheik, The (film)   328, 330, 331
sheikh romance   333–334
shipwrecks   3, 8, 56, 145, 283, 288, 311, 321, 327
Sicily   82, 88, 161, 242, 243
Siege of Corinth, The (Byron)   20, 324
Siege of Granada   320
Simonardottir, Guðríður   152

Singing girls (in al-Andalus)   59, 68–70, 73, 87
Sīrat Dhāt al-Himma/Delhemma   50, 57–58, 88
Sir Ferumbras   127–132, 134, 135
Sir Philip Sydney   266
Skin colour   11, 25, 150, 142–3, 195, 283, 312, 321
  religious conversion, and   26, 143, 144
Slave of Desire: Sex, Love, and Death in the 1001 Nights. See Beaumont, Daniel
Slavery   1, 4–7, 7–8, 11, 12–13, 14, 16–18, 18–19, 19–20, 21, 23, 24–25, 27–30, 44, 51, 62–64, 70, 75–76, 85, 97, 105–107, 149–155, 155–157, 159, 160, 165, 169–170, 175, 179, 186, 188, 194–198, 198, 205, 221–223, 253, 259, 272, 278, 284–286, 297, 305, 308–309, 312–313, 316, 318, 321, 323, 326, 328, 331, 332–333, 334, 337–338, 341–342, 345, 346, 349
  faith Slavery   149
  'Slave to Love' / Captivity and Romance   1, 8, 11, 20, 237, 274, 276, 283, 332–333, 337
  slavery and romance   11, 18, 19, 197, 198–199, 259–262, 316–319, 319–322, 326, 334–335, 341
  slave trade   5, 16, 23, 148–154, 156, 159, 185, 196, 282, 283, 332, 333, 339
  See also Captivity, and Chapter 3 passim
Song of Roland. See Chanson de Roland
Sosa, Antonio de   148, 166, 181–182
Southerne, Thomas. See Oroonoko
Spain   2, 9, 16, 19, 57, 84, 97, 99, 107, 108, 118, 122, 123, 132, 136, 168, 172, 176, 177, 181, 182, 199, 205, 212, 214, 215, 216, 220, 221, 224, 232, 242, 243, 252, 296, 305, 324
  Franks, and   125
  Islamic   58, 82, 83, 85, 88, 142, 199, 201, 203, 348
  literature of   8, 211, 231, 250, 285, 339
  medieval   89, 231
  Muslims and Christians in   10, 14, 46
  Muslim Christian frontier in   18, 142
  Muslim conquest of   115, 345
  Muslim expulsion from   148, 233, 258, 294, 338
  political boundaries of   206
  shifting alliances, and   124
  target of corsairs, as   149, 152
  See also Moorish Spain
Spectator Magazine. See Steele
Steele, Richard and Joseph Addison   321
stereotypes   42, 107, 195, 335
Story of O. See Réage, Pauline
Suleiman I, 'the Magnificent', sultan   113, 148, 186, 244, 261
Syria   9, 31, 32, 33, 64, 90, 281, 314, 317

Talavera (Archbishop Hernando de)   213–214
Talavera, city of   289
Tales of the Alhambra (Washington Irving)   21, 325
Tassy, Jacques Philippe Laugier de   17, 172–180
Tavakoli-Targhi, Mohamad, *Refashioning Iran: Orientalism, Occidentalism and Historiography*   38
Terence (Roman dramatist)   24
Teresa of Ávila, St   161
theology
  Christian   102, 161, 229
  Islamic   64, 78
Three Turk Plays from Early Modern England. See Vitkus, Daniel
Tiepolo, Giovanni Battista (painter)   264
Tinniswood, Adrian, *Pirates of Barbary...*   154, 294
Toledo   164, 213
Topografía, e Historia General de Argel   166–167
Tortosa   289
torture   56, 60, 64, 159, 165, 176–7, 179, 183, 189, 193, 215, 258, 277, 308, 309, 310, 328, 341, 342
towers   122, 132, 134, 137, 209, 227, 277, 304, Appendix 1 passim
tragedy   12, 34–36, 41, 92, 174–175, 223, 239, 260, 261, 262, 263, 266, 270, 276, 298, 299, 319, 320, 321, 323–325, 328, 336
  Jacobean Tragedy   223, 239, 262, 291
  Restoration tragedy   261, 270, 300
  revenge tragedy   323
  'she-tragedy'   266, 298, 299, 319
Tragicomedy   226, 262–281
  Jacobean tragicomedy   262–281
  Restoration tragicomedy   299
transatlantic slave trade   23, 53, 282

Trato de Argel, el. See Cervantes, Miguel de
traveller writing   6, 157, 281, 309
Travels of Ibn Baṭṭūṭa   111
Tripoli   57, 114, 148, 149, 153, 177, 178
troubadours   24, 64, 84–87, 108
True & Exact History of the Island of Barbadoes, A [1657] *See* Ligon
True and Faithful Account of the Religion and manners of the Mohammetans, A, with an Account of the Author's Being Taken Captive, (Joseph Pitts)   160
Tunis   19, 57, 114, 149, 161, 163, 177, 178, 181, 182, 272, 273, 276, 288, 304, 305, 308, 310, 311, 312, 324, 327
  Cervantes, and   181–2
  Cotton, and   302
  Massinger, and   276–7
  Tassy, de, and   177–178
Turk, Turkey, Turkish, 'Turkish'   16, 17, 36, 57, 88, 90, 138–139, 151–152, 157, 169, 173, 177, 187, 188, 193–197, 198–200, 209, 214, 216, 229, 242–243, 250, 254, 260, 269–274, 277, 279, 282, 284, 295
  costume   243–244, 257, 286, 316
  customs   195, 316
  family background   18, 156–157
  individuals   164, 174–175, 225, 251
  language   13, 113, 232, 261, 281, 314
  literature and   20, 51, 59, 75, 222–223, 259–261, 285–286, 296–299, 309, 313, 317, 319, 320, 323, 327, 328–329, 334–335, 336, 347
  rule, rulers   148, 170, 297, 332
  settings   198, 244–252, 313, 347
  sultans   8, 329
  synonym for Muslim   193
  titles   111, 153, 268, 271, 273
  'turn Turk'   158, 170, 189, 260, 273, 336
  women   195, 274, 309
  See also Ottoman
Turkish Embassy Letters. See Montagu, Lady Mary Wortley

'Umar Ibn al-Khattab (Caliph)   28, 50
'Umar ibn al-Nu'uman (character in the Tale of 'Umar ibn al-Nu'man)   39, 41, 92
'Umar ibn al-Nu'uman… , Tale of (*One Thousand and One Nights* story)   39–43, 47, 51, 55, 92, 335

Umayyad dynasty   9, 29, 57–58, 64, 72, 81, 115

Valencia   215, 216, 230, 304
Valladolid   161
Vega, Lope de, Félix. *See* Lope
Villedieu, Marie-Catherine de (Mme de)   286
Villegas, Antonio de. *See El Abencerraje*
Villiers, George, 2nd Duke of Buckingham   300
Virgin Mary   44, 48, 103, 136, 103, 136, 209, 214, 226, 228, 229, 232, 235, 240, 241, 247
  as guardian of men in trouble and, especially, captives   136, 235
  as inspiration and role model to young women   103, 214, 228, 229, 237, 241, 247
  as merciful saint, able to pardon transgressions   226
  as name of ransoming religious order   163
  as symbol of purity   232
  as unifying figure because venerated by both Christians and Muslims   214, 215, 247
Visigoths, Visigothic   9, 81, 345, 115
Vitkus, Daniel J.   158, 260
  Piracy, Slavery and Redemption…   152, 261
  Three Turk Plays   336
  True and Faithful Account of the Religion and manners of the Mohammetans, A   160
  Turning Turk   158, 260
Voltaire, François-Marie Arouet   336

Walid II, al-, poet-caliph   64
Wallada, princess and poet   62
Warner, Marina, *Stranger Magic: Charmed States and the* Arabian Nights   31
Warren, F. M., 'The Enamoured Moslem Princess … '   141
warrior women   51, 52, 57, 92, 111, 127, 271
Wasserstein, David, *The Rise and Fall of the Party-Kings…*   200, 201, 212
Watt, William Montgomery and Pierre Cachia, *A History of Islamic Spain*   200

Weever, Jacqueline de, *Sheba's Daughters; Whitening and Demonizing the Saracen Woman* ... 141, 142
Welch, Ellen R., *A Taste for the Foreign* ... 286
Wheatcroft, Andrew, *Infidels: A History of the Conflict between Christendom and Islam* 151, 215
Whitaker, Cord J, *Black Metaphors* ... 138, 140

Yiacoup, Şizen, *Frontier Memory* ... 206, 231, 285
Yusuf and Zulaikha 13, 52, 74–80

Yusuf and Zulaikha (Jami) 75–80, 190, 253, 349, 351

Zahra / Zara (character is Cervantes, *Los Baños de argel*) 229, 247, 337
   See also *Kitab al-Zahra* (Ibn Dawud)
Zaïde, Histoire espagnole. See Lafayette
Zegries (Granadine clan) 20, 207–209, 257
Zoraida (character in Cervantes, *La historia del cautivo*) 48, 211, 228, 229–232, 235, 240, 242, 247, 280, 337
   See also *Cantar de la Mora Zoraida*
Zwartjes, Otto, *Love Songs from Al-Andalus* ... 83, 84